The publisher and the University of California Press Foundation gratefully acknowledge the generous support of the Joan Palevsky Endowment Fund in Literature in Translation.

The Variae

The Variae

The Complete Translation

———

Cassiodorus

Translated by

M. Shane Bjornlie

UNIVERSITY OF CALIFORNIA PRESS

University of California Press
Oakland, California

Library of Congress Cataloging-in-Publication Data

Names: Cassiodorus, Senator, approximately 487– approximately 580,
    author. | Bjornlie, Michael Shane, translator, writer of introduction.
Title: The variae : the complete translation / Cassiodorus ; translated by M.
    Shane Bjornlie.
Other titles: Variae. English (Bjornlie)
Description: Oakland, California : University of California Press, [2019] |
    Includes bibliographical references and index. |
Identifiers: LCCN 2019003205 (print) | LCCN 2019010191 (ebook) |
    ISBN 9780520969735 (ebook) | ISBN 9780520297364 (cloth : alk. paper)
Subjects: LCSH: Italy—History—476-774—Sources. | Italy—Politics and
    government—476-1268—Sources. | Italy—Social life and customs—To
    1500—Sources. | Cassiodorus, Senator, approximately 487–approxi-
    mately 580.
Classification: LCC PA6271.C4 (ebook) | LCC PA6271.C4 A2 2019 (print) |
    DDC 945/.01—dc23

Manufactured in the United States of America

26   25   24   23   22   21   20   19
10   9   8   7   6   5   4   3   2   1

CONTENTS

Introduction

Sometime after 540, the former Roman magistrate Flavius Magnus Aurelius Cassiodorus Senator, or Cassiodorus, completed the collection of letters known as the *Variae*. He did so in the midst of the tumultuous conflict between the ruling Goths of Italy and the forces of the eastern Roman emperor, Justinian. This conflict, the Gothic War, would last eighteen years (536–54) and was the impetus for Cassiodorus's publication of an epistolary profile of his previous service under the Gothic Amal rulers. Probably less clear to Cassiodorus at the time was the fact that, like the Gothic War itself, the record of public service embedded in the *Variae* was a testimonial to a final stage in the unraveling of a tradition for imperial power in the former provinces of the western Roman Empire, making the *Variae* a palimpsest of momentous events, both of its own time and also of the extended history of the end of the western Roman Empire.

The end of the western Roman Empire and the emergence of "successor states" (Vandalic North Africa, Visigothic Spain and Gaul, Frankish and Burgundian Gaul, and Ostrogothic Italy itself) was a complex and protracted process that occurred for different reasons on a region-by-region basis over the course of the fifth century, but it is a process that had direct bearing on Italy's political position in Cassiodorus's lifetime. By the sixth century, the western Mediterranean was no longer organized by a single, coherent state apparatus. Political and economic

Portions of this introduction have been adapted from Shane Bjornlie, "The Letter Collection of Cassiodorus," in *A Critical Introduction and Reference Guide to Late Antique Letter Collections,* ed. Cristiana Sogno, Bradley K. Storin, and Edward J. Watts (Berkeley: University of California Press, 2016), 433–48.

structures had become regionalized and reoriented around nonprofessional military elites. Being Roman, too, had transformed in meaning and had yielded to more regional, and more relevant, kinds of identities. By contrast, imperial power in the eastern Mediterranean had become even more focused on Constantinople as a "new Rome." Although the fifth century had also imposed profound changes upon the political culture and social structures of the eastern Mediterranean, the eastern Roman Empire nonetheless preserved the administrative, fiscal, and cultural instruments of imperial power to a degree not seen in former western provinces in the sixth century. Thus, by Cassiodorus's lifetime, the western "successor states" and the eastern Roman Empire represented increasingly divergent historical trajectories. Nonetheless, the interconnectedness of the eastern and western Mediterranean should never be dismissed. The constant movement of ecclesiastical envoys, royal and imperial delegations, merchants and tradesmen, armies and migrant peoples, and even private entrepreneurs, ensured that political, religious, and cultural communication persisted between the western and eastern Mediterranean throughout the sixth century.

The position of Italy in this new matrix of what had been a centralized Roman provincial system was perhaps unique, in that it had become a frontier between the evolving "successor states," on the one hand, and the eastern Roman Empire, on the other. For centuries, Italy had served as the center stage of a vast empire and as a reservoir for imperial wealth and political talent. But by the beginning of the sixth century, Italy's control over western provinces had contracted considerably to include primarily the Italian peninsula and its Alpine hinterland, Sicily and the Dalmatian coastal zone. The consequent reduction in economic resources that attended the loss of a provincial system necessitated that the scale of imperial administration in Italy was proportionately, and substantially, reduced. These changes, however, were neither abrupt, nor even conclusively disruptive. The process of paring provinces away from Italy's control occurred mostly in the first three decades of the fifth century. By the time the Goths arrived under Theoderic in 489, Italy already had over half a century to accommodate itself to very different circumstances. New economic hinterlands and new channels of political patronage developed for the political elite, a process of regionalization that transformed Italy into a self-contained polity that was no longer dependent on provincial resources. Similarly during the fifth century, the detachment of the emperor's role as the ceremonial figure of state from the exercise of military power, visible particularly during the reigns of Honorius (393–423) and Valentinian III (425–55), had paved the way for the period of arriviste warlords in Italy that culminated in the reign of Odoacer as king of Italy (476–89). It was largely during the period following the death of Valentinian III that real governing power resided with a military class settled in northern Italy and ruling from Ravenna, while the traditional senatorial elite of Rome assumed a more or less ancillary role in the political culture of

Italy. Thus, when Theoderic arrived during the generation of Cassiodorus's father, the political, administrative, and economic patterns of governance over which he assumed control had already been set. Theoderic's primary innovation was to graft the army that had followed him from the Balkans (collectively known today as the "Ostrogoths") onto the military hierarchy of Italy's existing government.

Thus, the Italy reflected in Cassiodorus's *Variae* was liminal, both geographically and temporally. The nearly continuous (and always competitive) political dialogue that Italy had exchanged with the eastern empire since the early fifth century contributed to the maintenance of a political language that was the direct legacy of Roman Empire. In this sense, Italy maintained the pretensions of an imperial state to a degree far greater than other western regions. The ancient density of Italy's urban centers also contributed to a relatively complex late-antique administration. This maintenance of ancient tradition, so pronounced in the *Variae*, became the hallmark of the Amals, the Gothic ruling family, first under Theoderic, and then with his successors, Amalasuntha and Athalaric. At the same time, many of the realities imposed upon other regions of the postimperial West are visible in Cassiodorus's lifetime: diplomatic communication between royal courts that reveals the insecurity of political partnerships, new ideologies based on Romans as "civilians" and a culturally distinctive (and nonprofessional) military class, contracted economic and administrative horizons, and the increased importance of royal oversight to compensate for the increasingly inadequate reach of a professionalized administration.

For a region that is both an inheritance from Roman Empire and a legacy of its demise, Italy in the sixth century is notoriously difficult for modern historians to characterize. On the one hand, so many markers point to continuity with the previous imperial culture of Roman Italy—the maintenance of fiscal habits, relatively robust attention to urban fabric, and the appointment of traditional political offices such as consuls and praetorian prefects. On the other hand, capturing the essence of Italy in the sixth century requires carefully assessing the scope and character of what are often regarded as "imperial" features. For example, while there is ample testimony to tax collection, the evidence usually appears in response to the difficulty of sustaining regular collection with a reduced administration. Similarly, while it is clear that urban centers remained the focal point for economic and administrative activity in the sixth century, it is also clear that the city's role as a theater for these activities relied, in part, on the central administration, but also increasingly on the local church as civic benefactor. And where appointments to political office are amply attested, so too is reliance of the government on new roles, such as Gothic *saiones* (special agents of the royal court), to fulfill traditional administrative needs. Even the baroque style of a text like the *Variae* can be interpreted with completely different frames of reference—either in terms of stylistic continuity with a classical intellectual and governmental tradition, on the one hand, or in terms of rhetorical pretension in the face of insistent cultural change, on the other.

Compounding the difficulty of understanding sixth-century Italy is the nature of the sources. Although fairly abundant, textual sources describing Ostrogothic Italy can often be frustratingly myopic. Where sources for sixth-century Italy are rich, they can nonetheless sound like a chorus of half-utterances. The *Variae*, by contrast, provide perhaps the most holistic view of the region. As a collection of letters representing the concerns and activities of a late-antique administration, the *Variae* provide sometimes opaque, sometimes vivid perspectives of a startling range of life in the sixth century (diplomatic letters, administrative directives, the resolution of legal disputes, sentences for crimes against individuals and the state, military mobilization, attention to building projects, and appointments to military, administrative, and even honorary posts). As a whole, the collection offers the most fully elaborated and coherent expression of governmental ideology to survive from antiquity. Additionally, it informs our understanding of interstate relations, state administration and finances, land management practices, the church and religious culture, ethnic relations in Italy, literary interests, and the limits of "scientific" knowledge for the period. Furthermore, the collection offers tantalizing glimpses into the lives of women, children, the rural poor, and slaves—the frequently underrepresented voices of late ancient sources. The panoply of individuals addressed and mentioned in the collection is nothing short of a prosopographical treasure, with many persons of both high station and low who otherwise would have escaped the historical record. Thus, the *Variae* are an astonishing resource, providing not only a complete profile for life in Ostrogothic Italy, but also a frame of reference for both late antiquity and the early Middle Ages. The liminal quality of Ostrogothic Italy, and of the *Variae* as its putative witness, has ensured that Cassiodorus's collection figures prominently either as a source representing the end of antiquity or as a source projecting the beginning of the Middle Ages. Modern scholarship has accordingly availed itself of the *Variae* for *longue durée* studies of law and government, economy and the environment, the church and social history. In terms of sheer literary precocity, not to mention the impact of the collection on our understanding of an era as a cultural and historical setting, it would not be unreasonable to compare Cassiodorus's legacy to the impact of Chaucer on the modern understanding of fourteenth-century England, or William Shakespeare on the sixteenth and seventeenth centuries.

Of course, like any textual source of great compass, reading the *Variae* imposes considerable challenges. As a collection depicting the legal, administrative, and social life of Italy, the *Variae* have always enjoyed a particular legitimacy as "documentary" sources. Their authenticity as faithful "records" of the aims, interests, and policies of the Amal court has been almost universally accepted. This is partially the result of the assumed documentary nature of the letters and their potentially enormous historical utility, which has made them impervious to the same kind of literary analysis that has proven so useful to understanding the presentational aspects of epistolography in earlier classical settings. As a result, studies increasingly approach the *Variae* as highly rhetorical literary products that owe more to the compositional strategies and interests of Cassiodorus after he vacated his last official post. Assigning more agency to Cassiodorus as opposed to Amal policy has proven difficult because of the lacunose nature of the collection's historical context. The obscurity of important issues, such as the date of the collection's completion, Cassiodorus's relationship to actors in the great political and religious dramas of his day, and where he completed the collection, have made the *Variae* resistant to precise placement within political and social circumstances. Thus, whether the *Variae* should be understood as a "record" of Cassiodorus's efforts as amanuensis to individual Gothic rulers, as a "representation" of the ideological platform that Cassiodorus designed for Gothic rulers during thirty years of service, or as the "creation" of his authorial intentions after the fact, all remain a matter of debate.

The rich detail and impressive range of topics found in the collection encourage scholarship to treat each letter as an authentic response to a distinct historical moment, although the fact that the Gothic War dominated political life in Italy at the precise moment that Cassiodorus gathered the collection cannot be dismissed. Both the Gothic War and internal evidence for Cassiodorus's authorial intentions requires that scholarship take into account the extent to which the collection "performed" a carefully choreographed presentation of the Gothic government of Italy. The extent to which letters may be trusted as unadulterated witnesses to specific historical moments or as selective presentations adapted during the composition of the collection must be weighed carefully and on an individual basis. It is probably best to reach a compromise, in which the *Variae* are understood as a collection of documents that preserve the activities of the Gothic government, which Cassiodorus later revised for ideological coherence and consistency, to the extent of altering the content of some letters and, perhaps, in more specific cases, inventing others.

CASSIODORUS AS STATESMAN AND AUTHOR

Details concerning Cassiodorus's life (c. 485–580) are known almost exclusively through his own writing (most prominently, the *Variae*). The family of the Cassiodori seem to have originated in the eastern empire but sometime before the mid-fifth century had become large property owners in Calabria. The family's resources in land and horses likely brought them to the attention of imperial authorities and Cassidorus's great grandfather is noted for having mobilized these resources in the defense of Sicily and southern Italy against the Vandals.[1] Valentinian III honored Cassiodorus's grandfather with an appointment to the imperial bureaucracy as *tribunus et notarius*, in which capacity the famous Roman general Aetius entrusted him with a diplomatic expedition to Attila.[2] Although the family's political role during the troubled years between the death of Valentinian III and the deposition of Romulus Augustulus is unattested, Cassiodorus's father had a secure place in the administration of Italy, holding a succession of governorships and palatine offices first under Odoacer (476–89) and then under Theoderic.[3]

Cassiodorus probably first came to Theoderic's attention while his father held the praetorian prefecture of Italy (*Praefectus Praetorio Italiae*). At the time, Cassiodorus served his father as an aid (*consiliarius*) and had an opportunity to recite a panegyric in honor of Theoderic.[4] By the time his father received patrician rank as a reward for his service as *Praefectus Praetorio* (*Variae* 1.3 and 1.4), Cassiodorus had assumed responsibility for official state correspondence as *Quaestor*, an office that he held circa 507–11.[5] Cassiodorus's consulship in 514 was probably intended to sustain the connection between the Gothic court and the Cassiodori. Cassiodorus reciprocated in 519 by offering a panegyric to Theoderic's son-in-law, before the Senate, on the occasion of Eutharic's consulship and later by composing a history of the Goths at Theoderic's request.[6] When a member of a prominent senatorial family, Boethius, fell out of favor with Theoderic in 524, Cassiodorus was at hand to assume the condemned scholar's previous post as *Magister Officiorum*, an office that he continued to hold probably until 528, under Theoderic's successor Athalaric.[7] Cassiodorus's particular affinity with the Amal court continued after leaving this office. When the coastline of southern Italy had been threatened, presumably again by the Vandals, Cassiodorus abandoned literary retirement and, imitating his grandparents, assumed responsibility for the military mobilization of the region and provisioned Gothic soldiers from his own resources.[8] With the end of the military threat, Cassiodorus then assumed the primary role in restoring order to the region.[9] By the time of his appointment as *Praefectus Praetorio* in 533, Cassiodorus had already provided valuable service to the Gothic government in a variety of capacities, both officially and *ex officio*, for nearly three decades.

---

1. *Var.* 1.4.14; 1.4.17.
2. *Var.* 1.4.10–13.
3. *Var.* 1.4.3–6.
4. *Ordo generis Cassiodororum* 29–30.
5. *Var.* 9.24.3–5.
6. *Var.* 9.25.3–5.
7. *Var.* 9.24.6–7.
8. *Var.* 9.25.8–9.
9. *Var.* 9.25.10.

The period of Cassiodorus's tenure as Praetorian Prefect must have been the most difficult of his public career. Although Cassiodorus was doubtlessly intimate with the personalities and activities of palatine service at Ravenna, the years from 533 to 540 would witness a rapid succession of changes of royal personalities. Theoderic had died in 526, leaving his daughter Amalasuntha as regent over governmental affairs for her young son Athalaric. When Athalaric died prematurely in 534, Amalasuntha appointed her kinsman Theodahad as co-ruler. Internecine feuding among Gothic families and Theodahad's ambitions led to Amalasuntha's death in the following year (535). The murder of Amalasuntha, who had favored rehabilitating the relationship between the Amals and the Roman Senate, may have precipitated Justinian's attempt to conquer Italy. Soon after her fall, Belisarius crossed from Carthage, where he had recently toppled the Vandals from their control of North Africa, and initiated the Gothic War. Shortly thereafter (536), Gothic soldiers assassinated Theodahad on suspicion of betraying Italy in exchange for a lucrative settlement with Justinian. The Gothic soldiery elevated Witigis as the next king of Italy.[10] Based on the testimony of letters written in the name of Witigis (*Variae* 10.31–35), Cassiodorus probably continued to serve as *Praefectus Praetorio* until the capture of Ravenna in 540, whereupon Belisarius transported Witigis and the Gothic court to Constantinople. The Gothic War then entered a new phase, with the accession of the energetic Totila as king of the Goths. Eastern imperial successes in Italy became reversals and the war continued until 554.

For Cassiodorus and other Italians intimate with the Gothic government, the capture of Ravenna, which remained firmly in imperial hands throughout the war, represented the loss of a way of life. The *Variae* are carefully silent concerning the war, even in the two prefaces where Cassiodorus explains the purpose of the letter collection. However, later sources from Cassiodorus further removed from the war make it clear that the Gothic War represented a dramatic rupture in the social and political realities to which a generation of palatine elite had become accustomed. In the preface to his *Institutiones,* Cassiodorus recalled how peaceful endeavors had been abandoned on account of "raging wars and turbulent struggles in the Italic kingdom."[11] Sometime during the Gothic War, Cassiodorus collected, revised, and composed the letters that he called the *Variae.* An earlier generation of scholarship assumed that Cassiodorus assembled the *Variae* between 537 and 540, by which reckoning the capture of Ravenna figured as the terminus of his political aspirations, a view that has cast the *Variae* as mementos of a former public life and which, inadvertently, has obscured ambitions for the rehabilitation of the bureaucratic elite that Cassiodorus might have had after the fall of Ravenna. However, analysis of the political context suggests that Cassiodorus may have

10. Procopius, *Wars* 5.2–11.
11. *Institutiones divinarum et saecularium litterarum, praefatio* 1.1.

produced the *Variae* later in the 540s, in response to the vacillating fortunes of the Gothic War. In addition to the uncertainty concerning the date of the *Variae*, it is not known for certain where Cassiodorus assembled the collection. Individual letters do not disclose whether, as original documents, they may have been written on behalf of Gothic kings in residence at Rome, Ravenna, or, perhaps more likely, itinerantly as the court moved between the various estates owned by the Amal family throughout Italy. Similarly, a range of possibilities have been suggested concerning where Cassiodorus assembled the individual letters as a collection—at Rome after the siege of Witigis, at Ravenna either before or during the siege of Belisarius, at Cassiodorus's estates in Calabria (Vivarium), or perhaps when he was a political exile in Constantinople. The supradiction to the *Variae* addresses Cassiodorus as *Praefectus Praetorio et Patricius*, leading some to assume that he compiled the *Variae* while still in office. However, no mention is made of his patrician status within individual letters or the prefaces to the collection. Even *Variae* 9.24 and 9.25, which announce his appointment as *Praefectus Praetorio*, are silent on the matter of patrician status, indicating patrician status did not accompany this appointment. If he received patrician status upon leaving office (as occurred in the case of his father), this probably did not happen until Witigis set aside royal authority in 540. It then seems likely that Cassiodorus received patrician status from Justinian, who made a habit of awarding this particular honorary title as a conciliatory gesture during the Gothic War.[12] There is, therefore, a strong case for Cassiodorus having received the patriciate after 540 in Constantinople, where he commenced work on the *Variae* in particularly volatile political circumstances.

Regardless of the precise date and location of "publication," the *Variae* are a product of the Gothic War, a period in which the relative successes of Amal governance faced the revisionism of eastern imperial propaganda and the animosities of those political exiles, particularly the senatorial elite of Rome, who had reasons to disavow prosperity under a "barbarian" regime. From the report of Cassiodorus's *De anima*, a philosophical treatise that he appended to the letters, assembling the *Variae* had been a troublesome and lengthy process. The difficulty of completing the *Variae* should not be imagined in terms of the effort required to collect the 468 letters that Cassiodorus included in the collection. Cassiodorus's analogy for the completion of the *Variae* as being "received in the quiet of the harbor to which I had come, if not with praise, at least freed from care," implies having weathered at least the threat of social and political censure before arriving at sanctuary.[13] Whether the safe harbor that Cassiodorus imagined in the *De anima* was Constantinople, where sources locate him as late as circa 550, or at Vivarium, where

---

12. Procopius, *Wars* 5.8.3–4; Jordanes, *Getica* 313.
13. *De anima* 1.

Cassiodorus eventually retired and dedicated himself to religious scholarship, the context in which he produced the *Variae* was one of conflict.

The foundations for this conflict were complicated. First, it seems that the Amal family had come to depend upon the municipal elites of Italy as a source of bureaucratic manpower, as opposed to the senatorial elite of Rome who, although still the recipients of traditional honorary titles, were less frequently selected for offices with real political and judicial authority. The condemnation of Boethius was a case in point for the mistrust that existed between palatine and senatorial circles. Cassiodorus held senatorial rank, but his family's patrimonial base was provincial Calabria, where the combination of land, horses, and education had made several generations of Cassiodori indispensable to the government of Italy. It should be noted, however, that the emperor under whom the Cassiodori first became political participants (Valentinian III) was the last emperor to spend significant time at Rome; subsequent Cassiodori flourished under the patronage of rulers who preferred northern Italy to the senatorial seat of social and political interaction at Rome. The success of Amal "outsourcing" for administrative talent is evident in the intimacy of Cassiodorus's career with royal affairs. Panegyrics to Theoderic, Eutharic, and Matasuntha (Theoderic's granddaughter whom Witigis married) speak to open commitment to the regime. Similarly, the consistency in range of topics addressed by individual letters of the *Variae* implies that, contrary to the tradition of alternating public office with private retirement (*otium*), Cassiodorus was, more often, a permanent fixture among Amal rulers. Where it should be expected that the traditional competences of the *Quaestor, Magister Officiorum,* and *Praefectus Praetorio* would have differentiated the topics of letters in the *Variae,* it appears instead that Cassiodorus attended a similar range of legal, administrative and diplomatic duties in each office. The *Variae* even draw attention to Cassiodorus's having assumed the responsibilities outside of his current office as a token of his value to the court.[14] Cassiodorus may not have been unusual for having made a career of his dedication to the Amal court. Theoderic apparently requested the company of Cassiodorus's aging father out of respect for their shared affection.[15] Those who did not similarly bask in palatine preferment had cause for resentment. The *Variae* also draw attention to the alienation that Amal preferment had caused, making objections to Cassiodorus's appointment as Praetorian Prefect particularly rancorous.[16]

The events of the initial phase of the Gothic War only exacerbated prejudices and hostilities that were otherwise probably latent in Italy's political culture. Witigis' siege of Rome (then under Belisarius's control) and later Milan resulted in the

---

14. *Var., praefatio* 1.7; 9.24.6.
15. *Var.* 3.28.
16. *Var.* 11.1.18.

execution of senatorial hostages at Ravenna and, in the case of Milan, the profligate slaughter of civilians.[17] During the course of the Gothic War, members of prominent senatorial families from Rome found refuge and receptive audience with Justinian in Constantinople. It was during this period that the execution of Boethius and his father-in-law, the esteemed senator Symmachus, became a symbolic token for the injustice inherent in a "barbarian" government. Cassiodorus, whose own political career had advanced in the wake of Boethius's downfall, as *Praefectus Praetorio* of the last Amal king, was conspicuously vulnerable. It is not known precisely whom among the Gothic court Belisarius removed to Constantinople. Procopius reports that Witigis and Matasuntha were deported with a Gothic host of great size.[18] Provincial Italians who had constituted the majority of the administration in Italy (especially its most numerous branch under the *Praefectus Praetorio*) are not specifically mentioned, although Cassiodorus's residence in Constantinople is known from later sources.[19] The *Constitutio Pragmatica*, with which Justinian planned the postwar settlement in 554, maintains an ominous silence concerning the administration of Ravenna, while stipulating the privileges of the senatorial elite (among them, specifically, several relations of Boethius), the church, and the great landowners. The period from 540 to 554, therefore, was one in which the future of the former administrative elite of Italy was undetermined. As a record of that administration, whether authentic or partially fabricated, the *Variae* aimed at shaping the postwar settlement of Italy. Unfortunately, Cassiodorus's better-known reputation (particularly in the Middle Ages) as a Christian exegete, have overshadowed what was probably a period of great political urgency for both Cassiodorus and his former political dependents in the praetorian prefecture of Italy.[20]

THE *VARIAE* AS AN EPISTOLARY COLLECTION

Cassiodorus arranged the letters of the *Variae* in twelve books, perhaps in purposeful symmetry to the twelve books of his Gothic history which was in circulation during the Gothic War. The first five books of the *Variae* include letters written by Cassiodorus in the name of Theoderic. Books 6 and 7 comprise *formulae* for appointments to public office, honorary titles, and particular legal and administrative enactments. In Books 8 and 9, Cassiodorus included letters written on behalf of Theoderic's grandson Athalaric. The final selection of letters written in the names of Amalasuntha, Theodahad, and Witigis combine in Book 10. Cassiodorus

---

17. Procopius, *Wars* 5.26.1 and 6.21.39.
18. Procopius, *Wars* 7.1.1.2.
19. Vigilius, *Epistula* 14; Jordanes, *Getica, praefatio* 1.
20. Note the list of religious texts mentioned in the *praefatio* of Cassiodorus's *De orthographia*.

reserved Books 11 and 12 for the letters that he wrote in his own name as *Praefectus Praetorio*. Within each book, the content varies widely. Each book contains between twenty-five and fifty letters, with a considerable range in length of individual letters. Most letters fall between 200 and 250 words, with some barely managing a terse 50 words and other, more ornate letters swelling well beyond 1,000 words. In general, Cassiodorus observed a tendency to "bookend" by placing letters notable for the prominence of the recipient at the beginning and end of each book. Thus, books often commence and conclude with diplomatic letters to emperors or western kings, letters to the Senate or appointments of illustrious men to high honors.

Within each letter, Cassiodorus observed a particular regularity which generally conforms to the administrative style of the day. Most letters commence with a proemium that introduces the subject matter in a highly abstract form, often in terms of an ethical or legal principle, followed immediately by disclosure of the particular circumstance attracting the court's attention (for example, a complaint or report having reached the king), and then a decision for, or command to, the recipient of the letter (the *sententia*). Not infrequently, letters conclude with *exempla* or moralizing intended to further elaborate on the court's decision. Topics range from letters of appointment to honorary offices at Rome to clerical positions at the palatine *scrinium* of Ravenna; letters to the eastern Empire or other western states concerning conflicts and alliances; administrative letters concerned with taxes, the allocation of resources to the military and the maintenance of urban infrastructure; legal decisions concerning civil disputes and criminal cases; and formal edicts addressed to urban or provincial populations. Although most letters maintain consistency with respect to the formal structure of administrative letter writing, the level of detail within individual letters varies widely. Some letters, such as 5.39, which concerns fiscal arrangements in Spain, offer the kind of dense detail expected of a formal edict. Others, such as 3.35 to Romulus (perhaps the same Romulus Augustulus retired from the imperial throne in 476), offer only a few lines vaguely confirming the undisclosed decision of a magistrate. Still other letters were clearly intended to be literary works in their own right. A handful of letters in each book unfold lengthy disquisitions on encyclopedic topics (geography, nature, history, the arts, and the sciences) to an extent that, while providing fascinating insights into the intellectual culture of the sixth century, actually obscures the purpose of the letter.

Thus the formal and thematic structure of the *Variae* is quite complex, to which must be added the presence of two fairly elaborate prefaces, which Cassiodorus included at the beginning of Books 1 and 11. These prefaces are themselves sophisticated literary compositions. The first preface explains how Cassiodorus accepted the task of compiling the *Variae* at the request of colleagues, "so that the coming generation might esteem both the disinterested deeds of a clear conscience and the burden of my duties, which I had endured for the sake of common advantage."[21] The preface then elaborates the exchange between Cassiodorus and his interlocutors. Cassiodorus had declined his colleagues' request initially because the daily circumstances of public service had not allowed him to exercise the kind of style that would commend his reputation. His colleagues protested, citing the trust that Gothic kings had placed in him, the prestige of his office as Praetorian Prefect, and the enhanced value of letters written under genuine, as opposed to rehearsed, circumstances, "it will happen that those who are situated in more tranquil circumstances will more happily obtain the habit that you practiced while tossed about amid the dangers of various altercations."[22] Additionally, the preface claims that these colleagues reasoned Cassiodorus's letters would preserve a record of the probity with which he and those appointed by him served Gothic kings and, furthermore, that he should not fear censure from an audience that so approved his history of the Goths.[23] In response, Cassiodorus yielded out of affection for his associates, but refused others to model their future efforts on his own hurried writing. Hence, the preface explains that his twelve books represented a more polished version, entitled *Variae* as a token for the variety of materials contained within the collection.[24] The first preface ends with a discussion of the ancient precepts of literary style and their relation, in general terms, to the topics discussed in the collection.

The second preface, introducing Books 11 and 12, opens with the curious observation that a preface often allows an author to anticipate the objections of an audience.[25] Cassiodorus then continues the main theme of the first preface: the respective censure or approval that his style of writing might secure with different audiences. Cassiodorus notes that readers accustomed to more leisurely circumstances (*otiosi*) would be likely to reject his effort, while he anticipated understanding and a favorable reaction from those who were similarly occupied in public service (*occupati*).[26] The preface also alludes to how concern of censure had led Cassiodorus to represent "fewer things than done," but that in reporting what he had, he followed the advice of a trusted friend, Felix, whose discernment in such matters was proven by good character, knowledge of the law and refinement in style. It was at Felix's behest that Cassiodorus included the final two books by which his own voice in state service should be known.[27] The second preface ends on a note similar to the first, with a discussion of precepts of style, this time related to Cicero's recommendation concerning the relationship between reading and

---

21. *Var., praefatio* 1.1.
22. *Var., praefatio* 1.8.
23. *Var., praefatio* 1.8–11.
24. *Var., praefatio* 1.12–14.
25. *Var., praefatio* 11.1.
26. *Var., praefatio* 11.1–3.
27. *Var., praefatio* 11.4–5.

good composition. Both prefaces end with Cassiodorus excusing himself for having written at unseemly length and by inviting the readers to judge the collection on its own merits.[28]

In addition to their relative novelty among epistolary collections, the two prefaces are remarkable in terms of how they provide Cassiodorus with his own voice. In a collection where the majority of letters have been addressed in the names of various Gothic rulers, the prefaces have an important role in signaling to the audience that Cassiodorus's authorship went beyond merely acting as a collector and compiler of state documents. The topic of literary style addressed in both prefaces was particularly suited to anchoring Cassiodorus's authorship of the letters. Treatments of rhetoric had for centuries viewed style as an index of interior character. As Cassiodorus's interlocutors in the first preface reminded him, "it is scarcely possible that speech is found inconsistent with character," and, more pointedly, the letters contained "the image of your mind."[29] Similarly, the preface to Book 11 drew explicit attention to the authorship of letters that Cassiodorus wrote in his own capacity as *Praefectus Praetorio*, "so that I, who have acted as the royal spokesman in ten books, should not be considered unknown for my own role."[30] It is also noteworthy that the two prefaces mirror each other in both function and themes, despite the fact that they introduce letters written under the cover of different names. Both prefaces express concern about the style of writing, the collection's reception by different audiences, the manner in which the collection represents the moral integrity of persons involved in the Gothic government, and the extent that potential repudiation shaped Cassiodorus's presentation of the letters. Literary presentation and historical reality are carefully balanced in these prefaces, as befits a collection the purpose of which was to portray a particular ethical virtue as the active agency in government. As Cassiodorus noted, it was his interest to tincture the merits of those in state service "in some measure with the color of history."[31] Interestingly, this statement may reflect Cassiodorus's understanding of the function of epistolary collections. In his *Chronica*, written in 519, Cassiodorus referred to the epistolary exemplar, Pliny the Younger, as *orator et historicus*, whose talent was visible in the many works that had survived.[32] For Cassiodorus, letter collections had the moral imperative of classical historiography and, like classical historiography, were just as subject to rhetorical fashioning.

Some sense of that rhetorical fashioning may be visible in the arrangement of books in the *Variae*. In a collection intended to rehabilitate the reputations of the

28. *Var., praefatio* 1.18 and *praefatio* 11.9.
29. *Var., praefatio* 1.10.
30. *Var., praefatio* 11.6.
31. *Var., praefatio* 1.9.
32. *Chronica* 756.

palatine elite who served the Amals, Cassiodorus's own place in the collection, even when elusive, is purposeful. The two books of *formulae* (Books 6–7) separate the first five books written in the name of Theoderic (under whom Cassiodorus served as both *Quaestor* and *Magister Officiorum*) from those written in the name of Athalaric, whose accession occurred while Cassiodorus was still *Magister Officiorum*. Although Theodor Mommsen and others have attempted to differentiate letters of Cassiodorus's quaestorship from those written as *Magister Officiorum* under Theoderic, Cassiodorus nowhere signaled such a transition. In effect, the *Variae* have subjected the appointment that Cassiodorus received as a consequence of Boethius's execution to complete erasure. Even in letters for Athalaric which commence Book 8, where an informed reader may assume that Cassiodorus acted as *Magister,* the fact of his service in this office is undetectable. Mention of Cassiodorus as *Magister* appears only in the last letters written for Athalaric (*Variae* 9.24 and 9.25), which announce Cassiodorus's appointment as Praetorian Prefect. In effect, this completely disassociates the end of Theoderic's reign and the beginning of Athalaric's from Boethius's trial. Positioning the announcement of Cassiodorus's prefecture as the last letters attributed to Athalaric also has rhetorical purpose. Cassiodorus would have served as *Praefectus Praetorio* for more than a year before Athalaric's death, but the positioning of *Variae* 9.24 and 9.25 as the last letters attributed to Athalaric clearly signals Books 10–12 as representing the period of Cassiodorus's prefecture. It is in Book 11 that the reader first finds letters that Cassiodorus wrote in his own name announcing his elevation as *Praefectus Praetorio* (*Variae* 11.1–3). In the first (11.1) to the Senate at Rome, Cassiodorus attributed his elevation to the good governance and wisdom of both Athalaric and Amalasuntha, with an extended eulogy of Amalasuntha as the embodiment of all virtues possessed by previous Amal rulers.[33] Similarly, the first letter announcing his prefecture in the name of Athalaric drew attention to Cassiodorus's tutelage under Theoderic, suggesting that Cassiodorus's character as a servant of the state derived from an unbroken chain of Amal governmental virtue.[34] Book 10, the intervening space between Cassiodorus's appointment to the praetorian prefecture (*Variae* 9.24–25) and his acceptance of the office (*Variae* 11.1–3), offers a subtle portrayal of the rupture with that record of governmental virtue. The letters of Book 10 represent the reigns of Theodahad and Witigis as wholly inferior affairs. The report of Books 11 and 12, however, where Cassiodorus writes in his own name, represents continuity with the previous reigns of Theoderic, Amalasuntha, and Athalaric and suggests that Cassiodorus and his colleagues were capable of governing Italy irrespective of failed kingship under Theodahad and Witigis. The manufacture of this rupture through the placement of letters suggests that the gov-

33. *Var.* 11.1.
34. *Var.* 9.24.3–8.

ernmental virtue of the bureaucratic elite was something received from exemplary tutors and the extent of failed government represented in Book 10 rested on the shoulders of Theodahad and Witigis.

Cassiodorus's hand in the arrangement of the collection is also apparent at the level of individual pairs of letters. In many ways, the *Variae* is a study in contrasts and comparisons. In some cases, the themes linking otherwise unrelated correspondence are subtle, and in other cases, quite deliberate. For example, in Book 3, Cassiodorus pairs two letters which deliver sentences for unrelated violent crimes, but with very different results intended to portray the ability of the court to discern what the justice of the day required in different circumstances: on the one hand, *Variae* 3.46 reduces a sentence of exile for the rape of a young woman, and on the other hand *Variae* 3.47 imposes permanent exile in a case of murder. In Book 4, Cassiodorus presents a series of letters, with one (*Var.* 4.29) addressed to the *Praefectus Urbis* at Rome who embezzled instead of built, while the following letter praises a dutiful senator for undertaking the patronage of a new building project, and the next sought to remind an otherwise forgetful bishop of his promise to complete an aqueduct. At times, thematic links may be explained in terms of Cassiodorus's own reading at a given moment. For example, in Book 5, the opening diplomatic pieces (*Var.* 5.1–2) to completely different nations appeal to familiarity with Tacitus on the part of the collection's readers. But at other times, it is clear that Cassiodorus intended for his audience to locate good and bad *exempla* through the comparison of letters. Thus, in Book 2, two elaborate letters explore the theme of filial devotion, with one (*Var.* 2.14) ordering a trial for a possible parricide, and the other (*Var.* 2.15) elevating a son to office as a legacy of his father's support for the state.

The art of depiction in the *Variae* is also present in the encyclopedic knowledge that forms a major theme throughout the collection. Cassiodorus positioned letters representing aspects of *enkyklios paideia* (encyclopedic learning) in each book of the collection: histories of different disciplines of the liberal studies, explanations of geography and natural history, and digressions into the importance of various arts and sciences. Although not present in every letter, the theme is present enough to draw attention to important persons (such as Boethius and Symmachus) and to invite comparisons (such as between Theoderic and Anastasius or Theodahad and Theoderic). In as much as *enkyklios paideia* drew from a coherent intellectual tradition that capitalized upon a discursive presentation of knowledge, Cassiodorus's strategy of selectively scattering encyclopedic content throughout the collection conformed to an established mode for representing universal knowledge. Importantly, representations of *enkyklios paideia* in the wider tradition of the literature were often tied to moral, and therefore ideological, representations of the world. The extent that the *Variae* participate in this literary tradition is tied to the ideological presentation of the government of Italy as "enlightened" and informed by universal ethics. In the case of each digression, the unfolding of a topic from the encyclopedic tradition in a particular letter relates to the justification of the government's actions or decision in a particular case. Particularly prominent are the themes of *natura* and *antiquitas* that Cassiodorus wove into the various encyclopedic discussions and digressions, creating a network of legal, governmental, and philosophical ideals based on the legitimating force of tradition. Thus, Cassiodorus paints landscapes of local geographies in order to explain the fiscal capacities of particular regions;[35] the flocking habit of birds sets the example for civil order in Italian towns, the constancy of sea snails demands the regular production of the dye used to produce imperial purple, and the regularity of the Nile provides for the mirrored regularity of court documents produced on papyrus;[36] the perfection of mathematics demands precision in the payment of soldiers, and the long history of land surveying anticipates the preservation of property rights.[37] Many of these excursuses are performances of *reverentia antiquitatis,* in which the letter not only discusses the antiquity of a topic, but refers to the ancient authorities for that topic.[38]

The sheer variety of the collection allowed Cassiodorus to weave the quotidian concerns and functions of the state together with sometimes passing, at other times profound meditations on the virtues, ethics, the balance of nature and the inheritance of the past. The philosophical basis of this matrix of concepts comes into high relief especially in the connection between the *Variae* and the *De anima.* The second preface to the *Variae* explains how Cassiodorus's colleagues again compelled him to embark upon another project after completing the collection of letters.[39] This new project (the *De anima*) would speculate on the substance and the capacities of the human soul, with particular interest in the soul as that instrument by which Cassiodorus had been able to declaim so much in the *Variae.*[40] The introduction of the *De anima* reiterates the completion of the *Variae* and makes it clear that the topics apprehended by the soul which so interested Cassiodorus's interlocutors were the same as those found in the digressions of the letter collection—that is, the encyclopedic topics, particularly natural history, which the *Variae* mobilized so prominently to represent a government based on the observance of natural law. According to the *De anima,* only a soul of good moral conscience was capable of the kind of perspicacity that would perceive the secrets of nature and allow an individual to lead a truly ethical life.[41] Thus, the *De anima*

---

35. *Var.* 4.50, 11.14, 11.39, 12.4, 12.12, 12.14, 12.15, 12.22.

36. *Var.* 1.2 (snails), 8.31 and 9.2 (birds), 11.38 (Nile).

37. *Var.* 1.10 (mathematics), 3.52 (land surveying).

38. For references to *scriptores antiquissimi, Var.* 1.27, 1.39, 1.45, 2.22, 3.47, 3.53, 4.30, 5.2, 5.4, 5.17, 5.21, 5.34, 5.42, 6.3, 6.5, 7.5, 7.15, 7.18, 7.46, 8.12, 8.13, 8.20, 12.5, 12.28.

39. *Var., praefatio* 11.7.

40. *Var., praefatio* 11.7.

41. *De anima* 1.

reinforces the notion that Cassiodorus and his colleagues had acted with moral probity in supporting the Amal government of Italy.

The literary nature of the *Variae* runs much deeper than the mere adoption of a particular style of exposition. A number of studies have located the *Variae* within a tradition for the late-antique administrative style, at least at the level of orthography, syntax, and epistolary structure. Nonetheless, the *Variae* also represent something entirely novel in late-antique writing. Cassiodorus combined the concept of an epistolary collection with the administrative style of the late-antique chancery and the longer tradition for encyclopedic exposition. The differences of the *Variae* from other epistolary collections is apparent enough: two elaborate prefaces, supposedly official documents as opposed to personal letters, the first body of *formulae* in antiquity and the appendage of a philosophical treatise on the soul which acts as an hermeneutic for material embedded in the letters. Similarly, the encyclopedic interest present in the *Variae*, although something that is visible to less-pronounced degrees in other epistolary collections, is comparatively absent from a tradition for administrative writing. Some pretense to enlightened learning may be found in the *Novellae* that follow the *Theodosian Code* and in Justinian's *Novellae*, but nothing to the scale of topical treatments found in the *Variae* such as would warrant calling encyclopedism a habit of administrative writing. Far from it, the *Theodosian Code* and various successor codes produced in the West clearly privilege a more restrained and direct style of exposition. If the *Edict of Theoderic*, the *Collectio Avellana*, and the *Epistolae Austrasicae* represent the administrative style of the day, then the idiosyncratic features of the *Variae* represent something unique to Cassiodorus's authorial aims.

NACHLEBEN

Cassiodorus had a habit of leaving paper trails for his readers. In the first preface to the *Variae*, he acknowledged having previously written panegyrics and a history of the Goths (the *Variae* do not mention his *Chronica*).[42] The *De anima* opens by looking back to the completion of the *Variae*, while the *Expositio Psalmorum* discusses the *De anima* as the thirteenth book of the *Variae*.[43] The *De anima*, the *Expositio Psalmorum*, and the *Institutiones* all express a particular gratitude for having finally left behind the turbulence of public life at Ravenna.[44] The *Ordo generis Cassiodororum*, the provenance and purpose of which remain unresolved, notes the works associated, in particular, with Cassiodorus's public life—the panegyric to Theoderic, the history of the Goths and the *Variae*. Afterward, the *Variae*

---

42. *Var., praefatio* 1.11.
43. *De anima* 1; *Expositio Psalmorum* 145.2.
44. *De anima* 2; *Expositio Psalmorum, praefatio* 1; *Institutiones, praefatio* 1.

seem to lose their historical currency. The *De orthographia* that Cassiodorus composed at the end of his life mentions only the six previous works that, beginning
with his *Expositio,* expressed more direct theological interests. Interestingly, the
De anima did not number among these later religious works, possibly because of
its relationship to the politically charged purpose of the *Variae.* Among the various
bibliographical sources of the early and later Middle Ages (for example, the *Ety-
mologiae* of Isidore of Seville and the many Latin florilegia in the West; the *Bibli-
otheca* of Photius and the *Suda,* in the East), there is not so much as a whisper of
the *Variae.* Even the various formularies which became so popular to early-
medieval administrative culture show no direct evidence of familiarity with the
Variae. It seems Cassiodorus's epistolary collection was a text specific to a particular historical moment and purpose.

The robust manuscript tradition for the *Variae,* at first glance, seems to offer
evidence to the contrary. Theodor Mommsen examined one hundred and eleven
manuscripts in producing his edition for the *Monumenta Germaniae Historica* and
Åke Fridh could add a previously unknown manuscript to Mommsen's list.[45] Most
of these manuscripts are still extant and their earliest dispersion pattern (primarily
Italy, France, Germany) suggests maintained interest in the content of the *Variae*
in regions having contact with Carolingian intellectual circles. The earliest manuscript dates (probably) from the late tenth century, although a rash of copying
produced a copious number of manuscripts, as is the case with many medieval
sources, in the twelfth century. The two best copies (the *Codex Leidensis Vulcana-
nus* 46 and the *Codex Bruxellensis* 10018–10019) both date to the twelfth century. It
is, of course, logical to assume that the *Variae* had continued to be copied steadily
in scriptoria since the sixth century. But the purposes for copying may have little
to do with contemporary early-medieval administrative needs. Some manuscripts
(such as Mommsen's *classis tertia*) show a particular interest in the *formulae* of
Books 6 and 7, indicating interest in their use as administrative exemplars. The
majority of manuscripts, however, have deliberately excised the *formulae,* possibly
owing to the lack of utility of late-Roman offices in medieval administrative con-
texts, but also possibly owing to their lack of utility in supplying actual history for
the end of the western Roman Empire.

Literary audiences of the late-sixth through twelfth centuries remembered,
recorded, and reimagined the final stages of the Roman Empire in Italy via the
lively transmission of texts from late antiquity. The codicology of many early-
medieval manuscripts suggests that these later audiences excavated knowledge of
the fifth and sixth centuries from late-antique literary sources and reconfigured
that knowledge in new narrative structures. Manuscript transmission was a selective process in which writers reconstructed "authoritative" versions of the past for

---

45. Mommsen, *Auctores antiquissimi,* xxxix–cx.

a contemporary readership. At times, such as frequently occurred with the *Variae,* writers selectively excerpted only portions of original texts for transmission based on criteria specific to the narrative function of the manuscript. At other times, writers copied whole texts (as also occurred with the *Variae*), but included them within a manuscript in highly individualistic arrangements with other texts (the codicological context) that communicated, again, a particular narrative when combined with other late-antique texts. The number and diversity of manuscripts containing the *Variae* present an unexplored opportunity to study how later audiences fashioned narratives for earlier centuries through the creation and transmission of manuscripts. Some manuscripts certainly suggest that select dossiers of letters from the *Variae* were included in a given manuscript with other works which, when read as a whole, communicated a particular programmatic purpose. For example, the *Vulcanus* 46 manuscript combines the *Gesta* of Theoderic with Books 1–7 of the *Variae* and a later *Didascalion* that treats secular and spiritual learning. Other manuscripts from Leiden combine select books of the *Variae* with the *Collectanea rerum memorabilium* of Iulius Solinus (*BP Latina* 124) or the letters of later Frankish kings (*BP Latina* 93). Manuscripts housed at the Vatican likewise demonstrate a range of readership tastes including the combination of select portions of the *Variae* with excerpts from the *De moralibus* of Gregory the Great (*Palatinus* 272) or the exegesis of anonymous verse (*Palatinus* 273). Although the *Variae,* as Cassiodorus constructed the text, seem to have lost their relevancy after the Gothic War, it is clear that later audiences were using the *Variae* to construct their own historical narratives and meaning.

THE *VARIAE* IN TRANSLATION

The *Variae* are crucial to understanding Ostrogothic Italy and its distinctiveness from other regions of the sixth-century Mediterranean; nonetheless, previous English translations of the *Variae* have offered limited utility. The first English translation, by Thomas Hodgkin (*Letters of Cassiodorus,* 1886), was doubtlessly a courageous work. Mommsen had as yet not published the authoritative collation of manuscripts that would become the *MGH* edition of the *Variae* (*Auctores antiquissimi,* vol. 12) in 1896, and Hodgkin's translation provided only a paraphrase of the complete collection that failed to reproduce the style of the *Variae* and even omitted much material Hodgkin deemed unnecessary to a student of sixth-century Italy. By contrast, the more recent translation by SJB Barnish, for the Translated Texts for Historians series (*Cassiodorus: Variae,* 1992), offered a masterful rendering of the spirit and letter of Cassiodorus's collection, but with the limitation of being a partial translation that included only 110 letters. The choice to translate a selection of the *Variae* naturally prevents the student of the period from reading as Cassiodorus intended, the entire collection from start to finish. A selection negates many of the purposeful ligatures between individual letters of the collection and renders understanding the overall structure of the collection impossible for the casual reader unable to undertake a full reading of Cassiodor-us's Latin. Similarly, although many of the letters appearing in Barnish's translation are duly famous (e.g., Theoderic's letters to Boethius), much that is important to legal, religious, economic, literary, and cultural historians did not find a place in his version. More recently, the massive collaborative project under the direction of Andrea Giardina (*Cassiodoro Varie*, 5 vols., 2015–17), provides scholars with the first complete translation of the text with full commentary. Here, however, the translation of the text into Italian, and the decision to provide both the full Latin and a commentary for individual letters (expanding the work to five volumes) naturally limits the ease with which Anglophone scholarship may consult the *Variae* in academic libraries outside of Italy. The present volume offers the first complete translation of the *Variae* into English in a single volume.

Cassiodorus's style is both literary and bureaucratic. It is arguable that his was a style totally unto itself—partly a construct of learned reading meant to genuflect to a kind of received classicism, partly a construct of a world of legal and administrative language that had to be rendered understandable to the wider intended audience of the collection. Cassiodorus, thus, wrote within two distinctive received traditions. Late-antique bureaucratic style, on the one hand, conveyed consistency of meaning by preserving mainly legal habits of expression. By contrast, literary correspondence was often purposefully ambivalent in order to invite the reader's exploration of a range of interpretations. As an author, Cassiodorus had at his disposal exemplars of Latin that ranged, on the literary side, from the classical golden age of Cicero to the late silver Latin of Tacitus; and on the legal side, from third-century jurists to Theodosian and Justinianic *Novellae* of the fifth century and sixth centuries. And while Cassiodorus does classicize by drawing from authors that were "ancient" by his day, he was also an author embedded in the contemporary professionalized use of Latin by sixth-century civil servants. Thus, translating Cassiodorus's late-classical Latin into English requires sensitivity to several registers of meaning (classical literary and sixth-century bureaucratic). Although his Latin may appear "idiosyncratic," it is important to note that, for Cassiodorus, all Latin usages, whether ancient or contemporary, probably collapsed into the great fecundity of the *lingua Latina* that he had inherited and that he continued to modify. In terms of his own contribution to the administrative writing represented in the *Variae,* one may make simple note of the incidences in which Alexander Souter's, *A Glossary of Later Latin to 600 A.D.*, relies exclusively on examples from the *Variae*, an indication of the extent to which the text represents a unique development in late-classical Latin. Even where Cassiodorus has a propensity for contemporary usage of vocabularies, there are notable cases where he is inclined to the classical sense, such as *debitor* as "one obliged to an oath" (as opposed to the postclassical sense of "sinner") and *pietas* as "familial obligation" (as opposed to the later "piety"). Additionally, Cassiodorus's Latin achieves what may be thought of as syntactical "irregularities" by the inclusion of rhythmic *clausulae,* or phrases ending with intended cadence, the likes of which were not standard composition in late-antique administrative writing.

The course followed in the present translation renders Cassiodorus's text word for word, as closely as possible, according to the meaning best suited to a given script of Latin. In most cases, care has been taken to preserve Cassiodorus's sometimes baroque syntactical structures in order to convey something of the voice and assumed grandeur of administrative writing for the period. At the same time, certain verbal constructions, such as Cassiodorus's penchant for the future perfect and perfect infinitive, have been substituted with more readily legible English usage. Conversely, the present translation eschews the translation of specific terms where an English equivalent would be unsatisfactory. For example, terms such as *imperator, princeps, comitatus, regnum,* and *imperium* have only vague equivalents in English, for which reason these terms have been given in Latin. Similarly, Cassiodorus at times uses the demonstratives *ille* or *illa* to substitute for specific information, such as the names of envoys who would have delivered a letter, or for the names of unspecified properties or indiction years. The current translation reproduces these "place holders" in the original Latin. The titles of offices and ranks have also been left in Latin in order to allow scholars of social and administrative histories to disambiguate between terms that would otherwise be vague in English.

Dates assigned to individual letters are often given as a range of years that was assigned on the basis of the reign of the ruler named as the originator of a letter, the prosopographical information known from external sources about the recipient or mentioned individuals, rarely the mention of specific events, and more precisely, when available, the mention of indiction (tax cycle) years. Indictions occurred in a repeating fifteen-year cycle, with a given indiction year commencing on September 1 and ending on August 31, thus dividing the common era year. Where indiction years are mentioned, it must often be assumed that the letter concerns actions to be taken in preparation for the mentioned indiction year, usually in the weeks or even months immediately preceding the commencement of an indiction year.

The text of the *Variae* is translated from the edition produced by Theodor Mommsen for the *Auctores antiquissimi* series of the MGH in 1894. This has proven to be the most durable and frequently consulted Latin edition of the text. Aka Fridh's edition for the *Corpus Christianorum Series Latina* (1973) offers several lexical emendations that have been consulted throughout the translation, but I have preferred Mommsen's text for the simple reason that scholars and students reading the translation will find it easier to consult the Latin in Mommsen's edition. Additionally, Mommsen's edition was reprinted by MGH in 1980 and is generally more available in academic libraries than Fridh's edition.

CHRONOLOGY OF KEY EVENTS

425–55	Reign of Valentinian III as emperor in the west
	Cassiodorus's grandfather appointed *notarius et tribunus;* leads embassy to Attila
453	Death of Attila
454	Defeat of Hunnic confederation at Nedao
	Theoderic born in Pannonia
473	Accession of Theoderic as king of federated Goths in Pannonia
476	Deposition of Romulus Augustus as western emperor
	Odoacer becomes king in Italy
	Vandals cede Sicily to Odoacer
	Cassiodorus's father holds office as *Comes Sacrarum Largitionum* until 490
481	Clovis becomes king of the Salian Franks
484	Theoderic appointed consul, patrician, and *magister militum* in east by Emperor Zeno
	Beginning of the "Acacian" schism between churches of Rome and Constantinople
485	Possible year of Cassiodorus's birth
487–88	Odoacer campaigns against the Rugians along Danube
489	Theoderic enters Italy with the Goths
491	Accession of Anastasius as eastern emperor following the death of Zeno
493	Surrender of Ravenna and death of Odoacer
	Theoderic becomes king of Goths and *Princeps* in Italy
	Theoderic marries sister (Audofleda) of Frankish king Clovis
496	Consolidation of northern Gaul under Clovis
498	Contested papal election between Symmachus and Laurentius
500	Theoderic secures peace with Vandals by marriage of his sister Amalafrida to Thrasamund
	Adventus of Theoderic at Rome
	Possible date of Cassiodorus's panegyric to Theoderic
503	Cassiodorus's father holds office as *Praefectus Praetorio* until 507
	Cassiodorus serves his father as *consiliarius* sometime between 503–7

	Unknown volcanic eruption disrupts agriculture in Italy and much of the Mediterranean
536	Theodahad sends Pope Agapetus as envoy to Constantinople
	Belisarius captures Naples
	Theodahad assassinated and accession of Witigis as King of Goths in Italy
	Witigis marries Matasuntha (daughter of Amalasuntha) for which Cassiodorus performs a panegyric
	Belisarius enters Rome
537	Witigis lays siege to Rome for a full year until March of 538
	Latest datable letter in the *Variae*
540	Ravenna captured by Belisarius and Gothic court sent to Constantinople
	Cassiodorus in Constantinople
	Cassiodorus composes the *De anima* and *Expositio Psalmorum* sometime after 540
541	Accession of Gothic King Totila extends war in Italy
	Arrival of the "Justinianic" plague in the Mediterranean
552	Approximate date for Cassiodorus's composition of *Complexiones in Epistolas Apostolorum* and *Historia tripartita*
554	Justinian's "Pragmatic Sanction" signals the end of the Gothic War in Italy
	Cassiodorus's retirement at Vivarium in Calabria likely commences and as does his composition of the *Institutiones*
568	Invasion of Italy by Lombards
578	Cassiodorus composes *De orthographia* in his ninety-third year
580	Probable death of Cassiodorus at ninety-five

INDICTIONAL YEARS RELATIVE TO CASSIODORUS'S TENURE IN PUBLIC OFFICES

Quaestor (c. 507–11)

15th Indiction	September 1, 506–August 31, 507
1st Indiction	507–8
2nd Indiction	508–9
3rd Indiction	509–10
4th Indiction	510–11
5th Indiction	511–12

Magister Officiorum (c. 523–28)

1st Indiction	September 1, 522–August 31, 523
2nd Indiction	523–24
3rd Indiction	524–25
4th Indiction	525–26
5th Indiction	526–27
6th Indiction	527–28
7th Indiction	528–29

Praefectus Praetorio (c. 533–40)

11th Indiction	September 1, 532–August 31, 533
12th Indiction	533–34
13th Indiction	534–35
14th Indiction	535–36
15th Indiction	536–37
1st Indiction	537–38
2nd Indiction	538–39
3rd Indiction	539–40
4th Indiction	540–41

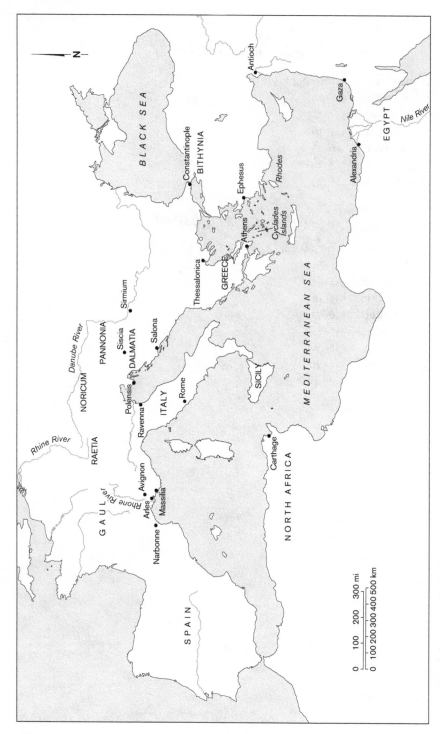

MAP 1. The sixth-century Mediterranean.

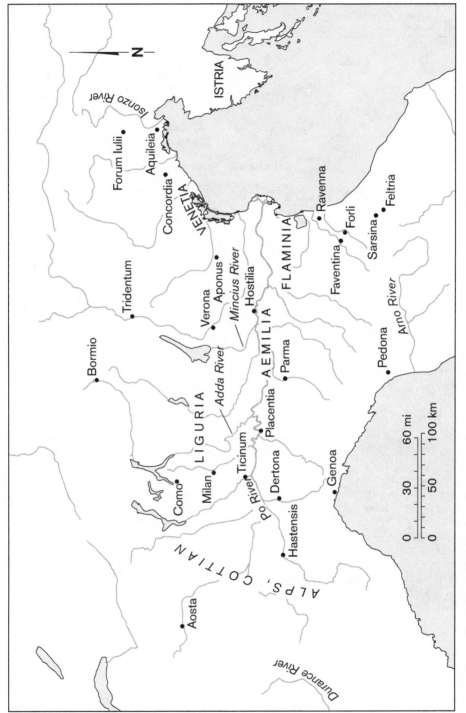

MAP 2. The northern region of Ostrogothic Italy.

MAP 3. The southern region of Ostrogothic Italy.

The *Variae*

Book 1

PREFACE (C. 538–54)

Cassiodorus's preface to the *Variae* in Book 1 is unique in ancient and late-antique epistolary collections. The topics treated, particularly concerning rhetoric and public life, parallel his preface at the beginning of Book 11.[1] Written as Cassiodorus's recollection of a discussion held with certain learned individuals (*diserti*), the preface provides a glimpse of his former service to the Gothic Amals, in addition to an explanation for his decision to compile the *Variae* in spite of the potential censure of his readers. The very fact that Cassiodorus would explain his collection to an audience speaks to some of its novelties.

Preface to the Variae

1. Although I have garnered the favor of the learned, either owing to shared conversation or to genuine kindness, but certainly not owing to any real merit, they nonetheless prevailed upon me to gather into one collection these words of mine which I had often supplied in offices for explicating the nature of public affairs, so that the coming generation might esteem both the disinterested deeds of a clear conscience and the burden of my duties, which I had endured for the sake of common advantage. **2.** I said that their esteem would in fact be injurious to me, since that manner deemed acceptable on behalf of the entreaties of petitioners afterward may seem

---

1. By comparison, for example, Pliny the Younger and Sidonius Apollinaris introduced their collections with letters to dedicatees, but not formal prefaces.

foolish to readers. I added that they ought to reflect upon the words of Flaccus,[2] who advises what danger hasty speech might incur. **3.** You see that everyone expects promptness in responding, and do you believe I would publish something that must be regretted? Speech that is either unaccompanied by meaning chosen through deliberation or that is unfolded with the least appropriate selection of words is always uncouth. The ability to speak is granted to all: only he is distinguished who discerns unlearned speech. **4.** Nine years are allowed to authors for writing;[3] for me, not even a span of hours is allowed. As soon as I have begun, the writing is harried by outcries and driven by excessive haste, no undertaking is carried out with care. One man taxes me with the frequency of his petty interruptions, another fetters me with the load of his miseries, others circle round with the raving contention of their disputes. **5.** Amid all this, why do you demand the eloquence of formal composition, where I am hardly able to hold a full conversation? Impracticable cares fill even my nights, lest cities lack their food supply, which the people demand above all else, favoring their bellies, not their ears.[4] Hence it is that I am forced by resolve to go through every province and constantly investigate my commands, because it is not enough to command civil servants to perform their duties, unless the constant presence of the magistrate should seem to demand it. I beg you not to show your esteem for me by wishing for such an injurious undertaking. An exhortation that holds more peril than appeal ought to be declined. **6.** But instead these colleagues were wearying me with arguments such as: "Everyone knows that you hold the rank of *Praefectus Praetorio*, for whom the preoccupations of public office always attend as though servants. For indeed, from this office are required military expenses; from it, the food supply of the people is demanded without consideration for the season; to which is added the onus of judging legal cases, itself alone a burdensome duty; for which reason the very laws seem to impose an immense burden, since almost every case prefers to affix the distinction of a high office to the judgment. For what leisure are you able to steal away from public duties, when whatever is required for the utility of the common good combines in one breast? **7.** It is added, moreover, that as *Quaestor*, demands repeated with oppressive frequency often deprive time for leisure, and the *Principes* seem to set upon you those affairs from other offices which their own magistrates are unable to unravel, as though you were wrestling with an ordinary burden. However, you accomplish these things, not by selling your services, but in the example of your own father, you accept from hopeful petitioners only toil. Thus, by offering everything to petitioners freely, you traffic everything with the gift of moderation. **8.** And even the illustrious official correspondence of kings is known to occupy you for the

---

2. Horace.
3. Thus the dictum of Horace, *Ars poetica* 385–90, "nonumque prematur in annum."
4. A reference to the oral and auditory nature of literary study in this period.

greater part of the day on behalf of the public good, so that you are known to sustain by continuous labor what would be distasteful to expect from those inclined to leisure. But this is more likely to ensure for you a vote of praise, if under such disparate circumstances you could succeed in producing something worth reading. Then will your work be capable of educating, without offense and by means of studied eloquence, those unlearned men who must be prepared for public office, and it will happen that those who are situated in more tranquil circumstances will more happily obtain the habit that you practiced while tossed about amid the dangers of various altercations. **9.** Consequently, because you are unable to conceal in good faith such kindnesses as you have enjoyed from kings, you would prefer, in vain rather, that they should be attributed to indulgent haste, if you permit them to be ignored. We entreat you not to allow that those who deserved to receive illustrious honors by your endorsement should be recalled to the obscurity of silence. Indeed, you have undertaken to render them with true praise and to tincture them in some measure with the color of history. If you would pass on to the following generation a record of those who must be honored, after the custom of our ancestors, you will have fittingly preserved those perishing from oblivion. **10.** Furthermore, you set straight perverse practices with the authority of a king, you shatter the impudence of the transgressor, and you restore respect for the law. And for how long do you hesitate to publish what you rightly deem suited to such use? Moreover, you conceal, I would say, the image of your mind, where each age to come would be able to admire you. Indeed, it often happens that the father begets a son different from himself, while it is scarcely possible that speech is found inconsistent with character. Therefore such an offspring is plainly a more reliable witness, for what is born from the secret of a man's breast is considered a more truthful representation of its source. **11.** You have also recited orations to kings and queens, frequently to the applause of all; you have composed a history of the Goths in twelve books, selecting from the record of their prosperity.[5] Since the outcome of these pursuits was favorable for you, why do you hesitate to give this to the public also, you who are already known to be successful in reciting less mature works?" **12.** I admit that I am defeated, to my own shame. I was unable to resist so much wise reasoning, when I saw myself reproved out of affection. Now forgive me, readers, and if there be some careless opinion, lay the blame more on those urging me, since my decision clearly depends upon those who failed to censure me. **13.** And therefore, what I was able to recover, being written by me in various public vocations as *Quaestor, Magister Officiorum,* and *Praefectus Praetorio,* I have compiled in an arrangement of twelve books, so that, although the attention of the reader is hastened along by the diversity of

---

5. Mommsen included fragments from two panegyrics in his edition of the *Variae;* the *Ordo generis Cassiodororum* includes *laudes* recited to Theoderic and a *Gothic History* among Cassiodorus's works.

subject matter, nevertheless, the mind is held more securely when it reaches the end.[6] **14.** But I have not been content to permit others to endure what I often experienced in bestowing offices; that is, speeches written hastily and without polish, which were demanded so suddenly that it seemed hardly possible to write. And thus, I have included *formulae* for all the official posts in the sixth and seventh books, so that however late I might take care for my own reputation, I may assist my successors in the near future. Thus what I have said concerning past offices applies to future ones, since I have described the suitability, not of the persons, but of the offices that they were deemed fit to hold. **15.** I have disclosed the title of the books accurately, with the name *Variae* as an indication of endeavor, a precursor for the contents, and a condensed name for the entire composition, since it was necessary for me to employ not one style of writing where I undertook to instruct a variety of people. For a topic is treated in one way for those glutted with much reading, in another way for those sustained by a moderate appetite, and in another way for those persuaded by a meager flavor of literature, such that they would avoid the kind of style that pleases learned men. **16.** Consequently, it is thus fitting to mention the admirable manner prescribed by the ancients, so that you would be able to satisfy the audience with desires already held. For not without reason did ancient wisdom determine three styles of discourse:[7] the humble, which seems to lumber, after the habit of common speech; the moderate, in which expression neither swells itself in greatness nor diminishes in poverty, but remains between both, enriched by a suitable loveliness but contained within its own bounds. The third manner is that which is elevated to the highest peak of oratory by carefully crafted sentiments. Clearly, as the diversity of audience determines the appropriate expression and, granted that it flows forth from one breast, it nonetheless emanates from diverse channels. No one obtains the distinction of eloquence, except one who is girded with these three styles and vigorously prepared for all manner of circumstances that may rise. **17.** Thus it happens that I am seen to speak at times in a manner for kings, at times in a manner before a council of magistrates, and at times before the common people, for some of whom it sufficed to pour forth words in haste, while for others it was permitted to employ language with forethought, so that what was composed in such a diversity would merit being called *Variae*.[8] Would that, even as I have deemed to take such usage from ancient precepts, thus would they transfer the same merits to the promised composition. **18.** Wherefore, I promise to render the humble style modestly and the mediocre style not brazenly. But the lofty style,

6. A vague expression urging his readers to form a final opinion only after reading the complete work.

7. Cassiodorus here genuflects to the three styles advocated by Cicero, to whom Cassiodorus returns when discussing matters of style again in the preface to Book 11.

8. This, of course, contradicts the earlier objection that he wrote without regard for style.

because it is reserved for elevated composition, I do not believe myself to have attained. But rather, since I am to be read, let indecorous presumptions abide in silence. For it would be inappropriate for me to conduct a discourse concerning myself, a discussion that I would better sustain according to your judgment.

LETTER 1.1 (C. 508)

Theoderic greets the eastern emperor Anastasius with a request for peace. Mention of previous hostilities, perhaps a reference to Amal annexation of Sirmium in Pannonia (504–5) and eastern reprisals along the Italian coast, provide a context for the elaboration of a political ideal envisioning two Roman republics, eastern and western, with Italy genuflecting to Constantinople. Theoderic's characterization of other former western Roman regions as "barbarian" kingdoms is also worthy of attention.

King Theoderic to Imperator Anastasius

1. It is fitting for us, most clement *Imperator,* to seek peace, we who are known to have no reason for wrath: any time someone is perceived to be ill-equipped for just things, that man is already considered at fault. Indeed, tranquility ought to be desired in every *regnum,* where the people profit and the weal of nations is preserved. For peace is the graceful mother of good arts: she increases resources, multiplying humanity in renewed generations, and she cultivates proper habits. Even one who is considered ignorant of such great matters knows at least to pursue peace. **2.** And therefore, most dutiful of *Principes,* it is becoming to your power and dignity that we ought to strive for harmony with you, the means by which we have thus far increased in love. For you are the most sublime dignity of every *regnum,* you the beneficent defender of the whole world, whom other rulers rightly admire, since they recognize something special to dwell in you. We especially know this, who by divine providence have learned in your republic by what manner we are able to govern Romans equitably.[9] **3.** Our government is an imitation of yours, the exemplary form of the only good *imperium* set on display: however much we follow you, so much do we surpass other nations. Often you have encouraged me to esteem the Senate, to embrace gladly the laws of *Principes,* so that I might unite all parts of Italy. In what way would you be able to separate from imperial peace one whom you have not allowed to disagree with your own habits? Additionally, there is affection for the city of Rome which must be respected, from which those people who have conjoined themselves in the solidarity of its name cannot be separated. **4.** Consequently, we have determined that *ille* and *ille* must

---

9. Theoderic was a political hostage at the court of Emperor Leo in Constantinople, subsequently elevated to imperial dignities by Emperor Zeno.

be appointed to your most sublime piety in the capacity of envoys, so that the integrity of peace, which is known to have been spoiled by causes now becoming evident, may endure thereafter firmly restored with grounds for dispute erased. For we do not believe you will suffer any discord to persist between both republics, which had always been proclaimed to be a single entity under ancient *Principes*. **5.** It is not only fitting that these republics be conjoined one to the other with easy affection, but also it is seemly to be supported with shared strength. Let there always be one will, one mind in the Roman *regnum*. And however we are able, may it attain your commendation. **6.** On which account, offering the dignity of a greeting, we ask with humble intention that you not suspend the ennobling affection of your good will, for which we ought to hope, even if it would not seem possible to grant to others. We have committed other matters to the bearers of this letter which must be brought to the attention of your piety by spoken word, as it could not be rendered more expansively in epistolary speech, nor would we be seen to have overlooked anything to our advantage.

LETTER 1.2 (C. 507–11)

A directive seeking to redress the delayed shipment of costly royal garments dyed with the *purpura* of harvested shellfish (specifically a kind of murex). The recipient is otherwise unknown, although his senatorial rank as *spectabilis* suggests a notable from Calabria holding a monopoly on shipments of royal vestments from workshops in Hydruntum (modern Otranto). Of interest is the elaborate natural history provided for *purpura* production and its relation to imperial authority, which frames a notable contrast to the deference given eastern authority in *Var.* 1.1.

King *Theoderic to Theon,* Vir Spectabilis

1. We have learned through the report of the *Comes* Stephanus that the production of royal vestments,[10] which we wanted to be completed with necessary haste, has been suspended instead by disrupted labor: for which, by detracting from recurring practice, you will become aware that neglect brings what instead must be avoided. For we believe that someone has caused this neglect, for either those milky fibers, having been steeped at least two or three times in the fleshy draughts, would glow in the lovely saturation, or the wool will not have absorbed the costly substance of the prized murex. **2.** For if the huntsman of the sea,[11] at Hydron, had stored the purple dye with careful consideration in the proper time, that harvest of Neptune, the begetter of an ever-purple bloom, the raiment of regal power, having been steeped in plenty of water, would have released a princely rain of fiery liquid.

---

10. Probably *Comes Sacrarum Largitionum*; cf. *Var.* 6.7.6.
11. A flowery phrase for professional divers (*perscrutator maris*).

The pigment abounds with exceeding pleasantness, a darkness blushing red, it distinguishes the one ruling with ensanguined blackness; it makes the master conspicuous and demonstrates this to humanity, lest it should be possible to mistake the *Princeps* on sight. **3.** It is amazing that this substance exudes a bloody matter made from its own death after such a long period of time, because it is accustomed to flow from wounds in living bodies. For, when the substance has been separated from the vital strength of its preferred sea for even six months, it fails to disturb perceptive noses, and naturally, lest noble blood should breath something repulsive. As soon as this substance adheres, I know not how it is able to be removed without destroying the garment. **4.** But if the quality of the shellfish is constant, if there is a vintage from its press, the blame will undoubtedly lie with the workers, from whom the supply has not arrived. However, when a skilled worker tinctures white strands of silk in those reddened fonts, it ought to have the most faultless purity of body, since the inner nature of such a substance is said to flee from pollution. **5.** If all of these conditions remain unaltered, if regular practice is overlooked in no way, I marvel that you recognize your own peril less, when it would be sacrilegious to stand accused of negligence and to sin against such vestments. For what have so many workers to do, so many crowds of sailors, so many troops of rustics? You who also command so many for transport to the *comes,* defend yourself with the presumption of the very title, so that, while you are believed to conduct royal business, you are seen to command your citizens in many affairs. **6.** Therefore, your inactivity both neglects that for which you were commissioned in the province and has managed to come to the noble attention of the *Princeps.* But if anxiety has not thus far deprived you of your ability to act, since the outcome touches upon your health, make ready to come with haste before the appointed day, to bring yourself with the purple, which you have been accustomed to deliver to our chamber each year. For now we send to you, not a supervisor, but one to exact punishment, if you should believe this a matter worth delaying in mockery. **7.** Indeed it is read how the substance was discovered with such ease and short work! When a dog, excited with hunger, crushed in his jaws the shellfish cast upon the Tyrian shore, naturally his mouth overflowing with the ensanguined moisture was stained with the wondrous pigment.[12] And so it is that the occasion led men to an unexpected skill and those following this example made the substance to give *Principes* an honored distinction which is known to have a humble source. Hydruntum is for Italy what Tyre is for the East: producing royal wardrobe not only preserves ancient rule, but continually supplies the new. Therefore beware, if you suffer to accomplish anything less than what you know us to expect as necessary.

12. Julius Pollux attributed this to the hound of Hercules (*Onomasticon* 1.45–49)

LETTER 1.3 (C. 507)

The first of many elaborate letters of appointment, here advancing the father of Cassiodorus to the rank of patrician. The letter describes Cassiodorus senior's merits and his previous services to the state, especially as *Praefectus Praetorio*. This letter should be considered a companion to *Variae* 1.4, which announces the prestigious elevation to the Senate at Rome. *Variae* 3.28 later summons this same Cassiodorus to attend the Theoderic's court as an advisor.

King Theoderic to Cassiodorus, Vir Illustris *and Patrician*

1. Although what is laudable by nature enjoys its own particular nobility, lest the rewards of outstanding character be wanting, when it begets distinction for the soul—for indeed, everything good is conjoined to its own benefits, nor is it possible for virtue to be acknowledged which is detached from its reward—nonetheless, the summit of our judgment brings eminence, since he who is promoted by us is deemed abundant in outstanding merits. **2.** For if one whom a just man would appoint must be regarded as fair, if one whom the temperate man would adopt must be regarded as endowed with moderation, then clearly the one who earns the opinion of the judge of all virtues is capable of every merit. For what is wanted more than to have found a witness to praises where partiality cannot be suspected? Indeed the decision of the king obtains its judgment by virtue of deeds alone, nor does the mind of the ruler deign to be flattered by the influence of gifts. **3.** Certainly what brought you to my attention should be recollected, so that you might enjoy the fruit of your labor, when you know each merit to have pleasingly ingrained itself in my mind. Already devoted at the very first of my *imperium*, when the inclination of the provinces wavered with the tide of events and novelty itself permitted an untried ruler to be disregarded, you diverted the minds of mistrustful Sicilians from a hasty resistance, directing them away from fault, and removing from us the necessity of punishment. **4.** Edifying persuasion accomplished what impetuous severity would have been able to correct. You gained for a province reprieve from a condemnation that it did not deserve to experience by reason of its devotion. There, protecting civil law in military dress, uncorrupted as a judge you weighed private and public interest, and while neglecting your own property and avoiding the stain of personal profit, you restored the wealth of high character. You denied an entrance to accusers and a place for detractors. And there, where it is hardly the custom for silent forbearance to be practiced, the voices of praise took up arms for you. For we know, from the testimony of Tullius,[13] how the nature of Sicilians is suited to quarrels, so that from habitual practice they would accuse their governors even on mere suspicion. **5.** Not for the extent of your

---

13. Cicero.

praises did I grant the privilege of governing Bruttium and Lucania,[14] but lest the fortune of your native country should alone not know that good which a foreign province had earned. But you, rendering your accustomed devotion, have placed us under obligation by affectionate service, where we had thought to discharge all obligation to you; hence you have increased the debt where we had thought it to be absolved. You have acted, in every matter, the part of the judge exempt from error, neither oppressing any man out of jealousy, nor elevating another in gratitude for blandishments. Since this conduct would be difficult anywhere, it becomes glorious in one's own country, where it is the case that either relations call out for favors or long-standing animosities provoke hatred. **6.** It therefore pleases us to revisit the deeds of your prefecture. A most celebrated blessing to all Italy, you demonstrated, by accomplishing matters with every provident arrangement, how easy it could be to pay taxes under a magistrate of integrity. No man reluctantly proffers what is distributed with equity, since nothing contributed according to proper arrangements is considered a loss. **7.** Enjoy now your blessings and receive multiplied those benefits which you despised out of concern for public regard. For this is a glorious model of life, for rulers to be witnesses and for citizens to bear praise. **8.** Therefore, urged on by such abundant praise, we confer upon you in just remuneration the distinction of the patriciate, so that what is payment to others, for you would be the return of good deeds. Congratulations, honored man, for your praiseworthy fortune. You have compelled the mind of your lord to this declaration, that we confess we believe these benefits to be more correctly your own. May these blessings be providently lasting, so that, while we pay this as remuneration, we may next time demand better achievements of your talents.

LETTER 1.4 (C. 507)

A more detailed companion to *Variae* 1.3 announcing to the Senate at Rome the elevation of Cassiodorus's father to the rank of patrician. This letter reads like panegyric, extolling the virtues of Cassiodorus senior's services to the state and digressing on the interesting fifth-century background of the family. Both *Variae* 1.3 and 1.4 serve to frame the family's commitment to an extended tradition of service to the Roman state that continued under the Amal Goths.

King Theoderic to the Senate of Rome

1. We truly desire, conscript fathers, that your garland be painted with the blossom of diverse distinctions. We desire that the spirit of liberty should see a Senate favored and thronged. Indeed, such a gathering is the honor of those ruling, and whatever reflects upon you with joyful thanksgiving, likewise applies to our praise.

---

14. This was regarded as a single province in southern Italy.

2. For all that, we have been especially desirous that ornaments of worth should adorn your assembly, when those who have increased in palatine influence rightly confer benefits on the homeland. Our attention scrutinizes these men, and we rejoice in those found with the treasure of good habits, in whom the grace of our countenance is imprinted just as in the modeled likenesses given for an office. **3.** Hence it is that we have bestowed the patriciate upon the grand and *illustris* Cassiodorus, upon a man esteemed for his most noted distinction on behalf of the republic, elevated in recompense so that the merits of one serving are proclaimed with the mark of a great title. He is not one who hurtles to the peak of offices with unexpected succession through the ranks, projected to a tenuous fortune by a game of fate; rather, just as virtues are accustomed to increase, so has he ascended to a position of great renown through deserved ranks. **4.** For as you know, his first entry to administration was set in the toil of the *Comes Privatarum*, where, neither faltering with the weakness of inexperience nor wandering unknowingly into the errors of novelty, he instead lived by an example to be imitated along the firm path of restraint. Soon after he rose to accept the honor of *Comes Sacrarum Largitionum* with common praise for how much he had deservedly accomplished. **5.** Why mention the discipline restored to the provinces, or the edifices of justice administered for men of diverse condition? He has lived with such self-control that he could instruct equanimity with firmness as well as teach by example. For a blameless magistrate is the advocate of probity. It would be a shame not to possess correct habits under one with such praiseworthy reputation. For who would avoid crime, who observes it implicated in the heart of the elevated? He adopts a hollow demeanor of feigned severity when the man tainted by money opposes bribery, when the unjust man decrees in law what must be obeyed. He does not possess the spirit of fairness, who does not administer authority with an unimpaired conscience, since excesses are held in dread only when they are believed to displease the magistrates. **6.** And so trained in these practices under the preceding king,[15] he succeeded to our court with a veteran's commendations. For you will recall, and in this the memory of recent events assists you, with what moderation he took his seat on the praetorian summit and thus, born aloft on high, he spurned the faults of good fortune all the more. **7.** Indeed, in no way did he raise himself up in the pretensions of great power, elevated by the favor of fortune, as is the habit of many, but having conducted everything with equity he reflected nothing hated back upon our favor to him. He caused greater things to be bestowed upon him, while within the bounds of modesty he restrained greatness. For here is the most pleasing benefit of an upright conscience, that although he was able to obtain heights, nonetheless he is judged by all to merit more. He aptly joined our revenues to a communal happiness, being liberal with the public treasury and justly meritorious

---

15. Odoacer, king of Italy, 476–93.

in expenditures. **8.** The republic then experienced a man from the assembly of Romulus who was free of blame, who was permitted to make himself glorious by self-restraint; he nonetheless conferred something greater, in that he left behind, to those who would follow, an example of good works. For it disgraces one to sin who is able to follow after such praiseworthy deeds. He has been, as you know, fear-inspiring to public servants, gentle with the provincials, greedy for giving, full of loathing for receiving, a hater of accusations, and a friend to justice. It was not difficult for him to act as a guardian, who demanded himself to refrain from the property of others. For it is the mark of an unconquered spirit to esteem the advantage of reputation and to instead despise profit from litigation. **9.** But those who are not familiar with the lofty characters of his father and grandfather rightly marvel at him. Indeed, fame celebrates these former Cassiodori. Even if the name may be known among others, nonetheless, it remains peculiar to his family. An ancient line, a praised stock, honored among citizens, exceptional among courageous men, since they flourished both in vigor of limbs and in height of body. **10.** For the father of this candidate bore the praiseworthy dignity of *tribunus et notarius* under the *Princeps* Valentinian,[16] an office which was then given to the outstanding. At that time, such men in whom it was not possible to find the blemish of recrimination stood for selection to the most privy of imperial affairs. **11.** But as kindred spirits are always accustomed to prefer each other, he was the greatly cherished associate to the patrician Aetius in the governance of the republic, that Aetius whom the ruler of state at that time followed in every matter of advice on account of his wisdom and the glorious labors undertaken on behalf of the republic. Therefore, not in vain was he sent with Carpilio, the son of Aetius, in the capacity of legate to the formidable warrior Attila.[17] He beheld without fear one whom *imperium* feared and, relying on truth, he remained above those terrible glares and threats, nor did he hesitate to stand in the path of argument with that man, who, overcome with I know not what fury, seemed to expect mastery of the entire world. **12.** He found a proud king, but left him pacified, and he overturned the king's false accusations with such honesty that the king sought to ask for clemency, when it was advantageous not to have peace with such a wealthy *regnum*. He encouraged those fearing Attila with his own steadfastness; nor were those known to be armed with such legates believed to be unwarlike. He brought back a peace thought untenable. What his delegation produced is commonly known; it was accepted as gratefully as it was sought after. **13.** Already decorated, the fair ruler first offered him office, then gifts of revenue. But this richly blessed man, with his native restraint, instead accepted a leisured dignity in place of remuneration and sought

16. Valentinian III, western Roman emperor, 425–55.
17. Attila, king of the Huns, 434–53.

out the pleasantries of Bruttium.[18] It was not possible to deny that preferred solitude to one who had brought safety from a hostile enemy. With sadness, he released from his employ one whom he knew had been essential. **14.** Now the grandfather, a Cassiodorus girt with the honors of gleaming rank, which it was not possible to withhold from that family, freed Bruttium and Sicily from the incursion of the Vandals by armed resistance, so that he deservedly held the first place of honor in these provinces, which he defended from so cruel and unexpected an enemy. And thus the republic owed it to his strength that Gaiseric did not so devastate those neighboring provinces with the rage that Rome afterward endured.[19] **15.** These Cassiodori, moreover, also waxed in praise of relations in regions of the East. For Heliodorus, whom we saw administrating the prefecture with distinction in that republic for eighteen years, was known to be related to them by blood. A family elevated on both sides of the world, it is aptly fixed to twin Senates as though conspicuous with two lamps, it shines with the purest brilliance. For where do you find nobility extended further than this, which merits being exalted on both sides of the world? **16.** And this Cassiodorus has lived in his province with the esteem of a governor and with the peace of mind belonging to a private citizen. Superior to all men by his nobility, he drew the hearts of all to himself, so that those who by right of their privilege were unable to be subdued, instead became pleasantly bound to him more by the increasing advantages of his association. **17.** Moreover, he is so endowed with the abundance of his own patrimony, that among other good deeds he surpasses *Principes* in herds of horses, and by often making gifts of these, incurs no jealousy. Hence it is that our candidate always equips the Gothic army and, improving on the beneficial arrangements that he received from his forebears, he preserves hereditary bounty. **18.** For which reason we have conveyed everything in order, so that anyone may understand that one who chooses to live according to an elevated rule of life may be able to recover the reputation of their family through our praise. And therefore, conscript fathers, since the honor of good men is advantageous to you and your assent attends our judgment, let the elevation of one who has sought to take upon himself the service of all be supported by good fortune. For it is rather by remuneration than by gift that those who have honored you with worthy deeds should be thanked with reciprocal favors.

LETTER 1.5 (C. 507–11)

The first of letters more typical to the collection, *Variae* 1.5 is brief and spare of background details, concerning a property dispute in which Theoderic has denied

18. The region of Calabria in modern Italy.
19. Geiseric, king of Vandals, 428–77; the Vandals sacked Rome in 455.

appealing the ruling of a local Gothic *comes* who may have served in place of a civilian provincial governor.

King Theoderic to Florianus, Vir Spectabilis

1. It is not fitting for a settled dispute to drag on without end. And what if peace is given over to wrangling? Should comfort not be found in lawful decisions? For only one safe haven among tempests of human conjuring is provided, which, if men should ignore with raging willfulness, they will always wander astray into surging tides of brawling. **2.** And for that reason, we declare to your excellency in the present proclamation, insofar as the case remains as it was entreated by those present, the quarrel over the estate at Mazenis has been decided with lawful statutes in the judgment of the *Comes* Anna, nor shall anything that has been decided be judged by appeal. **3.** Because just as we would not want to deny justice to the oppressed, thus should we not offer assent to unreasonable quarrels. For one who would reject being peaceful on account of his own vices ought to be compelled to be peaceful. Even so does the skilled doctor often cure the uncooperative patient, where the will is unbalanced by burdensome desires, so that the patient grasps after that which is onerous rather than that which is perceived to be a healthful choice.

LETTER 1.6 (C. 507–9)

The first of many letters dealing with public building projects and the maintenance of antique heritage, here directing the *Praefectus Urbis* to send marble workers from Rome to Ravenna for the construction of a new annex to Theoderic's palace. The *Praefectus Urbis* should assume responsibility for the cost, presumably from the municipal accounts. The building is otherwise unattested.

King Theoderic to Agapitus, Vir Illustris *and* Praefectus Urbis

1. It is fitting that the *Princeps* should consider which efforts would enrich the republic, and it is worthy indeed for a king to adorn a palace with edifices. For it is not fitting that we should yield to the ancients with respect to adornment, when we are not unequal to the prosperity of those ages. **2.** Therefore, I have commenced the massive undertaking of the Basilica of Hercules in the city of Ravenna, to which antiquity contributed a suitable name. We eagerly delegate to your greatness whatever should be secured in the palace for praiseworthy admiration, so that, according to the brief affixed below, you will send to us from Rome the most skilled marble workers, who may bind select pieces with fine seams, such that they would counterfeit in a praiseworthy manner a natural likeness conjoined with intertwining veins. From this skill comes that which may surpass nature. The variegated surface of marble is woven with a most pleasing variety of figures. Because it will be graceful and refined, such a thing is prized always. **3.** For this endeavor you will furnish the materials and transport, lest our *imperium* burden anyone, which we wish to be known for its advantage to each and all.

LETTER 1.7 (C. 507–11)

This letter summons a senator to Theoderic's court to answer for his role in the mishandling of an inheritance. The property had been awarded to a parent by Theoderic and it subsequently passed to the children. It seems the addressee claimed property on behalf of his wife, the sister of the underaged child entitled to the property (Plutianus). The following letter (*Var.* 1.8) offers further detail.

King Theoderic to Felix, Vir Clarissimus

1. We know that you have been entangled in litigation with respect to Venantius's guardianship of the inheritance of Plutianus, in a manner unbecoming, to the extent that he whom you ought to have assisted at your own expense, you have instead harmed with the loss of property. Indeed, costly consolations ought to have been testimony to your relationship to him. Therefore, what kind of deed would it seem to be between those conjoined by blood, which would be judged criminal between strangers? **2.** And therefore, we resolve by the present injunction that whatever property you know that wanton Neoterius has not so much shared as stolen with willful prodigality you must restore fully intact to our agent without any delay, lest you compel us, who up to this point have tempered everything with mildness, to avenge a deed of this sort by turning to the law. For we do not permit what we have bestowed upon parents with our praise to be taken from the ward. It is indeed most grievous to steal through chicanery what was conferred by the beneficence of the *Princeps*. **3.** Now, in regard to the remainder of the property, which you will assert on behalf of your wife had been divided in a share contrary to the path of justice—if somehow that division which stands widely known under the original judgment must be addressed—hasten yourself to approach our *comitatus,* so that in your presence we may arrange that which accords with justice. For it is unjust that, from one property by which succession occurs in equal portion, some should prosper abundantly while others should groan with the misfortunes of poverty.

LETTER 1.8 (C. 507–11)

This letter delegates the inheritance dispute initiated in *Variae* 1.7 to an agent of Theoderic's court.

King Theoderic to Amabilis, Agent of the Court

1. It is in our heart to protect everyone in common, but especially those whom we know have been unable to protect themselves. For thus the scales of equality are served, if we liberally bestow assistance upon those without means and, on behalf of children, we instill the insolent with fear of us. A lesser fortune requires a *Princeps,* since those who would subvert a gift made publicly encounter our censure. **2.** And so we have learned through the tearful petition of Venantius, the legal guardian of Plutianus, that his own brother Neoterius, having forgotten the condition of brotherhood, has attacked the property of this child with hostile madness. This matter has moved us to act severely on behalf of his affairs, since our beneficence, which we would have stand as a statement of our public duty, seems to have been replaced by an illegal audacity. And since it is not doubted that a waste of time would especially result in a repetition of offense, therefore, let your devotion, by our firm command, cause the required property to be restored to the aforementioned guardian without delay, if there is nothing that is reasonably able to interpose punishment. **3.** But if there is anyone who may oppose this with the intention of retaining their own portion, by preceding with a legal surety, they should hasten to approach our *comitatus,* so that we would judge with proved representatives according to the custom of our equity.

LETTER 1.9 (C. 507–11)

This letter offers judgment in a treason case against the bishop of Augustana. As his superior in the ecclesiastical hierarchy, the bishop of Milan is directed to restore the accused to his congregation and ensure his safety.

King Theoderic to Eustorgius, Venerable Bishop of Milan

1. The well-being of subjects is preserved, where it thrives under the fairness of those ruling; nor is it fitting for one, by whom I have established policies that must not change, to be dragged down by uncertain rumor. Indeed, we gather faith in matters from reason, which is never concealed from those searching after it, if it is carefully followed according to its own evidence. **2.** And therefore, what we hold to be most agreeable to your blessedness, in the present statement we declare the bishop of the city of Augustana to be accused of treason against the homeland on false accusations;[20] restored by you to former dignity as bishop, let him hold every right that he held. For nothing in such a dignity must be presumed from rash thinking, wherefore, if something is believed by report, the silent man is excused from harm. Similarly, openly criminal deeds should hardly take faith in such matters; moreover, whatever is said out of jealousy is not deemed true. **3.** Indeed, we want to strike down his assailants with righteous punishment, but since these very men perform in the name of clergy, we commit all that must be arranged to the

20. Augustana is probably Augusta Praetoria, or the modern Aosta; cf. *Var.* 2.5 for this location.

judgment of your sanctity, whose role it is to establish probity of behavior in such persons and to preserve ecclesiastical discipline.

LETTER 1.10 (C. 507-11)

One of several justifiably famous letters addressed to the philosopher and senator Boethius. Here concern for timely and proper payments to the palace guard, reported to Boethius presumably during his tenure as *Magister Officiorum*, opens an opportunity for a lavish excursus on measures and mathematics. The other letters to Boethius (*Var.* 1.45, 2.40) are similarly propaganda pieces.

King Theoderic to Boethius, Vir Illustris and Patrician

1. It is fitting for the people that justice must be weighed out to all in common, by which it thus obtains dignity in the meaning of its own name, if it delivers measured equity to the powerful and humble; nonetheless, those individuals more boldly expect this equity who do not shun service in the palace. For it is something bestowed with leisurely ease from the beneficence of a *Princeps;* the habit, moreover, is expected as a kind of payment by those serving faithfully. **2.** The *domestici* of both the foot and horse divisions, who are known ever to keep vigil in our palace, because it is customary to arise out of serious grievances, have complained to us loudly in a unanimous petition concerning their accustomed salary that they do not receive *solidi* of full weight from the *arcarius praefectorum,* and they incur upon themselves a severe loss in value of coin. Therefore, let your wisdom, learned as it is from well-read instruction, cast out this criminal falsity from the company of truth, lest anything should be profitable in detracting from the integrity of truth. **3.** For that which is called arithmetic has established a sure rationale among the uncertainties of the world, just as we know it has in the heavens—a visible ranking, a sweetness of arrangement, a recognizable simplicity, a changeless body of knowledge—which both serves the earthly and gives dimension to the celestial. For what is there that has not measure or transcends weight? Each thing has compass, all is measurable, and hence the universe attains a sublimity, since we recognize everything by its own measure. **4.** It delights to observe in what manner the measure of the *denarius* both revolves upon itself in the manner of the heavens and is never found lacking. Its calculation always increases according to its own amount by adding itself back with each change so that while the *denarius* does not seem to be diminished in itself, it has the capacity boundlessly to combine into a greater amount. This process may be repeated often by bending the fingers on the hands and continued indefinitely by reextending the fingers. Unfailingly, the calculation leads back to its own beginning in amount, just as it increases all the more by the same. Sands of the sea, drops of rain, stars of the clear sky are each delimited within a quantifiable number. Indeed, every created thing is enumerated from its own beginning and whatever comes into existence is unable to transcend such a condition. **5.** And since it delights us to speak on such mysteries of learning with knowledgeable persons, although coins by themselves seem base from their frequent use, nonetheless attention must be given to the extent of reason with which coins were amassed by the ancients. They intended six thousand *denarii* to equal one *solidus,* namely so that the circularity formed with shining metal should correspond suitably to the ages of the world, like a golden sun. In fact, the *senarius,* which not without merit learned antiquity defined as perfect and indicated by the name of the ounce, which is the primary base of measurement, with twelve reckoned in a pound, would correspond similarly to the twelve months computed in the course of the year. **6.** O revelation of the wise! O foresight of the ancients! Such a thing is carefully worked out, which both naturally adorns human usage and so symbolically contains the secrets of nature. Thus it is rightly called a *libra,* which weighs with such consideration of matters. Therefore, does it not seem a cruel and wretched mangling of truth itself to want to so confound certitudes of nature and to violate such mysteries. Let an exchange of value be practiced in commerce; let people buy cheaply what they sell even more dear; but let the weights and measurements remain credible to the people, since everything is thrown into disorder if rectitude becomes mingled with deceit. **7.** Certainly what is given to those toiling ought not to be corrupted. Rather, the compensation by which faithful service is derived should stand out as inviolable. Give a *solidus,* by all means, and thence draw away from it, if you are capable; hand over a pound, and diminish it, if you can. The provision against such an act would remain fixed in the name itself:[21] whether you would give pure or not, you may not unbind it from that by which it is called. This is in no way possible. You may not bestow the name of purity and also effect criminal reductions. Therefore, see to it that the custodian of the treasury should hold his own just practices and that what we intend for those deserving well should be obtained by them through uncorrupted reward.

LETTER 1.11 (C. 507–11)

Instructions to the military commander of the province of Raetia to intervene in the abduction of slaves by the Breones, a people with some connection to local military service. The letter insinuates that liberties taken by the Breones have been tacitly condoned by the *dux.*[22]

King Theoderic to Servatus, Dux of Raetia

1. It is fitting that the honor which you bear in title, you should demonstrate in habits, so that throughout the province in which you preside, you should suffer no

---

21. That is, reducing a *solidus* or pound changes its name and value.
22. The Breones are not otherwise attested as a people.

violent actions to occur, except that it is exacted for the justice whence our *imperium* flourishes. **2.** Therefore, we have been asked in a petition of Moniarius to stir you with the present statement, as it seems you have been aware that the Breones have unreasonably born away with slaves legitimately his. These Breones, being accustomed to military service, are said to threaten civil harmony by arms and on account of this they despise yielding to justice, since they continually direct themselves toward warlike acts. While I know not for what reason, it is difficult to preserve a measure of good conduct with these constantly threatening. **3.** Therefore, with that impudence which is able to be adopted on the presumption of strength having been removed, let you cause the aforementioned property to be restored by them without hesitation, lest the petitioner should be seen to despise his victory on account of the inconvenience of delay by the Breones.

LETTER 1.12 (C. 507–11)

This letter elevates a former *Quaestor* to the office of *Magister Officiorum*.

King Theoderic to Eugenitus, Vir Illustris and Magister Officiorum

1. The solemn celebration of the deserving is a royal prerogative, since we know not how to dispense anything except to the worthy. And although we want, with God's favor, everything to be associated with our authority, nonetheless our desire is measured by reason, so that we value it more to choose what is worthy of the approbation of all. **2.** Hence it is that we have found you, long since attaining the height of *Quaestor*, commendably pursuing the study of learned philosophical principles, such that the distinction of letters, for you, has become the reward for noble service. For what is more adorning than duty in legal service which, if it is conducted honestly, attracts the legal affairs of others to its own annoyance, so that it may provide relief to the labor of others? In this field of exercise, you graduated through a course of services to the honor of our notice. **3.** However, not content with one reward, our generosity doubled, it extended increased gifts and in its zeal prepared yet more, as if to bestow everything that it ought. Take, therefore, the badges of distinction of *Magister Officiorum*, enjoying every legal privilege that it was proper for your predecessors to hold. And therefore, with such a judgment joyfully rendered, you who earned honor on behalf of your worthy labors now accept another. For what we have perceived concerning the earlier reward, we declare increased by the second dignity. Branches properly cultivated retain the nature of the tree and shoot forth again; thus *fasces* are sprung from *fasces*. **4.** Indeed, may this compensation not satiate you, lest the praise created by our judgment give rest to your labors. Nay, on the contrary, let respectability be more desirable, when it attains a reward, and then anxious labors become more pleasing to have been perpetual, when you know their reward to have found you. Therefore, what honors you take from legal writ, give back from your merits. Know well with what eagerness it pleases us, you who arrive from the inner chambers of our very council. Remember that however much the blameless are praised in our presence, so much do we bestow good acts in turn. By your speech, we shall pronounce our judgments; by your mouth, we speak to rouse with distinguished examples. Be a temple of innocence, the sanctuary of restraint, and the hall of justice. Anything profane should be absent from the mind of the judge. Let a pious *Princeps* be served by a kind of priesthood.

LETTER 1.13 (C. 507–11)

Confirmation of the elevation of Eugenitus as *Magister Officiorum* (cf. *Var.* 1.12), with an address to the Senate at Rome.

King Theoderic to the Senate of Rome

1. The distinction of office, conscript fathers, when it comes to an unknown man, is a gift; when it comes to the experienced man, it is as payment for just desserts. Of which, the one is dependent upon judgment, while the other is obliged to partiality. For we elevate some in estimation, to others we show gratitude, and to all our kindness extends itself as a path to blessings. But we recall by beholding your affection how much is said in your assembly which is appraised on the basis of the celebrated virtues. For if anything is the flower of the human race, it deserves to be the curia, which, just as the citadel is the prominence of a city, is the jewel of other ranks. **2.** And therefore, we have elevated the *illustris* Eugenitus, shining with the reputation of learned philosophical principles, to the honor of *Magister Officiorum,* so that he may bear in title that dignity which he claimed by desserts. For who could be so ignorant of his public service, which he accomplished not with meanness of spirit, but which he attended with the respect of an obligation? And so we grant a role equal to such high distinctions, so that, shining with the grace of both, each might adorn the other with the pleasantness of its nature. Here he is who long ago as *Quaestor* and jurist clung to our side, whom no cloud of jealousy ever darkened, nor did he with venomous feelings seek devices for harming others out of devotion to malevolence: he obeyed us honestly with a hidden purity of heart, and he offered his own faultlessness to devotion to commands. For a troubled mind does not follow the decision of one ruling, but it would rather accomplish its own inclination. **3.** You clearly know our opinion on this account, that after the highest honors of this office, he would climb to yet another dignity. Nor would we allow one to be at leisure whose merits do not permit him to remain a private citizen: it is appropriate that he should be considered with regard to the nature of the bright sun, which having accomplished one day, nonetheless illuminates another with the same pleasant brilliance. Here then, conscript fathers, let your approbation welcome one shining so completely with merits. For you are thoroughly indebted to those serving, just as the approval of your praise accompanies them. For if the pace of horses is hastened by the acclamation of spectators and driven by the clapping of their hands, and thus speed is drawn from dumb animals, so much do we believe it possible to stimulate men, whom we find particularly fitted by nature to an eagerness for praise.

LETTER 1.14 (C. 507-11)

Addressed to the *Praefectus Praetorio* who was ultimately responsible for the collection of taxes, this letter approves a request from a municipality to pay its taxes in one installment, as opposed to the customary schedule of three portions.

King Theoderic to Faustus, Praefectus Praetorio

1. With pleasure do we extend our complete consent, so just is the voice of those petitioning, since it is hardly possible for a favor to be difficult when it does not diminish liberality. **2.** And therefore, in regard to the manner of the *tertiae* which is born by the Catalienses,[23] let your lofty splendor cause it to be paid in total as a single annual tax, nor hereafter should those petitioning endure any requisition beyond this share. For what does it matter, under what name the landowner bears a responsibility, provided that he pays what is owed without reduction? And thus we remove from them the mistrusted title of the *tertia* and by our mildness we banish discomfort from the payers.

LETTER 1.15 (C. 507-11)

This letter orders a patrician to provide *tuitio,* or legal patronage, over the household of a fellow patrician acting on Theoderic's behalf at the Vandal court in North Africa.

King Theoderic to Festus, Vir Illustris *and Patrician*

1. It is pleasing to us that, however so much an appraisal of the extent of your merits increases, thus too should you be entrusted as the guardian of the absent and the patron of the weak. For, on that account, you formerly deserved to be on the Senate, so that you would illustrate the consideration of justice to those following. Thus it happened that good opinion of you increased from the example of glorious legal acts. For never was your own advantage increased by abandoning another, except that it was decided properly from good conscience. **2.** To which, we have decided in the present injunction concerning the household of the patrician

---

23. Possibly the Catali, a people of Venetia or Istria.

Agnellus, who, departing for Africa, will serve our advantages by petitioning the *regnum* of another king. This household would do well with your guardianship with respect to sound legal matters, lest, lacking the protection of a master, it endure any violent attack. For there are always opportunities for harm to the resources of those absent from home and the occasion appears by whatever means to drag into litigation what the attention of the traveler is not able to deter by resistance. **3.** And therefore, let your eminence, which is a blessing to have nearby, uplift the humble, rescue those otherwise oppressed, and, what is rare among the influential, benefit everyone, because you are more eminent than all.

LETTER 1.16 (C. 507–8)

This letter grants a deferment of rents owed by tenants (*conductores*) on state property for one tax period (*indictio*). The deferment is couched in the language of reciprocity so common to descriptions in the *Variae* about the relationship of governmental authority to the obligations of the governed.

King Theoderic to Julianus, Comes Patrimonii

1. Let us share more fully, to our own benefit, in what we grant on behalf of human misfortune. For the resources of the ruler would then become more enriched, when it remits something and acquires a distinguished treasure of more noble coin by means of denying parsimony. Hence it is that we extend means to the weak and a hand to the overburdened, so that, stirred by the humanity of our policy, those who sink under the calamity of their own fortune may rise up by the remedy of our devotion. **2.** Not long ago, the *conductores* of Apulia complained bitterly to us in a sorrowful petition that their crops had been burned in enemy raids,[24] requesting that they, for whom the substance of payment has been reduced, not be compelled to make full payment of rents owed. Therefore, we declare on behalf of what must be considered out of innate kindness, that we are unable to accuse those of idleness whose fortune we deem must be restored. For now, we wish to assume their regular debt, whence subsequent payments should occur at the appropriate time. **3.** And therefore, we order that your eminence diligently inquire into this matter, so that, however much less it will be determined for them to have sold, you should detract this with accustomed moderation from the remaining payment on the first indiction. Nevertheless, let no fraud be associated with our beneficence, lest you should be obliged to restore anything overlooked, you who have always pleased us by your inclination to foresight, because just as the losses of supplicants touch us, so ought their profits be payments to us.

---

24. The proximity of Apulia to ports of the eastern empire makes it more likely that these are eastern imperial attacks, although Vandal attacks are also plausible.

LETTER 1.17 (C. 507–11)

This letter exposes some of the interesting features of Ostrogothic military culture. The inhabitants of Dertona (modern Tortona), in Liguria, are ordered to fortify and relocate to a nearby site in preparation for time of war. Noteworthy is the fact that both Goths and Romans in the area are expected to shoulder this burden as a community. For a similar directive, see *Variae* 3.48.

King Theoderic to All Goths and Romans Settled at Dertona

1. Stirred by reason of public advantage, for which we are continually and willingly concerned, we instruct you to strengthen the fortress situated near you, since preparation for war is properly arranged however well it is managed at a time of peace. Indeed, a particularly strong defense is prepared then, when it will have been strengthened by long-thought planning. Anything erected quickly is carelessly done, and to seek a site for building then, when danger already threatens, is bad. **2.** Furthermore, that same mindset already agitated by various cares will not be well disposed to bold action. The ancients rightly designated this an *expeditio*,[25] since the mind given over to battles must not be occupied by other considerations. Therefore, a goal that is addressed in advance out of consideration for the commonality must be embraced, nor is it appropriate to bring delay to a command which is known to especially assist devoted citizens. **3.** And therefore, we decree by the present order that you should eagerly construct homes for yourselves in the aforementioned fortress, making recompense for our attention to these matters, so that, just as we determine what must be done for your own benefit, so would we feel you have adorned our reign with the most admirable structures. For then you will want to assume expenses suited for your personal homes and it will be a dwelling not unpleasing to you, in which the very architecture is worthy of compliment. **4.** I ask, what will it mean to be in your own households, then, while the enemy is known to endure the roughest accommodations? Let him lie exposed to the rains, while roofs cover you. Let want consume him, while abundant stores refresh you. Thus, with you favorably disposed, your enemy will suffer the lot of being despoiled even before the outcome of battle. For it happens in a time of need that the man who does not divide himself among many concerns is proven the most valiant. Who would judge him to be wise, if he begins giving attention to the service of construction and to storing provisions then, when it behooves him to conduct war?

---

25. One of several obscure etymological references in the collection, here seemingly referring to the single-minded preparation involved in a military campaign.

LETTER 1.18 (C. 507–11)

This letter addresses two outstanding legal issues, one requiring a general decision applicable to the entire kingdom, and the other applying to a specific case. In the first instance, Theoderic rules against soldiers assuming ownership of property subsequent to the initial settlement of 489 (see *Var.* 2.16, for similar reference). The second matter concerns a man's assault against his brother.

King Theoderic to Domitianus and Wilia

1. It is fitting that you who have undertaken to advocate impartiality on behalf of the people should honor and defend justice, while it is unfitting for one who is entrusted to restrain others under rules of impartiality to commit a crime, lest someone acknowledged as chosen for a praiseworthy purpose should become a corrupt example.[26] And therefore, we have taken the care to offer a response to your question, lest you should be allowed to err through uncertainty—unless, on the contrary, you wanted to deviate. **2.** If, from the time when we first crossed the River Isonzo and by the grace of God undertook the *imperium* of Italy, a presumptuous barbarian has occupied the estate of a Roman without the writ of any assignor,[27] let him restore the dispossessed property to the previous owner without delay. But if he is found having occupied the property before that assigned time, since he is then proven to obviate the thirty-year limit, we decree the petition of the plaintiff to be nullified.[28] **3.** For we want those cases led back into full view which have taken place in our reign; since we disapprove that a condition for accusation not be abandoned when the obscurity of a long time has passed. **4.** Concerning the man accused only of assaulting his brother, and not also of killing him, although he is condemned by the common law of all and only parricide would exceed so tragic a crime, nonetheless our humanity, which finds evidence for itself in an instance of criminality as much as an instance of devotion, determines by the present order that monstrosities of this nature should be driven beyond the borders of the province. For to whomever the company of family is detested, the society of citizens should not be deserved, lest the pleasant serenity of a pure civic body be polluted with dark blemishes.

26. Regarding the addresses of this letter: Domitianus's office is unknown; Wilia is also addressed in *Var.* 5.19–20 as *Comes Patrimonii.*

27. A *pittacio delegatoris,* which would have assigned newly arrived military personnel allotments of land.

28. The *praescriptio trecennii* usually acknowledges the status quo of property ownership after thirty years; the statement here seems to align the limit with Theoderic's entry into Italy in 489, and hence the settlement of 489 should be assumed to have legal force *similar* to a *praescriptio trecennii,* rather than a literal sense, in which case the letter would have to originate sometime after 519 (Cassiodorus is assumed to have held the quaestorship until 511–12, after which he did not assume office again until c. 523).

LETTER 1.19 (C. 507–11)

One of many letters addressed to various forms of fiscal corruption, in this case, Theoderic responds to a petition from the *curiales* of Adriana, where it seems some citizens have spurned the assessed payment, with the result that the difference has fallen disproportionately to poorer landowners.[29]

King Theoderic to Saturninus and Umbisuus, Viri Spectabiles

1. We wish to protect the legal advantage of the fisc, since our generosity is known to be maintained by means of our own property, and just as we desire to burden no one, so we ought not to lose debts owed to us.[30] We justly avoid want, which it is a pleasure to exceed, while poverty in one ruling is a ruinous state. And here moderation must be praised. For why should a censurable carelessness descend upon one's own property or an execrable greed extort from another? **2.** And therefore, we instruct you in the present order that with respect to the petition received from the curia of the city of Adriana, whoever declines to pay to the fisc of the Goths, him you should constrain to the equity of redress, lest the poor man be compelled to pay from his own property because the other man held back the appropriate amount without paying. With this evident reason observed, such that if anyone should prefer to impede our command with criminal obstinacy, since he could gain much because he will not need to submit the obligatory amount, in a just age let bald temerity not be left unpunished with such an indecently impudent spirit.

LETTER 1.20 (C. 507–11)

The first of several letters addressed to the unrest attending the popular chariot races at Rome, this letter assigns two leading senators to act as patrons for the Green Faction and to select a pantomime for that faction. The two men may have been brothers, since the letter mentions their responsibility as patrons as having been passed from their father. The problem seems to escalate later at *Variae* 1.27, 1.30–33.

King Theoderic to Albinus and Avienus, Viri Illustres *and Patricians*

1. It is fitting that the least portion from among the honorable cares of the republic and the salubrious tide of concerns for governing should be that the *Princeps* speak concerning spectacles, yet nevertheless it is not distasteful to enter upon this topic for the sake of love for the Roman republic, since from this we are able to demonstrate what we believe worthy to our way of feeling, especially when the blessing of

---

29. Agents assigned to collect revenues from a particular area were concerned only with the total amount assessed for that municipality; withholding tax payments could force the agent or local curia to exact the difference owed from poor landowners with less ability to resist.

30. The official appointments of this letter's addressees are unknown.

the times would be the happiness of the people. For by the grace of God it contributes to our labors, that the common populace know themselves to be at leisure. **2.** And so we have learned in a petition introduced by the Green Faction (and it has been remarked that the people clamor on behalf of this faction) that disruptive outbursts are agitated by the most nefarious types of individuals and that the state of public happiness has been thrown into frenzied turmoil. As it stands, it is not possible for the comeliness of celebration to have a distinguishing quality if it will not deserve to hold peace for all. And therefore, it is also worthwhile that our clemency examine these factions, so that it will be possible to illuminate the probity of good habits everywhere. For we do not dwell upon the idle products of popular banter, but we cut out the seed of harmful discontent. **3.** For this reason, by the recommendation of this present command, let your illustrious greatness kindly assume the patronage of the Green Faction, which your father of glorious memory managed. For it ought not to be reckoned injurious to rule the people and to govern Romans. For if it would be considered the cause of all honors, those who deserve to receive the most glorious honors will be chosen on behalf the utility of others. **4.** Therefore, assemble the spectators, and between Helladius and Thorodon,[31] whichever will have been thought most suitable to public delight, with the turbulence of the people subdued, let him be confirmed by you as the pantomime of the Greens, to the extent that we may be seen to bear for those chosen an expense which we shall pay on behalf of entertainment for the city. **5.** The ancients named this the silent accompaniment to the musical discipline which indeed one speaks with a closed mouth by means of the hands and which by certain gesticulations make understood what is hardly able to be expressed by spoken word or the written text.

LETTER 1.21 (C. 507–11)

This letter requires two senators to audit the accounts used to fund the workshops (*fabricae*) at Rome which produce materials for the maintenance of public buildings. The order concludes with a short excursus from natural history.

King Theoderic to Maximianus, Vir Illustris, *and* Andreas, Vir Spectabilis

1. We are called forth for the improvement of the city from an active zeal for its citizens, since nobody is able to esteem what he knows the inhabitants do not love. For each person, his own native city is more precious, since, beyond anything else, he seeks safety, where he had lingered from the time of the very cradle. Therefore, we are induced by similar sentiments to make a gift which, however much we

---

31. Helladius is mentioned again at *Var.* 1.32; these actors are otherwise unattested.

should willingly contribute, we will have redoubled gratitude. And therefore, it would not be harsh to anyone to give an account of moneys allotted for Rome's architecture, since a pure conscience would desire to prove itself when it obtains the fruit of its own labor, provided that it knows prosperity has reached us through its efforts. **2.** On which account, we have decided in the present dictate that you ought to inquire of the workshops of Rome, whether the labor of the project agrees with the expenses; or, if it should happen that the money remains idle among some, in which case it has not been paid out to the workshops, let him return what must be paid out for the allotted purpose. With this matter clearly expressed, send to us the most faithful account, so that you who have been chosen to track down the truth of the matter may be seen to comply with our directive. For we believe that nobody wants to be cheated from our generosity, when we have deemed him to be capable of managing this kind of business for his own support. **3.** The very birds roaming the sky love their own nests, the wandering beasts hasten to the thorny den, delightful fish crossing watery fields follow along practiced trails to their own fastnesses, and every kind of animal knows to take itself back where they have been wont to settle for generations. What ought we to say now concerning Rome, which it is even more appropriate for her own children to love?

LETTER 1.22 (C. 507-11)

This letter appoints a man to the post of *advocatus fisci,* or legal representative of the treasury. The legal training of the appointee receives due attention, but also interesting public-relations advice concerning the desirability of an acceptable amount of loss to the fisc.

King Theoderic to Marcellus, Vir Spectabilis *and* Advocatus Fisci

1. Praise is the gold standard of regal generosity, however much indulgences combine with good judgment, nor does the balance of good administration dare to make a faulty appointment, since where offices are affixed to merits, nothing ought to be uncertain. For we bear no regard for the uncultivated, but rather we approve of the most upstanding. **2.** Indeed, as a man of reputation you have honed your talent with the whetstone of a richly varied legal career and you have nurtured eloquence in the exercise of legal cases. You have become skilled, in the way that devotion bears sweet fruit, just as that very devotion also would win over the hearts of those ruling. Our intuition, that espier of virtues, sees this quality in you. You have succeeded in pleasing those among us possessing discernment, so that you, who heretofore have managed private cases with integrity, stand out as worthy to take up cases for the state. **3.** Take, therefore, those cases that must be handled for our fisc, following the example of your predecessors in enjoying the advantages of your post. And so, as a man of moderation, walk the middle path of justice, so that you neither load false accusations on the innocent nor unburden those restrained by just complaints. For this we deem to be true wealth, which we discern with the support of integrity. Therefore, we shall not inquire after how often you succeed, but rather by what means you prevail. **4.** Favoring impartiality will please us. Let it be that you seek victories, not from our influence, but rather from the law, since that most praiseworthy aspect of the fisc is lost when justice is lost. For if the master should win, it is begrudged as oppression. Equity is truly credited if it should happen that the suppliant prevails. Thus, we do not pursue cases with small losses, where our reputation then gains, when the unfair advantage is restrained. For that reason, occasionally allow a case to go poorly for the fisc, so that the *Princeps* may be seen to be good. Indeed, we lose a greater advantage if victory should favor us without loss.

LETTER 1.23 (C. 507–11)

This letter assigns two senators of patrician rank to settle a dispute between three other senators. It was standard policy for the Amals to avoid direct involvement in the affairs of Roman senators, as indicated by the paucity of details concerning the case and the greater attention to the dignity of senatorial rank.

King Theoderic to Caelianus and Agapitus, Viri Illustres *and Patricians*

1. It is fitting that concern at a royal height preserve the harmony of the general populace, since it adds to the praise of the one ruling, if peace should be loved by all. For what is there that speaks in favor of us better than a peaceful people, a Senate in accord with itself, and the whole republic enrobed in the respectability of our habits? **2.** Hence it is that we have decided by the present dictate that the dignified patricians Festus and Symmachus should, by your judgment, make an end to the case which they claim to have against the *illustris* patrician Paulinus. With these claims taken up according to the measure of the laws and settled, if the extent of the law should permit it, then let Paulinus produce in his own turn whatever case he may claim himself to have against the aforementioned dignified persons. We do not want the judgment with respect to either party to be delayed, but we would want everything to be decided and nothing else remaining between them except what should be owed out of good will. **3.** Take heed, therefore, that you have been chosen as arbiters for such a great legal case. Take heed of our expectation to demand fair justice. You would bear a rich bounty of gratitude if this present controversy should not prove those believed worthy to be unequal to the task of judging it. Indeed, there ought to be especial care taken with respect to such men who are able to provide clear examples to junior men. For whoever neglects a legal quarrel that must be eliminated from among the ranks of the highest men, encourages others to imitate the same without hesitation.

LETTER 1.24 (C. 508)

This letter calls Goths enrolled in the army to muster on June 24 for military campaign in Gaul. The Frankish defeat of the Visigoths under Alaric II at Vouillé and Alaric's marital connection to Theoderic initiated the Amal annexation of southern Gaul. This letter announces the initial muster under the direction of a *saio* prior to the army's departure for Gaul. The sentiments of the letter disclose something of the military culture of Ostrogothic Italy.

King Theoderic to All Goths

1. It is more fitting that battles must be known to Goths than that they must be advised by Goths, since it is a delight to be established from warlike stock. Indeed, one who covets the glory of martial excellence flees not from toil. And therefore, with God's blessing (the source from which everything prospers) and for the common weal, we have determined to send the army to Gaul, so that at the same time you will have an opportunity for advancement and we shall offer what we are known to confer on the deserving. For praiseworthy bravery lies hidden under leisure and the full light of deserving deeds is overshadowed when it lacks the place for proving itself. **2.** And thus we have given attention to what must be advised through our *saio* Nanduin, so that, in the name of God, you should set out for military duty sufficiently equipped with arms, horses, and all necessary gear according to customary practice on the eighth day before the calends of this July. With God's favor, display in yourselves the excellence that had been your fathers' and successfully perform our command. **3.** Bring your young men forward to the practices of Mars; let them see under your attention what they should strive to represent to posterity. For what is not learned in youth remains unknown at a mature age. The very raptor whose meal is always had from the spoils of battle casts its own young from the nest, feeble with inexperience, lest they should become accustomed to prefer leisure. The raptor buffets the unmindful with its wings, compelling the tender young to flight, so that they must come forward as the kind of offspring maternal devotion should demand. You, however, whom nature stirs and love of reputation goads, strive to leave behind such sons as your fathers prepared to have in you.

LETTER 1.25 (C. 507–11)

This letter combines fiscal auditing with urban ideology by commanding that the river front of Rome be returned to its intended purpose of housing the brickmaking industry that contributed to, among other things, the restoration of the mural fortifications. The letter loses no opportunity to vaunt the role of the Amal government in preserving Rome's ancient urban heritage.

King Theoderic to Sabinianus, Vir Spectabilis

1. It advances nothing to firm up the beginning of a project, if lawlessness will prevail to destroy what has been arranged. For those things are robust and long-lasting which wisdom commences and care preserves. And so, there is more security in conserving something than in arranging its furnishings at the outset, since fame is owed to an invention from its beginning, but praiseworthy completion is acquired through preservation. **2.** Not long ago, it was established by our order that the port of Licinius should be repaired with allotted revenues, so that it should produce twenty-five thousand roof tiles as an annual contribution to the walls of the city of Rome, where it will ever be an unending ambition to expend our efforts. Moreover, at the same time, the nearby docks which of old had pertained to that site now have been overwhelmed by usage of various sorts. **3.** Therefore, the entire shorefront is to be returned without delay to its intended obligation. Although it is fitting that our commands should be scorned in no way, on account of the reverence they are due, nonetheless, we especially want to preserve those mandates by which the appearance of the city is known to be adorned. For who would doubt that by this provision the miracle of architecture is preserved or that, by the covering of roof tiles, rounded vaults of overarching stone are protected? And so the ancient *Principes* rightly owe the praise that is given them to us, who have given a lasting youth to their buildings, so that they may be resplendent in their former newness, which until now had been blackened by an idle old age.

LETTER 1.26 (C. 507–11)

Vague in detail, this letter nonetheless illustrates a classic case in the devolution of fiscal integrity. An immunity to taxation donated to a particular church has been extended either to other persons or other church properties, for which reason the *Praefectus Praetorio* has been commanded to restore former obligations to the fisc.

King Theoderic to Faustus, Praefectus Praetorio

1. It is shameful that trust in a former gift has been diminished for those whom it often happens are shown our generosity in other matters. But even though on one occasion we agreed that this gift deserved not to be rescinded in perpetuity, nevertheless those who obtained our generosity by moderate requests ought not to have transgressed the limits we set for this donation with their immoderate presumption. **2.** Whence, because we were reminded of the deference owed to religious studies, some time ago we offered to the venerable gentleman of the church, Bishop Unscila, what we deemed should endure in perpetuity. But now we find that your *illustris* magnificence must be reminded how long the aforementioned church has not felt the burden of annual property taxes, on account of this donation, which had been discharged with consistency and pure trust for us from the time it was released from obligation by the magnificent patrician Cassiodorus.[32] 3. Let that property, which indeed has been transferred by some persons from the time of the donation to our church, now know the burden of payment common to all landowners and let it be subject to the fulfillment of that which it is the right of the master to obtain. In no other respect will this gift from us be increased for someone who profits from loss to the fisc. Let the payment of rent satisfy the landowner; taxes are for the ruler, not the private citizen. Wealth obtained by deceit is dangerous; how much better to conduct everything moderately, which no man would dare to accuse!

LETTER 1.27 (C. 509)

This letter responds to a petition from the Green Faction at Rome which claims two senior senators have harassed its members. Similar to *Variae* 1.23, the injunction takes into account the esteemed rank of those accused by delegating the inquiry to men of equal rank. The letter also offers thoughts on the appropriateness of senatorial involvement in public spectacle.

King Theoderic to Speciosus

1. If we moderate the conduct of foreign nations under law, if everything connected to Italy observes Roman statutes, how much more fitting is it that the very seat of civil harmony may possess more deference for the laws, so that the grace of dignified appearance should shine through the example of moderation?[33] For where may a restrained disposition be sought, if violent acts would bring shame upon patricians? 2. And so it has been brought forward to us in a petition from people of the Green Faction, since they have arranged to come to our *comitatus* seeking the accustomed redress, that savage attacks have been committed against them by the patrician Theodorus and the *illustris* consul Inportunus,[34] so that one among them is mourned as dead. 3. This, if it is true, moves us by the very savagery committed, that armed fury should persecute harmless citizens whom civic affection ought to cherish. But since the condition of lesser people justly implores the assistance of one who rules, we have decided that the above-mentioned *illustres* are to be advised by the present command that, by your urging, they should not delay to send informed representatives to the court of Caelianus and Agapitus, likewise *illustres,* to the effect that the familiarity of these men with the laws may bring closure with a weighed sentence. 4. But lest the gossip of the people perhaps

---

32. Cassiodorus's father.
33. Speciosus is addressed as *comitiacus* at *Var.* 2.10.
34. Inportunus and Theodorus were brothers.

offend these great men, an end to such presumption must be had. Let whomever impudently brings insult upon a passing reverend senator be held at fault, if he intended evil, when he ought to speak well. **5.** Nevertheless, who expects serious conduct at the games? The Catos knew not to gather at the circus. Whatever is said there by a celebrating people should not be deemed an insult. It is a place that excuses the excess of those for whom, if chatter is patiently indulged, it is shown even to adorn *Principes*. Let those who are occupied by such eagerness answer us without ambiguity: if the senators desire theirs to be peaceful opponents, clearly they want them to be the victors, since they will leap to insults then, when they blush to see themselves bested dishonorably. Why, therefore, do they choose to become enraged at what they know themselves without a doubt to have desired?

LETTER 1.28 (C. 507–11)

This is a general decree requiring the transportation of unused stone to local cities for use in fortifications. Presumably, the order would equip local magistrates with the authority to enforce such labor as a compulsory service or *munera*.

King Theoderic to All Goths and Romans

1. Construction is worthwhile in that city which promotes royal attention, since the restoration of old cities is the celebration of an age, in which both the adornment of peace is acquired and the necessary precautions of warfare are prepared. **2.** And so, by this present command, we decree that, in the future, if anyone has stones lying about in his field of any kind that would benefit the walls, in a charitable spirit he should hand them over without any delay. He will then take possession of what is more genuine than many things, since by this he would then contribute to the utility of his own city. **3.** Indeed, what is more agreeable than to witness the increase of public beauty, wherein the common advantage of all is embraced? And should stones of little worth be brought forth, it is fitting that what returns to their owner should be great in advantage: indeed, more is given back to him because of what is received on behalf of the greater good. For man often embraces his own gain, when by necessity he donates according to the needs of the time.

LETTER 1.29 (C. 507–11)

Similar to *Variae* 1.28, this seems to be a writ addressed to a local magistrate (here titled *vestra devotio*), charging him to restore lands used to maintain horses of the public post (*cursus publicus*) which have been claimed by local landowners (*possessores*). The letter pertains more broadly to the attention given to communications in northern Italy (cf. *Var.* 2.31, 4.47, 5.5, 5.17, 5.20).

King Theoderic to All Lucristani Settled on the River Isonzo

1. There is no doubt that the protection of the public post pertains to the advantage of the republic, a service through which the swift enactment of our proclamations is made public. And therefore, as greater provision must be made for the horses, so that the post should continue without interruption, let them not wither with unsightly neglect, lest, thin and overcome with weakness, they should succumb to their labors and a means designed for speed should become affected by delays. **2.** Therefore, mindful of the present command, let your devotion restore to the use of their way stations the tracts of land that formerly had been permitted to the horses, duly claimed from the landowner, so that land lost in small quantity should not harm him and land recovered should be sufficient for the horses.

LETTER 1.30 (C. 507–11)

This letter addresses the ongoing problem of maintaining civil order during the pantomime performances that attended chariot races at Rome. Senators are reminded that members of their households have been implicated in outbreaks of violence, seemingly in retaliation for various indignities to which senators have been subject during the games. The Senate is reminded that they may not shelter individuals from the discipline of the *Praefectus Urbis* and that the urban populace will be made aware of their right to appeal to the *Praefectus* (cf. *Var.* 1.31–33).

King Theoderic to the Senate of Rome

1. Our mind, conscript fathers, aroused by cares of the republic and scrutinizing the assemblies of diverse nations, is struck often by the complaints of the people of Rome, which, originating in events of celebration, nonetheless vomits forth severe excesses. For, it is lamentable that extremes of danger should transpire on account of the pleasure of the games, so that, with consideration for law driven hopelessly under foot, a slave's armed fury could harass the innocent. And what our kindness has bestowed upon them for the sake of delight, punishable audacity has turned into sadness. We restrain this with the accustomed foresight of our generosity, lest by gradually relaxing we would be compelled to punish a more severe offense. Indeed, is it not for a benevolent *Princeps* to prefer to punish faults, rather than to destroy, lest, either he is thought excessively harsh for punishing or he is considered lacking forethought for acting mildly? **2.** And therefore, we have decided in the present decree that, if the servant of any senator will by chance become involved in the assault of a free-born person, let that senator deliver the assailant to the law, so that with the particulars of the case having been discussed, a fitting sentence may be justly pronounced. If indeed the master should in bad faith fail to present to judges a man accused of such a deed, let him know himself to be liable to a fine of ten pounds of gold and, what is far more grievous, liable to enter into the danger of our displeasure. **3.** But, so that the honor of each man should be settled by justice and the esteem for civil harmony should come together with restored conduct, we also direct to the people our instructions, which we have enclosed to be openly shared with you, so that broken concord among citizens may be mended through one of several considered opinions. Accordingly, we have withdrawn the joy of the games from nobody, but we have torn out the seed of dissension, root and all. **4.** Let it therefore be decided between your splendid reputation and more base habits: avoid such servants as would be the bearers of injury, who would strive to ascribe to their love for you what they commit in crime, and who, while they desire to exercise their own willfulness, work to entangle your respectability. You, for whom solemnity has always been seemly, are not given to answer the empty words of the people with hostility. If the insult is such that it should deserve punishment, bring it to the notice of the *Praefectus Urbis,* so that the fault may be restrained by laws, not through vigilantism. For what distinguishes the man who strives to avenge himself to the point of excess from the one transgressing? For the citizen, it is revenge that comes by means of law that will not be regretted, and he who is known to have triumphed loftily over insult is the one proclaimed victor by the judge. **5.** As you know, the first battles were not between armed adversaries, but a contest, however incensed, resolved itself with fists, whence also comes the word *pugna.* Afterward, Belus first produced the iron sword, for which it was pleasing even to be called *bellum*: a savage assembly, a cruel assistance, a bestial disputation.[35] For even if to easily overcome the unarmed was first given a name by him, what posterity was thence wont to abolish must nevertheless be considered a crime. Therefore you should not permit members of your households to do against citizens what even now ought to be deplored against enemies.

LETTER 1.31 (C. 507–11)

This is a companion piece to *Variae* 1.30, concerning the civil disturbances attending the pantomime shows and chariot races at Rome. Citizens are reminded to respect the dignity of senators who attend the games.

King Theoderic to the People of Rome

1. We want the pleasure of the games to be a joy to the people, nor ought what was established for the diversion of the spirit provoke a motive for anger. For we have undertaken such a burden of expenses for that very reason, that your assembly should not be brazen in sedition, but rather adorned by peace. Reject such foreign

---

35. Cassiodorus here offers ironic exaggerations for the concepts of *pugna* ("quarrel") and *bellum* ("war"), to illustrate how some behaviors have no justification, however described.

behavior; let the voice of the people be Roman, which delights when it is heard. Do not let rejoicing give rise to violent insult, nor let it be engendered out of celebration. It was certainly this that you faulted in foreigners. Do not in any way aspire to adopt the disruptive life which you have observed others to follow.[36] **2.** And therefore, we have determined by public proclamation that, if an unjust voice should presume to commit outrageous injury to any of the senators, he will find himself hearing the law from the *Praefectus Urbis,* so that in response to the particulars of the case having been discussed, he may justly receive a public sentence. **3.** But so that every planted seed of discord should be extracted, we have ordered the pantomimes to practice their arts at assigned locations; but the arrangements given to the *Praefectus Urbis* will be able to instruct you. And thus it is that you should enjoy the delights of the city with composed minds. For there is nothing that we want to preserve for you more eagerly than the discipline of your forebears, so that what you always held to be praiseworthy in antiquity should increase more under us. **4.** For you have become accustomed to fill the very air with a sweet cry and to speak with one voice, which it delighted even the beasts to hear.[37] Let you produce voices sweeter than a musical instrument and thus resound among yourselves that certain harmony of the cither in a vaulted theater, so that anyone will be able to apprehend musical notes rather than discordant shouts. For what could be seemly amid such brawling and enflamed strife? Let rejoicing cast down raving, let revelry exclude wrath. For even a foreign disposition is able to be tempered when your applauses are sweetly heard.

LETTER 1.32 (C. 507–9)

This letter treats the civil disturbances of *Variae* 1.30 and 1.31 by addressing the *Praefectus Urbis* as the official ultimately responsible for maintaining order in Rome. Here it becomes clear that contention over the popularity of pantomime performers has played a role in the disturbances.

King Theoderic to Agapitus, Vir Illustris *and* Praefectus Urbis

1. It is fitting for the president of the most exalted city to be the custodian of peace. For from whom should moderation be expected more, than the one to whom Rome was entrusted? Indeed, that mother of all dignities rejoices that men of virtues preside over her. And therefore, you ought to be equal in disposition to your exalted position, so that what you have acquired from our favors would be credited to your merits. It is fitting that you constantly be on the watch, lest any cause for disturbance arise during the games, since a tranquil people is your public reputa-

---

36. Perhaps a reference to circus riots in eastern cities?
37. Presumably a reference to interaction between audience and animals in the amphitheater.

tion. Let moderate behavior be cause for triumph, so that an honorable license should not squander liberty nor should discipline lack good conduct. **2.** On which account, just as we have instructed the highest rank and we have decreed the people to be advised by our proclamations, so by this we recommend your greatness to observe, that, if there is an insult to a senator from any kind of indiscretion, brazen temerity should be punished immediately by the severity of the law. But indeed, should a senator, unmindful of civil harmony, cause any free-born citizen to be harassed by execrable assault, being immediately apprehended by a summons sent from our court, let him anticipate much trouble. **3.** For everyone should be mindful to thus separate factional politics from the zeal for the games, as there ought to be concord in the homeland, nor should disorder be displayed for its own pleasure, from which hostile wrath would begin to seethe. But lest hereafter anything will again be able to provoke outrageous strife, introduce Helladius to the public eye.[38] Let him offer pleasure to the people and hold equal place among the pantomimes of the other factions. **4.** Moreover, we declare by the present dictate that, because it incites frequent riots among the people, that Helladius's followers should assign a free opportunity for others to watch him, whom we have selected to dance in public without favor to any faction. Even if the fickle inclination of the crowd should gravitate in favor of one faction, let the people thus enjoy its enthusiasm in the circus as in the theater, from the faction which it loves, so that if it presumes to pursue prohibited disturbances, the faction itself may be judged.

LETTER 1.33 (C. 507–9)

Following upon the concern in *Variae* 1.32 for the role of pantomimes in maintaining public order during the games at Rome, this letter directs the same *Praefectus Urbis* to support the pantomime of the Green Faction with public funds.

King Theoderic to Agapitus, Vir Illustris *and* Praefectus Urbis

1. A judgment of our serenity, once published, knows nothing of uncertainty; nor may that which has been settled by prudent arrangements be altered by the deception of any opportunity. Pursuant to that, not long ago we gave instructions to the patricians Albinus and Avienus, to the effect that they should select the pantomime of the Green Faction who would befit the games most excellently, which, having been accomplished, they had disclosed to us in their own report. **2.** And therefore, we have now decided in this present writ that it be confirmed: to whomever the above-mentioned distinguished men have chosen, you should pay without reduction that monthly salary owed to the Green Faction, so that what our

---

38. Helladius appears at *Var.* 1.20.4, but is otherwise unattested.

foresight has determined for the sake of eradicating disorder should not become an opportunity for riots, but for peace.

LETTER 1.34 (C. 507–11)

This letter directs the *Praefectus Praetorio* to regulate the amount of grain being shipped from each province in order to ensure local inhabitants have proper provisions.

King Theoderic to Faustus, Praefectus Praetorio

1. The harvest of grain first ought to supply the province in which it was sown, so that the local inhabitants are sustained by their own fruitfulness, which is drained dry by the eager greed of foreign merchants. Indeed, that which is surplus ought to be assigned for other regions and should be intended for foreign lands afterward, when the amount for local needs has been satisfied. **2.** And therefore, your distinguished *illustris,* let those who are known to have the administration of the shores in each port be advised that nobody should load grain onto merchant ships bound for foreign shores before they determine the amount most suitable for public distribution.

LETTER 1.35 (C. 507–11)

One of the more fascinating examples of natural history in the collection, this letter fulminates against the *Praefectus Praetorio* for delays in the shipment of taxed grain for which nature herself could offer no excuses.

King Theoderic to Faustus, Praefectus Praetorio

1. Although the dryness of the current year, which customarily ravages this region in certain seasons has hardened the inland areas with excessive heat, it is not so much that it produces a harvest of crops that must be abandoned as that it brings forth only partial fruitfulness. This crop, which is normally expected even in abundant times, now must be demanded with greater eagerness. **2.** And therefore, we are irritated not to have received in the autumn, in any manner, the public grain, which is customarily to be sent in the summer from the Calabrian and Apulian shores by your *cancellarius.* With the course of the sun rushing back to southern skies, the measured arrangement of nature revives the tumultuous storms with an agitation of the atmosphere, which is given from these same months in order to know when preparation for the amount of rains to come should be suitably undertaken. Why, therefore, such a delay? Would not ships sent out into such calmness be swift? Would not the clear position of stars dipping into the sea invite sails to swiftly spread and would not faith in calm skies fail to deter the promise of hastening? **3.** Or, perhaps, with a favorable southern wind and oarsmen assisting, remoras fetter the course of the ships,[39] delayed even now among the waves? Or do the conches of the Indian Sea fasten their lips to the bottoms of the ships to similar effect? It is said that the gentle hold of these restrains a vessel more than the disturbed elements are able to propel. Thus, a winged ship would stand unmoving with swollen sails and have no course. Even though the wind should be favorable, it stands fixed without anchor, fettered without ropes; and so a small animal holds it back more than the assistance of fair weather may compel it. Thus, while submissive waters prepare the course, it happens that the hull of the ship stands transfixed beneath the sea and by a marvelous means is restrained, swimming motionlessly, while the water is driven along by innumerable waves. **4.** But let us mention another kind of fish: perhaps the sailors of the aforementioned ships languish on account of the paralyzing touch of the eel, by which skilled hands are weighed down by such fixedness, that it thus corrupts the hand as though stricken through by a spear (to which it would be vulnerable), to the extent that a portion of the living body is stunned and immobile without any feeling. We believe that these sailors who are unable to move themselves have acquired such an affliction. But for them the impediment of the remora is venality, the bite of the conch is insatiable greed, the eel is the pretense of fraud. Indeed, these very men have fabricated delays with a perverse eagerness, so that opportunities for embarking should seem adverse. Let your greatness, you for whom it is especially important to be concerned about such things, cause this to be corrected by the most expedient emendation, lest the poverty native to this region seem not to be so much from the bareness of the season as from negligence.

LETTER 1.36 (C. 507–11)

This letter grants a man of senatorial rank a public post of undisclosed title. More attention is given to the recipient's first duty, which is to provide legal guardianship (*tuitio*) for the surviving sons of the man who previously held the position.

King Theoderic to Ferriolus, Vir Spectabilis

1. The utility of good men in leading roles ought to be to renewed by their successor, lest any interrupted office should suffer a loss through the inability of its ministers. And therefore, we bid you to undertake the place, by our authority, once held by Benedictus in the city of Pedona,[40] so that, setting forth everything with diligent care, you should merit the increase of our gratitude. You should also direct your attention to those surviving Benedictus, since we are eager to recompense the

---

39. Remoras are opportunistic passengers that fasten themselves to larger fish and ocean vessels.
40. Located on the Ligurian border with Gaul.

relations of the deceased whose good faith we are unable to forget. **2.** Moreover, we recall this out of the habit of our duty, because the good memory of loyal servants does not flee from us. Thus, let you cause those sons of the aforementioned Benedictus, who was known to obey us with sincere devotion, to be protected by legal guardianship, to the extent that, fittingly alleviated from cares by your protection, they would rejoice to have been conferred security from their father's servitude. What was able to be distinguished by the devotion of one man would, therefore, profit the son, since it is fitting that we contribute more than we are seen to receive from our servants. Here fairness is not equal, but our portion is weighed most justly when it is burdened more by making recompense.

LETTER 1.37 (C. 507–11)

This letter attempts to resolve the delicate issue of an honor killing. The accused is absolved of the previously imposed exile provided that he can demonstrate adultery as the cause of murder. Examples from nature are offered to substantiate the standing of chastity in natural law. The sentence also offers protection against any harassment that the defendant or his legal guarantor (*fideiussor*) may suffer.[41]

King Theoderic to Crispianus

1. However much more the ears may revile the crime of homicide and the eyes may avoid the cruel hand of the guilty, since the path inclined toward misery is always apparent to those with good intentions, nonetheless, homicide must be weighed by the consideration of justice, since for some injury may become a necessary crime.[42] If a man should prove himself innocent, then, by twist of fate, this curse of all humanity will be something different. For who could endure leading to the courts a man who has striven to violate the rights of matrimony? **2.** It is innate for wild animals to defend their own marriage bond from foreign attention, since that which is condemned by natural law is inimical to all animals. We have seen the bull to defend its herd in horn-locked combat, rams to rage headfirst into foe on behalf of its ewes, the stallion to assert its claim to mares with blows and bites. Thus do those who are not swayed by coyness array their passions for their consorts. **3.** Moreover, how much more should man bear to leave unavenged an adultery which, to have overlooked it, would become known to his everlasting shame? And therefore, if you are cheated in the least with respect to the veracity of the petition sent against you and you have washed the blemish on your marriage bed

---

41. For different treatments of adultery, *Var.* 2.10, 2.11, 4.40, 5.32–33.

42. Crispianus is otherwise unattested, although his *fideiussor* Agnellus had patrician rank; that the letter refers to Crispianus's exile also indicates he was himself of high rank, otherwise capital punishment would have been warranted.

with the blood of the discovered adulterer, lest you toil under the appearance of a bloodstained mind on account of honor, we order you released from the exile that you had been sentenced to, since for a married man to draw steel on behalf of his love of chastity is not to trample the laws under foot, but to honor them. **4.** Nonetheless, in case a lawful accuser would appear, you should be proven by a hearing concerning the nature of your deed so that, if you come through innocent, the crime will be reduced to a civil penalty. If you have separated the intimate embraces of the adulterers by wrongful death, let it be considered a crime rather than punishment. **5.** If, however, anyone has caused the injury reserved for the guilty on you or your legal guarantor Agnellus, as you say, if it has happened that money has been wrenched away by the *Vicarius* or his office, by our decree let a second hearing restore the obstructed laws. Indeed, we do not want property to be destroyed for anyone whom our sentence is known to free from penalty. In the same way, we offer you the guardianship of similar protection against the lawless attacks of Candac,[43] so that he should neither drag you into the courts nor may he again belabor you contrary to common rights.

LETTER 1.38 (C. 507–11)

This letter manumits a young Goth from the legal protection of his uncle and demands the restoration of his legal inheritance, citing both precedent from natural history and the military obligations of young Gothic soldiers.

King Theoderic to Boio, Vir Spectabilis

1. That which is bestowed upon the unwilling is not a favor; nor will anything seem useful which is granted with hostile intent. Whence, let your *spectabilis* know we have come upon serious complaints of your young nephew Wiliarit, to whit, that you detain the property of his father, not for the sake of improving, but for abrogating a vow. Therefore, whatever you know yourself to have held back by previous right, restore now without any delay, so that he may dispose of the property of his parents according to his own discretion, because he also seems to us to be a suitable person who would profit by assuming the prerogatives of a master. **2.** Bold eagles nourish their own pullets for a long time by measuring out the morsels of food, until with the more tender plumage gradually disappearing they become fledged in an adult's estate. As their flight becomes steady, new claws become habituated to delicate spoils; nor do those who are able to be satisfied by their own game need to live by the labors of others. And thus with our own young men, who

---

43. Note that Cassiodorus's Latin may indicate that Candac had been offered to Crispianus as protection (*tuitio*), possibly as a *saio*, although it is equally likely that Candac was a relation of the man slain by Crispianus.

are deemed fit for the army and thought capable of waging war, it is shameful that they should be called feeble in arranging their own lives and deemed unable to manage their own homes. Among Goths, excellence determines the age of majority, and whoever is capable of striking down an enemy ought to defend himself from any slander.

LETTER 1.39 (C. 507–11)

A curious letter refusing the request of a man serving at court (*nostri palatii*) that the sons of his brother be restored to their hometown of Syracuse. The letter orders an *illustris* senator and patrician to maintain their custody at Rome. Possibly related to *Variae* 2.22, which rescinds a similar order. See also *Variae* 4.6, for an almost identical request from another Syracusan *spectabilis*.

King Theoderic to Festus, Vir Illustris *and Patrician*

1. We gladly embrace the reasonable requests of supplicants, we who consider not only the rights of the petitioner. For what is more worthy than that we are wrapped in constant deliberations both day and night, so that just as arms protect our republic, equity too would preserve the state inviolate? And so the *spectabilis* Philagrius abiding in the city of Syracuse, being long detained by the duties of our court, entreats that those sons of his brother whom he presented at Rome in order to study should be returned to him at their home. **2.** Let your *illustris* magnificence situate these sons, retaining them by our order in the above-mentioned city; nor should it be permitted for them to depart until such a time that we have decided upon the matter with a second order. For thus is the advancement of character acquired by them and for us a measure of advantage is preserved, by which a delay can be beneficial, when one who is able to acquire wisdom would occasionally seek to avoid his homeland. Only by chance had Ithaca concealed, in his own home, that Ulysses whose wisdom the noble song of Homer especially claims, because he wandered among many cities and peoples, where those men wiser than himself always dwelled who were considered learned from their frequent dealings with many men.[44] For indeed, just as human nature is instructed by hard work, thus lethargy is inspired by leisure.

LETTER 1.40 (C. 507–11)

This letter orders a military *comes* to procure arms for soldiers stationed in the province of Dalmatia and offers interesting justification from natural history and military theory.

44. Possibly a reference to Homer, *Odyssey* 1.3.

King *Theoderic to Osuin,* Vir Illustris *and* Comes

1. Our preparation should not be impeded by delay, lest that which depends upon being advantageously arranged encounters an obstacle through the fault of tardiness. And therefore, arms must be distributed before necessity can demand it, so that, when the occasion requires, those more prepared should overcome the unprepared. For the art of waging war is a skill that, if it is not trained beforehand, whenever it should become necessary, it will not be at hand. Consequently, by our order, your elevated *illustris* will procure all necessary arms for the soldiers of Salona, so that the capacity for warlike expeditions will have been made available to them, since the true security of the republic is an armed defender. Let the soldier learn in peace what he will perform in war. They will not rouse their courage for arms in a crisis unless they entrust themselves to what is suitable to that very activity beforehand. Bull-calves wage battles, by which they satisfy the requirements of a more vigorous age. Puppies play at unfamiliar hunts. We begin lighting fire in our very hearths with tender kindling, but should you apply full wood to the first sparks, you would extinguish the small fire which you strive to encourage. Thus the courage of men, unless they are first accustomed gradually to that which you intend, will fail to be suitably prepared. All beginnings are fearful and timidity will not be overcome by other means, except when unfamiliarity with inevitable things is removed.

LETTER 1.41 (C. 507–9)

This letter announces to the *Praefectus Urbis* the award of senatorial membership to a young man, with interesting commentary on the heritable nature of the senatorial order and an oblique comparison to the eastern Senate of Constantinople.

King *Theoderic to Agapitus,* Vir Illustris *and* Praefectus Urbis

1. An especially protective concern for your order leads me to prefer deliberation, and the Senate's accustomed state of honor compels me to investigate whoever must be admitted to an assembly requiring such deference. We want the Senate to increase, not only by the number of its members, but especially by the brilliance of those deserving membership, with which it is adorned. Let another order accept mediocrities by mistake; this Senate rejects those not proven to be exceptional. Therefore, we seek in a colleague that nobility which is better than nobility of the blood, which may produce morals inconsistent with itself, some worthlessness that hides in the blood. And therefore, concerning Faustus, the adult son of the *illustris* Faustus, let your *illustris* magnificence determine what the venerable order has dictated to be allotted concerning those who would be brought into the curia. For in this request, we diminish no precepts concerning the customary authority of the sacred order, since it is a greater glory to behold the decision of leading men after a royal decree. Indeed, it is an honor for those very same men, if we bid what they are accustomed to choose for themselves, and if we should grandly demand what is sought from them daily.

LETTER 1.42 (C. 509–10)

This letter elevates Artemidorus to the office of *Praefectus Urbis*. Perhaps unlike his predecessor, Agapitus, the letter indicates that Artemidorus's advancement had been preceded by a period of official service at Theoderic's court.

King Theoderic to Artemidorus, Vir Illustris *and* Praefectus Urbis

1. The remuneration of deserving service produces for the one ruling a just *imperium,* within which anything attained through labor knows naught of ruin. For if we grant rewards unexpectedly, in what way would we be able to deny what we owe? Every devotion that is obtained resides in safe keeping with us and one who knows himself to have been obedient to us in any way gathers a doubled harvest. 2. Indeed, often you have deserved to have from us what would be more costly than an office, as you were worthy to remain close at the side of the throne. Our affection contrived to detain you. You have obtained promotion more slowly for the sake of one who cherishes you, so that after a taste of consecrated friendship, you would advance to honors even more adorned. And now, indeed, everything from whence refinement gets its renown sits congenially in you—birthplace, lineage, noble instruction. Of which, if only one should comprise nobility, summed up in you they should render more, you who gleam in the good fortune of your native sun no less than you are furnished with the glory of pedigree and excellence. 3. Hence it is that now, on the third indiction, we have raised you auspiciously to the pinnacle of the urban prefecture, conferring the *fasces* upon you in that city where honors are everlasting. We, who calculate our rewards more modestly, will certainly admit that you deserved much in our judgment, so that you will preside over that assembly which you know to be revered by all humankind. 4. What is it to govern a palace and manage your own household? A post acquires more according to its importance. Such is not the case for undertaking the care of a wine cellar, but rather to serve as guardian over a precious jewel. We bestow this post on those best suited for preserving, which we believe preferable, and on those from whom we need not suffer recrimination. We attach this post to those with truly the most faithful intentions. If Rome has an equal, then judge us to have entrusted similar honors upon others; but if it is a singular honor, then we have made you the governor of exceptional wealth, which we hope to always increase.

LETTER 1.43 (C. 509–10)

This letter to the Senate confirms the appointment of Artemidorus as *Praefectus Urbis* (cf. *Var.* 1.42), with additional insight into his origin in the eastern Senate of

Constantinople. Of note is the intimacy that Artemidorus seems to have had as an advisor to Theoderic before being sent to Rome.

King Theoderic to the Senate of Rome

1. You know, conscript fathers, your genius to be the peak of honors; you know it to be advantageous to yourselves that it falls to us to bestow the dignity of the *fasces*. For whenever an honor is taken up by someone, it is the Senate that gains. For you recognize what we value concerning your assembly, when we bestow this reward upon men truly accomplished in long service, so that they deserve to be colleagues of your body. **2.** Here, indeed, is such a man, who has preferred to cleave to us while forsaking the sweetness of his native sun. And although he would be permitted distinction in his native country, nonetheless he chose to support our own fortune, passing over power with the greatness of his generous nature, this man enjoyed the company of the *Princeps* Zeno,[45] not as a faithful servant, but as a relation by marriage. And what favors could he not have obtained from his family in that republic, which so readily favors foreigners? But much beloved, he despised all these benefits, so that rightly we should be amazed that so many desirable advantages have been scorned by one man, and it is for us that he is known to have done this. **3.** This man, beyond this exceptional fidelity, has shared with us the comfort of his conversation, so that he would sometimes disperse with the sweetness of his speech the stormy cares of the republic, which we undertake according to the necessity of emerging affairs. Flattering in his encouragement, a faithful patron of those seeking assistance, never thinking to blame, but only enjoying to commend. This man has made himself famous by the great purity of his intentions, so that when he deserved from us the dignities of court, he satisfied himself with the pleasant duty of arranging the spectacles, so much that he seemed to willingly prefer serving under the guise of pleasure, even to the extent of withholding himself from duties, but estranging himself from us in no portion. **4.** For even as a cheerful dinner companion, he has adorned the royal table, here striving to attach himself to us, where we are most able to take pleasure. But what more must be said concerning his morals, which suffice to thoroughly demonstrate that he has always deserved our affection? To be deserving is not greater than finding the favor of a ruler; for those who are known always to select the deserving, it is natural to seek the best among all men. **5.** And therefore, making payment for his labors, we have bestowed the *fasces* of the urban prefecture on the *illustris* Artemidorus. Therefore, conscript fathers, favor one surpassing in so many and such remarkable merits with your acclamation; favor him with your collegiality. He will also be a commendation for your good will, so that, when you measure esteem with honors, you would spur others to his example.

---

45. Eastern emperor from 474–91.

LETTER 1.44 (C. 509-10)

This is clearly a supplement to the previous announcement of Artemidorus's appointment as *Praefectus Urbis* (*Var.* 1.42–43), here stating more forcefully the direct authority that he will have over civil disturbances at Rome.

King Theoderic to the Senate of Rome

1. You will be able to recognize the special esteem that we have for you by the very same cares for which we are seen to be so disturbed, that we should permit no admonition to be disregarded. Affection promotes caution and what we prize most eagerly, we watch over with greater regard. **2.** Hence it is that we gave the ruling *fasces* of the urban prefecture to the *illustris* Artemidorus, who has been long educated in our service, so that, since civic harmony has been overturned by the lawless rioting of certain persons, the innocent should have a witness of pure conscience and the errant should be subject to a just punisher. We, who are delighted by the guiltless, have decided what must be given preference for the reputation of all concerned, lest anyone should presume unexpectedly to go beyond accustomed punishment. **3.** On which account, you will want to transfer such matters to us through the aforementioned man, so that, if any disorderly person comes forth, he would meet with the impediment of our mandates on the spot. And although the laws have conceded this authority to the *Praefectus Urbis*, we have nonetheless transferred that authority to him in particular, so that he would be able to accomplish more confidently what had been permitted to two. **4.** He will, therefore, stand bold before the most outrageous persons and by our authority overthrow the unreasonable with public punishment. Let the rage of the most disruptive minds be at rest. Why should the blessings of peace, which by the grace of God you have earned through our labor, be spoiled by lawless rioting? The traditions of your forebears have never been more in danger of harm, than when Roman seriousness is at fault. And so let an honorable city restore its restraint. It is shameful for the most prominent citizens to have degenerated, especially at a time when you know yourselves to have the kind of *Princeps* who confers rewards on the well deserving and punishment on the disruptive.

LETTER 1.45 (C. 507)

The second of three letters addressed to Boethius, this letter requests that Boethius prepare clocks to be delivered by envoys to the Burgundian court of Gundobad. Like *Variae* 1.10, this letter provides an opportunity for an elaborate disquisition on engineering. And like the third letter addressed to Boethius (*Var.* 2.40), which prepares for envoys to the Frankish court of Clovis, this letter says less about Ostrogothic diplomatic culture than interest in Boethius's legacy as a philosopher.

It is also worth noting that the letter discourses at far greater length than does the letter to Gundobad (*Var.* 1.46), for whom Boethius had been consulted. A similar disproportion prevails in the next pair of letters to Boethius and Clovis (*Var.* 2.40 and 2.41).

King Theoderic to Boethius, Vir Illustris *and Patrician*

1. Favors requested out of presumption by foreign kings should not be scorned, since acts of little consequence may succeed in accomplishing far more than the greatest riches would be able to obtain. Indeed, what arms often fail to accomplish, the pleasantries of kindness impose. Therefore, while we seem to trifle, it is also on behalf of the republic. For in this way we seek after delights, so that we may accomplish something earnest. **2.** And so the master of the Burgundians has avidly requested from us that a clock, one that observes limits by the rhythmic measurement of flowing water and one that designates completed hours with the illumination of the full sun, ought to be sent to him with instructors for such devices. By enjoying such sought-after delights, what is quotidian for us would seem miraculous to them. Indeed, it is fitting that they should desire to gaze upon what has astounded them in the reports of their own legates. **3.** We have discovered that you are known as one gorged on great learning, so that concerning those arts that men commonly practice without understanding, you have imbibed from the very source of their instruction. For you entered upon them, having abided long in the schools of Athens, mingling the toga with the crowds of Greek tunics, so that you made Greek philosophy become Roman learning. Indeed you have learned with what depth speculative theories may be considered in their own categories, by which each is learned within its respective divisions by active reasoning, passing on to the senatorial heirs of Romulus everything extraordinary about the world that the heirs of Cecrops produced. **4.** In your translations, the Italian reads Pythagorean poetry and Ptolemean astronomy; the Ausonian hears the arithmetic of Nicomachus and the geometry of Euclid; the children of Quirinus discuss the theology of Plato and the logic of Aristotle; you have even given back to the Sicilians a Latinate mechanics of Archimedes. And whatever learning or arts Greek eloquence has produced through multiple men, Rome has received in its native speech from your single authorship. To those famous men you have restored such a great splendor of words, to men already remarkable you have added such great propriety of language, that those who have read both works would be justified in preferring yours. **5.** You entered upon the aforementioned art, known from famous teaching, by way of the fourfold doors of mathematics. Situating these matters in the inner sanctum of nature, summoned forth in the books of authorities, you have come to know clarity of spirit, you, whose purpose it is to know difficult practices and to display wonders. It is stirring to display that which men have come to wonder at, and in a marvelous manner this thing draws faith in an event from the reversal of nature, even while it offers proof to the eyes. Such knowledge causes water drawn from below to fall headlong, fire to course with its own weight, instruments to sound out with unnatural voice, and fills pipes with traveling wind, so that trifles may bewitch by their very artifice. **6.** By its means, we have seen the fortifications of once tottering cities suddenly rise up with great strength, so that the despairing man is rendered greater who finds strength by the assistance of machines. Buildings steeped in seawater are drained; while what is firm may be loosened by ingenious contrivance. Metal objects bellow, a Diomedes trumpets heavier in bronze, copper snakes hiss, the likenesses of birds chirp, and that which is known not to have its own voice is proven to emit the sweetness of chatter. **7.** We shall mention a little concerning that by which it is lawful for the heavens to be imitated.[46] Here Archimedes caused a second sun to traverse in its sphere; here he forged another zodiac wheel by human deliberation; there with artifice he demonstrated the moon, restored from its own waning illumination; there a small machine pregnant with the world, a portable heaven, an abbreviation of the universe, a mirror to the likeness of nature in the upper world that flies with its own incomprehensible movements. Thus a constellation, for which we are permitted to know the courses, we nevertheless do not discern to advance before deceived eyes: standing, it crosses through the stars and what you know by true reason has coursed swiftly along, you would not behold moving. **8.** How wondrous it is for humanity to devise that which is hardly able to be understood? Because published fame in such matters adorns you, send the clocks to us at public expense and without any loss to yourself. Let the first be one where the indicator is designed to show the hours by its own slender shadow. And so a small and motionless spoke, accomplishing what that wondrous span of the sun traverses, it matches the flight of the sun, the motion of which it always ignores. **9.** If the stars were sentient, they would envy such an accomplishment, and would perhaps turn away from their own courses, lest they should be cast under such ridicule. What unique miracle is in the light of approaching hours if even a shadow reveals them? What is the distinction of an unfailing rotation, if even a metal device that remains continually in place accomplishes it? O the inestimable excellence of the craft, which succeeds in making the secrets of nature common, when it claims itself only to play! **10.** Let the second clock be where the hours are recognized without the radiance of the sun, dividing even the night into portions, so, as though owing nothing to the heavens, it converts the reckoning of the heavens instead to the flow of water, by which it shows with motion what revolves in the heavens and by bold presumption artifice confers measure upon the elements, which a stipulation of creation denied. The whole of the disciplines of learning, every endeavor of the learned, as far as they are able, seeks to know the power of nature; it is only mechanics which attempts to

46. The famous astrolabe of Archimedes of Syracuse.

imitate nature by contrary means and, if it is proper to say so, to a certain extent it even strives to surpass nature. For this is known to have made Dedalus fly; this caused the iron Cupid to be suspended in the temple of Diana without any fastenings. It is this art that today causes mute objects to sing, the inanimate to live, and the immovable to be moved. **11.** The engineer, if it is proper to say, is practically a colleague with nature, revealing secret things, controlling the palpable, tinkering with the wondrous, and thus simulating the sublime, so that what is known to have been arranged by craft is nonetheless valued as real. Since we know you have studiously read in this art, will you as quickly as possible hasten to send the aforementioned clocks to us, so that you would make yourself noted in that part of the world, where otherwise you would not be able to travel. **12.** Let foreign nations recognize in you the kind of nobles that we have, who are chosen as authorities. How will they manage to disbelieve what they will have seen? How often will they attribute this reality to a pleasurable dream? And when they have recovered from their stupor, they should not dare to call themselves equals with us, in whose presence they know learned men have thought upon such ingenious devices.

LETTER 1.46 (C. 507)

This letter is a companion to *Variae* 1.45, where Boethius has been asked to equip a delegation to the Burgundian court with clocks. Here, Gundobad is greeted and encouraged to order the lives of Burgundians according to a civilizing arrangement of time. Gundobad was king of the Burgundians from 473 to 516.

Theoderic to Gundobad, King of the Burgundians

1. Gifts that are proven entirely useful must surely be embraced, especially when what can fulfill a desire is not objectionable. For whatever price attaches to a thing, so much does the attention of the one desiring incline toward it, so that it should be fulfilled. Therefore, greeting your prudence with the usual kindness by carriers, *ille* and *ille,* we have determined these amusements must be dispatched—clocks with their own regulators. The one, in which human ingenuity seems to be gathered, is known to compass the extent of the entire day; the other knows the course of the sun without its presence and delimits the span of hours with drops of water. **2.** Possess in your country what you formerly have seen in Rome.[47] It is fitting that your pleasure, which is conjoined to us also by marriage, should enjoy our blessings. Let Burgundy learn under you to contemplate the most finely wrought things and to praise the inventions of the ancients. Through you, Burgundy sets aside the habit of a foreign nation and when it reflects upon the foresight of its king, it rightly yearns for the accomplishments of the wise. Let Burgundy mark off the

47. Gundobad had briefly served as *magister militum* in Italy from 472 to 473 or 474.

span of the day according to its own determination; let her establish the most fitting passage of hours. **3.** A confused order of life is driven headlong, if its very
divisions are not understood according to the actual nature of things. Indeed, it is
the manner of beasts to feel the hours according to the hunger of their bellies and
not to hold as certain what is well ordered in human practice.

Book 2

This letter addresses the delicate issue of selecting a candidate for the annual consulship in Rome. By the sixth century, it had become tradition for two consuls to host annual celebrations, one in Rome and the other in Constantinople. Communication between rulers concerning consular appointments were diplomatic opportunities to negotiate other agenda. In this case, Theoderic has chosen Felix, a man from a leading Gallic family, illustrating one strategy to bring southern Gaul under Amal authority following the conflict with the Franks (507–11). Letters announcing the appointment to the candidate and Senate follow (*Var.* 2.2 and 2.3).

King Theoderic to the Most Dutiful Imperator Anastasius

1. The custom of annual celebration reminds us to give a name to the calendar year, that adornment particular to Rome, the earthly distinction of the Senate, so that the grace of offices may continue according to the passage of years and so that the memory of the age is consecrated by the generosity of the *Principes*. May a fortunate year take good omen from its consul,[1] and by such a name, let the year named after him enter the gates of days and let the good fortune of its beginning favor the remaining portion. **2.** For what could be better accepted by you than that Rome should gather back her own fosterlings into her bosom and that she should count the Gallic Senate among the assembly of her own venerated name? The curia knows well the distinction of Transalpine blood, which not just once has decorated

---

1. Here *felix annus* offers a play on the consul's name of "Felix."

its own crown with the blossom of that nobility. Among other offices, the curia knows to choose men from there as consuls. This man is a natural claimant to honors by right of antiquity, from which he is lead to the senatorial robe by a long pedigree. For who does not know Felix to be natively endowed with good qualities, a man who from the very first indications displayed that merit which is known to hasten to the homeland of virtues.[2] Prosperity follows upon good judgment and he increased in promotions with independence. We could not permit one to remain unglorified, who has deserved to attain public office in the republic. 3. He is plainly worthy of our generosity, who in the very flower of childhood curbed a perilous time of life with mature habits and, because he is a man blessed with uncommon restraint, when deprived of a father, he became a son to seriousness. He subjugated that cupidity so hostile to wisdom, he despised the allurements of vice, and he ground underfoot the vanities of pride. Thus with excesses overcome, he was already seen to hold the consulship with respect to his morals. 4. Therefore, we would recompense that good moral foundation which tested probity confers and offer this candidate the curule fillets,[3] so that we may be able to prompt the desire for excellence by rewards, since eagerness will not fail for an office which holds the most liberal reward. And therefore, you, who are delighted by blessings to both republics without preference, lend your support, attach your assent. A distinguished man who deserves to be raised to the very *fasces* is selected by the judgment of us both.

LETTER 2.2 (C. 511)

Announcing the appointment of Felix as consul, this letter is part panegyric and part exhortation. Although the candidate's moral qualifications are emphasized, it is clear from the tone of the letter that Felix was selected to entice support for the Amal regime among Gallic nobility. The letter's emphasis on generosity accurately reflects the financial obligations of a consul to host spectacles at Rome.

King Theoderic to Felix, Vir Illustris *and Consul*

1. We love that our favors should double, nor should generosity demonstrate reluctance once conferred. Those men more frequently rouse us to rewards who deserved to receive the auspices of our gratitude. You know that judgment is certainly weighed; nevertheless, it is pleasing that a favor be demonstrated. For indeed, it is not becoming for the judgment of a *Princeps* to remain fixed, since former accomplishments recommend themselves to later gifts and every unhesitating decision is strengthened with repetition. Recently, we granted an honored

2. *Ad patriam virtutum,* meaning Rome.
3. The ornaments of the consulship.

rank to you,[4] and now, we confer the height of a dignified position. And in this way, we are seen to have deservingly bestowed former favors and, with these to follow, our kindness is considered to have remained constant. **2.** For we do not permit those who have been marked by the fame of their birth to remain without glory. On the contrary, when the favor of offices continues through the family, good fortune of every kind should prosper under the rule of a good *Princeps*. For who would despair of promotion, where it is given in affection and to demonstrate purpose? You hold yourself to have proven evidence of this kindness when, with the blessings of your native sun abandoned, you had traveled to an ancient homeland as though a kind of *postliminium*.[5] Our affection awaits you; the hand fills with advantages and causes what you sought from our *imperium* to be vowed. Thus it was fitting to elevate one who clearly chose better things. Indeed, fortune changes with each master, and what the subject acquires, prospers in the praise of the ruler. **3.** But you have demonstrated something of this generosity in yourself. For, enriched with the distinction of an *illustris*, you bore yourself with such great maturity, as evidenced by the fact that you had endured fragile years under a weight that the most potent strength of character would not be able to overcome at a mature age. For when enriched by paternal property which new heirs always waste, you conserved that wealth, since you instead attained an eagerness to labor for it. For it is natural that what has been acquired without difficulty should easily be squandered. **4.** You have increased your patrimony by constant application. For what better indication would be sought as testimony for the consulship than good management? By this very ability, you have merited what could hardly be obtained with a ruined patrimony. Thrift in private matters nourishes public generosity. You have transcended the glory of your father by praiseworthy conduct and what that man was unable to undertake, you have accomplished from the use of his resources.[6] The triumphal carriage does not reach heights except with great boldness, while it is even loftier to wish for a generous spirit. **5.** Self-confidence makes a man daring, since nature expects him to stand out who does not permit himself to be obscured. Through you the consulship returns to a Transalpine family and you have invigorated parched laurels with a green shoot. Behold the sacred city glittering with your good wishes. Hold, therefore, the high ground of praiseworthiness, so that your forebears, whom you restore to distinction, you would transcend in virtue. And so, take the regalia of the consulship for the fourth indiction and comport yourself as worthy of such great auspices with immediate generosity to those in need. **6.** Here is truly the place where an office merits extravagance and

4. More than likely his senatorial rank as *illustris*.

5. *Postliminium* was the restoration of full legal rights to a Roman citizen after residence in non-Roman territory.

6. The father is otherwise unattested.

where it is a kind of virtue not to prize one's own property, where however much one is deprived of resources, so much does one attain reputation. Behold yourself upon the shoulders of all and fluttering from mouth to mouth. Present yourself as the kind of man you would deem worthy of his origins, worthy of the city, worthy of our judgment, and worthy of consular raiment.

LETTER 2.3 (C. 511)

A lengthier companion to *Variae* 2.1 and 2.2, this letter provides more detail concerning the family of the consul designate.

King Theoderic to the Senate of Rome

1. Rejoice, conscript fathers, that a payment in offices has returned to you; rejoice that the provinces, unaccustomed to such practices after a long period, now send you men to esteem as consuls. And look forward to even greater things from such a sign. Often do beginnings portent better things, which, while they originate in insignificance, they consequently elevate themselves to great admiration. **2.** A noble race lay idle under the suspension of Gallic courts and, deprived of its own honorary offices, it returned a stranger to its homeland.[7] At length, by divine providence, those burdened were relieved; they chose to recover Rome in glory and to recover the ancient laurels of their ancestors from the honored grove of the curia. For who would be able to refuse a kind of duty one would regard as treasure deposited in a citadel? Indeed, the consulship of a prior Felix still thrives in common banter,[8] since good character is known to endure after the man and what he gloriously accomplished will not be bound by the end of time. **3.** Satisfied with the rich quality of his forebears, let us move from the ancient family to that most noble father of the candidate, who,[9] still before the eyes of all, shone forth in the curia with the torch of wisdom, so that he was rightly considered brilliant among so many other luminary dignities. Indeed, dedicated to the study of letters, he gave over his entire life to the most learned disciplines. Not with, as they say, a light kiss did he pursue eloquence, but he sated himself fully in the spring of the Muses. **4.** An ardent debater over books, a delightful declaimer of stories, and an extraordinary producer of words, in prose he was equal to the merits of those authors whom he had often read. Moreover, he advertised the blessings of intense study

7. Here, with *peregrinabatur in patria,* the letter plays with the estrangement of Gallic nobility from Italy as the source of Roman government.

8. Probably consul of 428; use of the phrase *antiqua prosapia* strongly suggests this was a direct ancestor.

9. The father is unattested, although his description *in oculis . . . in curia* indicating he was known among senators at Rome, despite the rhetoric of the letter which suggests repatriation of the son from Gaul.

through the mark of kindness; he knew that ignorance was blown all the more by the airs of pride, which expels empty winds because it grasps not the root of virtues. He was indeed the Cato of our times, who by abstaining from vices, educated others by his example. A thorough investigator of the reasons of natural history, he fattened himself with the Attic honey of Cecropian teachings.[10] For him, knowledge which always embraced something healthful to the soul was clearly worthwhile, in which the honorable mind may find repose. For him, nothing unrewarding ever occurred, when one for whom fickle fortune did not compel found each and everything of the known world worthwhile. It suffices for you to remember everything else concerning him, when there is no time for occupied men to explicate the good works of such a man. 5. Now turn your attention to this candidate, so that you may recognize the imprint there to be that of a praiseworthy father, lest the father should be thought to have passed to him only physical likeness rather than the mark of his virtues. For as you know, he lives among us not with foreign customs, but with Roman seriousness. Indeed, having entered upon his own childhood from the very beginning with distinctions, which is the most certain indication of probity, he always followed with emulated seriousness the company of the most honored men, so that after examples of virtue at home, he would adopt firmness from public authority. And although he might have pursued the favors of anyone by indiscriminate selection, since rarely is it possible to be chosen from among the great, he nonetheless adorned himself with the affection of the patrician Paulinus, so that thence he would give an indication of that remarkable conscientiousness which is known to hasten an excellent man. 6. Indeed the coveted friendship of influential men confers distinction, which association with good habits teaches by practice, when one strives to be equal to the agreeable affection that so delights. Therefore, conscript fathers, offer the brilliance of your favor to a man outstanding in ancestral blessings as well as his own accomplishments. One who descends from such a splendid stock is not unworthy to approach the insignia of the curia. 7. For Rome has often selected the *fasces* from among Gallic cities, nor would Rome despise something distinguished, to its own loss, any more than excellence would yield to proven dishonor. Therefore, let the noble curia fill with those good men of the provinces, men for whom anything known to be outstanding is characteristic. The very father of time also arranged the year for himself in four divisions, lest longing should take hold, if the year should not have the charm of newness.[11] Therefore, conscript fathers, favor our decision with your support. For if a candidate will be adorned, he now receives what is deserved from you.

10. Cecrops was the legendary first king of Athens, who bestowed what would become ancient customary practices upon its citizens.

11. The year commenced with a new consulship, here described in parallel with the natural transition of the seasons.

LETTER 2.4 (C. 507–11)

The recipient of this letter, addressed as "honorable gentleman," apparently possessed neither rank nor title and should be regarded as a familiar at the Amal court. The letter awards him with the administration of sales taxes, including the support of a *saio*, a Gothic retainer of the king, for which reason the addressee is warned not to abuse the mandate of the present writ.

King Theoderic to Ecdicius, Vir Honestus

1. We are delighted by the inventions of antiquity and we gladly embrace the following of established rules, since however much established practices are safeguarded in accordance with reason, a place is not allowed for deceitful practices. And therefore, we decide in the present mandate on a course suggested by your petitions, so that whatever pertained to Antiochus concerning the administration of titles to the *monopolium* or *siliquaticum* taxes, by our order should be transferred in similar measure to you, now fortified with sound fairness by the present mandate against the treachery of any false claimants. Moreover, our authority solemnly assigns you to have the support of a *saio*, for the purpose of assuming the aforementioned titles. Nevertheless, your legal protection thus should become less entangled with private business. For what we have granted for support should in no way be perceived as contrary to justice, since the *saio* reasonably regards you as beyond blame, if, through your influence, he should feel another whom you request to be brought before you to be injurious to himself.

LETTER 2.5 (C. 507–11)

This letter orders the *Praefectus Praetorio* to arrange the *annona* payment for soldiers stationed along the defensive network of the Alps (*Claustra*).[12] The payment must have been delinquent as soldiers typically received rations and salary distributions on a thrice annual schedule. Noteworthy is the court's attitude toward foreign incursion, for which the state depended upon reliably paid soldiers.

King Theoderic to Faustus, Praefectus Praetorio

1. When our kindness is known to search out a suitable occasion for munificence and it may sometimes lavish desired gifts on persons less intimate with the affection of our mildness, how much more it delights to spend on the weal of the republic, where whatever is contributed multiplies the utility of the one giving. Therefore, we order your *illustris* magnificence by the present dictate to immediately

---

12. Augustana in the letter is probably Augusta Praetoria, or the modern Aosta, which was part of the fortified defensive network protecting Liguria and northern Italy; cf. *Var.* 1.9 for this location.

present without any delay the *annona* to the sixty soldiers settled at the fortress of Augustana, just as has been determined for others also, in order that the weal of the republic, which is supported by wages paid from taxation, should be supplied from a willing spirit. **2.** It is indeed appropriate to think on behalf of the payment of a soldier who is known to toil on behalf of the common peace on the farthest frontiers, and who is deemed to bar, as though a kind of gate, the passage of peoples from the provinces. He who strives to hold back barbarians will ever be girt for battle, since he alone represses that dread, which promised fidelity does not restrain.[13]

LETTER 2.6 (C. 509–11)

This letter appoints the former *Praefectus Urbis* to a delegation being sent to Constantinople. The skill needed to negotiate with highly educated officials at the eastern capital receives emphasis.

King Theoderic to Agapitus, Vir Illustris *and Patrician*

1. Our deliberative council requires the service of discerning men, so that the administration of what is useful to the public may be fulfilled with the assistance of wisdom. And therefore, your *illustris* greatness, let it be known that, God willing, we have determined to send a delegation to the east, for which, judging you to be suitable, we nominate you by this present dictate, so that thus equipped you should increase our estimation of you and that through you the business required by us should be advanced. **2.** And granted that any delegation would require a wise man who would be wholly committed to protecting the standing of the *regnum* and the advantage of the provinces, it is nevertheless now necessary to choose the most prudent man possible, who is able to dispute with the most sophisticated men and thus maneuver in the company of the learned, lest some invention of clever learning be able to prevail over the undertaken cause. It is a great skill to speak against clever men and to plead any case in the presence of those who consider themselves to have anticipated every argument. Therefore, take cheer in such high estimation, that you had been able to prove your native character even before you accepted the gift of this delegation.

LETTER 2.7 (C. 507–11)

This letter appoints a *comes* to supervise the collection of masonry for use in mural fortifications, with a warning not to appropriate materials from private property.

---

13. Referring to treaties the Ostrogothic kingdom maintained with peoples outside Italy which nevertheless relied upon the maintenance of military strength.

Whereas *urbs* usually indicates the city of Rome, *quaequam urbs* ("any city") renders the location indeterminate.

King Theoderic to Suna, Vir Illustris *and* Comes

1. It is not appropriate for anything to lie unused which might increase the grace of the city, since it is unwise to despise anything beneficial to the future. Therefore, let your *illustris* nobility arrange for the blocks of marble which lay torn down and neglected throughout the city to be culled by those known to be attached to this work in the building of walls, so that a venerable fortification may return something to public beauty and so that stones cast beneath ruins may adorn. Nevertheless, let this quarrying from collapsed public buildings be managed by you with clear discernment, since, just as we do not want the adornment of any city to be befouled by recklessness, thus do we condemn corruption befalling private property.

LETTER 2.8 (C. 508)

Damage to private property frequently attended the movement of armed forces, and this letter entrusts fifteen hundred *solidi* to a local bishop to compensate property owners for the passage of the Gothic army (probably to Gaul).

King Theoderic to Severus, Venerable Bishop

1. What man is better delegated to the rights of equity than one clothed by the priesthood, who, because of affection for justice, knows not how to judge for personal advantage and, delighting in everyone alike, does not abandon a case to deception? Therefore, considering the task well suited to your merits, we declare that we have sent fifteen hundred *solidi* to your sanctity in the care of Montanarius, a sum which you should distribute to the provincials according to what you learn concerning any loss suffered during the passing of our army this year, with careful estimation of the damage, so that nobody should receive from our generosity anything beyond what his own losses aggravated. For we do not want to bestow liberally, in a confused manner, what is more fittingly distributed with reason, lest what we determined should be sent to the afflicted out of need should be paid unnecessarily to the uninjured.

LETTER 2.9 (C. 507–11)

An order that the *Praefectus Praetorio* should increase the monthly salary received by a popular charioteer.

King Theoderic to Faustus, Praefectus Praetorio

1. Our kindness wants to be inclined toward those entreating us and, for the love of devotion, not even to observe the limits of the law. Indeed, it is proper for the kindness of a generous *Princeps* to exceed the bounds of fairness, when it is only to compassion that every other virtue may honorably not refuse to yield. **2.** Indeed, some time ago we had made over the monthly allowance of one *solidus* to the charioteer Sabinus for what we appraised of his merits. Now, however, this performer has moved us ever so much with a respectable petition, claiming that one who has risen as an agent of public entertainment ought not to be weighed down by such grievous poverty. And therefore, we determine by the present dictate, that the above-mentioned horse driver should receive one additional *solidus* per month, which ought to be paid from the public accounts. For we rejoice at how much the pages of expenses are overburdened by these entries, since it is the greatest advantage to us when we bestow something upon the needy in any circumstance.

LETTER 2.10 (C. 507–11)

This is the first in a dossier of letters (cf. *Var.* 2.11 and 4.40) resolving a case in which a woman of senatorial rank had been seduced (or abducted) and thereby induced to alienate property pertaining to her marriage.[14]

King *Theoderic to Speciosus,* Vir Devotus *and* Comitiacus

1. It is the royal purpose to relieve those burdened by injustice, just as the punishment of a wicked man should cause justice to be loved more. Nor can that by which the wicked man lives be concealed from a healthy community, such that the cherished association of the marriage bed should endure professional seducers and that sacrament belonging to the engendering of humankind should be polluted by a profane crime. **2.** Therefore, having been moved by the petition of the *spectabilis* matron Agapita, who revealed her own secret sin to diverse witnesses— that these men even threatened the violent death of her husband, by whom rather they rightly deserved to be snuffed—we have decided in the present decree that from the time when that deeply shamed woman abandoned the conjugal bond, with respect to any contract which is unable to be valid by virtue of unstable mental state, by which the principle of the laws having been compromised, whatever will be determined to have been claimed by detainers you should cause to be restored without any delay, lest criminals should prevail to defend the advantage of their frauds to the derision of justice. For it is exceedingly absurd that those who deserved to be consumed by punishment should even attempt to defend profits thereby gained.

---

14. For different treatments of adultery, cf. *Var.* 1.37, 5.32–33; a similar case concerning property and marriage is at *Var.* 4.12.

LETTER 2.11 (C. 507–11)

This letter elaborates on the case of Agapita (cf. *Var.* 2.10 above) by directing strong language at the patrician Probinus. According to the complaint, men associated with Probinus were responsible for Agapita's loss of property. Although the letters hint that Agapita may have been a willing party, the case clearly fits the legal description of *raptio;* nonetheless, the court offers the senior senator involved an opportunity to restore the status quo. Probinus was a former consul of 489.

King Theoderic to Probinus, Vir Illustris *and Patrician*

1. Among other burdens of the human condition, conjugal affection provokes its own particular anxiety: and not without merit, since the source of posterity's renewal deserves to be held in high regard. Every indecency follows its particular author, while the mistake of a mother transfers to her sons, and in a particularly strange case of misfortune one's own disgrace becomes the sin of another. Therefore do husbands take such great precautions that the marriage bond be safeguarded either by divine or public sanction, so that it would be a great flaw of character not to respect the affection shared between others. **2.** And so the *spectabilis* Basilius has complained in petitions that his own wife, Agapita, had been led away from their own home by the seduction of certain persons, since the female sex lies exposed to the faults of inconstancy. Moreover, the confession of the above-mentioned wife in her own petition has confirmed this to us, adding that when she had sought refuge within the precinct of a holy church, unknown to her husband and with all reason set aside, she transferred the estate Arcinatina to your magnificence.[15] And now, having tasted of such burdensome wantonness, she deplores what she has done to herself, condemning her own acts, so that she would make restitution even as a poor wretch to the wealthy man, a deceitful woman to a chaste man and as a fool to a wise nobleman. **3.** Now cast away the prize, which clearly does not commend an honorable demeanor, since it is instead more fitting that you acquire that which may increase your reputation. Hence, the order we had issued the first time, we now repeat with a second dictate, so that you will surrender the above-mentioned property without any delay. For the alienation of property requires a firm judgment, and certainly with respect to Agapita's change of heart in these matters, she is shown to have squandered good counsel. For what respectable man will she be able to find, who has abandoned a husband who has no obvious faults?

---

15. It was not uncommon for elite estates to have names. Unfortunately, nothing further is known about this property.

LETTER 2.12 (C. 507–11)

The agents who regulate commerce and ports in Italy are forbidden to allow the export of cured meats. The *siliquatarii* were customs officers.

King Theoderic to the Comes of the Siliquatarii and to the Agens Curas Portus

1. If foreign commerce serves our needs, if foreign obedience is attained with offered gold, how much more ought Italy abound in its own goods, since it is assumed no obstacles to obedience would be tolerated? And therefore, we command that under no circumstance should any kind of cured meat be sent to foreign regions,[16] but that it should serve higher purposes in our use, lest it be evident that criminal neglect has diminished what is produced in our realm. **2.** Therefore be warned, lest the smallest opportunity should present itself for blame, knowing well the severest consequence if you should strive to support this injunction only half-heartedly. The sin is a matter of kind, not quantity. Indeed, injury requires no measure. If even some small measure of *imperium* is despised, then it is violated in every portion.

LETTER 2.13 (C. 507–11)

Ulpianus complains that Venantius defaulted upon his debt to the public taxes, for which Ulpianus is now responsible as *fideiussor* to Venantius. This letter acts as a warrant for a *saio* to compel Venantius to pay.

King Theoderic to Frumarith, Saio

1. We are indeed moved to the complaints of supplicants by a zeal for duty, but especially in that case which involves losses to the innocent, such as when those who must not be compelled to payments are subject to severe loss by paying. It is manifestly not appropriate to the justice of our reign that the contempt of one man should burden another, and that he should be accused by the innocent for the disregard of others. Indeed, Ulpianus submitted in a tearful petition that, during his own tenure in office, he bound himself as guarantor to the public debt in the amount of four hundred *solidi* at the request of Venantius.[17] For which, with Venantius scorning to fulfill his pledge with the presumption of uncultivated rustics, the mentioned amount of *solidi* has burdened the petitioner. **2.** And therefore,

---

16. *Laridus* translates as either "cured pork" or "lard"; *species laridi* is even less specific. Cured meats were crucial sources of protein in periods of scarcity.

17. This Ulpianus is otherwise unattested, despite the reference to his having held public office; Venantius should not be confused with other men of that name in the *Variae;* cf. the index of individuals.

we have decided that the aforementioned Venantius, who often animates the plots of many such crimes, being designated also in the complaints of other citizens, should be called upon in the present case, so that legally convicted, he should satisfy what he had promised to render without the delay of any evasiveness, since outrageous acts curbed by the weight of law are always better heeded and, when dread is instilled in such great men, a license for sinning is not allowed.

LETTER 2.14 (C. 507–11)

The great patrician and father-in-law of Boethius, Symmachus is asked to investigate a case of possible parricide and to exact punishment if necessary. Digression upon the nature of duty between children and parents occupies the greater part of the letter, perhaps reflecting the significance of Symmachus's devotion to Boethius, for which both were executed in 524 and 526, respectively.

Letter Theoderic to Symmachus, Patrician

1. Who could now find fault with anything else, if promises of familial devotion are deemed to be unfeeling? The man accused of a trivial matter is ignored when a great tragedy of crime clamors, nor does anyone strive to avenge what is equitable, if the highest order of travesties are seen to escape. The very nature of his intent displays an enemy to be savage: you may even find a colleague more wrathful, but decency does not allow the disobedient son to deflect punishment. **2.** Where is that moral vigor of nature that fastens to offspring in the embrace of kinship? The whelps of wild beasts attend to their parents; shoots do not disagree with their own seedbed; the tendril of a vine retains its own origin; and should a man, once begat, quarrel with his own origins? What shall we say for that kindness that can bind even persons foreign to a family?[18] From infancy, children are tended to and riches are made and accumulated for them. And when anyone should believe that what he possesses abounds for himself, when to that point it had been acquired from fathers, he sins more on behalf of the new generation. Oh, the grief! Do we not deserve the affection of those for whom we would not refuse to undergo utter ruin? The cares of a father do not flee from the very ocean when it is stirred by savage storms, so that he might attain through foreign commerce what he may leave behind for his offspring. **3.** The very birds, for whom life is continually concerned with food, do not defile their own nature with perverse behavior. The stork, continually the harbinger of the returning year, expelling harsh winter and harkening the delights of the spring season, provides a great example of devotion. For when parental wings have become weakened with ripening age, nor may they suitably find the necessities of their own sustenance, the offspring restore warmth to

---

18. Slaves are implied here.

the cold limbs of the parent with their own plumage and revive weary bodies with victuals. And until the elderly bird returns to its former vigor, in a dutiful change of roles, the young return what they had received as children from their parents. And therefore, those who do not abandon the responsibilities of devotion rightly preserve a long lifespan. 4. Moreover, it is the custom with partridges to replace a broken egg with one taken from another mother, so that by the adoption of an alien offspring, they amend the misfortune of their bereavement. But as soon as the hatchlings begin to confidently move about, they venture into the fields with the foster parent; when they are stirred by the call of the natural mother, they would rather seek the birth mother of their egg, even though they were reared by others as stolen hatchlings. 5. Therefore, how ought men to behave, when this devotion is recognized also in birds? And so, bring to our court this Romulus, who,[19] tainted by the egregiousness of his own deed, befouls the name of Romans. And if it is determined that he laid hands upon his own father, Martinus, let him immediately feel the lawful punishment. Thus we have chosen your probity, since you would not be able to spare the cruel, not when it is a kind of piety to confound those who are shown to have involved themselves in criminal acts against the order of nature.

LETTER 2.15 (C. 507–11)

This letter promotes the son of a prominent senatorial family to the office of *Comes Domesticorum*, the commander of the palace guardsmen. The post is honorary only (*honore vacantis*), but enough to elevate the recipient to the *illustris* rank of his father. The main theme of this letter and the announcement to the Senate (*Var.* 2.16) is the service of the father and the reward that it brings to the family. This Venantius is most certainly not to be confused with the Venantius of *Variae* 2.13; this may be the western consul of 507.

King Theoderic to Venantius, Vir Illustris

1. It is in the interest of foresight to prepare future merits at a tender age and to determine the succession of the offspring according to the virtues of the parents, since those blessings are certain whose very origins confer trust, when a shoot that has been habituated to springing from the root knows nothing of divergence. Moreover, native vitality is carried in the continual flow of the spring and everything proceeding from the well sustains this condition, so that the flavor that derives from the source, unless it is spoiled perhaps by accident, knows not how to deny the stream. 2. Hence it is that we have elevated you to the honorary title of *Comes Domesticorum*, out of consideration for the service of your magnificent

---

19. Not the Romulus of *Var.* 3.35.

father,[20] so that you who are outstanding in your birth should shine with the nobility of your office. For who could not consider that those qualities would be certain in you, when he recollects the official duties of so glorious a father? That man, inflamed with knowledge of wisdom, thus was accustomed to unexpected events, almost as though one could imagine he had been instructed by setbacks. **3.** For he discharged the duties of the prefecture, a most noble burden filled with every possible anxiety, which by itself would have been praiseworthy to accomplish, together with the care of our army, so that neither did the assessment of provincial taxes fail, nor did the provisioning of the army detract from his own resources. He tirelessly succeeded at everything with unimpeded prudence; he guided barbarian customs to peace. He moderated everything that we promised so that it would thus prove sufficient for all receiving, lest those giving should find grounds for complaint.[21] But so that little should suffice for the needs of many, he practiced the very policy with regard to himself, so that posterity would adopt untested options from his example. **4.** For all that, among achievements of the kind that are especially comely in the most admirable of nobility, you are not found lacking the support of your own merits. If indeed, diligent and thorough, you pursue the study of letters, which is worthy by virtue of its assistance to every kind of office, you will sweetly add a natural disposition for eloquence to a distinguished family record. Therefore, by applying yourself to such studies, you will recognize in yourself a vessel for repayment, so that you too may promote our judgment with your advancement. For you should only expect from us as much as you recognize yourself to be intent upon good service.

LETTER 2.16 (C. 507–11)

Nominally an announcement of Venantius's promotion (cf. *Var.* 2.15), this letter shows more interest in the career of his father, Liberius, who had successfully transitioned from the reign of Odoacer to Theoderic. Ideologies of personal integrity, political loyalty, and the cohabitation of Romans and Goths are the dominant theme.

King Theoderic to the Senate at Rome

1. It is our passion, conscript fathers, to confer remuneration for upright accomplishments and excite men of natural talent to a better purpose with the fruit of

20. Liberius, a figure of great interest who served the regimes of Odoacer, the Amals and Justinian in Italy.

21. The phrase *ne dantes locum querimoniis invenirent* refers to the initial distribution of Roman land to the Goths upon Theoderic's arrival in Italy. Venantius's father, Liberius, supervised this process (cf. *Var.* 2.17.5).

distributed benefaction. For the examples of the most excellent men nurture the virtues, nor is there anyone who would not strive to attain the heights of good habits, when what is praised by a witness of good conscience is not left unremunerated. **2.** Hence it is that we elevate to the honorary title of *Comes Domesticorum* the *illustris* Venantius, just as resplendent in his own merits as in those of his father, so that the inborn splendor of his native qualities should be rendered more distinguished by the attainment of offices. Indeed, you recall, conscript fathers, the patrician Liberius had been praiseworthy even in his rivalry with us, when he thus offered unwavering service to Odovacer,[22] so that after he was known to accomplish so much against us as an enemy, he was even more worthy of our esteem. For he neither crossed over to us in the mean state of a deserter, nor feigned hatred for his former master, so that he might procure for himself the affection of another. With integrity, he awaited the outcome ordained by God, nor did he allow himself to seek a king, until he had first lost his ruler. **3.** Thence, because he acted thus, we gladly bestowed a reward upon him, since he had assisted our enemy faithfully. However much this man was then known to be hostile in opposition to the fall of his patron, so much did he become acceptable to us. Then, with his master nearly defeated, he bent to no fear. Unwavering, he endured the downfall of his *Princeps*; nor was the change of circumstance able to discomfit him, something which even quelled native courage.[23] Wisely he followed the prevailing outcome, so that, since he steadfastly endured divine judgment, being more commendable, he obtained humane kindness. **4.** We have demonstrated the fidelity of this man. Grieving, he accepted our rule; overcome, he changed his disposition; not, however, because he had been defeated, but because he decided upon it. Soon after, we granted to him the dignity of *Praefectus Praetorio*. He managed the affairs entrusted to him with such great integrity, anyone would marvel that one who had been known to be so fervently opposed to us could be so single-mindedly devoted. Then, with tireless focus, he was seen to administer the taxes under the esteem of a multitude, which is the most difficult kind of virtue. With thoughtful diligence, he properly repaired the property assessment, conducting it not for expanding, but for saving a tax system that until then had been managed poorly. We noticed the increase of collections; you knew nothing of additional taxes. He thus accomplished both feats admirably, so that he increased the fisc and advanced public weal without loss to private concerns. **5.** It pleases us to have restored any proportion at all to the assignment of the *tertiae*, and he has bound both the property and dispositions of the Romans and the Goths. For, although men may accustom themselves to conflict over neighborly boundaries, these same people may be inspired by the sharing

---

22. King of Italy from 476 to 493.

23. Here *ferocitas gentilis* may refer to either the native courage of Italians opposed to Theoderic, or the ferocity of federated peoples who had supported Odoacer.

of property as a reason for concord; for thus it happens that both peoples, while living together, converge with a single will. Behold a new and wholly praiseworthy creation—the popularity of landlords is conjoined by the division of soil, through loss they increase in the friendship of peoples, and a defender has been acquired by the portioning of fields, so that the security of property may be preserved without loss. One law and one fair discipline embraces them. For it is necessary that sweet affection should increase among those who would continuously preserve duly established boundaries. Therefore, the Roman republic owes its tranquility to the aforementioned Liberius, who has transmitted the love of community to such distinguished peoples. **6.** Consider carefully, conscript fathers, whether we ought to leave unremunerated this offspring, the father of whom we recall has accomplished so many outstanding deeds. May the heavens favor this selection, so that, just as we invite the virtues through the distribution of blessings, thus may we show noble good conscience to enjoy increased honors.

LETTER 2.17 (C. 507–11)

Addressed to all citizens directly involved in the collection of taxes (*tertiae*) at Trento, this letter resolves issues arising from the tax immunity granted to a local priest (for similar immunity, cf. *Var.* 1. 26). The letter absolves the community from the amount that Butila's property had previously contributed to the calculation of total taxes owed from the municipality.

King Theoderic to the Honorati, Possessores, Defensores, and Curiales of the City of Trento

1. We want our beneficence to stand out as a loss to no man; nor should what is conferred upon one man be applied to the expenses of another. And therefore, be aware by the present dictate that nobody ought to make payment from the calculation of fiscal revenues for that portion which, in our liberality, we have applied to the presbyter Butila, but in that payment the amount of *solidi* owed is satisfied. Consider it to be removed from your collection of the *tertiae*. Nor do we want anyone to be responsible for what, in our kindness, we have removed from another person, lest, it is criminal to say, a gift for the well-deserving should happen to become an expense for the innocent.

LETTER 2.18 (C. 507–11)

An undetermined number of citizens from Sarsina (in Umbria) have taken refuge on the property of a bishop, possibly of the same town, to avoid municipal duties. The letter advises the bishop to return the citizens to their allotted duties or to prepare for a legal contest.

King Theoderic to Bishop Gudila

1. The authority of ancient laws dictates what must be revered, just as it is not by any means possible for one born of the curial class to escape the municipal duties of his own ancestral home, nor may anyone prevented by the allotment of birth be drawn into another office of the republic. Because, if the laws have forbidden them to cross over even to honored positions, to what extent does it seem contrary for a *curialis* to serve shamefully, with the privileges of the republic lost, and afterward continuously hold that status which antiquity has called a lesser senate?[24] 2. Your reverence will, therefore, take heed that your own colleagues have claimed your church has unreasonably harbored citizens of Sarsina by your own will. Thence, let your prudence disperse what enters into a legal dispute with the truth examined, and, for the sake of the integrity of your office, if the claims of those petitioning should hold to truth, permit them to return to their own curia for the sake of fulfilling municipal duties. 3. If, however, you believe anything reasonably supports them on your land, send to our *comitatus* a person briefed in every detail, who should be able to obviate the claims of the other party. Because, if you doubt the nature of this case, it agrees with the priestly canons that, rather than the litigation, you should give more thought to justice which, as the victor in the case, you would abandon for the sake of a sentence. Then again, it is not fitting that a man who is known as a lover of equity should be defeated in a public court.

LETTER 2.19 (C. 507-11)

This sentence declares the servants of a murdered master to be outlawed. Although the place of the murder is undisclosed, addressing the letter to Goths and Romans at ports and border towns suggests the assailants intended to flee from Italy.

King Theoderic to All Goths and Romans or Those Who Preside at Ports and Border Fortresses

1. Indeed, we rightly detest all crime, and the indulgent man is repulsed upon hearing anything that is perverse, but our censure especially rouses itself against what is polluted by the letting of human blood. For who would bear for danger to have a place in an inviolable household and to have found the end of sweet life there, where assistance ought to have arisen in defense? 2. And so we command in the present dictate that you should detain by the severity of the law those from the household of Stephanus who, in a crime deserving punishment, slaughtered their

---

24. The letter here discloses that some among the *curiales* of Sarsina have abandoned their privileged position by seeking the protection of the bishop. *Curiales* were legally debarred from entering higher, palatine offices and the letter contrasts this with the assumption of degraded status, presumably as "tenants" of the bishop.

own lord, and, by leaving him exposed, defiled his burial. Look to it that those who would be roused to the most evil deeds would be enclosed by punishments. For the sake of grief! Familial devotion is found among the birds, which are separated from the human condition. **3.** The very vulture, for whom nourishment is the carcass of another creature, having a stature of such great size, is not hostile to lesser birds, but rather strikes down for others the hawk, that bird keen for the lives of feathered creatures, tearing at it with beak and striving with its entire bulk to subdue the dangerous creature. But men know not how to spare those whom they recognize to be kindred to themselves. A man should not wish to snuff out the one by whom he had been fed; yet these servants prefer to murder one who was accustomed to nourish those around him. Let them, therefore, become nutriment for the pious vulture, whoever is so cruelly capable of desiring the violent death of a shepherd. Let one who paid his master with an uncovered death get instead a tomb of that kind.

LETTER 2.20 (C. 507-11)

An order that a *saio* requisition grain at Ravenna for delivery by ship to Liguria, where the *comitatus* of the king has strained the resources of the local area.

King Theoderic to Wiligis, Saio

1. It is fitting that all men generously reflect upon what would be possible to expend on the common weal, when it is necessary that the limbs feel what is felt by the whole body. And therefore we decree in the present dictate that, however many small boats you can find in the city of Ravenna, bring them all the way to us loaded with the grain from taxes, to the extent that the public distribution of grain, duly relieved by such a provision, ought not to endure the inevitability of scarcity. Let Ravenna return to Liguria the abundance that it is accustomed to receive from that very province. For whatever province endures our presence ought to receive in return the comfort of many things. Indeed, our *comitatus* draws crowds of attendants and, while it hastens to bestow favors, a necessary abundance is required by the people.

LETTER 2.21 (C. 507-11)

Theoderic had granted a contract to two men of senatorial rank to drain a swamp near Spoleto, in Umbria. The present letter responds to complaints from one of the partners that his colleague has withheld resources for the completion of the project and illustrates state concerns for land management. For announcement of a similar reclamation project, cf. *Variae* 2.32. An *apparitor* was a civil servant assigned to the staff of a public official. It is not known to whom Johannus was assigned.

King Theoderic to Johannus, Apparitor

1. It is especially serious that a most diligent man should be cheated from the fruit of his own labor, and that which ought to be conferred as a reward for earnest application should be endured as an unjust expenditure. This matter particularly concerns our own liberality, where no kind of neglect ought to be permitted, lest we should seem to have sanctioned less for things that would be useful. **2.** In respect to that, some time ago our generosity bequeathed to the *spectabiles* Spes and Domitius lands in the area of Spoleto where, unprofitably occupied by muddy flows of water, the deserted depths of waters had swallowed pleasant land in no way beneficial for use. The ground lies shipwrecked in a squalor of messy marshland, and, having been subjected to loss of two kinds, had not gained the liquid purity of water and had lost the distinction of earthly firmness. **3.** Now it is our intention to change all things for the better, and we granted this land to the abovementioned men on the condition that, if the unsightly flood should be drained by their labor and application, they should gain the liberated countryside from that very work. But a number of the agents of Spes report in a petition the fault of the *spectabilis* Domitius. While unmindful of the order, he firmly withholds the outlay of expense. The work of the laborers is called back at its commencement, while already the soft face of the ground had gradually dried and hardened and an unaccustomed sun kindled an appetite hidden in the ground for so long. **4.** In no way should we suffer this to be ignored, since anything begun well is destroyed by unfavorable inactivity. Thereupon, let your devotion call upon the aforementioned Domitius with moderate means, so that either he should come forth as the assiduous agent of a project already begun, or if he has found it too expensive for himself, let him yield his portion of the project to the petitioners. For it is fitting that, if he himself is unable to execute the requirements, he should permit a sharing of the favor to fulfill the glory of our reign.

LETTER 2.22 (C. 507-11)

Possibly related to *Variae* 1. 39, which ordered a patrician to detain the nephews of a Syracusan *spectabilis* at Rome in order that they would finish their education while the uncle fulfilled obligations to Theoderic's court. This letter rescinds the previous order, releasing them to return home (*ad patriam*) to attend the death of their father. Both letters use Homeric lore as justifications.

King Theoderic to Festus, Vir Illustris *and Patrician*

1. It is fair that royal devotion should accommodate itself to an unintended wound for the aggrieved, since those individuals deserve to be supported more who have suppressed the adversities of their own lot. And therefore, we declare in the present dictate that your magnificence should order the sons of Ecdicius,[25] who at first we had decided should reside in Rome, to return to their native country for their father's funeral (indeed, a longed-for return, but on a bitter occasion), lest their wound should be joined to the affliction of denied desires and, what is abominable to say, we who have ever blotted away the darkness of the grieving with our fair weather, should now be seen to deny pious tears to the miserable. **2.** Indeed, that grief is unquenched that is not permitted to take part in the interment of the body; while he always deems himself indicted, who does not offer just observances to the dead. How many entreaties did Priam make to redeem Hector for burial? He asked one who was driven mad,[26] he bent in supplication to one in arms, and he even preferred to put aside his own life, in order that he would not neglect those duties owed to the corpse. And because the duties of devotion between these persons are mutual, it is unjust that a son should not render to the father in gratitude what the father brought about with a great sum of money.

LETTER 2.23 (C. 507–11)

A contract to three officials for the management of the pottery works, confirming protection against suits that would transfer the contract to others or transfer the competence of the officials to other endeavors.

King Theoderic to Ampelius, Despotius, and Theodulus, Viri Spectabiles

1. It befits the discipline of our reign that those who provide service to the common weal should not be loaded with burdens. Nor is it right that the jealousy of any person should harm arrangements made by our intention. On that account, apply yourselves energetically to the operation of the pottery works granted to you by royal authority: nor should you fear that it is possible to be passed on to other offices, from which we trust you have been disentangled already by the present order. Therefore, the shameful presumption of bad persons around you will cease and our authority will destroy anything caused by concealed treachery. For he is hated in vain, to whom the kindness of a *Princeps* has been offered as protection.

LETTER 2.24 (C. 507–11)

In tenor quite different from the carefully crafted deference shown to the Senate elsewhere in the collection, this letter offers a scathing rebuke of senators who have avoided paying taxes, for which citizens of lesser means are burdened instead.

---

25. Possibly the Ecdicius awarded a tax monopoly at *Var.* 2.4.
26. Achilles.

The letter also informs the Senate that the court has informed the public about its resolution in an edict (*Var.* 2.25).

King Theoderic to the Senate at Rome

1. It stands that the Senate has projected for the people a standard by which one must live; for the name Roman adorns what is chosen by you as established practice. For this reason were the fathers so named in the beginning, since a way of life was arranged by you as though for children. For you decreed the devotion owed from the provinces and you decreed rights for private persons. And you have taught your subjects to gladly obey every aspect of justice. And it is therefore not fitting to bear the mark of contrariness, where once an example of moderation could blaze forth. Our kindness, which passionately assays the measure of every affair, entrusts to your attention what must be accomplished, lest a transgression should be nourished more from ignorance in those for whom good conscience is not permitted to be perpetually in error. **2.** Accordingly, we have learned from a report of the provincial governors sent to his magnificence, the *Praefectus Praetorio,* thus some time removed from the first occurrence, that nothing or very little may be collected from the senatorial houses, alleging that the weak, whom it would be better to relieve, are oppressed by this difficulty, for it happens that the balance owed to the revenue officials, when it is despised by the influential, weighs instead against those of slight means and that man who is devoted to his own duties instead pays for another person. Moreover, they add what is more bitter, that each according to his own will deems to cast forth anything to the collectors, which loss they nonetheless claim to be entirely inflicted upon the *curiales,* and those who had been restored to public service by our own provision have been torn to pieces by this contumacious disregard. **3.** And therefore, conscript fathers, you who ought to strive for the republic equally with us, arrange it thus fairly, that whatever each senatorial house should be assessed, let it be paid in three installments to the revenue agents sent to the provinces. **4.** Or certainly, what you have become accustomed to ask in place of a favor, if you choose, send the complete amount to the treasury of the vicar's office, lest it become necessary for the *curialis* to assume, in place of your own slender obligations, a loss to themselves through complicated and inefficient labor of the assembly, and lest it should result in a detestable situation, so that a loyal man who had barely been able to bear his own taxes is then weakened, squeezed by the burden of another. **5.** We are unable to conceal this for the sake of sound civil harmony, so that even without the bitterness of war the oppressed are stripped of their own property and those who hasten to obey the republic perish more. Moreover, you will know that we have sent notice by the proclamation of an edict to all provinces, to the effect that whoever knows himself to be oppressed by the weight of another's taxes may freely come forth and accuse him in public. The fruit of justice will soon return to us, we who know to offer protection to the weak.

LETTER 2.25 (C. 507-11)

This general edict declares the intent to correct abuses of elite citizens in the payment of taxes. Town counsellors (*curiales*) and landowners (*possessores*) are invited to report abuses, as announced in the previous letter, addressed to the Senate. Senators here are not specifically indicted.

Edict of King Theoderic

1. Although the voice of grief may be contentious, although the threatened may not restrain themselves and a wounded soul may be fed on shouting, nonetheless, the voice that is relieved under our authority calls out more freely. For we despise that the lowly should be degraded. We are even stirred by the afflictions of those not complaining, and what the shame of the suffering conceals comes to our attention more quickly. When the injuries of everyone reflects upon us, rightly do we then feel as a loss to ourselves any cause for the middling person which we know has escaped our devotion. **2.** And so, we recently learned by report from the provincial governors that certain houses of the very powerful have not fulfilled their own obligations to regular taxes. Hence it happens that, when the amount of payment due is sought, typically the greater portion is exacted from people of slender means. Then, with the arrogance of *conductores,* the imminent hand over the scheduled *solidi,* not in due manner, but by casting forth coin of substandard weight; nor do they yield according to standard practice the common *siliqua,* which they had been accustomed to pay. Consequently, it is the case that the *curiales,* for whom we have wished to act as guardian, experience severe loss from the coercion of the collecting agent; and if it is even proper to admit, since they are compelled by harsh collection agents on account of the debts of others, they are impoverished by the loss of their own properties. **3.** Because this offense must be cut off, we have sent instructions to the most reverend Senate and we have now determined by this proclaimed edict that, whoever—whether of the *curiales* or of the landowners—feels himself to be loaded by the payment of another's taxes, may hasten to approach the court of our serenity, where he will learn former excesses have wholly displeased us, when he sees the benefits that follow. Therefore, the arbitration of a just *Princeps* is open to you, even though it would ever be declared by many signs. Now, either conceal your resignation to grief in silence or lay bare a just path with a voice. Now, the focus of this counsel will be on you, which is at hand to determine what you believe will disentangle you.

LETTER 2.26 (C. 507-11)

This letter responds to the corruption of agents in charge of the public grain (collected as taxes), who have charged merchants with unregulated commissions. The letter also addresses other problems related to the taxation of sales. The problems described could have deleterious effects on local municipal finances by discouraging merchants (the sale of grain was the means by which taxes collected in kind became commuted to coin revenue).

King Theoderic to Faustus, Praefectus Praetorio

1. We are pleased by no kind of unjust profits, nor should what departs from the grace of probity be associated with the spirit of our devotion. Indeed, the republic has ever increased by right of equitability, and when moderation is prized, benefits swiftly follow. **2.** And therefore, your *illustris* magnificence, being greatly stirred by a petition of the merchants of Apulia and Calabria, we decree what must be done so that, concerning the grain which the above-mentioned merchants have bought on the public market, no amount of *solidi* should again be required from them in the name of a commission. For if you should not maintain a reasonably legitimate appearance with respect to public expenses, then the measurement of grain charged may be appropriately drawn from your office. The accounting of fiscal affairs has a record that is known to reject what has been unjustly imposed. Indeed, it is especially unseemly that one who serves the other *imperium* should endure this expense.[27] **3.** And those assessing the *sextarius* in the same manner, whose merchant is known to come from the same province, let no impudent person dare to exact a continually condemned price. And in order that we may check such abuse more vigorously, we have imposed a penalty of thirty pounds of gold on the office of your prefecture, if anyone attempts to move against this most healthful edict with dishonorable daring. Moreover, the staff of the office will find itself bearing a loss in the amount of ten pounds of gold, if it presumes to maintain prohibited practices. **4.** And in this way our clemency extends to the weak, so that if the merchant should offer payment to the *siliquatarius* for the proper entitlement, he too should enjoy use of the grain monopoly. If the *siliquatarius* truly deems this entitlement must be removed from merchants, he may exact no payment from them, since it is thoroughly absurd that one who does not have the remuneration of a legal right should be afflicted with an expense. **5.** Henceforth, let the ancient usage be observed by the *aurarii,* and let its observance apply only to those whom the authority of antiquity wanted to practice this entitlement. Therefore, our favor extends protection in every way to those merchants who are properly confirmed with contracts from your office, lest the kind of man who lives by profit should be able to catch his death from financial loss.[28]

---

27. The merchants extorted for commissions were from the eastern empire.

28. Cassiodorus here inserts a play on words, describing the merchant as someone who both "lives by profit" (*vivit lucris*) and "dies from financial loss" (*ad necem pervenire dispendiis*).

LETTER 2.27 (C. 507–11)

This letter touches upon the delicate issue of the government's relation to Jewish communities living in Italy. Imperial law since Constantine forbade Jews from expanding the urban fabric of synagogues, and here the letter concedes to a request from Jews in Genoa to restore damage to a synagogue, while at the same time illustrating the minimal level of tolerance for a non-Christian group (cf. *Var.* 4.33 and 5.37).

King Theoderic to All Jews Settled at Genoa

1. Just as we desire to demonstrate the righteousness of concord when called upon by entreaties, so too we dislike that offenses to the law should occur through our favors, especially in that portion of the laws that we believe concerns divine reverence. Therefore, let those puffed up with pride and destitute of divine grace not be seen to behave insolently. Wherefore, we decree in the present dictate, that you should erect a roof over only the ancient perimeter of your synagogue, obliging as much license to your petitions as divine constitutions have permitted. Nor would it be proper to add any adornment or to stray beyond bounds by enlarging the building. **2.** And you will know the severity of the ancient sanctions to waver the least, if you should to refrain from illegalities in this matter. Indeed, we grant license only for covering or strengthening the walls of the building, if the thirty-year limitation is not able to prevent you. Why do you request that from which you ought to flee? We verily grant permission, but to our own praise we disapprove of the desires of those so erring. We are unable to command religion, since nobody may coerce the unwilling to believe.

LETTER 2.28 (C. 507–11)

A classic example of the ideology of public service, this letter elevates a former *princeps*, or head of a governmental bureau, to senatorial rank. Given the legal nature of duties described, the recipient was likely a chief within the departments of *exceptores*. Remuneration includes exemptions from fiscal obligations. This Stephanus is not to be confused with others of the same name in the *Variae*.

King Theoderic to Stephanus, Comes Primi Ordinis *and Former* Princeps of Our Officium

1. Compensation of the first order must be paid for work performed well, since service that passes unremunerated is looked upon as having been reproached. The palm designates the athlete as a victor before the people. The civic crown bears witness to exertions in war. Even horses await their own reward, and such is the strength of justice, that a fee should be given unhesitatingly for those services that are not found wanting. **2.** Because, if these things are true, it is worthwhile to return something to a man who is recognized for pleasing with honorable obedience. For you have held a firm course of upright service among so many dangerous uncertainties of the courts, and, as happens rarely among those serving, the alternation of judges around you never altered your course. Nor was there in you any jealousy for the judgment received by another, even when an opponent restored the verdicts of your predecessors in office. Indeed, you have managed to please all, since you have ever been a watchman to what is most cherished, a confidant in secrets, effective in legal cases, and constantly at the work of public office. And what the frequent vices of men have made a blessing of rare self-control, while you offer dutiful respect to many, to none would you sell your service. **3.** You have smeared the name *princeps* with no filth, protecting the dignity of the title with the application of virtue.[29] Hence it is that, in the present dictate, we confer upon you the dignity of *spectabilis* rank, which antiquity rightly designated for those scrubbed clean by the sweat of public service. So that you may at length end the vigils of your labors, know yourself now secure in remuneration as *Comes Primi Ordinis*. **4.** And because a dignity should not be joined to the gratitude of a *Princeps* as though naked, nor that something experienced with no utility may be called a favor, we have also added to that generosity the same privileges which the divine constitutions had intended to be granted to former heads of your corps. Nor should you fear anything in these benefits, which would perhaps be attempted in a novel usage. Thus, ancient mandate has discharged you from every exaction and base labor. **5.** But, although we rightly free you from any obligation with this present remuneration, we nonetheless promise to have greater hope for future service. But since favors are cheap that do not offer something for the future, the foresight of a *Princeps* will add to it, so that those whom we have found worthy of our good will, we should also heap with the greatest distinction. Truly since the blessing of kings ought not to be concealed, let the present elevation come to the attention of the provincial governor, to the effect that the intentions of all may recognize your proper elevation to the rank of *spectabilis* by our testimony, and that respectful observance for your discharge from the duties of public service should be preserved inasmuch as it agrees with praise for our reign.

LETTER 2.29 (C. 507-11)

This letter advises a military *comes* assigned to Sicily to be mindful of the protection (*tuitio*) accorded to the estates and clergy of the church of Milan in that region. Like the church of Rome, the church of Milan owned extensive properties in Sicily, which provided revenues and required intensive land management.

---

29. Note that the letter here describes how Stephanus preserved the dignity of his rank as *princeps* of an *officium,* not the king as *Princeps;* elsewhere in the letter, *Princeps* refers to Theoderic.

King Theoderic to Adila, Vir Spectabilis *and* Comes

1. Although we do not want anyone whom our devotion is known to protect to endure any great burden, since the leisured peace of the subjects is the glory of the ruler, nonetheless we especially desire foreign churches to be delivered from any injury.[30] When fair treatment is offered to the church, the mercy of divine authority is acquired. **2.** And therefore, having been stirred by a petition from the blessed bishop Eustorgius of the church of Milan, we remind you by this present address that you may be eager to offer protection for the property and persons of this church situated in Sicily in a spirit of sound civic harmony, lest, against sacred law, you should allow to be oppressed, by anyone of any origin whatever, those for whom it is fitting to be elevated by considerations of divine authority. It is nevertheless true that they should not postpone answering to public and private suits which may have been reasonably brought against them, since, just as we in no way want them to be oppressed by anyone, so too we would not permit them to be found exempted from the path of justice.

LETTER 2.30 (C. 507–11)

This letter grants permission for the church of Milan to appoint a purchasing agent who would be exempt from taxes imposed on other merchants so that he might obtain the resources needed for the church's care of the poor.

King Theoderic to Faustus, Praefectus Praetorio

1. A personal exemption should not prejudice civic responsibility, since it is fitting that a *Princeps* be generous, lest royal munificence is able to be confined within rules of procedure. Let fickle wrath be coerced by heavy regulations; let impatient ambition be curbed by law. Kindness has no need of law, nor should liberality follow narrow strictures, because it is fitting to be lauded without limit. **2.** And therefore, the *defensores* of the patrimony of the holy church at Milan desire that one from among the merchants of their city be made available to them who would have authority in the office of a purchasing agent, being exempt from the impositions placed on merchants so that he may fulfill what he undertakes on behalf of the resources of the poor, which are squandered under an increase of profit.[31] For they remind us in a reasonable petition that we granted to the church of Ravenna that example of our piety which they now entreat also be transferred over to their own advantage. **3.** And therefore, your lofty and *illustris* magnificence, with public advantage secure in regard to other merchants, by which the civic body is accustomed to be supported, authorize one, whom

---

30. The phrase *ecclesias alienas* should be understood as a reference to the church property owned by Milan in Sicily.

31. The phrase *sub lucre exaggeratione funduntur* describes the inflation which impacted the purchase of resources for the care of the poor.

they will have elected from among themselves, so that he might exercise the trade of a merchant, to the extent that he should not pay any fee for the monopoly, the sales tax, or for the exchange of gold;[32] nor should he bear any burden whatsoever from having been permitted access to the market. For why should we delay assenting to this, where it is not possible that we would experience any loss?

LETTER 2.31 (C. 507–11)

The oarsmen of state vessels (*dromonarii*) on the Po River are ordered to assemble and transport the couriers (*veredarii*) of the public post in order that they may receive their salaries. It is not clear how often this may have taken place; by comparison, Gothic soldiers assembled once per year for the distribution of the donative. For other letters concerning naval resources, cf. *Variae* 5.16–20, 12.24.

King Theoderic to the Dromonarii

1. Those who claim the name of civil servants ought to toil on behalf of the public. For what may a man accomplish, if he should fail his avowed obedience, so that he neither finds private profit nor acquires glory from vigorous application? And therefore, our authority has prevailed upon the *Comes Sacrarum Largitionum*, so that you ought to be gathered in place at Hostilia,[33] to the end that you would make an expedition along the Padus River, in customary fashion with the state couriers, in order to be refreshed by the treasury's kindness. Thus, by a division of labor, it ought to assist the public couriers, since your path will not wear away, you who set out upon a watery course. For it does not happen that you, who travel by means of the strong arm, would become lame with excessive toil. Your conveyance feels no injury, nor does that which is carried instead by flowing waves suffer failure.[34]

LETTER 2.32 (C. 507–11)

Announcement of a project to reclaim swampland (cf. *Var.* 2.21), this letter serves to provide legal notice that the lands will have been reclaimed for public use (*auctoritate publica*), but under the purview of the senatorial patron who sponsored the project.[35]

---

32. The *monopolium, siliquaticum,* and *auraria* were taxes levied on merchants, as discussed in *Var.* 2.26.

33. Modern Ostiglia, located east of Padova on the Po River.

34. Cassiodorus is here comparing the services of the oarsmen, who row "by means of the strong arm," to the currier service (*cursus publicus*) that employed horses and was prone to delay caused by the exhaustion of, or injury to, the animals.

35. Inscriptions recovered from the vicinity of Terracina also relate to this project; *CIL* 10.6850 and 10.6851.

King Theoderic to the Senate of Rome

1. Devotion freely expended on utility to the public is pleasing to us, conscript fathers, since when we approve the laudable intentions of citizens, we then find an occasion for just rewards. For what is more beloved among senators than if one among them should weigh out affection for the utility of the public, so that he will be able to work for the betterment of the homeland to which he has been born? **2.** And so, the grand gentleman and patrician Decius,[36] bound by glorious love for the republic, has made a resolution beyond a marvel, which hardly would have been possible to impose under a directive of our authority. He has promised in an open statement to drain away a swamp, a hostile expanse of pitfalls laying waste to the vicinity of Decemnovium.[37] This infamous wasteland of our age has sat with impunity as a muddy sea for an interminable time, and since it is hostile to cultivated places, it overflows favorable land with flood waters, likewise commingling with wild growth. Enriching nothing of use under its waters, it has robbed the earth of its fruit, which ever since has been obedient to the marshes. **3.** And therefore, we marvel at this man of old-fashioned determination that, what virtue fled publicly for a long time, he takes in hand privately. He has, therefore, committed himself to follow upon this bold labor with praiseworthy completeness, so that, by destroying the ruinous abyss of water, those lands which had been lost should go to waste no longer. Hence, he has requested from our serenity injunctions beyond this notice, so that this exceptional accomplishment, which will be to the advantage of all traveling, may fall under public authority. **4.** But we, conscript fathers, whose intention it is to assist a good desire with supportive ordinances, assent in the present dictate, that you should direct to the very site of Decemnovium two from your assembly by whose witness the extent of overflow that the flood covers with its marshy assault may be marked with fixed boundaries. In this way, when the promised work has been completely accomplished, the restored land might benefit its own liberator, lest anyone should then presume to claim something which for such a long time he has been unable to defend from invading waters.

LETTER 2.33 (C. 507–11)

This letter confirms the notice sent to the Senate regarding the reclamation of swampland by Decius (cf. *Var.* 2.32), with the added proviso that Decius should allow others to share in the project's labor and profit.

King Theoderic to Decius, Vir Illustris and Patrician

1. It is a matter of justice that good fortune from mandates should follow upon a praiseworthy request, and that what was undertaken from good will also should be

---

36. Also consul of 486.
37. A settlement in southern Campania bordering on the Pomptine Marshes.

completed with royal exhortations. And thus, by the present dictate, we grant that fitting desire to which you had committed yourself, that with regard to the pools and swamps of Decemnovium, drained without contribution from the fisc,[38] you may claim possession over the soil in the reclaimed countryside. Nor should you fear to produce any cultivation on these liberated lands, which we have freed under testimony of an edict. **2.** We have, moreover, sent this decree to the most honorable Senate, so that, with the extent of the region now delimited, what has been freed from fetid waters may pass to your own sweet ownership. For it is equitable that each man's labor should profit him, and just as he will know inconveniences by expending effort, thus may he attain increased profit from a completed project. In addition, we who are ever-enthusiastically watchful on behalf of the republic have decided that, if anyone should choose to assume this work jointly in cooperation with you, he should have available to himself that land in proportion to the work which he has undertaken, to hold by right as his own, so that you should not strain alone under the weight of such an immense undertaking and so that what is undertaken with the assistance of a colleague should not provoke animosity. And so it may happen that what is friendly in the greatest of undertakings would then be free of troublesome jealousy. **3.** In this way, act vigorously upon these glorious desires, lest it prove injurious to your reputation to have weakened in assumed endeavors. Indeed, bear in mind the eyes and attention of all turned upon you; reflect that the judgment of our serenity hangs suspended over the outcome of the planned work. However much you apply yourself successfully with winged spirit, thus will you be judged to have emerged from such an undertaking a man worthy of everyone's praise, now and ever with admiration.

LETTER 2.34 (C. 509-10)

This letter orders the *Praefectus Urbis* to correct the abuse of the accounts intended for the maintenance of Rome's walls, which have been diverted to other uses. This appears to have been an ongoing problem (cf. *Var.* 1. 21).

King Theoderic to Artemidorus, Praefectus Urbis

1. Our judgment rejoices to have flourished in you. We are pleased to have elevated a worthy patron for the fortifications of Rome, you who with generous intentions would not bear to secretly conceal a friend's fraud, lest either the crimes implicate you or a sense of safety rather encourage greater offenses. And therefore, that public account, which was set aside for Roman builders and according to the report of your magnificence remains perjured, since it neither explains expenses nor has it

---

38. The phrase *sine fisco* is elusive, possibly describing lands that Decius liberated without financial support from the treasury or possibly his right to ownership without obligation to the fisc.

returned to its original condition, let it be restored without any delay and let it be applied again to the walls of Rome by your arrangement. For it is scandalous, and not without reason, that Rome should long for those funds stolen from it which have passed to other uses. **2.** And so we ought to strike down with unreserved punishments those embezzlers of delegated funds who defraud our generosity in such a manner. But that governess clemency is always at hand and conjoined to our intentions, lest we should strike out severely, with unseemly punishment against one urging justice. Let it suffice that the greed which motivated him should not be satisfied. Nor shall the rod of punishment be permitted to extend further, when what he had shamefully decided to take possession of, having been restrained, must seem just as the loss of his own property.

LETTER 2.35 (C. 507-11)

A curious letter, again illustrating concern for Roman cities, this time ordering an investigation into the loss of a public statue at Como. The nature of statue is not discussed, merely its importance to antique heritage, the loss of which provoked an edict (*Var.* 2.36). Compare a similar concern for public statues at Rome, elaborated at far greater length with *Var.* 10.30. Tancila, addressed in the letter, is probably a *comes.*

King Theoderic to Tancila, Vir Spectabilis

1. It is exceedingly grievous that the accomplishments of the ancients diminish in our times, we who desire to increase the adornment of cities daily. Wherefore, we urge you in the present command, that with full devotion you carefully inquire after the bronze statue at the city of Como, which happens to have been lost. Promise even one hundred *aurei,* if anyone will see fit to expose this disrespectful theft, to the extent that the promise of our kindness may invite those anxious for hope of forgiveness, which an edict sent to you also explains. But nonetheless, after you have published the command, if the crime thus far has remained secret, after Sunday, bring together the craftsmen from all the shops, to inquire from them under threat by what assistance the crime had been accomplished. For the overturning of a statue would not be accomplished easily by those unskilled in these matters, unless the help of experience had dared to change its location.

LETTER 2.36 (C. 507-11)

An edict issued at Como for the restoration of a stolen public statue, pursuant to the previous letter, which offers both reward and pardon for the return of the statue.

Edict of King Theoderic

1. Although an eased punishment may be quite sufficient for revealing the crime, a gift for boldness may not be enough to deflect the fear of punishment; nonetheless, we have added a reward that innocence is accustomed to enjoy, not because the deeds committed have been forgiven, but because it delights us to be liberal in manumission from punishment. **2.** Therefore, by the authority of the present edict, let it be known that anyone will be promised one hundred *aurei* from our generosity, if he should produce whomever has seized the statue from the city of Como, and concerning his own complicity, what the guilty person will especially seek, he will know himself to have been considered forgiven. We assign a golden price to a bronze commodity, and we bestow a metal far more precious than what we have been able to find. To those ransoming the statue for the sake of this generosity, that which is established as illegal may not become common practice. **3.** Who, therefore, would be afflicted by such blindness of stupidity that he should fail to come forth, when he will discover sanctuary and acquire a reward for his confession? However, if anyone has perhaps trusted in concealing the crime and our serenity uncovers him by some evidence of the truth, he will know himself to be given over to the most severe punishment. For it is unworthy that anyone should reject our forgiveness after human kindness would vote in favor of those revealed.

LETTER 2.37 (C. 507–11)

After lengthy preamble on the relation of liberality to good governance, the *Praefectus Praetorio* is ordered to release another *millena* of taxes to support the maintenance of public baths at Spoleto.

King Theoderic to Faustus, Praefectus Praetorio

1. The advancement of our reign ought to emulate benevolence, so that however much human kindness enlarges rewards, thus would the republic receive increase. For we would not otherwise be able to safeguard a praiseworthy manner of life, except that we should inspire a design for the contemplation of our administration. For among so many daily blessings from God, the advance of parsimony would be a vice eager for meager liberality. And therefore, let your *illustris* magnificence know by the present dictate that another *millena* beyond the customary amount must be allocated to the maintenance of baths for the citizens of Spoleto. For we desire to freely spend upon what we know pertains to the health of the citizens, since the proclaimed happiness of the people is praise for our reign.

LETTER 2.38 (C. 507–11)

Responding to a petition from merchants at Sipontum (in Apulia, on the eastern shore of Italy), this letter orders the *Praefectus Praetorio* to suspend compulsory purchases (*coemptiones*) and debts owed until the merchants may restore property damaged during an attack by the enemy (*depopulatione hostium*), referring perhaps to Vandal or Byzantine raids along the Italian coast. For a similar complaint concerning foreign attack, cf. *Variae* 1. 16.

King Theoderic to Faustus, Praefectus Praetorio

1. We desire our wealth to be increased by a treasury of devotion, cursing advantages to us that have been acquired by the misfortunes of troubled people. That payment which is lamented burdens our clemency, since whatever attaches to the reputation of the one receiving is measured by happiness. **2.** And so the merchants of Sipontum claim that they have been devastated by a raid of the enemy, and since we would rather appraise our wealth in terms of solace to the needy, let your *illustris* magnificence cause those named to be troubled by no compulsory exactions for two years uninterrupted.[39] **3.** But since it profits nothing to have relieved the downfallen, if another burden of payment should then accrue, let your eminence be advised concerning those of the aforementioned merchants who are known to have borrowed money, lest within this span of two years someone should think the amount owed must be demanded. Thus, under the provisions of this judgment, they should be able to restore the money given and in some measure the property of the debtors should be sound enough to be restored. For what does it profit the creditor to goad himself, when he strains to compel the destitute in vain? We foresee a greater advantage for them, if we cause them to collect a loan by extending it.

LETTER 2.39 (C. 507–11)

A fascinating letter ordering the court architect to supervise the restoration of baths at Aponus, but which digresses at great length on the healing and spiritual qualities of the natural springs.

King Theoderic to Aloisius, Architect

1. If we want to join the wonders heard of the ancients to praise for our clemency, with nothing diminished under our care, since fame is the prosperity of a king, , with what zeal should that which often happens to come before our eyes seem fit to be restored? Indeed, it is a delight to recall the efficacy of health-bearing Aponus.[40]

---

39. *Nuncupatos* here may refer to a list of exempt merchants that had been attached to the original letter.

40. Hot springs located near modern Padua.

For this reason, as you know, we desire to make new what has not been able escape our memory. **2.** We have beheld the cerulean spring, seething with the shape of the curved mouth of a wine jar, and the burning craters of exhaling waters wreathed round with polished rim in the fitting arrangement of nature. As befits warm water, these exhale a billowy vapor, which nevertheless reveals such a pleasant transparency to human inspection that any person would desire to reach for its charms, all the more since it knows not how to burn. Domes of water in the likeness of spheres swell beyond their own bounds in the ample openings, whence the smooth waters flow so tranquilly, as though gliding along with great stillness, so that you would not think it is moving, except that you notice something passing thence with a hoarse murmur. **3.** The waters pass from such boiling heat along cooling channels, so that after winding lengths that have been made more extensive by engineering, they return the fullest warmth. O the ever miraculous genius of its creator, that the heat of a natural passion should thus be restrained for the advantage of the human body, so that what would be capable of causing death at its source, thus moderated by learning, should bestow both health and delight! It delights to behold a mystery: fluids exhaling burning clouds, harmless burning issuing unfailingly from waters, and heat to come from a coursing stream, whence it is customarily extinguished. The philosophers rightly speak of the elements, which are known to war among themselves in a variety of oppositions, as being bound to each other in changing combinations and to be united by miraculous alliance. **4.** Behold a wet substance arranged to produce a fiery cloud, which then travels to the comely buildings of the baths, the tumult of waters decreasing in heat warms even the air with its own attribute and becomes more manageable to the touch, when it has been received in bathing pools. Whence not only a charming pleasure is attained, but also so many caressing medicinal cures are conferred. One hears of cures given without pain, remedies given without torture, health exempt of penalty and libation given against the diverse ills of the body. Therefore antiquity has called this blessing Aponus in the Greek language, so that the ill should recognize it as the source of so much relief, since no doubt could be had concerning such a name.[41] **5.** But among the other blessings of this very place, we have learned something else that must be marveled at, that waters with one nature are seen to be suitable to diverse ministrations. For by continually coming into contact with the rock, the churning waters of the first chamber absorb a quality that produces sweat. From there it descends, having exchanged the threat of scalding for soothing warmth, and it softens to a gentler temperature. The water thus produced winds about in the area with some delay and cools to a much more alluring temperature, until, finally forsaking even its very warmth in the Neronian pool, it attains a coldness as extreme as the heat first felt. **6.** Not unduly sharing a name with its author, the pool is festooned with the green

41. *Aponus* literally means "without suffering."

of gems, so that the very greenness too would stir the waters to a kind of trembling with the transparent stillness of a glasslike substance. But even as this very pool becomes calmer, arrested as though by the discipline of restraint, the waters, by which men may be refreshed, if a woman should enter, boil over. And on that account, the appropriate display of either one or the other sex has been assigned, evidently, lest they would not believe the place to have the most enriching of hot waters, whence so many blessings are bestowed, if both sexes should make use of one gift at the same time. **7.** This constancy of the water provides evidence of its perception, by flowing from a great depth, by secret courses, through heated veins of the earth, the refreshing purity of the boiling waters bursts forth in breaths. For if it would have been a fire of natural origins, it would not exist without being extinguished by the consumption of its substance. But the sentient substance of the water, just as it attracts foreign heat, thus does it easily return to its native cold. **8.** And this strength offers another kind of medical assistance. For near the head of the shimmering fountain, provident nature has formed a certain path for itself. Here, above its established seat, which is pierced through in the likeness of an arch of human contrivance, it takes up the harmful product from the interior moisture. While the weak will repose here in great weariness, refreshed by the delight of these vapors, the enfeebled flesh of the body is restored and harmful elements are leached from the beneficial humors by an infusion of vital dryness, and as though from some desirable nourishment, the ailing are immediately restored and made more vigorous. Thus, that which heats by sulfur and that which dries by salt come to the medicinal property of the waters. Not to pass such a wonder to posterity is to sin grievously against a whole generation. **9.** For that reason, the ancient stability of the buildings here should be restored, so that, whether in the underground passages or in the baths there will be something requiring repair, it ought to be rebuilt by you immediately. Also, the harmful thickets springing up with impunity should be torn out of the lawns and born away, lest the gradually swelling tendrils of roots should penetrate the body of the buildings and they should nurture offspring with the nature of a serpent, contrary to their own fecundity, whereupon the seams would burst asunder. **10.** Also strengthen with persistent care the palace that has been shaken by a lengthy old age. Clean away the scrubby woods from the span that intervenes between the public hall and the beginning of the heated pools. Let a comely disposition smile with grassy blossoms in the level areas. Let it, moreover, rejoice in the fertility of warmed waters and, by wondrous means, while nearby waters produce a sterile salt, let them also nourish verdure. **11.** But not by these benefits alone should Antenorean ground be fruitful;[42] there are others even greater by which you would be astounded. This soul, as I shall call it, in conversation with the solitude of the mountains, disarms contentious business. For if someone, by

---

42. Antenor was a character from the Trojan War famous for the number of his children.

chance, should presume to steal a sheep in the fashion typical of local bandits, it would be necessary for the stolen pelt to be immersed continually in the burning waters so that it would boil away before he should succeed at cleaning it. Oh, how the waters must receive due reverence for their secrets, when they not only possess feeling, but also stand possessed of righteous judgment, and what fails to be resolved in human altercations is given over to be decided by the equitability of the pools. Silent nature speaks here, and when it judges, it pronounces by certain means a sentence that prevents the falsehood of the one denying the charge. **12.** But who would fail to protect such a place, when he may become soiled more by parsimony? Indeed, what is singularly honored by the whole world adorns the *regnum*. And therefore, concerning the money that has been given to you, if you have not been able to complete the work undertaken, indicate to us in a short letter however much you know still must be spent, since we are not burdened to spend, in order that we might be seen to watch over so great a city of the countryside.

LETTER 2.40 (C. 507)

Among the lengthiest in the collection, this letter requests Boethius to select a cithara player to accompany envoys to the Frankish court of Clovis. Boethius does not seem to have formal office, but his reputation for learning has instead commended him for the task. The letter's digression on music (the bulk of the letter) blends natural history, philosophy, mythology, and Christian ethics. It is noteworthy that the request to Boethius is far more elaborate than the letter to Clovis (*Var.* 2.41), on whose account Boethius had been consulted.

King Theoderic to Boethius, Patrician

1. While the king of the Franks has sought from us the player of a cithara with great entreaties, being allured by the fame of our banquets, we have promised this to be fulfilled for the sole reason that we know you to be accomplished in the learning of music. For to select one so instructed falls to you, who with difficulty have been able to attain station in the very same discipline. **2.** For what art is more outstanding than this, which keeps time with celestial mechanics by means of sweet resonance and encompasses the arrangement of nature, dispersed everywhere, with the grace of its own virtue? For anything of measurable dimension that arises into being does not draw back from the moderation of harmony. Through this we think properly, we speak sweetly, and we move pleasingly. However often it reaches our ears, it directs melody according to the law of its own discipline. **3.** The practitioner of music changes dispositions when heard, and this most powerful pleasure, while it advances from the mystery of nature, as though it is the queen of the senses adorned with her own melodies, she causes everything to divert course and other thoughts disperse, so that she would delight that only she is heard. The musician brings pleasure to hurtful grief, disperses swollen rage, caresses cruel savagery, excites the idleness drunk with lethargy, returns healthful rest to the sleepless, calls spoilt chastity back from shameful love to an ardor for honor, restores a weary mind ever adverse to good thoughts, turns pernicious hatred to grateful assistance, and, what is a blessed kind of restoration, expels the maladies of the mind with the sweetest of pleasures. **4.** He softens the incorporeal soul by means of a bodily sense, and by merely being heard he leads to what he wants, to accomplish what would not prevail by word. Silent, he calls out by the hands, he speaks without voice, and by the obedience of unintelligible notes, he succeeds in exercising mastery over the senses. Among men, this is accomplished entirely by five scales, which are named according to the individual provinces where they were discovered. Indeed, while divine compassion made everything for its own greater praise, it sprinkled favors on specific places. The Dorian mode bestows foresight and is the author of chastity. The Phrygian excites aggression and inflames the will of rage. The Aeolian calms the agitated mind and lends sleep to those already agreeably disposed. The Iastian sharpens the intellect for the dull-minded, and as the agent of blessings grants an appetite for heavenly things to those burdened with earthly cares. The Lydian acts against excessive cares of the soul, and it was discovered that it may restore fatigue with rest and enliven amusement. **5.** A corrupt age caused this scale to be noted for dances, turning an honorable remedy to shame. Herein the five scales are arranged into three divisions. For each scale possesses a high and a low; moreover, each of these are joined to a middle range. And since they are unable to exist without each other, each returning back to another in alternating changes, musical theory was profitably invented, that is, discovered by the work of musicians on various instruments, by which the fifteen modes would be arranged. **6.** Adding something greater to these properties, human ingenuity assembled through learned inquiry across the world a certain agreement of sounds, which is called a diapason, evidently from all the modes assembled, as though virtues, which together are able to comprise melody. In this, a marvelous unity is bound. Hence, Orpheus, by being heard, persuasively directed inarticulate animals and enticed wandering herds from disdained pastures instead to the banquet. By that song, the Tritons came to love dry earth, Galatea danced on firm land, ambling bears deserted the forests, lions at last abandoned the thicket of reeds as a home, the prey rejoiced beside its own predator. Contrary natures were gathered together into one assembly and with the lyre singing in faith, every creature entrusted itself to its enemy. **7.** And so Amphion, conqueror of Dirce,[43] is said to have founded the Theban walls by singing to strings, so that when he would rouse men enfeebled by toil to a zeal for work's completion, the very rocks were thought to have abandoned their craggy purchases. The powerful tongue of Virgil celebrated even Musaeus, the son of Orpheus, in both

---

43. Here given as *Amphion Dircaeus,* according to Euripides' now lost *Antiope,* Amphion and his brother executed Dirce for tormenting their mother.

craft and nature, saying he was placed on a fortunate eminence among the dead, because he delighted happy souls throughout the Elysian fields with the thrumming of seven strings, indicating that the loftiest reward is to be enjoyed by one who happens to feast upon the sweetness of this discipline. **8.** But all these things are seen to be accomplished by human fondness for music produced by the hands. The natural rhythm, however, of the living voice is recognized as its accompaniment, which then governs fair melody, when it remains silent at the right moment, when it articulates appropriately, and when follows with a suitably arranged voice a path marked by musical feet. And even the forceful and captivating speech of orators was invented for the purpose of stirring the mind, so that judges might either become incensed at criminals or have pity for mistakes. And whatever the eloquent man is able to bring about, it is no doubt attained by the glory of this discipline. **9.** Moreover, according to the testimony of Terentianus,[44] to the poets have been attributed the first two principle meters, the heroic and the iambic, which the one rouses, while the other soothes. From these, diverse means have arisen for amusing the attention of the audience, and just as with the scales of a musical instrument, so too in the human voice does a pregnant meter give birth to various emotions of the soul. **10.** The inquiries of antiquity claim sirens to have sung in a wondrous fashion, and although the waves would direct ships away and the wind would billow the sails, those soothingly charmed would choose to rush upon the crags, lest they should suffer being torn away from such sweetness. Among these, only the Ithacan evaded the snare, who adroitly blocked the seductive song from the hearing of his sailors.[45] This most prudent of men contrived a felicitous deafness to the dangerous charm, and thus, what the sailors would not have overcome by understanding it, they prevailed all the more by not turning their attention to it. But he bound himself with tight knots to an immoveable beam, so that he might be able to test the famous song with unfettered ears, and having been conquered by the dangers of the charming voices, he nonetheless escaped from the grasping waters. **11.** And indeed, that we might pass beyond such temptations in the example of the wise Ithacan, let us speak concerning that Psalter descended from heaven, which a man worthy of song throughout the world so composed and measured for the salvation of souls, that by these hymns the wounds of the mind may be healed and the singular grace of divine authority may be sought. Behold what this age should marvel at and believe: that David's lyre drove forth the devil, the sound commanded the spirits, and by singing to a cithara, a king was restored to freedom who had been shamefully possessed by an internal enemy.[46] **12.** For it is fitting that many instruments of such delight have been tested; nonetheless, nothing more efficacious to stirring the soul has been discovered than the

---

44. The Roman poet Terence.
45. Odysseus or Ulysses.
46. A reference to David's ministrations to Saul at 1 Samuel 16:14–23.

pleasing reverberations of the hollow cithara. Moreover, we believe that chord to be notable which easily moves the cords of the heart.[47] Here so many voices are gathered under a diverse harmony, so that once the cord has been struck, it causes trembling spontaneously in the neighboring cords, which nothing has touched. For such is the force of harmony, that it causes an insensate object to move itself, since its partner happens to act. **13.** From here come diverse voices without language; from here the most pleasing chorus produces a variety of sounds. This one is exceedingly sharp with tension, that one heavy with a certain laxity, the middle most pleasing from an adjustment at the neck of the instrument. Even men may not succeed at attaining such unity among themselves, such a social concord which these strings arrive at while lacking reason. For here a certain string sounds out sharply, another heavily, one harshly, and another with purity, and others with diverse differences, which are assembled together as though in one ornament, even as a diadem shines before the eyes with a variety of gems: thus it is pleasing for the cithara to be heard with a diversity of sound. **14.** The loom of the Muses speaks, with copious warp and singing thread, in which is woven with a lively pick that which is sweetly heard. Thus Mercury is said to have invented this in imitation of the variegated tortoise, which, because of its utility, astronomers have supposed it courses among the stars, since they believe music is celestial, when they are able to perceive the shape of the lyre located among the constellations. **15.** Indeed, the harmony of the heavens cannot be explained adequately in human speech. Reason has given this only to the soul, but nature has not transmitted it to the ears. For they say it ought to be believed that heavenly beatitude is to be fully enjoyed through those pleasures, which neither finish at an end nor falter with any kind of interruption. Indeed, the celestial beings are said to live in the presence of this sensation, the heavens to enjoy these very allurements, and those heavenly beings cleaving to such contemplations are enclosed in their delights. **16.** They would have indeed considered rightly, if they had been able to assign the source of heavenly beatitude, not to sounds, but to the creator, where there is truly joy without end, ever abiding eternity without any weariness, and the mere contemplation of divine authority brings it about that any greater happiness is not possible. This truly bestows everlasting life, this heaps up pleasures; and just as no creature may exist outside of that very authority, so too it is not possible to possess an unalterable happiness without it. **17.** But, whereas this digression is pleasurable for us, since it is always pleasing to discourse on learned matters with knowledgeable men, let your wisdom select at this time the one whom we said had been requested from us, the best cithara player, who would accomplish something like Orpheus, when he has tamed the savage hearts of foreign people with sweet sound. And however much this will have been pleasingly done for us, just as much will be returned

---

47. *Chordam . . . corda.*

in our fair compensation to you, who both obey our command and accomplish what is likely to make you famous.

LETTER 2.41 (C. 507)

Following from the request to prepare a delegation to the Frankish court of Clovis (cf. *Var.* 2.40), this letter invokes the ties of marriage that bound the two kingdoms in order to appeal on behalf of Alamannic refugees that had fled to Italy from war in Frankish Gaul.

King Theoderic to Clovis, King of the Franks

1. We take joy indeed in our splendid bond with your excellence, because you have successfully roused the nation of the Franks, resting in its old age, to new battles, and because you have subdued the Alamannic people, who, with their bravest cut down in heaps, have bent to your victorious right hand.[48] But since the transgression is always seen in the authors of an execrable treachery, nor ought the fault of blameworthy leading citizens be the punishment of all, temper your intentions toward the exhausted remnant, since those whom you have seen fleeing to the protection of your parent deserve to escape by right of indulgence to us. Consider these men forgiven, who have fled as fugitives to our borders. **2.** It is a memorable triumph to have belittled the bravest of the Alamanni, so much that you have witnessed him bend in supplication for the gift of life.[49] Let it suffice that their king has fallen, along with the arrogance of his nation. Let it suffice that an innumerable people has been subjugated, some by the sword, some by servitude. For when you continue to belabor the remaining people, no one would believe you have overcome all of them. Listen to one often experienced in such cases: those wars have turned out successfully for me that achieved a moderate end. Indeed, he conquers continually who knows how to be moderate in everything, while a pleasant outcome favors those instead who do not become unyielding with excessive severity. And so, gracefully concede to our inclination what concern for family is accustomed to yield by well-known example. For thus it happens, that you should be seen to give satisfaction to my requests, nor should you be overly concerned about that territory which you know pertains to us.[50] **3.** Wherefore, greeting you with respect and good will, for which it is appropriate that we have sent to your excellence with the usual affection our legates *ille* and *ille,* through whom we would

48. Clovis defeated the Alamanni in 506, although the refugees associated with that conflict may have sought asylum in Italy later.

49. A reference to the king of the Alamanni.

50. The phrase *ex illa parte* apparently refers to the region inside the Gothic boundary with the Franks to which the surviving Alamanni had fled.

inquire after both the fulfillment of our requests and indication of your well-being. Indeed, we have entrusted to the bearers of this letter certain matters that have come to our attention on behalf of your advantage, which must be introduced to you by spoken word, so that, being made more cautious, you might steadily fulfill the desired victory. Indeed, your health is our glory and however much we know about your happiness, that much do we deem the *regnum* of Italy to prosper. **4.** Moreover, just as you requested, we have sent a cithara player learned in his art, who should attract splendor to your power with his hands and his harmonious singing voice. And therefore, we rather believe him pleasing to you, since you so ardently deemed he must be sent.

Book 3

Although letters in Books 1 and 2 already indicate Ostrogothic involvement in the conflict in Gaul (cf. *Var.* 1. 24, 2.1, 2.8), Book 3 opens with a series of diplomatic exchanges that would have been made immediately prior to the conflict. Here, a letter from Theoderic takes a paternalistic tone to restrain Alaric II from involving the Visigoths in conflict with the Franks. Although Alaric was Theoderic's younger kinsman by marriage, he was a king of perhaps forty-one or forty-nine years at the outbreak of war.

King Theoderic to Alaric, King of the Visigoths

1. Although the countless multitude of your family line grants confidence to your bravery, although you may recall that the might of Attila wavered before Visigothic strength, nonetheless, since the hearts of a fierce people have become tame in the course of long peace, beware sending into danger so suddenly those who have not had practice in war for such a very long time. **2.** Battle is dreadful for men if it is not frequently practiced, and, unless it is adopted as a matter of habit, those entering the fray will immediately lose heart. Let it not happen that some blind indignation would carry you away. Provident is the moderation that protects a people; rage, however, often precipitates recklessness; it is only a practicable measure to rush to arms then, when justice is unable to find a place among adversaries. **3.** Therefore restrain yourself, until we should direct our legates to the king of the Franks, so that the decisions of friends may remove your grievance. For we do not want anything to happen between two conjoined to us in marriage, whence it may be that one of you would be found weaker.[1] The spilled blood of kinsfolk has not inflamed you, nor has an occupied province galled you grievously. Thus far, it is only a small contention of words.[2] You will settle this easily, if you do not incite your mind to arms. Although you are bound to us in kinship, we array before you distinguished nations, and justice, which the most powerful kings wield. One who perceives such armed against him should quickly change heart. 4. And therefore, we have decided that that the aforementioned legates, *ille* and *ille*, must convey to you the honor of greetings. Let our admonitions influence you sufficiently through these men and let them hasten further, with our directive, to our brother Gundobad, and to the other kings as well, lest you should be found laboring under the opportunity of those who malignly delight in the conflict of others. Indeed, may divine providence prevent that this injustice should overcome you. We deem your enemy to be a common threat. For that man who strives to be hostile to you will rightly endure me as an enemy.

LETTER 3.2 (C. 507)

Following the intent of *Variae* 3.1, this letter announces the arrival of legates to the Burgundian court of Gundobad and the intent to muster support for mediating the conflict between the Franks and Visigoths.

King Theoderic to Gundobad, King of the Burgundians

1. It is grievously wrong to see hostile intentions between royal persons dear to us, and to watch while ignoring that something might arise for the destruction of one. It is not done without our displeasure, if he should contend to the ruin of kinsmen whom we support. You have had every pledge of great gratitude from me; we are inseparable, one from the other. If anything should be wanting in your realm, you cause me severe grief.[3] 2. It is for us to restrain young kings with opposing reason, since, if they should notice that what they wrongly desire rightly displeases us, they would be unable to follow upon the rashness of their own desires. They respect men of experience, even though they may be flushed with the passions of their time of life.[4] Indeed, it is fitting that we should speak harsh words, lest our

---

1. Theoderic was married to Audofleda, the sister of Clovis; Alaric II was married to Theodegotha, daughter of Theoderic by his first wife.

2. Gregory of Tours claims a conflict over religion (*Decem libri historiarum* 2.37), but cf. *Var.* 3.4.4, which suggests external influence.

3. The letter here departs from the characteristic self-reference in first-person plural (*noster*) to *me* in order to use *noster* in the sense of "Theoderic and Gundobad."

4. Probably intended to encourage Gundobad to adopt a similarly paternalistic perspective, it is nonetheless worth noting the maturity of the respective kings: Gundobad and Theoderic were certainly senior, at perhaps fifty-five and fifty-three years respectively, although Alaric and Clovis, at forty-one years (perhaps forty-nine for Alaric), were not flushed with youth.

relations be permitted to reach an extreme.[5] **3.** And so, we have decided that the legates *ille* and *ille* must be sent to your fraternity, so that, if it will be permitted by our son Alaric, they should direct the king of the Franks, with support of our allied nations, to reasonably set aside, with friendly mediation, that case which churns between them. For it should not come to pass that such great kings would pursue lamentable quarrels among themselves, such that they would wound even us with their own downfall. **4.** For that reason, let your fraternity strive with me, with additional eagerness, to mend the concord between them, since nobody would believe that they arrived at this war without our consent, unless it would be wholly clear that our battle had rather been that they should not reach conflict. We have committed certain things that must be made known to you in speech to the bearers of this letter, so that your prudence might thereby arrange all necessary matters, however it should be accomplished with God's blessing, upon which one should be accustomed to reflect most carefully.

LETTER 3.3 (C. 507)

A letter apparently sent in duplicate (*epistula uniformis*) to the kings of the Herules, Thuringians, and Warni. The intention was to muster the support of peoples bordering on the Frankish realm from across the Rhine in opposing the conflict between Clovis and Alaric II (cf. *Var.* 3.1 and 3.2). The proper names of the kings to whom the letter is addressed are not given.

A Common Letter of King Theoderic to the King of the Herules, the King of the Warni, and the King of the Thuringians

1. Common consensus ought to harry the pride that is ever so hateful to divine authority. For whoever would want to overthrow a renowned nation with willful injustice is not prepared to preserve justice for other nations. It is an evil habit to despise truth. If it should happen that an exalted man prevails in execrable rivalry, he would expect all nations to yield to him. **2.** And therefore, you, whom a knowing virtue elevates and whom the idea of detestable presumption incites, send your legates to King Clovis of the Franks, together with mine and those of our brother, King Gundobad, so that either, with equity considered, he would hold himself in check concerning conflict with the Visigoths and appeal to the laws of nations, or he may endure an assault from all nations who deem the arbitration of such matters to have been despised. What further should be asked of him, to whom unconditional justice has been offered? Let me speak what I feel plainly: one who desires to act without law prepares to shatter the *regna* of all people. **3.** But it is better that the adoption of a pernicious habit should be restrained at its inception, so that

---

5. Clovis was related to Gundobad by marriage to his niece, Clothild.

what could be a war for each nation may be accomplished without toil by any. For recall the disposition of the elder Euric,[6] with how many gifts he often assisted you, how often he held back from you the looming wars of neighboring nations. **4.** Concerning this, we have sent to your excellency greetings in epistolary speech through our legates, *ille* and *ille,* who are also bearers of matters to be spoken of with you, so that you, who should follow our arrangements with God's blessing, may embrace a single consensus and that you may accomplish this from abroad, lest you should have to contend in your own province.

LETTER 3.4 (C. 507)

Addressed to the Frankish king, this is the last in a sequence of letters aimed at resolving hostilities in Gaul between the Franks and the Visigoths. The war finally erupted with the Battle of Vouillé in the summer of 507; the Frankish victory was short-lived, with Theoderic's army thereafter securing possession of Visigothic Gaul on behalf of Amalaric, his grandson by Alaric II and his daughter Theodegotha.

King Theoderic to Clovis, King of the Franks

1. The divine law of marriage has been wont to grow among kings for the purpose that a peace desired by peoples may come forth through agreeable intentions of those bound together. Indeed, this is a sacrament that is not permitted to be violated by any ill feeling. For in what pledge is faith to be had, if it is not trusted among kinsmen? Are not lords closely related, so that divided nations ought to be glorified by a single disposition and so that, as with certain streams united one to the other in concord, the desires of peoples should be able to conjoin themselves? **2.** And since it should be like this, we marvel that your aggression has been incited thus for the sake of petty causes, so that you would want to engage in the harshest conflict with our son, King Alaric, so that the many who fear you may rejoice over your strife. You are both kings of distinguished nations, both in the prime of life. Not lightly will you shake your *regna,* if, with affairs given over to factions, you come into open conflict. Let not your strength become the unexpected calamity of your homeland, because in trivial matters, the great hostility of kings is the grievous ruin of the people. **3.** Let me speak freely what I feel, let me say it pointedly: the feeling that stirs arms immediately at the reception of the first embassy is impetuous. Let what is claimed by your kinsfolk be sought with chosen arbitrators. For among such men as you would want to make mediators, it will be pleasing to yield. What would you think about us in this matter, if you thought we had ignored your claims? Let that conflict fail, where one among you will be prone to suffer pain.

---

6. Euric, the father of Alaric II, was king of the Visigoths in Gaul and Spain from 466 to 484.

Discard the sword. You would choose to fight against my reproach. **4.** Even by the right of a loving father do I forbid you. That man who will have deemed such admonitions to be worthy of contempt will endure our opposition and, we do not merely conjecture, that of our friends. Therefore, we think it very important that our legates, *ille* and *ille,* must be directed to your excellency, through whom we have also sent our letters to your brother, our son King Alaric, so that in no way may foreign enmity plant obstacles between you.[7] Rather, by insisting on peace, you ought to appease each other in matters which are concluded through friendly mediation. **5.** Moreover, through these legates we have committed certain things which must be said to you by word, so that peoples who have flourished under your kinfolk in a long peace ought not to be wasted by sudden violence. Indeed, you ought to trust those whom you know to favor your own advantage, since it is certain that one who would want to send another to a reckless downfall would not advise faithfully.

LETTER 3.5 (C. 509–11)

This letter elevates a young man of the Decii family to patrician rank. The promotion seems to have followed his consulship (509), which like the consulships of his three brothers, was awarded in deference to his family name. Although the letter praises his moral deportment, far more attention is given to the distinction of the family in general.

King Theoderic to Inportunus, Vir Illustris *and Patrician*

1. If nobility of birth alone decorated you, or you only possessed such great influence in the estimation of praiseworthy men, we would perhaps suspend conferring these dignities with justifiable delay, lest great rewards should become debased at the very same time that each poured forth. Now, however, all these things accompany you with well-ordered accomplishments, nor does what is celebrated in many men lack in your one person. It agrees with our justice, that, since you have come forth with abundant blessings, the generosity of a *Princeps* may satisfy you richly. **2.** Indeed, this rank to which you advance is not for many men. A man of mediocre virtue is deemed to be advanced gradually, when someone is acknowledged with more difficulty because he has become prepared slowly. Your prosperity has extended itself with a kind of leap, and only a state of fruition is expected of you, since many blessings came into being with your birth. Indeed, the dignities of your family have been painstakingly accumulated over a long duration, dignities which have resided in your family like *lares* in a familial shrine. **3.** For let us

---

7. The reference to *aliena malignitas* is curious and may indicate influence from outside of Gaul was suspected as the *casus belli.*

mention the former age, which has been sufficiently recognized for bringing forth men of distinction. Conspicuous do you gleam in the twin stateliness of your father and uncle,[8] who were not only the ornament of their family, but also lent their decorum to the Senate itself. They adorned the modern age with olden manners; endowed with goodness, glorious in steadfastness, open to friendship, and resistant to taking offense. Thus, what is the greatest kind of good fortune, while they had been judged to be men of great influence, it happened that they had not the jealousy of those following after them. 4. On the contrary, the anxious concerns of the city hung about them, public affection increasing beyond that of private citizens. The Senate followed upon their disposition, the crowd their intentions. And it was inevitable that what they decided at Rome the collective seemed to desire, and by a miraculous outcome of prosperity, the wandering will of the people maintained firm approval for them, which we deem to be a special reward among other dignities. For if love from the few is indeed justly glorious, what enthusiasm is able to hold the acclamation of such a city? Consequently, just as anything unrecognized becomes obscured, so are those things chosen with public approval elevated. 5. Therefore, decorated with the praise of your family and conspicuous in the brilliance of your habits, after the deserved post of the consular *fasces,* take the insignia of the patriciate, the fullest token of your dignities, and bind youthful locks with the fillet of a shining honor, you who have overcome the requirements of age by the praise of worthy men. For why should rewards come forth lately to one for whom so many examples of family approve? Indeed, the praise of birth and the glory of achievement is found in you; and although you may draw many blessings from men of old, you deserve to win approval with regard to your own. 6. Indeed, from the very beginning of life, what is accustomed to be rare among the flock of youth, you have striven to demonstrate belief in celebrated virtues. And therefore, hold fast to the path of your manner of life, so that one who has pursued distinction in youth, may increase with glorious honors in the prime of life. Mark well, then, with how much preliminary praise you are adorned. It is a kind of crime not to have conferred upon you what is the highest honor. Indeed, many better things ought to come from your maturity, which we know to have been predicated in you at a tender age. For we believe that neither the instruction of your family nor our judgment should be able to fail concerning you.

LETTER 3.6 (C. 509–11)

An announcement to the Senate concerning the elevation of Inportunus to patrician rank (cf. *Var.* 3.5). More details are offered concerning the young man's family,

---

8. Fl. Caecina Decius Maximus Basilius iunior, consul of 480, and Caecina Mavortius Basilius Decius, consul of 486, respectively.

the Decii, especially the role of his mother (unfortunately not named) in raising four senatorial sons after the death of their father.

King Theoderic to the Senate of Rome

1. It is indeed pleasing to us, conscript fathers, to lead forth young men to the heights of offices. It delights to introduce men of foreign stock to the bosom of liberty, so that the hall of the Senate should put forth shoots of varied virtue. For such a crowd adorns the assembly and a numerous assembly thus honored turns a bright face to the public. But it has proven much more gratifying to us, how often we restore to dignities those who have been born to that very brilliance of the curia, since our usual scrutiny does not pertain to you, when you, who excel with a deserved brilliance, transfer anticipated blessings from one generation to the next. The very stock is already glorious; praise has its origins in noble birth. The advent of life, for you, is likewise the beginning of public office. For the fullest honor, to which the Senate arrived at hardly a young age, is brought forth with you.[9] **2.** And while it is permitted that we truly believe this concerning all of you, just as the happiness of senators binds the spirit of the order, the blood of the Decii, which has gleamed with the same brilliance of virtue for so many continuous years, glows especially in the sight of our serenity. And although distinction may be rare, it is not known to be thus divergent in the entire family line. This noble blood has produced men of the first order since its own beginnings; it knows nothing of mediocrity born of itself. As many are proven good as are born, and, what is difficult to accomplish, they are both abundant and select. Behold a fourfold crop sprung from one germination—grace, the honor of citizenship, the distinction of the family, and the enrichment of the Senate—although they shine forth in a communion of merits,[10] you may still find one whom it is possible to praise concerning his own accomplishments. **3.** Behold a young man, pleasing indeed in grace of form, but more in the sweetness of his character. The face recalls the distinction of his blood. Through his countenance, the nature of the soul is made known and with fairness of the body he even clears doubt from the mind. But this blessing of nature is adorned with the insignia of learning, so that, having been ground to a refined edge by the whetstone of the great arts, he gleams all the more in the inner chambers of the mind. He has learned of the ancient Decii in the books of elder writers, a noble race living on by the service of glorious death.[11] **4.** Indeed, it was the happiest labor of studies in which he happened to learn poetry of the ancients

---

9. In other words, the current generation is the apogee of the Senate.

10. Here referring both to the fourfold distinctions already enumerated and also to the four sons of the current generation.

11. As noted by Barnish (1992), this is a reference to the legend of three Decian generals who consecrated themselves as sacrifices for victory in battle.

from family and to polish the introduction of a tender breast to the praise of ancestors. It is pleasing to recall how then, at a great event, the attention of the entire school turned to him, as though when it heard the name of the family, it immediately strained to seek the heir, so that it would be possible to find agreement with what it had heard the author say through his very likeness. **5.** For just as an unworthy posterity might efface the songs sung of an ancient line, thus does a distinguished posterity confirm the admirable things said about its patrimony. Everything that is read concerning this family is believable, since a vein of virtues present now teaches the renown of the ancients by rekindling the flames of genius in workshops of scholars. Indeed, he was reared according to these examples, but he was more fruitfully advanced by household rule. **6.** For having lost the comfort of the husband, the glorious mother undertook the burden of governing, a woman whom neither the ample cares of the patrimony, nor the tutelage of so many sons, could agitate. She provided them with nourishment, increased the patrimony, adorned them with honors, and she returned to the curia as consuls as many young men as she produced for the family.[12] Therefore, our intuition, the examiner of morals which even enquires into the good of domestic virtue, looks upon these things to enable the awarding of honors of praise for both public and private merits. **7.** And therefore, conscript fathers, we have indulged the *illustris* and magnificent Inportunus with elevation to the patriciate, so that, just as your assembly sprouts from the lot of birth, thus will it also be able to increase with public offices. Show gratitude for this kinsman and add your assent. It is your own native character which you approve. You will certainly have what you may grant to yourselves with genuine praise, if you would make this decision publicly binding with your esteem and if what is thought to be conferred by our commands should be extended on account of natural affection.

LETTER 3.7 (C. 507–11)

A plainly written letter admonishing a bishop to pay a vendor for oil that has been delivered for lamps in the church. The letter weighs the pettiness of the dispute against the bishop's reputation for justice and his standing in the eyes of God.

King Theoderic to Januarius, Venerable Bishop of Salona

1. Certainly we presume everyone will observe and cultivate justice, but especially those who are raised up to divine offices, so that the nearer they come to heavenly grace, the further they will then be from earthly greed. And so Johannus stirs us with a tearful allegation that your sanctity had accepted from him sixty jars of oil

---

12. The name of the mother is unknown, although she is described in terms similar to the great Republican model of maternity, Cornelia Africana.

for filling the lamps,[13] the cost of which he claims should fittingly be restored to him. This would indeed be a good desire, if nothing untoward should be associated with this matter. **2.** For it is proper that justice ought to be safeguarded everywhere, and it is especially important in these matters, which are offered for divine observances, lest we suppose God to not know from whence he receives offerings, whether he has received them fraudulently. And therefore, if you know the complaint of this petition to be true in consideration of justice, which you preach in the sacred law, do what, by right, ought to be restored without delay. Let no man groan over a loss having been born for you, for whom it is rather more fitting to offer assistance. Therefore, take heed, so that one who is unaccustomed to transgress on account of weighty matters, should not be seen now, what would be worse, to sin in an insignificant matter.

LETTER 3.8 (C. 507–11)

This letter admonishes the governor of Lucania and Bruttium to collect the *bini et terni* (a portion of the land tax probably collected in cash) according to the established schedule (*canonicaria*), lest already burdened debtors should fall further into arears.

King Theoderic to Venantius, Vir Spectabilis *and* Corrector
of Lucania and Bruttium

1. The principle of justice advises that what happens to be inflicted upon one should be required from everyone. It also advises to vigorously demand taxes, lest a negligent collector should overburden the debtor. For if remission from taxes should come to corrective measures, it is inevitable that a contemptible man would entangle all others. And cruelty would be born, to a certain degree, from piety, if you should afterward compel that person to pay whom you had failed to admonish. It is therefore useful to warn caution, both when an opportunity for failing to pay draws near and when a place for illegalities must be amended. **2.** With respect to this, we have discovered from the report of the *illustris Comes Sacrarum Largitionum* that not long ago the collection of the *bini et terni* had been delegated to you, pursuant to ancient custom. Concerning this, we advise in the present communication, that you ought to accomplish it within the established period of time, according to the fidelity of the *canonicaria,* lest you should be compelled to pay from your own resources whatever the public will have sustained in lost moneys, you by whom respect for such a command has not been observed, nor devotion to your promise fulfilled.

---

13. Johannus is otherwise unattested.

LETTER 3.9 (C. 507–11)

A theme previously rehearsed at *Variae* 1. 28 and 2.7, this letter requests that citizens of Aestuna transport derelict masonry to Ravenna to facilitate construction there. The location of Aestuna is unclear, although it must have been within a reasonable distance from Ravenna.

King *Theoderic to the* Possessores, Defensores, *and* Curiales *Settled at Aestuna*

1. It is indeed our intention to build new things, but also to protect ancient things even more, since we are likely to acquire no less praise for the preservation of things than for their foundation. Consequently, we desire to erect modern buildings without diminishment to those of previous rulers, for it is not deemed acceptable to our justice that anything should occur through disadvantage to others. **2.** And so, we have learned that columns and marble stone cast down by the envy of great age, now lie without use in your town. And since it profits nothing to protect things cast aside carelessly, those stones ought to rise up, renovated for embellishment, rather than to point out sorrows from the memory of the preceding age. **3.** And therefore, we have decided in the present dictate, that, if the testimony of those reporting is true, that none of the material is deemed now suitable for public adornment, let the above-mentioned columns and marble slabs be gathered for transport by any means to the city of Ravenna,[14] so that, by a lovely craftsmanship, the forgotten form may be restored again from sunken quarries and so that what had been blackened with decay should be able to reclaim that quality of shining antiquity.

LETTER 3.10 (C. 507–11)

Whereas harvesting fallen masonry for reuse at Ravenna was a local effort for the citizens of Aestuna (*Var.* 3.9), the transport of building materials from Rome to Ravenna required the influence of a leading citizen (the patrician senator Festus).

King *Theoderic to Festus,* Vir Illustris *and Patrician*

1. It is fitting for your prudence to obey royal directives in the enrichment of buildings, since it is most noble of a citizen to have regard for the betterment of his own homeland, especially when it would be proposed from our enthusiasm, which everyone is known to obey without personal loss. **2.** And therefore, we declare to your greatness in the present reminder that the marble, which happens to have fallen

---

14. The gerund *devehendas* suggests water transport, perhaps along the Po River.

from the Pincian residence,[15] should be directed by your arrangement to the city of Ravenna by means of the muleteers. But we have arranged the conveyance for immediate attention, lest either a delay to our plans should arise, or those toiling to this end should experience any personal loss.

LETTER 3.11 (C. 510–11)

This letter announces the elevation of a new *Praefectus Urbis* and provides some interesting insight into the standing of this official in comparison to senatorial peers.

King Theoderic to Argolicus, Vir Illustris *and* Praefectus Urbis

1. We have decided to hasten an entire day fully sated with our generosity; we have decided to radiate our favors everywhere, since that which the liberality of a *Princeps* will indulge lives in eternity. For what so befits kings than to have thoroughly bestowed upon one who would marvel at himself having attained elevation and to have made that man happy? These are indeed gifts which dignify *regna,* and that ruler is able to increase liberty unendingly, if he should strive after glorifying his own subjects. With this, the ambitious intention of our habits, since we cherish everyone alike with paternal affection, we bestow upon you with abundant generosity the fillets of the urban prefecture for the fourth indiction, so that bright succession to familial honors may delight and so that whoever deserves to succeed in our reign should be able to prosper under us. **2.** Be mindful, therefore, how great it is that aged Rome was able to be entrusted to your entry to public life, so that, in that great assembly, you should be seen to stand out from the height of a judge, where it would be difficult even to maintain parity. For that reason, take care that you are able to accomplish what you know we have advertised concerning your ability. Flee from greed, pursue justice, cherish the moderate path, and despise the wrathful course. **3.** What will be sweeter than to have pronounced a noteworthy judgment in that crowd of the most elevated men, where the hearts of so many patricians are excited to gratitude, should a good deed be celebrated in the words of the wise? Virtue is never practiced with greater praise, than when Rome is properly governed. Let you consider what wealth would be more becoming than to bear the precious purity of good conscience in the eyes of the Senate and not to have been held captive by any vice at the very bosom of Liberty? **4.** We have seen with what renown other offices may be appraised: the urban president is esteemed above other offices.[16] This distinction is not allowed to perpetrate what the noble crowd

---

15. The phrase *de domo Pinciana* seems to indicate a specific residence, possibly an imperial residence on the Pincian Hill of Rome.

16. *Praesul urbanus:* the *Praefectus Urbis* acted as president of the senatorial assembly at Rome.

typically overlooks. Situated in the midst of all, the *Praefectus Urbis* draws attention to himself, and his reputation among the people pronounces sentence on his entire life. That study of letters, which you have formed through the instruction of undoubtedly learned men, and whence you have recognized everything that is fitting and advantageous to a glorious life, causes you both to express from the heart and to unfold matters clearly and worthily in our presence. **5.** Therefore, let your instruction avoid crime. It is the unlearned mind that is drawn to crime. One edified with books does not abandon to injustice that standing acquired in tender years which is preserved by mature age. Let the deeds of your predecessors encourage you along a path of rectitude, let the authority of reading advise you, so that you, the glorious choice of our judgment, will be able to claim greater things from us then, when you will have learned to fulfill that to which we have entrusted you.

LETTER 3.12 (C. 510-11)

Following from *Variae* 3.11, this letter announces the elevation of Argolicus to the office of *Praefectus Urbis*. Here, the letter dwells at greater length on the achievements of the candidate's family.

King Theoderic to the Senate of Rome

1. We cherish, conscript fathers, the exceptional dignities begotten by our liberality. For the mind of the ruler is the source of public distinction and such as the judgment of the master will be, thus does it give rise to the image of liberty. It is easier, if it is proper to say, that nature would err than that the *Princeps* would be able to shape a republic dissimilar to himself. Hence it is that we desire that you should flash with the radiance of unending honors, since whatever opinion utters about you attaches to our policies. For since you have earned every eminence, it touches our indignation if by chance anything will have been wanting for you. **2.** Thence, that it may be hallowed with blessed auspices, we have promoted the *illustris* Argolicus to the dignity of *Praefectus Urbis,* so that he may be furnished with *fasces* and so that the adornment of so great a judge would detract from you the least. For you know men from this family have often struggled toward prominence.[17] Recall that grandfather of accomplished promotion,[18] enriched by the distinction of philosophical learning, in whom the courts marveled for his innocent eloquence. Because he overflowed with eloquence, he was especially anxious,

---

17. The implication of this and the previous statement seems to be that members of the Senate would be ruffled the least by someone holding the office whose family thus far had not posed serious competition for distinction, although it appears, in the following statements, that the grandfather and father each held high offices in the *comitatus.*

18. The grandfather is unknown.

knowing that one skilled in speaking ought to be conspicuous in purity. With these merits, he was led forth to the heights of the offices. He warded the sacred largesse with faithful custody,[19] even fulfilling the dignity of *Magister Officiorum* with the learning that he had received. He was so celebrated in both offices that he was believed to be the best in each. **3.** Moreover, that most renowned father of the candidate,[20] who never profaned the fillets of the *Comes Privatarum* with the grievousness of deceit, who, striving after the advantages of reputation ignored the increase of wealth, and, what is a rare example of virtue, practiced moderation throughout his career, during which time, the stain of avarice touched him not. For he caused the resolve of the *Princeps* both to disregard officials and to love the virtues. Accordingly, laying out the proofs of so great an origin, let us admit the blessings of noble birth, since praiseworthy blood preserves its source and passes faithfully on to posterity what he deserved in ennobling transmission to himself. Therefore, conscript fathers, favor one consecrated by your dignities, so that you, whom we have stirred by the example of rewards, would rouse a greater desire for the virtues.

LETTER 3.13 (C. 507–11)

This letter reveals some of the difficulties of maintaining administration between civilian and military populations by appointing Sunivadus to resolve disputes between Romans and Goths in the province of Samnium. The man is presumably Gothic, although the exact nature of his appointment (as *comes* or perhaps *saio*) is not disclosed and his mandate must be understood as deriving from intimacy with the king.

King Theoderic to Sunivadus, Vir Spectabilis

1. The long service of your labors and the extensive evidence of tested devotion have led us to this decision, that you, who have restrained your passions, now should be offered for the conduct of others, and that you, who have cherished self-control in private life, should offer discipline to a province. For one is able to rule others well, who has practiced conducting himself with grace. And so, having been moved by the entreaty of the Samnians, we have decided to relieve their suffering with this remedy, if we should appoint your *spectabilis* to attend to ending these altercations. **2.** Now make yourself conspicuous there, so that you may answer a good directive with praiseworthy judgment, and show yourself aptly suited to our command, you who thus far have been so easily agreeable in your own affairs. And so, if in the province of Samnium any case emerges, whether a Roman against

---

19. He was *Comes Sacrarum Largitionum.*
20. Also unknown.

Goths, or a Goth against Romans, let you adjudicate with consideration of the laws, lest you should permit those whom we want to protect with one will to live according to separate laws. Therefore, assess what is friendly to justice in every case, since one who would intend upon pure equitability knows not how to recognize individual persons.

LETTER 3.14 (C. 507–11)

A remarkably short letter responding to a complaint that a bishop's dependents (possibly tenants on church property) have assaulted the wife and property of another man. The status of the victims, whether tenants of church property or free landowners, is undisclosed, but their vulnerability is evident, as is the state's position in relegating the case to the care of the bishop.

King Theoderic to Aurigenes, Venerable Bishop

1. Although we may believe that any wickedness would displease your judgment, we especially trust that what would assail the condition of legal matrimony must be condemned by you. For with what hostility is it received by the faithfully married that it is even execrated in the curses of the laity? And so Julianus has complained to us in a tearful petition that his wife and property have been ravaged in an unjust attack by your men. Whence, if you know the claim of the petitioner to be true, once struck, the crime is not reasonably dismissed. Restrain the author of the deed without any delay. For, when a wicked deed remains unpunished, it increases, and a hastened corrective for the transgressor is a healing boon.

LETTER 3.15 (C. 507–11)

Another example of *ex officio* conflict resolution (cf. *Var.* 3.13 and 3.14), this letter charges a member of the royal family (the future king Theodahad) to bring an accused man to court. The defendant is presumably a dependent of Theodahad's, probably either as a tenant of Theodahad's property or as a member of his personal retinue.

King Theoderic to Theodahad, Vir Spectabilis

1. Outraged justice is indeed an insult to us, since we rightly take upon ourselves the profaning of those causes that we cherish. Whence, we especially do not permit anything standing in open contempt of an order of ours to remain unpunished. For what provocation deserving punishment would not be dared, if the fear of a consecrated right is despised? And so that man, whom some time ago we decided to summon to the court of the *illustris* Suna and who hid himself away with well-practiced cunning, we commit him to be judged in your presence, so

that you may give an end to a dispute deserving punishment that has been pro-longed by artifice. And so, have regard for the concern of the court, so that the reputation of your justice may increase, when unresolved quarrels are entrusted to you for the sake of remedy.

LETTER 3.16 (C. 508)

This letter appoints a *Vicar Praefectorum,* or an assistant to the *Praefectus* in Gaul, the southern portion of which had recently come under Ostrogothic rule. Although Liberius later will be appointed as *Praefectus Praetorio Galliarum,* subordination to a senior prefect is not mentioned in this letter or in the announcement to pro-vincials in Gaul (*Var.* 3.17), indicating that the court at Ravenna had not yet made the important senior appointment.

King Theoderic to Gemellus, Vir Spectabilis

1. Our judgment is decided, for which an example is at hand, nor is there room for ambiguity, where credible experience approves. We have tested your ability through diverse stages of difficulty, but you, equally proven on various assignments, have earned like praise in each. **2.** Hence it is that, at the present time, our authority sends you to Gaul, now subject to us by God's will, as *Vicar Praefectorum.* Whence may be seen what sort of opinions we hold concerning your measure, when you would be sent for guiding those people, whom we believe especially to have gar-nered our praise. The glory of a *Princeps* is costly and it is necessary to be even more protective concerning those victories whence we have found ourselves arriving at an increase of triumphs.[21] **3.** Therefore, if you desire our esteem for you to advance, take this commission. Cherish not controversy and avoid avarice, so that an exhausted province may find you to be the kind of judge that it would expect a Roman *Princeps* to send. United by its own defeats, the province desires distin-guished men. Make it so that the province would delight to have been conquered. Let it experience nothing like what it had endured, when it would long for Rome. Let it leave behind all the sadness of ruin; let a darkened countenance finally brighten. Let it happen that Gaul now rejoices, upon arrival at its own desires.

LETTER 3.17 (C. 508)

Presumably sent to the municipal assemblies of southern Gaul, this letter announces the appointment of Gemellus as *Vicar Praefectorum* in Gaul (cf. *Var.* 3.16). The letter

---

21. A convoluted way of saying that Theoderic wishes to be protective of the means by which his military glory has increased, with the *illis . . . unde* referring either to the "victories" whence the recent triumphs arrived, or the Gallic people over whom Gemellus has been sent.

assumes the tone of a return to Roman civilization for Gallic provincials, the efficacy of which in terms of diplomatic relations may be questionable.

King Theoderic to All the Provincials of Gaul

1. You should gladly yield to Roman ways, to which you have been restored after long duration, since the return to where your forebears had their first advancement is welcome. And therefore, having been recalled by God's will to ancient liberty, clothe yourself with togate habits, move beyond barbarity, cast off a cruel disposition, since, under the equity of our reign, it is not fitting for you to live with foreign customs. **2.** Hence, thinking about your needs with the gentleness innate to us, what is said happily, we have decided that the *spectabilis* Gemellus must be directed to you as *Vicar Praefectorum,* for the purpose of arranging matters in the province for us with diligence and good faith. We hope that it would be in no way possible for him to fail in his duty, he who knows that wrong-doers severely displease us. **3.** Therefore, follow his administration by our command, since we believe he has determined what would be in your best interest. Return to lawful habits gradually. A novelty which is righteous could not be harmful. For what could be more fortunate than that men trust only in laws and do not fear continued misfortunes? The certitudes of public order are the safety of human life, assistance for the weak and a curb to the powerful. **4.** Cherish these, and security will come and good conscience will prosper. For foreign manners, thrive upon self-gratification, where one who is able to take what he pleases more often finds his own death. Show yourselves now secure in riches. The blessings of your forebears, now recovered from long neglect, are brought forth into the light, since, however much one reflects the gleam of upright morals and brilliant dignity, the more celebrated he will be. **5.** For this reason we have directed a *Vicar Praefectorum* to you, so that we may be seen to have settled a means of civil conduct with that very kind of office. May you enjoy the likes of which you had only heard. Come to know men who prefer not so much bodily strength, but rather the force of reason, and know that those who are able to demonstrate righteousness to others wax deservingly in good fortune.

LETTER 3.18 (C. 508–11)

An example of the patronage with which Theoderic hoped to garner the loyalty of the Gallic elite, this letter orders the restoration of possessions to a man who presumably had sided with the Franks in the recent conflict. His properties had probably been seized by other Gallic provincials at the outset of the war.

King Theoderic to Gemellus, Vir Spectabilis

1. Those who are known to approach our clemency deserve blessings, inasmuch as we are able to show that they chose correctly by their own prosperity. But if it is proper for such men to be sought for public munificence, how much more right is it for them to possess their own, which is deemed to be a reward universal to justice? **2.** And so the *spectabilis* Magnus, recalling that he was born in Roman *imperium,* has rejected his association with the enemy and repatriated. He claims that, in his absence, it happened that his property had been allowed to be squandered. And therefore, we confirm in the present decree that, however much property or slaves, whether urban or rustic, or whatever belonging to him that he should now be able to prove lost by whatever means, let him recuperate without any delay, while, by our authority, retaining every right of ownership which he had possessed. Nor do we want him, for whom it is our intention to furnish even new blessings, to endure suit concerning the legality of his claim to former properties.

LETTER 3.19 (C. 507–11)

This letter appoints a craftsman to superintend the production, sale, and disposition of marble sarcophagi at Ravenna. The appointee's obligation to prevent corruption is couched in terms of duty to the bereaved.

King Theoderic, a Notice to Daniel

1. It is fitting that we reflect upon just deserts for those serving in our palace, since public duty ought to be most advantageous, so that, although willing obedience should rightly be owed to us, nonetheless, we provide enticement for service by means of moderate payment. And therefore, having been delighted by the skill of your craftsmanship, which you practice so carefully by carving and adorning marble, we grant in the present dictate that the sarcophagi, which are arranged for the disposition of burial remains at the city of Ravenna, should be administered according to your own reasonable management, by which benefit corpses are interred above ground, no small consolation for the bereaved, when so many souls depart from worldly association, but the survivors may not abandon once sweet countenances. **2.** Hence, the grieving agree to any price, and profit from commerce in human dead increases with the wretched lot of the devoted. Nevertheless, let the appraisal not be unjust under this circumstance, lest the wretched would be compelled to bemoan the loss of their means in the midst of the bitterness of painful grief, and they would be forced to acts contrary to devotion, either being pressed upon to lose patrimony on behalf of the dead, or, instead, for the grieving to cast a beloved body into some base pit. Let the cost be at the inclination of those making the request, when lamentation itself reveals those counterfeiting grief. For he ought to be outraged less, who is known to be cheated more on account of duty to piety.

LETTER 3.20 (C. 507–11)

An order to a *saio* and a tax official (*apparitor*) to restore properties that had been seized by the *Praefectus Praetorio* without proper warrant. The letter is redolent with the language of Christian and Roman ethics regarding the protection of the helpless and the abuse of power.

King Theoderic to Trivuila, Saio, *and to Ferrocinctus,* Apparator

1. Among the glorious cares of governing the republic, which, by God's will, we continually turn over in our thoughts, solace for the lowly is close to our heart, so that we have erected the obstacle of our devotion against the might of the proud, lest any audacity may be permitted in our reign, whose purpose it is to grind down the proud.[22] **2.** Therefore, having been moved by the tearful misfortune of Castorius, whom the deadly treachery of various persons has harassed up to this point, he provides an opportunity for a salutary decree, so that the assistance of our devotion shall prevail rather than the iniquitous cunning of corrupt men. And therefore, we have decided in the present dictate that, if his magnificence, the *Praefectus* Faustus, has either burdened with legal contract or detained through private seizure the property that Castorius owned, by your close supervision the estate should be returned to him immediately with another of the same worth from the transgressor, so that we might console one afflicted by cruel losses with the salve of our devotion. **3.** If, however, anyone else is discovered involved in this audacity, if he should be unable to suitably reimburse to the property that which has been ordered, lead him to us bound in chains, so that the punishment may be satisfied by one whose means do not suffice for revenge. Thus may the violent impulse of an unjust mind then be put to rest by so great a deterrent that one would seem to attack, not Castorius, but rather our will. **4.** Now, if afterward, that notorious fraud should attempt to harm the aforementioned Castorius on any occasion whatever, let him immediately be smitten further for fifty pounds of gold, and let it be a greater punishment for him to behold untroubled by torments the very one whom he desired to see afflicted. Behold that this deed may immediately restrain all others and let it correct the powerful. It is not permitted for the *Praefectus Praetorio* to rage in attack on the lowly. The power to harm the poor is removed from one raised up by us. Hence, let all men know by what love of equity we are delighted, so that we would even rather threaten the efficacy of our judges, to the extent that we would be able to increase the blessings of good conscience.

---

22. An interesting conflation of Christian and Roman ethics, with the one concerned with the care of the *humiles,* and the other concerned with restraining the *superbi.*

LETTER 3.21 (C. 507-11)

This may or may not be addressed to the *Praefectus Praetorio* of *Variae* 3.20. In the case that it is, this may be a politically polite way of removing the former *Praefectus* from office. The letter responds to a request for a sabbatical from Rome in a tone that verges on the ironic. Terms such as *indutiae* ("armistice") and *regressio* ("retreat") suggest failed military enterprise, a not uncommon metaphor for public life.

King Theoderic to Faustus, Vir Illustris

1. It is the way of human custom that adornment would attract more, and although distinctions may be held in legal right, anything that satiates desire may introduce aversion. Thence, you claim that you ought be granted a hiatus from constant residence within the sacred walls,[23] for the sake of arranging affairs to your own advantage, not because such a lofty dwelling would be wearisome, but by which a renewed return might become all the more sweet. And therefore, your *illustris* greatness, our devotion bestows a leave of four months for the purpose of withdrawing to your province, on the condition that you would hasten to return to your home within the same amount of time, so that your home in Rome, that most prized of lands, which we want to be frequented by numerous assemblies, should not become thinned by the loss of inhabitants. And, moreover, we deem it most agreeable to you, when it would be possible for a Roman senator to be delayed elsewhere only with resentment. For where else is there that charm of kindred? Where else is such great beauty to be observed within city walls? It is a kind of sacrilege that those who are able to dwell in familial homes at Rome would make it overly distant from themselves.[24]

LETTER 3.22 (C. 510-11)

This letter summons the former *Praefectus Urbis* to join the royal *comitatus*, probably at Ravenna. A similar summons was received by Cassiodorus's father (*Var.* 3.28), after completing the post of *Praefectus Praetorio*. In both cases, the men probably remained at court to serve as *ex officio* advisors. The new *Praefectus Urbis* was appointed at *Variae* 3.11 and 3.12.

King Theoderic to Artemidorus, Vir Illustris

1. It is fitting that we should adorn our *comitatus* with the most celebrated men, both so that their desires should be fulfilled and so that the benefits of public offices should equip our court. Thence we, who do not hesitate to be most grateful to you, call your greatness to our presence with these summons, so that you, who

---

23. The phrase *sacris moenibus* more than likely means "at Rome."

24. The use of terms such as *lares* and *penates* for "home" intensifies the sentiment in this last statement of sacrilege against family.

have associated with us for many years, may be selected for the sweetness of our company. Indeed, he who hastens to the *Princeps* is able to find only what is favorable; for it is fitting for one who shares our conversation to trust the reward to be heavenly. Therefore, we do not delay a request for one whose appearance we desire. We trust that you whom we eagerly await would come rejoicing.

LETTER 3.23 (C. 507–11)

This letter appoints a *comes* to govern Pannonia Sirmiensis with careful instructions to temper provincial administration with civil, not martial law. It is noteworthy that the letter characterizes the provincials as *gentes* ("foreign peoples"), not Romans, with the implication being that the Goths had restored Roman order to the province. Whereas other appointments appear in paired letters to the appointee and to the Senate, this letter is followed by an announcement to the provincials of Pannonia (*Var.* 3.24).

King Theoderic to Colosseus, Vir Illustris *and* Comes

1. It is a comfort to entrust those things requiring proper disposition to proven men, and indeed, the decision to appoint such men is a delight and the property of people that has been entrusted to such approved men is secure. For just as we select him to be the one who would be acceptable; thus do we take care that one who will be acceptable would stand out in merit. **2.** Consequently, commencing with favorable portents and being girt with the dignity of an *illustris* belt, set forth to Pannonia Sirmiensis, the former seat of the Goths,[25] and protect with arms the province entrusted to you; arrange matters according to law, so that a province which knows that it obeyed our forebears happily will be fortunate to receive again its former protectors. **3.** You know with what integrity you may commend yourself to our company. Your only path to pleasing us would be if you should imitate that which we have accomplished. Cherish equity, and defend the innocent with virtuous spirit, so that you would be able to represent the justice of the Goths amid the perverse practices of various peoples. They have ever been set in the middle course of honor, as they had adopted the wisdom of Romans and possessed the strength of foreign nations. Roll back the detestable customs that have appeared. Pursue legal cases not by arms, but rather by words. Do not allow the affairs of family members to end in death. Let the fraud repay what he stole from another, not his life. Nor should the interests of the community exact more than wars would consume. Let shields be raised against the enemy, not kin. **4.** And lest, perchance, poverty may be seen to sentence anyone to death, take a completely honorable loss for the sake of such persons. You would elect a bountiful profit of gratitude from

---

25. Goths settled in Pannonia after the breakup of the Hunnic Empire with the Battle of Nadao in 454.

us, if there you could graft an example of civility and the true dignity of our judges, and if the judge would accept loss to himself, in order that one about to perish should acquire life. Therefore, let our habits be implanted in uncultivated minds; thence may the cruel disposition become accustomed to live in a refined manner.

LETTER 3.24 (C. 507–11)

This letter announces to the provincials the appointment of a *comes* as governor of Pannonia (cf. *Var.* 3.23). The emphasis placed on the loyalty of the provincials and the maintenance of order may indicate that the province was not thoroughly integrated under Amal authority.

King Theoderic to All Romans and Barbarians Settled throughout Pannonia

1. Our foresight will not fail your needs, since it continually arranges the future welfare for subjects, so that those who recognize us to have taken pains for them would be stirred to greater devotion. **2.** Hence it is that we have entrusted your governance and protection to Colosseus, an *illustris* great by name and in strength, so that one who has already given much proof of his virtue may increase yet in deeds to come. And so now show your obedience, so often proven before, to this same man, to the extent that he will commence upon these affairs which must be accomplished for the advantage of our reign according to reason, and so that they may be accomplished with devotion worthy of approval, since constancy renders good faith and that man proves the integrity of his own intentions who persists in perpetual obedience. **3.** Additionally, we feel you must be reminded of this as you may prefer us to rage not upon you, but on the enemy. Let not small matters lead you to extreme dangers; acquiesce to that justice which the world enjoys. **4.** Why should you who do not have a corrupt judge return to trial by combat? You who have no enemy, lay aside the sword. Worse, you raise your arm against kindred, for whose sake it should happen one would rather die honorably. What use is the human tongue, if the armed fist settles litigation? Where is it believed that peace would exist, if it is battered along with civil harmony? Let yourselves openly imitate our Goths, who know to wage wars abroad and to exercise restraint at home. We want you to live thus, by that very means that you perceive our kin to have flourished, with a distinguished master.

LETTER 3.25 (C. 506–7)

This letter appoints a *comes* to govern the province of Dalmatia. In comparison to *Variae* 3.23 and 3.24, where it is clear that the governor would be required to maintain military discipline, this appointment is more concerned with the assessment of taxes and the management of the province's mineral resources. Based on the indiction periods given, this was to be a three-year appointment.

King Theoderic to Simeon, Vir Clarissimus and Comes

1. We love to involve in public affairs those officials conspicuous for the probity of their habits, so that the increase of utility may grow through the obedience of those faithful to us. Thence, knowing the purity of your mind through outstanding testimony, our mandate entrusts to you the title to the *siliqua,* which we have granted for the lawful assessment of state taxes on the first, second, and third indictions in the province of Dalmatia. Thus, wheresoever by your examination the trail of fraud will have revealed a loss to public taxes, let it be born by our treasury without penalty, since it is not so much wealth that we seek, so much as we hasten to comprehend the morals of our subjects. **2.** Additionally, we order you to examine the ironworks of the aforementioned Dalmatia with the shaft of truth,[26] where softened earth brings forth the rigidity of iron and it is baked in fire, so that it is altered to a hard substance. Whence, God willing, comes the defense of the homeland; whence utility is derived from the fields and it extends the convenience to human life in countless uses. Iron lords over gold itself and compels the wealthy to serve the stoutly armed peasant. And so it happens that this substance is carved out with careful searching, by which both our wealth is produced and destruction is purchased for our enemies. Therefore, be eager regarding the previously discussed administration and be moderate with public resources, so that our reasonable gain will be able to procure an advantageous means for your own increase.

LETTER 3.26 (C. 506–7)

This letter announces to the resident *comes* of Dalmatia the arrival of another *comes* assigned to manage fiscal matters and mining (cf. *Var.* 3.25, above). Presumably, the existing *comes* had been assigned primarily to military concerns, as was apparently the case at *Variae* 3.23 and 3.24.

King Theoderic to Osuin, Vir Illustris and Comes

1. Although it may be necessary for your prudence to offer protection to those assigned to public administration, we nonetheless heap admonitions upon admonitions, so that it may become more firmly rooted where respect ought to accommodate itself to our commands. And so, we have sent to the province of Dalmatia the *clarissimus* Simeon, whose fidelity to us has been recognized for a long time and whose devotion is proven, for the administration of the *siliqua* and also the

---

26. The phrase *cuniculo veritatis* ("mine shaft of truth") is an obvious pun on the subject of mining.

ironworks according to our direction. You should not deny any comforts sought by him. In this way, your eminence may become more highly valued by us, when it hastens to display itself for the sake of public affairs.

LETTER 3.27 (C. 507-11)

Another letter addressed to the fraught praetorian prefecture of (probably) Faustus (cf. *Var.* 3.20, 3.21), here offering the governor of Campania sureties of protection against the prerogatives of the more senior *Praefectus*. The assurance also holds the edge of threat against the governor's own malfeasance, now that the oversight of the *Praefectus* has been removed. It is worth noting that the title of *Consular,* here refers to the office of governor; a former *consul* would hold senatorial rank as an *illustris,* not as a lesser *spectabilis.*

King Theoderic to Johannus, Vir Spectabilis *and* Consular *of Campania*

1. It is the intention of royal devotion to sever opportunity for unjust hatreds and to repress the arrogance of armed might with respect for commands. The offenses of a superior are indeed dangerous to the lowly, since he is drawn to glory when he should exact punishments on men of middling means. Consequently, having been cast about for a long time by various persecutions, it is hardly in vain that you, claiming the most prominent *Praefectus* has terrorized you, have flown to the protection of our devotion, lest private grievances against you should be sated through public punishment. **2.** But we, who wish those dignities bestowed to serve justice, not resentment, girt you round with our protection against illicit outrages, so that the rage of burning desires may shatter upon its own hazards by the opposition of royal majesty and so that impudence may take punishment more from itself, when it is restrained and harmless. Indeed, so long as he is called a judge, thus he should be deemed just, since that name, which is obtained from equity, is not held for the sake of pride. **3.** It remains now that you should complete the office assumed as governor and that you, diligent and devoted, should attend to the public administration that your predecessors agreed to perform, and you will be protected by us as much as you hasten to obey moderation. For if you will enjoy gladness, because you know the threat of the *Praefectus Praetorio* has been removed from you, who are appointed to be under him, what do you suppose you would suffer for comporting yourself wickedly?

LETTER 3.28 (C. 507-11)

Similar to *Variae* 3.22, which summoned the former *Praefectus Urbis* to the royal *comitatus,* this letter requests the company of Cassiodorus senior, presumably to act as *ex officio* advisor after serving as *Praefectus Praetorio.*[27]

---

27. For a possible comparison, cf. *Var.* 11.1.16, where Liberius has received *praesentaneam dignitatem.*

King Theoderic to Cassiodorus, Vir Illustris *and Patrician*

1. The sight of those who settle in our thoughts with glorious deeds is always pleasing to us, since those who are proven to strive for virtue in our presence have given a lasting surety of their affection. Thence, by the present command, proven as you are by glorious service, we summon your greatness to the *comitatus,* so that, adorned by you it may increase with respect to royal service, and you may prosper in our presence. **2.** For it is all the more fitting that you, who have caused our reign to be uncommonly popular, should be missed. You have adorned the palace with the purity of good conscience; you have given the deepest peace to the people. Hence it is that you were made more famous than anyone because the one who wanted you placed in a position of authority did not know you personally, but those present in court knew you for a judge without any fear of loss; you were made dearer to all because you could be bought at no price. Who would not want to behold such a man, to whom it remains for us to publicly return our gratitude? For we who have striven to suppress another magistrate have instead praised you with the entire palace as witness.[28] Take the step and hasten your approach.[29] It is fitting for one who knows himself to be expected by a *Princeps* to come eagerly.

LETTER 3.29 (C. 510–11)

A letter giving a senator rights to restore and manage particular granaries at Rome for his own use. Provided the granaries have no current function, it is deemed better to release public claim to the structures for the purpose of ensuring the restoration of derelict buildings. *Variae* 3.29, 3.30, and 3.31 all concern aspects of urban infrastructure at Rome.

King Theoderic to Argolicus, Vir Illustris *and* Praefectus Urbis

1. Who does not know that the profit of petitioners is our remuneration and that what kindness is able to offer with generosity increases with a good *Princeps?* For in this way, royal gifts are seed which, having been scattered, flourish in the field; having been forced into one hole, they are wasted. Therefore we choose to distribute gathered rewards among many, so that our favors will be able to take root everywhere. **2.** And therefore, concerning the petition received from the representatives of the magnificent *illustris* and patrician Paulinus, which is included in

---

28. Possibly contrasting the failed prefectural tenure of Faustus (cf. *Var.* 3.20, 3.21, 3.27) with that of Cassiodorus senior.

29. Note that *gradus* ("step") can also be understood as an "official post," in which case Cassiodorus senior's *adventus* ("approach") may be thought of as a ceremonial arrival to undertake the position of advisor to the king.

the attached below,[30] we grant to the above-mentioned man, with unrestricted use for himself and all his associates, those granaries ruined by the extent of long time, to which antiquity had affixed the names *illud* and *illud*, if they are now demonstrated to be unnecessary to public need and if there is no amount stored there which pertains to the fisc. In this way, let him arrange freely for his own future use what he has taken on to repair and pass on to posterity, since anyone who wants to undertake the necessary restoration of ruined buildings confers a greater gift on the republic, especially in that city where it is fitting that every building gleam, lest the ruin of stones from mangled buildings should be visible among so many ornaments of the city. Indeed, the least among other cities have maintained beautiful buildings; certainly in this city, which is praised above others in the voice of the world, nothing mediocre should be permitted.

LETTER 3.30 (C. 510–11)

This letter announces to the *Praefectus Urbis* the appointment of an official to superintend the sewers of Rome. The letter is notable as a partner with *Variae* 3.29, both of which concern maintaining the urban infrastructure, but with different strategies: *Variae* 3.29 relied on a private citizen assuming responsibility for a project, while the present letter introduces a public official for the purpose.

King Theoderic to Argolicus, Vir Illustris *and* Praefectus Urbis

1. Concern for the city of Rome always keeps watch over our attentions. For what is more worthy than to demand the restoration of that place which we ought to maintain and which, thus adorned, serves to unite our republic? Consequently, your *illustris* dignity should know that we have sent the *spectabilis* Johannus to the city of Rome on account of the remarkable sewers,[31] which bestow such amazement upon observers, that they are able to surpass the wonders of any other city. 2. There you may see floods enclosed, as though within hollow hills, rushing through prodigious, plastered channels. You may see, among the waters, torrents being navigated by vessels assembled with the greatest precaution, lest it should be possible to sustain a maritime shipwreck in the headlong torrents. Here, Rome, is it possible to understand how much singular greatness is contained in you. For what cities would dare to contend with your towers, when they are unable to find an equal to your deepest foundations? And therefore, we order you to offer the assistance of your office to the above-mentioned Johannus, since we want officials to implement our public administration, thereby removing the private hands that are so brazenly immersed in illegalities.

---

30. The letter included the original petition from Paulinus's agents.
31. Johannus may be the same man mentioned as governor of Campania at *Var.* 3.27.

Similar to *Variae* 2.24, this letter takes a censorious tone announcing to the Senate a full-scale investigation into the exploitation of public buildings for private use, particularly the misappropriation of aqueduct resources, the spoliation of valuable materials from public buildings, and the demolition of monuments for which restoration had been ordered. The Senate is not directly implicated in condoning these abuses, but a royal agent (Johannus from *Var.* 3.30) has been appointed to prepare a detailed report disclosing individuals involved.

King Theoderic to the Senate of Rome

1. Although we may desire to expend indefatigable care on the entirety of our republic, and, with the favor of God, we may be eager to restore everything to its former state, nonetheless the vexatious improvement of the city of Rome constrains me, where whatever is spent on the comeliness of the city is displayed for the common delight. And so, through the report of many it has come to our attention, which cannot ignore corrupt practices, that detestable confiscations have brought many places in Rome to ruin, so that, what we desire to assign to the peak of our attention endures lawless corruption. **2.** Therefore, we bring our decrees to your attention, who, we trust, are displeased even more by the loss to your city. Therefore, it is said that concern for private gain has diverted the water of the aqueducts, which it would be more fitting to protect with the greatest attention, instead for the purpose of operating mills and irrigating gardens. It is shameful and wretched that what is scarcely permitted to take place in the countryside would happen in this city. **3.** And since we are unable to correct this kind of crime beyond the measure of the law, lest we should destroy the edifices of law while we seek to benefit buildings, if the instigator of this abominable crime is protected by the limitation of thirty years,[32] let him pay an accepted price compensating his error, so that he should no longer presume to offer harm to public buildings, lest what we now correct with generosity, afterward we punish most severely. **4.** If, indeed, any such misappropriation has been attempted recently, let it be abolished without hesitation. For the common advantage, which can seldom be obstructed even for the sake of justice, ought to be considered before the corrupt desire of one man. Indeed, we know the service of slaves set aside for the aqueducts by the provision of *Principes* has passed into the control of private persons. Moreover, no small quantity of bronze and, what is easier for spoliation, soft lead, are reported to have been removed from the ornaments of the city, materials which their own authors dedicated to posterity. Indeed, King Ionos of Thessaly discovered bronze, and Midas, the ruler of Phrygia, discovered lead. And how wretched it is, that

---

32. For other instances of the thirty-year limitation, *Var.* 1.18.2 and 2.27.2.

where the foresight of others acquired fame, we may be found to have incurred a reputation for negligence. Even the temples and public places, which we have assigned for restoration at the request of many, have instead been sold for demolition. **5.** And since we delight in the correction of corrupt practices, lest permission seem to have been conceded out of silence, we have sent the *spectabilis* Johannus, chosen by our justice for investigating the matters that we recounted above. Thus, everything examined according to its own circumstance will be brought to light by the service of a report to us, whereupon we shall decide according to the habit of our justice what best would be done concerning individual cases and their perpetrators. Now take heed, give consideration, so that you may be seen to satisfy with a pleased disposition an investigation that you ought to have requested.

LETTER 3.32 (C. 510)

This letter cancels the collection of taxes from citizens of Arles for one year, citing the loyalty already shown by their resistance during a siege of the Franks and Burgundians. Numerous letters in Books 3 and 4 attest Theoderic's attention to Gaul after the collapse of Visigothic power in the region.

King Theoderic to Gemellus, Vir Spectabilis

1. It does not agree with us that the service of faithful men should go to waste, but having expended their effort in harsh circumstances, they receive good fortune in better. And so for the citizens of Arles, who for our sake preferred enduring the penury of a famous siege, our kindness has released them from taxes for the fourth indiction, so that they may return to their accustomed payment at a future date. In this way, we shall be known to have made a good exchange for the deserving, and, when the situation requires, the customary devotion will not be denied by them. **2.** Let those who, for our sake, preferred to go hungry in precarious situations, be sated in freedom; let those be happy who faithfully preferred grief. It is not fitting that one who was barely able to avert the previous hardship should immediately after be disturbed over taxes. We require such from those at peace, not from the besieged. For what might you compel from the owner of a field that you know has not been cultivated? They have already yielded to us the costly toll of their loyalty. It is unjust that base money should be exacted from those who have offered up the glories of good conscience.

LETTER 3.33 (C. 510-11)

A letter of appointment, announcing the elevation of two men as *referendi curiae,* representatives of the royal court to the Senate. The appointment is commended by the learning and legal experience of the men, as well as the persuasive eloquence of the senior candidate. The appointments may be connected to what seems like a recent breakdown in relations with the Senate (cf. *Var.* 2.24 and 3.31).

King Theoderic to Argolicus, Vir Illustris *and* Praefectus Urbis

1. It is pleasing to us that our wishes should accomplish improvement to the sacred order. We are delighted that such men emerge who would deserve to shine in senatorial brilliance, so that the grace of official appointment may be passed down to those conspicuous in praise. For the curia stands open to the instruction of the ancients. It is not possible that one who is a fosterling of the liberal arts should be deemed a foreigner to the Senate. And therefore, your *illustris* magnificence, let that office which shining antiquity called *referendi curiae* be offered to the *clarissimus* Armentarius, and his son, Superbus. **2.** For he is that well-known Armentarius who is commended to us both by the good fortune of his family and by his own native character, one who, striving by his merits rather than his wealth, hopes for official dignity. For what is more worthy than if the orator's occupation is clothed even in senatorial distinction,[33] so that he would dare to pronounce an unrestrained opinion among that crowd of learned men, lest one whom the laws of eloquence encourages to have a voice may be curbed by the terror of inexperience. **3.** And furthermore, a knowledge of letters is glorious, first because it purifies morals in men, but secondly because it lends the grace of words. Thus, remarkably adorned with both favors, he is both restrained and persuasive. Therefore, let those lauded according to their own worth be led to the inner sanctum of Liberty, adorned with our judgment, to belong without question to a most grateful Senate, for whom it is an art to procure good will from wrath, assenting opinion from conjecture, mildness from severity, and favor from adversity. Therefore, what would he not be able to accomplish with senators, who has prevailed to bend the heart of a judge?

LETTER 3.34 (C. 508–11)

This letter advises the citizens of Massilia (modern Marseilles) that a *comes* has been appointed for the defense and administration of the city. Like the case of Arles (*Var.* 3.32), this letter is also sensitive to the impact of the recent war on the community.

King Theoderic to the Citizens of Massilia

1. It is our purpose to send officials of proven strength and moderation for your defense and administration, so that both the interests of the provincials may be

---

33. The phrase *togata professio* ("togate profession") is likely an antiquated reference to the legal profession.

alleviated and public weal may increase for good governors. **2.** Thence, we have determined that the *Comes* Marabadus, a man known to us for his equity, must be sent to the city of Massilia, so that, with God's blessing, he may accomplish whatever pertains to your safety and civic harmony, and, mindful of our gratitude, he may give attention to justice, bring comfort to the vulnerable, restrain the harshness of his own punishment of the arrogant, and finally, that he may permit no man to be oppressed by lawless presumption, but compel every man to justice, whence *imperium* always flourishes. **3.** As for the man designated for these matters, about which he will have instructed you for the sake of public weal: obey him with open minds, so that your loyalty, which has already been demonstrated in former trials, will also be declared in subsequent proofs, since that obedience is most pleasing which is preserved through continual devotion. Nonetheless, we, who are unable to forget the cost of good service, know how to return opportunity in exchange.

LETTER 3.35 (C. 507–11)

This is a compressed and curt address to a person who may be the former western Roman emperor, Romulus Augustus, advising him that the terms of his arrangements with Liberius (cf. *Var.* 2.16) remain fixed. Romulus had been deposed from office in 476 by Odoacer and retired to an estate in Campania, apparently with an annual pension.

King Theoderic to Romulus

1. It is fitting that our generosity maintain firm constancy, since the will of a *Princeps* ought to be unshaken, nor ought that which is known to be strengthened by our injunction be torn apart by the design of wicked men. And therefore, we have determined in the present order that whatever the patrician Liberius decided to allocate to you and your mother from our administration, per the deed, ought to stand firm on its own; nor should you, who possess the strength of our favor, fear an unreasonable challenge from anyone.

LETTER 3.36 (C. 507–11)

This letter orders a *comes* to arrange a hearing to determine the legality of claims made against a well-known patrician by a certain Firminus. The nature of the complaint is not explained. The fact that the plaintiff is provisionally threatened with the penalty for slander indicates disparity in rank between the two litigants.

King Theoderic to Arigernus, Vir Illustris *and* Comes

1. It is the purpose of our devotion not to deny an audience to pitiable complaints, especially when it is our custom to refer everything to the laws, so that both the one complaining may merit action and nobody punished may bemoan himself to have been treated with prejudice. Thence, Firminus claims that he has a case against the magnificent patrician Venantius and that his formal complaints have been frequently scorned by Venantius. **2.** And since influence is always suspected in legal cases, when a powerful individual is assumed to want what he is thought capable of taking, we order the aforementioned man to be advised by you with due respect, so that he should place himself under a legal pledge to send to our *comitatus* an informed agent, who would be capable of offering an explanation for his intentions to judges selected by our inclination. This Firminus should be ready to receive a penalty for his own presumption, if he has maintained a case of falsehood against the magnificent Venantius.

LETTER 3.37 (C. 507–11)

This letter offers the bishop of an undisclosed city an opportunity to resolve a property dispute before the case is sent to the royal court. The petitioner claims that property belonging to his father had been detained; the father may have been a member of the clergy, in which case the property was probably willed to the church in part or in whole.

King Theoderic to Peter, Bishop

1. If it has happened that your blessedness has been inclined toward the welfare of others, so that the clamoring of litigants finds its repose in you, how much more ought that case be referred to you which finds you as its author? And therefore, let your sanctity know us to have been approached by a pitiable representative from Germanus, who claims to be the legitimate son of the late Thomas, saying that a portion of his father's property pertaining to him by law has been detained by you. **2.** If this petition is supported by truth, and you judge the property of his father to rightly pertain to Germanus, with full consideration given to that justice which you advocate, let what is owed be offered without the expense of long deliberation, since the nature of your cases ought to be determined by your judgment. More justice should be expected from you than would be imposed upon you; because, if your authority determines this case with less fairness, you will find the complaint of this petitioner being addressed at our court. For indeed, you teach that the voices of the poor should not to be denied what may be accomplished with justice.

LETTER 3.38 (C. 508)

A brief message intent on reminding an official of unspecified title to preserve order in Avignon. Because the letter does not seek to address specific problems, it seems this letter probably served as an appointment to a military post.

King Theoderic to Vuandil

1. Although it may be consistent with the intent of our devotion that where civility may be practiced, there too would moderation be practiced, nonetheless, we especially want matters conducted well in Gallic regions; both areas where the recent devastation did not convey harm, and areas at the very origin of the conflict, ought to instill the good report of our name. Therefore, let the safeguarded security of the subjects spread the reputation of the *Princeps* far and wide, and wherever the army is sent, let them reckon it done not for burdening, but instead for defending. **2.** And so, we have decided in the present dictate that you should permit no violence to occur in Avignon, where you take quarters. Let our army live in harmony with the Romans. Let the protection sent to them be to their advantage, nor permit those whom we have striven to free from enemy occupation to suffer anything from us.

LETTER 3.39 (C. 512)

This letter responds to a claim that charioteers hired for recent consular games in Milan have not been paid by the sponsoring consul. The consul is reminded that debts acquired in public munificence are their own kind of reward. The recipient had been appointed consul for 511 (*Var.* 2.1–3).

King Theoderic to Felix, Vir Illustris *and Consul*

1. The rationale of equity persuades that we should preserve the customs of antiquity by the observance of public celebrations, particularly celebration initiated by the consul, for whom it is the established purpose that he ought to be praised for liberality, nor should the office seem to promise one thing and a senator want to accomplish something else. Concerning which, it is not fitting to be found sparing in generosity in public opinion, since the shadow of parsimony darkens public fame for a consul. **2.** Therefore, your *illustris* greatness should know that we have been approached by the charioteers from Milan. That munificence, which ancient custom concedes, while in present day it would be as though law, was withdrawn from them during your tenure.[34] Thence, if these assertions are not spoiled by dishonesty, bring your loftiness to follow antiquity, which, as though a special kind of privilege, openly displayed for itself the debts that were acquired. It is not permitted that something which you know has been granted since antiquity should be denied by you.

LETTER 3.40 (C. 510)

Another in a series of letters responding to what seems to be deepening crisis in Gaul, this time expanding the remission of taxes previously granted to citizens in

34. This suggests the complaint was lodged after Felix had completed his term as consul.

Arles (*Var.* 3.32) to include all provincials in Gaul. Regions unaffected by the war will continue to support the military.

King Theoderic to All Provincials Settled in Gaul

1. Although a multitude of tumultuous considerations intrudes upon the perception of our devotion and would provide for the diverse interests of the *regnum* with the usual zeal, nonetheless, we have considered the remedy of your utility hastily, since in the view of our good conscience, it is a kind of injury to delay good things; nor are we able to consider anything as pleasant that will have been delayed by unwanted postponement. For an injury is allowed to rage and worsen when the medicine is deferred. **2.** And so consider the taxes for the fourth indiction suspended on account of the nature of injuries to you from savagery of the enemy's devastation, since we are not pleased to exact what an aggrieved contributor is known to offer. But nevertheless, military expenses should be assisted by those areas that remain unharmed, since duty ought not to abandon altogether those whom it knows to labor on its behalf. Because a meagerly provided defender is powerless, nor does the spirit aid bravery, when prowess has been deprived of bodily strength.

LETTER 3.41 (C. 508–11)

A letter ordering that grain shipped from Italy to support the military in Gaul should be transported to armed encampments along the frontier with the Burgundians and Franks through labor requisitioned equally among Gallic communities. The following letter (*Var.* 3.42) announces the same to Gallic provincials.

King Theoderic to Gemellus, Vir Spectabilis

1. Everything that is arranged by fair administration becomes bearable, since a burden shared in common is certain not to oppress subjects. Indeed, a very small portion falls upon any one person, when the total amount includes everyone. **2.** And so, the amount of wheat that our foresight sent from Italy to meet the requirements of the military, lest an exhausted province should be harmed by supplying all provisions, should be transported from the granaries at Masillia to the forts positioned above the Durance. **3.** For this reason, we order that the exertion of transporting the above-mentioned amount should be undertaken in common, to the extent that, what is known to be assumed by the application of everyone may be accomplished swiftly.

LETTER 3.42 (C. 508–11)

This letter assures provincials in Gaul that the Gothic army has been supplied with pay and provisions from Italy, thereby not increasing the fiscal burden on landowners. Not only does the measure intend to enhance the image of Amal rule in Gaul, but it also tacitly informs provincials that attempts by the military to exact support would be contrary to present policy.

King Theoderic to All Provincials Settled in Gaul

1. It should not befall the generosity of a *Princeps* that a remedy entangle subjects, since kindness precedes the entreaty and, in a miraculous way, desires become fulfilled before they arise. Indeed, recently we had been stirred by justice to order that certain unharmed regions of the province should offer available provisions to our Goths. But, since it is fitting that the *Princeps* always should reckon the greater good, because what will remain unchanged in respect to its benefit does not carry the vice of variability, and so that landowners should not be burdened by the least payment, we have sent military provisions from Italy, so that the army sent for your defense out of our kindness should be supported and the provinces should experience only assistance from so great an assemblage. **3.** Moreover, we have sent a sufficient quantity of money to the *duces* and to the *praepositi,* so that their salaries,[35] which had not been possible to convey, ought to be provided, without loss of any kind, since by our choice we do not want to impose that which, as we perceive it, you would have been able to offer.

LETTER 3.43 (C. 508–11)

This letter illustrates yet another consequence of the war in Gaul: the dislocation of property, including slaves. In this case, the letter alleges that slaves have used the confusion as an opportunity to abandon servitude and offer themselves to the patronage of others, probably to landowners offering better conditions. The letter orders the king's sword bearer, likely an honored position among *saiones,* to investigate and return runaway slaves. Uncorrected, the situation could impact agricultural production. A *spatharius* was usually the personal attendant or bodyguard of an emperor in the late imperial period.

King Theoderic to Unigis, Spatharius

1. We are delighted to live under the law of the Romans, whom we desire to protect with arms; nor is attention to moral behavior less of a concern to us than matters of war. For what does it profit to have banished barbaric disorder, except that life

---

35. The *dux* (a senior field commander) and *praepositus* (a senior officer ranked under a *dux*) each received a *praebenda* (regular salary). It is not clear whether the *praebenda* discussed here would also include regular Gothic soldiers.

is lived according to laws?[36] **2.** Therefore, since the time when our army, by the grace of God, entered Gaul, if any slaves turning away from their duties have carried themselves to others, for whom this seems agreeable, we order them to be restored to the prior masters without any hesitation, since laws ought not to be confused by dictating justice, nor is a defender of liberty able to favor the common slave. **3.** Perhaps the battles of other kings aim at either the spoils or ruin of captive cities. It is our intention, with God's blessing, to conquer so that subjects should lament that they acquired us so late as a master.

LETTER 3.44 (C. 508–11)

A letter promising funds to repair the fortifications at Arles and also the shipment of provisions from Italy, likely to relieve the impact of siege on agricultural production (for the siege of Arles, cf. *Var.* 3.32). Both the cost of urban repairs and relieving food shortages would have been factors key to the loyalty of the large landowners (*possessores*) to whom the letter was addressed.

King Theoderic to All Possessores of Arles

1. Although the first priority should be to restore the inhabitants of cities and then to offer an indication of our devotion to the greater extent of humanity, nonetheless, our kindness combines both, so that we both regard the interest of citizens, with the remedy of beneficence, and strive to lead ancient cities back to being habitable. For so it may happen that the happiness of a city, which rises in its citizens, be demonstrated also in the charm of its buildings. **2.** And so, on behalf of the restoration of the aged walls and towers of Arles, we have sent a determined amount of money. **3.** We have also prepared provisions, which should relieve your costs, so that they should be sent to you when the season for sailing has arrived. Now lighten your concerns and, being relieved by our promise, take hope in future abundance and have confidence in divine favor, for what is contained in our words is not less than what is contained in our granaries.

LETTER 3.45 (C. 507–11)

Another letter adjudicating confused property rights of the church, in this case the *defensores* of the church of Rome contest a claim that a house bequeathed by a former member of the church and currently used by clergy had been a "Samaritan" synagogue. It is not clear why this case had been addressed to the *comes* at Rome (Arigernus), and not to the bishop of Rome. At *Variae* 3.37, a similar matter had

---

36. The phrase *removisse barbarous confusos* should be understood in the sense of the political confusion that attended the war in Gaul, not Goths having abandoned "barbarian ways."

been handed to the bishop. Similarly, it is not certain whether this letter uses the term *Samaritan* as a generic reference to the Jewish community, or to a distinctly Samaritan community in Rome.

King Theoderic to Arigernus, Vir Illustris *and* Comes

1. It agrees with our justice that we should not allow chicanery to occur in regard to generous benefactions, and whatever is concealed through misleading interpretation, we would uncover from a fleeing cloud of lies. And so the *defensores* of the sacred Roman church have been complaining that formerly Simplicius, of blessed memory, had purchased from the acolyte Eufraxius, with documents drawn up according to custom, a house situated in the holy city, which, by right of no contest, the Roman clergy undertook to inhabit in the course of many years and transferred to other uses with security of ownership. **2.** Now, however, one hardened by the shameless effrontery of the Samaritan superstition has appeared, who would prevaricate with perverse intentions that the same place had been a synagogue, while to the contrary they may point to domiciles far and wide designed for human habitation, which this building calls to mind. For this reason, let your greatness dispense this case with diligent examination and according to the proven justice of your own good conscience, and, if you should learn the truth that comes out of this complaint, let it be decided with well-considered equity. For if trickery must be banished from human affairs, how much more we feel that matters judged to be practically an outrage to divine authority must be corrected!

LETTER 3.46 (C. 507–11)

This letter delivers a verdict in a case involving the abduction (and presumed rape) of a young girl. The petitioner claims that his confession of guilt was extracted under duress from the governor. The letter reduces the sentence to temporary exile, and revokes disabilities to his civil rights (*infamia*). Although the defendant's rank is not mentioned, the length and elaboration of the letter suggests a person of some importance.

King Theoderic to Adeodatus

1. The formal charge of a crime is the stuff of glory to a *Princeps*, since devotion would have no place, except when the opportunities for errant behavior arise. For what wholesome resolutions may be arranged, if the probity of good morals settled everything? Parched thirst longs for the blessing of moistening rain. Healthy strength has no need of alleviation from health-bearing hands, unless when sick. Thus, when one succumbs to feebleness, the cure may be suitably granted. Therefore, in cases of harsh misfortune, governance must be offered for the praise of justice, so that we neither allow the punishment to exceed the sin committed nor permit an unpunished crime to outrage the laws. **2.** And so, you have alleged in submitted entreaties that the bitter hatred of Venantius, the *spectabilis* governor of Lucania and Bruttium, has constrained you. Toiling for a long time in a place of confinement, the abduction of the young girl Valeriana was confessed by means of coercion, because a man will more gratefully expect the prospect of a quick death than endure the cruelties of torture. For amid the utmost constraints of suffering, the desire is to perish, rather than to live, since the wretched feeling of punishment excludes anticipation of sweet relief. Moreover, what is least amenable to justice, you claim further that the protection of legal representatives, so often demanded, was withheld from you, while your adversaries, being eloquent by nature, were able to bind you, as yet an innocent man, with the nooses of the law. **3.** This petition effectively set upon the inclination of our devotion and gradually bent the laws toward mercy, although a report sent from the governor of Bruttium has arrived, which enfolded the personal allegation of tragedy in his own voice, denying that a deceptive supplicant should be believed in opposition to public trust. **4.** And therefore, in our leniency we have softened the harshness of the punishment, ruling that, from the day of the sentence's publication, you should endure exile for six months, so that after our verdict, in no way may it be permitted for the stigma of infamy to oppose you under any sort of interpretation,[37] when it is the endowed right of the *Princeps* to scour away the stains of a rapist's reputation. But with this period of time completed, restored to your home and all properties, you may have every right of free men which you first possessed, since we deem that you should not groan with the brand of disgrace, whom we have decided to detain in temporary exile.[38] We threaten anyone who has attempted to violate our present decision, either by obstructing or otherwise interpreting it, with the penalty of no less than three pounds of gold. **5.** But since we do not want this decree to extend to the innocent unconditionally, lest the ignorance of anyone seem to have benefited them in the least, by this present dictate we free from fear those who will have been unknowingly involved in this case at any time or place. For one who has no knowledge of criminality resembles a man who is free from harm.

LETTER 3.47 (C. 507–11)

This letter sentences a *curialis* to permanent exile on a remote volcanic island for the murder of his municipal colleague. The letter presents an interesting study in contrasts with *Variae* 3.46, which similarly sentences a man to exile under less

---

37. The phrase *crimen infamiae* likely refers to a reduction in the defendant's civil status that would have otherwise attended conviction.

38. The *maculosa nota* and *adustio probri* refer to branding which convicted criminals could endure as part of their *infamia*.

severe terms. Also of note is the interest in the providence of nature, volcanism and the habits of the salamander, which offer philosophical justification for the sentence.

King Theoderic to Faustus, Praefectus Praetorio

1. A softened punishment is a reflection of devotion, and one who has mitigated a due penalty with considered moderation punishes out of kindness. The governor of Lucania and Bruttium reports to us that the *curialis* Jovinus has been stained with the shedding of human blood.[39] Having been incited to this in the passion of a mutual disagreement, he escalated a verbal altercation to the punishable death of a colleague. But being aware of his guilt in the deed, he refused to entrust himself to the punishment prescribed by law and fled within the precincts of a church. We have condemned him by permanent banishment to the Vulcan Islands, so it is clear that we maintain respect for the holy building; nor may such a criminal, who is himself believed to be unforgiving of the innocent, avoid punishment entirely. **2.** Consequently, because he would be overcome by deadly heat, let him lack a paternal hearth, there, where the bowels of the earth do not extinguish, when they are perpetually consumed for all time. Indeed, such earthly flame, which is nourished by the diminishment of some substance, when present, is not extinguished. The interior portion of the mountain continuously seethes unexhausted among the waves, nor is that diminished which is known to have been released. It is certainly on account of the inexplicable agency of nature that however much devouring flame reduces, an increase of stone restores. For by what means may stone remain intact, if it always melts away without increase? **3.** Indeed, divine providence thus causes the wonder of contrary natures to be perpetual, so that what purposes to remain fixed for all time, having been openly consumed, is reborn from the most obscure origins. Certainly, when other mountains boil forth with billowing clouds, they are not known by corresponding names. Therefore, it must be thought that this mountain is acclaimed by the name of Vulcan because it burns so severely. **4.** Hence, let the man condemned to capital punishment be sent to the aforementioned place. Let him lack the world that he enjoys, from which he has cruelly banished another man to exile, so that the one surviving would receive that which he inflicted with the result of death. He will follow the example of the salamander, which commonly passes its time in fire, for it is constrained by such a native coldness, that it finds burning flames to be temperate. It is a slender and sparing animal, related to the worm, and clothed in a yellowish color. It enjoys a life of heat that consumes all other mortal creatures. **5.** The conservators of ancient ages recall, however, that some many years ago this island erupted from deep

---

39. The governor may or may not be the same Venantius of *Var.* 3.46. Here, "governor" is given as *corrector*; at *Var.* 3.46, the title is *praesul*. Both titles could be used interchangeably.

within with a fearful churning of waves, at the time when Hannibal himself contended with his own veins at the court of Prusias, king of Bithynia,[40] lest so great a leader should come to the derision of the Romans. Thence, it is more remarkable that a mountain burning with such a great gathering of flames would be held concealed under currents of the sea, and that a heat should thrive there without end, which such great waves were known to overwhelm.

LETTER 3.48 (C. 507–11)

An order to Goths and Romans to prepare a local hill fortress under the direction of a *saio*, this letter is fascinating for its perspective on the physical attributes of topography, examples from natural history, and preparedness for political change. For a similar directive, see *Variae* 1. 17. The location of Verruca is unknown.

King Theoderic to All Goths and Romans
Settled Near the Fortress of Verruca

1. The provident command of one ruling ought to be the delight of everyone, when you see us providing what you ought to need. For what is more pleasing than that human affairs should always have the support of precaution, which is both necessary and does not burden when exceeding necessity? And therefore, we have sent our *saio*, Leodefrid, with this present order, so that according to his supervision you may build homes for yourselves in the fort of Verruca, which derives its name appropriately from its own position.[41] **2.** For in the midst of a plain, it is a rocky hill rising with a rounded shape; with steep sides and cleared of woods, the whole mountain effects the likeness of a lone tower, the base of which is narrower than the summit and expands above in the manner of a graceful mushroom, since it attenuates at the narrower portion. A rampart without rival, a secure stronghold, where no opponent may attempt anything surreptitiously and where one enclosed need not fear anything. Distinguished by reason of its defensibility and its charm, here, the Adige flows, honored among rivers for the purity of its pleasant current. A fort practically separated from the world, maintaining the defenses of the province,[42] for which it is therefore deemed to be more important, since it stands opposed to savage nations. **3.** Who would not desire to inhabit this miraculous haven, this so-called stronghold, which even foreigners are delighted to visit? And although we believe the province to be secure in our reign, with God's blessing, it is nonetheless wise to take precautions even for that which is not thought likely to

---

40. Hannibal committed suicide between 183–81 B.C., rather than be handed over to Roman authorities.

41. An etymological reference to the word *verruca* ("projection" or "hillock").

42. Also on the *Claustra* of the Alpine defensive network, *Var.* 2.5.

occur. **4.** Defense always must be commenced in time of leisure, since it would then be badly required when necessity should demand it. The gulls, whose name is derived from the fact that they share habitation with the fish,[43] being aquatic birds and naturally farsighted, seek dry havens for approaching storms and abandon their ponds. Porpoises dwell among the waves of the open main, fearing the shallows of the shoreline. The urchins, which possess a honey-like flesh, a succulence encased within hard ribs, that saffron-hued delicacy of the rich sea, when they become aware of an approaching storm, desiring to change position, embrace pebbles equal to their size, since they have no faith in swimming on account of the lightness of their bodies, and saved by the ballast of anchorage, they seek out those rocks which they believe will not be harassed by the waves.[44] **5.** The very birds change their native country with the approach of winter, requiring nests suitable to the harshness of the season. Should it not be the concern of men to anticipate what might be required in adversity? It is not a world without change: human affairs are shaken by mutability. And therefore providence dictates what should be carried out for the future.

LETTER 3.49 (C. 507–11)

This letter grants to the leading citizens of Catana (a port city in Sicily) permission to strengthen the city walls using materials quarried from an unused amphitheater. The letter seems to have been predicated by fear that spoliating a public monument without warrant would provoke official disapproval.

King Theoderic to the Honorati, Possessores,
Defensores, and Curiales *of Catana*

1. That obedience is pleasing and desirable to us that will have preceded a beneficial decree and a gift has been deservingly given if we are able to order what would be requested. Indeed, the happiness of the one ruling is that he seek out what those serving love, when the goal of our intention has been obtained, at the same time that our subjects arrange matters for their own future. **2.** And so, with the direction of your petition understood, whereby, from civic affection, you have undertaken the necessity of fortifying the city walls, we grant you unrestrained license in this matter; nor should you be anxious over anything concerning this matter, whence you ought to expect recompense from our gratitude. For your defense is no less than our strength and whatever grips you out of uncertainty attaches to the

43. *Mergi* ("gulls") derive from the verb *mergere* ("to plunge"), referring to the fishing habits of water fowl.

44. See Ambrose, *Hexaemeron* 5.9.24, for the same example, although Cassiodorus's treatment lacks verbal reminiscence that would allow firm attribution to Ambrose.

reputation of our protection. **3.** Therefore, those stones from the amphitheater which you report collapsed from long age and which now offer nothing to public embellishment other than displaying its shameful ruin, we grant freedom to you inasmuch as it applies to the public use of those stones. In this way, let the facade of the walls rise, which it would not be possible to bring about, if it should remain neglected. On which account, boldly undertake whatever precaution requires for defense, whatever adornment requires for beauty, knowing that however much gratitude you gain from us, it will have been elevated all the more by the gratitude of your city.

LETTER 3.50 (C. 507)

This letter grants warrant to provincials in Noricum (Roman province along the southern bank of the Danube, roughly modern Austria) to trade cattle with the Alamanni. These Alamanni may be the same settled under Amal rule after conflict with the Franks (cf. *Var.* 2.41), although it is more probable that official license for trading activities would be needed to exchange of cattle with Alamanni from beyond the frontier.

King Theoderic to the Provincials of Noricum

1. An order that assists the one giving and cheers the one receiving in time of need must be gladly undertaken. For who could think it a burden, where more is derived with a shared benefit? **2.** And therefore, we have decided in the present decree that it should be permitted to exchange the cattle of the Alamanni, which are more valuable on account of their ample bodily size but have become weak from lengthy travel, with your own, which, although of lesser stature, nonetheless are better suited to labor. Thus, their task should be assisted by healthier animals and your fields should be furnished with larger cattle. **3.** It thus happens that their beasts acquire the robustness of strength, yours more outstanding stature, and what is accustomed to occur rarely, you both will be seen to attain the desired advantage in the same transaction.

LETTER 3.51 (C. 507–11)

An order to confirm the salary of a charioteer, this letter is a carefully crafted digression on the history and customs associated with chariot races at the Circus Maximus in Rome. The letter ends with a subtle nod to the political expediency of continuing spectacles at Rome. It is noteworthy that a similar letter (*Var.* 2.9) to the same *Praefectus Praetorio*, ordering the increase of a charioteer's salary, warranted far less attention.

King Theoderic to Faustus, Praefectus Praetorio

1. However rare constancy and respectable inclination may be among performers, it is so much the more valuable, when genuine good will is demonstrable among them. For it is precious for a man to have discovered something laudable where he had not thought to find it. Now, not long ago, a reasonable portion of the *annona* was bestowed by our consideration upon the charioteer Thomas, who arrived from eastern regions, until we should judge his bravery and skill. But since he is known to hold first place in this contest, and having abandoned his own country, his inclination has chosen to support the seat of our *imperium*, we have reckoned he must be confirmed in a monthly allowance, lest we should now make an ambiguous return to him, whom we know has been elected the dominion of Italy. **2.** For as a victor, this man flutters in the talk of diverse throngs, conveyed more by reputation than by chariots. He immediately supported that faction of the people in decline and to whom he himself had brought grief, labored to once again return them to a more fortunate state, surpassing other charioteers by means of his skill, just as he by-passed them with the speed of horses. Sorcery is often said to make him victorious, and it is known to be a great mark of distinction among them to have attained such an accusation. For it is unavoidable that a victory that cannot be ascribed to the merits of the horses should be attributed to the perversity of witchcraft. **3.** Spectacle expels respected manners, invites frivolous disputes, makes honorability hollow; a spring watered with brawls,[45] which even antiquity held sacred, but which contentious posterity caused to be ridiculous. For it is said that Oenomaus of Asiatic Elis was first to have brought them into the world, which afterward Romulus, not having yet founded the city, presented to Italy in rougher mode at the abduction of the Sabine women. **4.** But the master of the world, Augustus, added an undertaking to his own prestige, raising up in the valley of Murcia a structure wondrous even to the Romans, so that he bound a massive construction, girt firmly around with mountains,[46] where symbols of great importance were enclosed. They positioned twelve gates for the twelve signs.[47] These were thrown open abruptly in unison by ropes weighted with herms, proclaiming, as they used to suppose, that everything was guided by design there, where the image of the head is known to have influence.[48] **5.** Moreover, the colors were contrived in a fourfold division in place of the seasons. Green was said to be for the

---

45. Cassiodorus here seems to be alluding to the parentage of the "inventor" of spectacles, the mythic Oenomaus, who was descended both from Mars and, on the maternal side, from the god of a spring.

46. The Circus Maximus, located at the base of the Palatine and flanked by the Aventine hill.

47. The twelve signs of the zodiac.

48. The "head" is a reference to the previously mentioned "herm," usually a bust mounted on a block of stone.

verdure of spring, blue for the clouds of winter, russet for the heat of summer, and white for the frost of autumn, so that the entire year was signified, progressing as though according to the twelve signs. Thus it happened that the offices of nature were imitated in the ordered confabulation of the spectacles. **6.** The two-horse rig was invented as though in imitation of the moon, the four-horse rig of the sun. The horses of the acrobats, by which the attendants of the circus, having been sent out, would proclaim the names of those about to be released from the gates, mimicked the swiftly advancing course of the morning star. Thus it happened that, when they thought themselves to worship the constellations, the public performances simultaneously profaned their own religion. **7.** White lines, not far from the gates, were drawn to both sides of the podium, as though by a straight ruler, from which the contest between the chariots might spring at the outset, lest, while they attempted to hastily thrust out between each other, they should not deny the people the pleasure of watching. The whole contest completed seven courses in simulation of the recurring seven-day week. The very circuits themselves follow the zodiacal divisions,[49] hold three markers, past which the chariots speed just as the sun. **8.** Stars of the East and of the West designate the boundaries.[50] A channel imparts the likeness of the glassy sea, where sea-loving dolphins pour water. Also, the great lengths of obelisks have been raised to the heights of the heavens, but the greater is dedicated to the sun, the lesser to the moon, where, as though in letters, the sacred rites of the ancients are indicated in Chaldaean symbols.[51] The partition barrier depicts the fate of unfortunate captives,[52] where Roman generals treading upon the backs of the enemy receive adulation for their labors. **9.** Now the napkin, which is seen to give the signal for the races, converged with custom in this way. While Nero reclined at his meal and the people, eager to see the spectacles, as it was accustomed, demanded haste, he ordered the napkin, with which he had wiped his hands, to be cast from the window, and in this way unleash the demanded contest. Hence it has been continued that the openly displayed napkin should be seen as a promise of races to come. **10.** The circus is so called from its circuitous course, and the *circenses* as though from a circuit of swords, on account of the rusticity of ancient times, which had not yet brought the spectacles to the adorned state of buildings, when they were held on green swards between swords and the river. Nor is it happenstance that the outcome of each contest is decided in twenty-

49. The *decani zodiaci* was based on astrological practices that divided signs of the zodiac into thirds.

50. The unusual *Eoae Orientis et Occidentis* may also refer to images of two of the horses that pulled the sun's chariot.

51. A reference to the hieroglyphs etched into obelisks brought to the Circus Maximus from Egypt: the first was erected by Augustus in 10 B.C. and the second by Constantius II in 357 A.D.

52. The partition barrier was the *spina* running down the center of the course; the *euripus,* or water channel, probably flowed down the middle of the *spina*.

four heats, so that with that very number the hours of the completed day and night would be included. Nor should it be thought without significance that the completion of courses is marked by the removal of eggs, when the very act, pregnant with many superstitious beliefs, openly confesses itself about to give birth to something after the example of the egg. And therefore, it is made clear that the flighty and inconstant behavior that applies to mother birds is engendered at the circus. **11.** It would require a long explanation to recount everything else concerning the Roman circus, especially when everything seems to pertain to separate causes. Nonetheless, we find it bewildering in every case, that here, more than any other spectacles, the passion of madness is embraced with seriousness left unheeded. Should the Greens prevail, part of the populace mourns; if the Blues lead, a crowd of citizens is stricken all the sooner. They hotly cast insults, achieving nothing; they are grievously wounded, having endured nothing. And they thus fall to petty contentions, as though it were a labor for the standing of an endangered homeland. **12.** It is rightly understood that this has been dedicated to a multitude of superstitions, where one happens to depart from respectable behavior. We are endeared to the games, by the demands of a threatening people for whom it is the wish to gather for such an event, where they are delighted to cast aside sober thoughts. **13.** For reason leads few, and a genuine purpose pleases even fewer. The crowd is led instead to what was clearly invented for escape from cares. For it is thought that whatever must pertain to its enjoyment also decides the happiness of the age. Therefore, while we grant the expense, we do not always give out of better judgment. It is at present advantageous to act foolishly, so that we are able to contain the rejoicing desired by the people.

LETTER 3.52 (C. 507–11)

This letter has much in common with *Variae* 1. 45 and 2.40, which request that Boethius locate experts in various learned fields. In the present letter, an *illustris* senator is being consulted to locate a land surveyor (*agrimensor*) to settle a property dispute. Less is said about the legal dispute than about the relationship of surveying to other sciences. Any official capacity the recipient of the letter may have had is not specified. This letter may be considered a partner with *Variae* 3.53, which discourses upon the need for a water surveyor.

King Theoderic to Consularis, Vir Illustris

1. As we have learned from the exceedingly hostile petition of intermediaries, a boundary dispute has arisen between the *spectabiles* Leontius and Paschasius, such that they have decided that the resolution of their case must be determined, not according to laws, but with violence. Hence, we marvel that what should clearly be defined by witnessed boundaries, mountain ridges, river shores, a surveyor's landmark, or some other visible sign, will have conflicted with such animosity. **2.** What would such men do, if they possessed land in the country of Egypt, where the enormous tides of the Nile erase markers of boundaries with rising flood of the river and leave the face of the land unmarked, where mud is known to cover everything? Therefore, they must not now rush to arms, if the aroused suit should fail without any enduring satisfaction. For this matter is so carefully expressed according to the calculation of figures and the surveyor's discipline, just as every speech is given shape by words. **3.** Indeed, the Chaldaeans are recorded to have first discovered geometry, as this race is the most intelligent and inquiring of men, who, generally surmising the extent of this very discipline, had then demonstrated it to be applicable to astronomy, music, engineering, architecture, medicine, logic, or anything else able to be defined by types of figures, so that, without it, it would be possible to attain a true understanding of nothing in these disciplines. **4.** Later, the Egyptians, similarly excited by mental ardor, transferred geometry to the measurement of land and to restoring the shapes of boundaries, on account of the Nile's growth, a desired inundation that they endure once yearly, so that what had been subject to the confusion of litigation became determined by a science. **5.** Therefore, let your greatness employ nothing less than the most skilled surveyor, whose name is derived from his art,[53] so that he ought to show according to visible evidence everything that has now been marked off by manifest calculation. For if this wondrous discipline has accomplished this, so that it may separate undefined land with clear reasons, how much more clearly ought such a man to demonstrate everything that is already found defined according to its own boundaries? **6.** Indeed, in the time of Augustus, the Roman world was divided into properties and delineated according to the census, so that the property of no man should be considered unclear with respect to the amount that he would assume for paying taxes. **7.** The author and scholar of measurements, Heron, redacted this learning in a composed treatise, such that the most eager student may learn through reading what he ought to demonstrate with perfect clarity to the eyes. Let men learned in this art see what public authority feels concerning this very matter. For of all the celebrated disciplines in the whole world, none have this distinction. If you demonstrate mathematics, there is a lack of listeners. Geometry, even when one argues concerning the heavens, is explained only to the most eager to learn. Astronomy and music are learned for the knowledge alone. **8.** But a recent dispute of boundaries is entrusted to the land surveyor, so that he may cut short the scandal of legal contention. He is certainly the judge of his own art. Abandoned tracts of land are the courtroom of such a man. You would believe him possessed, whom you will have observed wandering along winding tracks. Indeed, he inquires after the markers of property among the rough woods and thorn brakes; he does not walk according to

53. An *agrimensor*.

the common manner, his own reading determines the way for him. He demonstrates what he claims; he proves what he teaches. He discerns the rights of those disputing by his own wanderings and after the fashion of a vast river, he bears away open spaces from some and grants countryside to others. **9.** Therefore, with the support of our authority, choose such a man before whom these parties may blush to quarrel with shameless arrogance, such that the rights of landowners should not be confused, for whom it is necessary that cultivation apply to their own affairs.

LETTER 3.53 (C. 507–11)

A companion piece to *Variae* 3.52, this letter instructs the *Comes Privatarum* to offer a water surveyor a public salary so that he may assist the water needs of the region surrounding Rome. More attention, however, is given to the art of water divining than to the needs or role of the surveyor, who is curiously not named.

King Theoderic to Apronianus, Vir Illustris *and* Comes Privatarum

1. We have learned in the report of your greatness that a water surveyor has come to Rome from the provinces of Africa, where that skill is cultivated with great eagerness owing to the dryness of the region. This man is able to allow deeply hidden waters to arid lands, so that he may cause a region dry from excessive drought to be habitable from its own abundance. **2.** Know this to have been pleasing to us, inasmuch as this craft had come to us already approved, having been set forth in the books of the ancients. Indeed, he properly infers the proximity of water by the signs of green growth and by the height of trees. For in those lands where fresh waters are not far underground, the fruitfulness of certain shoots always responds favorably, such as water-thriving grass, the hollow reed, the hardy blackberry, the happy willow, the verdant poplar tree, and other kinds of trees which, nonetheless, grow abundantly to a height fortunate beyond their own natures. **3.** These and other things are the evidences of this skill. When with nights approach, dry wool is placed on ground already chosen and is left, covered with an unglazed pot; then, if the proximity of water is sufficient, the cloth will be found moist in the morning. Moreover, even areas under a clear sky are observed by careful practitioners and where a swarm of the smallest gnats are seen flying together above the earth, there they promise with rejoicing what has been sought out. They also add that a sort of slight vapor will be visible in the likeness of a column, which they recognize as having extended to a height that will be equivalent in measure to the depth at which the waters lay hidden, so that it is miraculous how, through this and other diverse signs, a definite measurement is predicted for what depth the sought water should be expected. They even predict the taste of the water, so that bitter waters should not be sought with wasted labor, nor that sweet and advantageous waters should be disdained. **4.** This knowledge was passed down fittingly to subsequent scholars by a certain man among the Greeks,[54] and by Marcellus among the Latins, who carefully treated, not only subterranean streams, but also the location of wells. For they claim the waters that spring forth to the east and the south are sweet and clear, and found to be wholesome in their own lightness. But water that flows to the north and west is deemed exceedingly cold, and also unbeneficial from the density of its own weight. **5.** And therefore, if your wisdom will detect in the afore-mentioned man that which is indicative both of the reading of treatises and of experience in the science, you shall alleviate his poverty and his travel with the appropriate salary deducted from the public funds. The man accepting this fee will bestow the gifts of his own art. **6.** For although the city of Rome abounds with irrigated waters and it may be felicitous in springs and in the abundant flow of aqueducts, nonetheless, many suburban estates are found that clearly need this skill, and one is rightly employed, who is acknowledged as essential for this region. Nevertheless, an engineer should be closely involved so that the waters, which the surveyor will find, the engineer may raise, and by his art he may bring support for that which is unable to rise naturally. Therefore, let this water surveyor be reck-oned even among the masters of other arts, lest the city of Rome would be unable to maintain under us what would be deemed desirable.

54. Only *apud Graecos ille* is given.

Book 4

This and the following letter demonstrate a general policy of strengthening ties with peoples north of Italy. In this instance, alliance with the Thuringians has been formed with a marriage between the Thuringian king and Theoderic's niece. The alliance would have been pivotal to influencing Ostrogothic relations with the Franks. Description of the union includes attention to the receipt of horses as a bride price at Theoderic's court.

King Theoderic to Hermanfrid, King of the Thuringians

1. Desiring to associate you with our family, we join you, with the blessing of divine authority, by the dear pledge of our niece,[1] so that you, who have descended from royal stock, may now gleam even further with the brightness of Amal blood. We send to you the jewel of a royal home, the boon of a people, the comfort of faithful advice, a wife delightful and most pleasing, who, with you, should fittingly complete your dominion and arrange your nation with a sweeter manner of living. **2.** Fortunate Thuringia will have that which Italy has nourished, learned in letters, polished in behavior, charming not only in lineage, but even the extent of her feminine dignity, so that your country may glitter in her very habits, no less than in its own triumphs. **3.** Therefore, greeting you with due pleasure, we confirm having received, with the arrival of your envoys, the agreed-upon gifts, indeed priceless, but

---

1. Amalaberga, Theoderic's niece by his sister Amalafrida, and the sibling of Theodahad, the third Ostrogothic king in Italy.

according to the custom of nations, horses fitted with silver trappings, such as would befit nuptials. The breasts and legs of these horses are distinguished by appropriately rounded flesh; the ribs extend with that particular breadth; the waists are confined to a trim dimension; the head gives the impression of a doe, and they imitate the swiftness of those creatures they are seen to resemble. These creatures are mild from extremely abundant care, fleet from their great size, pleasant to look upon, and gratifying to ride. Indeed, they step with a light gait, those seated do not tire with senseless exertion; one reposes upon them rather than laboring, and, having been trained with careful moderation, they know how to endure with continued agility. **4.** But you nonetheless acknowledge that this noble herd, these obedient beasts and other things that you have sent, are greatly inferior, considering that she who plentifully supplies charm to kingly power, by right, surpasses everything. Therefore, we have indeed sent what the rank of *Princeps* requires, but we have paid nothing more than what we gain by conjoining you with the distinction of such a woman. Let divine providence witness your marriage, so that just as the cause of affection has bound us, so too may familial regard oblige our posterity.

LETTER 4.2 (C. 507–11)

Here extending an alliance to the Herules, a people living north of Ostrogothic Pannonia and the Danube, this letter formalizes the relationship in terms strikingly different from *Variae* 4.1. Rather than diplomatic marriage, the letter describes the bonds of martial virtue and loyalty. The Herules and other trans-Danubian peoples, such as the Gepids, contributed to Theoderic's campaigns in Gaul and probably also provided leverage with the eastern empire (cf. *Var.* 4.45, 5.11).

King Theoderic to the King of the Herules

1. It is widely considered among nations to be commendable to become a son by virtue of arms, since one is not worthy of adoption, unless he deserves to be considered the bravest. We are often disappointed in offspring; however, those whom judgment has brought forth are not known to be ignoble. For these men owe gratitude, not to nature, but only to their own merits, when they become obligated to a stranger by a bond of affection. And there is such great strength in this impulse that they would prefer to die before anything harsh should be inflicted upon adopted fathers. **2.** And therefore, with this present gift, we adopt you as a son in the custom of the nations and in masculine bond,[2] so that you, who have become known for your warlike nature, are fittingly reared through arms. We therefore

---

2. The term *condicio* often refers to a marriage bond, hence the letter emphasizes the masculine character of the relationship with *condicio virilis.*

bestow upon you horses, swords, shields, and other gear of war; but what is in every way greater, we bestow our approval upon you. For you, who are accounted in the judgment of Theoderic, will be reckoned to be the greatest among nations. **3.** And so, take these arms for your benefit and for mine. That man who arranges to defend you the most seeks your devotion. Prove your bravery and you will not have a taxing obligation. Such a man adopts you, whose nation you otherwise would have dreaded. For the assistance of the Goths, with God's blessing, is known to the Herules. We have offered our arms to you; formerly, however, nations would only extend promises of courage to each other. **4.** Thence, greeting you with due pleasure, we entrust other matters to the native language through our envoys,[3] *ille* and *ille,* who may clearly explain our letters to you and may assist in strengthening that gratitude which must be spoken.

LETTER 4.3 (C. 509)

This letter promotes to the office of *Comes Patrimonii* someone with long intimacy with the Amal court and emphasizes previous loyalty to official policies and the promise of further promotion owed to upright service. This particular office traditionally managed the revenues produced on properties owned by emperors, and hence by the Gothic king, which could be used to contribute to governance in diverse areas—military expenditures, public building projects, and the maintenance of the royal household. The appointment is followed by an official announcement to the Senate (*Var.* 4.4). The address to the letter suggests that Senarius held the office of *Comes Privatarum* either directly before or in conjunction with the new elevation as *Comes Patrimonii.*

King Theoderic to Senarius, Vir Illustris *and* Comes Privatarum

1. We believe that to elect persons suitably fitted to their offices pertains to the prestige of the palace, since the fame of rulers increases from the brilliance of those in its service. For it is truly fitting for the *Princeps* to promote such persons, so that, however honored he sees his own nobleman become, so much does he know himself to have had correct judgment. For one who is given to be an example ought to be conspicuous in his conduct. It is easy for someone to act on their own behalf, but the one selected for office should rather be inspired for the many. **2.** Therefore, let your *illustris* take the dignity of *Comes Patrimonii* for the third indiction, which royal authority deservingly grants to you. Indeed, for a long time, balancing combined roles by our appointment, you had been a partner to counsel and you performed the necessities of governance with commendable application. Often have you assisted the duties of a difficult embassy. Not unlike a public

---

3. The phrase *patrio sermone* seems to imply the Gothic language.

advocate did you stand resolute before kings, compelled to display our justice even to those who were barely able to perceive reason through their harsh obstinacy. Royal authority incited by contentions did not terrify you; rather, you subjugated boldness to the truth and, obedient to our orders, you swayed barbarians to your own way of thinking. **3.** And what should we say concerning your enthusiasm, fueled by long nights of study, and the faultless loyalty of your continual service? You are practiced in the talented employment of outstanding eloquence; your own opponent, so delighted, lends his support, since when you begin to speak, you state the case better. Your declamation used to sway our decisions, since you changed the minds of claimants whenever the attention of those deliberating could be worn down. There was also another praiseworthy aspect of your life, in that you locked away our secrets with the probity of good morals, being privy to many things; but nevertheless, you did not make public the many things that you knew. You have accrued gratitude and you have pleased your betters with your humility. **4.** Thus, a single opinion shared among a great diversity of people has been forged in your favor. You pluck the most agreeable fruit of an approved institution; when thus promoted, you will be able to accomplish every happiness, so that everyone may find their desires fulfilled in you. Therefore, preserve that amiable character and that remarkable constancy, and supported by the authority of our household, eagerly seek after a gratitude equal in blessings to the number of offices you consider yourself able to attain. Henceforth, confine your succession to better things with good deeds, knowing that our favor always increases for those who desire to be found worthy of obtaining eminence.

LETTER 4.4 (C. 509)

A companion to *Var.* 4.3, announcing to the Senate the promotion of a new *Comes Patrimonii*. Again, the emphasis is placed on an array of services that the candidate provided from an early age at the royal court.

King Theoderic to the Senate of Rome

1. It is indeed most glorious for us, conscript fathers, to dispense offices far and wide, but it is more praiseworthy to bestow dignities on the well-deserving. For whatever we grant to such persons, we bestow rather upon the common good. Indeed, the man advanced in office who clings to virtue benefits all men; nor is the office abandoned to injury, when he conveys the order of discipline to good men. **2.** And so, according to this lofty desire, we have elevated the *illustris* Senarius to the dignity of *Comes Patrimonii*. This is a man who would disperse the clouds of corruption with the light of good intention, who takes no joy in deceit, who, supported by the authority of the patrimony, would not use a fear of us to his own advantage, but rather, would be able to maintain fair justice in other ways, by which he knows that public servants please us. This fidelity in former years promises blessings he will produce in the future. **3.** Indeed, he entered our palace in the very flower of youth, already mature in merits, and because he also busied his robust years, when he returned to the judgment of the one ruling, being misled by no error of inexperience, he displayed the effects of good instruction. He was first worthy of the assembly, then suitable for court cases, even chosen often for the office of envoy, from which he returned to us many times clearly distinguished. For a man by whom so many good things are clearly accomplished should not be assigned to one office. **4.** Moreover, his humility, which is as distinguished as it is rare, commends this decision more amply. For it is unusual to preserve modesty under the affection of a *Princeps,* since happiness ever animates pride; for that moderation which is more commonly found in the company of afflictions rarely extends to affluence. **5.** But in addition to the wonder of his attainments, he also shines with a similar brilliance in his origins, so that you would be confounded as to which portion would be the richer, when he possesses both so copiously. Distributed singly, these blessings are exceptional; held conjoined, they are wondrous. Therefore, conscript fathers, let Liberty, grayed with age, rise to young entrants. It detracts nothing from your native spirit, when the novelty of those newly arriving is honorably received. You are appointed parents of the state with regard to your kindness; let two reasons call you to generosity: a man commencing his career should merit your gratitude, and having been promoted, he has earned your support.

LETTER 4.5 (C. 508–11)

For reasons probably connected to the ongoing war, famine in Gaul has necessitated that this letter order a *comes* to mobilize the *navicularii* (bonded shipping agents) in Italy to transport food stuffs for sale.

King Theoderic to Amabilis, Vir Devotus *and* Comes

1. It is fitting that nobody should grudgingly undertake our commands, which are better known to increase the advantages of the loyal. Therefore, we know there to be a shortage of food stores in the Gallic territories, to which commerce hastens, always eager that goods bought at a cheaper price may be sold for a greater one. Thus it happens that our foresight may both satisfy the merchant and assist those in need. **2.** And so, by the present dictate, let your faithfulness know that all shippers at Campania, Lucania, and Tuscany ought to entrust themselves to suitable bondsmen, so that they may set out only to Gaul with various kinds of food, possessing free rein to sell as would agree between the buyer and seller. **3.** The remuneration for bargaining with those in need is great, when famine is wont to despise all costs, so that it might fulfill its own wants. For he provides a service to his own reputation, who, having been asked to sell, is seen to give away at an almost moderate price. It is a struggle to approach the well-supplied with goods; however, one who is able to carry food to the hungry may ask a price according to his own judgment.

LETTER 4.6 (C. 507–11)

This letter refuses a request to release the sons of a man from their studies at Rome. Almost identical to *Variae* 1. 39, both letters originate with different *spectabiles* from Syracuse; although the refusal is couched in terms of concern for the education of the sons, this is probably a strategy by which enforced *tuitio* ensured the loyalty of leading Syracusan citizens.

King Theoderic to Symmachus, Vir Illustris *and Patrician*

1. We willingly embrace the reasonable petitions of those entreating, we who reflect upon just deeds, even when not asked. For what is more worthy than that we should churn over in constant thought, both day and night, how untarnished equity may preserve our republic, just as arms protect it? And so the *spectabilis* Valerianus, living in the city of Syracuse, has petitioned that his sons, whom he had brought to Rome for the sake of their education, be returned to their home. **2.** Let your *illustris* magnificence see to it immediately that, by our order, these children should remain in the aforementioned city; nor may it be permitted for them to depart unless our approval should assent to it. For thus the advancement of studies is acquired for them and respect for our commands is preserved. **3.** Therefore, he should not consider what he owed as a vow to have been imposed upon him. Let Rome be displeasing to no man, that fertile mother of eloquence, that temple replete with every virtue, which it is not possible to call foreign. Let what is apparent be openly acknowledged: one to whom so great a home is offered should not be thought lacking in gratitude.

LETTER 4.7 (C. 509–10)

Possibly related to *Variae* 4.5, concerned with the transport of grain to alleviate famine in Gaul, this letter orders that the grain lost in shipwreck from Sicily to Gaul should be credited to the public accounts of the agents involved (*prosecutores frumentorum*).

King Theoderic to Senarius, Vir Illustris *and* Comes Privatarum

1. It is the purpose of our devotion to alleviate the fortunes of those unjustly stricken, since we are unable to find fault with what happens to be imposed by adverse force. For it is unjust that what is not under a man's control should be attributed to his own fault, and that what is rarely possible to avoid should be charged against the stricken. **2.** And therefore, let your loftiness be aware that the agents of the grain, who were sent to Gaul from Sicily, have moved us with a woeful petition, to the effect that, at the time that they had advanced their cargo to the open sea, it was overcome by hostile weather, where, with the seams of wooden beams sundering, the violence of the waves consumed everything, nor was anything returned to the poor men from the expanse of sea except their tears alone. **3.** Whence, advised by the present dictate, let your *illustris* loftiness bring it about that the allotment of grain, which has manifestly perished in this misfortune, should be credited to the accounts of the aforementioned agents any without delay. For it is a kind of cruelty to want to exact punishment harsher than shipwreck, and to compel to payment those men from whom the monstrous elements are known to have stripped a comfortable life.

LETTER 4.8 (C. 507-11)

Frustratingly spare of detail, this letter orders the leading citizens of Forlì to organize the collection and transport of timber to another settlement for unknown purposes.

King *Theoderic to* Honorati, Possessores, *and* Curiales *of Forlì*

1. What has been decided by our command should not seem grievous, since we know how to reckon what is fitting for you to accomplish. Indeed, to be protected reasonably by that power of ours which has assisted you is not burdensome. Thence, we have decided in the present dictate that, without any delay, your devotion should transport timber to Alsuanum from your area, being recompensed with an acceptable price, inasmuch as it is possible to accomplish according to our instructions and with wages paid for labor, lest you should appear to have sustained a loss.

LETTER 4.9 (C. 507-11)

A letter ordering a *comes* to provide *tuitio* for two orphaned children who have become targets for unspecified legal suits.

King *Theoderic to Osuin,* Vir Illustris *and* Comes

1. It is the role of the innocent to seek our court, where no place is given to violence, and where the injuries of greed are not tolerated. And so Maurentius and Paula, stripped of the assistance of a father, claim they have been exposed to the attacks of many. Their youth is deemed an opportunity for misfortunes, especially when it would be easy to steal from young orphans. And therefore, they deserve our protection, because the conniving of the wicked would not restrain itself from them. Thence, your loftiness, recognizing the intention of the present order, if any litigant in a legal contest prefers to vex the above-mentioned youths, they must be sent to our *comitatus,* where, it will be known, the innocent may find refuge and plotters may find the severity of law.

LETTER 4.10 (C. 507-11)

A lengthy letter addressed to a provincial governor, demanding that discipline be restored to the management of personal debts. In particular, the main issue is the practice of distraint, or the forcible seizure of goods and property in satisfaction of debts owed to private citizens. The province (Campania) was an enclave of senatorial land holdings.

King Theoderic to Johannus, Vir Spectabilis *and*
Consularis *of Campania*

1. It is scandalous to give free rein to private animosities in the face of public laws, nor must the heedless rage of pride lay claim to its own arbitration. Indeed, it is the exceedingly unjust man who delights in wrath. Enraged men feel no right, because, while so stirred that they rage in vengeance, they do not seek moderation in their acts. Hence it is that the sacred reverence for laws was founded, so that nothing would be done according to its own whim, nothing by violence. For what separates tranquil peace from bellicose chaos, if litigations are decided according to force? **2.** Accordingly, we have learned in a petition of the provincials of Campania and Samnium that, with the discipline of the times neglected, some men have eagerly given themselves over to practicing distraint, and, as though by the revocation of an edict, license to criminality increases among the general public. Joining to this a far more grievous charge, some are induced to the payment of others' debts, and with the only likely justification that a certain property should happen to be near to that of the debtor. Oh, unjust error of judgment! The legal cases of brothers are separate. The son is separate from the obligations of his father, if he does not happen to be the heir. The wife does not retain the debts of the husband, except through the bonds of inheritance. And audacity drags unrelated persons to payment, when the laws absolve those conjoined as family. Thus far, our ignorance has perhaps permitted this to happen; now, it is necessary that it should have a remedy by laws that will be able to come to our attention. **3.** Thence, with the intent of our published edict understood, let your respectability bring it to the attention of all people, so that whoever will have taken the opportunity to purloin with the practice of distraint, let him lose that which ought to have been restored according to the letter of the law, nor may it be permitted that a pledge of security on property may be taken by anyone according to his own desire, except that it has instead been legally mortgaged. But if he prefers to distrain one man's property on behalf of another, which is shameful to say, let him restore twice what he seized by force, since loss of property restrains criminality more, and those who have managed to toss shame aside consider only the consequences. And should the shameful protection of poverty excuse him from this restitution, on account of the type of crime committed, let him be absolved by the capital punishment of cudgeling. For what we know is not permitted, we shall not allow to remain unpunished.

LETTER 4.11 (C. 509-10)

A simple order to adjudicate a dispute between *curiales* and *possessores* of Velienses (possibly Velia in Lucania). The dispute was probably fiscal in nature, in which case the letter demonstrates the flexibility of magisterial competence, as the jurisdiction of the *Comes Privatarum* pertained primarily to royal estates.

King Theoderic to Senarius, Vir Illustris *and* Comes Privatarum

1. It is the hope of supplicants to submit their true desires for a remedy to the judgment of wisdom, so that the uncertainty of confusion may be removed by the gift of a ruling. Therefore, let your greatness, whose jurisdiction is known to pertain to this ruling, investigate the case between the landowners and the *curiales* of Velienses with careful scrutiny, to the extent that the quarrel between them may be quelled by you with open justice. For it is not fitting that a case should drag on after a hearing with you, by whom cases ought to be heard after other judges have failed.

LETTER 4.12 (C. 508-11)

An interesting case entrusted to the care of two leading officials in Gaul, the *Comes* of Massilia (*Var.* 3.34) and the *Vicar Praefectorum* (*Var.* 3.16), making this a local Gallic affair. A woman had abandoned her husband for another man, and the mother of the previous husband has filed suit in order to recover properties claimed by her former daughter-in-law. For a similar scenario concerning marriage, fidelity, and property, compare *Variae* 2.10, 2.11, 4.40.

King Theoderic to Marabadus, Vir Illustris *and* Comes, *and to* Gemellus, Vir Spectabilis

1. It is our intention that, just as we defend with arms the provinces subject to us, by God's will, so too should we govern them with laws, since the observance of justice ever increases a *Princeps*. However much one lives according to an approved institution, so much does it contribute to further heights of advancement. **2.** And so Arcotamia, a woman of *illustris* rank, groaning lamentably, has cried out over the calamity of her own grandson with such great complaint, since the concern of one's own grandmother is always more tender. She claims that her own daughter-in-law Aetheria, with the love of her husband set aside, has bound herself in a covenant of marriage to a certain Liberius, and, since she wishes to display her new marriage bed more lavishly, she hastens to ruin the resources of her first husband, claiming herself to be endowed with the inheritance of her sons, for whom it would be more fitting the property remain intact. **3.** And therefore, we who have been accustomed to refer the desires of supplicants to the statutes of divine sanction,[4] so that we neither deny a petitioner access to a hearing, nor condemn the case of the opponent with gullible ease, commit this case, deserving the audience of the law, to the judgment of your loftiness. In this way, with all discord dispersed by the presence of the holy gospels, and with three *honorati,* whom the consensus of the parties will have chosen and who should have familiarity with laws, you may produce something settled between them with the grace of venerable law and decided with the discipline of our reign. For it is not fitting that violence should settle anything between those who deserve to attain our governance.

LETTER 4.13 (C. 509-10)

This letter responds to a shortage of supplies faced by soldiers in Pannonia. Although the directive is vague, it seems to require the *Comes Privatarum* to send provisions to the *Comes* of Pannonia, presumably from the resources of the royal estates that the *Comes Privatarum* managed.

King Theoderic to Senarius, Vir Illustris *and* Comes Privatarum

1. It is not right that gain should be lacking for those who toil, since the way to good things in the future should be apparent and the hardships of diligent men should be concluded with just compensation. And so, know that our foresight, which surveys all territories of the republic with heavenly favor, has arranged things so that provisions gathered in the established manner may be provided for the *illustris* Colosseus, who was sent to Sirmiensis Pannonia on behalf of those struggling and distinguishing themselves there. Inasmuch as necessities should have been prepared for the aforementioned man, the opportunity has been lost to unjust corruption. **2.** A hungry army is unable to preserve discipline, especially when the armed man always seizes what he lacks. Let him have what he may purchase, lest he be compelled to consider what he may plunder. Necessity does not respect moderation, nor is it possible to order the many to preserve what the few cannot protect.

---

4. That is, Roman imperial law (*statuta divalium sanctionum*).

LETTER 4.14 (C. 507–11)

This letter assigns a *saio* to compel Goths settled in Picenum and Tuscany to pay taxes owed on land. Because soldiers received an allotment of land immune to taxation as a part of the emoluments of military service, it should be assumed that these were properties purchased by wealthier Goths in addition to their allotment. The behavior described here resembles senatorial disdain for tax payments on display in *Variae* 2.24.

King Theoderic to Gesila, Saio

1. The greatest kind of sin is for one man to be overburdened with the debts of another, so that one who is able to be compelled should not deserve to receive a hearing. Let debts reflect upon their owners and let the man who is known to have the advantage of property pay the tribute. And so, we have elected you by the present dictate, so that the Goths settled throughout Picenum and the two Tuscanies should be immediately compelled by you to pay the taxes owed. 2. For this digression from lawful practice must be restrained at its very origin, lest shameful imitation should, like an unsightly disease, gradually take hold of the rest of men. Therefore, if anyone relying on his boorish nature casts our commands aside, using the strength of our resources, you will lay claim to his homes with their documented pertinences, so that, one who is unwilling to justly pay a small amount can reasonably expect to lose much more. Who, indeed, ought to be more zealously dedicated to the fisc than one who has seized the benefit of the donative,[5] especially when much more is received from our kindness than is demanded in payment by law? For if the taxes are managed for the sake of our generosity, it is rather we, elevating the fortunes of all men, who pay voluntary tribute.

LETTER 4.15 (C. 507–11)

Addressed to an untitled official superintending the personnel of ships (*dromonarii*), probably those ships assigned to grain transport along the coasts, this letter finds fault with the official for allowing the number of oarsmen to fall below the established complement. This was a common form of peculation throughout the history of empire, by which officials collected salaries for vacancies.

King Theoderic to Benenatus, Vir Spectabilis

1. We have learned from the report of the great and *illustris Comes Patrimonii* that twenty-one oarsmen in public service have fallen from the established number on account of accidental death. Whence, our foresight, in whose interest it is to

---

5. The bonus paid to soldiers annually at Ravenna; cf. *Var.* 2.31, 5.16, 5.26, 5.27, 5.36.

recover by plan of action what has been lost to misfortune, knows to arrange this,[6] so that you hasten, without any hesitation, to replace the above-mentioned oarsmen with those who could be found suitable for this task. **2.** For the work of the oars demands the most active vigor of mind and body, since confidence of the mind is able to make way through stormy waves. For what is more daring than to enter so wide and faithless a sea with a small ship, which only the presumption of desperation causes to be surmounted? On that account, by our order, let it happen that you take this precaution, so that you will not provoke a complaint from an enfeebled assemblage of oarsmen, when you know that we had demanded the most robust of men for the task.

LETTER 4.16 (C. 509–11)

An announcement appointing a *comes* to manage the affairs of the Senate at Rome. Although this responsibility had previously fallen to the *Praefectus Urbis* (cf. *Var.* 3.11–12), it seems that corruption had not abated. Somewhat ominously, the letter emphasizes the military discipline of the candidate during his previous assignment in Gaul.

King Theoderic to the Senate of Rome

1. For the sake of public weal, to which our attention always gives consideration, we had thought some time ago that your citizen, the *illustris Comes* Arigernus, must be sent to Gaul, so that the hearts of the wavering might be fortified by the maturity of his counsels. Indeed, he caused the nervous inexperience of the province to embrace wise governors, so that, just as order will fashion every manner of life, thus may devotion hasten instruction. With these affairs arranged to our satisfaction, he both restored the glory of civic harmony and, displaying what he learned in your presence, brought back the trophies of battles. **2.** We have returned this man to your assembly, as we judged this to be your wish, so that one who had already pleased you for a long time would now become even more pleasing, since additional blessings now commend him. For this reason, let the Roman Senate restore itself to the discipline of the aforementioned man and let what is instructed by an affection for peace be fulfilled in a dutiful spirit, to the extent that leave for corruption is abolished and, what is especially important, no place should be found for feuding. **3.** And so, if anything blameworthy advanced during his absence, correct it among yourselves with consideration for justice, so that one for whom probity is always pleasing may come to work with your nobility. Know him to be intimately bound to us, so that any erring behavior that has not been emended by its own authors will be cut short by the punishment of the laws. Therefore,

---

6. A similar syntax and vocabulary used in the dispositive statement at *Var.* 4.13.1.

conscript fathers, let him be obeyed, a man already approved for such a long time, for whom it is a necessity to pursue anything requiring admonishment. This man thus far has conducted himself in your company with the praise of all, and, in so great an assembly, has encountered a hostile opinion from none.

LETTER 4.17 (C. 508–11)

An order to a military commander in Gaul to protect the properties of the church from illicit seizure, indicating the degree of disorder caused by the conflict and also the role of military personnel in preserving civil order.

King Theoderic to Ibba, Dux and Vir Sublimis

1. We want no policy settled by a former king, especially which had been decreed in agreement with reason, to falter with any kind of ambiguity, since it is fitting that what had been established by a just command should remain firm. For why should we topple previous arrangements, where there is nothing that we ought to correct? **2.** And so we advise you in the present dictate, following the instructions of that Alaric of excellent memory,[7] that should the properties of the church of Narbonne be held by any kind of occupation by squatters, let you restore them with a mind toward equity, since we do not want illicit seizures to be stirred in loss to the church, when it would befit our reign to calm confusions. **3.** Be the kind of man thoroughly roused against such things, so that you, who are distinguished in war, may also return as one outstanding in civic harmony. And so, should you struggle to preserve justice for people of modest means, you strengthen your arms by the blessing of God. For it is not possible for the mischievous to resist what the powerful do not excuse, when they willingly yield everything to you, whom they recognize as glorified in the battles of war. The coward will be able to direct nothing brave for the daring; no man better controls the presumptuous than one whose own deeds commended him.

LETTER 4.18 (C. 507–11)

This letter orders a *comes* to investigate claims that a local priest has plundered wealth interred with the dead. Clergy were responsible for maintaining the precincts of the dead and it is not known where this may have occurred, although it may be connected to a similar command to a *saio* in *Variae* 4.34.

King Theoderic to Anna, Comes and Vir Spectabilis

1. It is the practice of our kindness to entrust issues requiring action to fidelity that has been proven to us, so that, when we choose judges endowed with a mature

---

7. The late Visigothic king, Alaric II.

discernment, craven thievery may not find a foothold. Indeed, not long ago it reached us through the report of many that the presbyter Laurentius has been searching among corpses of men for funerary riches by exhuming the remains, and he has inflicted harm upon those dead who ought to be shown respect from the living. It is claimed that such corrupt contact has not been withheld from hands dedicated to the sacred rites. It is reported that he sought gold in an execrable manner, one for whom it would be more fitting to bestow his own wealth, or at least wealth properly collected, upon the needy. **2.** We order you investigate this matter with careful inquiry, so that, if you find that the claims hold true, conclude your surveillance of the man only with that end, lest he should be able to conceal those things that were illicit for him to find. For we believe that this crime, which we leave unpunished on account of the dignity of the priesthood, must be punished by something weightier.

LETTER 4.19 (C. 508–11)

An order to suspend the collection of the *siliquaticus* on the sale of grain, wine, and oil at the ports of Gaul; further indication of efforts needed to restore order following the conflict.

King Theoderic to Gemellus, Vir Spectabilis

1. It is fitting that princely forethought refresh what is exhausted, so that the gentleness of commands may lessen the harshness of hardships. For a disadvantage is not felt, if the gift of good fortune will offer assistance for what is known to be oppressive on account of adversities. **2.** For that reason, we command that the obligatory payment of the *siliquaticus,* which the foresight of antiquity prescribed for transacting business of all kinds, need not be paid at the present time on grain, wine, and oil. In this way, the remission of payments will be able to provide a surplus to the provinces and, to some extent, the exhausted may be restored by the curative of the present decree. **3.** For who is not more fully hastened to commerce than one for whom the accustomed expenses are reduced? Let the ship approaching our ports not fear, so that it would be possible to have a secure haven for sailors, if the hand of the collectors may not attack those whom taxes afflict more often than they are accustomed to be stripped bare by shipwreck. This may, perhaps, be tolerated in a time of peace; now, however, since we desire to be distinguished before the provincials, we have, for the time being, taken consideration for the masters of commerce.

LETTER 4.20 (C. 507–11)

An order to restore properties seized from a local church which had been donated earlier by emperors. The location of the church and the official capacity of the addressee (presumably a *comes* or *saio*) is not known.

King Theoderic to Geberic, Vir Spectabilis

1. If we have desired to find an opportunity for benefaction, so that we may raise the reputation of our devotion, how much more would we, who desire to bestow our own largesse without regret, want the favors granted by another to be preserved intact, especially when what was bestowed from the fisc on a former occasion reflects upon our good conscience. Thence we have learned from a petition of the venerable bishop Constantius that a *iugerum* of land belonging to his own sanctified church,[8] conferred by the devotion of former *Principes*, is now held by the violent seizure of certain persons. **2.** But since we want no man to enjoy the fruits of his own scheming, especially when, with despicable intention, it hinges upon loss to the poor, we have decided in the present dictate that the aforementioned church should take possession of those properties that had been formally set aside by the kindness of former *Principes*, without any reduction, and moreover, with impending punishment for the transgressor who is proven to have violated both an imperial donative and an advantage to the church.

LETTER 4.21 (C. 508-11)

Frustratingly bare of context, the point of this letter is simply to remind the *Vicar Praefectorum* in Gaul to preserve Theoderic's commands in all things. It is impossible to infer what may have prompted such admonition.

King Theoderic to Gemellus, Vir Spectabilis

1. Although we know that your efficiency dwells upon our injunctions and carefully avoids what you know displeases us, nonetheless our admonition will not fail one already attentive, so that you may be rendered even more prepared, when you would act upon instructions on short notice. Thence, our provision ought to seem displeasing to no man, when the necessity of the moment excuses the burden of obligation. **2.** And so be roused by our decrees, since it is fitting that they are always applied, especially since their preservation in time of need is beneficial. Thus warned will you obey, so that, thus, you will be able to accomplish with the provincials whatever you believe we would want to give them. In this way, you would act assured of our gratitude, provided that you have assiduously avoided giving consideration to anything of a craven intention.

LETTER 4.22 (C. 510-11)

This letter addresses charges of sorcery against two prominent senators by appointing the *Praefectus Urbis* to judge the case in consultation with a traditional panel

---

8. A *iugerum* is approximately two-thirds of an acre.

of five senatorial colleagues (*iudicium quinquevirale*). The *Praefectus* is furthermore notified that the *comes* assigned to Rome will be at hand to ensure civil order.[9]

King Theoderic to Argolicus, Vir Illustris *and* Praefectus Urbis

1. That transgression is intolerable which effects injury against supernal majesty and, forgetful of piety, repeatedly follows the barbarism of error. For what chance of pardon will he hope, who despises that author deserving reverence? Let profane rites now depart from our midst; let the punishable murmuring to the spirits fall silent. It is not permitted in Christian times to be entangled in magic arts.[10] **2.** And so, we have learned from the report of your greatness that Basilius and Praetextatus, already long polluted by contact with perverse arts, have been brought to indictment under your examination by the accusation of certain persons. You claim to observe our decision over this matter, so that what the authority of our piety recommends may happen more confidently. **3.** But we, who know not how to differ from the laws and whose intention it is to hold moderated justice in every way, have decided in the present dictate that you should consider this case by lawful examination with five senators, that is, with the honored patricians Symmachus, Decius, Volusianus, and Caelianus, as well as the *illustris* Maximianus. And with procedure of law observed in everything, if the crime that is maintained has been found substantiated, let it also be punished according to the stricture of the very same laws, so that hidden and secret members of this art, those whom uncertain information cannot drag before the laws, may be restrained from such crimes by the nature of its punishment. **4.** We have sent instructions to the *illustris Comes* Arigernus concerning this affair, so that, with the violent reaction of any person restrained, he may bring the accused to court, if they should conceal themselves, and sitting with you in this trial, he may give assurance that the innocent have not been oppressed and that the guilty may not evade the law.[11]

LETTER 4.23 (C. 510–11)

This letter communicates the content of *Variae* 4.22 (in some places verbatim) to the *comes* in charge of maintaining civil order during the trial and of maintaining custody of the accused, who apparently escaped those charged with confining them. The *comes* is reminded that the trial must be impartial.

9. The trial is later mentioned by Gregory the Great in the *Dialogues* 1.4.

10. This could be a reference either to the continued (and at this time illicit) practice of rites associated with former public "pagan" religion or to the less formal substratum of common, non-Christian ritualistic practices thought of as "magic."

11. Given that a *comes* has been mobilized to maintain order in Rome, it is safe to assume that this was a high profile case with active partisans.

King Theoderic to Arigernus, Vir Illustris *and* Comes

1. Although it may be expected that the discipline of Rome, having been entrusted to you, should be safeguarded in any situation, nonetheless, in this matter, which you know has been delegated to you by our authority, you ought to be especially diligent, so that gratitude may increase concerning your protection of justice, and you, who have thus far pleased us with your integrity, would claim profit from our judgment. 2. Therefore, the *Praefectus Urbis* has declared to us in his own report that Basilius and Praetextatus have been attacked by the accusation of many for being involved in magical arts. He reports that these men have escaped by a lapse of judgment of their captors. We order you to lead them from wherever they may be found to the *iudicium quinquevirale,*[12] which our authority has chosen for the present case and where we want you to preside, so that, with the violent reaction of any person restrained, you may bring this case to be considered and closed with respect to the laws. 3. And, if they are convicted for the kind of crime of which they have been accused, let them submit to a sentence that the limits of the law have sanctioned. If indeed their innocence has been attacked by a detestable plot, for no reason may you tolerate them being oppressed, because we want what increases the reputation of our piety to happen in every dispute with consideration for the divine.

LETTER 4.24 (C. 507–11)

This letter donates unused public space adjacent to a local bath to a member of the clergy at Milan. It is not explicit what purpose the deacon intended for the space, but it involved the renovation of architecture, probably for religious purposes.

King Theoderic to Helpidius, Deacon

1. Those things that are fittingly conferred upon the deserving yield a profit, and more is acquired by the very act of giving away, when just desserts are bestowed on the best recipients. Thence, we have learned from the tenor of your petition of an area in Spoleto, which the decay of great age has already concealed for a long time with grime, and which awaits the splendor of restoration, so that, in a kind of confusion, the face of novelty is returned to something mature with antiquity, and from your beneficence something renewed would rise forth, which had fallen to ruins with the decline of many years. With regard for your accomplishments and for the long duration of your thankless service, we grant what must be assented to with a free spirit, so that a just outcome may be conferred upon the wishes of those beseeching and so that the adornment of restoration may augment the city. 2. And so we grant strength to your petition with the present kindness, so that you may

---

12. The panel of five senatorial peers constituted by the *Praefectus Urbis* in *Var.* 4.22.

gain possession of the portico behind the Baths of Torasius, generously given with its precinct, if it still serves no public function, since, with permission to restore buildings, we receive a gift rather than giving one. Therefore, supported by this decree, take faith in building upon the aforementioned places; nor should you fear any complaint in the future, since, on account of you, both the utility of the city is maintained and the desire of the *Princeps* has been respected.

LETTER 4.25 (C. 510–11)

This letter inducts a man into the senatorial order at Rome. By comparison to letters of appointment to high office for *illustres,* little is said about the accomplishments of the candidate, although inclusion within the Senate required *illustris* rank. He later became western consul in 516.

King Theoderic to Argolicus, Vir Illustris *and* Praefectus Urbis

1. It is a given that one who desires to attain the fillets of the sacred order is known for his character. For striving for a desired blessing confers merits and an honorable intention can be recognized in this kind of desire. For what man ignorant of the arts of the *palestra* would enter the stadium for competition? Or who would be involved in a legal fight when he was not advised by the good conscience of virtue? Contests that are not assisted by the reputations of the meritorious do harm to the very persons striving to win. **2.** Therefore, to have sought after the assembly of the greatest men is a declaration of public praise, and one who seeks the rank of exalted dignity reports a good opinion of himself. Therefore, our devotion gladly indulges itself concerning these requests. Moreover, we elevate enfeebled wishes with hope, so that, while advancement is sought, eagerness for probity is loved even more. **3.** Thence, let your *illustris* magnificence hasten Peter, conspicuous in the glow of his family and already a senator in his very demeanor, to be added to ranks of the sacred roll following ancient custom, so that, enumerated in such a great assembly, he may prosper, and adorned with membership in the sacred order, he may advance further.

LETTER 4.26 (C. 508–11)

This letter cancels tax payments for the citizens of Marseille for the remainder of the year, illustrating the strategic importance of a major port city to the control of southern Gaul. The letter is perhaps unusual in that it is not addressed to the *Comes* of Marseille (cf. *Var.* 4.12 and 4.46).

King Theoderic to All Inhabitants of Massilia

1. With a giving spirit do we safeguard those favors formerly granted to you, since we desire to bestow new ones for your advantage. Indeed, kindness knows not how to observe limitations, and it is fitting that benefits restored after so long a time may encourage new ones. **2.** Thence, we grant you, by this dictate, an exemption which applies to your territory, following the special grant of former *Principes,* nor shall we permit any new kind of requirements to be imposed upon you, whom we want to be protected from all burdens. Let the generosity of a *Princeps* release you from the property tax for the remainder of the present year, so that you will be able to receive what you have not demanded. For it is the very perfection of devotion that knows to have regard for troubled things even before they are shaped into prayers.

LETTER 4.27 (C. 508–11)

An interesting case of *tuitio* gone awry, this letter orders the arrest of a *saio* for attacking and extorting his delegated ward. The addressee, another *saio,* is ordered to work with a *comes* (and likewise *saio*) to resolve the matter.

King Theoderic to Tutizar, Saio

1. Any insult is certainly detestable, and whatever has been permitted contrary to the laws is justly sentenced to condemnation. But where the harm of every wickedness is deemed to have reached the furthest extent, assistance is believed to advance. For diverted cruelty heaps blame upon the hostile party, and an unexpected betrayal is a greater burden for the accused. **2.** And so the *spectabilis* Peter has complained to us in a remarkable deposition that the protection of the *saio* Amara,[13] which we granted to him against violence, has instead been twisted about, such that only the intervention of doors could stop the blow of a sword being plunged into him. He has been subject to a wound of the hand, which, as it had not been completely severed, the hard wood of the doors prevailed against the blows. Even when the attack had been exhausted, the extremity of his body attested to the glittering sharpness of the blade. **3.** Oh, execrable crime! His own protection has assaulted the man and, with the beneficial comfort of protection removed, harm increased from his defense. He even affixed a more grievous crime to this, almost as though hostility came at a price; his own crime was thus appraised with an enormous tribute. And therefore, the wrath of our devotion justly rises up against these men, who have transformed liberal commands into a savage practice. For what refuge is there for supplicants, if even our favors cause wounds? **4.** Thence we have decided in the present order, that whatever the above-mentioned Amara received in the name of payment for the representation of the same petitioner, bound by you as though he himself were the unwanted assailant, let him be

---

13. The term *tuitio,* in this instance, indicates that the protection of the *saio* had been a legally formalized patronage.

compelled to pay double to Peter, since it is proper that what happened to be extorted by means of willful impudence should be restored as a punishment. 5. Moreover, concerning the blow that the brash outlaw inflicted with a drawn sword, let him come, by your compulsion, for a hearing at the court of the *Comes* Duda, also appointed a *saio,* so that it may be settled without any delay following the precedents of edicts that will have clarified the crime committed. Indeed, you will demonstrate protection for one requiring it against unlawful attacks, with civil harmony preserved by our injunction, not by the example of one condemned, but by the thoughtful consideration of one properly delegated.

LETTER 4.28 (C. 507–11)

This letter addresses the *comes* who would have authority in judging the case of the errant *saio* from *Variae* 2.27. Interestingly, the letter is far less elaborate than *Variae* 2.27, which was written to the *saio* deputized to arrest his colleague (and presumably of lower rank than a *comes*).

King Theoderic to Duda, Vir Spectabilis *and* Comes

1. We have approved the good conscience of one to whom we have entrusted matters that must be decided, since he who is seen to impose a standard of his own on legal deliberation is worthy to determine consequences among other men. And so the *spectabilis* Peter claims that our *saio,* Amara, who, to the contrary had been chosen only for his protection, has wounded him with a drawn sword and has offered the kind of protection that an enemy would hardly be able to dare. We want you to investigate this matter with a legal inquiry and to close the case with a fair sentence, to the extent that no man should dare to attempt that which he knows to displease us.

LETTER 4.29 (C. 510–11)

A serious charge of peculation and obstruction of justice brought against the *Praefectus Urbis,* which the present letter addresses with a strong warning, perhaps indicating the precarious diplomacy needed to maintain control of Rome, but also shedding light on what appears to be the more prominent role of the *Comes* at Rome (cf. *Var.* 4.16 and 4.23).

King Theoderic to Argolicus, Vir Illustris *and* Praefectus Urbis

1. If the authority of your position should be reflected upon, and concern for the reverence due Rome, you ought to have striven further in those affairs for which you are now censured. For how in the present age would you be able to value your own profit as much as that of the Senate at the capital, when what that sacred order

acquires increases the reputation of its president? **2.** But it is declared in the report sent by the *clarissimus* Armentarius how much,[14] to the contrary, you pursue profits with a shameful ambition for delaying those improvements for which you clearly ought to wish. For what could be more obviously inconsistent than for you to attempt to obstruct the entreaties of petitioners from our ministrations, and after the pronouncement of a sacred decree, if it is right to call it such, to have even obstructed royal judgment? **3.** But we, whose desire it is not to unyieldingly require punishment after the first offense, would rather apply injunctions toward correction, lest our discipline, which a weak patience should not surpass, may seem excessive. And therefore, we have decided in the present dictate that no clever delays may be endured by our orders, since one who fails after being duly warned will have no ground for pardon.

LETTER 4.30 (C. 507–11)

Similar in theme to *Variae* 4.24, this letter grants a patrician permission to renovate a portion of the Republican Forum at Rome.

King Theoderic to Albinus, Vir Illustris and Patrician

1. It is indeed fitting that each person consider the increase of their own country, but especially those whom the republic has obligated to itself with the highest honors, since it is the nature of things that one who is seen to undertake greater things necessarily ought to accomplish more. **2.** And so you have asked in a submitted petition that permission be granted for building workshops at the Portico of Curva, which fittingly encloses the Forum in the manner of a courtyard, being situated near the Domus Palmata, so that a building for private habitation may be extended and the appearance of newness may arise from the ancient city. Thus it happens that what had been able to decline from neglect may be sustained by the diligence of inhabitants, since the ruin of buildings is easily accomplished by removing the careful attention of residents, and what the presence of men does not look after quickly sunders with the ripening of age. **3.** Thence we, who desire the city to be arranged with the brilliance of rising buildings, grant the requested opportunity, provided that the project impede neither public weal nor its comeliness. For this reason, expect to commence untroubled by legalities, so that you may appear a worthy patron to Roman workshops and the completed work may commend its author. For there is no undertaking by which one is better acknowledged for both the inspiration of wisdom and practice of munificence.

---

14. Assigned as Theoderic's delegate to the Senate at *Var.* 3.33.

LETTER 4.31 (C. 507–11)

This letter exhorts the bishop of Vercellensis (Vercelli) to complete the repair to a local aqueduct, a form of public munificence more traditionally undertaken by a secular magistrate. The reference to the project's official sanction (*nostra auctoritate*) may indicate that the court had subsidized the project in some manner.

King Theoderic to Aemilianus, Venerable Bishop

1. That which the intention of wise men is seen to have undertaken ought to be completed, since, just as the completion of something gives rise to praise, so too something unsound which is abandoned in the midst of completion produces censure. For having failed in endeavors, one has proved either to have wavered in plans or fallen short of strength. Therefore, let your sanctity, foregoing any particular objections, quickly bring to completion that charge undertaken by our authority for the satisfactory restoration of the aqueduct. 2. For what is more fitting than that a blessed bishop should provide water for a thirsting people and that human foresight should sate those who moreover ought to be fed with miracles? Indeed, you would imitate that most ancient Moses, who brought forth abundant streams from a sterile stone for those Israelites, long parched with thirst, and who, by fulfilling a miracle, caused clear waters to rush where there had been dry hardness. You, however, if you lead forth waters channeled by the construction of stone, would bestow upon the people with your own labor what Moses had by his miracles.

LETTER 4.32 (C. 507–11)

This letter orders a *saio* to act as the royal representative in an inheritance dispute brought before the governor of Campania. A condemned man's property has apparently passed to the control of his family when a strict interpretation of the law would see the inheritance as forfeit to the state.

King Theoderic to Duda, Saio

1. Since we wish to preserve justice in any legal case, because the love of equity is the distinction of a *regnum,* in those cases especially that are put forth in the name of our fisc, detestable deceit should in no way attach scandal to those ruling. Indeed, we allow ourselves to be overruled by sound equity through law, just as we are always able to be conquerors amid arms. For one whom the subject overcomes easily does not wage war as an adversary. 2. And so we have learned in the report of Marinus that the property of Tufa was formerly entrusted to Johannus according to an issued contract. And because it is apparent that what had belonged to a proscribed man pertains to us, we have therefore decided in the present dictate

that you should bring the wife of the aforementioned Johannus and his son, Janu-arius, to a fair hearing. **3.** If they recognize themselves to unjustly possess intestate properties, let them restore it with due consideration for equity. At the very least, let them approach the governor of Campania for a legal hearing, with a commit-ment to appear sent in advance, so that, with the parties publicly arraigned by your insistence, the form of punishment may be determined.[15] Nevertheless, let inno-cence be burdened with no prejudice, with no insult, and with no punishment, lest your indignation should be seen to cause the harm of another accusation.

LETTER 4.33 (C. 507–11)

One of several letters addressed to Jewish communities in Italy, this brief rescript affirms for the Jews of Genoa the state's commitment to maintain the rights accorded to Jews under former imperial law. The reason that warranted such an assurance is not clear from the letter.

King Theoderic to All Jews living in Genoa

1. The maintenance of the laws is the hallmark of civic harmony and reverence for prior *Principes* also testifies to our sense of duty. For what is better than for a peo-ple to want to live under the precepts of justice, so that the assembly of many may be a union of free wills? For this draws people from the life of a savage to a model of human concourse. This separates reason from beastliness, lest those who want to be ruled by divine counsel should wander to the arbitration of chance. **2.** And so, you have demanded in a submitted petition that those privileges ought to be preserved for you which the foresight of antiquity decreed for Jews in the institutes of law. We willingly consent to this, we who desire that the laws of the ancients be observed for our own reputation. And so we have decided in the present dictate that whatever the statutes of law proposed concerning you, they should be pre-served undiminished, to the extent that what is known to have been devised for the conduct of public harmony may be maintained with continuous devotion.

LETTER 4.34 (C. 507–11)

This letter orders a *saio* to investigate and recover gold and silver deposits at a burial site. The contrast with *Variae* 4.18, which orders a *comes* to investigate grave robbery, is noteworthy. The letter seems to draw a distinction between returning buried wealth for use by the living and damaging burial structures, which has not been sanctioned.

---

15. The phrase *forma sanctionum divalium* refers specifically to articles of imperial law that define penalties.

King Theoderic to Duda, Saio

1. It is the inclination of wisdom to recover for human use coins hidden in the earth and for the commerce of the living not to have contact with the dead,[16] hidden in the earth and for the commerce of the living not to have contact with the dead, since things buried are lost to us and profits are lost to them in no measure. Indeed, the circulation of metal coins is the comfort of men. For if it lies neglected it is similar to veins of rich gold abandoned in the earth; it increases in value with use, when what is enclosed in greedy hands becomes properly disposed among the living.[17] **2.** And so, we have decided with a measured decree that you should convene with a public notary at that place where much wealth is accumulated near the surface, and if, as it is said, gold or silver may be uncovered by your searching, you may faithfully lay claim to it for public profit. Nevertheless, you should restrain the hand from the ashes of the dead, because we do not want to seek that wealth which is likely to be discovered by grave robbers. Monuments cover the ashes, and columns and marble adorn the graves; let those who have abandoned the commerce of the living not retain wealth. **3.** For gold is rightly removed from graves where an owner is not in possession. On the contrary, it is a kind of crime to uselessly abandon to the secrets of the dead that from whence the welfare of the living is able to sustain itself. It is not greed to rescue what no owner would grieve to lose. In fact, Aeacus is said to have first discovered gold, and Indus, king of Scythia, discovered silver, and they passed them down to human usage with the greatest praise. We ought not to neglect this example to the contrary, lest, just as hidden wealth is brought forth with praise, these discoveries would seem to be ignored with criticism.

LETTER 4.35 (C. 507–11)

A young senator has been led to make ill-considered contracts, and his legal representatives have appealed to the court, for which reason this letter offers to nullify any contracts made while the client was a minor.

King Theoderic to the Agents of Albinus, Vir Illustris

1. The foresight of antiquity has deliberately decreed that minors would not have the freedom of entering into a contract, as they are ensnared by the deceptions of schemers, and an insecure age assists their mistakes. Indeed, innocence is overwhelmed if bold vigil should be eased, and every man would be eager to deceive if the fraud of plotters should succeed at bringing profit. **2.** And therefore, you allege

---

16. The use of *talenta* for "coins" is unusual and suggests ancient, possibly preimperial currency.

17. The phrase *apud vivos sepulta sunt* has intended irony with the use of the verb *sepelire*.

in a petition submitted in a respectable manner that your patron, being a minor, has accrued losses to his own resources, since ignorant childishness guides to the contrary whatever he will have considered advantageous, and that now we, adducing his age to have acted thus, should be able to amend a fault of ignorance, so that our kindness may also bestow what the laws have assigned. **3.** And furthermore, if your petition does not deviate from the truth and he lives within that span of years for which the sacred laws offer this benefit, and nothing is claimed contrary to this right, then our authority also permits your patron to be duly restituted in full with respect to the considered case. Nonetheless, let everything be carried out according to justice and the laws, since we want to consider entreaties thus, so that we do not burden your adversaries unjustly.

LETTER 4.36 (C. 509)

Another response to the general crisis created by war in Gaul, this letter cancels the payment of taxes for landowners of the Cottian Alps, to which the Gothic army apparently caused considerable damage in transit to Gaul.

King Theoderic to Faustus, Praefectus Praetorio

1. It is the most perspicacious *Princeps* who releases the grievously weakened from the payment of taxes, so that those who would fail to pay, being pressed by the harshness of losses, may be refreshed toward fulfilling the customary dues with renewed effort. For, if a burden is lifted in the least manner from the weary, the man leveled by necessity is resolved to leap up. It is better, therefore, to disregard a present loss than to lose a continual advantage on account of a negligible profit. **2.** And therefore, let your *illustris* greatness know that we have untied the provincials of the Cottian Alps from payment of taxes for the third indiction. The passing of our army, in the manner of a river, even while it irrigates, has also burdened them. For it is fitting that it will burst forth with a united roar for the common safety; nonetheless, in passing it wasted the cultivation of the very same people. For a flood always erases its own course, and, while it is expected to gently enrich the vicinity in its progress, nonetheless leaves barren that place where it has flowed in confinement. **3.** Whence it was necessary to extend a helpful hand to those cast aside by civic disruption, lest they say that they alone suffered without thanks for the defense of all; instead, let those who offered a route for defenders from Italy be confounded with delight. For the downcast, through whom I have happily acquired new tributaries, should not be compelled to make tribute. Let our intention dictate on their behalf what the subject is hardly able to expect from a king. We purchase the prosperity of the Goths with our taxes; we offer the necessary things, so that an enemy may be conquered without injury.

LETTER 4.37 (C. 507–11)

Addressed to a woman of the royal family, this letter advises that measures be taken to close a litigation between two persons. It may be inferred that at least one of the litigants was a dependent of the addressee, as the letter draws attention to the impact that the case may have on her own resources. The precise relationship of the woman to the Amals is not known.

King Theoderic to Theodagunda, Femina Illustris

1. It is proper for your wisdom to apply careful supervision to the legal cases of your subjects, since anything able to demonstrate royal connection ought to occur through your arrangements. For thus we believe, since, mindful of your birth, you have cast all wrongdoing from yourself and you are able to delight only in that which you also know us to love. The examples of our ancestors would perhaps be blotted from memory, if the deeds of so old a people were honored less, but the sons already follow the same renown of the fathers. **2.** And so Renatus has complained to us in a pitiable petition that representatives chosen by you obtained judgment in his name against Inquilina after a long interval of time, and that they then anticipated your justice in settling his losses and protection. Nonetheless, the malicious accusations of the litigant have not ceased, while he pursues the vulnerability of the petitioner with renewed litigation, so that it seems he pursues not so much the desire to win as the ruin of his opponent. **3.** For this reason, if you know the provisions of this case have been adjudicated by your orders, do not permit them to provoke further legal controversy. Let a case closed by law remain closed by your own strength of character, lest the long quarrel of litigants not so much increase your patrimony, but ruin it, and what happens because of immoderate desire for wealth, would seem to become a cause for loss.

LETTER 4.38 (C. 507–11)

This letter responds to a petition from two groups of people (it is unknown whether these are citizens of a municipality or farmers of estates), claiming that the tax assessment is not appropriate to the low yield of production. It is decreed that they should return to the tax assessments paid in the time of Odoacer.

King Theoderic to Faustus, Praefectus Praetorio

1. While we desire all regions of our republic to be enriched equally, yet the increase of fiscal tribute must be considered with the fairest possible judgment, since an increase of revenue is diminishment to those serving, and however much one region produces, it detracts as much from its own strength. But the ever-harmful increase of taxes must be prevented by us, who want the utility of a stable fisc to be well established for all time, lest by swelling with its own increase, the fisc should begin to weaken the larger it seems to grow. **2.** Thence, let your *illustris* greatness be aware that the citizens of Gravassius and Pontonis have petitioned us, that they have been burdened with unjust assessments by Januarius, and also by Probus, the auditors, while the excessive unfruitfulness of their estates permits no surplus to accrue to them. Because any amount of hard work yields to the resistance of nature, it does not profit to expend the effort of toil which the fertility of the place is known not to support. Where cultivation will produce, there the census may be increased. Thereupon, even tribute is variable, because the fertility of the fields is not consistent. **3.** And so we have determined the former practice must be restored for them, so that the tribute they paid in the time of Odoacer may now be a service by them to public weal. And if anything is shown to have increased, we would yield more in favor of their depleted resources. For we do not want any such thing proclaimed that would later be necessary to remove.

LETTER 4.39 (C. 507–11)

The second letter addressed to Theoderic's nephew (cf. *Var.* 3.15), again in censorious tone. This letter orders Theodahad to release properties that had been seized by his personal dependents at great risk to the reputation of the Amal family.

King Theoderic to Theodahad, Vir Illustris

1. Among other things by which human kind is vexed, a shameful ambition for another's property is an allurement that must be avoided especially, since properties cast far and wide are seized if the practice is not curbed by the weight of justice. And moreover, it is testified even in divine readings that avarice is the root of all evils, which is punished by so great a fate that, although one may seize much, one always has need of more. It is a vice that we do not want to increase in your heart on account of the propinquity of our kinship, such that we would not even overlook the beginning of it. **2.** For what do those with filthy intentions bring to the luster of birth? It is more fitting that you elect what is able to adorn us. It is not fitting that greed should cheapen a man of Amal blood, since the family finds itself ennobled with purple. And so we correct you with the incentive of public renown, you for whom as of yet we ought not to be vexed. **3.** And so the *spectabilis* Domitius complains in a petition given to us that estates legally his, that is *illa* and *illa,* have been taken over by your men with disregard to the law. It would be proper for this to be corrected with all due civility, if it has been demanded rightly. **4.** But since we will not permit obscurity to be cast upon you for long, you who blaze with the brilliance of your family, we have decided in the present dictate that, if the conditions of the exchange are favorable, you should cause those recently occupied properties that have been seized, together with all pertinences, to be restored to the plaintiff without any delay and with our *saio* Duda present. **5.** And if you believe it is possible that anything concerning your party agrees with the law, let it happen that you send an instructed person to our court, so that a decision may be pronounced with the positions of the parties discussed according to equity, a decision that authority dictates with respect to the laws. Indeed, it is agreeable that well-bred men accomplish everything under the rubric of civic harmony, since, however much the outrage of insult increases among the powerful, it is also believed that one who is demonstrably lesser in fortune is more likely to be oppressed.

LETTER 4.40 (C. 507–11)

A continuation of the dispute involving the property of a married senatorial woman, Agapita (*Var.* 2.10 and 2.11), who appears to have been seduced or raped by agents of the patrician Probinus. Here, the patrician has refuted the allegations, and the letter advises his legal counsel that Agapita's husband has been required to send his representatives to court.

King Theoderic to the Agents of Probinus, Vir Illustris

1. We are compelled by the love of justice to issue certain commands more strictly, while the precepts of our heart are much more lenient concerning lesser matters. For one who is vulnerable attracts mercy, and he holds the blessing of his own mediocrity, just as at times he may move from a favorable judgment to grief, but jealousy oppresses the powerful and cruelty elevates the humble. **2.** And so, recently the respectable Basilius earned our judgment with his submitted petitions of complaint, so that the estate Arcinatina, which your patron had bought with due formalities of the law from that man's wife, Agapita, should be returned to the aforementioned husband without delay and with all articles of sale. Meanwhile, the wife lamented in a tearful complaint concerning her seduction from her own marriage bed. Later, after the habit of our justice, we added an injunction that, if your patrons would represent themselves in this kind of case, they should quickly petition the court, so that they would be able to receive that judgment which issues forth as though from a font of justice. **3.** Therefore, if Basilius and Agapita are indicted by no false claims, we have decided that Basilius should be advised by the office of our court, so that, if there is anything that he is able to offer on his own behalf, lest it be disregarded in this case, he should hasten to respond to your accusations, whether he should prefer to come to our court or to contend in an agreed-upon court, because we shall impose the hardship of great distance on no persons, except those who know how to settle the matter to their own advantage. Indeed, we grant our presence in place of a favor; and thence, that which deserves to be preferred ought not to be imposed on the unwilling.

LETTER 4.41 (C. 507-11)

This letter orders the restoration of certain rights that the court physician lost in a legal suit after his accuser retracted his claim following a change of heart. The letter furthermore assigns a patrician to provide legal patronage (*tuitio*) for the beleaguered physician.

King Theoderic to Johannus, Archiater

1. It is the royal intention to assist those pressed hard by disgrace with the remedy of blessed piety and to alter the grievous troubles of injury with a sweeter lot. In fact, you have complained in a submitted petition that the *spectabilis* Vivianus, exalted by the artifice of law in which he is experienced, harried your person with cast accusations and succeeded to the extent that, defenseless against the body of laws, you would be condemned by the sentence of the *Vicarius* of Rome. Now, however, he has disavowed worldly hatreds with the goodwill of a religious mind and, by his own admission, he regrets your predicament. 2. And so, if these assertions are not weakened by any protests, we shall not allow a scandal that has been found displeasing to its own architects to adhere to the wretched. Therefore, with the sentence which was settled by decree over this case by the *Vicarius* of Rome being annulled, our authority restores you to all the rights of your homeland; nor should you at any time fear accusation concerning this case. 3. But if, perchance, the punishable temerity of anyone should be able to prepare another attack of such boldness against you, let the deputed sponsorship of the patrician Albinus fortify you with sound legal advice, since we want nothing uncivil to occur, for which it is a daily labor to act on behalf of a common peace.

LETTER 4.42 (C. 510-11)

The last addressed to Argolicus as *Praefectus Urbis*, this letter perhaps culminates official dissatisfaction with the manner in which he managed his authority (cf. *Var.* 4.29). The letter censures the *Praefectus* for acting opportunistically to seize the theater seats of a dead senator. Tradition required these seats to pass to his young sons, and the letter waxes piously on the state's obligations to bereft sons of the senatorial order.

King Theoderic to Argolicus, Praefectus Urbis

1. It is well that the kindness of the *Princeps* support those whom paternal devotion has forsaken, since the loss of a father ought to be felt less under a public guardian. Indeed, abandoned and defenseless children rightly hasten to us, by whom the offspring of all men advance. 2. Therefore, the complaint of the young *clarissimi*, Marcian and Maximus, has moved us, when on Easter day they had been stricken

with the wound of paternal mourning, and in that very time of rejoicing they were compelled to endure grief alone, that they neglected their own advantage with pious contempt, when, even at a sober age, it seems a kind of insanity to consider such affairs amid tears. For ambition for profit ceases when it is given over to lamentation; nor does the mind grasp anything whatever, when the mood of devotion has so occupied it. 3. They add that, at this time, undertaken in cruel stealth and with detestable calculation, the seats of their *illustris* father at the circus and amphitheater had been claimed by your office. The good will of humanity has never recalled treachery of this kind; no similar grievance has threatened; it has burdened defenseless children, for whom it is rightly considered to be a loss of decency not to assist. 4. But we, who serve the rules of the ancients and opportunities for devotion, have decided in a salubrious decree that if Volusianus, the noble patrician and father of the supplicants, formerly possessed the above-mentioned places according to common right, these should not be lost by the sons, especially when we desire to nurture the seed of senators with new favors, so as to restrain the aspirations of the young age, at its very beginning, from any sort of scandal. And so your *illustris* greatness, if any such deed is known to have been committed, know it must be corrected on the spot, lest that crowd of the senatorial order so deserving veneration should be disgraced by unjust presumption.

LETTER 4.43 (C. 509–11)

Another letter illustrating the strained relations between Christians and Jews at Rome (cf. *Var.* 3.45), the present address to the Senate responds to an outbreak of violence, apparently involving Christian slaves and Jewish masters, to which the urban populace responded by burning a synagogue. The Senate is charged with investigating and bringing to trial the principal parties.

King Theoderic to the Senate of Rome

1. The celebrated reputation of Rome must be preserved at the very least by its own practices, lest it adopt strange vices which it has ever before dispersed with the probity of conduct. Indeed, it is not Roman to want the disorder of sedition and to invite arson in that very city. And therefore, discipline of deeds must be preserved among the authors of laws, lest the detestable appearance of arson compel the hearts of the common people to imitating what must be execrated. 2. And so we have learned from the report of the *illustris comes* Arigernus that the complaint of the Jews was roused because the unruliness of slaves had erupted in the slaughter of masters. Although the deed could have been punished for the sake of public discipline, with the contention being immediately enflamed by the populace, they caused the synagogue to be utterly consumed in a reckless fire, punishing the faults of men with the ruin of buildings. If any Jew had been proven to transgress, he

himself would have been subject to injury. However, it was not right to rush to the horrible act of rioting, or to hasten to the burning of buildings. **3.** But we, whose desire it is to correct wrongly committed acts, by the grace of God, have decided in the present dictate that you should become acquainted with the above-mentioned case by lawful inquiry, and that you should restrain with the accustomed punishment the few agents of this conflagration whom you are able to discover. In this way, everyone will be able to participate in pleasing conduct. For we do not want anything detestable to occur, whence Roman prestige deservingly may be dishonored. **4.** Evaluating the case with equal measure, so that, if anyone will reasonably believe something supports him against the Jews, let him come to be heard at our court, so that whomever the offense will have implicated may be condemned with censure. Know for certain, this has displeased us exceedingly, that such fruitless intentions of the people have accomplished so much as the destruction of buildings, in a place where we want everything to be arranged with beauty.

LETTER 4.44 (C. 507–11)

A case very similar to other property disputes with local churches (cf. *Var.* 3.37), this letter orders the bishop of Pula to investigate the claim that the house of a man has been illegally seized by dependents of the bishop. The relationship of the petitioner to the church is not stated, but it seems likely that the relationship had been reinterpreted upon the accession of the new bishop.

King Theoderic to Antonius, Venerable Bishop of Polensis

1. A complaint against one for whom the right of reverence must be observed is scandalous, since I know not what should be credited as a serious trespass, where silence is not held against men of such station. Therefore, Stephanus has complained in a tearful petition that the house owned by him legally for a long time, under your predecessor and the predecessor before, has been overrun for nearly nine months by men of the church over which you preside, with the manner of civil harmony disregarded. If you know this to have been done, restore the house to the supplicant with due consideration for the importance of justice. For it is fitting that what should not be done by members of your household should be corrected by you. **2.** Nevertheless, if you know justice favored your party in this case either formerly or presently, with the case first diligently investigated and traced, because it does not befit a bishop to protract an unrighteous case, then send a person instructed in the laws to our *comitatus*, where the nature of the case may be ascertained and concluded. Therefore, do not let the mind of your sanctity be burdened, nor be grieved at being accused by false words. An exonerated reputation is much better than if, with the ceasing of the complaints, the case had not been tried.

LETTER 4.45 (C. 507–11)

This letter orders the preparation of transportation and provisions for Herules visiting the Ostrogothic court at Ravenna. The reference to the Herules as petitioners (*supplices*) suggests envoys seeking an arrangement with the Ostrogothic kingdom. *Variae* 4.2 strongly suggests that a treaty involving military support had been formalized. It is not clear why leading citizens at Ticinum (Pavia) would facilitate the travel of Herules (typically associated with the Danubian region) westward to Ravenna.

King *Theoderic to the* Comites, Defensores, *and* Curiales of Pavia

1. We have ordered Herule petitioners to come to our *comitatus* according to our provisions, by the authority of God, for which conveyance by ship must be arranged, lest they seem to toil in vain, coming from their own province all the way to our country. And so be advised by the present decree, and without any delay prepare for them the use of a ship to Ravenna and provisions for five days, lest you should cause them to lack any necessities, to the extent that, with the discovery of abundance, they may realize that they have left behind a destitute province and that a foreign land would be more fruitful to them than their native country.

LETTER 4.46 (C. 507–11)

A letter to the *Comes* of Marseilles, directing him to assemble a jury to consider the property dispute of *Variae* 4.12. The *Comes* had previously judged the case, apparently outside of formal procedure, provoking complaint, although royal censure seems mild. The litigants are also offered the opportunity to send representatives to Ravenna.

King *Theoderic to Marabadus,* Vir Illustris

1. It is fitting that our devotion directs the petitions of supplicants to wholesome arrangements, since the hearts of subjects are relieved, however much the complaints of the aggrieved are settled. And so the *spectabilis* Liberius has reported to us in a lamentable petition that his own wife has been oppressed by your judgment, contrary to the provisions of the law. If this is so, let the case be tried in your presence and according to the laws among arbitrators removed from partiality whom the consensus of both parties has chosen. But if it is not possible to reach an end to this case in this way, we would not deny the parties permission to hasten instructed persons to our *comitatus,* if they still chose not to come themselves. Here, perhaps bribery would not be suspected, nor could treacherous deceit cause harm.

LETTER 4.47 (C. 507–11)

A lengthy letter to a *saio* charged with regulating the usage of the public post (*cursus publicus*). The letter seeks to remedy a number of abuses which had been common since the high empire.

King Theoderic to Gudisal, Saio

1. Those things known to be placed under constant use must be revived with careful attention. Given that, how might the conveyance of the post-horses suffice for the necessary task if they are permitted to be used beyond measure? Truly, a neglected stewardship is an inducement to wrongful presumptions. **2.** And so we have learned, from the report of our envoys,[18] that the post-horses are weakened by frequent misuse and that which we wish to preserve for public necessity, we know has been taken for use by private inclination. And therefore, we order you to reside at Rome in the command of the *Praefectus Praetorio* and the *Magister Officiorum*, whom public need will advise, so that you should permit neither Goth nor Roman to set out thence on public mounts, except those whom the *vices agentes* of the aforementioned offices will have sent forth.[19] **3.** And, because it is reported to us that this misappropriation occurs frequently, if anyone has perhaps attempted to claim post-horses from those unwilling agents to whom this care has been entrusted, whether it would be on account of his birth or rank, let him be compelled to bear the fine of one hundred *solidi* per horse, not because the harm to a single beast of burden is deemed so great, but because insolent abuse must be reprimanded by considerable loss. **4.** Henceforth, you should permit none of the *saiones* to make excursions, except for a purpose that has been ordered. He is permitted to travel and return only by one route. On much longer routes, let frequent changes of horse occur. **5.** Moreover, let none of the packhorses exceed a load of one hundred pounds. For we want those who must be dispatched to hasten unimpeded; we do not expect them to travel widely. Whoever carries many things with himself produces his own slothfulness; nor does one who prefers to haul himself about in luxuriously outfitted travel understand anything of speed. When the storks are about to cross the ocean, they clutch small pebbles in the claws of their feet, so that their lightness may not be pulled by excessive winds, nor is their native swiftness overburdened by unsuitable weight. Should not one who knows he has been chosen for public needs imitate this? And so let anyone who supposes a packhorse must bear more than one hundred pounds incur a further fine of fifty *solidi*, not only the courier, but also the muleteer. **6.** Moreover, we additionally expect you to have regard for those of the office of the post who are present in the city, to

18. *Legati*, apparently the envoys who used the *cursus publicus* most regularly.
19. *Vices agentes* were deputy assistants.

the extent that any digression from these mandates that is detected should be punished by your action according to the above-cited measures. However, if any intemperate person prefers the fine, we want the amount collected by the *vices agentes* to be applied to the purchasing agents of the changing stations,[20] so that the postal circuit might have a remedy where thus far it had assumed only inconvenience. 7. Thus, in worldly affairs prosperity often emerges from adversity, and when men desire to cause damage, they often impart something good. But fulfill everything thus, efficiently and diligently, so that, incited by your good accomplishments, we ought to entrust greater things to your devotion.

LETTER 4.48 (C. 507-11)

This brief letter grants a senator a leave of absence to Lucania for a period of eight months following the completion of his official duties in Rome. Eusebius is the future *Praefectus Urbis* of 523–24.

King Theoderic to Eusebius, Vir Illustris

1. After the tiresome anxieties of the bustling city and the burdensome troubles of official duties, your greatness desires to be refreshed by provincial pleasantries, claiming at the present time that you have extricated yourself from the requirements of your post, during which escape you desire to enjoy rural sweetness. 2. And since what is granted by our order is truly peace of mind, when the duration of your post has been completed, we grant by our authority a sabbatical of eight months in the pleasant retreats of Lucania. Let it be reckoned from the time when it happens that you set out from the city with divine favor. When those days have been spent, and with the anticipation of many people, hasten to return to your Roman home. You must return to the assembly of nobles and to a concourse worthy of your character.

LETTER 4.49 (C. 507-11)

A curiously short letter announcing the appointment of a man (probably as *comes*) over the Pannonian provinces of Siscia and Savia. Maintenance of order in this region seems to have been a recurring problem (cf. *Var.* 3.23–24). The reference to long-haired (*capillati*) *defensores* of the provinces may indicate that the *defensores* of Balkan provinces had assumed roles other than the traditional urban duties suggested for Italy elsewhere in the *Variae;* at the time, the Frankish kings were also styled as *capillati.*

---

20. Presumably for the purchase of new horses.

King Theoderic to All Provincials, the Long-haired Defensores, *and*
Curiales *Living in Siscia and Savia*

1. Strict observance of a royal decree ought never be undermined, so that dread
may restrain the audacious and that hope for future blessings may restore the
afflicted. For often, announcing a warning accomplishes more than punishment
settles. And therefore, with God's guidance, we have decided to set Fridibad over
your territories, one who may compass the rustlers of livestock with legal severity,
cut away homicide, condemn theft, and offer you, in place of criminal daring, a
peace which excessive presumption now rends to bits. Live in a well-ordered manner. Live instructed by good morals. Let no claim to birth or to distinction be an
excuse for public standing. It is necessary that one who falls in with depraved habits may be subject to the rod of punishment.

LETTER 4.50 (C. 511)

The last of the letters comprising the dossier of Faustus as *Praefectus Praetorio*, this
letter requests that Faustus assess the extent of damage done to agricultural production in Campania by the eruption of Vesuvius (c. 511). On this basis, he is to
reduce the tax burden for the province, although the natural history of volcanism
supplied by the letter suggests limited tolerance for revenue reduction in one of the
most productive provinces in Italy.

King Theoderic to Faustus, Praefectus Praetorio

1. Campanians have poured forth entreating tears to our clemency concerning the
devastating violence of Mount Vesuvius, to the effect that, being stripped of produce of the fields, they would be relieved from the weight of the payment of taxes.
Our devotion acquiesces to what ought to happen deservingly. **2.** But since unsub-
stantiated misfortune of any kind is doubtful to us, we order your magnitude to
send a man of proven devotion to the territory of Nola and Naples, where that
crisis threatens like a kind of domestic assault, so that with the very same fields
carefully inspected, the productivity of the landowner may be alleviated in the
amount that he has suffered: let the amount of the kindness be conferred, then, in
proportion to the measure of harm that is accurately assessed. **3.** For the province,
shorn of verdure of the soil, suffers this one evil, for which it is frequently agitated
by bitter fear, lest it should otherwise enjoy perfect happiness. But this harsh event
is not totally unbearable: it sends ahead pregnant signals, so that the adversities
may be endured more tolerably. **4.** For the orifice of this mountain murmurs, by
nature contending with the great mass, so that like a kind of disturbed spirit, it
terrifies the neighboring region with deep groaning. Then the airs of this place are
darkened with noisome exhalations and it is recognized throughout almost all of

Italy when this displeasure is stirred. Heated cinders fly for great distances and with earth-filled clouds blown aloft, it even rains ashen drops upon provinces across the sea. What Campania is able to endure is proclaimed when its misfortune is felt in other parts of the world.[21] **5.** You would behold ash moving as though a kind of river and, just as a liquid torrent, coursing in a boiling and sterile rush of sand. You would stand amazed at the furrows of fields suddenly filled over all the way to the highest tops of trees, and at fields suddenly wasted with doleful heat which had been painted with the most graceful verdure. But even while this perpetual furnace vomits forth pumice, fertile earth, which granted will be dry and burnt for long, having enclosed seeds, will soon produce varied shoots and restore even this great expanse which only shortly before had been wasted. Is this singular exception the reason that one mountain rages thus, so that it may be known to cause dread by the perturbation of the atmosphere in so many regions of the world and thus to disgorge its own substance everywhere, as though it seems to feel no loss? **6.** It bedews with ashes far and wide, although it belches shapeless heaps on nearby areas and a mountain that is exhausted by such great expenditure has been known for so many centuries. Who would believe such huge chunks, having fallen so far upon the plain, had boiled up from such a deep orifice and, escaping from the mouth of the mountain in the manner of a wind, projectiles spew as though mere chaff? **7.** Elsewhere nearby, great crags of earth are seen to glow with fire; it is given that these fires are noticeable nearly anywhere in the world. Therefore, for what reason should we not believe from the local inhabitants what may be known from testimony across the world? Therefore, as it has been said, let your prudence investigate this remarkable matter, and let you both confer assistance upon the afflicted and not provide grounds for fraud.

LETTER 4.51 (C. 507–11)

The last and most elaborate of Book 4, this letter addresses the father-in-law of Boethius, who would later become implicated in the treason trial against Boethius and executed. Here, the patrician is asked to undertake the restoration of the Theater of Pompey (originally built 61–55 B.C.), although the main purpose of the letter seems to be a learned disquisition on theater architecture and arts. The skepticism about the moral content of the theater may be understood either as the parroting of traditional ethics or a parody of how a great Roman senator ought to allocate his patronage. A similar attitude may be seen at *Variae* 5.42 with respect to wild animal hunts staged in the arena (*venationes*).

---

21. This may be a reference to the eruption of 472, which appears in Constantinopolitan sources such as the *Chronicle* of Marcellinus Comes.

King Theoderic to Symmachus, Patrician

1. Since you have so devoted your attention to private buildings that you may behold a kind of city having been made in your own home, it is right that you should be known for clothing Rome in the same marvels with which you have charmingly adorned your houses; you, who are a distinguished founder of buildings and an outstanding embellisher of the same, since to arrange their foundation aptly and to adorn existing ones agreeably both derive from wisdom. 2. For it is noted with how much commendation you have drawn Rome into its own suburb, so that, one who happens to enter these buildings does not feel himself to be beyond the city, until he recognizes himself to be in the midst of the pleasantries of the country. A most attentive imitator of the ancients, you are the noblest instructor of moderns. The buildings indicate your character, since no man is acknowledged for being attentive to them, except one who is found the most steeped in their nature. 3. And therefore, we believe the structure of the theater, pulling away from itself in a great mass, must be strengthened with your advice, so that what was granted by your founders as an adornment to the homeland should not seem diminished under a better posterity. For what may old age not unravel, which has already shaken such a strong structure? The mountains are reckoned to give way more easily than this solidity would be disturbed, so that, since the entire mass was thus derived from cliffs, except for the addition of refinements, it would also be considered to be natural. 4. We would perhaps be able to deny this, if it had not happened that we saw such a thing: those apsidal entrances of vaulting stonework thus arranged with structural supports concealed in a stately manner, so that you would believe them to be the grottos of lofty mountains more than you would think them to be anything fabricated. The ancients made a place equal to so great a people, so that those who were seen to obtain mastery of the world would have the most preeminent spectacle. 5. But since we deem this to be discourse with a learned man, it is fitting to trace back how it is read that rough antiquity founded these structures. When, on festal days, the cultivators of fields would celebrate the rites of diverse divinities throughout the groves and villages, the Athenians first gathered a rustic beginning to the urban spectacle, naming the place for observing with the Greek word *theater*, so that the gathering crowd might see without any hindrance to those standing at a distance. 6. However, the front of the theater is called a *scaena* from the dense shadows of the grove, where songs of various sorts were sung by the herdsmen at the commencement of spring. There, musical acts and the words of the wisest age flourished. But gradually it happened that the most honored disciplines, fleeing fellowship of a more degraded sort, withdrew itself out of consideration for modesty. 7. Tragedy is named for the vastness of the voice that seemed to produce the type of sound strengthened by hollow echoes, so that it could scarcely be believed to come from man. It is, however, based on a goat's

meter, since anyone among the herdsmen who pleased with a voice of such quality was given a goat in reward. Comedy was so called from the country village, for the country village is called the *comus,* where playing rustics used to mock human activities with joyful songs. **8.** To these was added the troop of garrulous pantomimes, talkative fingers, silent clamor with soundless expression, which is said to have been discovered by the Muse Polymnia, when she demonstrated that men could even declare their will without speech of the mouth. Indeed, in the eastern tongue the Muses are spoken of as the *homousae,*[22] because, just as the virtues, they may be seen to be reciprocally necessary to each other. Therefore, peaks of gentle feathers are depicted on their brows, since their perception meditates on lofty matters, uplifted with speedy thought. **9.** Then, when the pantomime, named for his many-faceted imitations, first advances onto the stage invited by applause, the harmonious chorus, skilled in various instruments, assists him. Then the hands of sensation display before the eyes a song of melodies and through composed signals teaches the appearance to the audience as though by a kind of writing, and in it they read the meaning of things and not by writing do they accomplish that which texts clarify. The same body depicts Hercules and Venus, a woman present in a man; it makes a soldier and a king, renders an old man and a youth, so that, in one person, you would believe there to be many, each distinctive by various performances. **10.** Moreover, the mime, who is now only considered with derision, was devised with such great care by Philistio that his performance was set down in writing, to the extent that by trivial thoughts it would calm a world seething with consuming cares. **11.** And what of the jingling of the *acetabula?* What of that melody carried on the varied strokes of sweet sound? It is listened to with such esteemed pleasure that, among other senses, men consider hearing to be the highest gift conferred upon them. Here the subsequent age has dragged this to vice, mixing the invention of the ancients with obscenities, and impelled what was discovered for the sake of honorable delight to the bodily pleasures of rash minds. **12.** The Romans, inanely incorporating these rites, just as other customs, into their republic, founded an edifice conceived from a lofty idea and wondrous generosity. It is rather from this that Pompey is not undeservingly believed to have been called the Great. And therefore, whether it could be held together with inserted rods or so great a building could be renewed with the application of new construction, we have taken care to send the funds to you from our private treasury, so that the fame of a fortunate undertaking may thus be acquired by you and antiquity may seem pleasingly renewed by our reign.

22. Of the same substance.

Book 5

Similar to previous books in the collection, this letter commences Book 5 with a diplomatic exchange, in this case with a little-known Germanic people of northern or central Europe. The interest in a local commodity offered by the Warni (swords of native manufacture) pairs with the following letter (*Var.* 5.2) to the Haesti. Interestingly, neither letter addresses a named individual. Both may owe to Cassiodorus's reading of Tacitus's *Germania,* which may offer first mention of the Warni.[1]

King Theoderic to the King of the Warni

1. With the pitch-black furs and slave boys glowing with foreign fairness, your fraternity has sent us swords of iron, more precious than the cost of gold, that cleave even armor. On them, a polished brightness gleams, so that the face of the admirer reflects with true clarity; their edges taper to points so evenly that they may be reckoned as fashioned, not with files, but in fiery furnaces where they were molded. Their mid-lengths seem to have been hollowed with a kind of elegant furrow, etched with curling patterns, where reflections of such great variety play that you would well believe clear metal has been blended with various colors. **2.** Your whetstone has carefully honed them and your finest sand has so meticulously polished them that it makes the steely light a kind of mirror for men. The sand has been bestowed by the native generosity of your country for the purpose that it would bring you special regard for this kind of work. The blades, by their very excellence, may be thought to be those of Vulcan, who was known to refine simple

---

1. Tacitus, *Germania* 40, on the Varini.

tools with such grace that whatever was fashioned from his hands was credited, not to mortal but to divine craftsmanship. **3.** Thence, through our envoys, *ille* and *ille*, who repay you the affection of an owed greeting, we declare that we have gladly accepted your arms, which have conveyed your concern for the blessings of peace. Our envoys offer a gift in exchange out of consideration for your expenses. Having arrived, may they grant as much satisfaction to you as yours were pleasing to us. Let divine providence bestow harmony, so that, achieving these things between us with good will, we may conjoin the will of our peoples and, in turn, be roused to obligations of mutual advantage.

LETTER 5.2 (C. 523-26)

A curious diplomatic letter to the Haesti, a people presumably settled along the Baltic shore. Like *Variae* 5.1, to the Warni, the basis of the exchange seems to be a native commodity (in this case, amber). In both cases, *Variae* 5.1 and 5.2 seem indebted to Cassiodorus's reading of Tacitus, here explicitly so.

King Theoderic to the Haesti

1. By the arrival of your legates, *ille* and *ille*, we have learned of your great eagerness to reach our attention, so that you, who are settled on the shores of the Ocean, have been conjoined to our intentions. Audience with them is both pleasing and quite flattering to us, in that our fame would have reached you, whom we have been unable to reach by any attempt. Enjoy the affection of one now known to you, whom unknown you sought by wandering course. For it is not an easy thing to arrange a route through so many nations. **2.** And therefore, being desirous of the amber that you have sent with carriers, we acknowledge you with affectionate greetings; your gifts have been received with a grateful disposition. And just as your report has maintained, the falling waves of the Ocean convey this lightest substance to you; but from whence it may come, which you have received in your country, offering it to all men, the bearers claim you to have no knowledge. It is read in the writing of a certain Cornelius that,[2] flowing from the sap of a tree, whence it is called *sucinum,* on the inmost islands of the Ocean, this substance gradually hardens in the heat of the sun. **3.** Indeed, it becomes a perspired metal, with a transparent delicacy, sometimes glowing red with golden tincture, sometimes enriched with flaming brilliance, so that, by the time it has floated to the bounds of the sea, cleansed and deposited by alternating tides,[3] it is surrendered

---

2. Cornelius Tacitus, *Germania* 45, attributes the collection of amber along the seashore to the Aestii.

3. The *aestus* of *aestu alternante purata* refers both to the heat of the amber's appearance and the tumult of its supposed conveyance on the ocean.

to your shores. On that account, we decided that this must be related, lest you should think what you consider to be your secret has completely escaped our notice. Thence, seek us more often along that route that your desire has opened, since the search for riches always procures harmony among kings, who, while they are comforted by small gifts, always provide greater things in compensation. Moreover, we have committed certain matters to words for you through your envoys. These things that we have sent ought to be pleasing.

LETTER 5.3 (C. 524)

This letter announces to the recipient his elevation to the office of *Quaestor*. At the time, Cassiodorus, who formerly held the same office (507–11), served as *Magister Officiorum*.

King Theoderic to Honoratus, Vir Illustris, *and* Quaestor

1. It is indeed a good practice that the deserving receive our gifts, but you have arrogated to yourself the favors of the *Princeps* by right of heredity. Accept the office of your brother, since you are both twins in wisdom. We do not drive away from the same blessings one whom we similarly approve. The parents have now gone and the sons emulate their study of the good arts with the incentive of resemblance. We have made it a new law in you to succeed family in administration.[4] Here, a promoted man is not lost and exchanged. Since it is fitting that a person should be chosen as a substitute, it is nonetheless not a loss that a most deserving brother should acquire the office. **2.** Oh, how faithfully have you been chosen for your merits and honored by the omen of your names![5] The parents had a certain foreknowledge in setting names upon the offspring, and since knowledge of the foreshadowed was furnished, the course of affairs to come is from the highest command of divine authority. It is claimed that we say what we do not realize we were aware of, but that after the fact, we become aware that what we had unknowingly said is true. **3.** Decoratus, therefore, was thoroughly demarcated in such a way; chosen, I say, and having been praised in our judgment, he associated with palatine offices, claiming that dignity which we are accustomed to give to the wise, clearly obtaining what he was able to achieve beyond others subsequently chosen. He was indeed bold under the scrutiny of our patronage,[6] but he stood reverently at our side, silent when appropriate, fully spoken in need, a distinguished comfort

---

4. Succession of family members in public office was obviously the norm, but perhaps is remarkable here for having someone succeed to the same office of his brother, although Boethius's two sons had been consular colleagues in 522.

5. Here referring both to Honoratus and his brother Decoratus, names synonymous with being ennobled by high office.

6. Here *genius* is translated as "patronage"; Cassiodorus's use of the term is rare.

to our cares, and he would have been enriched by the indulgence of our authority, except that, contented more with praise of character, he counted himself among ordinary men. He lives among us in the recollection of good men, since the fidelity of men knows not how to fail with death. He concealed our secret counsels as though he had forgotten them. He upheld our commands as though he had written them line for line, serving without avarice and seeking our gratitude with the greatest zeal. **4.** Indeed, we rightly turn to praises of a deserving man, but adopting an economy of speech, when we refer to him, we teach you. He was undoubtedly pleasing, because he has not ceased to be in our presence even after death. Sadly do we seek for one whom we are grieved to lose. But he has softened the bitter event because you succeed him with substituted excellence, since no man feels he has lost what he knows has been found in another. You, for whom such great familial honors have been familiar, do not follow an unknown example. You are Decoratus through him and he is Honoratus through you.[7] Merits unite with one another when their names conjoin them together so. **5.** For we rightly expect better things from you who follow, since the imitator is ever more assiduous than the original, when it is fitting to choose blessings from precedent and to accumulate new ones. And therefore we elevate you to the dignity of *Quaestor* for the third indiction and we cause an Honoratus man to thrive in the brilliance of our court, so that you may now commence being what before you had been called. Act now by cleaving to justice, so that we who grant honor to the untested may confer better things upon you when you are proven.

LETTER 5.4 (C. 524)

This letter to the Senate confirms the elevation of Honoratus to the office of *Quaestor* (cf. *Var.* 5.4).

King Theoderic to the Senate of Rome

1. It is certain, conscript fathers, that your assembly flourishes with wise men, but it is considered remarkable also because the distinction of letters has mingled with your company. For we deem each man whom we raise to the peak of *Quaestor* to be most learned, the kind of man for whom it is proper to be a prophet of the laws and a partner in our counsels. We speak of that distinction that is found neither among riches nor in birth alone, but only that wisdom which is possible to attain when combined with learning. For it is permitted that we would confer favors upon the various offices, hence do I always consent. This portion of our cares is truly happy; it crosses the threshold of our thoughts; it is acquainted with our

---

7. Again a play on the names of the brothers, literally, "You are adorned through him and he is honored through you."

heart, in which cares are commonly enmeshed. **2.** Consider what ought to be thought concerning a man who would become a partner to such intimacy. Experience in legal matters is demanded of such a man, for there converge the wishes of supplicants, and, what is more precious than any treasure, the fame of our civic harmony rests in this man's keeping. The privy confidence of the innocent becomes secure with a righteous *Quaestor,* the desires of the untoward return only anxieties, and when the expectation of filching is taken from the wicked, a zeal for good character is invited. **3.** He protects the rights of everyone as his own, being restrained with money, profligate with equity, he knows not how to cheat, but is the most prepared to assist. He protects with the nature of a *Princeps* what he lords over all. He is known to speak in the voice of the very one to whom no man may be found equal. Is it not worthy that a colleague of yours be one who is able to discharge this office in our presence, free from vice and full of virtue? You know well by what stock this candidate is glorified. **4.** Recall, therefore, Decoratus, toiling at the labors of the advocate, by what probity he bound himself to the cause of any good man. He was at hand as an orator, faithful to our causes; pleading important trials, he represented the intention of the one judging to the seats of those approved to sit in court, for which merit he often attained honors, since he wisely attended to matters requiring delegation. For those who conduct themselves first according to the law know not how to bear the sacrifice of decency. Inferior to former consuls in rank, he presented himself as their patron, and when he was considered unequal to your offices, a patrician is said to have retained him for a celebrated trial. **5.** It is especially rare, conscript fathers, to speak firmly, and, when one needs to say many things, to avoid protraction. This was most certain in Decoratus, and this you approve even in advance of our own opinion. For who in his own tenure was able to ignore him, as though he were a governor over legal controversy? One who did not seek his assistance truly had little use for the laws. We do not complain over his swift death now; a brother has sprouted from that fertile stock of his. For one who was first covered by the shadow of a brother, with the latter removed by the law of nature, has fully extended the rays of his own fame into the open. **6.** Indeed, the one who prevailed to be first in order of birth, ripening prematurely, fittingly bore a shoot of good fruits; but that noble germination has preserved in a successor that fruit which it lost in the predecessor. The branch harmonizes with that family, that ennobled man who ever springs to mind in the poem of Virgil, "Even with this one torn away, the other golden branch fails not, and it puts forth leaves of the same metal."[8] And indeed, this man has nurtured a facility in legal advocacy. Yielding to the reputation of his brother at Rome, he preferred to involve himself in the legal affairs of the citizens of Spoleto, an affair acknowledged the more difficult as it was removed from your wisdom. He was certainly most accomplished at affixing

8. Virgil, *Aeneid* 6.143.

righteous judgments to men of good character; but exceedingly difficult with provincials conducting themselves with inconsistent license. **7.** He seems to have persuaded the moderation of law, where even the very judges regularly plundered with shameful cupidity and whenever they saw something among men of middling means that especially pleased them, they could not bear to be obstructed from their own desires. It is difficult to punish in courts such as those and for the strength of great conviction to recall the corruption of judges to the design of rectitude. Therefore, conscript fathers, gladly accept our judgment and with rejoicing take Honoratus to your bosom, elevated to the peak of *Quaestor.* For it is right that one who has deserved to be found equal to such offices should be esteemed by you.

LETTER 5.5 (C. 523–26)

Restricting abuses in the use of the public post (*cursus publicus*) required constant effort, and this letter orders a *saio* to police the use of mounts for the postal system with strict oversight. The letter seems to be a reiteration of demands made earlier at *Variae* 4.47.

King Theoderic to Mannila, Saio

1. It is praiseworthy to strengthen stewardship in that portion of the administration which has been established with great care for the necessities of the republic. For through this, both utility for envoys and the speed of our commands is managed. Moreover, here it assists, by varied commands, tasks accomplished by powerful courtiers; there it enriches our treasury with frequent dues, so that hardly anything is undertaken in the republic that is not completed with the assistance of the post. Consequently, it is fitting that what is deemed appropriate for the public advantage should always be prepared, lest, what was devised for speed should introduce an unsuitable slowness rather than haste. **2.** And therefore, whereas the *Praefectus Praetorio* and the *Magister Officiorum* may assign those contracted on behalf of the public advantage, we order you to curtail the wrongful abuse of those transgressing use of the post with such a severity that, if anyone, whether Goth or Roman, should presume to attain a mount without our requisition, or that of those officials whom it concerns, he should be compelled by you to pay, on the spot, one hundred *solidi* per horse. And we also demand the same severity concerning those who presume to claim postal mounts beyond the number requisitioned. **3.** But we also command that not more than one hundred pounds should be loaded onto a packhorse. For it is exceedingly absurd that a creature from which swiftness is demanded should be oppressed with a great weight. The very bird becomes slow with a burdensome load. Ships which do not feel their toil move more ponderously when full. What might a beast of burden accomplish, when, burdened to excess, it succumbs? Moreover, if anyone will be found to hold only a slight measure more than the limit, let him bear the fine of two ounces of gold. **4.** We warn that this important demand ought to be executed immediately, just as it has been arranged in former edicts, through the office of the postal ministry. For it is right that this abuse, from whence it is known that the public horses have been badly overburdened, should be coerced to pay. Let the man who does not want to be hastened by his own will be unfettered by his own loss. In addition, we remind that you should not presume upon the prerogatives of the *praepositi*,[9] nor should you disgrace by any seizure that which hallowed antiquity has sanctioned those in power to have. For we want to strengthen stewardship through you, not to remove the precautions of ancient custom.

LETTER 5.6 (C. 523-26)

This letter orders the restitution of overdue rents from an individual who had contracted to manage several royal estates (*praedia nostrae domus*). A *comitiacus* is ordered to assign a lien on the individual's private property in satisfaction of the debt. Because the matter concerns royal estates, the *comitiacus* was an agent of the *Comes Patrimonii*. Further details concerning the case appear at *Variae* 5.7.

King Theoderic to Stabularius, Comitiacus

1. A measure must be taken that does not act contrary to public advantage and that seeks a remedy encompassing the desires of private individuals, so that these concerns may not seem to produce a loss to us. And so we have learned in the complaint of the *clarissimus* Johannus that Thomas has taken responsibility for certain estates of our household, that is, *illud* and *illud,* and now has postponed the return of ten thousand *solidi* for our advantage and, through diverse ploys, does not pay the owed amount. This has also been made perfectly clear to us by the report of our court officials.[10] **2.** Therefore, we believe that provisions must be made for such a remedy that you ought to apply a lien to all the property of the aforementioned Thomas on behalf of a public debt, to the extent that, if, by the Kalends of September, less than what is reasonably expected will have been paid by Thomas, let the aforementioned property be deeded to the *clarissimus* Johannus, who has promised to pay the debt owed to our treasury. But if the aforementioned Thomas should somehow be able to pay his obligation within the predetermined time, let all property that has been taken from him be returned undiminished, so that thus, our fisc may not be seen to suffer a disadvantage and we may be known to offer the expected justice to our subjects. We would be able to delay even beyond this point

---

9. Military officers and heads of administrative bureaus.

10. Whereas Johannus was a treasury official in charge of balancing accounts (*arcarius*), the other officials confirming his report are here described as *proceres,* which is a general term ("court officials"), rather than a specific appointment.

if anything were produced in favor of this most irresponsible individual, whom we have ever found to be unwilling for such a very long period of time.

LETTER 5.7 (C. 523-26)

This letter assigns the property of a debtor to an official of the treasury (*arcarius*). As described at *Variae* 5.6, this official would have the right to claim the debtor's entire property, should he default on the debt, with the understanding that the treasury official would then be required to pay the debt. The letter also suggests that the official may have used this opportunity as leverage to marry the debtor's daughter.

King Theoderic to Johannus, Vir Clarissimus *and* Arcarius

1. It is proper to confirm a valid settlement to the wishes of those who prefer to maintain public advantage, nor do we permit those who secure us from loss to be troubled about their own loss. Hence, we have learned from your report that the estates of our patrimony situated in the province of Apulia, that is, *illud* and *illud*, were entrusted in a lease agreement for a previous indiction to the honorable Thomas, but that he has postponed payment to the public account for the indictions *illa* and *illa*, up to the amount of ten thousand *solidi*, on account of poorly administering the undertaken property. This man, frequently warned by our court officials to return the debt,[11] has disdained the demand with spiteful cunning. And lest any complaint should come forth against you in the future, you declare your wish to satisfy the amount owed to the public advantage under the condition that the estates of the above-mentioned debtor should be deeded to you in the form of a mortgage. **2.** Hence it is that we confirm your request in the present order, having been drawn up in the appropriate manner. First, let you fear no suit in the name of this contract. Furthermore, under these conditions, we award to you the entire properties of the debtor, Thomas, which he either holds now or was formerly in possession of when he then became hostile to our agreement, and which not long ago we had claimed with liens affixed in our name. **3.** We will relax this injunction only out of a consideration of kindness, if he should return the amount owed within the period before the kalends of September. If not, provided that, on the above-mentioned day, you will have brought the money that is owed to our *illustris Comes Patrimonii*, just as we have said, all resources of Thomas will be given for your profit. We do not hold it to be harsh for the one losing, when he is not seen to lose the property in whole, because it is known that he has acquired a son-in-law in you. For what you had been able to claim by right of succession, he will possess from you under the conditions of a purchase.

---

11. *Proceres;* see the previous note.

LETTER 5.8 (C. 523-26)

An unusually brief letter on a familiar theme, this letter orders a former consul and possibly governor to transport stone to Ravenna from Faventina (modern Faenza). The request for *quadrati* may imply quarried stone (cf. *Var.* 3.9, 3.10).

King Theoderic to Anastasius, Consularis

1. It is agreeable for your sublimity to offer assiduous constancy in obedience to our orders, to the extent that what has been arranged by wholesome planning is drawn to completion. Nonetheless, an unfulfilled command may be completed moderately and with wisdom, and a delegated task knows how to be managed by reasonable deliberation, without the blemish of ingratitude. **2.** And therefore, we order you to arrange public administration in the city of Faventina, so that stone blocks may be hauled to Ravenna, per our order, without harm or loss to anyone, to the extent that we may be pleased by the completion of our desire and an opportunity for provoking complaints may be preempted.

LETTER 5.9 (C. 523-26)

Similar to *Variae* 5.8, an uncharacteristically brief letter addressed to an important topic, in this case the construction of a new city in the region of the Italian Alps. The landowners (*possessores*) are ordered to share in the construction of portions of the new city wall (cf. *Var.* 3.48).

King Theoderic to the Possessores of Feltria

1. The public concern of many ought to be addressed with devotion, since it is not proper that few should undertake what stands to assist many, lest royal commands should weaken from disinterest, while a useful undertaking is delegated to those unfit for its completion. Therefore, our authority has ordered a city to be built in the region of Tridentum.[12] **2.** But since the scarcity of the region is unable to sustain the magnitude of the operation, our disquiet concerning this has ascertained that you, who are near the area, should each undertake an assigned portion of wall by agreeing upon a fee to be received, to the extent that what was known to have been perhaps impossible for a few may be completed more surely with relative ease. Let it be clearly defined with this stipulation, that no man may be excused from this duty, whence not even the divine household is excepted.[13]

---

12. The term *civitas* at least suggests an urban center with full municipal duties and amenities.

13. *Divina domus* probably refers to the imperial household (i.e., the household of the king), although it may also mean the local church.

LETTER 5.10 (C. 523-26)

A letter to a *saio*, ordering him to arrange transport for Gepid soldiers for the continued protection of Gaul. The soldiers have been awarded a stipend to prevent them from forcibly seizing needed supplies during the passage to Gaul. A shorter letter announces this provision to the Gepids at *Variae* 5.11.

King Theoderic to Veranus, Saio

1. While that most fortunate army is lead forth, with God's blessing, for the common defense, it must be provided for, lest either the very soldiers are worn out with unexpected lack of resources or, what is heinous to say, our provinces should be seen to endure a depredation. For the first step of prosperity is not to be harmful to one's self, so that, we should not seem to afflict the wealth of those for the benefit of whom we toil. **2.** And therefore, we have chosen your devotion in the present dictate, so that you might make the multitude of Gepids, which we have caused to hasten to Gaul for the sake of its protection, to pass through Venetia and Liguria with every restraint. Lest an opportunity is provided for destroying anything, our generosity has arranged a payment of three *solidi* for each household,[14] so that instead of a desire for pillaging our provincials, there would be the capacity for commerce. **3.** Our indulgence openly grants this to those laboring on behalf of peace for everyone, so that, if their wagons are stricken by the long route or if their beasts languish, having been worn out, they may exchange with landowners without any oppression, according to your supervision and guidance, so that they should be given animals better in size or quality, although they may be satisfied with animals of poor health, since life is uncertain for those who are exhausted with excessive fatigue. Let it happen thus, lest transports should fail their needs and any man should find himself in such a reversal of fortunes.

LETTER 5.11 (C. 525-26)

Following from the directive sent to a *saio* (*Var.* 5.10), this letter announces to Gepid soldiers the provision of a stipend from the *annona* to satisfy their needs during travel to Gaul.

King Theoderic to the Gepids Sent to Gaul

1. Indeed, it was by our arrangement that we ordered a means for spending the *annona* for your activities. But lest payment in kind should prove difficult either in

---

14. The word *condoma* appears elsewhere (Gregory the Great, *Epistulae*) as a measure of land; hence the phrase *per condamam,* used in reference to an unspecified number of soldiers, likely indicates a unit of Gepid soldiers travelling as a "household"; this was a one-time payment for travel expenses, not a soldier's salary.

itself or from spoiling, we have chosen to arrange a payment for you in gold, of three *solidi* per household,[15] so that you will be able to choose lodgings, and an appropriate amount of fodder should be available to you, and what is even more fitting for you, that you ought to purchase it. For this measure causes even the landowners to hasten, if it is known that you pay for necessities. Set forth with good fortune, travel with moderation. Let your route be the kind that befits those who labor on behalf of the health of all men.

LETTER 5.12 (C. 523–26)

Yet another complaint against Theodahad (cf. *Var.* 4.39), this letter orders Theoderic's nephew to restore a property seized by his men or to send a representative to court for a formal hearing. The petitioners are family of the deceased former *Praefectus Urbis* Argolicus.

King Theoderic to Theodahad, Vir Illustris

1. If we command all men to respect and cherish justice, how much more fitting is it that those who are glorified by relation to us should conduct everything in praiseworthy fashion, so that they would be capable of demonstrating the brilliance of the royal family? For it is an unquestioned nobility which is proven to be adorned by good character; it is the sweet advantage of fame to avoid the foul profit of money. **2.** And so the heirs of the *illustris* Argolicus and the *clarissimus* Amandianus have complained in a petition submitted to us that the estate Pallentiana, which our generosity had transferred to them as compensation, since by this benefit they were paid for the loss of the Arbitana house, has been unbecomingly assailed by your men for no apparent reason and thence to have caused the crime of illegal seizure where an example of glorious restraint ought to be provided. **3.** For which reason, if these claims are not repudiated as lies, let your grandness restore what has been taken. Furthermore, if you believe anything can be put forward on your behalf, send to our *comitatus* a representative instructed in the law to the fullest measure, so that a formal hearing may obtain an end with civility according to the laws. For certain, no matter what is decided in court there, it will be attributed to your deception and you will suffer great harm to your reputation, since such things are unavoidable in legal contentions. Here, however, cases are compared according to their own strengths and any common citizen is given a decision without partiality, when justice is prevailed upon in person.

---

15. *Per condamam*; see the note 14 above, at *Var.* 5.11.

LETTER 5.13 (C. 523–26)

Addressed to two individuals connected with the distribution of the *annona,* this letter orders the payment of provisions to the army. The location of the army is not indicated, but the officials are reminded that soldiers are wont to seize supplies when their daily needs are neglected. Note a similar order at *Variae* 2.5. Eutropius and Agroecius were probably attached to the *officium* of the *Praefectus Praetorio.*

King Theoderic to Eutropius and Agroecius

1. You ought to expend your enthusiasm for the republic with a cheerful disposition, since we have known well from experience how to offer many blessings to the deserving. For we promise an exchange in consideration of devotion, even when we arrange everything on your behalf. And so we believe that you must be reminded in the present order that you ought to offer the appointed *annona* to the army, to the extent that they should not be overlooked by an intention adverse to them, nor ought harmful plunder burden the provincials. For it is most advantageous that the army is restrained under the law of expenses, as it would waste everything if permitted. Rash seizure neglects to observe moderation, nor is it able to be restrained under any measure, for which license will have been granted. For which reason let the army obtain the designated amount of sustenance, lest on that account a region is permitted to endure the injury indicated.

LETTER 5.14 (C. 523–26)

Addressed to an *illustris* senator who probably held official position as governor in Savia, this letter directs attention to a wide range of issues plaguing the administration of the province. Fiscal corruption similar to that found at *Variae* 2.24 is the main focus, but also the abuse of the prerogatives of provincial officials and marriage between Romans and "barbarians." The sweeping problems facing provincial administration in Savia compare well to those illustrated by the letter concerning Spain (*Var.* 5.39).

King Theoderic to Severinus, Vir Illustris

1. The reason of justice urges to restrain those transgressing, so that it may be possible for the sweetness of peace to spread to all men. For by what means is equitability achieved if the resources of ordinary citizens are not permitted to increase? And so, we have often learned in the complaints of our provincials that the wealthy landowners of Savia have not only abandoned to a tenuous fate the duty of taxes on their houses, but next that they have even attached something of a criminal commerce to their own profits, so that public payments have become a private enterprise. **2.** We truly desire this to be corrected by as many officials as possible, but thus far it seems to have been delayed to your own glory, inasmuch as fidelity is considered more welcome when you so thoroughly prove your enthusiasm after the negligence of many. And therefore, we order you to investigate all landowners with the wisdom for which you are noted and with deliberate justice, and herein to measure the equity of the tax with reason, so that the public tax may be imposed according to the standing of the man and his property, and with that corruption that has been practiced by some thoroughly removed from everything. For thus is justice achieved and the resources of our provincials are supported. **3.** Those, however, who are found to have imposed a tax assessment without our instruction and who, according to their own pleasure, have cast the burden of certain obligations onto others, let the severity of the law follow hard upon them, so that they may mend every injury to those to whom they have heedlessly caused losses. We further order that this must be investigated so that the amount of tax payments among the *defensores,* the *curiales,* and the landowners may be ascertained and, likewise, whatever a landowner should prove he has paid beyond the contribution of *solidi* for the recently collected eighth indiction, lest it happen that he has not declared in correct measure the payment made to our treasury or for the expenses necessary to managing the province. Let unjust seizure be corrected to the fullest extent. **4.** Moreover, do not suppose that this measure should be ignored, so that if this expense which the accountant reckons is not reasonably disclosed in our privy chamber, let it be returned from the one unjustly withholding it. For is it not so absurd that our generosity, which we want to be of use to all, is now hampered by the profit stolen by a few? **5.** Also, the judges of the province, both *curiales* and *defensores,* are said to impose unwarranted expenses on the landowners as much for travel as for other matters. We order you to investigate this and to correct it under the measure of the law. **6.** Let the former barbarians, who have chosen to be associated with Roman women in the bond of marriage, and for whom it pleases to have sought legally documented estates, be compelled to pay the fisc for the ownership of land and to obey the imposition of extraordinary imposts.[16] **7.** Furthermore, let a Roman judge approach each town once per year, and, on account of expenses to the provincials, which are reported to burden the poor, they may be offered no more than three days' *annona,* just as they were provided by the precautions of the laws. For our ancestors had intended the circuit of the judges not as a burden but as an advantage to the provincials. **8.** The attendants of the *comes* of the Goths and also of the managers of the royal estates are said to have stolen certain things from the provincials by ingenious threats: with these matters

---

16. The "former barbarians" (*antique barbari*) are likely federated allies settled in the region, or their direct descendants, who previously maintained certain immunities from public obligations on account of their military service. This clause of the edict seeks to clarify their status and obligations to the state.

determined under legal inquiry, your justice will discover whatever has been done unjustly by this party and will arrange matters legally with delays avoided. **9.** Therefore, concerning these matters that pertain to both the provincials and public resources, we want you to conduct everything with investigations that, in every step, ought not to depart from our mild approach. Our foresight has reflected upon this matter sensibly, so that the public records may be ordered to be updated with everything found by your careful and diligent examination, to the extent that evidence may reveal your good faith and, after this, nothing that we would want to avoid may crop up from seeds of deceit.

LETTER 5.15 (C. 525–26)

This letter announces to the landowners (*possessores*) of Savia the appointment of Severinus (cf. *Var.* 5.14) to investigate widespread fiscal abuses. Primary attention is given to the trustworthiness of Severinus and his incorruptibility as the king's representative.

King Theoderic to All Possessores Living in the Province of Savia

1. It is permitted, God willing, that our *comitatus* may grant justice to all who toil and thence remedies descend from subjects to other members of the *regnum* as though from a living font; for all that, being moved to our native piety by your frequent petitions, we have determined both to grant equity to you and to dismiss the fatigue of long journey, since that assistance is sweeter which is obtained without obstacles. **2.** And so we have sent the *illustris* and great Severinus, a man instructed in our policies, so that he might accomplish among you what he knows has always been pleasing to us. For he has seen in our company how the just man may be regarded as respectable, how the blessing of our radiance may smile upon good acts. He practices to perfection what we joyfully hope to receive; rapacity cannot be cherished by a restrained *Princeps* who takes no pleasure in bribery. Therefore, let the tumult of complaints boldly converge on him. Let the oppressed man hope for some measure of relief from outrage. **3.** We have removed the hardship of quarrels from you, since crimes committed are cut short at their very origin. Let the man burdened with the baggage of another's taxes cry out without any trepidation, for he is about to receive that succor to be had from the laws. Thus have we indeed promised, since harm may not come to the innocent through those whom our policies have set in place. Truly have we ordered the kind of things that would be arranged in support of your peace and the equitability of the taxes; these, our decrees, which we have given to the above-mentioned *illustris* Severinus, are declared to the people, so that afterward, he may clearly acknowledge anyone who ought to petition.

LETTER 5.16 (C. 523–26)

A fascinating letter ordering the *Praefectus Praetorio* to assemble a fleet to serve Italy's commercial and military needs. Furnishing timber and sailors for one thousand light war vessels may be connected also to the deterioration of relations with either the eastern empire or the Vandal court at Carthage. A sense of these ambitions appears in a connected letter (*Var.* 5.17).

King Theoderic to Abundantius, Praefectus Praetorio

1. Although it is by continual habit that we ponder things profitable for the republic, and to that end we command what would be the most pleasing to all, since potential benefits are known to all, it must nevertheless be accomplished in such a way that the intention of the *Princeps* ought to appear onerous to none. For even things that have been very clearly considered, if not acted upon well, are unrewarding; moreover, only that which is praised both for its intention and its execution is said to have been perfectly accomplished. 2. Therefore, since it vexes our mind with frequent anxiety that Italy possesses no ships, where such a great abundance of timber would assist, so that she might export goods sought after even by other provinces, we have determined, with God's guidance, to take upon ourselves the immediate construction of one thousand dromonds, which would be able to convey the public grain and, if necessary, to oppose hostile ships. But we seek the completion of a project so great that we believe it must be administered by the attention of your grandeur. 3. And therefore, let instructed craftsmen seek throughout all Italy for the wood suitable for the work, and wherever you should find cypresses and pines near to the shore, let there be regard for a given price agreeable to the owners. For this is the only timber which may be designated by an assessed value; others are not needed to be appraised by virtue of their own worthlessness. 4. But lest our foresight should languish, abandoned in the midst of the endeavor, we order you at the same time to prepare, with divine assistance and with due moderation, a suitable number of sailors. And if someone considered necessary for this project happens to be the slave of another man, either hire him for service in the fleet or, if he should want more for this, grant the right of his own freedom for a price reasonable according to market value. If a selected individual enjoys his own freedom, let him receive the appropriate portion of the *annona* and a donative of five *solidi*. 5. And those who have put off their former masters must be likewise treated in this manner, since it is a kind of freedom to serve a ruler (for often it is thought by those enduring labor, whom the collar of a strict master has oppressed). Thus, for this reason, the above-mentioned sailors ought to receive from your office two or three *solidi*, depending on the quality of the man, in the name of a commission, to the extent that anyone, because he has been paid, ought to be prepared to present himself for duty. For certain, we conclude that fishermen

should not be included in this provision, since one who is retained for providing delicacies would be grievously lost, when it is the custom of one to furrow the teeming shoreline, and of the other to hazard the raging winds.

LETTER 5.17 (C. 525–26)

A sequel to the previous order to assemble a fleet (*Var.* 5.16), this letter congratulates the *Praefectus Praetorio* for the completion of his previous project and orders him to assemble the fleet at Ravenna. It is difficult to imagine construction of a fleet within the several years of Abundantius's tenure in office and the letter seems to equivocate between actual completion and desired completion.

King Theoderic to Abundantius, Praefectus Praetorio

1. You have eagerly taken in hand what required accomplishment, since the approach of completion has already occurred, when an anticipation already fulfilled prevented the weariness of the labor, and it is a great inducement to believe that these aims are completed. Truly not long ago, we ordered your grandeur to prepare a commission of sailors from the shores of Italy, so that a fully outfitted band of oarsmen should support the dromonds that you had prevailed to construct with industry. But you, in answer to our judgment and request, have produced what was sought and have shown how an unconditional completion could be accomplished by the most effective means. You have so soon reported as finished what could hardly be believed as begun, that the construction of the fleet has been completed with haste almost equal to the speed with which a ship is accustomed to sail. 2. Nor have words alone been the demonstration: you have so suddenly placed before our eyes a forest of ships, a town afloat, an infantry of sails, which would lack no labor, but which steadfast men may bring to the appointed anchorage, each a trireme that provides conveyance for such a great number of oarsmen but carefully conceals the faces of the men. We have read that the Argonauts first devised this. And it is deemed to be both fitting for warfare and suitable for commerce, so that, we who once gazed upon foreign fleets now may send both terror and enticement alike to other provinces. 3. You have furnished a restored republic with your accomplishment. What does the republic not have for which the Greek may fault us and the African insult us?[17] Envious, they see flourishing for us that means by which they had fulfilled their own desires at great cost. Now prepare the rigging for planned ventures, sails serving as the wings particular to ships, that winged linen, the very spirit of the headlong keel, the harbinger of the merchant, the silent helpmate of sailors, the gentle favor by which they conclude

---

17. Indication that the construction of the fleet was connected to relations with Vandalic North Africa and the eastern empire.

what is hardly deemed practicable for the swiftest of birds. **4.** Isis suspended a sail on the first barge, when, with the boldness of feminine devotion, she searched throughout the seas for her son Horus.[18] Thus, while maternal affection hastened her to fulfill her desire, she was seen to reveal something unknown to the world. And therefore, with divine assistance approving us, whose virtue it is to execute the wishes of men, let the entire host of ships assemble at Ravenna on the next ides of June, to the end that the endeavor may be brought rejoicing to the fullest conclusion at a close destination. **5.** But since, with God's blessing, we have wanted to increase the number of dromonds, if it will be possible to find any of the timber necessary for their construction along either shore of the Po River, we order it to be removed with no man's objection, since we only want any lumber thus found to be granted for the present operation without disadvantage to the owners. Let our Po send native ships to the open sea and let those firs, which he raised, nourished by flowing streams, learn to prevail over the mass of maritime swells. **6.** Moreover, we especially agree that what we learned has happened from your report must be dealt with, lest in rivers wandering through diverse territories that you would navigate, anyone should dare to confine the channels at any time for the purpose of fishing. Let those that have been disgracefully seized (that is, on the Mincius, Ollius, Anser, Arno, and the Tiber) be returned immediately. Let a river stand open to the passage of ships; let it suffice to seek out delicacies for human desires with the accustomed practices, not to entangle the liberty of the river with rustic inventions, lest, and it is criminal to mention it, private pleasure should seem to stand in the way of the common weal.

LETTER 5.18 (C. 525–26)

A brief and elliptical letter which seems to announce the official commencement (*adventus*) of the newly constructed fleet (cf. *Var.* 5.16 and 5.17), and furthermore orders the *Comes Patrimonii* to surrender timber harvested from royal estates for the shipbuilding effort.

King Theoderic to Wilia, Vir Illustris *and* Comes Patrimonii

1. Just as public advantage has regard for the preservation of all things, thus it ought to be accomplished with the devotion and labor of all men, since it is an occasion for great praise, if something is known to be fulfilled so singularly for the common cause. For even one who knows he has profited himself nonetheless should be commended for what he accomplishes for others. Consequently, recall that we commanded that ship masters should be sought out for our *regnum*. **2.** We ordered these men to assemble together, God willing, at Ravenna on the ides of

18. Given here as Harpocran or Harpocrates in some manuscripts.

June, so that the commencement of their newly constructed fleet might be appropriately offered, lest divided efforts would seem to produce a particular hesitancy and one would be like the other in finishing, unless the commencement should happen to involve all parties. **3.** Moreover, if any lumber suitable for constructing drommonds will happen to be found on royal estates along the shore of the Po, by granted permission, they must be removed by the great *Praefectus Praetorio,* Abundantius, for those craftsmen deputed for this project. For we want to set this example by our own estates, so that an order that constrains even the *Princeps* should be unbearable to no man.

LETTER 5.19 (C. 525–26)

This letter relates to other previous communications concerning the construction of the new fleet (*Var.* 5.16–18), by deputing a *saio* to assist with mobilizing the naval personnel needed to attend the first full assembly of the fleet.

King Theoderic to Gudinandus, Saio

1. Whoever effectively brings unfinished endeavors to completion causes himself to be entrusted to greater things, since it is without a doubt that something has been entrusted to a man approved of as the best, and his honorable selection is evidence of the favorable judgment of his superior. And therefore, we command you to hasten to that province under the supervision of the grand *Praefectus Praetorio,* Abundantius, and the grand *Comes Patrimonii,* Wilia, so that, following the former commands, you may urge those provided for as sailors, as much from the royal household as those living in other places, to hasten to Ravenna, with God's blessing, on the ides of June, to the extent that no delay may be tolerated with respect to such important orders. Take care, therefore, lest bribery should stain you, or the shame of neglect envelop you, and you would be constrained by the weight of ruinous consequence far superior to your authority, if you will have appeared unequal to such great and important matters.

LETTER 5.20 (C. 525–26)

The last in a sequence of letters written to facilitate the construction of a fleet (cf. *Var.* 5.16–19), here ordering a *saio* to superintend the removal of timber from private and royal lands and also to remove fence-works that had been placed across navigable rivers by fishermen.

King Theoderic to Aliulfus, Saio

1. We have ordered timber, suitable for constructing dromonds, to be found along both shores of the Po, and therefore we select you by the present order, so that following the arrangements of their magnitudes the *Praefectus Praetorio,* Abundantius, and the *Comes Patrimonii,* Wilia, you should unhesitatingly set out for the designated places with artisans and, whether it will have been found on royal domains or private property, you should arrange for it to be prepared without any delay, since we believe what is prepared by God's will and for the common good extends a burden to no man. **2.** Thus, we truly want you to execute this unfinished endeavor in such a way that nothing may seem to be eagerly sought to the detriment of the landowner, but only that may be claimed which is necessary for the sake of our utility. Let nothing be taken from an owner that afterward may not be deemed acceptable in public. We order the timber of woodlands to be felled, not that anything related to other resources should be impetuously seized. Such an endeavor is an advantage to us that does not cause a burden, concerning which, what the landowner does not seek in person, he should not believe himself to have lost. **3.** We have learned that certain men have cut across the course of rivers with fence-work, namely on the Mincius, Ollius, Anser, Tiber, and Arno Rivers, to the extent that it impacts application to sailing. We want you to clear these away in every instance, at the direction of his magnificence Abundantius, the *Praefectus Praetorio,* lest you should permit anyone to presume anything beyond such a deed, but so that the course of the riverbed should be left unimpaired for the passage of ships. For we know that fishing must be done with nets, not with fence-work. For thus also is a detestable avarice produced, such that it hastens to enclose only for itself what had provided passage for many.

LETTER 5.21 (C. 523–26)

This letter appoints the recipient to the directorship of a corps of public notaries (*rector decuriarum*), possibly the *apparitores*. The letter indicates the office is connected to the maintenance of public records at Rome, including testaments, legal verdicts, and record of public appointments.

King Theoderic to Capuanus, Vir Spectabilis

1. If our court had selected you as a raw recruit, if you had come unknown to scales of examination, we would think you must be advised as to the type of wisdom with which you should decorously conduct yourself. But you, who have deserved to be employed in the service of letters, are known to have knowledge of every virtue. Indeed, you, who have been seen to prosecute the desires of another man's case, consider with what modesty you ought to comport yourself. For if you felt the cruel mistrust of a judge, you corrected his opinion by the mild and insightful remedy of praising justice, obtaining with sweet persuasion what you had not been able to impose upon a superior. Who, therefore, doubts that what is certain to persuade the voice of the public would choose you! **2.** Proclaimed blessings hold no uncertainties; nor does the native talent of anyone lie dormant, such that what that person has been able to attain as a veteran would seem to be learned as though from something unrefined. Examining the authenticity of a submitted document, you used to demand with righteous voice whether the office of records maintained truth untainted. Now does the judge present to you what you would rush to attain for others. Act now, lest your voice betray you, since the weight of the most severe modesty is challenged by its own voice. Take, therefore, with God's approval, the directorship of the public notaries, that most truthful testimony of human deeds, the safeguard of ownership, a resplendent sanctuary of public faith. From this, you will acquire as much praise as public weal is preserved unsullied. **3.** Here, the will of the deceased may live on uninterruptedly for ages, here the decisions of parents may pass to posterity, here the peace of all men is protected by your records. Others may have honors and dread-inspiring *fasces;* the welcome guardians of human affairs are known to serve you. For here are the final decisions of mankind, the chains of legal cases, the bonds of litigation, the imprisonment of fury, about which the Mantuan prophet most truthfully said, "The doors of legal controversy are sealed, enclosed within, impious and begrimed rage bellows with gory mouth."[19] Therefore, hold the secretarial offices with judgment bound by merit, since it is not fitting to pronounce too easily what is of such great importance to the city. You may even enjoy, when it becomes necessary, the pronouncement of one greater by birth, one made more senior by so many forefathers, the voice of the Senate for so great a silent host.[20] Take heed what you receive from this office, that you would be the most eminent in speaking among such eloquent men, whom even we confess must be respected. Claim, therefore, what we determine to grant, what we agree to offer, so that you may open the doors of the curia for those whom our choice has ordered the chamber of Liberty to receive.

LETTER 5.22 (C. 523–26)

A more elaborate letter (cf. *Var.* 5.21), announcing to the Senate the appointment of an individual as director of personnel maintaining public records (*rector decuriarum*). The force of his eloquence and his humble background both receive attention.

King Theoderic to the Senate of Rome

1. It is fitting that one who must be elected should always be sent to you fully and carefully approved, since the very man whose public presentation is known to be considered is handed over for even greater testing. Nonetheless, we wish for these

---

19. Virgil, *Aeneid* 1.294.
20. *Vox senatus* here suggests partnership with the authority of *Praefectus Urbis.*

offices, which are affixed to the heights of Rome as though noble gems, to be associated with wise men. For where may an eloquent man prosper with more distinction than in a city of letters, so that he may be declared a man of worth there, where native talent is nourished? It is expected that any and everything good and praiseworthy should become shabby in its own place, unless it obtains a suitable position. The strong hand demands a fight, the courageous heart desires a ship; thus our secretarial office requires a reliable promotion, and thus an eloquent curia requires a learned man. Therefore, it is agreed that whoever is presented daily before your attention must be considered with much deliberation. 2. Hence, our interest looks to the *spectabilis* Capuanus, a man eloquent by nature who would proclaim the decisions of your curia with the authority of his senior and who would serve the secretarial office of the Senate with self-conscious righteousness, so that acting with his own refined integrity, he may represent those celebrated men who must be honored. It is a great charge, conscript fathers, to be selected for integrity, nor may the good conscience of one to whom the testimony of the ages is entrusted be only partially proven. For if anyone summoned as a witness would speak the truth in an ongoing case, for which he would be proven honorable, who could offer such certitude for all times? But, however much you may favor every distinction of your fosterling,[21] it is more helpful to recall what unanimous consensus may acknowledge. 3. A certain grace of speech always contributes to the choice; it soothes the ears, it attracts the mind, it enjoys the clarity of eloquence which fittingly emanates from a stainless conscience. For the speech of one acting in public is a kind of mirror of character; nor is it possible that there be a greater witness of the mind than the nature seen in his words. For even though we have described his qualities thus, he endures a bound tongue in minor matters; nonetheless, he speaks more forcefully at the point that he concludes these matters, and this is granted to him for pleasing by provident design, so that this man, whom you would see hesitating before the doors, would astound you with his eloquence in courtroom battles. 4. Truly that memory which justly is called the treasury of orators resides in him with such strength that you would assume anything heard from him has been recorded in writing. It is a great benefit not to know the defect of forgetfulness, and there is indeed a certain similarity to the coursing time of the heavens to always have matters at hand. We now make this clear, so that you would know that we consider the pleasing virtues of our subjects, and so that we may demonstrate that our judgment is formed, not according to casual whim, but from a process of selection. 5. Therefore, concerning these matters, conscript fathers, we have ordered Capuanus, a man endowed with good gifts, to be the director of the secretarial offices for the present indiction. Moreover, we elevate him to a prestige

---

21. The curious phrase *alumni vestri cuncta notissima,* may refer either to the Senate of Constantinople as Rome's "fosterling," or to candidates groomed by individual senators.

native to a superior office, so that, one who has conducted himself with gray-haired maturity of good character, the most ample kind of respect, should complement the dignity of age in your order. Enriched with a better appointment, he will increase eloquence, since one who dictates the decision which the supplicant seeks is much more eloquent. Liberty nourishes words; dread, however, often restricts their abundance. Let this man, who has held a public post so different that not long ago he even defended the fortunes of the humble and insignificant, now introduce former consuls to your curia.

LETTER 5.23 (C. 525–26)

A brief letter ordering the *Praefectus Praetorio* to release ships and rations (the *annona*) to a *saio*, who will organize the transport of archers to a *comes* for the purpose of training exercises.

King Theoderic to Abundantius, Praefectus Praetorio

1. We have determined that our *saio* Tata must be sent to the *illustris Comes* Wilia with the archers, so that an increased army may obtain greater strength. Let our young men demonstrate in wars what is said of manliness in the gymnasium. Let the school of Mars send a throng. One who accustoms himself to practice in leisure is prepared only to fight in sport. And therefore, we have decided that your *illustris* magnitude should offer them ships and the *annona* following the established practice, to the extent that, with God's blessing, they ought to be prepared for travel. We have indeed given the effectiveness of our order into your care, since it is acknowledged that what is begun, with God's blessing, by your arrangement may in no way be forsaken.

LETTER 5.24 (C. 525–26)

This letter directs the governor of Dalmatia to investigate claims that unrelated persons have claimed the property of a recently deceased woman. The property is ordered to be brought under the control of the fisc unless legitimate claims arise.

King Theoderic to Epiphanius, Vir Spectabilis *and* Consularis *of Dalmatia*

1. It is maintained that Johanna, who succeeded her former husband Andreas by award of the law, has been deprived of life, with no declared heirs and no existing relations. It is added that her property has been occupied by the willful seizure of diverse persons supported by no legitimate right, and since the measures of the law have determined that her legacy should join our fisc, we advise you in the present message that, with the veracity of this matter determined, if it should be true that either no heir survives in her will or has succeeded by right of relation, let it be delivered to us, to be attached to the body of our fisc with its advantages. Since the declaration of our innocence is just, in whose presence deceit is never able to find a home, it is just not to deny our advantages. **2.** For it is not fitting that the *Princeps* is asked to be cheated in such a matter, since it is a crime of negligence to ignore unlawful seizures that the laws have arranged to prohibit. However, if you should discover anything to the contrary, allow peace to the owners, since our patrimony is greater by those properties which our subjects possess legally.

LETTER 5.25 (C. 523–26)

This letter appoints the recipient as *Tribunus Voluptatem* ('tribune of spectacles') in Milan. Unusually, the letter confers this office for life, out of respect for the recipient's advanced years. For this office, see *Variae* 7.10.

King Theoderic to Bacauda, Vir Spectabilis

1. Our generosity invigorates the wearied years, to the extent that it causes the waning generation to feel none of the detriments of poverty. If indeed the excellence of young men is animated by seizing an undertaking, the only way of life for old men is to find the comforts of peace. And so, moved by your petition to be appointed *tribunus,* we have decided that the care of affairs that must be assiduously attended in Milan should pertain to you, so that, what is new in service to the republic, for as long as you live, the punishable presumption of anyone may never grant a successor to your post, to the extent that, with the assistance of our kindness, you may continually enjoy the care of this duty to offer public pleasures. And, as a comfort to your generation, you possess both things, the opportunity of an office and the delight of pleasures.

LETTER 5.26 (C. 523–26)

A general summons for all Goths from Picenum and Samnium to assemble for the annual distribution of the donative. The letter at least suggests that by this date some among the military class may have never had audience with the king. Neither this nor the following companion letter (*Var.* 5.27) specify the location of the muster, although Ravenna may be assumed.

King Theoderic to All Goths Settled in Picenum and Samnium

1. Although our generosity may be most pleasing to all people everywhere, nonetheless we believe what is conferred in our presence is far more gratifying, since the people gain something more from viewing the *Princeps* than the benefits that they obtain from generosity. For one who is ignorant of his own master is almost like one dead; nor does he live with any kind of distinction, whom the fame of his own king does not defend. **2.** And therefore, we command in the present order that on the eighth day before the ides of June,[22] God willing, you ought to come before our presence. You will receive the royal donative according to custom, if you hasten to come immediately. It is nonetheless necessary that we advise that none of those coming will be permitted to make detours, lest you should ruin the fields or meadowlands of landowners, but rather, hastening with every restraint of disciplined precaution, will your gathering be pleasing to us, since thereupon we would willingly take upon ourselves the cost of the army, so that civic harmony may be preserved intact by armed men.

LETTER 5.27 (C. 523–26)

A companion to *Variae* 5.26, this letter orders a *saio* to supervise the assembly of the Gothic military from Picenum and Samnium for the distribution of the annual donative. The letter suggests that the assembly also involved a review of individual military merits. The same *saio* is addressed at *Variae* 5.30 as a *dux*.

King Theoderic to Guduin, Saio

1. Concerning the practice of royal generosity, we order that our Goths ought to be granted the customary donative. And therefore, let your devotion advise the commanders of the provinces of Picenum and Samnium without any delay,[23] so that you may influence those who obtain the reward of our good will each and every year to hasten unhesitatingly to the *comitatus* in order to receive the donative, to the extent that those who have truly deserved it from us may be gratified with greater generosity. **2.** For it is necessary that one who knows he must stand before the *Principes* should live blamelessly; indeed, praise accompanies good men and complaints the wicked. It is fitting, moreover, that we seek on this occasion the deeds of singular note, so that it would not be possible to overlook what any man has accomplished in battle. For if the army anticipates a regular assembly, it cannot neglect the love of excellence. Let the man who does not recall having done anything bravely learn to come before the judge fearfully, so that one who prefers to avoid the wounds of our censure will be more capable of rising impetuously against the enemy.

LETTER 5.28 (C. 523–26)

A letter similar to *Variae* 3.22 and 3.28, this letter summons to the presence of the king a man who has apparently distinguished himself with a public career. Unlike

---

22. June 6.

23. The *millenarii* are named as military commanders, presumably of units of a thousand soldiers each.

previous letters of this type, the invitation was preceded by a request for summons by the recipient.

King Theoderic to Carinus, Vir Illustris

1. The merits of good public agents enjoy this glorious prejudice, that those who have become noted for upright actions are unable to become numb with leisure. And therefore, being so pleased with your request, and because we have held you to be an intimate associate, we summon you with the present order, to the extent that our services may be embellished with the most distinguished men and that through you we may be able to set right what we believe to be advantageous to us.

LETTER 5.29 (C. 523–26)

A fascinating letter ordering an investigation into the case of a former Gothic soldier who had been reduced to servitude by two other men. The Goth was blind and therefore unable to defend himself. The recipient of the letter was likely a Gothic military commander. The letter is paired thematically with *Variae* 5.30, which also treats abuses against Gothic soldiers.

King Theoderic to Neudes, Vir Illustris

1. An entreaty poured out by Anduit has sincerely moved us. Once decorated, he now returns as a more wretched man, bereft of his own sight. Indeed, it is unavoidable that his calamity should stir us more amply when seen, rather than heard. For lingering in perpetual night, he has hastened to our consolation with the assistance of shared sight,[24] so that he who is unable to see should at least feel the sweetness of kindness. Indeed, he clamors that, irrespective of his own birth, the condition of slavery has been imposed upon him by Gudila and Oppas, when not long before he had followed our army freely. **2.** We marvel that such a man has been dragged into servitude who deserved to be discharged from service by a true master. It is a strange ambition to harass the kind of man whom you would dread and to call a servant one whom you ought to serve out of pious consideration. He adds still that the false accusation of these men has been refuted by the investigation of the celebrated *comes* Pitzia. Now, however, restrained by the difficulty of his own infirmity, he cannot avenge himself with the hand once deemed a protector to stand in battle with strong men. **3.** But we, for whom it is fitting to preserve equitable justice between men of equal and unequal standing, have decided in the present order that, if he has formerly proven himself to be freeborn in the opinion of the above-mentioned Pitzia, immediately censure those falsely accusing him.

---

24. Likely a servant.

Let those, for whom it was already fitting to be condemned by their own desire to injure, not dare to mistreat him any further with hostile attacks.

LETTER 5.30 (C. 523-26)

This letter censures a *dux* for subjecting two Gothic soldiers to unspecified duties deemed unsuitable for men of their station. The addressee is named a *saio* at *Variae* 5.27, and the letter serves as an interesting companion to *Variae* 5.29, both treating abuses against Gothic soldiers.

King Theoderic to Guduin, Vir Spectabilis

1. We elect those men as *duces* to whom we may at the same time apportion the weight of legal equitability, since we desire you to be made resplendent not as much by arms as by the execution of justice. Therefore, Costula and Daila, while, by the grace of God, they enjoy the liberty of our Goths, plead that you have yoked them with demeaning tasks, which it is neither fitting for them to endure, nor is it permitted for anyone to impose upon them. If you know this position to be the case, may you cause it to be changed without delay, lest a more egregious complaint next be brought to us and a returning suit should incline our attitude to be severe with a *dux*, for whom it is more fitting to accomplish the kind of things that we would delight to hear.

LETTER 5.31 (C. 523-26)

This letter discloses a simple case of dealing with delinquent tax payers in the provinces of Apulia and Calabria. The relationship of the letter's addressee to the fiscal or judicial process is unknown. As a *vir devotus*, he was simply someone trusted by the king.

King Theoderic to Decoratus, Vir Devotus

1. The *clarissimus* Thomas has complained that several among the provincials of Apulia and Calabria owe the full amount of money for the *siliquaticum* for the first, second, eighth, ninth, eleventh, and fifteenth indictions,[25] which, he reminds us, pertain to his own management. And since it should not happen that the public advantage should be discredited with continual derision, let your devotion therefore undertake the present decree and summon the presbyter Mark, Andreas, Simeonius, and others, whose signature is indicated at the bottom of the brief, with civic harmony preserved in each case, so that, if they will be manifestly determined as owing property to the fisc, and not through any false accusation, let them

---

25. Indicating arrears spanning from 507 to 521.

pay without any delay the amount that has reasonably been determined. **2.** For this must be carefully attended, lest the spirit of obstinate persons seem to bring any disadvantage to public affairs. Let those who have truly acknowledged the warnings least come to the appropriate court by your threat, so that what agrees with equity, the case may be settled with the allegation of each party reviewed with respect to sound laws.

LETTER 5.32 (C. 523–26)

One of a pair of letters treating a domestic dispute between the households of two Gothic soldiers, this letter censures a man for the conduct of his wife, who has assaulted the wife of another man. In the following letter (*Var.* 5.33), the source of the conflict is revealed as adultery between the two households.

King Theoderic to Brandila

1. Patza has sent the same complaint to us time and again, claiming that, while he was occupied on a very successful expedition, his own wife was mutilated with three blows from your wife, Procula, with the result that she had escaped only by the grace of sheer chance, since at that time she was believed, not to have been exhausted from blows, but to be dead. This audacity, at which we especially marvel in a woman, if indeed it is true, we shall not permit to occur unpunished. **2.** And so we advise you in the present decree, that, if you openly acknowledge the deed, reflecting upon your own sense of honor, censure the disclosed charge with a husband's severity, to the extent that a just complaint should not return to us concerning the same case. Furthermore, you know it is possible to restrain with laws what would be fitting for you to correct with domestic severity. **3.** But if you perhaps want to say more, charging a case of unfounded slander, removing any excuses for delay, hasten immediately to our court with the aforementioned wife, there in due course either to be punished for wrongful presumption or vindicated of a wife's bad behavior.

LETTER 5.33 (C. 523–26)

This letter requires a military *dux* to resolve the dispute initiated at *Variae* 5.32 between the households of two Gothic soldiers. In the present letter, it becomes apparent that the source of the conflict had been adultery and a bigamous marriage conducted while one of the soldiers had been on campaign in Gaul.

King Theoderic to Wilitancus, Dux

1. The intimate complaint of Patza weighs on our sense of forbearance. While Patza was absent and engaged in the Gallic campaign, Brandila is reported to have launched an attack against him, so that Brandila led his wife, Regina, to share his company as his own wife, and in an adultery injurious to our reign, he legally contracted the semblance of marriage. In no way shall we permit these charges, if they are true, to pass unpunished. For when would anyone hold anything dear, if he should be vulnerable to a crime then, when he will have fought for the well-being of all men? **2.** Consider, O shameless woman, the most chaste species of the cooing turtle-doves, which, if it becomes separated from its mate by accidental death, it confines itself to a perpetual rule of abstinence. It does not seek out again the delights of marriage, which it lost. Patza served in good faith, while Regina ignored praise of chastity, and what is honored by no association with widowhood, she was detected speculating on his death. **3.** Wife, take heed of your peril! For those who fail to hold vows, reason urges chastity, the punishment of law imposes it, and the terror of a husband demands it. Good habits wither away completely if they are not proven by those circumstances which are tempered by reason and affection. And therefore, let your loftiness cause those sought out to hasten to your scales of justice and, with the truth of the matter examined in full, just as our laws demand, censure the adulterers in favor of married men, since those who were conjoined in criminal presumption did not want a defender of the republic to return. **4.** Those who attempted to use the laws for scandalous acts had desired all these deeds to be concealed without suspicion. But it is better that the intentions of the wicked be corrected with the condemnation of a few, since every marriage would be abandoned to uncertainty when the husband was away, if such a respected institution should be sinned against without any fear.

LETTER 5.34 (C. 523–26)

This letter offers a vivid indictment against a former official convicted of embezzling public funds, for which the *Praefectus Praetorio* has received the order to arrest him. Of particular interest is the mobilization of natural history in building a case against the culprit.

King Theoderic to Abundantius, Praefectus Praetorio

1. It was reported to us in frequent claims that Frontosus, a testament to his own name,[26] had frittered away no small amount of the public funds. We caused the man to be examined in just investigation by various judges, lest perhaps, as it often happens, not the truth but rather prejudice should condemn him. Having confessed the crime, that man claimed he was capable of restoring everything, if the judges should grant him a generous period of time. With judges frequently exhausted, unmindful

---

26. A *fronto* was a person with bulging forehead; this seems to be a specimen of Cassiodorus's fascination with the moral import of physiology, for example, as seen in the *De anima*.

of his own promise, he hastens ever unprepared to the agreement, not even knowing how to flee, but ignorant of his own guarantee, forgetful when he fails, trembling when he is apprehended. He changes words, varies the arrangements; not satisfied with the nature of his own promises, he alters them with a diverse array of ploys. **2.** Rightly should he be compared to the chameleon, which, similar in form to a small serpent, is distinguished only by a head of gold and in the rest of the body by pale green. This creature often attracts human attention, and since the speed of flight is denied it, confused with excessive timidity, it alters its own colors with a many-sided nature, so that it is possible to be found now light blue, now vermilion, now green, and now dark blue. **3.** Whence it is a marvel to behold such diversity in one likeness, which not without merit we have said to be very similar to a sparkling gem,[27] in which it is not possible to contain but one brilliance. When the stone is held still, it fluctuates with wavering appearances. For what you see at one time, if you inspect more closely, you presently change it to something else. Thus what you know no man has laid hold of, you nonetheless believe to have changed. **4.** The mind of Frontosus is found to be similar to these considered permutations, a mind that does not hold faith with its own claims, which will produce as great a variety of words as it contains. Rightly, he must be associated with the stories of Proteus, who, once seized, never maintained the form of his own substance. In order to conceal his human form, he either roared as a lion, hissed as a snake, or was dissolved into ripples as liquid. **5.** And thus, since he is well known, when he should present a face at your court, first harry him, lest he should promise anything, then threaten him, lest he should decide upon anything, since it is easy for the character of a fickle mind to promise what it does not plan to fulfill. Having been confined, let him pay, then, without any delay whatever he will be able with considered fairness, since, after so many falsehoods, his own cleverness will be able to reflect upon what he knows he has so frequently ridiculed.

LETTER 5.35 (C. 523–26)

The first of two letters addressed to the administration of Spain (cf. *Var.* 5.39), this letter orders the *comes* and a senior senator (possibly governor) to exact payment from ship owners who have absconded with grain destined for Rome. With the death of the Visigothic king Alaric II, Theoderic had assumed control of Spain in the name of Amalaric, Alaric's heir and Theoderic's grandson.

King Theoderic to Liuvirit, Comes, *and to Ampelius,* Vir Illustris

1. Since poverty strikes Roman households with its taut visage as the consequence of uncertain events, and, however rare, it nonetheless seems to be the most

---

27. The type of gem named (*pandia*) is not otherwise attested.

wretched time for so beautiful a city, we have ordered stores of wheat from Spain to be offered there at a reasonable price, so that under our rule Rome should receive its ancient tribute more happily. Indeed, the industry of the *spectabilis* Marcianus served our commands with commendable praise, but with equal diligence, what had clearly been prepared with the best possible care has been corrupted. For those who had undertaken the conveyance of the grain, not bearing the tedium of delays, are said to have sold the designated grain in regions of Africa for their own profit. **2.** Although this should pass unpunished by no means, as the love of our own advantage should suspend the starved pleas of so many people, nonetheless, since it is our nature to relax punishment which we are able to correct with circumspect measures, we have seen fit that the vigorous Catellus and Servandus must be sent, so that, since the ship owners are reported to have received 280 *solidi* from the grain and 758 *solidi* in passage fares, if the truth of the matter has become familiar to you, let the sum of the computed amount, that is, 1,038 *solidi,* be paid by them, so that we, who have rescinded punishment, might feel the least loss. Thus, let your sublimity diligently employ yourself in that region, so that you may be seen to satisfy both justice and the public weal.

LETTER 5.36 (C. 523–26)

This letter grants discharge from military service for a soldier who has grown infirm with age. The *spectabilis* rank of the recipient indicates some status, probably a minor military command. The letter offers interesting insights into the conditions of military service and is an interesting comparison to *Variae* 5.29.

King Theoderic to Starcedius, Vir Spectabilis

1. You affirm that a body worn with continuous labors has brought a feebleness of the limbs to you, so that you, who formerly had been suited for military decorations, are now scarcely fit for a leisured life. You therefore request that you not be compelled to those fortunate expeditions, from which you would be lead not by will, but from necessity. And because you have requested with your petitions for too long and, having been convinced of the truth in this matter, we grant you an honorable release with the present order, since the wretched misfortune that excuses you is not the fault of cowardice. **2.** But even though we grant your return to civilian life, thus, by the present dictate, we deprive you of the donative, since it is not fair that, while you are recognized as deserving regarding your request, you should receive while at leisure the wage of those toiling. Therefore, as a free man with our protection, enjoy a life secure from the plots of various persons. Nor should anyone accuse you of the disgrace of desertion, when those who happen to be suspended from military service for the sake of illness must be regarded on the basis of former deeds and must be respected by law. For it is not fitting that someone who has deserved to be released from duty by our judgment should be reproved by anyone.

LETTER 5.37 (C. 523–26)

This letter, addressed to the Jewish community of Milan, ensures the preservation of its legal rights in the face of hostility from the local Christian church. The exact nature of the dispute is not disclosed, but it seems to have required reiterating legal distinctions between the two communities. For other letters addressed to Jews in Italy, see *Variae* 2.27, 3.45, 4.33, 4.43.

King Theoderic to the Jews of Milan

1. We have gladly assented to that which is requested without injury to the laws, especially since, for the sake of preserving civic harmony, the benefits of justice must not be denied to those who thus far have been known to err in faith. And in this way may they learn the sweet taste of good conduct, so that, those who strive to attain human justice may begin more eagerly to consider divine justice. **2.** Consequently, since several of you have often claimed to be wounded by infringements, and you claim that rights have been rescinded which pertain to your synagogue, let the requested protection of our kindness bring assistance to you, to the extent that no man of the church, which rightly contends with your synagogue, may incite with violent disruption; nor may he involve himself in your affairs with troublesome hostility. Instead, just as there is separation in the observance of religion, let the performance of celebrations be separate.[28] Nonetheless, we grant the benefit of royal assistance in this matter with moderation, so that you should not attempt to disruptively appropriate what the court has determined to pertain to the aforementioned church or to its religious offices by right of law. **3.** On that account, the thirty-year prescription, which is preserved for the protection of all mankind, should rightly be preserved for you; nor do we unreasonably order you to endure the loss of usury practices, so that your petition may enjoy freedom from illegal prejudices by the walled defense of our piety. We therefore grant what you have requested in the usual habit of our kindness; but why, O Jews, thus supplicating, do you seek earthly peace, if you are unable to find eternal rest?

LETTER 5.38 (C. 523–26)

This letter orders all landowners (*possessores*) in the vicinity of Ravenna to provide labor for the maintenance of the city's aqueduct. It is worth noting that the state had maintained slave gangs for regularly removing vegetation that would crumble

---

28. The phrase *conversatione actuum* is vague, but suggests the celebration of holy days.

the carefully balanced architecture of aqueducts at Rome. Other urban centers depended upon the seasonal conscription of the agrarian labor force organized by large landowners.

King Theoderic to All Possessores

1. A particular concern for the aqueducts admonishes us, so that we must quickly clear away what has been allowed to grow harmfully, to the extent that, God willing, the strength of the aqueducts should be preserved intact; and, because this pertains to young trees, this would be an easy undertaking for you. For what are now only shoots, would become, if ignored, even stronger. For such saplings which are dislodged with the ease of uprooting, later will hardly succumb to blows from axes. And therefore, you ought to attend to this with shared haste, so that you may avoid with present diligence the troubles of future toil. For without opposition, this is the ruin of civil order, a sundering of buildings as though from a battering ram. **2.** For this reason, we order all trees that grow dangerously close to the walls along the aqueduct of Ravenna to be ripped out at the root, so that the restored structure of the plastered channel may decant water for us of such a purity as is possible to have from springs. Then will the production of water be the embellishment of the baths, then will the fish paddle in glassy pools, then it will be that water washes, not pollutes, after which it would not always be necessary to bathe. Moreover, if waters sweet for drinking should flow, everything would be rendered acceptable to our palate, since no morsel of human fare is made pleasing, when the clarity of sweet water is not available. For if we desire to bathe in the cleanest water, how much more should we hasten to be sated by such? If these things are now accomplished for the future, the labor that is undertaken for the delight of all men will cause distaste for none.

LETTER 5.39 (C. 523–26)

This letter, similar in many respects to the problems of administrating the province of Savia (*Var.* 5.14), illustrates those difficulties at the outset of Ostrogothic involvement in Spain. The two recipients of the letter, a prominent Roman senator and a Gothic *comes,* have been instructed to address a wide scope of corruption including tax fraud, misuse of the public mint and public post, unrestrained violence, and extortion imposed upon the locals by Goths sent from Italy.

King Theoderic to Ampelius, Vir Illustris, *and to* Liuvirit, Vir Spectabilis

1. It is fitting that the provinces, now subject to our rule by God's will, should be arranged according to laws and good character, since truly is the life of men bound by the order of law. For it is the practice of beasts to live by chance; they fall prey to unexpected mishap while engaged in a cycle of violence. And so the experienced cultivator clears his own field of thorny scrub, since it is to the credit of the careful cultivator if something wild should be made pleasing from its sweet fruits. Likewise, that delightful peace of the people and the tranquil management of a region is deemed to be the reputation of those ruling. **2.** And so we have learned of the complaints of many in the province of Spain that, what is the worst among moral crime, the lives of men are despoiled by random lawlessness and many fall, ground down by chance of unfounded litigation. And thus they are ruined by a corrupt kind of peace, as though it were sport, to the extent that they could hardly expect to fall under the duress of wars. Furthermore, the fortunes of provincials are not allowed to be subject to public records, as is customary, but to the authority of those in a position to compel. It is a species of obvious plunder to give something on account of the personal inclination of one hastening to compel something more to his own advantage. **3.** On which account, wanting to assist with royal foresight, we have decided that your sublimity must be sent throughout all Spain in official capacity, so that nothing of their accustomed behavior will be permitted under the novelty of your administration. But so that, in the manner of physicians, we may grant a hastened remedy to cruel sickness, let our cure commence where the harm is known to be the greatest. **4.** We order the crime of homicide to be restrained with the authority of the laws; but, however much more severe the penalty, the inquiry ought to be considered with that much more care, lest the innocent seem to endure harm to life on account of a zeal for punishment. And so, let the guilty alone fall for the correction of many, since it is even a kind of piety to imprison the crime in its infancy, lest it should increase with maturity. **5.** Further, those collecting the public tax are said to burden the property of landowners with inconsistent weights, so that it seems to be not so much a payment as plunder. But so that every opportunity for deceit may be removed, we order all tax payments to be weighed on scales from our privy chamber, which at present have been given to you. For how much more execrable is it that lawlessness should be permitted to sin even against the very nature of scales, so that what has been accorded its own innate justice is known to have been corrupted by fraud? **6.** We have decided that the contract farmers of the royal domain, from whatever family they may be descended, should pay as much in correctly assessed rent as our estates are determined to produce. And lest the burden on each property seem unprofitable to anyone, we want the rents to be set for them by your equity, according to the quality of the property leased. For if the measure of payment occurs according to the inclination of the one being contracted, the farms must not be called ours, but theirs. **7.** Furthermore, we order you to attentively collect the import duties, where no small amount of fraud is reported to have befallen the public advantage, and to determine the amount assessed according to the quality of the goods, since a useful corrective to fraud is to know what has been imported.

8. Next, we have learned that the coin minters, who happen to have been established for collecting taxes, have changed practice for the profit of individuals. Concerning the perpetration of this illegality, let them devote themselves to the public assessments according to the capacity to pay. **9.** Moreover, may you take care that the annual tribute of the customs house is not corrupted by any kind of private use, but so that it may show a regulation useful to business, censuring those abusing their freedom in commerce with a measured fairness, lest the ambitious appetite of the collectors extend itself indefinitely. **10.** Further, we order that the administration of Laetus,[29] whose best intention is stricken by unpopularity, should be investigated with our usual equity, so that fraud may not be concealed with clever intrigues, and nor may the innocent be burdened with false accusations. **11.** Indeed, let anyone whom you find to have been involved in illicit activities return the concealed money in place of possessions, according to your estimation. But if this property will happen to be dispersed among others, let those who knowingly permitted themselves to be involved in such an affair be nonetheless held liable for punishment, for even those who had not committed the act of theft have shown themselves to be accessories to the crime. **12.** The prescribed distribution of salaries, which our kindness has granted to various persons, is reported by the provincials to be an intolerable cause of loss, when it is exacted in kind and then brazenly demanded in money. Such acts are evidence of detestable greed conspiring to exhaust itself and soon to increase the shamelessness of the one making demands. What is seen to be exceedingly corrupt is also exceedingly foolish, that they would both ignore our policies and be found harming the property of tax payers who must be supported. Let them, therefore, be satisfied with the predetermined measure, whether fixed in kind, or all the same, converted; let them hold power over the free man to expect only one of the two, while they should not burden the property of others with a double exaction. **13.** It is also said that the liberty of the collectors wrenches much more from the provincials than happens to be paid to our privy chamber. Having dispelled this with careful inquiry, we have decided that you should refer to the exaction of the taxes that happened to be collected in the reigns of Alaric and Euric.[30] **14.** And so we have learned from the complaint of provincials that those who have assigned horses demand the conveyance of extra pack-animals. You should permit no man to take this entirely for granted, when the landowner is worn down by the most shameful transactions and even the speed of those traveling is impeded. **15.** We also utterly removed the kind of stewards that they lament having found to the ruin of their wards, as much with respect to private property as to public, since it is not protection when it is offered to the unwill-

---

29. Otherwise unattested, this was probably Theoderic's representative sent to administrate the province.

30. The previous Visigothic kings of the region.

ing. It is noteworthy that the unwilling have endured. For it is a blessing in a real sense, if something is accepted without complaint. Therefore, we have decided to dispense with the services that they had offered uselessly to the Goths posted in cities. For it is not fitting that those whom we have sent to fight on behalf of liberty should seek servitude from native born citizens.

LETTER 5.40 (C. 524)

This letter appoints the recipient to the office of *Comes Sacrarum Largitionum,* an office with responsibilities over the mint and circulation of currency. The candidate's qualifications are related to former legal service and to experience gained as an envoy to the East.

King Theoderic to Cyprian, Comes Sacrarum

1. Although we may rejoice to bestow benefits beyond the desires of supplicants so often, and, what is especially difficult, we would at times surpass the prayers of human ambition, we nonetheless gladly embrace what we may boast to have done according to just deserts. Truly must the one to whom the scales are passed be weighed for a long time, and such a man ought to be chosen by a *Princeps* who could be approved by the law itself. The value of gems is prized in a band of shining gold,[31] and they capture the grace of beauty, since they are not soiled by the presence of anything unworthy. **2.** Hence, good deserts, coupled with honorable posts, are each assisted by high reputation and the appearance of a single thing becomes lovelier from association with grace. Now, concerning you, we who have often been pleased by your observable deeds have entrusted nothing to purchased praise or to babbling rumor. In fact, you are accustomed to relate the confused quarrels of agitated claimants with a particularly well-defined and clear summary. Those who have been unable to disclose their own grievances have managed to be entrusted to your assistance, and lest the irregularity of some favor should be suspected, you pressed the claims of supplicants in their very presence. **3.** The desires of disputants combined in your speech and, what is the most unlikely kind of gratitude, you pleased each party with your impartial respect, a feat that even evaded the very orators. For when the purpose was for orators to speak the protracted pleas of a single party, it was always important for you to declare both sides of an unanticipated case. Also to be considered is that most resplendent weight of the royal presence, under which it happened that you disentangled cases with such ease, so that what orators could hardly obtain from judges with the most carefully constructed rhetoric, you were proven to obtain from the *Princeps* by clear pleading. **4.** The verdict of our serenity was proclaimed indisputably to the public good, since it endured no delay

---

31. The phrase *venae auri fulgore* may be a figurative description for a gold ring.

in deciding the case. For why delay the end of a case, when, having been reviewed, it has already been narrated by you, and you have summed the possible verdict with clear brevity. We believe that you have learned to judge by serving in our court. Thus, what is the most effective kind of apprenticeship, you have been instructed by acting rather than by reading. 5. Hence, as a man instructed by such distinguished training, you assumed the office of envoy to the East, even being sent to men of the highest degree of experience. But you were not bewildered with anxiety in their presence, since after serving us, nothing could seem extraordinary. Reared in the three languages,[32] Greece had nothing new to show you; nor did that subtlety, with which she abounds, surpass you. 6. More precious than all praise, fidelity is added to your merits, which divine providence cherishes and human nature venerates. For among the tossing storms of the world, where may human frailty shelter itself, if resolve of the mind does not attend our actions? It promotes friendship among associates, it serves its master with pure integrity, it grants the respect of pious faith to the majesty of heaven, and, if you seek widely for the blessing of such a virtue, everything that is conducted well in life becomes permanent through faith. 7. Take, therefore, by the grace of God, the office of the sacred largess for the third indiction. Make use of those teachings appropriate to your birth. Thus far, you have deserved that we should grant the insignia of office. Conduct yourself now, so that, in our gratitude, we may confer upon you nothing less than the loftiest honors.

LETTER 5.41 (C. 524)

A letter announcing to the Senate the promotion of a new *Comes Sacrarum Largitionum* (cf. *Var.* 5.40), with more attention to the candidates family and the intimacy of his interaction with the king.

King Theoderic to the Senate of Rome

1. Although the generosity of the *Princeps* has often sired candidates for you and our fruitful indulgence would be second nature for you, now you truly have a man, whom we ought to have chosen and whom it should happen that you would accept. Just as it was fortunate for him to be elevated by us, so will it be praiseworthy for him to be associated with your assembly by the law of offices. Nonetheless, it happens more fortunately for the curia, because even an unpolished recruit serves us, while the Senate does not receive anyone, unless he is already found honored with offices. 2. Therefore, your order, which is always drawn together from the most upstanding men, is appropriately adduced to be the most distinguished. For the entrance there is not unbolted to the uninitiated, but only such men are permitted to enter there as are seen to leave. And so take a colleague whom our palace has proven by long expe-

---

32. Presumably Latin, Greek, and Gothic.

rience, one who has served our voice unshaken, so that he would often explain our commands in our presence and with our commendation. **3.** You know well of whom we speak. For who among you has been turned away from the devotion of Cyprian? For whoever sought his services had already received our blessings. He more often obtained while hunting with us what was usually pleaded in the former imperial assemblies. If ever indeed it was permitted to relieve a fatigued mind from the cares of the republic, we would seek exercise on horseback, so that the firmness and vigor of the body might restore itself by that very change in activities.[33] Then this pleasing advocate would present a multitude of cases to us, and his report would not be spurned by the weary mind of the judge. **4.** When thus this pleasing advocate would pore over a multitude of cases for reviewing, a mind kindled by eagerness for generosity was restored. Therefore, the candidate who thus ministered to our mind remained steadfast in these duties, so that no discredit burdened him. We would often grow wrathful at unjust claims, yet the speech of the advocate could not displease us. We would condemn a case, while, at the same time, its proponent appeased us. And the one who claimed the influence of our gratitude frequently endured the brunt of our consternation. **5.** He is, moreover, not ennobled by the light of foreign birth. For his father, just as you recall, was Opilio, a man from an inferior era,[34] but who nonetheless was selected for palatine offices. This man should have been able to advance more fully, except that his fidelity lay in the barren ground of a parsimonious patron of rewards. For what could an impoverished lender confer? If he was not enriched, he nonetheless became well noted, since to have earned even mediocre reward during the impoverishment of the republic is wealthy and praiseworthy. **6.** This man has surpassed his own forebears by the fortune of the age, and, because he has been promoted more fully,[35] it must be attributed to our reign. Indeed the difference between the masters will be the measure of those promoted among the subjects. On that account, conscript fathers, we have elevated the aforementioned Cyprian to the brilliant peak of the sacred largess on account of his own merits and the splendor of his birth, so that your number may increase and the devotion of those serving may be inspired. Consider, most reverend fathers, what we expect from your order, when we have commended those whom we feel must be added to your number with a laden announcement.

LETTER 5.42 (C. 523)

A fascinating letter, presumably given on the occasion of the recipient's consulship in 523, when he would have offered public spectacles at Rome. The letter, however,

---

33. A rare glimpse of an intimate royal setting.
34. Under Odoacer.
35. Opilio, in fact, held the same post as *Comes Sacrarum Largitionum*.

does nothing to congratulate the new consul, but rather dwells upon the gross moral error of paying performers to court death in the arena with wild animals (*venationes*). In this sense, the letter should be understood as satire, much like *Variae* 4.51, to Symmachus. Both Maximus and Symmachus were relations of Boethius.

King Theoderic to Maximus, Vir Illustris and Consul

1. If those who wrestle with supple and anointed bodies may invite consular generosity, if the award of prizes is made for performances with a musical instrument, if a merry song comes to a reward, with what payment must the huntsman be satisfied who labors toward his own death so that he might please the spectators? He offers pleasure with his own blood and, constrained by an unfortunate lot, he hastens to please the people, who do not wish him to escape. A detestable act, an unlucky battle, to want to contend with beasts, which he does not doubt he will find stronger than himself. His only boldness is therefore in deceiving, his one comfort in trickery. **2.** If he should not prevail to flee the beast, at times he will be unable to find proper burial; while the man stands, his body perishes and before it is rendered a cadaver, he is savagely consumed. Caught, he becomes a morsel for his enemy, and that man—oh, the horror!—satisfies the appetite of the one whom he had hoped to dispatch. A spectacle so elevated by its edifice, but debased by its performance, was founded in honor of Scythian Diana, who used to rejoice in the flow of blood. **3.** Oh, to have desired to venerate that error of wretched deception, she who was placated with the death of men! First with the prayers of country folk in the groves and woods and with dedications to hunting, they fashioned this tripartite deity with false images, depicting her to be the very moon in the heavens, the matron in the forest, and Persephone in the netherworld. But perhaps only as a power of Erebus did they reckon her correctly, when, deceived by such falsity, they passed living into deep darkness with their error. **4.** This cruel sport, a blood-stained pleasure, godless observance, and human bestiality, as it should thus be called, the Athenians first introduced to the rites of their city, providing it divine sanction, so that what the celebration of false observances had discovered would transfer to the mockery of the spectacle. **5.** The royal power of Titus conceived to commence this edifice, with a flowing river of wealth, whereupon the capital of cities could partake in it.[36] And when a theater, which is a hemisphere, as it is called in Greek, appears joined as though two into one, a place for watching is rightly called an amphitheater. It encloses the arena in the shape of an egg, so that it is given an appropriate space for races and the spectators may view everything with ease, since that accommodating roundness has gathered everyone together.

---

36. Here describing the purpose of the Colosseum, begun under Vespasian in 72 and completed by his son Titus in 80.

6. They therefore go to such affairs that human nature ought to avoid. The first man, trusting in a slender beam, rushes upon the mouths of beasts, and he is seen to head for that which he hopes to evade with great impetus. Both predator and prey hasten upon each other in equal speed; nor is it possible for the one to be safe, except that he should meet in that spot the beast that he desires to escape. Then, with an elevated leap of the body, his upward prone limbs are cast into the air, as though the lightest of cloth, and poised in a kind of corporeal vault above the beasts, the onslaught of the animals passes under him, while he makes a delay of descending.[37] **7.** Thus it happens that the animal reckoned to have been mocked can seem much less fierce. Another man flees not by veering away; holding four-part screens distributed in a circle with angles arranged on a rotating mechanism, he does not escape by holding himself at a distance, but pursues the one following him, bringing himself nearly to his knees, so that he might avoid the mouths of bears.[38] Another man, suspended from a narrow beam on his belly, taunts the deadly animal and except that he is endangered, it is not possible that he obtain there a means to survive.[39] **8.** Another man encloses himself against the most savage of animals with a portable wall of reeds, hidden away after the example of the hedgehog, who, withdrawing under his own back and gathered up within himself, thus hides, his body is not visible, while he never runs away. For just as the one, having rolled into a sphere against an approaching enemy, is protected by natural spines, thus the other, girt with a sewn-together wicker work, is rendered more defended with the fragility of reeds. **9.** Three others, just as I shall describe, each positioned at an assigned portal, dare to call upon themselves the waiting fury, hiding themselves behind lattices in the open arena, now showing their faces, now their backs, so that it is a marvel that you should behold them dodging and dashing among the claws and teeth of lions. **10.** One man is offered to the beasts on a lowered wheel, while another is raised aloft on the same, so that he is born away from the danger. Thus does this machine, formed in the likeness of a treacherous world, restore some with hope, torture others with fear, but nonetheless smile upon all in turn, so that it might deceive them. **11.** It would be tedious to digress in words on every species of danger. But what the Mantuan said concerning the netherworld is aptly appended here, "Who could comprehend all the kinds of crimes, who could peruse every name for punishment?"[40] But you, for whom it is necessary to exhibit such sights to the people, shower rewards generously and with an open hand, so that you may make these offerings to the wretched. Otherwise, it is

37. Here describing pole vaulting over animals.

38. The performer here seems to wear a harness supporting rotating screens which he must continually shift on a frame to interpose contact with the animal.

39. This seems to describe a tight-rope performance, probably on a flexible reed, above the animals.

40. Virgil, *Aeneid* 6.625–27.

a kind of savage compulsion to withdraw customary gifts and to order spiteful deaths. **12.** And therefore, grant to the supplicant, without any delay, whatever customarily occurred for a long time with respect to ancient liberality, since it is a case of homicide to be frugal toward those whom your advertisement has invited to death. Alas for so harmful an error of the world! If there would be any consideration for equity, as much wealth ought to be given for the life of men as seems to be poured into their deaths.

LETTER 5.43 (C. 511)

This letter provides a glimpse into the interconnected state of diplomatic affairs in the western Mediterranean and the continued consequences of Alaric II's death in the confrontation with the Franks. Because the eldest son of Alaric, Gesalic, was not related to Theoderic, as had been his younger brother, he proved unsuitable to Ostrogothic interests as a prospective ruler of the Visigoths. The assistance that Gesalic received from the Vandal king threatened to destabilize relations between North Africa and Italy that had been tentatively secured by the marriage of Theoderic's sister (Amalafrida) to Thrasamund.

King Theoderic to Thrasamundus, King of the Vandals

1. Although, with God's guidance, we have given both our daughters and granddaughters in marriage, as they are sought out by diverse kings for the sake of confirming peace, we have nonetheless reckoned to confer nothing upon any man equal to our sister, that unprecedented distinction of the Amal family, whom we have made your wife. A woman equal to your wisdom, who not only deserves respect from the *regnum*, but who is also wondrous in her giving of advice. **2.** But I am dumbfounded that you have become bound by these favors to Gesalicus, a man who, even while he was associated with us and supported by us, was hostile to us. This man has thus been taken into your protection, so that, while he had come to you deprived of property and destitute of means, he suddenly appeared, having been sent to foreign nations and endowed with a wealth of money. And while this, with God's blessing, is able to cause no harm, nonetheless, it has uncovered the nature of your intentions. **3.** What could laws expect of strangers, if kinship merits this? For if he was received in your *regnum* for the sake of pity, he ought to have been held there. If he had been expelled by us, it was not fitting that he should be sent with riches to foreign nations, which would unreservedly wage battle against us, unless they should gain your hostility. Where is your habit, nourished with such great reading, of teaching others good character? If you had wanted to accomplish this with our sister, she certainly could not have assisted you, since she would neither permit her brother to be harmed nor cause her husband to be discovered in such affairs. **4.** And therefore, we send duly respectable salutations through our envoys, *ille* and *ille,* so that your deliberation may study this injustice, lest the disposition of your kinsman, agitated for obvious reasons, should be compelled to attempt something that would see peace destroyed. Indeed, that insult wounds grievously which happens unexpectedly and if deceit should appear there, where assistance was expected. We have committed further things that truly must be imparted to you by spoken word through the bearers of these letters, so that considering everything, your foresight may reckon upon whatever would be fitting to happen in such circumstances, since it is not lightly that wise men sin against the foundations of peace.

LETTER 5.44 (C. 511)

Following the diplomatic rupture of *Variae* 5.43, this letter congratulates the Vandal king for restoring the conditions of peace. The restoration of peace seems to have been predicated by Gesalic's defeat in battle in Gaul (earlier in 511), rather than Thrasamund's apology, which the letter acknowledges.

King Theoderic to Thrasamundus, King of the Vandals

1. You have shown, most prudent king, that advice from wise men can be of assistance after error has been committed, and that you love not the fault of obstinacy, which is known to take hold in brutish men. You have obliged our disposition by changing so rapidly to something better. For when a king makes restitution, he resolves all difficulties whatsoever, since thus is honorable kindness among *Principes,* however hateful boasting may exist among lesser men. **2.** We recently reproached you for the departure that the former king Gesalicus made with deceitful preparations, but you, mindful of your nobility and honor, have declared the matter to us truthfully. Whence, however honorable it is for a ruler to expiate himself so quickly, thus will it not be reprehensible that a man had given rise to grievous suspicion. For the man who could be coerced the least does not suffer passions to violate sacred trusts. **3.** For which, we accept your sincere apologies with pure intention, returning a change of heart inasmuch as we are able. But we have not retained the gift of gold sent to us, so that you may know our cause was motivated by justice, which no venality may realize. We have both acted in royal fashion: we have thus prevailed over the tyranny of greed, just as you have clearly conquered error. Let the gifts return to your privy chamber, only the gesture of which will be known to be pleasing. Let gold be forgotten where the prize of good conscience has been chosen. Let it be permitted to spurn at times that which always dictates to greedy kings. Let such an act now come to pass between our families that a dear kinsman would not avoid fault and that wounded pride would spurn money. **4.** Thus may it happen that what was usually sought in war will be declared contemptible out of an eagerness for affection. Let kinsmen know there were such men who were incapable of being roused out of a desire for avarice. Affection has indeed prevailed over everything. Complaints arrive at a conclusion all the more when a stricken man does not permit objections to be denied. Therefore, take back a gift received in spirit, not in hands. It will be sweeter to us to return such a gift than to have received anything more magnificent. Now be warned in similar ventures, be attentive to coming events, since a mind is granted instruction for the future when it is advised by the examples of the past. Therefore, we have extended the fullest affection of salutation by returning your envoys, *ille* and *ille*, wishing that divine providence grant your safekeeping, of which we know the strongest sort to be allied intentions.

Book 6

First among *formulae,* presumably because of its place in constitutional tradition, the consulship is here described with a sixth-century flavor. The titular nature of the appointment, and its lack of official power in the face of kingship, is portrayed as a virtue for a leisured nobleman, while at the same time, nothing is said concerning the partition of twin consulships between Rome and Constantinople. For examples of this appointment, see *Variae* 2.1–3, 9.22–23.

Formula *for the Consul*

1. In the opinion of the ancients, such a man would be consul, then, when it was known to all that he alone deserved to have, among all the distinguished honors of the world, the palmate robes that good fortune was accustomed to grant; the spoils of conquests were the names of the year, a singular compensation for one to whom all was owed.[1] The right hand of a brave man defended the standing of the Roman republic, his resolutions protected free citizens and the fortunes of all; and for so many great services the only recompense was the return of this dignity, bestowed for adorning freedom, invented for common rejoicing. **2.** Fortunate Rome always supported this office, through which, no doubt, the standing of imperial power continually increased. Long ago, he rightly held a kind of *imperium;* one who defended the homeland from an enemy rightly held power over all other citizens. Ordering public weal with equity, he furthermore claimed the right of capital

---

1. Even in the sixth century, the year was customarily named after the consuls, here referred to as a distinction conferred on only one individual (*sola compensatio*).

punishment; but the power to kill was only entrusted to one who was also the source of safety. **3.** Hence it is that the rods and axes were previously bound with such great strength, so that, since they were separated with difficulty, they would cause delay for considering whether something deserved the punishment or execution of a man. Thus, since everything was drawn from his deliberation, lest he would become haughty with pride, he is called consul from the necessity of deliberating. **4.** Likewise, such great largesse flowed from that right hand, which so copiously shed the blood of enemies, as would flow to citizens from a font of health. Thus, the good fortune he had achieved through war, he discharged in the exertion of largess. Moreover, in confirmation of public glory he released those servants from the yoke of servility who had surrendered to the liberty of so great a city. **5.** But now you undertake such affairs more fortunately, when we hold the labors of consuls and you the joys of distinction. Thus indeed, your palmate robes are conferred by our victory and you grant manumission to servants in the peaceful circumstance of prosperous times, while we grant security to Romans through waging war. And therefore, we decorate you with the insignia of the consulship for this indiction. **6.** Shade your broad shoulders with the varied color of palmate robes, ennoble a capable hand with the triumphant staff, take the curule chair out of respect for the magnitude of the many steps ascended, so that as a private citizen in leisure you may merit what we in ruling have obtained after the greatest labors. **7.** You who have known no wars conduct the business of victories; we rule with God's favor, we deliberate and your name designates the year. You who exercise the highest honors and do not bear the toil of ruling surpass *Principes* in good fortune. Therefore, raise your bold spirit; it is fitting for consuls to be great-hearted. You have no interest in private wealth, you who have chosen to claim public gratitude by giving. **8.** For hence it is that we elevate even those magistrates not exercising power, although we promote only those desiring to be consuls, since you alone who know yourselves equal to such expenses may arrive at this largesse. Otherwise it would not be an honor, but rather a burden, if we should impose anything unexpected upon noblemen. Therefore enjoy fittingly what you have chosen. This is an ostentation that is approved. Be outstanding to the world; we prosper by your imitating prosperity for posterity.

LETTER 6.2

Similar to the *formula* for the consulship (*Var.* 6.1), this letter describes a titular dignity intended to honor the senatorial class without granting specific legal authority. The letter skirts the political influence that acknowledgment as a patrician conferred, and also the reliance of the king's court upon such individuals in dealing with the Senate and the eastern emperor. For examples of this appointment, see *Variae* 1.3–4, 3.5–6, 8.9–10, 8.21–22.

Formula *for a Patrician*

1. If we examine the record of antiquity for the origin of the distinction, the college of patricians is known to have been proclaimed by Jove, so that worship of the highest god, as he was supposed, would connote the foremost position. But since it is fitting for you to attain something extraordinary and the very name was joined to greatness by its reference to senatorial fathers, with superstition abandoned the name has shifted to your assembly in the best circumstance, since the celebration of something priestly could rightly agree with the good conscience of the Senate. **2.** Thus you even read of kings instructed by the college of augurs, not unjustly, since it is fitting that one who had been able to arrogate public law would come from such important design. Hence it is even a laureate distinction, although it is empty, having no jurisdiction and not conferring the belt of the judge. The good fortune into which it is born is perpetual, since it fears not the candidacy of a successor. For as soon as it has been granted, it becomes coeval with the remaining years of the man's life; an individual adornment, a faithful trapping which never departs before the man leaves the world. **3.** I believe it similar to the pontificate, a distinction fashioned from the office whence it had come. Priests do not lay aside sacral authority, except when the gift of life abandons them. It is added that the laws confer such reverence upon them, as though placed in sacred office, that when a man has been girt with this honor, it may be divested of connection with paternal power only if it should be abrogated specifically by a *Princeps*. This is known to be founded with the purposeful reason that one who assumes the fullest expression of precious liberty would not have a servile condition among those in office. **4.** It surpasses prefects and noblemen of any other dignity, yielding to be celebrated before only one other office, which is presently known to to be held by us. Consequently, know that this honor is praised for its importance, lest either we seem to have given too little or you behave negligently, if you should believe that you have received anything commonplace. Therefore, elevated by our gift from this indiction, rise to the peak of the patriciate, which some magistrates wanted to be named after the fathers; you are about to become endowed with everything that had deserved such reverence. For although our clemency confers great things, you may covet what you have received thus far, if you strive to comport yourself in an upstanding manner.

LETTER 6.3

This *formula* introduces the chief appointed office in sixth-century Italy among those that held real administrative and judicial power. The office is described as a kind of partnership with the king, which is traced to a confabulated biblical origin. For examples of this appointment, see *Variae* 8.20, 9.24–25.

Formula *for the* Praefectus Praetorio

1. If the origin of any honor is praiseworthy, if a good beginning can proclaim what will follow, the *Praefectus Praetorio* is ennobled by an author who is deemed both the wisest in the world and especially agreeable to divine authority. For when Pharaoh, the King of Egypt, was vexed by portentous dreams concerning the danger of future famine, nor had human advice been able to explain such a vision, the blessed Joseph was found who could both predict the future accurately and who providently relieved the people from danger. **2.** This very man first consecrated the insignia of this office; he first mounted its carriage as a venerated official; he was raised to this pinnacle of glory, so that he would confer to the people through wisdom what the power of the king was unable to offer. For even now this official is called a father of *imperium* from that patriarch; and today the voice of the herald imitates this man, directing the judge, lest he should permit himself to be dissimilar in nature. It is with merit that one to whom such power had been granted should always be found carefully admonished. **3.** Indeed, certain privileges of this office are shared with our position. For it holds jurisdiction over a great distance without specific warrant, it punishes offenders of many kinds, it manages the public account according to its own discretion, it grants access to the public post with like authority, it claims intestate property, it punishes the transgressions of provincial governors, it pronounces final verdicts. What may not be considered resolved for one whose very speech is a judgment? It is almost as though he can establish laws when reverence for him is able to settle disputes without appeal. **4.** Having entered the palace, he is commonly adored after our own manner, and such office is known to perform what would cause others to stand condemned.[2] No public distinction, therefore, is equal to his power. He judges everywhere in place of consecrated authority. No public servant enjoys sanction from the authority of his court except from the staff of the *Magister Militum*.[3] I believe that antiquity conceded something to those who were known to wage war on behalf of the republic. He even inflicts corporal punishment on *curiales,* whom by law are acknowledged a lesser Senate. **5.** On his staff, he holds privileged authority, and he is known to command men of such high distinction whom even provincial governors may not dare to despise in any way. The staff which thus acts upon his commands is clearly esteemed, effective, well-ordered, and capable, with a thoroughly firm disposition, so that commands are not delayed by hesitation. **6.** He confers the rank of *tribunus et notarius* upon those discharged from public service, and makes his own officials equal to those mingled among the leading men subject to our immediate presence.

---

2. Note how this contrasts with Cassiodorus's report of the tedium, labor, and disrespect that he endured as *Praefectus Praetorio* in the *Praefatio* to Book 1.

3. The *magister militum* was the senior military commander, an office exercised in Ostrogothic Italy by the king.

Gladly do I confirm what he has accomplished; reverence for him even constrains us so that we may enact without delay what we know he has decreed; not without merit, when he sustains the palace by his attention, provides the *annona* for our household, brings cultivation, moreover, to his own officials, and satisfies demanding legates from foreign nations with his arrangements. And while it is fitting that other offices should have prescribed jurisdictions, almost everything is handled by his office, whatever is accomplished with fair moderation in our rule. **7.** Finally, I place fittingly upon your shoulders, from the present indiction, the bulk of every noble concern that would be prosperous to us, useful to the republic, and which you may sustain with your native virtue which you may endeavor to accomplish with the greatest loyalty. However much this office is bound by diverse anxieties, the more fully celebrated it triumphs. **8.** And therefore, may such light of glory invest your actions that it may both brighten our palace and reflect back from distant provinces. May your prudence be equal to your power; may the fourfold virtues guide your good conscience. You will know your court has been made so lofty that, placed there, you would think nothing mean and abject. Consider what you ought to speak, because it will be received by such distinguished people. **9.** Let the public records contain what nobody would blush to read. A truly remarkable leader has no part in scandal. Unless he is assiduously engaged in something noble, he incurs blame even for leisure. For, if we recall that aforementioned and most blessed author, to discharge competently the office of *Praefectus Praetorio* is a kind of priesthood.

LETTER 6.4

This *formula* for the *Praefectus* of Rome emphasizes the delicacy of acting as advisor and judge to the Senate, a role that letters of the *Variae* tend to corroborate, in addition to hinting at a small host of ceremonial, administrative, and commercial duties. For examples of this appointment, see *Variae* 1.42–43, 3.11–12.

Formula *for the* Praefectus Urbis

1. While the praise conjoined to officials is always valued according to the dignity of the office, and the appointee must be considered more capable than those who he is known to supervise, nobody is known to be elevated more handsomely than one to whom Rome has been entrusted. It is indeed grand to be a leading citizen, but even grander to render judgment over leading citizens. This Senate, glorious by its remarkable reputation, is acknowledged to have a president whom the world beholds preserving the laws. And there it happens that those men enjoying complete power in the Senate tremble to pronounce their own cases in your presence. **2.** Indeed, it is also known that this honor must be made public, so that they would choose to bind themselves to the laws that are known to have been established by them. This relation to the law is identical to our own station, but with the singular difference that we who appoint judges are not subject to another. **3.** Behold so many learned men and consider what it would be to advise them in anything, much less to dread the shame of transgression. You settle great disputes among those you know to be your betters. Thus do you derive your office, so that all men of that noble congregation may acknowledge you as judge. And above all show deference to former consuls. You render an opinion first and you will appear as one who must be respected in that chamber of Liberty, where you will be deemed fit to convene the foremost assembly of the world. **4.** What would he then think about the dark stain of vice, who knows himself to be among so many lamps of virtue? Would you not recoil from enmity? Separate the desire for favors from yourself. It is necessary that you have the love of the public if you would promise nothing as a bribe. It would be an exceptionally great and singular commendation, if anywhere there are those who compete to offer a large payment, the judges would not accept. **5.** Not only Rome is entrusted to your authority, although it would seem the universe is contained in that city, but ancient laws also permit you to extend your authority to one hundred miles from the city, lest the mural rampart restrain the judge of such a city, while Rome possesses everything. Moreover, you decide appeals to the law from designated provinces. **6.** Because it is not difficult to find orators in such a country, where masters of eloquence are always heard, learned advocates serve you. You are conveyed through a noble populace by carriage, public prayers accompany you, grateful acclamations proceed you with accordant voice. Act well, because it is fitting even for the populace to remain calm at your approach. You prosper abundantly if you draw the gratitude of such a city to yourself; hence, let diverse goods be sold with no venality, let the warming and healthful maintenance of the baths not grow tepid with the burning desires of theft; let the spectacles, which are offered for pleasure, not be a cause for litigation. For whoever deflects injustice in the struggles of factions knows the people to be pleasantly agreeable. **7.** For such is the strength of honorable truth, that equity is desired even in matters of the theater. Therefore, according to the stipulations handed down, we adorn you for the present indiction with the raiment of togate dignity, so that, clothed in the attire of Romulus, you will be obliged to pursue Roman law. For if you prove equal to such an office, you may expect anything from us. For if the Senate praises your performance, you will be no less worthy for any honor with such support. For trust in ability is complete where the approving witnesses are acknowledged as the most eminent men.

LETTER 6.5

A lengthy *formula* describing the post of *Quaestor,* the magistrate charged with crafting official communication. More is said concerning the intimacy of the office with the reputation of the ruler, especially as his representative to other subjects; hence, the *formula* dwells more on the importance of maintaining good reputation, as opposed to legal or administrative duties. For examples of this appointment, see *Variae* 5.3–4, 8.13–14, 8.18–19, 10.6–7.

Formula *for the* Quaestor

1. If offices are more prestigious the more they enjoy our witness, if the frequent attention of the ruler demonstrates affection, then no magistrate is able to be more honored than one who has received a share of our deliberations. For to some we entrust the administration of taxes, to others we grant the hearing of legal cases, and to others we have delegated the management of our patrimony. We retain the *Quaestor*, whom we deem to be the voice of our pronouncements, for our innermost counsel. 2. This office is by necessity attached to our most private thoughts, so that it may speak what it knows that we feel: it resigns the opinion of its own will and thus willingly assumes the intent of our mind, so that what it pronounces would be judged more to come from us. Oh, how difficult it is for the subject to adopt the speech of the ruler, to be able to pronounce what may be assumed as our own, and, being advanced in public distinction, to enact a noble falsehood! 3. Consider how you would have both burden and distinction in equal measure. If I doubt something, I seek it from the *Quaestor*, who is a treasury of public reputation, the armory of the laws, ever prepared on short notice, and as Tullius, the master of eloquence, has said,[4] nothing "seems more remarkable than the ability of speaking to hold the minds of men, to attract their inclinations, to impel them to where it wants, and to lead them whence it wills." 4. For if it is innate to the orator to speak seriously and ornately so that he would be able to move the opinions of judges, how much more eloquent ought one be who is known to admonish the people with the words of the *Princeps,* so that they would delight in upright behavior, despise the perverse, praise good men without end, and oppose the worst without hesitation. Let it be almost as though discipline is on holiday where the strength of eloquence prevails. Let him be the wisest imitator of the ancients, let him both correct the morals of others and preserve his own with due integrity. 4. And finally, it is fitting for the *Quaestor* to be the kind of official as would deserve to bear the likeness of the *Princeps*. For if we, as is usual, should happen to hear a case from the transcripts, what authority will a tongue have that is able to play the role of the royal presence in the hearing of others? Knowledge of the law and cautious speech ought to be present in him, so that no man may challenge what the *Princeps* happens to decide. Moreover, a steadfast spirit will be his fortress, so that he may be led astray from the path of justice by no threats or bribes. 5. Indeed, for the sake of preserving equity, even we, whom it would nevertheless be fitting to

---

4. Marcus Tullius Cicero, *De oratore* 1.8.30.

obey, permit ourselves to be contradicted. But take heed that you only defer to learning, to the extent that you would expound reasonably and thoroughly informed. Indeed, other offices may seek the assistance of advisors, but your office provides counsel to the *Princeps*. And therefore, prompted by the reputation of your eloquence and wisdom, with God as witness, we make you for this indiction *Quaestor*, the glory of letters, the temple of civil harmony, the nurse of every honor, the residence of self-restraint, and the seat of all virtues, so that, however you may act, you would strive to be equal to the aforementioned conditions. **6.** For to you, the provinces send their pleas; from you, the Senate seeks assistance with the law; from you, the learned may confirm what they know, and, as often as it happens that a legal solution is required from us, it will be necessary for you to be involved. But, while you accomplish all this, you may be carried away with no self-exaltation, you may take annoyance at no insult, and you may not delight in the misfortunes of others, since it is not possible that what is hateful to the *Princeps* would agree with the *Quaestor*. Exercise the power of a *Princeps* with the rank of a subject. Thus glorified by our authority, make pronouncements so that you may hold yourself accountable to our court, where the blameworthy man receives a change of fortune and a praiseworthy man acquires the glory of good intention.

LETTER 6.6

This *formula* provides a detailed description for the responsibilities of the *Magister Officiorum*. The attendance of the *Magister* upon the king was similar to that of the *Quaestor*. Where the *Quaestor* handled official communication, the *Magister* supervised the routines and resources of the departments (*scholae*) of palace guards and servants. For examples of this appointment, see *Variae* 1.12–13.

Formula *for the* Magister

1. Whoever receives the name of *Magister* assumes a distinction requiring respect, since the title always comes from experience and what must be assumed concerning the character of the office is known by that name. To him especially pertains the discipline of the palace: he addresses the stormy dispositions of unruly palace guards with the promise of his own moderation. So many departments are arrayed without any confusion, and he bears the weight of everything that host conducts individually. Thus, he discharges his office with the seriousness of his title and adorns the government by his actions. **2.** Through him, the arriving senator is presented to our inspection: he urges the nervous petitioner, guides the expressive, and is even accustomed to interject his own words, so that we may hear everything in proper order. A trustworthy intermediary for obtaining the royal presence, he is the honored facilitator of our counsel, almost a kind of morning star for the palace court: for just as that star promises the coming day, thus does he assign the appearance of our serenity to those in need. Moreover, with full trust do we place the greatest portion of legal cases in the attentive folds of his robe, so that alleviated by his faithful ministrations, we may be more actively involved in the public weal. **3.** But he also protects, by the discipline of his industry, the preparedness of the post-horses, the condition of which is always in motion, so that by the assistance of speed, he liberates our responsibilities, which he aids with advice. **4.** Through him, to the glory of our republic, hospitality is arranged for those from foreign nations; and those whom he has received lamenting depart unwillingly. Through him, indeed, the arrival of legates is announced to us in advance, however hastened they may be; through him, the public post is assigned in our name, and what is felt to be so important is entrusted chiefly to this man. **5.** Moreover, with these labors in mind, antiquity decreed great power to this office, so that none may assume the *fasces* of a provincial governor, unless this very man has decreed it. Antiquity has subjected the judgments of others to his appeal, so that what another is known to have rendered is referred to him. At least he does not have the vexation of collecting taxes, but he enjoys the benefit of widely assigned power, I believe so that an office founded for the solace of the *Princeps* should gather its bouquet from a diverse field of entitlements. **6.** Furthermore, he designates agents for the distribution of public rations in the royal city,[5] and creates an official for a matter of such importance. For this man offers rejoicing to the people, and adornment to our reign, when he appoints over the public bounty men of such quality that a querulous urban populace may be sufficiently fed and know nothing of riots. **7.** Even his staff is decorated by privilege of such splendor that one who has completed the duties of service is adorned with the rank of *Princeps,* and by miraculous means, those who rendered humble obedience to you may be found in first rank among the cohorts of the *Praefectus Praetorio* and the officials of the *Praefectus Urbis.* Thus, a certain injustice comes from laws in deference to a great office, when one who had been appointed to serve elsewhere is made *praepositus* over the personnel of another office. **8.** Moreover, the personal aid to the *Magister* is admitted to our presence, so that with a transferred share of kindness, we may distinguish the mainstay of one who offers us faithful service. Therefore, for the present indiction, with due seriousness, we appoint you to govern an office distinguished by so many entitlements, so rich in insignias, that you may be seen to act as the "master" in everything that you accomplish, because if (may it not be the case) one with such maturity should err, nothing may be entrusted to the character of others in state service.

---

5. *Peraequatores victualium rerum in urbe regia,* presumably Ravenna, although this may apply to any city in which the king was resident, such as Milan, Verona, or, more rarely, Rome.

LETTER 6.7

The first of three describing the great nonmilitary *Comites,* this *formula* describes the sundry administrative (primarily commissarial) duties of the *Comes* of the "Sacred Largesse." In addition to supplying funds for urban spectacles, for which the *Comes* maintains control of the mint, the regulation of foreign trade and luxury goods fell under his purview. For examples of this appointment, see *Variae* 5.40–41, 8.16–17.

Formula *for the* Comes Sacrarum Largitionum

1. Those titles that signify prompt action are wholly pleasing, since any ambiguity is removed upon hearing it, when what is done is encapsulated in the term. For the words testify to the nature of the office, the *Comes Sacrarum Largitionum* presides over royal gifts. How truly charming it was, carefully planned in every way, to make an office on behalf of the distribution of royal gifts and to call it someone else's honor, when it would be ours to bestow the gifts. A harmless performance, a pious duty to always attribute to this office that by which the reputation of the *Princeps* is able to increase itself. **2.** It is a truly great felicity to serve with the gifts of kings and to hold an office for public munificence. Other magistrates perform a mere shadow of the ruler's virtues; it is this office alone that assists so completely on occasions of public devotion. For no punishment is enforced through this office, nothing severely grave is judged, but whenever entreaties gush upon us, then it complies. Through you, we raise the welfare of suppliants; we bestow gifts abundantly on the New Year, and rejoicing is your public service. **3.** Indeed, you adorn this, our liberality, with another service, so that the form of our countenance is impressed upon metal currency and you make a coin that will remind future ages about our reign. O great invention of the wise! O praiseworthy institution of the ancients! That even the likeness of *Principes* should be seen to gratify subjects through commerce, for which our deliberations do not cease to watch over the welfare of all. **4.** But in this case, to the distinction of distributing largesse, as I would call it, a herald of our generosity, a proclamation to public prosperity, we attach the role of the *Primicerius* as well, so that we may also grant honors through you, through whom we confer the liberality of our wealth.[6] Deservingly, when both offices are shown the same favor and they seem conjoined by equal praise, they ought to be administered by one magistrate. **5.** This, however, is not enough, because magistrates of the provinces submit to your office; furthermore, you confirm appointment for even *Proceres Chartarum,* since it will not be considered complete unless it is finalized by you with due process. **6.** Also, the sacred vestments from antiquity are customarily

---

6. The *primicerius* was the head of an administrative department; holding this rank would presumably allow the *comes* to furthermore appoint a staff of subordinates who could then advance through departmental ranks.

entrusted to you, lest anything that pertains to the splendor of kings should submit to anything less than your administration. **7.** You also maintain care of the coasts with respect to import duties. By this, it is clear that merchants, who correspond to the necessities of human life, are subject to your authority. For whatever in garments, in bronze, in silver, and in gems is able to hold value in human interaction complies with your administration, and whatever should arrive from the farthest parts of the world pertains to your authority. **8.** Not unfittingly, antiquity has also allotted to you the trade of salt, along with that of silken garments and precious pearls, so that it should display your wisdom clearly, a purpose which such select species of wealth would serve. **9.** Therefore, for the present indiction, we confer upon you the dignities of the *Comes Sacrarum Largitionum* and *Primicerius,* so that you, who will have been girt with numerous distinctions, would be adorned with much praise. Enjoy, therefore, your entitlements with due solemnity, and if any practice departs from the ancient prerogative of the office, thoroughly abandon what you certainly ought to avoid, especially when the honorable care of twin offices, even though it is a laborious responsibility, attaches to you the abundant fruits of distinction, should they be cultivated with upright character.

LETTER 6.8

This *formula* describes appointment as *Comes* of the "Private Properties," the primary involvement of which was with revenues of imperial estates. These properties were the legacy of confiscated and intestate land that had passed to emperors over the centuries and should not be confused with the personal property of the royal family, which the *Comes Patrimonii* administrated (*Var.* 6.9). For examples of this appointment, cf. *Var.* 4.3–4.

Formula *for the* Comes Privatarum

1. The *Comes Privatarum,* just as the title of the office implies, is held to superintend certain private properties of the *Principes* through the care of accountants.[7] And because the exalted rank of a magistrate is unable to operate among men who have stooped to such sunken standing, the office also receives from provident consideration other entitlements, lest a Latian dignity seem in any way to have purpose among servants. Instead, the office now occupies itself more happily with urban duties, whereupon it properly lays aside the concerns of uncultivated men. **2.** For what would public law accomplish among slaves, who by law lack personhood?[8] No

---

7. *Rationales.*

8. *Rationales* were originally slaves who served as estate managers for elite households; in the eastern empire, the distinction between officials trained in law (*exceptores*) and less-educated accountants (*scriniarii*) was pronounced and Cassiodorus here seems to reflect the same prejudice.

legal advocate represented there, nor did their factions struggle with each other in customary litigation. Sanctuary for them was confused with rude sedition and judgment was improperly forced where words of wisdom were not adhered to by parties. Now the office profits from the legal conflicts of free men and a lawful patron is properly obtained when the case is felt to concern the welfare of the free-born. **3.** Your first duty is to protect, like a parent assigned to the public, against unnatural lusts and appetites inappropriate to humankind, lest anyone should pollute themselves in disgraceful intercourse, while disregarding reverence for kindred blood. For public dignity discerns with sound reasoning between the sanctity of kinship and the grace of marriage, because the extent to which we can indulge in concupiscence is restrained by a particular distance of natural kinship. You will be elected as a singular and restrained judge against these offenses, so that, while you pursue such upright matters, you model the celebration of chastity. **4.** Sound laws have even committed the sacred repose of the dead to your good conscience, lest anyone should strip the burial accoutrements of their marble, lest anyone should claim with irreligious temerity the grace of columns, lest anyone should lay bare for criminal examination another person's ashes, whether just consumed in gluttonous flames or left to the remoteness of time, lest a body, having already abandoned earthly vexations, should again endure human crime. For even though a concealed corpse feels nothing, one who is revealed as having stolen something from the dead is deemed foreign to all sense of devotion. Behold what has been entrusted to you: the modesty of the living and the security of the dead. **5.** You also possess no less a responsibility throughout the provinces with respect to the continued exaction of tribute. You command the *canonicarii*,[9] you admonish the landowners and you distribute immoderate duties among other magistrates. You do not permit unclaimed properties of good quality to remain vacant. Thus what the opportunist might seize, you make a just profit to obtain for our fisc. You prefer, by due legality, the relatives of the dead to us, because in such a case the status of the *Princeps* is always second, for we do not wish to acquire abandoned goods when they ought to possess them. **6.** Hoarded moneys, too, the rightful owners of which are long-lost to antiquity, are added to our treasury by your inquiry; since we permit everyone to own their own property, they ought to gladly offer us the properties of strangers. Indeed, one who had not lost his own property parts with newly discovered wealth without loss.[10] **7.** Thence, to increase the blessings of fortune, we adorn you for the present indiction with the office of *Comes Privatarum*, which the laws have decreed to be equal even to the prefecture.[11] For this princely authority should rightly be esteemed by

---

9. Agents tasked with assessing and collecting taxes; although note the *canonicarii* also fall under the authority of the *Praefectus Praetorio* (*Var.* 11.38, 12.4, 12.7).

10. Here referring to landowners who discovered buried hoards on their property.

11. Presumably the *Praefectus Urbis*, given the overlap in urban jurisdiction.

our palace, an authority which you will cause to increase beyond its own bounds if you manage the assumed office with restraint.

LETTER 6.9

Unlike the previous administrative *Comites* (*Var.* 6.7 and 6.8), which have complex portfolios of responsibilities, the *formula* for appointment as *Comes* of the royal patrimony describes only the management of private estates which provided victuals for the royal table. Nonetheless, the post is described as enjoying the kind of intimacy with the king as did the *Quaestor* and *Magister Officiorum*. For examples of this appointment, see *Variae* 4.3–4.

Formula *for the* Comes Patrimonii

1. The appropriateness of ancient custom persuades us to initiate with written documents those who accept offices sent from a great distance, so that edifying reading would admonish those whom we are unable to instruct in person. But you, whom royal privilege chose for the responsibility of our estates, we need not instruct with sent precepts when we have educated you in the enjoyment of the most edifying conversation.[12] Since indeed our discourses were, for you, lectures in justice, then you observed that what arrives from divine injunction is pleasing to us. **2.** Consequently, we believe that, for you, our estates would facilitate alleviating the fortunes of individuals, not burdening them. For if you wish to understand the nature of our tranquility, introduce an appreciation for a kind of humility to the servants of our household. Indeed, an unjust master strives by whatever means to arrogate his own advantages; on the other hand, one who is known to strive after a good reputation is always more burdened by his own better judgment. The rustics, who so deem themselves permitted by free will, claim an immoderate kind of liberty, since they are said to pertain to our property. Therefore, be for them a man moderate with lofty authority. Likewise do we show a mild disposition toward one upon whom we are able to bestow it. **3.** Consider with what distinction the received office ought to be managed, an office through which you have merited having, beyond other magistrates, the familiarity of the *Princeps*. For just as the rising sun reveals the colors of objects upon night's flight, thus will the quality of your character not conceal itself from the careful scrutiny of the *Princeps*. Your mind will lay itself bare to our eyes and ears. We recognize the character of servants in their countenance and in their voice. If an expression is tranquil, if the voice is calm, we believe the reason to be the most morally upright. For we do not consider anything that is said confusedly to be just. Therefore, your consideration

---

12. As a *formula*, this may indicate that this post was typically reserved for persons intimate with the court.

of the one ruling will be thought to speak, since those who are able to put forth their own speech are unable to conceal their own intention. **4.** Indeed, the words of men are the mirror of the heart, for it is demonstrated that what accords with good character is itself read in its very actions. The proud man is apparent by his swaggering gait; the wrathful man is declared by the seething of his eyes; a crafty man always prefers the view of the ground; a fickle man possesses a wandering of the eyes; the greedy man is revealed by hands hooked inward as though they are talons. And therefore be attentive to this: pursue virtue, for no man is able to deceive the *Princeps,* who is proven best at investigating the nature of things even in you. **5.** Therefore, with God's blessing, we promote you for the present indiction to *Comes Patrimonii Nostri,* so that our palace may provide testimony to a magistrate removed from greed whom we have judged worthy of advancement. For what should you desire more than to know that the speech of nobles praises you? Elsewhere unjust magistrates are dreaded greatly; here where remedy is sought in our presence, a judgment rendered is not feared. Resolve the complaints of landowners without extortionate measures. If indeed every just act transforms into an advantage with convenient celerity and returns it in payment, the reward is considered with great gratitude. **6.** Those properties of ours, because they are immobile, may not be extended beyond their constituted bounds, lest what is not permitted to move into an unlawful condition happens to be extended by unlawful practices.[13] Moreover, pass to your servants the purity of soul that you would prefer to be followed, since that man may be called just under whom it is not possible to part ways. Therefore, happily enjoy the privilege of office conferred upon you by the authority of God. Let the desire of good deeds that you know so well rouse you, since I shall be judge and witness to the things you do. **7.** For even if you manage our resources with careful arrangements, not only are you rendered distinguished in our palace, but importantly, you are rendered more outstanding even to people of foreign nations. For legates arriving from almost every part of the world, when they share meals with us, admire what is found abundantly, which they know to be most scarce in their own country. Moreover, they marvel that such a crowd of servants is required to satisfy the abundance of only one table, so that they assume the items consumed have been regenerated from wherever it is that such plenty is thought to have come. They openly consider what they may say in their own country, when they desire to tell their kinsmen what they have seen. **8.** Thus, the man who is found attentive to our splendor is rendered nearly the most celebrated man in the entire world. In addition, our opportunities for festivity are your counsel chambers, when the breast is rendered foreign to troubles and an opportunity is offered to you for making suggestions then, when the king is removed from all

---

13. A warning not to increase the patrimony by illegal means.

others. And rightly, as the heart sweetened by victuals should concede to you, who are magistrate over such great resources and over such sumptuous food.

LETTER 6.10

This *formula* awards men with *codicillos vacantes* ("empty titles") or titular appointment as *proceres* ("courtiers"). Although the title did not confer real authority or entitlement to a role in the administration, it did allow leading men who otherwise had no role in government to be recognized through association with the royal court. The appointment provided social prestige and presumably easier access to the king.

Formula *by Which Men Become* Proceres *by Titular Appointment*

1. Men of good character would be grievously endangered, if offices were offered only to those with wealth alone or to those with excellent physical qualities, while you would find that many flee from palatine rank who are more capable of shining with praiseworthy habits. For many, capability does not itself suffice for success; for many, vigor of the body is drawn from philosophical studies. It would often be the case that wise men would remain unacknowledged, because men could only succeed to posts in court service. It is rare that many good things coincide in one, although the devotion of a ruler should assist everyone. 2. What if a poor nobleman should dread the expenses of the consulship? What if a man distinguished in wisdom should fail to endure the turmoil of a prefecture? What if the man of flowing eloquence should fear the duties of the *Quaestor*? What if other offices should be avoided because of the irksomeness of difficulties rather than the appeal of rewards? If such distinctions should be avoided by great men, would not public offices draw a particular repudiation upon the integrity of our goodness? How much more just it is for a good *Princeps* to leave nothing unremunerated that nature has made praiseworthy! It is wisdom that deserves public honors, the exterior quality arrives at something totally different. It is prudence alone that is preferred to other qualities when it is fortunately found in a man. In our presence, may even the consular be untouched by wealth, may even the most distinguished men abide without long labor; let court service have its own reward, but let such a man as is furnished only with merits have an honored rank. 3. For not mistakenly do the sacred laws permit those whom the fame of good reputation may commend to claim distinguished eminences by titular appointments. Even if real power may avoid them in furnishing such an honor, recognized excellence does not hide. Men who were accustomed to despair of their own good fortunes are animated for such distinctions. Thus the one most able is honored for his labors, while the other, weak in body, is honored for his praiseworthiness. For all men are proclaimed with a variety which the name of various distinctions embraces, and, for what reason

more I know not, the man most full of distinction is thought to have been tormented while the most disengaged man is felt to have deserved the lot of those toiling. **4.** And so by the present writs, for the present indiction claim for yourself this title by the grace of divine authority, so that in the considered judgment of our reign you may obtain the sought rank of honor. Nevertheless, those who succeed by great exertion in our presence will be preferred in every manner. For it is necessary that one among two so honored, being surpassed, should yield position. Indeed, all men would be able to strive for quiet offices if those laboring were esteemed less than those in leisure. Those who are able pursue the other course, nor should such as we grant you be disappointing. Thus are both excited by gratitude and, while those are able to hasten to our palace, the joys of being chosen for distinction accompany you.

LETTER 6.11

Similar to *Variae* 6.10, this *formula* grants a titular appointment for senior senators. The *illustris* order was itself always titular, indicating the highest degree of senatorial rank and access to appointments with real authority, although itself not relating to governmental duties nor requiring attendance at the king's court. The *formula*'s inclusion of appointment to *Comes Domesticorum*, a commander of the palace guardsmen, in this case is honorary and not a necessary function or entitlement of *illustris* rank. For examples of this appointment, see *Variae* 2.15–16.

Formula *for a Titular* Illustris

1. The republic that gleams with the ornament of many citizens happens to be fortunate. For just as heaven returns its brilliance in the stars, so do cities shine back with the illumination of public dignities. It is not that a man may become better than another with honors, but because he has been proven more moderate, a better manner of habits is expected from him. For who would want to attract something scandalous to himself when it is his reputation that is especially known to have been selected for praise? Indeed, honors glorify one whose very life commends him. For it is not appropriate for a *Princeps* to abide with a bad appointment, when the people are wont to speak secretly even about him, whose personal habits nobody dares to impute in public. **2.** Therefore, on account of your faithfulness and labors, take the titular *illustris* office of *Comes Domesticorum*, so that you may appear adorned even among citizens, and, what is most gratifying to good intentions, you may perpetually attain your own advantage. For what would be more fortunate than to cultivate fields and to shine in that city, where an achievement delights its own author (unless anything is found wanting), while the granaries are heaped with pleasant labor? For this reason, we grant you a delightful honor, a dignity associated with influence, for both are conjoined together. The one depends upon the other; scattered seeds do not quicken, unless the quality of the earth had been tilled. You would soon have a copious harvest from our gratitude, if we learn that our opinion of you had been well supplied.

LETTER 6.12

This *formula* confers the status of *Comes* "of the First Rank" as an honorary title. The title did not bear responsibilities of office, but like *illustris* status, confirmed rank in the social and political hierarchy. The same rank is bestowed at *Variae* 6.13 for continuous service, thus offering an interesting insight into the politics of honor. For a possible example, see *Variae* 2.28.

Formula *for* Comes Primi Ordinis

1. It is considered great and honorable to many men to be involved in public offices with upright actions on behalf of the public weal; but how much more fortunate is it to take a splendorous honor without difficult conflicts? For occasionally strenuous labors may bring both public honors and even ingratitude; while human frailty quickly becomes accustomed to endure discomforts, even what was first thought worthy of pursuit, afterward is felt necessary to avoid. But it is much more outstanding to be in the presence of the king and to be removed from troubles, to have the esteem of the post and to avoid abuses from duty. Thus it is sweet to deserve something that nothing is able to disturb with anxiety, since something is rendered much more pleasing where only the joys of prosperity are felt. **2.** Therefore, you regard this honor as much an elevation to leisured compensation as, in ancient usage, it was known to have been a call to arms for those laboring excessively. Governors, hailed for the service of a year, to whom provinces confessed that they owed much, would attain such eminence with difficulty.[14] The legal advisors to prefects,[15] distinguished by good conscience and prominent in service, who are seen to wield such eloquence that you would believe them another *Quaestor* for furthering the public weal, also take this rank with the completion of the prefecture. And from this rank we often select magistrates, since we deem them the most learned. **3.** Therefore, consider what may be gained from such an honor, when accomplished men have found rewards of distinction on account of such praiseworthy administration. And rightly, it is conferred with such great display that it is deemed even appropriate for the splendor of the senatorial order: the resplendent

---

14. The past tense suggests this is a rehearsal of the history of the rank and that it was not currently conferred on governors in the sixth century.

15. *Consiliarii Praefectorum.*

rank of *spectabilis,* dignified by access to our *consistorium,*[16] which find entrance among the *illustres* and is announced among the *proceres.* A rank girt with the honor of a leisurely belt,[17] which is known to offend none and burden none and, beyond all other blessings, does not incite jealousy. **4.** Wherefore, urged by your character, we bestow upon you from this indiction, with the blessing of grandeur, the rank of *Comes Primi Ordinis,* so that, whenever summoned, you may enter our *consistorium,* which, thus praised for your character, you might adorn. The first honor is reserved for the *illustres,* while it holds a place second to none. Let it delight those who follow you in rank to imitate you. **5.** You will achieve an important and honorable position if you conduct yourself with restrained habits. Let it be a true admonishment that the rank you have assumed is weighed by the name of "first rank," at least because all those who follow you are adorned with the rank of *spectabilis.* But take heed that anyone who follows you in rank does not precede you in reputation. It is otherwise a grievous burden of jealousy to gleam with the belt of distinction and not to shine with the light of good character.

LETTER 6.13

This *formula* confers the rank of *Comes Primi Ordinis* for a *comitiacus* upon completion of services under a *Magister Scrinii* (the head of an administrative department). This *formula* therefore offers an interesting perspective of state service via comparison to *Variae* 6.12, which offers the same rank as an honorary title to someone without experience in service.

Formula *for What Is Given to a* Comitiacus *When He Completes Service for a* Magister Scrinii

1. If public distinction is frequently deferred to leisure, if sometimes nobility is chosen for position or a reward is granted only for something owed, with what zeal must one who attained advancement for his own public labor be remunerated? Public service must be considered in respect to the type of labor entailed and from this the remuneration must be determined. Indeed the estimation of these matters comes from its opposite, since such a gift ought to be given to obedient servants as would be a challenge for the impious. **2.** The duties which servants of the court endure are abundant: they compel contumacious litigants to be obedient, they track fugitives to their own lairs with shrewd cunning, they impose the restraint of equitability on the overbearing. Thus, whatever is easily pronounced by magis-

---

16. An archaic term, by this point, for the imperial high council, referred to elsewhere in the collection with more consistency as the *comitatus.*

17. The *cingulum otiosum* is a parody of the military belt worn by many magistrates to mark official rank.

trates, is fulfilled by them with servile exactitude. The danger they endure when they are sent to execute a court order is well known. If he should act tardily, the plaintiff complains; if harshly, the condemned cries out. Thus in both cases, it is rare for praise to find voice. **3.** We speak with respect for magistrates, but it is far easier for a magistrate to restore a praiseworthy man than for a civil servant to execute his injunctions without causing offense. For it is one thing to pronounce the law, it is another to bring justice to its completion. Indeed, a just ruling is rightly pronounced, but fulfilling legal verdicts is much more glorious. The sentence is only declared by judges, but the execution is claimed by court servants. After each case, they are subject to dangers, if the inconvenienced complain about anything with seeming truth. **4.** Often it is also the case that even the legitimacy of a sentence is unknown to others. For many sentences, if only because they are bemoaned in execution, the magistrates will rescind afterward. And they often unknowingly offend those whom they must later obey, and while they preserve duty to another's legal case, they meanwhile incur threats to their own safety. Is it not a wonder in these circumstances that the public servant justly avoids commendation? **5.** Accordingly, compensation must be granted to men so greatly deserving, so that we may rouse those exhausted from excessive labor with compensatory favors. Therefore, boldly enjoy whatever munificence the laws bestow upon veterans of civil service; you who have conducted yourself with purest habits must be subject to no humbling duties.[18] **6.** And so according to imperial statutes, claim for yourself the rank of *Comes Primi Ordinis,* which venerable antiquity deemed for those accomplished in such service. **7.** You will indeed follow this according to the kindness of the ancients, but you are fortified by our name against uncivil attacks and the usual exaction of annual taxes, so that public service, which is a servitude to our commands with its own particular difficulties, may seem something to be deserved more amply by other civil servants. And so we order that so many pounds of gold must be parted with if anyone finds pretext of any sort for violating our statutes.[19] Nor do we permit anything to prevail against you that would be attempted by deceitful contrivance.

LETTER 6.14

This is a *formula* by which provincials from outside Italy (*germen alienum*) may be restored to the Senate. It is unusual among the *formulae* in that it refers to a specific recipient for this honor.

---

18. The elevation of rank conferred by this promotion would make the recipient immune to certain compulsory obligations owed by other citizens.

19. *Multa tot librarum,* indicating that the amount of the fine would vary depending on circumstances.

Formula *for Those Who Must Be Restored to the Senate*

1. It is certain that we want the curia of the Senate be filled with an ample and natural fertility and that its offspring increase so much that (what is the most troublesome kind of longing) it may be known to fulfill the wishes of the parents. But to seek something less from whence it is possible to increase ranks in number is not a fuller kind of love.[20] A farmer cherishing the coming shoots assists the heavenly rain and irrigates beforehand the young trees that deserve beneficial rain. Moreover, striving to improve the shoots of the trees, he conditions the breeding with diverse seeds, so that he may sow the supply of his own garden with the increased sweetness of variety. Thus do we desire to bring the sweetest praise of virtue to bear upon the distinction of Gabinius,[21] so that a foreign seed gathered to the embrace of a grateful curia may grow with good habits. **2.** But this cultivation is greatly dissimilar. For what is thought better for the trees is grafted on; the stranger comes to them, so that they may grow sweeter. To you, however, they are offered so that the rustics may improve. For although the flame may shine forth in the night, it is nonetheless obscured in the presence of the sun. Hence it is that nothing outstanding may be offered to this order, except that which would be increased by it. And therefore, may the lamp of the Senate, burning prudently with the heat of its native character, receive one conspicuous in the splendor of his birth. Thus far, he was distinguished with his own merits; but now he will be resplendent with your brilliance. **3.** Offer the curia; take the candidate; one to whom we have conferred the dignity of the *laticlavus* is now fated for the Senate.[22] It is necessary for the fathers to be a liberal public assembly, because this word is dedicated, not only to its own offspring, but also to the eager desire for the common good.

LETTER 6.15

This *formula* announces an appointment as *Vicarius* (or deputy) to the *Praefectus Urbis* at Rome. Of note, the *formula* devotes more attention to the relationship of the *Vicarius* to senators, rather than the *Praefectus Urbis*. For examples of this appointment, see *Variae* 3.16–17.

Formula *for the* Vicarius *of the City of Rome*

1. It is the custom of deputy magistrates to submit to the authority of magistrates,[23] since they lack public distinction of their own. Instead, they sparkle in alternating light, they shine with dependent strength, and in those who have no right to their

---

20. Referring to a presumed reluctance among senators to accept new membership.
21. Otherwise unattested.
22. The *laticlavus* was the broad scarlet stripe on a toga or cloak that indicated senatorial status.
23. *Vices agentium.*

own illumination, there seems to be a certain reflected image of the true office. You, however, will be titled *Vicarius* and you will not relinquish your privileges while it remains within your jurisdiction, which is granted by the *Princeps*. For you have a particular relation to *Praefecti*. Litigants quarrel in your presence before praetorian assistance. You pronounce sentence in a sacred office and, what is a particular mark of honor, you commit the deeds of men to inscriptions, which is a precious thing among mortal affairs. **2.** Furthermore, laws do not permit you to be saluted without the military cloak, so that always being seen in military dress, you would never be recognized as a private citizen. But we intend all these privileges to be conceded to the glory of the prefecture, so that one who should grant such great things to the post of the *Vicarius* should not seem overshadowed by it. Let one who is conveyed with such grand presence display the kind of consideration given to your appointment. One deprived of criminality is not stripped to a harmless capacity. For what crime may be attributed to you, if anything lost would be charged to your own account? Furthermore, you are conveyed by carriage in the same manner as the loftiest men. You preserve the laws within the fortieth milestone of the most sacred city. At Praeneste, you proclaim the games, sitting in place of the honor of the consul, claiming the dignity of a senator, and those halls are extended to you which are deemed to be reserved for the loftiest men. **3.** Hence it is that in the hall of Liberty you hold a seat of the fathers and there, where it is an honor to enter, you have earned free access. Indeed, even the very senators who precede you in rank are known to request certain unavoidable services from you. You possess what you offer to your superiors, nor without reason must you, who are able to either assist or harm men of consular rank, be consulted among men of the highest rank. Direct your mind with the spirit of modesty. However elevated the public office, such is the inclination of those assisting it. Nothing is servile that is conducted on behalf of the republic, unless it becomes corrupted by bad character. For if the equitability of humble private citizens is pleasing, how much more pleasing is it to preserve equitability at the peak of power? Such equitability maintains moderation with difficulty, when it hastens to its own inclination. **4.** Thence, after the appraisal of our serenity, we confer on you the office of *Vicarius*, which you may thus administrate at Rome, so that you may cause your own good conscience to be recognized as the most distinguished in such a city. You will enjoy every privilege that your predecessors held, because just as we have required the practices of the ancients from you, so do we not deny you the long-standing rights of your dignity.

LETTER 6.16

This *formula* appoints the recipient to the office of *notarius*, a legal secretary, for whom the completion of service admits senatorial rank as *primicerius*. Of note is the importance of discretion in this office, especially as pertains to royal policy.

Formula *for the* Notarius

1. There is no doubt that servants furnish the privacy of the *Princeps,* when important matters are considered worthy of entrusting to nobody except those who have been fortified with great trust. Indeed everything that we do is public, but many things must not be known beforehand until, by God's will, they have been completed. However much it would be desired that such matters be revealed fully, they ought to be hidden even more. 2. It is fitting that the deliberation of the king knows only the most serious men. These ought to imitate a chest of drawers containing a full record of documents that only divulges whatever information is specifically sought from it; the rest, however, ought to be concealed as though unknown. For whatever is kept silent is often revealed through expressions to those searching carefully. Let there be an appearance of innocence that protects everything, since it is fitting that royal words be stored in an expressionless disposition. 3. But since that huntress of good habits has revealed to our scrutiny your instruction in upright character,[24] we appoint you to be *notarius* from the present indiction, so that in the course of service you may happily attain the rank of *primicerius.* This honor, which grants the rank of a senator who is admitted to the hall of the fathers, is not burdensome; for whoever serves our cares with assiduous and constant work is rightly seen to enter even the hall of Liberty. 4. There is added, moreover, another reward for completed service, which is that, if by some means this official also has merited attaining the rank of *illustris* or a titular office, he may be preferred to all those who have been adorned with the rank of *illustris* by titular appointment. Hence the *primicerius* is completely provided with the merits to enjoy the gift, since with one and the same title, dignities similarly bestowed are unequal.[25] You ought, therefore, to be attentive to your work, when you see such a reward prepared for you as the best men would rejoice to have found for themselves.

LETTER 6.17

This *formula* appoints a *referendarius,* an official practiced in rendering summaries of ongoing legal disputes brought before the king. A role similar to that of the *Quaestor,* who formulated official language broadcast to the public, the *referendarius* formulated language communicated to the court. The *formulae* for both stress intimacy with the person of the king.

24. "Huntress of good habits": an interesting expression, *venatrix bonae conversationis,* perhaps an expression for the *anima,* which is described in Cassiodorus's *De anima* as the instrument that reveals moral character.

25. See the description of *illustrates vacantis per codicillos* at *Var.* 6.11.

Formula *for the* Referendarius

1. Although any public office may be only as resplendent as the presence of our gaze may illuminate it, when one who fittingly acquires our attention always receives honored distinction, nevertheless, no man deserves our conversation more than one who would be worthy to be a *referendarius*. Through him, the disposition of legal cases are explained to us; through him, we learn the desires of petitioners and we give responses to them, so that we might unwind entangled legal proceedings. **2.** It is a great man who serves wisdom in this original public contest and thus represents the grievances of others in crisis, so that he may be known to satisfy the wishes of those petitioning. For what kind of case would we allow to be complicated with any confusion in tumultuous proceedings or to be obstructed in the least with such clamor? It is his concern to seek in disordered accounts what he could relate to us in reasonable terms and to report more clearly what he had been able to hear. **3.** It is indeed arduous to collect the words of agitated men and to report them accurately; the intermediary fears nothing in these legal cases so much as the danger he himself may sustain in its telling. If he should relate anything less than he ought, he is declaimed as hostile and is decried for bribery. The protagonist of a case is able to change his own words by pleading from fear, while it is not permitted for the intermediary to alter anything. Truly, our decisions must be preserved by such precautions of memory that nothing may seem to be less or more than the truth. When you attempt to explain the cases of others, you must speak fully and in our presence and, constrained in a difficult circumstance, you are vulnerable to our judgment. **4.** Therefore, it is our choice to make you *referendarius,* but apply the purity of good conscience and the language of truth to our sentences. Indeed, our discourse with you acquiesces to bedazzling erudition which, while it arranges the affairs of others through you, reveals the quality of your mind. It is not permitted for those under us to be incompetent, when, as with the passing of a whetstone, we create something inherently resplendent that we hone with constant application to legal cases. **5.** Therefore, report everything we have commanded to all, just as you ought and as you have received it. Thus do you commend our acts if you repeat things appropriately. Cherish what glorifies us. Let your will be what you recognize as our intention. We desire you to reside at such a height that we might even correct magistrates through you. We exact a certain peculiar tribute from you, so that just as we share intimate conversation with you, thus may our reputation particularly deserve to be protected by you.

LETTER 6.18

A fascinating *formula* that combines history and myth to promote the reputation of maintaining the *annona* at Rome. The continued operation of annonarial provisioning at Rome had been the key factor in maintaining what was the largest urban population in antiquity, possibly even as late as the early sixth century.

Formula *for the* Praefectus Annonae

1. If public offices must be assessed by this measure, that one may hold as much distinction as he is known to have benefited citizens, then certainly the one worthy to be selected for the alimentary resources of the Roman people ought to be the most gloried. It is indeed by your attention that the *annona* of this most sacred city is furnished, where the abundance of bread may overflow and so great a people may be sated as though at a single table. You hasten nourishment to and from the guilds of the millers, you enforce the correct weight and purity of bread, nor do you deem it demeaning why it is that Rome is able to praise you, and rightly so, when the affection of this city is a singular glory. **2.** And lest anything that you do is thought somehow peripheral, you ascend the carriage of the *Praefectus Urbis* with shared gratitude. You are found seated next to him at public games, so that the urban mass whom your diligence feeds may know that you are honored as a tribute to itself. For if complaints over the bread are provoked, as is customary, you, as the guarantor of plenty, settle civic dissension with immediate satisfaction and through you it is planned, lest anything is wanting for a complaining popu-lace. **3.** Not without reason it is reported that Pompey attained the summit of pub-lic life with foresight for the extent of alimentary resources, since it is rightly the singular desire of a people that it will be free from want. Hence that man earned popular applause and gratitude; hence was he always singularly loved and, in the gratitude of every citizen, he surpassed the deeds of the greatest men. Out of appreciation for this role, he was even called "Great," lest he might be spoken of with any dishonor.[26] **4.** May this example encourage you to success, when that man whom blessed Rome admired is known to have acted in the role of your office. However, lest anyone should suppose you to rule over abject men, the laws over bakers, which were most widely used across diverse regions of the world, are also subject to you, lest what supplies Roman abundance with praiseworthy servitude should be cheapened by causing scarcity.[27] The pork butchers, also, devised for the sake of Rome's plenty, are known to be delegated to your administration. **5.** You have acquired privileges in which to glory. Your tribunal is not among lesser offices when you enjoy the gratitude of Rome and you send commands to the provinces. But so that we may scrutinize in whole the efficacy of these deeds, the

---

26. Cassiodorus was apparently unaware of Plutarch's claim that Sulla had given Pompey the cog-nomen "Magnus."

27. Those engaged at the lower levels of alimentary provisioning, such as bakers, were regarded as having sordid professions; this passage seems to suggest that the *Praefectus Annonae* could mitigate the legal disabilities of bakers to encourage continued employment.

Praefectus Praetorio procures the supply of wheat; but to manage the approved distribution is not an honor less than collecting the grain, when, regardless of the abundance, complaints do not fail if the refinement of bread is not served. **6.** Similarly, Ceres is said to have invented grain, whereas Pan first determined to bake the moistened grain, whence bread is called after his name.[28] And thus Ceres discovered that by which she is honored and Pan, who fittingly applied it to consumption by human means, is praised. **7.** And therefore, knowing your diligence, which is always a friend to wisdom, we choose to confer upon you the office of *Praefectus Annonae* for the present indiction. Give these matters your attention now, since it is not appropriate that anything be stolen from the people. For what is done to the detriment of the city may not be concealed in silence. The populace knows not how to be silent when sometimes it even decries what has been perpetrated by no one. Be an equitable judge, correct fraudulent abuses, maintain the weight of bread. That by which the Quirites live is weighed more carefully than gold,[29] because the happiness of the Roman people is more agreeable to us than an abundance of the most precious metals. Consider well what we say. Consider what would be sweeter for you to prefer than to seek from that people the gratitude that even we desire?

LETTER 6.19

This *formula* provides appointment for the late-antique equivalent of the "Surgeon General," who not only attended personally to the king's health, but also resolved professional disputes among other physicians.

Formula *for the* Comes Archiatrorum

1. Among the most useful arts that divine providence has granted for sustaining the needs of human frailty, none seem to offer anything similar to what the handmaiden medicine is able to confer. For she always lends maternal kindness to those in danger of sickness, she strikes against ailments on behalf of our feeble nature, and she strives to raise us up then, when wealth and public dignities are unable to relieve us. **2.** Laurels of victory are accorded one skilled in legal cases, when the public interests of individuals have been well represented; but how much more glorifying is it to expel what brings death and to restore health to the threatened, for which a publicly active man would have despaired! It is an art that finds more in a man than he knew of himself, strengthens the imperiled, invigorates the stricken and does not withhold knowledge of future conditions from the healthy, since the sick man will distress himself with present infirmities. The physician

28. *Panis* is the Latin for bread.
29. *Quirites* was an archaic and hence poetic name for Romans.

understands what he sees more fully, trusting more in reading than in the eyes, so that what is gathered from reason is considered by the ignorant almost a prophecy. **3.** Should not ignorance of human mortality be deemed as a judge lacking legal skill? And since pleasures of wanton nature receive a *Tribunus*,[30] has not this art earned a more eminent position? And so, let this art have a president, to whom we entrust our safety; let those who undertake laboring on behalf of human health know that they are assigned an office. Let it be called an art, not for what it will do in each case, but for what it reads; otherwise, would we be instead exposed to dangers, if we subjected ourselves to changing opinions. It suffers immediately if it but hesitates. **4.** The health of humans is exceedingly obscure, remaining constant by a tempered mixture of contrary fluids; whenever any one of them will have separated from the others, the body is immediately drawn toward infirmity. Hence it is that, just as weakened strength is restored with the appropriate sustenance, what is administered incompetently is poison. And so, for the well-being of all, physicians have a master even after the schools; let them have leave for books, let them delight in the ancients. No man has a right to read more carefully than one who will practice on behalf of human health. **5.** Set aside, O practitioners of healing, the professional bickering harmful to the ill, since when you do not yield to each other, you are instead found squandering your learning. Consider what you would be able to discover without scandal. Every wise man seeks advice, while that man is easily acknowledged more learned who is shown to be more cautious from frequent inquiry. Indeed, at the very beginning of this practice, oaths consecrate you as though a kind of priest; for you promise your teachers to despise carelessness and to adore purity. **6.** Thus it is not easy for you to willingly fail, for whom the mind is compelled to yield before certain proof of knowledge. And therefore, the most careful man seeks what troubles the afflicted and what strengthens the feeble; for as I see it, although rashness may excuse an error, it is the crime of homicide to be mistaken in regard to the health of a human. But now we believe it suffices when we place you in a position to admonish such misdeeds. **7.** Therefore, we decorate you at this time with the distinction of *Comes Archiatrorum,* so that you alone among the teachers of health may have eminence and all others who would torment themselves in the course of mutual contention may yield to your judgment. Be the arbiter of an exceptional skill and strip from them the contentions that performance alone was accustomed to decide. In this way do you care for the ill, if you judiciously prune the harmful contentions from physicians. It is a great gift to have wise men close at hand and to become honored among those who are revered by others. **8.** Let your appearance be the safety of the ill, the restoration of the weak, and certain hope for the exhausted. The untutored whom the ailing visit

---

30. Cf. *Var.* 7.10, for the *formula* for the appointment of a *tribunus voluptatum* to superintend public spectacle.

may inquire if the pain has ceased, if sleep comes; let the sick man ask you concerning his own faintness and may he hear from you more verily what he has suffered. You have certain verifiable witnesses whom you are able to question. Indeed the pulse of vessels announces to the skilled physician what nature suffers within. Even excretions are offered to the eyes so that it would be easier to ignore the voice of the crying patient which feels symptoms of the least significance. **9.** And so, commit yourself to our palace; have the freedom of coming, which is accustomed to be furnished as a great reward. For it is fitting that others may serve a subject with authority: you provide rulers of the state with observations from study. It is lawful for you to weary us with fasting; it is lawful to sentence what is contrary to our desire and on behalf of assistance to dictate what would torment us for the celebration of health. And finally, know that you have the kind of license with us that we have not deemed to grant others.

LETTER 6.20

An interesting *formula* for the appointment of a provincial governor (*consularis*), this letter takes greater interest in the moral probity necessary for governing a province than in the duties that attend the post. The ideal of virtuous poverty has replaced the former use of governorships for personal enrichment.

Formula *for a* Consularis

1. Although the evidence of the very name would seem to declare your public office derived from the consulship, nonetheless even such insignia surround you so that no man would be able to doubt that you shine with the distinction of that same brilliance. For the axes and the rods, which antiquity ordained for that high office, are known to be set aside for your ornaments, so that a silent or rather understood authority is exercised over the provinces. For what kind of thing should you have that would ornament the celebrated curule chair? Indeed, even the appearance of those ruling announces the joyous procession of obeisance, so that you are adorned by not only the highest magistrates, but also heaped with the respect of the leading men. **2.** Oh, discovery of great moderation! Most kind of men, you are sent forth in the name of the consul and dreaded for your likeness to *Principes*. It is even the case that in certain provinces, adorned with a military cloak, you are also decorated by the conveyance of the state carriage, so that it is declared by many tokens that you mark the alternation of lofty office through fashioned images of distinction. Note that what you undertake is great, and you will be corrupted by the degradation of no crime. The origin of your title is announced by conferring many benefits. Conduct yourself in such a way that you should be accused of no greed, so that if you lack the resources to give, then certainly hasten to be moderate in will. For the man next best to one giving is considered to be one who continually abstains from the property of others. For it is certainly a crime of the most wretched hypocrisy to have a name for generosity and to intend thefts. **3.** May that which you proclaim elevate your soul to praise. You will truly make yourself unequaled if you trample the faults of the ugliest ambitions. For to overcome harmful weaknesses and to prevail over defamatory vices is itself, in a real sense, to be begotten from the morals of the consulship. For not superfluously did the wisest of the ancients impose such a name for public affairs, when they sent a consular president of great restraint to the provinces. Celebrate public law, be strong enough to bestow justice and imitate from a position of strength one to whom you are attached by proximity of name. The middling man may lack money, but one who is just is unable to lack wealth. **4.** Fear not the liberal hand of the consul; good men and poor alike have their own riches. Therefore, what is sought from you is what is born in the human breast, not what is contained in the bowels of the earth. How much better it is to triumph from a treasury of the heart, whence nothing penurious is born, because you do not accomplish little when you concede much, but rather, the more you are known to scatter the blessings of good conscience, the more you become an enriched man. Therefore, enticed by praise of your reputation, we conjoin you to execute the office of the consular in this province for the present indiction, since that which is deemed hostile to the laws would not be acceptable to you. Esteem all the more this office, which the laws of equity commend. **5.** Bolster your name with upright actions. Console the exhausted and then will you truly be called a consular.[31] But so that everything may be considered with equitable restraint, determine not to find money and you will find yourself having earned abundant rewards. For divine providence fixed this circumstance in human affairs, so that the man who is innocent of wishing for shameful gains is able to become richer. Ignoring vice, those who conduct themselves well receive more, since it follows that while the ambition of wicked men is despised, more is gained in heavenly remuneration.

LETTER 6.21

Also a *formula* for appointment as provincial governor (cf. *Var.* 6.20), this office differs from that of the *consularis* perhaps only in terms of rank, with the *rector* holding second position. The same emphasis on avoiding corruption prevails, but with more emphasis on judicial activity.

Formula *for the* Rector Provinciae

1. Antiquity providently determined to send magistrates to the provinces, lest the modest means of one coming to us should burden him. For who could bear the

---

31. More etymological gymnastics, *Consule ... consularis.*

boldness of brigands, if they knew that order resided at a distance? Force is permitted to have completely free reign if the one complaining is thought to be heard only lately. But how much better it is to repress weakness in its very cradle, than to vanquish hardened criminality. We expel the profit in wickedness if we cause justice to be at hand. For who would dare to sin when he knows punishment hangs above his own neck. **2.** And therefore, our decision sends you to this province as *rector* for the present indiction, so that, in a real sense, you will strive to correct those whom you know to be entrusted to you. Behold as though at a distance, among other things, the broad stripes of your chlamys, which you know have been placed there not without reason, except that when public officials should discern the purple, they might always admonish with the vigor of a *Princeps*. Joyous garment, pleasing vestment, which Venus is said to have woven for her son Priapus, so that the son, so singularly adorned, might bear witness to a mother of exceptional beauty. **3.** Behold how much the laws grant, and exert yourself to the extent of your authority. The trusted exaction of fiscal tribute is appointed to you. It is proven that whatever emerges in the provinces has been entrusted to your fidelity to report to the *Princeps*. You are, moreover, bid to give audience to the senators residing there; you protect with good conscience the servants of the *Praefectus* himself; your name is to be preferred to provincial *honorati* in the documents that they sign. Whatever your estimation would be is determined by those many whom the nobles have been able to neglect. **4.** It is added that you are called a brother by the *Princeps,* so that you have been elevated above the cheapness of accusations by the distinction of an esteemed name. Take heed that the reputation of such a man has been entrusted to you. Your good character is the fame of our reign. Be restrained in yourself, so that you will be able to be a judge to others. It is equitable that the eminent first control themselves, so that the criminal ought to fear one whom they fail to find similar to themselves. For no culprit fears a fault in himself which he knows the witness to have, when he assumes that nothing displeases someone acting wickedly except good character. No man condemns his own actions in another, since it is the nature of the human heart to instead strive to vindicate what the man recognizes he has committed. **5.** Oh, what freedom it is to sit upon the tribunal and not be harmful to your own client, lest he happen instead to become the one who redeems you.[32] Let the magistrate fear the disciplined man, let him fear the restrained man, may he not give audience to flattery. Decree so that he would be able to strengthen a stiff sentence. Avaricious judges do not know the extent of their transgressions; for when they receive payment for another's crimes, they cause themselves to become sinners. Therefore, be roused, so that we may hear only praise for your good actions. You will surely receive from us whatever

32. Presumably the client would redeem the reputation of the governor by vouching for his good character.

you have accomplished, since we will confine your remuneration to whatever amount of peculation we know you to have avoided.

LETTER 6.22

This *formula* appoints a *comes* to act as senior magistrate (*praesul*) for the city of Syracuse. The tenor of the letter suggests this *comes* was expected to operate with much personal discretion, given the distance from Ravenna. It was also clearly a military appointment, for which the necessary discipline of soldiers is emphasized. For a similar appointment, see *Variae* 3.23–24, 3.34, 4.16.

Formula *for the* Comes *of Syracuse*

1. It is the providence of a king to select men of such standing to be magistrates as would have no need for coming to our court, whose interest it would be to remain in distant regions. For there is no public business that could bear such travel expenses from Sicily, when it would be more advantageous to lose the case than to have won anything through such cost. For we do not want complaints to come from Sicily, but rather praise, since the conduct of a leading magistrate weighs upon us, if petitions can accuse him from such a distance. For a grievance is not believed to be false, when the exertions of such a voyage are undergone. And for that reason, affairs must be conducted with greater care, whence ill will is feared more. **2.** Thence, with the blessing of divine authority, we appoint you *comes* of Syracuse for the present indiction, so that you may thus strive to accomplish all things in such a way that we would recognize you to have been successful. We support the pleas of cases from nearby areas; but we also look beyond, to where we feel it would be difficult to reach us. You have what ought to distinguish you, if you arrive there purified with good conscience. **3.** Numerous soldiers attend you at our expense. You will be received as a jovial man among arms; your procession is furnished as though girt for battle. Use the army for peace, nor do you undertake the dangers of war so that you may be embellished by their trophies. But among these duties be mindful of civil order. You may not permit the soldiers to be abusive to landowners. Let them enjoy their own *annona* with moderation; they may not become involved in unrelated legal conflicts.[33] May one who is glorified by arms know that he has been chosen for the security of all. We want neither that the privileges of your office should be diminished, nor do we grant them to be exceeded. Let it suffice for you to manage as much as your predecessors had been able to reasonably accomplish.

---

33. It was common for locals to defer to soldiers for arbitrating local conflicts.

LETTER 6.23

Interesting especially as a comparandum to *Variae* 6.22, this *formula* offers appointment as the chief official stationed at Naples. The post was clearly military, although more is said concerning the challenges of administrating such a large population. The following *formulae* (*Var.* 6.24 and 6.25) announce the appointment to leading citizens of the city. For examples of a similar appointment, see *Variae* 3.23–24, 3.34, 4.16.

Formula *for the* Comes *of Naples*

1. Among the admirable rewards of public administration and the other inventions of antiquity, this deserves to be singled out for praise from all, that the decorated appearance of diverse cities should be found adorned with appropriate services, so that an assembly of nobles may be convened for a celebrated event and the knots of controversy may be resolved with discussion of law. Whence we also know that we have no less glory, we who renew the accomplishments of the ancients with annual solemnities. For what discovery would advance, if it lacked constant protection? **2.** Resplendent public offices stream from us as though rays from the sun, so that safe-guarded justice might shine on every part of our realm. For thus we sow conditions so favorable to profits that we may reap the security of the provinces. Our feast is the peace of all, which we are not able to imagine otherwise, except that the subjects seem not to have lost anything unreasonably. **3.** And therefore, we gladly appoint you *comes* of Naples for the present indiction, so that, as one who weighs with scales, you may hold public business in balance and you may guard your practices and reputation with maturity, to the same extent that you might recognize that you would displease that people with overly capricious punishments. It is a city adorned with a multitude of citizens, abounding in delights of land and sea, such that there you will think yourself to have found the sweetest life, provided you would not become involved in anything acrimonious. Your office will fill the praetorian residence and crowds of soldiers will protect it. You sit at a fortunate tribunal, but however many soldiers you would think to place around you, you will be exposed to as many witnesses. **4.** Moreover, by granted right, you ward the shores up to the predetermined point. Traveling merchants obey your will. You determine your own price for those buying and what the greedy merchant acquires profits you. But among these remarkable privileges, it is fitting to be the best kind of magistrate, when one who is known to dwell amid a crowded populace is unable to conceal himself. Your deeds will be the conversation of the city, since what happens to be practiced by the judge is conveyed through the mouths of the people. **5.** Crowds of men have their own revenge, should anything adverse be said, and whatever is sounded out with the assent of the many is considered a judgment on the judge. Against this, what is better than to behold this people grateful to you, who preside over them? How great it is to enjoy the favor of the multitude and to receive those acclamations which delight even gentle masters to hear! We grant you the material for being successful; it is yours to act upon, so that it would delight the *Princeps* to increase your blessings.

LETTER 6.24

A short companion to *Variae* 6.23, this *formula* announces to the leading citizens of Naples the appointment of a new *comes*.

Formula *for the* Honorati, Possessores, *and*
Curiales *of the City of Naples*

1. You do indeed pay us tribute with annual devotion; but in a better exchange we return to you decorated public offices, so that those who comply with our directives may protect you from the ruin of attacks. Your peace will be our joy; should you lack disturbance, it will be a sweet payment. Pass the time with proper conduct, so that you may live with idle laws. What need is there to cause anyone to rush upon punishment? Let the judge inquire into your affairs and find none. **2.** Let reason direct your actions; you know yourselves to be reasonable. We send a judge for poor character and a witness to good character, so that no man may feel himself compelled, except one whom a series of lawful procedures may charge. And therefore we have appointed *ille* as *comes* of Naples for the present indiction, so that a man commended for your governance may merit another public office from our judgment. It is fitting for you to obey him, since it is praiseworthy in both cases, that a good people may make a magistrate generous and that a mild judge may unite the greatest people with fair reckoning.

LETTER 6.25

This *formula* announces to the head of public staff (*apparitores*) at Naples the appointment of a new *comes*.

Formula *for the* Princeps Militum *Concerning*
the Above-Mentioned Comes

1. It is fitting that each office of public servants should have its own judge; for the opportunity to serve is denied to one whose president is removed.[34] But we, whose intention it is to maintain all administration in its own place, designate *ille* as

---

34. Presumably referring to the promotion of the former *praesul*.

comes of Naples, with God's assistance to those receiving him, so that the solemnity of public service may not perish for you with the annual succession of new magistrates. Therefore, render suitable obedience to the designated man, so that, just as you would not suffer to lose the advantages of your privileges, thus even by obeying you ought to protect ancient custom.

Book 7

LETTER 7.1

Taking great care to describe the temperance needed with martial authority, this *formula* announces an appointment as *comes* of a province. It is not clear from this or other *formulae* whether the authority of a *comes* substituted that of civilian governors (*consularis* or *rector*) or complemented existing gubernatorial authority. It is also worth comparison to *formulae* for *comites* assigned to individual cities (*Var.* 6.22, 6.23, and 7.3). For examples of this appointment, see *Variae* 3.23–25.

Formula *for the* Comes *of a Province*

1. Although the duties of every public office are excluded from military service and those who are instructed to manage public discipline may be seen clothed in civilian garb, only your office is equipped with threats that are girt with sword of war even in peaceful affairs. Behold by what judgment you enjoy this promotion, when we may seem to entrust the vigor of the *fasces* to others; to you, however, by these very same laws it is permitted to extend iron. They surrender ensanguined business with a pacified heart, so that both the guilty fear greatly and the stricken rejoice for a deserved punishment. On the other hand, the ancients were reproved if all things were not done with restraint. But since you know yourself chosen for a measured governance, do not lightly covet the ruin of men. **2.** He is called a defendant who would be judged. Know that the remedy of punishing has been given to you for the well-being of many. Such arms belong to law, not to rage. Without a doubt, such a display is deployed against injurious men, so that terror may correct more than punishment would consume. One who deflects mild offenses with words is not compelled to follow upon more hardened deeds with the sword. Such is a civilian dread, not military, which you would thus cause to be glorified, provided it is not deemed excessive. **3.** Moreover you still have a bloodless sword. Let those who stir plots of slight crime be bound with knots of chains. One who decides the issue of a life ought to be a procrastinator; another sentence may be corrected, crossing over from life is not permitted to be changed. Let cattle rustlers dread your insignias, let thieves quake with fear, let brigands shudder, only let innocent deeds look to happy ends, when that which the discipline of the law conveys anticipates that assistance will come from you. Let no man turn your will with bribes. The sword is despised where gold is taken. You render yourself unarmed if you replace a manly spirit with greed. **4.** For which reason, we grant you the dignity of *comes* in this province for the present indiction, so that as a praiseworthy man you may pursue your entitlements by maintaining civic harmony. Nor should you presume to do anything except what you would be able to defend by law as a private citizen. For it is this very kind of upstanding governance that is defended without force, so that a man is deemed to have been just when an adversary may oppose whatever he wants. **5.** For all that, you need not abandon your aspirations in distaste; for if you should preside well over provincial administration, the laws have rightly consented that you may hope for the fullest distinctions. Whence, what is known to have been promised to you by such authority already seems almost a debt.

LETTER 7.2

This *formula* is an appointment to provincial command as *praeses*, an office indistinguishable from that of *consularis* or *rector* (cf. *Var.* 6.20 and 6.21), except perhaps in excellence of rank. Like other titles for provincial governor, the *praeses* was an administrative position devoid of military authority.

Formula *for the* Praeses

1. Wisely in every respect did antiquity observe that public offices in the provinces should be renewed in annual succession, so that one man would not become haughty from continual power and the advancement of many men would meet with rejoicing. Only one year is necessary to ruin a praiseworthy man, since soon the duration of power is complained about as overly long, when scandals from shortcomings become unavoidable. For it is miraculous to avoid such a thing even in a short period, since even those who set aside provincial authority in haste are often dragged back to their responsibilities. An entire year suffices for making known the blessings of a good conscience, and such a man more easily guards himself from temptation. It would be your place to undertake governance for only one year; it is for us to increase the duration for the deserving, since we do not desire to lightly remove those men whom we feel to be just. **2.** For that reason, encouraged by your good character, we proclaim you, by the grace of divine authority, *praeses* in this province for the present indiction, so that you should act accordingly and whatever the landowner pays you for taxes would seem gratitude. Follow the good examples of your predecessors; distance yourself from imitation of corrupt men; not every custom is considered upstanding. You must be careful, not to follow foreign mistakes. One who follows something condemned effects the fault of stupidity. But that thing is better chosen whence the reputation for excellence is praised with admiration. **3.** Behold how full your province is of respected men. Consider those who ought to speak well of you and those who may presume to detract from you, since there is no power able to keep the nature of your reputation from the mouths of men. On the contrary, it is the benefit of a commendable reputation to travel through neighboring provinces and to find true praise there, where you command no power! Furthermore, we shall not leave unremunerated what we hear you have accomplished in upstanding manner. Fear vice and you will deserve the affection of the *Princeps*. You have the royal will in laws; submit to these and you will know that you have fulfilled our mandates.

LETTER 7.3

Whereas *Variae* 6.22 and 6.23 appointed *comites* for specific cities, this *formula* serves more generally for other (presumably less important) cities. Here, the ideology of separate legal jurisdictions for Goths and Romans is more clearly articulated, although this should be understood as the traditional imperial distinction between the military and civilians. Unlike the previous examples, this *formula* is addressed to both the *comes* and to the citizens of the *civitas*.

Formula *for the* Comes *of the Goths of a Particular City*

1. Since we know that, by God's blessing, the Goths live intermingled with you, lest any trouble should arise among partners, as is accustomed to happen, we deemed it necessary to send you a *comes* who, being a man lofty and hitherto comported with good character, ought to decide litigation between Gothic parties according to our edicts, and even if any kind of dispute will have arisen between a Goth and a freeborn Roman, by summoning to himself a wise Roman advisor, will he be able to disarm the dispute with fair reason. Between two Romans, however, let those Romans who we have sent to the provinces as legal representatives hear the case, so that each may be served by his own laws and a single justice may embrace all people under a diversity of judges. **2.** Thus by the grace of divine authority may both people enjoy sweet prosperity and a shared peace. Know, though, that for us there is but one equal affection for all men; but that man who cherishes the laws with a moderate intention will be able to commend himself more amply to our heart. We have no love for anything uncivil; we condemn wicked arrogance with its authors. Our piety execrates violent men. In legal cases, laws have force, not arms. For why would those who are known to have courts at hand elect to seek violent measures? For that reason have we granted salaries for judges; for that reason have we maintained so many staffs with diverse donatives, so that we should not allow anything to increase among you that pertains to hatred. **3.** Let one desire for living embrace you, by which there is permitted one *imperium*. Let both peoples pay heed to what we cherish. Just as the Romans are neighbors to your properties, so should they also be conjoined to you in affection. You, however, O Romans, ought to cherish with great enthusiasm the Goths, who in peace make you a populous people and who defend the entire republic in wars. And so it is agreeable that you obey the judge sent by us, so that you may fulfill by any means necessary whatever he will decide for preserving the laws, to the extent that you would seem to have satisfied both our *imperium* and your own interest.

LETTER 7.4

Unlike *Variae* 7.3, where the emphasis had been on preserving civil order among a settled urban populace, this *formula* appoints a *dux* to govern a province where military readiness and campaigns were more important to stability. For an example, *Variae* 1. 11.

Formula *for the* Dux of *Raetia*

1. Although the distinction of *spectabilis* rank would seem to be of one sort, nor is it customary that anything would be required for that rank except a certain time in service, nonetheless, with the nature of the matter carefully weighed, it seems more should be credited to those who have been allotted the borders of the people, since pronouncing the law in peaceful regions is not the same thing as providing protection from hostile nations, where not only crime is anticipated, but war, not only the voice of the public crier sounds out, but the blast of the war-horn often assaults. **2.** For the Raetians are the rampart of Italy, and the gates to the provinces, for which, not without reason, we deem them to be named,[1] when they are arrayed against fierce and uncivilized nations as though a kind of obstacle to floodwaters. For there, foreign raids are intercepted and the raging presumption is chastised with hurled shafts. Thus foreign raids are your quarry and the campaign that you wage successfully you know has been done in vigorous sport. **3.** And so, for the present indiction, knowing you to be capable in both skill and strength, we

---

1. This is a reference to the phrase *claustra provinciae* ("gates of the provinces"), terminology used to describe the defensive network of the Alpine region of which Raetia had been integral since the time of Augustus.

make you *dux* of Raetia, so that you may both command soldiers in peace and with them patrol our boarders with careful attention, since you know that you are entrusted to no small matter, when the tranquility of our *regnum* is protected by your care. Nevertheless, let the soldiers entrusted to you live with the provincials according to civil law, lest armed arrogance should become overbearing, since that shield of our army ought to offer peace to the Romans. Therefore, it is fitting for those stationed there, that within the province a more fortunate prosperity may be harvested with assured liberty. **4.** Therefore, answer our injunction, please us in fidelity and diligence, so that you would neither receive foreigners without careful consideration nor recklessly send our men against foreign nations. Indeed, it rarely comes to the necessity of arms where a carefully planned strategy is enough for defense. By our injunctions will you truly preserve the privileges of your office.

LETTER 7.5

This *formula* appoints a director to care for the physical fabric of the palace, probably at Ravenna. Much like a general contractor, the director is charged to supervise the contributions of various artisans to the maintenance of the palace, with the difference that he is expected to be versed in theory of architecture handed down from the ancients. For an example, see *Variae* 2.39.

Formula *for the* Curator Palatii

1. Just as our palace is known to be constructed by skilled planners, thus ought the precautions of learned men be diligent in its care, since that wondrous grace, if it is not continually restored, may be destroyed by creeping senectitude. These are the delights of our power, the charming face of *imperium,* the proclaimed testimony of those ruling; these are demonstrated to legates with admiration and, at first sight, the kind of man the lord is believed to be is confirmed by his residence. And therefore it is a great pleasure for a prudent mind to continually rejoice in the fairest of habitations and amid public cares to refresh an exhausted spirit with the charm of buildings. **2.** The Cyclopes in Sicily are said to have first established the most ample residences in an expanse of caves, after which, in caverns of a mountain, Polyphemus suffered the wailing bereavement of his single eye on account of Ulysses. It is read that, thereafter, the skills of building had been transferred to Italy, so that what was discovered by such great and remarkable founders, that emulator posterity might safeguard for its own advantage. **3.** Hence it is that we deemed that you, a *spectabilis,* ought to receive the care of our palace for the present indiction, so that you may both maintain in brilliance the ancient things of former men and that you may produce new things similar to antiquity. Just as it is fitting that a decorous form is clothed in a single color, thus ought the same brilliance extend to all appendages of the palace. You will thus be found apt for this, if you would often read the geometrician Euclid, planting in your mind's contemplation those plans of his, described with such marvelous variety, so that in time full knowledge may serve your recollection. **4.** Archimedes, too, that most discriminating artificer, with Metrobius, may ever assist you, so that you, who should be esteemed as learned in the books of the ancients, thus fully prepared, may be turned to new things. For it is not the least concern that has been delegated to you, when you are recommended to satisfy with the assistance of your art the eager desire in our heart for building. For if anywhere we should want either to restore a city or found a new fort, even if the charm of building a lodging should flatter us, what is found in our thoughts is produced for the eyes by your design. It is a stewardship of elegance, to set a wholly glorious accomplishment in such long ages, whence admiring posterity may be able to praise you. **5.** For whatever the builder of walls, the sculptor of marble, the caster of brass, the turner of vaults, the plasterer, or the mosaic worker may not know, he wisely asks you and that great army of builders rushes back to your judgment, lest it consider anything ill-advised. Behold, therefore, how much one who is able to instruct so many ought to know. You will certainly receive a rich reward for your careful plans, since you will be praised for their labor, if you meticulously demonstrate their accomplishments to them. Therefore, we want whatever pertains to you to be explained so fittingly and so clearly, that only the newness of the buildings should distance them from the work of the ancients. **6.** You only make this possible if our gifts have not been misused by any greed. For one who does not permit the worker to be cheated of his proper payment controls the workers effectively. A generous hand nourishes the genius of the arts, when one who has no anxiety over his sustenance hastens to fulfill orders. Consider also what you will accomplish with their obliging behavior, so that decorated with a golden wand you might be seen to process first before the royal feet among a throng of attendants, and so that by the very testimony of that proximity to us, we acknowledge that the palace has been entrusted to you.

LETTER 7.6

This *formula* appoints a *Comes Formarum* for the supervision of the aqueducts at Rome. A rare treat among *formulae,* this appointment offers a full digression on the wonders of aqueducts, but says little concerning the actual administration of water at Rome.

Formula *for the* Comes *of the Aqueducts*

1. Although the collected buildings of Rome are hardly able to be considered distinct from one another, since the entirety that is seen there is known to be designed for causing wonder, nevertheless, we are convinced there is a difference between what may satisfy necessary utility and what is dedicated only to beauty. To see the

Forum of Trajan even frequently is a marvel; to stand on the lofty Capitoline is to see human genius surpassed. But what is nourished by these monuments? And is bodily health refreshed in any way through delight in them? **2.** In the aqueducts of Rome, however, both utility and beauty are pronounced, so that the structures are wondrous and the wholesomeness of the waters is unparalleled. For so many rivers are led there, as though across fabricated mountains, you would believe through natural channels with the firmness of stone, when such a flood of water was capable of being firmly supported for so many ages. Hollowed mountains are frequently undermined, the course of rapids are dispersed, and this work of the ancients is not destroyed, if it is served by diligent support. **3.** We may consider how much the abundance of water offers to the improvement of Rome. For what would be of the beauty of the baths, if the city lacked that certain wet charm? The Aqua Virgo courses with the purest delight, which is believed to be named thus because it has been stained by no filth. For while other courses are polluted by an excess of rain commingled with earth, this gliding flow with the purest water is mistaken for perpetually clear sky. Who is able to describe such a thing in appropriate speech? **4.** The Aqua Claudia is marshaled to the peak of the Aventine on such a mass of arches, that when it falls there, tumbling from on high, it seems to water that lofty peak like a deep valley. The Egyptian Nile, swelling in certain seasons, rises boisterously under clear skies, with the flood channeled over level fields; but how much fairer is Rome's Claudia, sending the purest waters over the highest peaks of such dry mountains and through a bounty of pipes to houses and baths. It flows thus continuously, so that the desired amount is never able to be diminished! For when the Nile recedes, there is mud; when it arrives unforeseen, a flood. Who, therefore, would not consider the rivers of our city to be superior to the famous Nile, when its waters either terrorize in coming or utterly forsake in receding? **5.** We have not related these matters in gratuitous digression, but so that you should note what kind of diligence is expected from you, to whom such a great wonder has been entrusted. Concerning which, after much consideration, we have appointed you *Comes Formarum* for the present indiction, so that you may strive with the greatest effort to accomplish what you expect to be advantageous for such noble and great works. **6.** Harmful trees, which bring ruin to buildings, are akin to inexorable battering rams against walls. We suggest at the very outset that they be torn out at the root, since no injury may be avoided unless it has been destroyed at the source. If anything, however, has fallen to the consummation of old age, let it be repaired with dutiful celerity, lest a cause of expense to us should spread from increasing neglect. The management of the aqueducts is the source of your prosperity; should you strengthen them, you will remain unvexed. However much you are proven in devotion to these, you will advance in our presence. Therefore, act with skill and good faith, so that the structure may endure undiminished and the distribution of the waters may be diverted by no venality of the attendants.

LETTER 7.7

This *formula* appoints a *praefectus* for the command of Rome's *vigiles*. Rather than a military garrison, this was primarily an urban police force that patrolled the city. The *praefectus* is clearly described in terms of reduced authority, including the absence of judicial authority. See *Variae* 7.8 for the same post at Ravenna.

Formula *for the* Praefectus Vigilum *of Rome*

1. Although your title ought to rouse you to the security of the city, so that you would be able to fulfill that for which you are called, nonetheless, it does not detract from the customary precaution of our wisdom that we may also sweetly encourage those whom we designate for holding a public position to obey. For what would be more attractive to you than to zealously expend the pains of your diligence in that city, where such distinguished witnesses are seen to reside? Indeed, your guardianship, as soon as it becomes apparent, will course back and forth in the mouths of consuls and patricians; should barely anything happen with care and you will hear the nobles praise you with admiration. You direct a modest post and you revolve in the highest reputation. You will direct the guards of Rome, since you defend the city from an internal enemy. 2. Therefore, be vigilant for thieves. Even the laws, which advise you not to punish in any way, nonetheless did not revoke the license for finding them. I believe this is because, while thieves are detestable, nevertheless, because they are called Roman, the laws subject them to a magistrate of greater dignity. Enjoy, therefore, office as *praefectus vigilum* for the present indiction. The horror of inflicting punishment is removed from you, not the authority; for the law wishes the wicked to be seized by one whom it deems they fear more. Therefore will you be the security of sleepers, the fortification of homes, the protector of locks, an unseen investigator, a silent judge, for whom it is right to deceive plotters and a glory to cheat them. 3. Your activity is the nocturnal hunt, which by wondrous means is first unperceived, then felt. You bring greater theft to the thieves when you strive to circumvent those whom you know are able to ridicule everyone else. What you do is a kind of deception, that you are able to ensnare the wiles of brigands. For we reckon it easier to understand the riddles of the sphinx than to discover the current refuge of a thief. How may a man be caught who, watching everything, restless for anything approaching, anxious for any kind of snare, and having no fixed seat, is distinguished by the nature of the wind? 4. Keep watch with the birds of the night; observation unfolds the night to you and even as the birds discover their meal in the shadows, thus will you be able to find fame. Now, be attentive to our injunctions. Corruption need not deprive you of that which diligence provides. For while it seems fitting that these things are accomplished in deep darkness, nonetheless, no deed is able to be concealed. And so protect with good reason the privileges deputed to your office by our authority,

since it is necessary that in such a great city, what one man may not accomplish must be done through diverse magistrates.

LETTER 7.8

This *formula* appoints a prefect for the maintenance of order at Ravenna. The value of the post to the community, and its limitations in the eyes of the law, receive emphasis much as had been the case in *Variae* 7.7 regarding the same position at Rome.

Formula *for the* Praefectus Vigilum *of Ravenna*

1. Although you will be decorated at the outset with the dignity of a great rank, since the prudence of the ancients was not able to grant a title approximate to either the highest or the lowest ranks, lest one office should pollute with cheapness the splendor that it had given to the highest. Nonetheless, it is known in this case what the authority of the ancients intended, when they determined to name as *praefectus vigilum* one who prowled ceaselessly on behalf of the general tranquility. For entrusted to you is the security of wealth, the adornment of the city, the weal of all, even though you would wage a peaceful war against domestic vagabonds, should you find one of the citizens who must be chastised. 2. Protect the wealth of all men. By your vigilance, a safe sleep is had and feels no disturbance. Situated in time of peace, you claim a victory over the nocturnal thief. By morning the city which, when it beholds the captives and then knows itself to lack concealed enemies, thus defended, it celebrates your laurels. You triumph daily if you keep watch well, and while the glory of battle in war may be rare, glory attends you continually with discovered brigands. O what a command to receive with the great affection of the citizens! You presume to search for robbers whom the property owner is unable to find for himself and, generous on two accounts, you both obstruct future thefts and you prevent their present occurrence. 3. How inexpressible is the gratitude of a city because one man has taken upon himself what is seen to entangle all! Rightly did wise antiquity select for you the glorious name of *praefectus*, since it would not have been possible to award such a title, except to one who loved the citizens more than his own interests. And so your office happens to be elevated by no small reward, when even the laws of jurisdiction have been extended for those who are known to serve for the safety of citizens. 4. Which matters being thus, encouraged by your good reputation, we grant you the office of *praefectus vigilum* for the present indiction, so that you may pursue in every way both the care of this office and your own fitting privileges. But while common consent harries that most hated reputation of thieves, nonetheless we command that no action be taken immediately or without deliberation that causes the loss of human blood. Follow moderation, you who condemn audacity. Prize restraint,

you who sentence the thief. Let those condemned by their actions hear something be said on behalf of salvation, since justice has not decided anything that is not deliberated. Indeed, let the laws that have been decreed be preserved for condemned and confessed criminals, since one who follows the laws with cruelty achieves nothing.

LETTER 7.9

This *formula* awards the command of the port city Portus to a *comes*. Given the emphasis of the *formula*, it seems that this appointment only concerned the administration of commerce, rather than the governance of the entire urban community, as was the case with other *comites* assigned to cities (cf. *Var.* 6.22, 6.23, 7.3).

Formula *for the* Comes *of Portus at Rome*

1. To execute the office of the *comes* of the port of Rome is a service more full of delights than toil. For there the burgeoning arrival of ships is awaited; there a sea full of sails sends traveling peoples with the diverse commerce of the provinces and in the midst of such a spectacle of sweet commodities it is your pleasure to greet those escaping danger. Roman delicacies are tasted by these gullets first, and as though via a throat, the goods that reach the markets of the city travel on the currents of the Tiber. **2.** What a well-devised office that is seen to furnish the Roman bounty. For what could be more attractive than to manage what is known to satisfy that population? O invention of the ancients! O perfection of wisdom! In that Rome was seen positioned at a distance from the shore, more would initially be held there, where the arrival of graceful ships lay. Indeed, the flow of the Tiber's course supports two cities, adorned like two lamps, lest what ministers to the needs of such a great city should lack from partiality. **3.** You bring abundance, when you have treated travelers justly. A greedy hand closes the port, and when it draws the fingers together, simultaneously furls the sails of ships. For rightly do all merchants avoid what they know is detrimental to themselves. In which case, immoderate seizure there is an adverse wind; for one who agitates the waves of cupidity injures a fair sea. Let every merchant, thus advised concerning customary practice, bring a voluntary gift. For such commerce is a gift, not a debt. One who takes from the poor obtains too much; and one who restrains bribery nurtures for himself the rewards of life. Therefore, it would be your particular concern not only to restrain yourself, but also to hold back the hands of other presumptuous persons, since it is no slight matter to obstruct that wealth which it is fitting for all people to want incessantly. Concerning which, for the present indiction, we decorate you with distinction as *comes* of Portus, so that just as the office administrates sweet luxuries, thus too may you leave behind a praiseworthy reputation for honor.

LETTER 7.10

This *formula* appoints a manager for public games. The *formula* grudgingly accepts the necessity of following tradition, although it clearly considers involvement in public spectacle a degraded profession. For an example, see *Variae* 5.25.

Formula *for the* Tribunus Voluptatum

1. Although arts of the slippery sort may be removed from honorable habits and the wandering lives of actors may seem prone to produce dissolute behavior, nonetheless antiquity has provided a governess, so that they may not completely run rampant, when even these affairs countenance a judge. For the display of public games must be governed with a certain discipline. If not true order, then at least let the semblance of a judge restrain the stage. Let this business be tempered by a kind of law, as though noble conduct could govern the ignoble, and those who ignore the road of correct living might live by some measure of rule. For they strive not so much for their own enjoyment as for the delight of others and, by perverse compact, when they surrender mastery of their own bodies, they instead have captivated the minds of the audience.[2] **2.** It will therefore be worthy for those who know not how to conduct themselves with proper behavior to accept a *rector*. Your position, then, is arranged as a kind of guardian for this flock of men. For just as additional precautions protect those of tender years, thus must hot-blooded pleasures be curbed by you with careful maturity. Manage with proper instruction what the ancients invented with exceeding wisdom. Even if capricious desire and modesty do not agree, predictable discipline will maintain due measure. Let the appointed spectacles be conducted according to their own set of customs, since they will find no gratification unless they imitate something like discipline. **3.** Therefore, our preference appoints you *Tribunus Voluptatum* for the present indiction, so that you may conduct everything in such a way that you would associate the wishes of the city with yourself, lest what had been established for delight, in your tenure should be found transformed to blameworthy conduct. Preserve your own good reputation with the infamy of the lowly. One to whom prostitutes are subject must esteem chastity, just as it was said with great praise, "He is a man who pursued the virtues when involved in public spectacles."[3] For we wish that through the governance of something frivolous, you should attain a more serious office.

---

2. This is a traditional view of acting, in which actors endure degraded status for submitting their bodies to the audience, and the audience, in turn, becomes enslaved to the performance.

3. Attribution for this quote is not known; given Cassiodorus's tendency to cite authors, this was probably an anonymous aphorism by his time.

LETTER 7.11

This appointment confirms the office of *defensor*. During the late empire, the *defensor* acted as "public defendant" for underprivileged citizens of a municipality. Based on the *formula,* it would seem *defensores* regulated prices and transactions at the local marketplace. They were likely selected from among the *curiales* by leading citizens.

Formula *for a* Defensor *of Any City*

1. If such a man who should be praised for good counsel and seriousness is selected for conducting business of any kind, how much more distinguished ought you be, who undertakes the business of the whole city? For if it is a danger to cheat one man, how would it be to appear unjust in the judgment of so many citizens? For deeds done well for the sake of many ennoble the reputation, when one who is trusted to act entirely according to proper intentions is felt to be favorable to common needs. **2.** And so, moved by the petitions of your fellow citizens, our authority grants you the title *defensor* of this city for the present indiction, so that you, who are solemnly announced by so important a name, would want to do nothing venal, nothing disreputable. Arrange commerce for the citizens according to the value of the day and with fair measure. Abide by the limits that you set, since it is not a burden to restrain the highest price for selling, unless the prices chastely preserve public statutes. For in a real sense, you fill the role of a good *defensor* if you neither suffer your fellow citizens to be oppressed by the laws nor to be consumed by want.

LETTER 7.12

This *formula* appoints a *curator civitatis* for a municipality in much the same terms as that for the *defensor* (cf. *Var.* 7.11), with particular concern for the marketplace. However, the relation of the *curator* to the *curiales* is here more explicit. The difference between the two may be in the rank of respective cities, with *defensores* holding more distinction.

Formula *for the* Curator *of a City*

1. Although one who seems to cause the least disquiet for his own city and enjoys great respect among his citizens, for whom the citizens profess love, on this account may be considered respectable, nonetheless, the only indisputable distinction is conferred by our choice, since anything appointed by the authority of a *Princeps* is considered to be furnished by good planning. **2.** And therefore, we wish that the care of this city pertain to you for the present indiction, so that you may wisely direct the honorable ranks of the curia, and you may cause regulated prices to be preserved for those who have an interest in them. Do not allow commerce to be only in the power of those selling; let fairness protect desired things in all matters. Indeed, this will even gather the most fulsome gratitude of the citizens if prices are maintained at a moderate level, so that you truly fulfill the duty of *curator* when your anxiety will be for the weal of all. Preserve, however, by our authority, the customary practices that your predecessors had in the same post.

LETTER 7.13

Assuming that the *formulae* have been arranged in rank of importance, it is unclear why the *comes* assigned to Rome did not appear before the *comites* of Syracuse and Naples (*Var.* 6.22 and 6.23), except that any administrative or judicial role would have been overshadowed by that of the *Praefectus Urbis*. As described here, the role of the *Comes Romae* seems ancillary to that of the *praefectus vigilum* (*Var.* 7.7), with the difference that the *comes* has been charged with protecting public monuments.

Formula *for the* Comes *of Rome*

1. If the least inclination is enough to steal into locked and fortified homes, how much more likely is it that in Rome some find costly items on the open street that may be borne away? For indeed a copious population of statues and, moreover, abundant herds of equestrian monuments, such great reminders of service that they are placed with such care, where, if there were any depth to human nature, only reverence, not the city watch, ought to safeguard the splendor of Rome. **2.** What shall we say about the marbles so valuable in their craftsmanship and about precious metals, which, if it were permitted to snatch them away, rare is the hand that would be able to restrain itself from such items? Where such things have been displayed which the commonwealth and the labor of the world had been able to produce, for whom may it be permitted to be negligent? Who is permitted to be corrupt in regard to such a matter, when it is possible to cause such grave loss to exceptional beauty? **3.** For which reason, for the present indiction, we have granted you the office of *comes* at Rome, with its privileges and rightful advantages, so that with great fidelity and straining effort you may seek the shameless hands and you would compel thieves, whether of private wealth or of public, to come to your court and, with the truth of the matter determined, they may submit to the appropriate punishment according to the laws. Since public grief justly punishes such men who spoil the grace of the ancients with the amputation of members, they ought to suffer that which they wreak upon public monuments. **4.** Admonish your staff and soldiers to stand watch by night instead; the city guards itself by day, for watching requires no further attention. Indeed, theft is thus invited. But the bold thief is easily taken then, when the approach of the guard is least detected. Nor are the statues completely mute, when they seem to call to the guards with the wringing of blows by thieves. Let us, therefore, know your diligence by praiseworthy devotion, so we may later confer assured distinction upon one to whom we have now yoked a burdensome duty.

LETTER 7.14

Similar to the *comes* of Rome (*Var.* 7.13), it is unclear why the *comes* of Ravenna did not warrant attention earlier in the hierarchy of offices and ranks, except that as described here, the *Comes Ravennatis* seems to have been charged principally with the administration of the port at Ravenna (cf. *Var.* 7.9, for the *comes* of Portus).

Formula *for the* Comes *of Ravenna*

1. If a public office must be valuated according to its toil, if the praiseworthy attention of those acting on behalf of the public obtains gratitude for those serving gladly, your position, which by its own necessity is proven to remove any delay from our proclamations, must possess the greatest satisfaction. For who knows not the copious quantity of ships that you care for at our behest? An order is scarce written onto a post warrant by the officers of our palace and already it is executed by you with the greatest speed. 2. For among the anxious haste of dispatches, hardly anyone else suffices to attend to what you so vigorously fulfill. Let you exact neither too much in customary duties from merchants, nor turn a blind eye because of venality. The appropriate amount would be whatever does not burden those laboring, so that, when you have managed a touchy business without provoking complaints, you will merit greater things in our estimation. 3. Thence, our clear conscience makes you *comes* of Ravenna for the present indiction, so that you may assume the toils and privileges of your office. Moderate your duty with consideration for fairness. For one who is employed in public duties always finds reasons for being both injured and exalted. But inasmuch as your administration works among those of middling means, it ought to deal as much in fairness, since one who is known to better protect property of slender means liberates the poor man to hold a fair portion. The suitably wealthy hardly feel a loss, while the poor are injured by slight loss, when it seems to the poor man who possesses the least that he has lost everything to injury.

LETTER 7.15

A variation among *formulae,* this letter informs the *Praefectus Urbis* about the appointment of an architect for the maintenance of Rome's urban fabric. In many terms, this *formula* is similar to the appointment of a *curator* for the royal palace (cf. *Var.* 7.5), except that more emphasis has been given to the care of Rome's statuary heritage. The *formula* includes an interesting digression on the Seven Wonders of the world.

Formula *to the* Praefectus Urbis *Concerning the Appointment of an Architect in Rome*

1. It is fitting that the grace of Roman buildings has a skilled guardian, so that this wondrous forest of structures may be conserved with relieving care and a modern appearance of work may be constructed with skilled arrangements. For our liberality does not fail this desire, that we should renew the accomplishments of the ancients by preventing their ruin, and that we should cloth new things with the glory of antiquity. **2.** Thence, let your *illustris* magnitude acknowledge this man to be given the post of architect of the public buildings of Rome for the present indiction. And since it is a fact that attention to the arts must be nourished by just rewards, we want whatever was reasonably fitting for his predecessors to pertain to him. He certainly will see structures better than those he reads about, more beautiful than he could imagine, such statues retaining even to now the images of their authors, so that, however long the praiseworthy reputations of famous people should survive, thus the image of the body will protect the likeness of a living form. He will descry the natural character formed in bronze, muscles swelling with a particular strain, sinews extended as though in stride, and thus men cast in diverse postures, so that you would rather believe them to have been born. **3.** The Etruscans in Italy are reported to have first devised this art, which, embraced by posterity, has given to the city a population almost equal to that which nature procreated. It is a marvel that even signs of excited passion have entered into the forms of horses. For with nostrils rounded and flared, with limbs bunched, with ears laid back, you would almost believe them to strive in the race, when it is known that metal objects cannot move themselves. What may we say about the slender height of columns? Such lofty masses of buildings are sustained as though by erect spears and rounded out with such evenness as though by hollow channels, that you would think them to have been poured from molds, you would deem them made from wax, because you would see a smooth and metallic sheen. You would say the joined veins of marble are natural, because, where the eyes fail, fame is thought to be discerned in miraculous features. **4.** Narrators of antiquity have attributed as wonders of the world only seven buildings: the temple of Diana at Ephesus; the splendid monument of King Mausolus, from which mausolea are named; the bronze likeness of the sun at Rhodes, which is called the Colossus; the image of Jove at Olympia, which was formed from ivory and gold with the greatest elegance by the foremost of craftsmen, Phidias; the house of the king of the Medes, Cyrus, which Memnon built with a skill profuse in its use of stone joined with gold; the walls of Babylon, which Queen Samiramis constructed with bricks baked in sulfur and iron; the pyramids of Egypt, of which the space of the construction is beheld not to exceed what its own shadow consumes in any direction.[4] **5.** But who would suppose these

---

4. Lists of the Seven Wonders of the world varied; in this case, Cassiodorus has substituted the lighthouse at Alexandria with the palace of Cyrus.

extraordinary when such stupendous things may be viewed in one city? They have distinction, since they precede Rome in time and whatever new emerges from a rude era is rightly considered exceptional in the report of men. Now, however, there is one truly spoken of as a wonder, if all of Rome may be a wonder. Therefore, it is fitting that the most skilled man undertake such great things, lest among the ingenious works of the ancients he should seem overly dull and not be able to understand, as they should be known, what that craftsman antiquity wrought in them. And therefore, let him give attention to books, let him be at leisure with the instruction of the ancients, lest he know anything less from those in whose place he is known to stand as substitute.

LETTER 7.16

This *formula* appoints a *comes* for a group of islands otherwise unattested in earlier or late-classical literature.

Formula *for the* Comes *of the Islands of Curitana and Celsina*

1. It is fitting that everything may be accomplished well where the role of an advisor has not been lacking. For everything without a leader is disorderly, and when anyone decides to live according to his own inclination, he is known to have abandoned the rule of discipline. And so, following the custom of ancient practice, our authority grants you the magistracy of the islands of Curitana and Celsina for the present indiction. **2.** For it is right that one who may arrange affairs according to correct reason should go to the habitation of those who have been separated from relations with the rest of man, lest it would be an almost fated injustice that those situated at a distance should ignore common practice. Be then, as said above, one who would be able to hear and conclude cases arising at your court. Moreover, if anything is decreed by our devotion, act with the same intention, since the place for error is removed when what you ought to obey is disclosed to you. We believe this office thus strives for good deeds, such that it is possible to receive increase from our gratitude. For it is necessary that the office should claim remuneration from us, if it may provide anything that is beneficial to you.

LETTER 7.17

The importance of lime production to building at Rome cannot be understated, and the award of the title *Praepositus Calcis,* as well as the playful description of elements in the *formula,* attests that importance.

Formula *Concerning the* Praepositus *of the Lime Kilns*

1. It is a glorious work assisting whence it is that Rome is adorned, when someone profits from us as much as he will have contributed to the aforementioned city with his own labor. There is no doubt that baked lime, which is colored like snow and lighter than sponge, is the most important material for building. However much it is dissolved in burning fire, it hardens the strength of walls; a soluble rock, a stony softness, a sandy pebble, which is quickened only when irrigated with copious amounts of water, without which neither stones are joined nor individual grains of sand made solid. And therefore, what is known to take first importance in the walls of Rome deserves to receive the greatest attention. **2.** For which reason our authority places your diligence, celebrated in the talk of many, over the baking and distribution of lime for the present indiction, so that, having been abundantly provided, it may suffice for public as well as private building and the ambitions of all may be stirred for building, when they see that what is needed has been provided. You will defend the ordinances of your post according to our commands, so that you should be able to merit better things, if you have nicely fulfilled those delegated to you.

LETTER 7.18

This *formula* appoints an official to supervise the weapon smiths (*armifactores*). The *formula* does not mention specific factories (*fabricae*), although those at Cremona, Luca, Mantua, Pavia, and Verona may have all been operational in the sixth century. Not mentioned in the *formula,* an official appointed over one or more *fabricae* would have held the rank of *primicerius*.

Formula *Concerning the Weapon Smiths*

1. Consider what you undertake and you will know that there is no room for you to be in error. For the intent to construct arms well provides the safety of all, since an enemy is terrified at the first appearance of these very instruments and he begins to lose spirit, if he knows that he does not possess similar equipment. And so for that reason, encouraged by the reputation of your character, from the present indiction we place you in charge of the soldiers and workmen of the arms factories, so that you may compel such important work from the craftsmen as you know would please us. Do not lead our security by your absence. We shall see whatever you accomplish. Know that we are able to detect at first glance the defects of craftsmen through the exercise of the very weapon, and by the subtlest investigation we are able to judge the best-wrought works with praise. **2.** Behold, therefore, with what diligence, and with what care, that which is the test of our future must be made. Act, therefore, so that you become mired in no corruption, no blame, since what is neglected in such an important matter is not pardonable, and you would be punished in proportion to how much you have sinned. This work begets death and salvation, the destruction of those sinning, the protection of the good, and always necessary assistance against the wicked. Phoroneus is said to have first offered this craft to Juno,[5] so that, as the ancients supposed, he had dedicated his invention to divine majesty at the very beginning. Such weapons are necessary in war and comely in peace; furthermore, they make fragile and weak mortals stronger than any beast.

LETTER 7.19

This *formula* provides notification for the appointment of a new *primicerius fabricae* (cf. *Var.* 7.18), and reminds the *Praefectus Praetorio* to supply the arms workers with rations from the *annona*.

Formula *to the* Praefectus Praetorio *Concerning the Weapon Smiths*

1. We have learned through the report of many that a man instructed by good character has been able to faithfully accomplish the affairs entrusted to him. For that reason, your *illustris* magnitude should know him to be chosen, so that he may preside over the soldiers and have command over the craftsmen of the arms, according to venerable custom, to the extent that they may thus fittingly fulfill their quota, and so that nothing inappropriate may be found in their operation. It is fitting that wherever fault may lie, if it neglects the instruments of war, it is severely punished there. Obviously, to steal what equips the army is a kind of treason. For which reason, your foresight will allot your customary attention to the craftsmen, so that, because a license for rations has been granted to them, the necessary materials may be vigorously demanded.

LETTER 7.20

A *formula* reminding a governor to submit a reckoning of the *bina et terna* (the land tax) to the offices of the *Comes Sacrarum Largitionum*. The *tituli binorum et ternorum* mentioned in the *formula* probably refers to the receipts of collection, or "accounts," rather than the submission of payment to the *Comes*.

Formula *for the* Bina *and* Terna, *If Collected by a Governor*

1. If we seem to attach obligations to you, it is because we believe it pertains to the nature of your office, since however generously someone has been paid, just as amply will he be shown to undertake the cause of serving. And therefore, you will hasten, through the care of your office, to send to the offices of the *Comes Sacrarum Largitionum* the accounts for the *bina* and *terna*, which ancient authority has determined to be exacted from the provincials, so that the entire amount for the

---

5. Phoroneus was among the earliest of Argive kings who, according to legend, invented the forge and dedicated its use to Hera.

present indiction may be duly accounted for by the Kalends of March, lest you should be compelled to render from your own property whatever you have neglected to collect. For it concerns your own injury, if another man is known to execute those accounts that the most sacred laws have determined pertain to you.

LETTER 7.21

This *formula* serves the same purpose as *Variae* 7.20, except in lieu of a governor taking responsibility, a magistrate's staff (*officium*) has been directed to work with two *scriniarii* sent from the staff of the *Comes Sacrarum Largitionum*. Whereas *Variae* 7.20 refers to a reckoning of accounts (*titulos*), this *formula* refers to payment (*illatum*), indicating that the actual movement of taxes occurred between the governor's staff and the *scriniarii* and warranted a separate layer of communication.

Formula *for the* Bina *and* Terna, *If Collected by a Magistrate's Staff*

1. Although ancient custom has ordained that the collection of the *bina* and *terna* pertains to you, nonetheless, lest manifold responsibilities should overburden you and doubled concerns should create obstacles for you, we have determined that the *scriniarii, ille* and *ille,* must be sent from our staff, so that they might supervise your staff for you, to the end that with their assistance the due amount may be rendered to the *illustris Comes Sacrarum Largitionum* by the Kalends of March, lest you should be forced to defend your public reputation, if you have determined the sacred largesse must be hindered by any delay. Thus, as you would not deem you must be removed from office, we believe you must be assisted. For if anything in the payment is less than would be appropriate, you will know this amount must be wrenched from your own resources.

LETTER 7.22

The final *formula* in a series pertaining to the collection of the land tax (cf. *Var.* 7.20 and 7.21), here advising two *scriniarii* from the staff of the *Comes Sacrarum Largitionum* to transfer the revenues collected in a particular province.

Formula *for Advising* Ille *and* Ille, *the* Scriniarii, *Concerning the* Bina *and* Terna

1. We do not doubt that a man is most pleased, when he is advised to fulfill an accepted duty, since it is a rather serious matter if a public servant should live an idle life. For him, public affairs is his purpose, a command of the *Princeps* his honor. He is one who would consider being abandoned to ignoble inactivity the same as being disarmed. Therefore, we order you to travel to this province for the

present indiction, so that when the amount of the *bina* and *terna* is duly collected by the governor and his staff, before the Kalends of March, you will send it to the offices of the *Comes Sacrarum Largitionum* without any delay. Thus, let nothing less than the customary amount reach our treasury; nor should the landowner pay beyond the measure of his assessment. And you should not doubt that danger attends our admonition, if we come to know any kind of activity contrary to standard practices.

LETTER 7.23

It is not apparent what distinguishes this appointment from the *formula* for the *comes* of Portus (*Var. 7.9*), as the jurisdictions described both pertain largely to the management of incoming commerce. It may be that circumstances dictated whether the senior magistrate for Portus should be a Goth with military competence (a *comes*) or a Roman official (the *vicarius*).

Formula *for the* Vicarius *of Portus*

1. Our kindness rewards your agreeableness particularly if we ascertain that you have reasonably accomplished what was entrusted to you. Indeed, you will not remain unremunerated if you adroitly welcome foreign travelers and you arrange our commerce with measured fairness. Rightly, wisdom is necessary everywhere, and in this case it seems particularly advantageous, when disputes continually arise between two peoples, unless justice will be protected.[6] For that reason, those whose characters are similar to the wind must be mollified skillfully, for unless their hearts are first tempered, they leap to the worst contempt according to their native disposition. Therefore, stirred by the reputation of your restraint, for the present indiction we have decided for you to have responsibility for this port, so that you may thus arrange everything pertaining to your post, however you may accomplish it for the best. For in small affairs is learned that by means of which better things may be claimed.

LETTER 7.24

Although a *princeps* typically served as the chief of a bureau for palatine officials, this *formula* appoints a *princeps* to a particular province, where he served as legal assistant to the provincial governor (here given as *iudex*), or perhaps as his substitute on occasions.

---

6. The reference to two peoples is obscure and was probably meant in a general sense of "locals and foreigners."

Formula *for the* Princeps *of Dalmatia*

1. Whoever conducts service with the title *princeps* is adorned with great prerogatives among his colleagues. For he is acknowledged to hold chief place, when a large portion of titles claim the excellence of office over human affairs. Moreover, this title is judged according to the example of your tenure, without which access to official chambers is not obtained, nor is the public declaration of complaint accomplished, and thus the entire role of the governor is entrusted to you by law, so that without you he would not be able to complete a legal case. **2.** It is true that power over provincials has been given to the *comes*, but to you the governor himself has been entrusted. You hold the rod threatening the wicked; you maintain order with laws; it is your right to punish public slander, which it is not even appropriate for the *praesul* to punish;[7] moreover, the record of every legal case is completed with your signature and your agreement is sought, according to which the ruling of the governor is explained. **3.** Act well, then, so that you who are set over such important matters may be perceived as fulfilling them correctly. And so we order you to set out for this province for the present indiction, so that, joined to the staff of the governor, you might accomplish deeds suitable to your post and you, who are sent out by us as a *princeps* will be accused of no corruption. For you will make yourself respected more than anyone, if what is assumed in regard to your title is perceived even in your habits.

LETTER 7.25

Whereas *Variae* 7.24 announced to a *princeps* his assignment to a provincial governor, the present *formula* announces to a provincial *comes* the appointment of two *principes* to his staff, presumably to serve as legal aides in disputes between military personnel and civilians.

Formula *for the Letter Sent to a* Comes *for Introducing the* Principes

1. Solemn custom encourages us both to send someone distinguished to your staff and to maintain the former rank of those keeping guard. For it is to our credit if you are attended by a Roman official, when with such important ministers you will be able to accomplish what is known to agree with the sanction of antiquity. For thus, by God's blessing, have we led forth our Goths, so that they may be both accomplished in arms and comported by fairness. This is what other nations have been unable to possess; this is what makes you exceptional, that accustomed to war, you appear to live with the Romans according to laws. **2.** Therefore, we have decided that *ille* and *ille* should be sent to you from our staff, so that according to ancient custom, they may restrain by the reasonableness of antiquity those who

---

7. *Insolentia perorantis* is an elliptical way of describing slander, which a *praesul* (presumably president of the local curia) apparently had no authority to restrain.

obey your orders. You will demonstrate to them, by our order, your agreeableness in managing the *annona* and your good conduct. For one who has deserved to be sent by us ought to be esteemed by you.

LETTER 7.26

Appointments to comital rank in other cities have a clear military character (*Var.* 6.22, 6.23, 7.3); by contrast, this *formula* seems intended for a magistrate holding senior judicial and administrative authority in a *civitas*.

Formula *for the* Comites *of Diverse Cities*

1. In this age, public distinction is the manifest approval of human character, since the candor of the soul always reveals its true nature, when one who knows how to attract others to himself despises to conceal himself. But this is the fortunate condition of human character, which the approval of its own advancement encloses within bounds of moderation and thus compasses the briefest span of fame, even as an appointed official may be granted esteem for all time. 2. For this reason do judges sometimes fall to flattery. For it is indeed laborious, but not impossible, to coax from mortal affairs the recognition that the favor of divine authority assigns to popular sentiment, so that even those citizens who are ignorant of law may nevertheless come to recognize the purpose of truth. For it is necessary that what is granted by nature may be pleasantly witnessed anew by the same gentle reminder. And therefore, you should not labor to impose upon the people what is fitting for them to feel in their own nature. For those who are able to be receptive to an advisor easily follow the meaning of another's words. 3. On that account, we bestow upon you, by the grace of divine authority, distinction as *Comes Secundi Ordinis* in this city for the present indiction, so that you may govern the citizens entrusted to you with equity and you may continually satisfy the dictates of public ordinances, to the extent that we may offer better things to you when we feel you have acted appropriately in the present capacity.

LETTER 7.27

This *formula* follows upon the appointment of a *comes civitatis* in *Variae* 7.26 by announcing the arrival of the new official to the key constituents of the municipality: men of distinguished rank (*honorati*), the major landowners (*possessores*), and members of the local town council (*curiales*).

Formula *for the* Honorati, Possessores, *and* Curiales
Concerning the Above-Mentioned Comes

1. It is always useful to select one whom the rest ought to obey, since, if the inclination of diverse people is left to wander, confusion, that companion of sin, is

encouraged. And so, know that we have installed this man as *comes* of your city for the present indiction, the advantage of which is wholesome obedience, so that he may bring remedy to your disagreements, and he may bring effective administration to public ordinances. Let it be known that, if anyone has comported himself with upstanding loyalty, it will hardly be in vain for him to request similar things from our better judgment.

LETTER 7.28

Like *Variae* 7.27, this *formula* follows upon the appointment of a *comes civitatis* (*Var.* 7.26), by announcing the arrival of the new official to the key administrators of his local staff. These *principes* may be understood in terms of roles discussed for *Variae* 7.24 and 7.25, albeit at a municipal, not provincial level. The consistent reference to *iudices* in plural suggests the regular rotation of visiting magistrates.

Formula *for the* Principes Militum *of the* Comes *of the Above-Mentioned City*

1. We trust it is pleasing to you when we send officials to your administration, since however often you enjoy the presence of a judge, then do you accomplish your duties. The very titles of office are related in meaning: if you remove the chief magistrate, you do not remain a public servant; for however much the authority of one in command is annulled, public administration is removed. Therefore we grant you a vocation when we send magistrates to you and however long we require you to serve the public, we shall send you judges. Nor should you consider this a slight benefit when, since you should be obedient, the selection of witnesses hastens to you. 2. And therefore, know this man has been sent as *comes* of your administration for the present indiction. He is one whom we deem will accomplish as much in public matters as in private, so that the best praise should accompany him. Solemnly obey one whose most righteous devotion will instruct you in these affairs, since we believe our dignity to be respected if we feel our judges have been well accommodated.

LETTER 7.29

This *formula* provides for the appointment of guards assigned specifically to city gates, presumably in cities such as Rome and Ravenna, where the central administration would have an interest in such matters.

Formula *Concerning the Guard of the City Gates*

1. Your loyalty is in no way doubted, for which you are chosen for the protection of the city, since what will be for the security of many must be entrusted to probity of good conscience. And so by our authority we grant you the care of the gates of this city, so

that entrance may not be permitted for the mischievous and good people should not be denied access. For if the gates should always remain closed, it would be as though a prison; if, on the other hand, they remained ever open, the walls would provide no defense. **2.** Therefore, let both be in measure, so that you may provide protection at night and you may not presume to close the city without reason. Undoubtedly, the passage of citizens and the entrance of commerce, clearly a friend to prosperity, which you want to enter, will be of particular concern. Take care, then, when you welcome those coming with goods. You may not despise what has been entrusted to you. You who are known to watch over arriving food should privilege certain things at the entryway of the city. It is fitting that you accomplish this without conflict, so that what we are able to witness in small matters, we would credit in larger.

LETTER 7.30

This *formula* is addressed to the inhabitants of a province, announcing the elevation of a *tribunus*, probably for the staff of the provincial governor or *comes*. This seems to have been an appointment of a leading citizen from the province, as opposed to one from the palatine hierarchy.

Formula *for a* Tribunus *of Provincials*

1. It is fair that anyone who may strive for an extended time only for the fruit of public service should also receive a reward for the labor commensurate with his deserts. Whence it is that, since the consideration of ancient custom urges that one who deserves to become your *tribunus* ought to be designated by us, we have decided therefore by this authority that the one whom the post seems to require would preside over you in the above-mentioned office, to the extent that, at the time when he has become vested in this office, he may obtain the greatest distinction. Such decisions are divine in nature, not human, so that the one whom heavenly providence preferred to produce at a designated time is rightly seen to have received a reward for his own labor. **2.** In that manner would the appropriate privileges follow upon their own guardians, since we do not want any man whom we know has arrived at chief importance without blame to be cheated of customary recompense. For this reason, obey the man arranging everything for public utility, since leading men claim the role of magistrate when it is required of them, but only if anything insolent may be removed from you.

LETTER 7.31

Unlike the *principes* assigned to a provincial governor or *comes* (cf. *Var.* 7.24 and 7.25), this *formula* appoints a *princeps* over the staff of the *Vicarius* (cf. *Var.* 6.15) at Rome during his absence.

Formula *for the* Princeps *of Rome*

1. Since we had decided to accomplish many things at Rome and it was necessary for a portion of the comital staff to be there, so that public needs may be satisfied, we prepared in advance with our usual manner so that, since we do not permit a post important to our service to lack a *princeps,* you ought to solemnly serve in his stead at Rome with the role of a *Vicarius,* to the extent that that man, having preeminence, may enjoy the fruits of his own labor and you would be able to learn in the office of another what you ought to happily exhibit in yourself. **2.** Moreover, if you, having need of our consent, should decide that any of the *comitiaci* must be sent to our *comitatus,* let it be subject to your judgment. However, those whom you deem must remain in Rome, let them enjoy a comfortable captivity. Nevertheless, you should moderate everything in turn, so that continuous labor should not wear down those on duty, nor again should the rust of leisure that the slothful must avoid consume them.

LETTER 7.32

This *formula* appoints an official for the management of the mint. Ostrogothic rulers minted coins at Rome, Ravenna, and Milan, although the reference to the ancient king Servius suggests this appointment was intended for Rome. The official's title is not given, although it was probably a *rationalis summarum* or a *rationalis vicarii.*

Formula *by Which the Mint Is Conferred*

1. Indeed every public service ought to be discharged with faithful action, since a wholly criminal deed is wrought, where the purity of good conscience is not had. Furthermore, the integrity of currency surely ought to be striven for, where both our image is impressed and common utility is found. For what would be unadulterated if the currency sins in our image, and if the sacrilegious hand hastens to violate that which a man of loyal heart ought to revere? Additionally, it is a corruption that disrupts everything, if the metal substance of coinage is spoiled, when it is necessary to reject anything corrupt that is offered for merchandise. Therefore, who would permit the advantage of one man to become a criminal loss for all, so that a detestable defect might attach to a price? **2.** Let what is attached to the image of our serenity be perfect; royal beauty admits no imperfection. For if the face of anyone whatever may be depicted in pure color, the grace of the *Princeps* is more properly protected with the purity of metal coinage. Let the fire of gold become dulled by the injury of no debasement, let the color of silver smile with the grace of whiteness, let the ruddiness of copper remain in its natural state. For if it is judged by the laws to be condemnable for injuring one man, what would that man deserve who has sinned against such a great multitude of humanity? **3.** We, therefore, order that the weight determined for the *denarius* ought to be preserved. This coin once used to be exchanged by weight rather than by number, whence antiquity elegantly named profit and expense, aptly drawing from the origin of the words.[8] For money, named by Gallic authors from the hides of cattle,[9] formerly was converted into coin without any demarcation. We do not suffer currency to become contemptible by adding impurities, lest it should be thought to return to the previous cheapness. **4.** Because praise for your integrity in administration has reached us, we order you to have custody of the mint for five consecutive years from the present indiction. This mint King Servius first instituted to strike bronze coins. Doubt not that you seek your own destruction if anything in this business will be found fraudulent. For just as you would encounter severe downfall if you should perchance trespass in any way, thus we shall not abandon you unremunerated if we feel you to have acted blamelessly.

LETTER 7.33

This is a *formula* for a *tractoriae,* a letter given to foreign envoys which would provide safe passage and provisions for a journey to foreign parts. Such a letter likely would be presented to proprietors of *mansiones* ("hostels") of the *cursus publicus.*

Formula *Providing for the Passage of Legates to Diverse Nations*

1. Who would doubt that it concerns the well-being of public utility that we confer gifts upon those for whom it is unseemly to sustain injury from travel, when such men do not cause harm to you from inconveniences and they know that they have been treated well? And therefore, you will offer, without any delay, the hospitality appropriate for legates of this nation, including the prescribed measure of fodder for the horses, so that they may not reach their own homes unrewarded, since speed is more pleasing to those hastening homeward than the magnitude of any kind of reward.

LETTER 7.34

A *formula* for a letter summoning someone to the king's court. Unlike *Variae 7.35,* the present summons is not intended to resolve a legal issue; rather, this is a summons to serve the king in an unofficial advisory capacity. For examples, *Variae* 3.22, 3.28.

---

8. Here Cassiodorus connects the "weight" (*pondus*) of the precious metal in coin to the Latin words for "profit" and "expense" (*compendium* and *dispendium,* respectively).

9. *Pecunia* ("money"), from *pecus* ("cattle").

Formula *for a Noncompulsory Summons to the* Princeps

1. We do not doubt that what is accustomed to be conferred as a gift, when requested, will be received with voluntary gratitude,[10] since being in the memory of a master always provides an increase in prosperity, nor is it possible that tokens of kindness from a *Princeps* would be meaningless. Therefore, we summon you by the present command to our *comitatus,* so that you may enjoy a happiness in no way commonplace. **2.** And so, hasten to come on *illa* day to *illa* villa for the delayed enjoyment of leisure, so that we may judge whether our presence has been pleasing to you, when we know you to have hurried. For our halls desire the presence of good men, since we do not recognize any other association to please royal wisdom, and it is confirmed by divine judgment, because that same man who offers what we ought to desire rules our heart.

LETTER 7.35

Petitioners could expect to receive a rescript—a formal response to a complaint concerning various grievances. This *formula* offers a generic summons to the king's court, in lieu of a rescript, whereby a petitioner may explain a grievance at greater length.

Formula *for a Summons Granted to a Petitioner*

1. It is evidence of good conscience to seek the presence of a just *Princeps.* Only a man who is reassured by the great purity of his intentions could desire this. Only clear eyes seek the appearance of the sun, because only those who have the purest vision are able to endure its fiery rays. Thus, those who already possess a sincere heart petition for the presence of the *Princeps.* **2.** Hence it is that we offer you assurance in coming to our *comitatus* with pleased disposition, lest the honor of a summons, which was invented for your glory, should be turned to injury when it is spoiled by any delay. On the contrary, we invite the requests of those coming, since thence do we increase more, if we gather noble men by our assistance.

LETTER 7.36

Senators of high rank and officials assigned to Rome were required to obtain a *commeatalis* in order to travel beyond the legal bounds of the city's hinterland. This *formula* provides such a "leave of absence." For an example, *Variae* 4.48.

Formula *for Leave of Absence*

1. Nobody may doubt that men are refreshed by sweet variation, since the mind has a great aversion to being continually engaged in business. Sweet honey

---

10. That is, an audience with the king, usually a gift, has been freely offered to the letter's recipient.

becomes dreaded when it is enjoyed excessively; such a fair substance, although greatly desired, nevertheless becomes avoided when obtained. Not without reason, provided that a man may be changeable, he desires to enjoy circumstances of his own inclination. **2.** And therefore, we permit you to tarry for so many months in the above-mentioned province so that, hastening to the abundance of provincial delights, you may be revived, since a confined man, for whom it seems not mere freedom to change, turns more or less hostile. Nonetheless, whenever you may complete the deserved suspension of duties with your master's blessing, hasten to return to your urban home. For if it is boring to continually live in the renown of the city, how much more would it be to spend the entire time in the country! Therefore, we freely grant leave for departing, not as Rome ought to be abandoned, but so that it may be more amply appreciated by absence.

LETTER 7.37

This *formula* bestows the second rank (*spectabilis*) of the senatorial order. Only the *illustris* was more esteemed, for which *Variae* 6.11.

Formula *for the Rank* Spectabilis

1. We want those subject to us by God's will to be glorified with varied tokens of public distinction; we seek to adorn the upright stock of men with a grace imprinted with distinction, so that each man may live more commendably, when he knows that he has received the most respected honors. For thus does he fittingly ascend even to the study of the virtues and the republic is cherished more by good citizens. And so we cloth you in the glow of a *spectabilis,* so that you may know that your thoughts must be acknowledged in public gatherings, when thus decorated you will sit among the nobles, and so that, if you have discharged this honor in a commendable manner, you may be promoted to sweeter rewards in the future.

LETTER 7.38

This *formula* bestows the third and lowest rank (*clarissimus*) of the senatorial order. This rank usually implied a hereditary connection to the Senate, although new members could receive the rank after holding a position of civil or military authority.

Formula *for the Rank* Clarissimus

1. It is fitting that the taste of good things is pleasant and that the path of honor followed through the increase of virtue is profitable. We feed this zeal with a provident liberality, so that the more the desire for rewards increases, the greater the cultivation of good character may be. Therefore royal prerogative grants you the

ornaments of our judgment, the honor of the *clarissimus,* which may provide testimony of a demanding life and may promise the increase of future prosperity.
Therefore, you who shine with *clarissimus* distinction are now permitted to accomplish nothing in obscurity. For indeed such an important testimony of life is not
spoken of as "distinguished," but "most distinguished," when almost everything
best is thought concerning one who is called by a superlative title of such brilliance.

LETTER 7.39

This *formula* provides an individual with a warrant for legal guardianship (*tuitio*).
More typically, *tuitio* was assigned to a member of the nobility who was vulnerable
for some reason, for example young age. In some cases, *tuitio* involved the physical
protection of a ward assigned by the king (usually by a *saio*). In other cases, the
king assigned a prominent senator to provide legal patronage for the property of a
ward.

Formula *for Legal Guardianship*

1. Indeed, it seems superfluous to seek protection individually from the *Princeps,*
who is intended to protect all alike. But since the execrable temerity of certain
violent men has threatened your safety, it is not inappropriate to be led by the
quarrels of aggrieved men to this role of duty, so that we may most readily confer
upon a supplicant what we desire to bestow upon all. And so with kindness do we
remove you from the attacks of various harmful men, for whatever reason you are
attacked, to the camp of our protection, to the extent that you may be seen to contend with your adversaries, not in the open field, but from behind a fortified
defense. Let it be thus that, pressed by cruel men, you are restored to the battlefield
made equal by royal assistance. **2.** Therefore, our authority confers upon you the
guardianship of our name, as though the strongest tower against both lawless
attack and contractual damage; nonetheless, thus protected from this lawlessness,
do not despise offering the lawful response and do not appear so contemptuous as
to trample upon public laws, you whom a reprehensible audacity oppressed first.
And since our precept ought to have able executors, lest it may not seem possible
to act upon what it is fitting for a *Princeps* to pronounce, by order of the present
kindness, let loyalty and diligence readily protect you, the one against Goths and
the other against Romans: since it is not a labor to defend what is feared to offend,
when it is dreaded that the more powerful patron should become displeased.
Therefore, enjoy our kindness; rejoice in the privilege received. For if you are
threatened with further civil disharmony by anyone, in a stronger position, you
will satisfy your desires concerning your enemies.

LETTER 7.40

Not all unions had "legitimacy" in the eyes of the law (or religion), particularly those involving a man and woman of different social status. This *formula* provides legitimacy for a marriage to a woman of lower social status and confirms the heritable status of the man's children with her.

Formula *for the Confirmation of Matrimony and Granting Legitimacy to Children*

1. An everlasting gift is one that has been conferred by the blessing of posterity; nor could it be more becoming to a king than that he should provide for human offspring. It is certain that one entering the light of day does not deserve to receive adverse misfortune, lest he should first incur the disability of limitations rather than discover the joys of heavenly light. **2.** And so, in the submitted petition you have presented as wife one whose loving embrace you have gratefully bound to yourself, who ought to be married in honorable matrimony by our award, so that the children born from her may obtain the name of legal heirs. For when a living bond willingly shares everything and what pleases seems to be proper to everyone, it is hard not to have unconditional liberty there, where children have been engendered. **3.** And so, this woman who, even though she was legally taken as wife, was not deemed to be equal in reputation, we decree to have become your legitimate wife and we want the sons from the same woman, whether they are now born or will come in the future, to share the rights of inheritance, so that you may cherish without any hesitation those whom you know perfectly well to be your future successors. For nature has bestowed sons upon you, but we have caused them to become more precious with this security.

LETTER 7.41

Fittingly following the *formula* for *tuitio* (*Var.* 7.39), this *formula* emancipates a minor from guardianship, whereupon they would assume all legal rights and liabilities appropriate to a legally mature citizen.

Formula *for Coming of Age*

1. Ambitious is the petition that requests the grace of maturity, when one claims to have attained that maturity of character which the years of life thus far have not provided. A minor from birth, you desire to be endowed by official recognition with the respect accorded to mature age. Thus, what is the boldest undertaking in a human life, you despise protection from the errors of youth in preference for the advantages of maturity. For this reason have you presented in the submitted petition that, since the measure of your wisdom may be proven, your official status should not remain unsettled, lest what stands firm by virtue of ability should remain impaired by law. We, whose intention it is to grant worthy desires, gladly assent to this request, since anybody who publicly avows himself to want to avoid illegal snares aims to hold free and binding legal contracts. **2.** And so, if it happens that the time has passed by which the laws agree that maturity is claimed, neither shall we deny freedom for what is fittingly desired, so that what the antiquity of the laws dictates must be observed in such cases should be duly acted upon in legal form, such that the authority of the provision should apply to properties that must be rendered to you both in the city and in the country, lest we may seem to injure the welfare of supplicants when we want to be elevated in reputation. Therefore, take by our gift a more capable period of life and exhibit in character what you promise. For the profession of maturity denies a place for immature deeds, when that fault is much more serious which authority assails with the promises of its own author.

LETTER 7.42

This *formula* provides the *Quaestor* with instructions for assigning a *saio* to a petitioner. Emphasis is placed on correcting abuses whereby *saiones* have been used to pursue the personal, illegal agendas of their wards.

Formula *for an Edict to the* Quaestor, *So That*
He May Sponsor One Who Deserves a Saio

1. We have learned that the *saiones,* whom we intended to be assigned by us from good intention, have repeatedly been troubled by extensive disputes. What grief that this has been spoiled. Calamity has separated our kindness from the medicine, when what our remedy had intended for petitioners they, from spite, instead have transferred to other uses. Whence it will be necessary for us to oppose noxious desires with a wholesome remedy, lest we should suffer the most corrupt of wrongful acts, while we are impelled to just kindnesses from a zeal for duty. **2.** And therefore we have determined by publication of an edict that whoever perchance desires to be awarded a *saio* against violent attacks on account of his own unavoidable vulnerability, should put himself under obligation to our court with a bond of security, so that, if with punishable negligence he has transgressed our instructions concerning the *saio* he was awarded, that man should give so many pounds of gold in the name of punishment and he must promise to pay whatever loss his adversary will have sustained, as much for penalty as for expenses. For while we want to suppress uncivil intentions, we should not aggrieve the innocent. However, the *saio,* who of his own will has transgressed the limits of our instructions, will know that he has incurred danger by being excluded from the donative and, what is more serious than any loss, from our good will. Nor will anything further be entrusted to one who has revealed himself to be a violator of our commands, of which he ought to have been the facilitator.

LETTER 7.43

This is a *formula* for a *probatoria*, or a document that approves employment in a bureau or department of an administrative branch of the government. In this case, the appointment is for a *chartarius*, or archivist of royal documents.

Formula *for Approving a Clerk for the Chancery*

1. It is fitting that a service that is known to be established by men of upstanding character should be discharged well, when such a man is able to open and read for himself what a judge would have admonished him to do: especially when such a man should deserve to reach the property of the divine house,[11] where it would not be possible for him to nurture disreputable greed. Then, since that most resplendent office shines with a particular censorial officialdom, and it would be shameful for those to be involved who cannot be approved by men of dignified character, it seems fitting to seek such men who would not displease us in any way. And so, having obtained a recommendation from the *Tribunus Chartariorum*,[12] under whose control the due reverence of the department is placed, we want you to take the title of *chartarius* from this day, so that you who promise us to act well in the future will have been confirmed with a commendable testimony. Avoid avarice; fly far from corrupt gains. One profits much more if one benefits from good deeds.

LETTER 7.44

Disused property could be granted to individuals for various commercial or even personal uses provided that the owner would improve the property in ways advantageous for the community. This *formula* supplies a reply to a successful *competitio* ("proposal"). For examples, see *Variae* 2.21, 2.32, 2.33.

Formula *Concerning Proposals for the Ownership of Public Property*

1. One who desires to own public land is known to commit himself to something important. For it is fitting that this should happen, whereby a squalid property is transformed into a place of better appearance and what had formerly lain uncultivated is recovered for profitable use. And so we grant your desires for this place with legal ownership, excepting metals, lead, or marble, if any will be found lying

---

11. The *divina domus,* or imperial (royal) house.
12. Department head of the secretarial office.

buried there. So act such that, through you, what had lain abandoned in negligent waste should acquire charm, to the extent that you would deserve to find the praise of good citizens, if you adorn the appearance of the city. Moreover, be assured that whatever is accomplished from your own labor will be transferred to your descendants, since anyone will take on such an endeavor more vigorously if he considers himself to have spent generously for his own family.

LETTER 7.45

The remission of taxes for individuals and whole communities is a well-attested phenomenon. Remissions could either cancel accumulated arrears, lower existing payments temporarily or permanently, or postpone payments until a predetermined time when property owners were more capable of paying. This *formula* provides the complete and permanent erasure of tax obligations owed for a single property. For similar examples, *Variae* 3.32, 3.40, 4.19.

Formula *by Which the Tax Is Remitted for One Possessing a Single House Too Heavily Assessed*

1. When profit thrives from the usefulness of a field and all other endeavors, it is certainly just for it to come from those sources. But you complain that the tribute assessed on your property in *illa* province is burdensome, so that the enormous maw of the payment consumes all means for yourself and whatever may be gathered with great labor from other sources seems to disappear into this obligation, the excessive payment of which exceeds the means, when it renders more to tax collectors than it offers to the careful cultivator. Therefore, we believe that you could avoid ruin if you would flee the ownership of such rural property, to which compulsory payment brings barrenness, lest you who deserve to be the master, should be enslaved by want in a miserable condition. **2.** But since the most sacred laws have determined this kind of benefit should be offered to men of slender means,[13] so that an owner of a single plot oppressed by unusually large debt who may not be assisted by the substance of another may be aided by a permanent arrangement, our magnitude, whose nature it is to think on justice, decrees by the present authority that if the case is thus, the payment you would thus make of so many *solidi* for the aforementioned property to those collectors assigned to it, according to the instructions given, is to be so thoroughly scoured from the public archives that a second copy of this duty may not be found, but that what has been settled once and for all will be observed without error for ages.

---

13. *Leges sacratissimae,* or imperial law.

LETTER 7.46

The regulation of the degrees of propinquity for married members of the same family was a long-standing concern in Roman law. This *formula* provides a "dispensation" by which first cousins could marry.

Formula *by Which Marriage to a Cousin May Become Legitimate*

1. An introduction to the instruction of divine law assists with human law, when a precept is read in the headings of those laws that should be ascribed to the two tablets. For the prophet Moses, educated in divine instruction, determined for the Israeli people, among other things, that pious persons related by closeness of blood should refrain from copulation, lest they should pollute themselves by returning to their own kinship, and lest they should not enjoy a prudent enlargement in foreign stock. Wise men following this lesson transmitted the chaste observance much farther into posterity, reserving only to the *Princeps* the benefit of conjoining maternal cousins in a relationship of marriage, understanding that what they had decreed to be determined by a *Princeps* should be enjoyed only rarely. **2.** We approve the invention and we commend in amazed contemplation the mildness of these laws that this decision was entrusted to the *Princeps*, so one who used to govern the morals of the people would himself relax even the measured limits of concupiscence. And therefore, moved by the tenor of your supplication, if you are related to this woman by blood only as maternal cousins, nor may you be proven closer by another degree, we rule she may be associated with you in matrimony and we order henceforth that no inquiry should be made concerning you, when our laws willingly consent that this be permitted and your wishes have strengthened the gift of the present decree. And so, with God's favor, a chaste marriage, gloriously commingled, and a posterity of heirs, are yours, since it is fitting that whatever is commanded by us is not liable to blame, but to praise.

LETTER 7.47

Status as one of the municipal *curiales* was determined by property qualification, but so too was their liability to state obligations, which legally debarred *curiales* from selling properties. This *formula*, addressed to the municipal council, allows a *curialis* to resolve outstanding debts by alienating a portion of his property for sale.

Formula *to the* Praefectus Praetorio, *So That*
the Property of Curiales *May Be Sold by Decree*

1. The greater part of mortal kind endures this unfortunate condition, so that, when something is supposed to harm, it may assist, and when it seems to assist, it may harm. But what is considered to be profitable is striven for more. For even poisons are taken, if they are thought to help; and that sweetness of eloquence, which is likely to incur oratorical attacks, must be avoided. Therefore, the goal of the wise man is to love what sets him free; thus one who strives to prosper does not regard the wish of a sick man. Likewise, prudent antiquity did not intend for the estates of *curiales* to be dissolved easily, so that they might better suffice for public needs if they had the assistance of more property. **2.** But antiquity again provided for this circumstance, so that, if unavoidable harm should appear among you, a separation from its own precepts would assist. For what does it profit, if someone may seem fit and is unable to be extricated from entangling contracts? One who is unable repay another is similar to someone lacking property; nor is he able to call his own the property that he is not free to sell. **3.** But, however much will have been granted by the authority of the laws to your power, nevertheless, lest you should endure any slander even for such an exceptional occurrence, moved by the petition of this town, we also permit your eminence with the present order, that with the truth having been determined with complete clarity, if contracted bonds may not be dissolved by any other means, the town may be freed to separate from his own estates whatever property he will have chosen according to his own will, so that he may thus pay the debt that is proven to have been incurred, lest, stained with the vice of gluttony, he may seem permitted to consume his own resources with debt. Let a credible cause for loss be permissible in your eyes, since we want one who is proven to be constrained by harsh troubles to be assisted; for whether it is to loosen the reigns of good conduct for wicked men or to ignore just complaints, both are blameworthy. Therefore, antiquity has providently arranged for you to decide such cases, for whom it is useful to preserve the curia. For by whom may the responsibilities of cities be sustained, if the tendons of towns appear to be severed indiscriminately?

Book 8

LETTER 8.1 (C. 526)

The death of Theoderic in August 526 found Cassiodorus serving in the *comitatus* as *Magister Officiorum*. In that capacity he wrote a series of letters, beginning with the present address to the eastern emperor Justin, announcing the elevation of Athalaric, Theoderic's grandson, as ruler of Italy and the western provinces under Ostrogothic control.

King Athalaric to Imperator *Justin*

1. I would be justly reproved, most clement of *Principes*, if without enthusiasm I should ask for your approval, which it happens my kin sought so ardently;[1] in what sense would I be a suitable heir, if I should be found unequal to my predecessors in such a matter of reputation? The purple rank of my forebears ennobles, and thus the royal seat elevates, only to the extent that your open affection celebrates us. For, if we feel this has been withheld from us in no way, we shall believe everything in our *regnum* is in perfect harmony. **2.** But as it concerns the reputation of your duty to cherish those whose fathers you have loved—for nobody is believed to have devoted pure kindness to the elders of a family unless he is shown to regard the offspring as his own—let animosity be buried with the deceased. Let wrath perish with the impudent. Friendship should not die with the dearly beloved, but who is found innocent in the quarrels of ruling must be treated more favorably.

---

1. This may be said of *Var.* 1.1 to Anastasius, but no communication between Theoderic and Justin survives; if Justin began serving among the palace guard under Emperor Zeno around 470, he may have known Theoderic, who was a diplomatic hostage at Zeno's court until approximately 472.

Consider what a successor to good men should deserve from you. **3.** In your city, you elevated our grandfather to the lofty curule seat; in Italy, you decorated my father with palmate distinction.[2] Through a desire for concord, one who was almost equal to you in years was also made your son-in-arms.[3] This honor, which you bestowed upon our elders, you would give more fittingly to a youth. Your affection should transfer the parental role now, for by the laws of nature the offspring of your son should not be considered unrelated to you. **4.** And therefore, I seek peace, not as a distant relation, but as nearest kin, since you showed me the favor of a grandson then, when you bestowed the joy of adoption on my father. We have arrived at a royal inheritance; let us also be admitted into your heart. To have the regard of such a great ruler is more important to me than ruling. And so, let our commencement deserve to have the support of an elderly *Princeps;* let the tutelage of friendship attend my youth and we who are propped by such protection will not be totally bereft of family. **5.** Let our *regnum* be bound to you by cords of gratitude. You will rule more in a realm where you order all things with affection. Therefore, we have determined that our legates, *ille* and *ille,* must be sent to your serenity, so that you may grant us your friendship in these arrangements, and by those conditions which your celebrated predecessors are known to have had with our lord grandfather of divine memory. Perhaps I merit something even more from sincerity, because my age is not experienced and my origin is already proven not to be foreign. We have, in fact, entrusted certain matters to the above-mentioned legates that must be revealed verbally to your most serene hearing. May you cause these matters to reach completion after the habit of your clemency.

LETTER 8.2 (C. 526)

The second in a series of letters (*Var.* 8.1–7) announcing the accession of Athalaric to the throne. Unlike the previous letter to Emperor Justin, this and following letters conclude by exacting an oath (*sacramentum*) of loyalty to the new king.

King Athalaric to the Senate of Rome

1. Acknowledging the rise of a ruler, conscript fathers, is known to be the greatest cause for celebration, so that one who is known to protect everything may be proclaimed for having attained the eminence of the *regnum*. The scale of rejoicing comes from the grandeur of the announcement, and however eager the spirit is for

---

2. This is not precisely true: Theoderic was appointed consul in the east by Zeno in 484, although Justin did appoint Athalaric's father, Eutharic, to the consulship in 519.

3. Cassiodorus may be conflating the facts here: Theoderic was nearly as old as Justin, but had been formerly adopted in arms by Zeno; Eutharic, whom Justin did adopt in arms, was thirty years junior to the emperor.

this, thus will there be reflection upon its importance. **2.** For if the promised delights of companionship stir wise men, if news of the well-being of friends comforts them, with what exaltation ought news be received that a ruler of all territories has happily come forth, whom chaotic sedition did not produce, whom seething wars did not beget, whose gain was not a loss to the republic, but who was thus elevated through peace, just as would befit the arrival of a founder of civic harmony! It is truly a great species of good fortune to become *Princeps* without conflict and for a youth to become master in that republic where it happens that many are found with seasoned character. For it is not by any means possible to lack the counsel of years, where it is known that so many parents to the republic may be found. **3.** Hope for our reign, therefore, has been carried on the good intentions of all men and that should be more readily believed concerning us than what has been assumed concerning others.[4] Since the distinction of the Amal family permits no insult whatever, and, just as those who are born to you become nominated as heirs in the senatorial order, thus one who advances from this family should be approved the most worthy for the *regnum*. The things of which we speak are proven by the facts at hand. **4.** For, when the sweet memory of our lord grandfather severely grieved you on account of the quantity of his kindnesses, it transferred the grandeur of his lordship to us with such swiftness, that you would have thought a garment had been changed rather than the *regnum*. So many leading men, renowned for their advice and strong arms, fostered no murmuring, as would be expected; but with great rejoicing they followed the decision of their *Princeps*, so that you would instead admit that divine will had converged there. Therefore, by the grace of God, we have introduced the need to make you more certain concerning the commencement of our reign, since the *imperium* should appear continued rather than altered when it passes to heirs; for in whatever manner that same man is thought to live on, his offspring is recognized to rule over you.[5] **5.** Your prayers had tended toward this, what was doubtlessly his decision, that he should leave an heir of his own good family who would be able to increase his kindnesses to you. It is proper to be formed in the affection of *Principes*, as though the fidelity to his likeness had been preserved in a bronze sculpture, to the extent that the incumbent offspring would resemble the author who had obligated the republic to himself with many kindnesses. But how much more authentic is one who lives as his posterity, through whom in a large part both the form of the body is returned and the vigor of the soul is prolonged. **6.** And therefore, you now ought to extend the fidelity of your noble order with greater enthusiasm, such that it would appear that former gifts had been conferred upon the deserving and that

---

4. Although vague, following from the earlier statements concerning rulers coming to power through strife and warfare, it should be assumed the letter is here making a similar comparison.

5. The reference is to Theoderic.

without hesitation we may bestow future gifts on those whom we feel to be the most mindful of past events. **7.** Moreover, we know that this was arranged by divine providence, just as the common consent of Goths and Romans receives us and they have also confirmed their inclination, which they offered with pure intention, with the bond of a sworn oath.[6] **8.** We doubt not that you would follow this example at a distance, but not by affection; for you are able to commence what we would anticipate from a distance. Indeed, it is fitting that the most outstanding senators are able to show so much more respect because they are known to have received distinction greater than other ranks. **9.** But so that you would be able to acknowledge the commencement of our benevolence toward you, since it is fitting to enter your curia with favors, we have sent our *illustris comes* Sigismer to you, with those who are directed to administer the oath, since we desire to preserve as inviolate what we have promised by public authority. **10.** If, however, you believe anything must be required of us, by which your peace of mind would be increased, let those, whose entreaties we are clearly known to encourage, seek us unhesitatingly to be advised. Indeed such a thing is more a promise than advice: for one who takes it upon himself to entreat such a venerable Senate is nonetheless able to obtain what he had set before them. It is now yours to hope for whatever would increase the common weal of the republic.

LETTER 8.3 (C. 526)

This announcement of Athalaric's accession to the urban populace of Rome was probably proclaimed and posted as an edict by the *Praefectus Urbis* or possibly by Sigismer (cf. *Var.* 8.2.9) as *Comes Civitatis Romae.* The oaths exchanged here are explicitly mutual between the king and the people of Rome.

King Athalaric to the Roman People

1. If an heir foreign to *imperium* had adopted you, perhaps you might hesitate, lest, by discovering that the successor had no love for what the former ruler had esteemed, since by some unknown means, when the successor strove to be praised more fully, he was diminished by the reputation of his predecessor. But now, when we believe that we act accordingly if we comply with the venerable judgments of my grandfather, the person alone has been exchanged, not kindness toward you. **2.** It is certainly of interest to our reputation that we should nourish the copious statutes that he so kindly defended, even with an abundance of munificence. Those who succeed ignoble *Principes* engaged in mediocre activity may intend to do less; such a man precedes us that we ought follow his path with carefully consideration of virtues. **3.** Therefore, whatever has been established by the arrangement of our

---

6. For this, cf. *Var.* 8.3–5.

glorious lord grandfather, with God's guidance, we pronounce to be thus for you, so that the sweetest consensus of Goths and Romans would obtain in our *regnum* and, lest any mistrust is able to remain concerning unresolved affairs, they confirmed their desire with the acclamation of oaths.[7] They submit themselves to our dominion with such great rejoicing, as though our lord grandfather seemed not to be removed from them by the lot of fate, so that they should be recognized to be devoted, not by words alone, but in the depths of their hearts. **4.** If you should do this, as we suppose you will in similarly willing spirit, we cause the bearers of this letter to promise you under the sanction of divine witness to protect justice and, with God's blessing, to protect the equitable clemency that nourishes a people, and that before us the law will be equal for Goths and Romans, lest anything become unfair between you, except that the Goths undergo the labors of war for the common weal, while you increase in the peaceful habitation of Rome. **5.** Behold, we commence our reign as *Princeps* by bending to the mildest condition of an oath, so that the people whom our blessed founder nourished may have no cause for doubt, nor any cause for dread. Behold, we restore the shining example of Trajan to your age. You swear by that which the *Princeps* swears to you, lest anyone is able to be deceived by that invocation which it is not permitted to assert falsely without punishment. Now, rouse your courage and with God's grace always choose better things, so that, just as we have commenced upon royal power with affection, thus by God will we pursue peaceful tranquility in following years.

LETTER 8.4 (C. 526)

The third in a series of accession announcements to the subjects of the Ostrogothic realm, this letter would have been disseminated to citizens of major towns and cities through all available channels of the administrative apparatus. Again, the reciprocity of giving and taking oaths of duty is prominent.

King Athalaric to Various Romans Settled throughout Italy and Dalmatia

1. We believe that what you are able to recognize in the testament of good reputation indicates something honorable. Truly, one who deserves the praise of kings may rightly consider himself to be well-proven, since it is the distinction of the subject to have earned the attention of one ruling, especially in that case where the hearts of all are known to be stirred in such a way that, if they do not recognize the ruler as prosperous, they always believe him to be hostile. For one who hears that *imperium* has changed nonetheless fears it. And in a real sense, I know not

---

7. Similar to *Var.* 8.2.7, the letter announces that the Goths and Romans (probably those attendant on the court) have already signaled their consensus for the new reign with oaths.

what anxiety must disturb a ruler who delays promising benefactions at the beginning of his reign. **2.** Therefore, excising any opportunity for ill-founded thoughts, we do not permit anything to be believed about us except what was accorded to our forebears. And therefore, what should be said by the grace of divine authority, by the arrangement of that glorious lord our grandfather, we have taken the oaths of a commenced *regnum,* as much for the protection of Goths as for Romans present at our court. We have decided that you should also do this freely, so that you, who were faithful to our forebears, should also serve us with similar devotion. **3.** For the one who remembers the author of his blessings delights the heir most pleasingly. But, so that the integrity of our benevolence might become known to you, we have made what would declare our purpose and ought to protect the hopes of all to be promised to you with the bond of a sworn oath.

LETTER 8.5 (C. 526)

A letter similar in content to *Variae* 8.4, but addressed to the Goths of Italy. The actual settlement of Goths in Italy is much debated, although documentary sources (including the *Variae*) suggest communities in Samnium, the Po Valley and sub-Alpine Italy.

King Athalaric to Various Goths Settled throughout Italy

1. We would indeed want to relate to you the joys of our lord grandfather's lengthy life; but since he has been removed from those cherishing him by hard circumstance, he has made us the heir to his *regnum,* by his own decree and according to God, so that, with the succession of his own bloodline, he would make perpetual those benefits conferred upon you by him, while we desire both to protect and increase those things that we recognize were done by him. As it thus stands in the royal city,[8] by his decree, the wills of all men have been united by the introduction of an oath, so that you would think one man promises what the commonality was seen to elect. **2.** Act on this now, following their example with like devotion, lest we should seem to have done anything less for those in our service, for whom it is believed that we satisfy everything possible. Indeed, we have ordered the *comes, ille,*[9] to render oaths to you verbally, so that, even as you reveal your most loyal intention to us, you may thereby hear the desires of our inclination. And so, reclaim a name always prosperous for you, the royal stock of the Amals, a source dyed in the purple, a child clad in regal hue, through whom our kinsmen have been appropriately advanced with God's blessing and who, among such extended ranks of kings, always attained increase. **3.** For we believe in the grace of divine

---

8. *Civitas regia,* probably Ravenna.
9. The *ille* suggests different *comites* were dispatched to each community.

authority which fittingly assisted our ancestors and now extends the grace of its favor, so that you, who under our forebears have flourished with full praise for your virtues, would also receive the sweetest fruit of happy affairs from our rule.

LETTER 8.6 (C. 526)

This announcement of Athalaric's accession is addressed to Liberius, who had been serving as *Praefectus Praetorio* of the Gallic provinces under Ostrogothic control since 510. His absence from earlier letters of the collection that treat the administration of Gaul is notable, as is the contrast between the present letter and the more lavish letters (*Var.* 8.9–10) addressed to the *comes* Tuluin, who maintained military control of the region.

King Athalaric to Liberius, Praefectus Praetorio Galliarum

1. We know your heart is vexed with harsh grief for the fall of our lord grandfather of glorious memory, since everything seems to gravely lament good things lost; for an esteemed master is missed more when he is removed. The man lost, however, releases the afflicted mind from its expression of devotion and comforts it with a compensatory remedy, since one who is not succeeded by a stranger is hardly felt to be absent. **2.** For he thus arranged it by God's own design, when even after death he would be the provider, that he would leave peace to his domains, lest any novelty disturb tranquility. He has made us master in the seat of his kingdom, to the extent that the grace of his descent, which flourished in him, should henceforth shine out in his successors with equal illumination. The desires of Goths and Romans have coincided in this ordination, such that under the bond of oaths they have promised to preserve their fidelity to our kingdom with devoted hearts. **3.** We have decided that this must be brought to the knowledge of your *illustris* magnitude, so that a similar example may be rendered by those who are devoted to the *regnum* of our piety in Gaul and, just as they do not want our consideration to make less of them, thus should they be held bound by the same conditions.

LETTER 8.7 (C. 526)

Following upon *Variae* 8.6 to the prefect of the Gallic provinces under Ostrogothic control, a somewhat more elaborate letter was delivered to the Gallic provincials, presumably via the municipal assemblies of towns and cities in the region.

King Athalaric to All Provincials Settled throughout Gaul

1. Although the downfall of our lord grandfather of glorious memory may seem sad to you on account of his outstanding merits, nonetheless, while he succumbed to the human condition, he left us for maintaining the governance that he had managed with such singular ability. Lest you should feel the loss of a good *Princeps,* his offspring is acknowledged as ruling over you. For no man loses in our presence what that ruler had promised him, but rather we will return his debts with the liberality of redoubled munificence, and for future loyalty we borrow kindness from our native devotion. 2. And therefore, he now conjures you to demonstrate the former fidelity with greater devotion, since one who serves well at the beginning of a reign anticipates the state of affairs in the future, since that very man who is felt to support the advent will be trusted to persevere throughout the remainder of the reign. Moreover, we have been indicated by divine favor, when we attain the eminence of *regnum.* Everything thus has turned out happy and tranquil for us, so that you would believe that what one man pronounced had resounded among the all the people,[10] nor could it be thought humanly possible that the will of so many diverse peoples was proven to have no disagreement. 3. Whence it is fitting for you to imitate the aforementioned wish, just as Goths offered oaths to the Romans and the Romans confirmed by oath to the Goths, make yourselves unanimously devoted to our *regnum,* to the extent that your integrity may become commendably known to us, and in return the promised concord may advance your prosperity. Let the tranquility set by laws go among you; do not let the strong cause disquiet for the weak. Harbor a peaceful heart, you who have no foreign wars, since thence you will be able to please us, if you first provide for yourselves by this measure.

LETTER 8.8 (C. 526)

The last of letters announcing the accession of Athalaric, here addressed to a bishop of uncertain provenance.[11] Given that it follows two letters aimed at securing loyalty in Gaul and is followed by two letters elevating a *comes* in Gaul, it may be reasonable to assume that this was an influential Gallic bishop.

King Athalaric to Victorinus, Venerable Bishop

1. Such public figures as are moved to the grief of the human condition by an adverse lot must be reminded of faith and constancy. For you, however, whom wisdom makes resolved and a religious disposition comforts, it is instead fitting to be invigorated by the prospect of uniting the provincials, since the sinner who is entitled to be judged by many may rightly become the arbitrator of others.[12]

---

10. Theoderic's designation of Athalaric as heir.

11. There was a bishop of Fréjus by the name of Victorinus, c. 500.

12. Although vague, this seems to be a reference to the reversal of roles in late antiquity whereby clergy (not infrequently self-described as "sinners") arbitrate both the spiritual and legal needs of the laity.

Therefore, it is right that we, greeting you with respect, announce with great pain what will be a source of grief to relate to you, the passing of our lord grandfather of glorious memory. **2.** But it is possible for your sadness thence to be tempered, since with divine grace he placed us on the throne of his own *regnum*, so that rising restored to you by succession, he may not appear wholly torn from your longing. Now you may gladly support our commencement with sacred words, so that the King in heaven may strengthen our human *regnum*, he may grind down foreign nations, he may absolve sins, and may propitiously confirm and protect what was fitting for our glorious forebears to bestow upon us. **3.** Therefore, let your sanctity admonish all provincials that they ought to be free of blame in all things, keeping harmony with one another in our *regnum*. For we desire to be restored to faith in the subjects, whom we are able to reward with great devotion.

LETTER 8.9 (C. 526)

Although technically not an announcement of Athalaric's accession, this letter elevating a prominent Gothic *comes* to the rank of *patricius praesentalis* should be understood in the context of securing support for the young king's succession. As a patrician "attending at court," the recipient assumes a position among Athalaric's key advisors. As a public statement, the letter masterfully weaves panegyric of Theoderic with the biography of the appointee.

King Athalaric to Tuluin, Vir Illustris

1. It is fitting that those whom divine providence would advance to the consecrated peak of power should enable the people to be appropriately ruled, when the age of the ruler does not hinder what heavenly might has provided; nonetheless, it is known that you, who also adhered commendably and unswervingly to the administration of our lord grandfather, have aptly applied your wisdom to relieving the apprehension of our flowering youth. Because if it was proper to make a man so distinguished and great for that purpose, how much more appropriate is it for us to seek the comfort that, up to this point, we understandably lacked on account of the flush of youth! **2.** In fact, that prudence which no single man has attained is so great and far-reaching, that it would not seem troublesome to seek it through others. Even old men learn wisdom in counsel and what is derived on behalf of the common weal is found in the communion of experienced men. Mature kings often attach to themselves the comfort of an administration and hence are thought better kings if they do not presume to do everything alone. Because if aged lords are assisted by the talents of their subjects, we soften the brief celebration of our youth with counsel, so that, increasing with growth, our youth may more prosperously rise with the strength to sustain the weight of *imperium*. **3.** And so at the urging of divine support, we promote you to the height of *patricius praesentalis*, so that on behalf of our republic a noble rank may elevate the seat of governance, lest wholesome decrees that would be fitting to obey with humility may seem to have come from a humble source. This is the distinction that both complements arms and decorates peace. That wealthy Greece, which owed much to our most glorious lord grandfather, obligingly paid him with this honor; she covered his strong shoulders with the chlamys, those particularly Roman boots decorated his calves, and he was known to receive out of kindness what he knew he had attained through military distinction. The eagerness of the eastern people for seeing our hero increased, when, I know not how, a man considered bellicose had become more loved for civil honors. **4.** Accordingly satisfied with this repayment of distinction, he labored with tireless dedication to foreign lands and it dignified one who was engendered from the line of such great kings to offer service to a *Princeps* with his own family. Thus, the benefits granted to great men always exalt them, so that they impose oaths of respect even upon those whom such men happen not to rule. Promoted men always delight the author of their own advancement, and those who are not beholden to such benefits do not understand the laws of good character. **5.** But it would take too long to speak sufficiently of the glory of one whom a prosperous age caused to be singular among nations. The toil of this very man instructed you that we ought to labor less. With you, he shared the certainties of peace and the uncertainties of war, and, what is a singular gift from wise kings, he most carefully extended to your safe-keeping all the secrets of his heart. You nonetheless taunted none with suggestive answers. **6.** You have cherished patience in listening and truth in conversing; often you corrected with eager rectitude whatever falsehood had reached him and, what is a rare kind of trust, you sometimes resisted the wishes of the *Princeps,* but only for his reputation for rectitude. For this man, unconquered in battles, allowed himself to be overcome on behalf of his fame and the reasonable contrariness of servants was sweet to the just *Princeps.* **7.** Love justice now that you are elevated, just as you delighted in it when serving. Show yourself to be the pupil of one who never labored in vain. You have been conjoined to the Amal family with the noblest wife. Indeed, royal kinship ought to encourage everything that is good. Be ready to act with practiced wisdom, so that you may be seen to attain a lofty rank for the praise of your character. **8.** Let the example of that probity of the Gothic race be exalted; that Gensimund,[13] songworthy the world over, was made his brother-in-arms alone, and thus joined himself to the Amals with such great devotion that he demonstrated a diligent kind of service to his heirs. Although he himself was sought for a *regnum,* he exercised his talents for others and he demonstrated to his very young children what may be conferred upon the most restrained of all men. And therefore does the reputation

---

13. Gensimund is not otherwise attested, although clearly described as a well-known and colorful figure.

of our household celebrate him; one who despised things that should be avoided at any time lives forever in memory. Thus, while the name of the Goths prevails, his renown is born in the recollection of all. Whence it is natural to expect the best things from you, who are known to enjoy kinship with our family.

LETTER 8.10 (C. 526)

The partner letter to *Variae* 8.9, here announcing to the Senate at Rome the elevation of a Gothic *comes* to patrician rank. This letter offers more biographical detail for the appointee.

King Athalaric to the Senate of Rome

1. Consider, conscript fathers, for what reason you ought to give thanks to a glorious *Princeps*, when we confer upon an outstanding man and our kinsman, Tuluin, the distinction of your shining order. For the genius of peace is increased from the display of resplendent arms, nor may a toga already girt for battle lie ungirt and neglected. Before, we conferred these honors upon you, but now we elevate distinction itself. The splendor that the *patricius praesentalis* possesses is certainly poured back upon all men, when it is the nature of such pure illumination that it glows even on those near it. **2.** So resplendent and unflagging in service, he clung to our lord grandfather. But although he would be for you the most noble of candidates, nonetheless, it helps to report what is known to concern the glory of his mentor. First, what is exceptional to have among any people, he is glorified by the noblest line of the Goths. **3.** He soon abandoned a childhood among parents, steadfastly carried out his uninstructed years in the shadows of the sacred bedchamber,[14] acting not according to his age, but instead as the position required. For it is granted that all services to a king must be conducted with discretion; hence the closer one draws to the king, the more full of trepidation one becomes. It is exceedingly difficult to be held in confidence by the *Princeps,* where it is dreaded even by those not so intimate with king that anything private should be revealed. An intermediary who draws royal tempests to himself without harm is dear to his superiors and always welcome to his colleagues, so that even now it would seem to presage great felicity that he deserved the gratitude of all. **4.** As he began to harden from a tender age of adolescent years to the virile boldness of his people, he was sent on an expedition to Sirmium,[15] so that what the words of the king had taught him about war, he would demonstrate on the open field. He fought victoriously against the Huns, among others, and auspicious with the praise earned from his first battles, he dealt death to the Bulgars, a people terrible over the whole

14. He was a royal paige.
15. In 504.

world. Our cradles send forth such great warriors; thus are hands prepared for war where the spirit is trained. Nourished in peaceful service he subjected hardened men and what he did not learn in practice, virtue easily completed. **5.** A young man, he returned to the *Princeps* already advanced as a veteran, so that he could be thought an assiduous student of arms, not of peaceful service. For this, that assessor of deeds and remunerator of good men, observing Tuluin's vigor, entrusted him to the royal household out of consideration for his virtue, so that one whose talents war had proven became involved in the counsels of the bravest king, a man subtle in discerning, robust in acting, and cautious in keeping confidence. He held a position in the service of public security: he sometimes arranged battles for the king, at other times he prepared the equitability of public business. And he adopted such similarity to the king's thoughts that you would recognize instances where he accomplished according to his own will what the king would have wanted. He assisted the defender of all with his own administration and by providing advice he governed the ruler himself. **6.** Let the Gallic campaign serve as reminder, where then sent among *duces,* he was most conspicuous facing dangers and acting according to his own wisdom in battles. Arles is the city situated above the flood of the Rhone, where at the outset of morning, he crossed the surface of the so-named river on a bridge of planks. Here it was necessary to both attack the enemy and defend our soldiers. Accordingly, at this point were roused the mightiest battles between Goths and Franks. **7.** The boldness of our candidate stood firm here in doubtful circumstances, where he fought in such a concentration of massed enemy, that he parted the enemy with his ferocity and he received wounds as tokens for his own deeds: wounds, I say, a permanent reputation, a badge without need of witness, the language of bravery unto its own, which are fittingly received in immediate danger and then decorate the remainder of one's life. For the uninjured body requires witnesses, it seeks others who would divulge things seen. A wound leaves no doubt about proven bravery, and is corroborated by distinguished testimony. The clash of brave men overwhelmed the exchange of missiles; nor was he who contended with numerous enemies ever safe from harm. Perhaps the thrust of one enemy is skillfully evaded, but one who confronts many enemies receives a wound from the direction he had not anticipated; for which reason, however great the danger endured then, so much now is the glory. Therefore, an example of good fortune assists in explaining the calm demeanor of a brave man, since it is not always the experienced *dux* that claims praise from fraught labors. **8.** Thus, with Franks and Burgundians locked in combat, he was sent back for the protection of Gaul,[16] lest a hostile hand should seize anything that our army had defended with costly labors. From the struggles of others, he acquired a province for the Roman republic without any difficulty, and he made peace our advantage,

---

16. In 523–24.

where we only had threats from bellicose contention. It was a triumph without battle, a trophy without toil, a victory without slaughter. Therefore, however much profit we have received, we owe to his glory. The judge of these affairs decided that his return must be followed with generosity, so that he became a lord of lands there, where he had provided for an increase in the public weal.[17] **9.** And we rightly recall, amid his prosperity, the storm at Aquileia, since this danger, when it ended happily, left the impression of the sweetest memory. When he attempted an open sea raging with savage winds and the froth of waves, the swelling of crashing waves engulfed the ship, permitting not one of the crew of oarsmen safety except this brave man. Then this very man escaped the doomed ship alone at a dear cost. **10.** Here was the love of a devout king, there was the proven merit of the one hazarding danger. When the king himself was hardly secure on the shore, he demanded to enter the waves again, so that he might prevail to save him from ruin. In that moment, danger to the king terrified one who knows not how to fear for his own safety. **11.** Does the one for whom the present occasion is prepared not seem, conscript fathers, divinely exempt from harsh misfortune? And so, because it is decreed by God's guidance, we elevate this man, trained in war, distinguished by fortune, proven in wisdom, to the summit of *patricius praesentalis*. Now favor the initiation of this candidate and open the hall of Liberty for our men.[18] It is fitting for the tribe of Romulus to have men of Mars as colleagues.

LETTER 8.11 (C. 526)

A curiosity among letters of the collection, this letter is addressed from the recent recipient of patrician rank (cf. *Var.* 8.9–10) to the Senate. It is plausible that Tuluin read this to the Senate following a reading of Athalaric's announcement, but, given the compressed complexity of the Latin, it seems more likely that *Variae* 8.10–11 would have been circulated for leading members of the assembly to read in private.

Tuluin to the Senate of Rome[19]

1. I trust, conscript fathers, that your attention ought to be stirred toward expressing gratitude of all kinds for such a good king, when you know my advancement had been conceived for the benefit of all. And so what had been desired on account of close relations should also be accomplished eagerly. It is indeed advantageous to

---

17. As a result of his second intervention in Gaul, Theoderic either awarded him with lands or perhaps made him *comes*.

18. The specific reference to the Senate house (*atria Libertatis*) and an entourage attending Tuluin (*viris nostris*), suggests Athalaric followed upon his accession to the throne by sending his most capable commander to Rome, probably with a sizable military following.

19. Mommsen's edition notes that this letter is addressed, "King Athalaric to the Senate of Rome," although the voice of the writer is clearly intended to be that of Tuluin.

all to follow the decisions of *Principes,* but that very person who gladly assists another's cause advances his own. **2.** You will remember that I always honored the assembly of the Senate, but now especially, when I am seen to enter your company. Appointment to the dignity of your order multiplies my gratitude, when I feel that I am among those whom I trust love me. Moreover, it is appropriate that the most welcome pledge of your affection, the aura of patrician rank, remains esteemed through our efforts,[20] when there is not a man of any nation who would consider what he sees honored in me to be cheapening to you. **3.** Furthermore, my preferences in the award of distinctions often were conjoined with yours under the *Princeps,* King Theoderic of glorious memory, so that it may be said that I approved in advance certain court offices for those to whom it would be fitting for me to offer gratitude. For the more reliable man is sought where he has hastened after receiving rewards. Often have I advanced consuls, patricians, and prefects with my customary intercession, striving to obtain for you what I have ardently hoped to receive myself. Rejoice now, conscript fathers, in my initiation; I have ever promoted your distinctions. **4.** Do you want to know with what affection I shall embrace you? Being joined to the royal family, I still want to share your habits. By the grace of God, you thrive secure, and what is the most fortunate kind of pleasantness, you revel with your children. Be eager, as always, to be praised for Roman character and to achieve the fame of good deeds in profound peace. It concerns our shared glory that we increase the number of those whom we are entrusted to protect by the grace of divine authority.

LETTER 8.12 (C. 526)

This letter may be considered the final in a dossier concerning the elevation of Tuluin as *patricius praesentalis.* Here, a legal advisor (and later prominent Christian scholar) is appointed *Comes Domesticorum* in order to act as a civilian counselor for the new *patricius.* A corresponding announcement of this appointment to the Senate does not survive.

King Athalaric to Arator, Vir Illustris

1. We deem the completion of necessary matters to be final if, however we have provided for the military portion of the republic by appointing a magnificent *patricius,*[21] we also reflect upon associating with him the most learned man of letters. For it is fitting for those to whom the highest power is entrusted to have the most educated critics, so that advantages planned for the republic may be deployed

20. The letter is very careful to refer to Tuluin with the first-person singular *me,* but here uses the plural *nos* to indicate "Tuluin and the Senate" together.

21. Tuluin.

without hindrance from a lack of worthy men. **2.** There are other offices which operate with the usual degree of oversight; but such an official whose duties do not have equal must be paired with a very diligent colleague concerning state security. And since you are no longer regarded as unproven, you will come to office early in years. The battlefield of legal advising trained you; the peak of our discernment elected you. For dedication to literary arts was so great in you, that we could not permit your talent to whither with age there. You have been initiated into public service, because you will be able to fulfill the role of legal advisor, and although eloquence may draw you to speak for the defense, equity nonetheless used to persuade you to produce judgments. It is a given that articulate ability armed with good character is useful. For just as it is ruinous for the learned to encourage criminal acts, thus it is a wholesome gift when charming speech knows not how to transgress the bounds of truth. **3.** But so that I may instead base your merits in commendable examples, it will help to recount the official embassy which you accomplished so thoroughly, not with plain speech, but with a flowing torrent of eloquence. For when sent from the region of Dalmatia to our lord grandfather, you thus represented both the needs of the provincials and the public weal in such a way that, before a man agitated with great concerns, you were both replete and did not move him to distaste. Indeed, your abundant words flowed forth with the sweetest charm, and when you reached the end, you were asked to speak further. By delighting and moving your audience, you satisfied the goal of the true orator more, when you abandoned the role of legal advocate. **4.** True, you were also assisted by the charm and character of your father, whose eloquence could instruct you, although you were not without books of the ancients. For he was, as we know, exceptionally learned in literary arts.[22] And so that we may speak on something scholarly with a learned man, common opinion holds that Mercury, the author of many arts, first assembled these letters from the flight of birds on the River Strymon. **5.** For even today the cranes, which flock in formation, describe the shapes of the alphabet by nature's inspiration. Transcribing these to a seemly arrangement, with vowels and consonants suitably combined, he discovered the cognitive means by which a mind seeking higher meaning is able to rapidly arrive at the inner chambers of wisdom. About this, the Greek author Helenus said much, expertly describing the form and character of letters in the subtlest detail, so that the bounty of great literature can be understood at its very origin. **6.** But so that we may return to our purpose, you who have not nurtured eloquence in the Roman Forum, must therefore be trusted to extend the talent from your father's example. O blessed teacher and most fortunate of pupils, who learned from affection what the terror of learned men has violently wrenched from others. **7.** From there, you discovered Roman eloquence, not in its own regions, and reading Tullius restored

22. Arator's father is otherwise unknown.

you to learning there, where the Gallic language once sounded.[23] Where are those who claim that Latin letters must be learned at Rome and nowhere else? If a former age had engendered this advance, Caecilius would have avoided the weight of shame.[24] Indeed, the force of that judgment on Latin learning has unraveled: even Liguria produces its own Tullii. **8.** Take heed of what we think about your merits, when you see yourself bound to the councils of that very man who manages the secrets of our *imperium*. Hence it is that we have decorated you as an *illustris* with the office of *Comes Domesticorum,* so that you rightly ought to aspire to greater things in our judgment, we who expect to find better things to come in you. You see the important business entrusted to you: whatever you do, the state will feel. For one who is able to sin against the common good is exceptionally glorious if he knows nothing of excess.

LETTER 8.13 (C. 526)

Perhaps indicative of a wholesale changing of key personnel following the death of Theoderic, this letter appoints a new *Quaestor* to Athalaric's court.

King Athalaric to Ambrosius, Vir Illustris *and* Quaestor

1. He would be assured of climbing to lofty honors, who had proven himself gradually in lesser functions and followed a sure course that was obtained steadily with an acceptable degree of ambition. Indeed, anything received suddenly is considered remunerated without merit, nor will that which appears unexpectedly avoid suspicion of being untried. By contrast, anything weighed with deliberation is solidly rooted, and one who is promoted according to the evidence of praise in service is believed to have obtained everything from good deeds.[25] **2.** Not long ago, you presided over the *fasces* of the private largesse, a man adopted from the schools of rhetoric by that inspector of merits, who could even foretell the future with his decisions. Except that he had resolved upon it for you, this was an inadequate honor which, by undertaking the patronage of deserving men, you thus increased to the gratitude of the ruler, so that he often entrusted to you what was not the concern of your post. Because, if it is commendable to be equal to even middling offices, it is so much more distinguished to have succeeded at a palatine office by virtue of good character. When you had managed this position with such praiseworthy judgment, you also found gratitude for the position of another man.[26] **3.**

---

23. Tullius is Cicero. Arator was trained in rhetoric by Ennodius, who claimed Gallic origins.

24. Caecilius Statius, an author of *fabulae* from the second century B.C., whom Cicero later criticized for having Gallic Latin.

25. Theoderic had appointed him *Comes Privatarum* at some point prior to the king's death.

26. He apparently assumed the duties of *Quaestor* in *ex officio* capacity after Theoderic dismissed the former *Quaestor.*

For, while employed in correspondence, you proved yourself, when the former official had been expelled for his offenses, and thus your talent preserved a suspended office, so that you did not allow the palace to lack a magistrate, the office of which, at that time, we had thought to remove. Our reign is not unequal to these functions; we have men following and even rivaling the ancients. **4.** Behold one rising again who becomes *Quaestor* by his talent. Pliny now returns and Trajan adopts him.[27] Consider what great matters you would pronounce, if you too would shine with similar eloquence. The reputation of our reign derives from both lawful and elegantly expressed decisions. Indeed, learned speech increases all good things, and what is adorned by the grace of speaking well is received in advance from us. Be ever prepared to suggest good policies to us and be constantly on guard against the wicked improbity of grasping men. Speak also what is wholly in accord with our hearing. A good *Princeps* is the one for whom it is a given to speak on behalf of justice, and who expects to hear the decrees of ancient legal opinion as opposed to the claims of tyrannical savagery. **5.** We have truly revived that most celebrated dictum of Trajan: take up the pen on my behalf if I have been good for the republic, and take it up against me if I have been bad for the republic. But understand what we expect from you, when we have not permitted anything unjust to be done on our behalf. Therefore, let our decrees echo the constitutions of the ancients, which find the sweetness of praise however much they claim the wisdom of antiquity. **6.** We do not esteem in other men anything extralegal that we would abhor. We oblige you to the commonality when we order you to observe the laws absolutely. We therefore say this now, so that we may be seen to encourage it in you for every circumstance. For it is right to admonish one in advance, lest in other circumstances we seem to want to correct you too late. Follow the example of good men and proceed mindful of your own nobility. It is expected that those who are born from contemptible stock return to the vices of their own kind. **7.** Therefore, with these admonishments for the public good, with God as witness, we happily grant you for the fifth indiction insignia as *Quaestor*. This is the office of wise men, the well-spring of every public distinction, since it precedes what the bounty of our generosity will have bestowed.[28] Act so that you, who have been appointed to our counsel, should be known to excel all others in wisdom and dignified comportment. For you behold what may be appropriate for you. When we may found laws, you will speak with the voice of the law. Incline toward faithful probity now, so that just as the first post had been worthy of providing another for you, thus may the second provide a third distinction.

---

27. This is slightly confused: Pliny the Younger was indeed *Quaestor Imperatoris*, but under Domitian; Trajan later appointed him to a consulship and to an appointment on his *consistorium*.

28. A reference to the role of the *Quaestor* in formulating pronouncements of appointment to office; cf. *Var.* 8.14.2.

LETTER 8.14 (C. 526)

This letter follows the established protocol of announcing palatine appointments to the Senate at Rome, in this case the appointment of a new *Quaestor* (cf. *Var.* 8.13).

King Athalaric to the Senate of Rome

1. Behold, conscript fathers, the judgment which the commencement of our reign has proclaimed, when those things that must be avoided are more fully understood, since a succession is regarded only as exceptional as its origin. For no man is deemed to be attentive to future events who is not known to be careful with the novelty of his own reputation. The insightful cultivator strives to furnish his own garden with fruitful plants, so that they might return the best yield that could be cultivated with careful effort; how much more fitting that a *regnum* be arranged with the pleasantness of peace at its inception, lest it seem to have the quality of an uncultivated field! 2. And therefore, we have thought to provide a *Quaestor* like a door for our favors, through whom the lofty eminences of offices to come would fittingly arrive. The things of which we speak concerning this candidate are certainly known to you, even when they are wholly contemporary.[29] For when the stricken hearts of subjects mourned the passing of our lord grandfather of glorious memory—it is true that a good man is loved more when he is missed—through this the blessings of your security and our commencement were made available. Take heed with what equity we bind future affairs, so that one who was made an advocate for protecting justice would become the guardian of laws for you.[30] 3. A seemly and eloquent orator, he attended to royal mandates, even coaxing at a glance those whom a hearing rendered agreeable. For it is fitting that men of the court should be of such quality that their natures reveal goodness at the appearance of their countenances, and, when seen, they would be recognized for their good characters. Indeed, it is a great shame for someone to remain silent if he is ennobled so greatly by speech; however, he only remains honored if his disposition is tranquil and the most serene appearance commends him. In short, by this very fact, we offer testimony to our own abundant wisdom, when such a man who is praiseworthy on both accounts is chosen for office.[31] 4. It is certainly unnecessary for a *Quaestor* to boast the blessings of eloquence, when he is known to be chosen especially for this, since he would commend the reputation of our reign by the quality of his speech. For other magistrates are entrusted with the payment of taxes in provinces, some are delegated the maintenance of our personal treasury;

---

29. An instance of Cassiodorus's use of the term *modernus*, here seemingly in contrast to the senatorial order's preference for tradition.

30. Here speaking about Ambrosius as *Quaestor*.

31. Physical charm and moral development.

with the *Quaestor,* however, tokens of the palace's renown are enshrined,[32] whence common opinion is vaunted across the whole world. We believe that it bears remembering by you, conscript fathers, that you should trust us to find the kind of men who would be beneficial both to our reputation and to your safety. Acknowledge, O learned men, the worthy wish of the *Princeps;* trust favors from one who is commended to regard the celebrity of letters. It is for the sluggish man to be inactive, when he may know that the masters of the world have invited him to advancement. **5.** For this reason, conscript fathers, let the blessing of your kindness choose the *illustris* Ambrosius to be celebrated on high as *Quaestor.* For there ought to be no doubt concerning one who has already merited being approved by your order in his first office.

LETTER 8.15 (C. 526)

This letter to the Senate confirms the appointment of Felix IV as bishop of Rome. Theoderic had earlier resolved a contested episcopal election in July of 526. His death the following August may have occasioned dissatisfaction with Felix's appointment, which the current letter seeks to quell. The senatorial elite at Rome were major power brokers influencing episcopal elections and, in the case of contested elections, they also influenced papal appointments made by royal fiat.

King Athalaric to the Senate of Rome

1. We profess from our heart the greatest gratitude that you have agreed with the judgment of our glorious lord grandfather in the selection of a bishop. For it was proper to hearken to the decision of a good *Princeps* who, investigating with prudent deliberation, even though involving a religion foreign to him, clearly selected such an excellent bishop, as would rightly displease no person, so that by this, especially, you may acknowledge his preference that the religion of all churches should prosper with good priests. And so you have received a man both fittingly instructed by divine grace and approved by royal examination. **2.** Let no man be held by former rivalry at this point. One whose desire has been overcome by the *Princeps* should not experience the shame of defeat. Indeed, to the contrary, one who esteems the bishop with pure intention accomplishes his own desire. For what would be the reason for grief, when the defeated party finds in this very appointment from the other faction what it had desired? These contentions are civil, battles without iron and disputes without animosity: such an affair is resolved by acclamation, not suffering. For even if a candidate has been removed, nonetheless nothing has been lost by the faithful, when the highest religious office has been filled. **3.** Therefore, returning your *illustris* legate Publianus, we quite naturally

---

32. Probably referring to public speeches and letters.

extend the highest praise of greeting to your assembly. For we delight with great joy, however much we exchange words with our leading citizens. And I doubt not that this will also be the most pleasant outcome for you; if you accomplished anything for the *imperium* of that former ruler, you would also know us to be very grateful.

LETTER 8.16 (C. 527)

This appointment to the office of *Comes Sacrarum Largitionum* was probably quite controversial. The appointee had been instrumental in providing evidence against Boethius. Upon his accession, it may have been necessary for Athalaric to appease opposed factions of the senatorial elite. The letter tactfully omits any mention of the candidate's former service under Theoderic.

King Athalaric to Opilio, Comes Sacrarum

1. It is indeed customary for those obtaining offices at the palace to be weighed by continuous examination, lest imperial judgment may seem to recommend anything of doubtful nature, when it is the glory of a king to find choice magistrates. But so often has a fortunate member of your family been promoted, so often has wisdom been declared by many appointments, it is clear that anyone who may chose you spontaneously would seem to do nothing uncertain. The fortunate man preserves the image of his own family in his veins, while one who fails to find qualities similar to his own line feels shamed at the lack of it. 2. Hence it is that the man selected for nobility is acknowledged better than someone made by good fortune, since the one man, encouraged by the deeds of his forebears, preserves his reputation thus, while the other man has no exemplar except whatever he has accomplished. Therefore, we believe it guaranteed in you that we rejoice to have committed so much to two of your family. Your father presided over these very *fasces*, while your brother shone with the same distinction.[33] It is almost as though the office itself has been enshrined in your household as a guardian spirit,[34] and public distinction is a household commonplace. 3. For you have learned the requirements of service from praise for your brother, to whom you are connected with shared affection. You fulfilled kinship with public duties and brotherhood with participation in counsels. Deciding what office your brother should accept pertained instead to you. A fortunate man, he reclined on this prop, boldly trust-

---

33. The father and brother were Opilio, who served as magistrate under Odoacer, and Cyprianus, about whom see *Var.* 8.21–22.

34. A *lar*, possibly understood in an elite Christian sense of being a "founding father" for the household.

ing in that particular ability of yours,[35] since he perceived everything would be completed by you. **4.** Behold the sweet loyalty of brothers and the ancient harmony of the present day. It is well to base judgment in such affections as are perceived to preserve good conduct naturally. Because if perchance the provincial leisure of pleasant retirement would have been pleasing, the anxious prayers of the aggrieved and crowds of petitioners hastened to you.[36] Among them you assumed the duty of the good judge and in a kind of presage hastening toward future events, you accomplished the office that you had received from us by the appointment of meritorious men. **5.** We, moreover, remember with what devotion you served us at the beginning of our *regnum,* when it is especially difficult to maintain faithful loyalty. For when, after the passing of our lord grandfather of divine memory, the will of the people was anxious with trepidation and the hearts of subjects were overwhelmed on account of such a great *regnum* with an heir thus far untested, fortunate harbinger, you announced our commencement to the Ligurians and strengthened by the address of your wisdom, they commuted the grief that held them at his death into joy for the rise of our *imperium.* The renewal of a king occurred without any confusion, and your care prevailed so that no man offended us. **6.** And so, instructed with such great lessons, we happily appoint you, by the grace of divine authority, to *Comes Sacrarum Largitionum* from the sixth indiction. You may enjoy all the privileges and rewards that pertained to your predecessors; for it would not be proper that those who are established by the strength of their own service should be shaken by any designs of corruption. For there was a time when even magistrates were harassed by detractors.[37] You who have had no errors may now put aside fear. You enjoy the fruits of your forebears in office, for what long-established custom granted to your two predecessors in the time of our lord grandfather, our indulgence now protects. **7.** We confer the post of your brother upon you, but you imitate the loyalty of his service. For if you should follow him, you will supersede many in praise. He was a man of exceptional authority and constant in probity, who both served a great *Princeps* without blame and exercised good judgment commendably. It is easy to estimate what he would have accomplished when his renown will not lack a grateful successor to palatine duty. And so it is not difficult to follow the good character of a brother, since those who are engendered from the seed of the same man agree even more in the fruit of their association.

35. This passage is particularly ambivalent: *astu quaedam neglegens praesumptione tui* may be read in an unflattering light, which may have also been the intent, given Opilio's role in the condemnation of Boethius prior to Athalaric's accession.

36. Opilio and his colleague Gaudentius had both been condemned to exile for corruption prior to providing evidence against Boethius; this seems to be a flattering way of indicating supporters had offered opposition to exile.

37. An ironic statement considering this is what Opilio had done to Boethius!

LETTER 8.17 (C. 527)

Partner to the previous letter (cf. *Var.* 8.16) announcing an appointment as *Comes Sacrarum Largitionum,* this letter perhaps required more delicacy than the previous because hostilities to the candidate would have been more keenly felt in the Senate, where some parties may have held him responsible for Boethius's death.

King Athalaric to the Senate of Rome

1. So great is the abundance of merits in this candidate, conscript fathers, that we fear he would be thought chosen later than could be proven by sound judgment. For when our grandfather of divine memory sought out the best possible men, a more prosperous fortune held him unremunerated for us. He obeyed the former ruler, he served him with great readiness, and it happened that he was abandoned by the most generous master of beneficence without any recompense.[38] I believe that compensation for one deserving has been delayed so that he would become more closely bound to us as a cause for celebrating. For our devotion doubles itself in accordance to the law of nature. It is just as worthy that a debt accrued by its author should be paid by his heir. For why would our munificence exclude him, when the established custom of his own nobility encouraged him to succeed? **2.** His father was distinguished for his strong arm and conspicuous for the great nobility of his character,[39] a man whom neither raging war deterred nor tranquil leisure overcame. Robust in body and firm in friendship, he acted in accordance with antiquity, even when enriched with distinguished offices in the degraded reign of Odoacer. His conduct at that time, when a *Princeps* had not been elevated, was exceptional. **3.** But why do we call upon the antique nobility of his father when it shines in the closer illumination of his brother?[40] I speak not of his blood relation to him, but rather what had been commendably joined to him in friendship. Thus he bound and associated himself with the virtues of his brother, so that one who was foretokened by the other, in this way could hardly be worthy of doubt. **4.** The brother offered loyalty to friends, but this man owes great constancy from oaths. The brother also was devoid of greed, and this man is proven alien to cupidity. Hence it is that they knew how to serve the trust of kings, since between them they equally knew nothing of falsehood. For where good character is easily proven, nature reveals it without restraint. Therefore, in what way would these who knew not how to ridicule colleagues be unable to serve their masters with pure

---

38. This almost makes it sound as though Theoderic had died before having the opportunity to advance Opilio, rather than Opilio having his public career delayed by scandal.

39. The father was also Opilio, who served in senior posts under Odoacer.

40. His brother was Cyprianus, for whom see *Var.* 8.21.

intention?[41] **5.** Chosen for such praise, he was associated with the Basilian family in marriage;[42] thus he came to be associated even more with noble merits. Consider him, if it pleases, for his family connections, since often with your ancestors such indications produced capable men. Hence it was that private life was arranged with such great restraint that it could neither become soiled with any parsimony nor likewise would it be troubled by excessive extravagance. **6.** He obliged foreigners to himself in conquest and Romans in legal verdicts, and where ingratitude often comes to offices, this man accrued friendships from his settlements. Behold what nature makes noble. Born from magistrates, he accomplishes in court what may not be attained by any means except by the probity of good character. For the necessity of power compels most men to obey public authority; only the probity of legal decisions causes them to obey a judge in private matters. Whence a patron is known to gain more praise from us when he is not chosen for court unless he is thought to be just according to his character. **7.** Therefore, conscript fathers, cherish him among your adopted sons and among our magistrates. This man who was born to a senator and is judged honorable for service in the court arrives at your curia favorably prepared.

LETTER 8.18 (C. 527)

This letter appoints a new candidate to the office of *Quaestor,* fairly soon after the predecessor in this office (*Var.* 8.13–14) had replaced a previous *Quaestor* who had been disgraced in office. This particular candidate would hold the post for only a year, not holding office again until selected as *Praefectus Praetorio* during the Gothic War by Belisarius, in essence replacing Cassiodorus.

King Athalaric to Fidelis, Vir Illustris *and* Quaestor

1. It is appropriate that judges deploy men skilled in law to be an attestation of justice, since one who understands equity is hardly likely to deny it, lest one cleansed by learning should easily become soiled with the shame of error. Some time ago the ruling eye noticed you toiling in court cases, nor was it possible to conceal with what devotion you acted upon your charge, with what brilliance you pleaded your cases. **2.** Your eloquence and good conscience both advanced at an equal pace. No client could want for what he fully obtained from you; no judge would be able to correct what he found in you. For both charm of countenance and purity of heart agree in you. Only your comely appearance showed your youth; wizened words flowed from a mouth in its first spring. The maturity of your mind

---

41. Here it seems Cassiodorus has conjoined Opilio to the reputation of his brother to deflect his role as Boethius's *delator*.

42. Opilio's wife is unknown.

contended with the youth of your years; but that quality prevailed instead which brings us to the glorious path of the virtues. **3.** Therefore, we have fitted a reward to your name and your deserts, so that, as Fidelis,[43] you may take upon yourself the secrets of the court and as an eloquent man you may obtain a lettered office. Now decide in full glory the legal cases that you used to plead commendably. Let your own learning and experience aid you. But it is certainly a blessed situation in legal cases when one who pronounces sentence is unable to ignore what he reads. For it is not fitting that a judge would be the subordinate of another's will, so that one whom so many servants follow should obey another man even more. If, indeed, a man must be supported in any way by others, it is especially shameful in the case of a *Quaestor,* where one who was chosen for the counsel of a prince would await the assistance of another. **4.** And therefore, that it may be declared with God's guidance, we confer upon you the office of *Quaestor* for the sixth indiction. But your distinction is a reproach to unexperienced men. For just as it is joyful for a good conscience to be promoted for its merits, so too does a man who recognizes himself to be unequal to follow such rewards lie under accusation. Consider those ancient men whom you ought to imitate. Surpass in reputation those whom you follow in office. **5.** For if private life trained your virtues, how much better will public advancement reveal you to be? You have claimed a name from your merits; protect it, so that you will always be glad for the aptness of the word. For when any name is clearly given in order to declare an intended purpose, it is exceedingly absurd to bear a name foreign to that purpose and to be called something other than what is able to be found in its habits. Let these words furnish good conscience,[44] since one who is continually admonished becomes doubted concerning his name.

LETTER 8.19 (C. 527)

An announcement for a recent promotion to *Quaestor* corresponding with *Variae* 8.18.

King Athalaric to the Senate of Rome

1. It is fitting that your assembly should always radiate with native splendor, although it is rendered more brilliant by whatever means it increases with the illumination of public offices. For heaven itself glows more with a greater abundance of stars and from that numerous beauty it returns a wondrous grace to those gazing at it. It is clearly ingrained in nature that an abundance of blessings delights more. Thus meadows are painted with innumerable blossoms; the fertile field is

---

43. *Fidelis,* of course, meant "faithful."
44. Here shifting from an etymology of *fidelis* to the words of the letter.

praised for denser grain. Antiquity caused you to be considered noble; we want the Senate to be esteemed even more for its numerousness. 2. Hence it is that we want to attach to you one whom we have found to be outstanding in every way. For while it is permitted that the Senate may be a nursery for you, nonetheless let one who is joined to your assembly also be engendered by our kindness. Every office of the palace bears fosterlings for you, while the *Quaestor* is verily the mother of the Senate, since it is derived from wisdom. For who is more worthy to become a member of the curia than one who cleaves to the counsel of the *Princeps*? But since restrained praise does not generally suffice for a man of wisdom, let us touch upon his fame and his own qualities. 3. Know, conscript fathers, that the practice of eloquence first commended our *Quaestor,* and thus by his advocacy he achieved repeated successes, so that triumphal selection adopted him for his own merits, to the extent that, consecrated with the blessed fronds of victory, he would grant us every kind of glory. Having been inducted into the school of law at the earliest age, he studied continually. With single-mindedness and by excessive toil he attained chastity of the body and noble modesty. 4. A learned orator and most serious patron, he supported cases undertaken at his own expense, for which such a man was found assisting unlikely cases that were not supportable. Would it not be a loss to the public to pass by such a man? For what would be more welcome to us, or to you, than to join to our side such a man who deserves to be approved in the work of the laws? It is easy to love these merits by which a learned man is made conspicuous, when he claims each and every glory for himself, lest the heart is able to forget for what reason he was associated with us. 5. Perhaps you believe, chief men, that his wisdom appears untried and unequal to the task? His origin defends the inheritance that he claims in letters, for thus his father shone in the court of Milan, so that he sprang simultaneously from the workshop of his father and the shrine of Tullius.[45] Thence, although this would be a family difficult to satisfy among peers of middling status, nonetheless it often deserved to find praise among those of the first ranks for eloquence of advocacy. He stood against the great Olybrius,[46] he attained fronds of victory over Eugenetus with the fertility of his speech,[47] and likewise he stands equal to those whom Rome recognizes as exceptional. 6. For what could be nobler than to have been considered greater than the chief men of letters? For if men are made noble through family and by the long-established transmission of wealth, how much more outstanding is the origin of one who was found in the treasuries of abundant wisdom. Therefore, conscript fathers, embrace our decision and this candidate for his own merits; when you thus extend the hand of kindness to a colleague, you rather assist yourselves.

---

45. Cicero; Fidelis's father is unknown.
46. *Praefectus Praetorio* before Cassiodorus's father (c. 503).
47. Former *Quaestor* and *Magister Officiorum.*

LETTER 8.20 (C. 527)

This letter appoints a new *Praefectus Praetorio*, replacing a previous prefect discredited for unspecified corrupt practices. Although a new appointment to a senior magistracy seems consistent with the political realignments of Athalaric's accession, this is a puzzling case in that the candidate's predecessor was likely Abundantius (cf. *Var.* 5.16–17, 5.23, 5.34), who received high praise in the *Variae* for service under Theoderic.

King Athalaric to Avienus, Vir Illustris *and* Praefectus Praetorio

1. It is a firm statement of one's merits to have been appointed to office after a judge charged with corruption, when the excesses of those preceding are not corrected, but the best successor is found. A medical cure often follows a virulent condition, for when vital warmth has been applied, then the cold of infection recedes. The very clouds are scoured away by the breath of winds, and the north wind returns a tranquil appearance to the heavens which the southern gale had disturbed. Thus have we driven off your predecessor out of a love for the commonality, so that you would approach as one bearing healthful assistance. **2.** Strive to accomplish what demands praise and to imitate what is opposite to your predecessor. That man was hated for his chicanery; strive so that you may be found acceptable for your justice. That man was rapacious; you be restrained. The easiest definition of everything good is to avoid what he accomplished, when what may not be approved in his judgment truly must be praiseworthy. Reflect, then, upon the public antipathy for this man and strive for everyone's love. May as many men give thanks for your good character as condemn the grievousness of that man's actions. Therefore, be stirred by the shame of your predecessor when, after that man's manifest wickedness, you must be praised for having abstained from bad deeds. For what kind of distinction would it be, should you confer upon the provinces such blessings as they have not enjoyed up to this point? Unaccustomed goodness is loved more and a preceding period of grief confers sweetness upon the rejoicing to follow. **3.** And so, with God willing, we gladly confer upon you for the sixth indiction the *fasces* of the prefecture, which, however much it was fearfully harmful then, so much now it ought to hold the kindness of leniency, since the wounds must be healed by your care. Let none be burdened by your hand or another's. For it is beyond all impiety that one who is trusted to heal the wounded should strike blows. Let the *Praefectus Praetorio* return to that ancient name praised over the whole world, which, if we were to seek its beginning, commenced with the blessings offered through Joseph. Not without reason, the *Praefectus Praetorio* is proclaimed by our laws as the father of provinces and even the father of *imperium*, since they call for him to act with justice and foresight, so that the laws would assume the reputation not of a harsh judge, but that of devotion to the people. **4.** Let our treasury increase through you with just payments and debts. We renounce gain that desecrates the protection of the laws. We want that money by which the scales of justice are supported. We do not permit our household to contain any wantonness, since we are unable to privately allow what we condemn in public. **5.** Listen, O magistrates, to what we cherish; attempt nothing harmful to the public. For whom would you expect to please with iniquitous policies, when you know that only what can agree with the dictates of justice pleases us? You would sin against your own good character if you later abandon such conduct. Although some, perchance, accomplish great things who arrive at great offices through kinsmen, you are predisposed to add something better after the commendable prefecture of your father, since one who follows always ought to be more careful, when we rightly desire to imitate and even hasten to overcome the good works of our parents. **6.** It also adds to your credit that you are thought to be steeped in the words of the wise. It is serious to find fault with a wise man, where it reveals the fault of the other. One who knows nothing of laws transgresses law greatly; it is entirely legitimate to seek law from you, whose origin is not known to be uninstructed. For you, the books of the ancients and the deeds of your forebears are the same. Justify your reputation and justify our decision, so that you would not be unequal to those distinguished men whose offices you equate with our generosity.

LETTER 8.21 (C. 527)

This letter appoints an *illustris* senator to the rank of patrician after his service as *Comes Sacrarum Largitionum*. His brother succeeded him to this office (*Var.* 8.16–17), and both had been implicated in the condemnation of Boethius. Like his brother's appointment as *comes*, elevation to patrician rank was likely politically sensitive.

King Athalaric to Cyprianus, Vir Illustris *and Patrician*

1. It is fitting that you have been praised both for the office bestowed upon your brother and for those frequently given to you; nonetheless, since the special quality of offices is not spent when they are assigned, it is as though we restore for the new candidate the office about which so many pronouncements have already been trumpeted. Whatever ought to be well attested with regard to merits and fidelity is proven in your case. But one who has satisfied himself with the probity of public service will rightly want to be praised when he aims at new endeavors. **2.** The true source of glory is the steady flow of an annual font; for just as the spring is not exhausted by flowing, thus honors are not desiccated by frequent announcement. Because, even if accomplishments should be passed over in silence, you, who have ever increased in age with merits, are known to accumulate what may be proclaimed as new distinctions. For you, the passing of years procures the increase of praise. Even should you grow old of body, you are rejuvenated in praise. The most profitable age has rightly favored you, in whom the stronger reputation is always found. 3. Under our grandfather of divine memory, you always held honored positions in both branches of service.[48] He saw you as the warrior against Danubian nations; the horde of Bulgarians that opposed us with the presumption of battle did not terrify you. It was you, especially, who advanced upon unyielding barbarians and cut down those fleeing in fear. You thus assisted the victory of the Goths, not so much in number of conflicts as in difficulty. 4. Afterward, what was no less than those same battles, you maintained the duties of *referendarius* during laborious difficulties. Indeed, you rendered civil and military services in the presence of a man who possessed every virtue. For who could competently offer a favorable account to that ruler would not also be able to wage war? He always demanded such resolve in spirit, such constancy in maintaining the truth of words, so that one who had been able to avoid error in that man's presence could rightly claim to have conquered an enemy. Hence it was that wise men rendered services to him, since his attention was attuned to manifest caution and whenever someone dreaded incurring blame, he strove to consult with learned men. 5. He also conferred the office of the sacred largesse, the duty best suited to your industry, which you thus fulfilled with pure and restrained intention, so that you could make yourself worthy of greater things, even though you had undertaken this as a great reward. Through these offices, he trained you in the flush of youth, but your maturity serves our reign. You are indeed better equipped in counsel, nor will you be known as someone fatigued with age. Thus have you attained the blessings of old age, even as you have not succumbed to its disadvantages. There are benefits that we believe must be extended to you, so that, just as you are endowed with good conscience, you are also granted honor as one who must be respected. 6. For even heavenly judgment is consonant with our favors to you, when nature itself has made you the father of such sons that you would seem to be a patrician. It would not be absurd to refer to their good qualities as renewed growth, when it is a more blessed fame to be praised for the probity of sons being reared. Their childhood was first noticed in the palace, which signaled the beginning of praise in no way inconsiderable. Thus your children, enduring royal eyes hardly out of the cradle, comported themselves after the manner of standard bearers. Moreover, they shine with the grace of your stock, nor do they cease to be steeped in the brave instruction of arms. 7. Boys of Roman lineage speak our language,[49] indicating in particular the future fidelity offered to us, which they are now seen to affect in speech. Thus, it is to you, fortunate father, who have offered us even the devotion of your sons, that we ought to bestow a reward. Therefore, we confer upon you, with God's

---

48. Civil and military.

49. As children learning to handle arms at court, they were also learning the Gothic language.

guidance, the dignity of the patriciate for your many labors, your great loyalty, and your proven constancy. It is indeed a lofty distinction, but you are proven its equal in merits. Therefore, enjoy the benefit of your upstanding instruction, so that when you have doubled your good qualities, you will likewise increase from our favors.

LETTER 8.22 (C. 527)

The companion to *Variae* 8.21, presenting a candidate for elevation to patrician rank to the Senate.

King Athalaric to the Senate of Rome

1. If it is worthy of your favor, conscript fathers, who at any time is able to obtain the royal approval that the eminent Cyprianus has earned, one who ought to have become all the more pleasing to you by the extent that he has received offices from us? The garland more often decorates contenders in the races, the palm frequently glorifies the Olympic races; thus are prizes frequently conferred upon those who are rendered more glorious even in trivial affairs. From the outset then, it is possible to be in doubt concerning promotion, when many attempt to deceive the heart of the *Princeps*, because it is easy to make sport of one whose wish it is always to exceed. But this man has shown such constancy of purpose, he has held such great designs for good things, that he always calls upon himself the reward of kings. **2.** Here is certain glory, here a doubtless decision, to deserve so often that for which men are known to be crowned. It is even fitting that those who have not determined their worth in their first offices may enter your curia; but when they have undertaken greater responsibilities, they nevertheless deserve greater rewards. Such men likewise adorn our judgment, when the one who is often approved by you is first believed to have been aptly chosen by us. The manifest constancy of a good man is prized by nature itself, since commencing something for the purpose of praise is less important than preserving the designs of good men.[50] **3.** Conscript fathers, you had men similar to the Decii in olden times—antiquity predicted this family with the Corvini.[51] For in no way did this man, about whom we speak, sway our decision in his favor. He was already known to be greatly pleasing to one *Princeps*,[52] for it is known he deserved even under the other ruler to be advanced by sound judgment in both branches of service.[53] Therefore, one who perceives anything of the truth

50. This vague statement must relate to Cyprianus's public service, often described as the preservation of traditions or the prosperity of the state.

51. Heroes of Rome's history during the early Republic, Publius Decius and Marcus Valerius Corvus both earned glory during the First Samnite War (343–41 B.C.).

52. Theoderic.

53. Civil and military, cf. *Var.* 8.21.3.

considers his whole career in sequence. He merited the authorship of his own advancement, so that he rightly found us to be his promoter. **4.** The former king formed in him the foundations of public distinction; we have formed the pinnacle of his dignities. And therefore, conscript fathers, we append to the *illustris* Cyprianus, already greatly distinguished by so many offices and so much praise, the elevation of the patriciate, lest he should be greater from his own merits than from our conferred honors. Now embrace as a colleague one whom you have often decorated as an outsider. One who already lays his offices to rest in the hall of Liberty returns to you secure in his accomplishments. **5.** Consider moreover how he would be rendered more acceptable to you when he offers such fosterlings to your curia. Concerning his children, although an ambitious father, he nonetheless surpassed his own desires. These children are not, as would be expected, fearful or speechless before one who must be answered; they speak uncommonly well in several languages and they share the company of mature men. Thus they have been well known to us since they passed beyond adolescence in the very first stage of youth. Let divine majesty illustrate that, just as we have extolled the name of munificence on behalf of their father, thus even through them will we increase the rights of our devotion.

LETTER 8.23 (C. 526)

This letter orders certain properties to be transferred to the king's cousin Theodahad. The properties had belonged to Theodahad's mother, Amalafrida, possibly as a gift from Theoderic after the arrival of the Amals in Italy. This would have justified Theoderic's confiscation of the properties at her death sometime after 523. Athalaric's 'restoration' to Theodahad probably represents a strategy for cementing familial support for the young king.

King Athalaric to Bergantinus, Vir Illustris *and* Comes Patrimonii

1. Granted that while it may be fitting for generosity of the king to radiate in daily brilliance and to continually do whatever would allow the largesse of the *Princeps* to manifest, nonetheless, it is also by that means that a debt of good conscience is paid, so much so that it may fairly be lavished on family. *Principes* are enriched by their gifts to others and truly do we restore to our treasuries what applies to the advantages of good reputation. For it would be inappropriate that we should deny our kinsmen what we are accustomed to protect for our subjects, when one who is conjoined to us in blood deserves more, nor is it possible for one who serves a well-regarded judge to be cheated of his own desire. **2.** And so we inform your *illustris* magnitude that so many *solidi*, comprising the value of all the estates together from the former patrimony of the grand lady, his mother, be restored to the distinguished and fully honorable Theodahad. In that portion which we have claimed, we grant complete right of succession to him, with the fullest sense of his ownership happily preserved. **3.** We vouch for his loyalty and integrity, so that from this time forward he should deserve what remains of the aforementioned patrimony with all its pertinences. For what could we deny such a man who would obtain even better things through his obedience,[54] even if he were not favored by kinship? This is a man whom the exaltation of his nobility has not inflated, a man humble with modesty and equally always wise. Extend to this man what he may earn from us, while we govern for our glory what we confess to be his own.[55] **4.** Therefore, apply yourself to satisfy this effort by fair decree, and with documents appropriately drafted by your office, transfer the determined sum to his agents without any delay, so that more amicably he might give greater thanks to us for this present gift by his shared affection.

LETTER 8.24 (C. 527)

The first letter of book 8 to address an actual petition, this letter reinforces with new penalties the requirement of clergy to have legal cases heard by their bishop prior to petitioning secular courts. Curiously, the letter is addressed to the clergy of Rome, not the pope, who is indicated as the arbiter of such cases.

King Athalaric to the Clergy of the Church of Rome

1. However great are the things that we receive from mortal affairs, we owe more to the greatness of divine authority. For what of similar value may one who gains possession of *imperium* recompense to God? While it is granted that nothing could compensate adequately for such a great gift, nonetheless gratitude is shown to him when he is honored by those in his service. **2.** And so, you have pleaded in a tearful petition that it had been established by long-standing custom that, if anyone would believe a servant of the sacrosanct church of Rome must be punished with any kind of legal action, the accuser would bring his case to the bishop of the aforementioned city, lest your clergy become profaned in public litigation, rather than being occupied in heavenly offices. It is added, also, that your deacon has been accused with such bitterness in court proceedings, including the insult of religion, that a *saio* believed he must be transferred to him for his own protection.[56] **3.** Indeed, you should defend a presbyter of the Roman church when he has

---

54. This seems fairly ironic in that *obsequia* are typically used to describe official military or civil service; prior to his becoming king in 534, Theodahad is not known to have held any office or command.

55. In other words, an exchange of property for loyalty to the kingship to which Theodahad might have aspired.

56. Mommsen accepts *saius* as the original, with much variation in manuscripts; as such, this represents the first attempt of a letter to render *saio* in Latinate form.

been attacked as a criminal for slight cause. On account of the innate reverence that we owe to our author, we openly confess this has displeased us, just as long ago, those who had merited serving the sacred mysteries, being exposed to wicked injury, were irreverently subject to legal indictments.[57] But the lamentable miscarriage of justice against others confers upon us an occasion for the fullest praise, as it offers an opportunity for excelling what would commend us to heavenly assistance. **4.** And therefore, both considering the honor of the apostolic seat and wishing to agree with the desire of those petitioning in some arranged manner, we have determined by the present dictate that if anyone believes that any clergy pertaining to Rome should be punished in court for whatever probable cause, let it happen that this man must first plead before the judgment of the blessed pope, so that either he may decide between the two parties according to the character of his own sanctity, or he may assign the case to be brought to close from an eagerness for parity. And if by chance, what would be impious to suppose, an agreement eludes the one seeking satisfaction, then let the one insisting on the quarrel hasten to the secular courts, when he has proven that his petitions have been denied by the above-mentioned episcopal court. **5.** But if any litigant should exist, so dishonest and contemptuous, with a disposition disrespectful to the judgment of all, who would despise showing reverence to so great a seat, and who supposes anything could be gained from our affection prior to the sentence of any assembly, let him bear the loss of ten pounds of gold, which having immediately been delivered to the officers of the sacred largesse, should be distributed to the poor by the hand of the bishop, and moreover, lacking a resolution to the case, let him be punished by his own loss.[58] For it is right that those who flaunt both divine reverence and our commands should be struck with a double penalty. **6.** But even you, whom our courts respect, must live according to ecclesiastical constitutions. It is a great evil to commit a crime that should not have currency in secular life; your vocation is the heavenly life. Do not allow humble desires to sink to the faults of mortals. Worldly men are compelled by human law; you obey sacred habits.

LETTER 8.25 (C. 527)

This letter confirms the legal gift of a house at Castrum Lucullanum. Theoderic had awarded the estate to his *referendarius,* a decision which Tuluin executed, but the recipient seems to have requested a confirmation of the gift from Athalaric. If this property is also identifiable with Castellum Lucullanum in Campania, it was the place of confinement for Romulus Augustulus (cf. *Var.* 3.35), and later the site of a monastery founded by Eugippius in 492.

---

57. Perhaps a reference to early Christian persecutions.
58. A litigant who attempts to circumvent the bishop's court would automatically lose the case.

King Athalaric to Johannus, Vir Spectabilis *and* Referendarius

1. It is certainly right to support the gifts of another to those to whom it would be appropriate for us to confer our own gifts. For how would it be possible to dispute liberality, when you know that you deserve from us what you had received from our predecessor? And thus we assuredly acknowledge the gift of the other, but only the swiftest generosity and forward-thinking mind of the *Princeps* had prevailed over our judgment.[59] **2.** Hence it is known that our clemency's grandfather of divine memory wanted the house situated at Castrum Lucullanum to be given as a gift, encouraged by the assiduity of your services. Pursuant to this arrangement, the patrician Tuluin afterward conceding this to our generosity, he transmitted the right to the aforementioned house to your possession with due legality. **3.** Therefore, our serenity confirms by the present dictate the desire of an incomplete will and Tuluin's execution of a most generous donation, so that the oft-mentioned house of the deceased patrician Agnellus, situated at Castrum Lucullanum, should remain in your possession and that of your heirs, with all properties pertaining to it. Whatever you would prefer to do concerning it, you will have full power, in case anyone of either public or private station should afterward stir a legal contest. And if something should happen, whether by accident or perhaps by inquiry into some ambiguity, let it be known by the judgment of our authority to be rejected. Enjoy your own properties, being confirmed by God's blessing and also by our authority. Indeed, others have bequeathed these legal rights to you; we confer the peace of possession and untroubled stability for all generations. **4.** But lest, perhaps, some scoundrel jealous of our special favor should come forward, anyone who attempts to move any litigation against this ruling, at any time whatever, whether on behalf of the fisc or private interest, we command that he give either to you, or to one whom you want designated to own the above property, so many pounds of gold on the basis of punishment, and we command him to abandon his claim as nefarious and obstructed. For one who is found to have sought anything contrary to our judgment deserves to acquire this as profit for his impudence.

LETTER 8.26 (C. 526)

This letter appoints a *prior,* or chief civil magistrate, to govern affairs for the cities of Reate and Nursia. The appointment had been petitioned by citizens just before Theoderic's death and, similar to *Variae* 8.25, Athalaric's order brings those plans to fruition.

---

59. "Forward-thinking mind" is another instance of Cassiodorus's use of *modernus,* here with *modernam mentem.*

King Athalaric to All Inhabitants of Reate and Nursia

1. Conceding to your desires, our glorious lord grandfather arranged to make Quidila, son of Sibia, your chief magistrate. But because he failed to fulfill these plans on account of the intervention of the mortal condition,[60] it is necessary for us to accomplish his will, lest such a great man should be thought capable only of uselessly planning good works. **2.** And so we order by the present dictate that you ought to take Quidila auspiciously as chief magistrate, and whatever he will arrange for the good of public order must be observed, especially where our advantage is protected in everything that you ought to obey, since you were thus instructed according to the character of our lord grandfather, so that you would willingly listen to both laws and judges. **3.** For this is what adorns our *imperium*, what amplifies your reputation among foreign peoples, that you would act according to such standards that are both acceptable to us and most pleasing to divine authority. For strengthened by good character, we vanquish our enemies, since heavenly power protects those who are incapable of a contrary temperament. For you will effectively contend in legal matters when you strive to embrace justice from our court. For thus do two people unite themselves in a mutual embrace;[61] those who cultivate equity possess the fruit of victory. **4.** For what need could compel you to injustice, when both your own happy lot nourishes you and our rewards enrich you with God's blessing? For even if something must be sought by anyone, let him trust the generosity of the *Princeps* rather than the presumption of strength, since it profits you that Romans remain peaceful. While they enrich our treasuries, they multiply your donatives.

LETTER 8.27 (C. 527)

This letter orders a *saio* and a *comitiacus* to investigate claims that the *possessores* of Faventia have been subject to unspecified abuses.

King Athalaric to Dumerit, Saio, *and to Florentianus,*
Vir Devotus *and* Comitiacus

1. Just as the severity of public discipline ignores the innocent, it is thus necessary that it impose the standard of its own punishment on criminals, since the diverse deserts of various persons do not always merit one judgment. Even the sick are treated with different concoctions of herbs; for some the physician calls for nourishment as the best remedy, for others the scalpel, and in each case the prescription is determined by the nature of the suffering. **2.** And therefore, let your devotion hasten without delay to the territory of Faventia, and if it is found that any Goths

---

60. That is, Theoderic's death.
61. The people of Nursia and Reate.

or Romans have involved themselves in plundering the landowners, inflict both fines and punishment according to an examination of the deed, since those who are trusted to be obedient to the *Princeps,* neither initially nor after just admonition, must be punished severely. The better course is to want to serve new masters,[62] so that, having been commended by good behavior at the outset, they would enjoy the gift of security for the remainder of their lives.

LETTER 8.28 (C. 527)

An answer to a petition from two men, possibly free-born *coloni,* who have been subjected to the fullest extent of slavery. The letter presents an interesting perspective of legal redress available to even vulnerable citizens and is perhaps comparable to similar cases involving Gothic soldiers (cf. *Var.* 5.29–30). The letter's recipient was possibly a Gothic *comes* and one of the individuals denounced by Boethius for corruption in the *Consolation of Philosophy.*

King Athalaric to Cunigastus, Vir Illustris

1. Our serenity has been stirred by the lamentable complaint of Constantius and Venerius, by which they plead a small estate, which is called Fabricula, has been removed from their legal ownership, with its livestock, by Tanca. They add that, lest they should dare to assert their own legal case for reclaiming the property, they have had the status of lowest servitude imposed upon them as free men. **2.** And therefore, pursuant to the present decree, let your magnitude order the aforementioned man to attend your court, where, with the whole truth of the case between the parties examined, you will deliver justice that is consistent and agreeable to your character. Because, just as it is grievous to separate masters from their own legal right, thus it is inimical to our reign to bend free necks with the yoke of slavery. **3.** If they seek the rights of transfer, let the seized property be returned for the moment, but only such that the legitimate party may not withdraw from resolving the case. Let violent seizure cease, so that the case may be surmised by the judgment of a magistrate and either Tanca may possess his refuted slaves with the pertinent properties or he may abandon them as proven free, unharmed and untouched. For it suffices that we relax the penalty to one who presumes to cause injury.

LETTER 8.29 (C. 527)

An interesting letter in which the citizens of Parma have been mandated to restore function to the city sewers. The degree of oversight for what must have been a local

---

62. Presumably *novi domini* refers to Athalaric's court.

issue is remarkable, although the letter attaches the fame of Parma's hydrology to Theoderic, who previously restored the flow of water to the city. The effort is further detailed in *Variae* 8.30.

King Athalaric to the Honorati, Possessores, *and* Curiales *of Parma*

1. It would be worthwhile that you should accomplish with a willing spirit what you know has been commanded for the benefit of your city. For what is proper to be undertaken at your own expense is known to bring great advantage to you. For indeed, our lord grandfather, with God's blessing, diverted wholesome waters to your city as it was in constant thirst. **2.** For which reason the mouths of the sewers should be widened now by your effort, lest, with the obstruction of filth ignored, reversed waters are thrust into your buildings and what ought to be cleansed is forced to enter those same buildings. For this task, although civic ardor ought to urge you, we have directed the *spectabilis* Genesius to supervise, so that you may inspire us to greater things, if you pleasingly accomplish what we have ordered.

LETTER 8.30 (C. 527)

Civic waters form an important theme in the *Variae* and this letter directs someone of senatorial rank, possibly a local notable, to restore the flow of water at Parma by clearing the sewers of debris. Compare *Variae* 8.29 for notice to this effect given to the leading citizens of the city.

King Athalaric to Genesius, Vir Spectabilis

1. Indeed, out of love for your city did our lord grandfather construct an aqueduct of ancient design from royal largesse. But it avails nothing to disperse an abundance of waters to cities, unless the proper flow of the sewers may now be provided for. The very wholesomeness of this project corresponds to the nature of human life, where what one takes into the mouth, once it is consumed, then flows out from another part of the body. **2.** And therefore, let your sublimity cause the citizens of Parma to set about this task with urgency, to the extent that they join together and carefully dislodge the ancient water channels, both subterranean and along the gutters of streets, so that when the desired water flows into the city as it should, you will be glad for it not to be delayed by any obstruction of filth, since water does not have grace except the kind that flows continually and always departs from sight. For it cheers us that what is ugly in lakes drains in sweet streams; for the swamp is neither pleasing to see, nor fitting for livestock. The element itself is certainly most excellent, but only when it is preserved in its natural purity. Without it, fields become rough and cities weary in dry airs, so that rightly did ancient wisdom dictate that those who must be separated from civic concourse should be punished with the prohibition of water. Therefore, the consensus of all ought to provoke eagerness for so useful a thing, since the citizen who does not maintain the grace of his own city does not have a soul.

LETTER 8.31 (C. 527)

This letter addresses what seems to have been an endemic problem in Late Antiquity: the retention of leading municipal citizens for civic duties. Here, the governor of Bruttium is obliged to encourage local *possessores* and *curiales* to return to urban residences, which they have apparently forsaken for rural estates. The topic allowed Cassiodorus the opportunity to wax indulgently about urban culture and the natural history of his native region.

King Athalaric to Severus, Vir Spectabilis

1. Since we believe that you learned everything that pertains to managing the affairs of the republic while commendably engaged with the counsels of the *Praefectus,*[63] you especially understand, polished as you are by literary arts, that a city proven to have a host of peoples has a splendid manner. For thus the adornment of freedom shines in them and the necessary support serves our ordinances. It is given for wild creatures to seek woods and fields, but for humanity to cherish above all their paternal hearths. **2.** Those birds that are gentle with harmless intention fly in flocks. The melodious thrush loves the congregation of its own kind; the incessantly noisy starlings similarly attend in armies; murmuring pigeons delight in their own cohorts. Whatever enjoys an honest life does not refuse the pleasantness of association. **3.** By contrast, fierce raptors, hunting eagles and other keen-sighted birds, above all covet flying alone, since, being violent predators, they have no need of peaceful assemblies. For those who do not desire to come upon their spoils accompanied by another roam in order to act alone. Thus, the disposition of humankind that is known to avoid human sight is generally detestable, nor is it possible to expect anything genuinely good from one whose life lacks a witness. **4.** Let the landowners and *curiales* of Bruttium return to their cities: those who endlessly cultivate the fields are *coloni*. Those to whom we have granted offices and to whom we have entrusted public affairs by pleasing appraisal should endure separating themselves from rusticity, and certainly in that region where luxuries arrive abundantly without labor. **5.** There Ceres luxuriates in great fecundity and Pallas too rejoices with no less liberality.[64] The plains smile with fertile pasturage, elevated slopes with viticulture. The region abounds in various herds of animals, but it especially glories in droves of horses, and understandably, when the woodlands are so springlike in the season of heat that animals are not vexed by the stings of

63. The *Praefectus Praetorio* is probably implied.
64. The personifications of grain and olive production.

flies and they are fully fed on the ever-green grasses. You would see among the mountain summits the purest running streams and, as though flowing out of the very heights, they rush down from the highest places of the Alps.[65] It may be added that, on both sides, the region possesses wealthy and frequent maritime commerce, so that it overflows with wealth of its own and is furnished by foreign provisions along its neighboring shores. There the rustics live on the banquets of townsfolk; middling folk, moreover, enjoy the abundance of the powerful, so that the least fortune there is shown not to be lacking in plenty. **6.** Therefore, do citizens confess that they prefer this province only on their own estates, not wanting to dwell in the cities? What does it profit for men so greatly fattened on the literary arts to lie hidden? Boys seek the association of liberal education, and as soon as they would be fit for the court, they immediately undertake the ignorance of a rustic lifestyle. They advance in order to unlearn; they become learned in order to forget; and while they delight in the countryside, they know not how to respect themselves. Let the learned man seek where he may live with glorious reputation; let the sage not cast off concourse with men where he knows he will be praised. Likewise, a good reputation is failed by the virtues, if their merits should be unknown among men. **7.** For what kind of desire is it to abandon interaction with citizens, when they may observe that even some birds want to mingle with human society? For the swallows faithfully suspend nests in the dwellings of humankind, and the intrepid bird feeds its chicks amid the commotion of residents. It is, therefore, exceedingly disgraceful to educate the sons of noblemen in the wilderness, when one may see the birds entrust their offspring to human society. Let the cities, therefore, return to their former dignity; let none prefer the allurements of the countryside to urban walls of the ancients. **8.** How is it possible to flee in time of peace from that place for which it is proper to wage war, lest it should be destroyed? For whom would the assembly of nobility seem the least pleasing? Who would not be eager for exchanging conversation with peers, visiting the forum, observing noble arts, representing one's own causes with the laws, being occupied occasionally with calculations of Palamedes,[66] going to the baths with companions, arranging dinners with shared preparation? One who wishes to spend his entire life with slaves will certainly lack all these pleasures. **9.** But, lest a mind tainted to the contrary should relapse further into the same habits, let landowners as well as *curiales* offer promises with collateral, with a penalty determined by the assessment of other men, to remain for the greater part of the year in cities that they have chosen for residence. Let it be thus, that they would neither lack the distinction of citizenship, nor should they be denied the pleasures of the countryside.

---

65. The Italian Apennines were considered a branch of the Alps.
66. A dice game (gambling).

LETTER 8.32 (C. 527)

This letter requires the provincial governor to examine the claim that bandits have plundered the stock of a man traveling en route to Athalaric's court. The victim's name, Nymphadius, seems ironically attuned to the main subject of the letter, which is a celebration of the miraculous spring where he was robbed. The letter's perspective of the cognitive agency of nature deserves attention.

King Athalaric to Severus, Vir Spectabilis

1. When the *spectabilis* Nymphadius had hastened to pursue his interests at our sacred *comitatus*, having completed some distance of the journey, he decided to rest at the fountain of Arethusa, situated in the region of Scyllaceum,[67] because here the area abounds in fertile pasturage and is lovely for its inundation of waters. For it is said that there is a fertile field at the base of a hill overlooking the sandy seashore, where a wide pool, issuing from a bed girt with reeds, wreaths the edge of its own shore with surrounding reeds in the likeness of a crown. It is entirely pleasant and remarkable for its reedy shade and for the character of these waters. **2.** For when a man approaches there, remaining silent and taking care to create no sound, he finds the waters of the refreshing font so untroubled that they seem not to flow so much as to lie still, like standing water. But should he produce the grating of a cough or perhaps sound out in a loud voice, at the very same moment, by what agency I know not, the waters immediately churn with excitement. You would see the surface of the pool boil up, grievously disturbed, so that you would suppose placid waters had assumed the heat of burning oil. Remaining still with an undisturbed man, they answer the noise and clamor of one speaking, so that you would be astounded at water so suddenly disturbed which no touch had excited. **3.** A remarkable force, an unheard of property that waters are stirred by the voice of men and, as though called, they would respond thus to the words projected in human voice, murmuring I know not what. You would believe some animal rests there prostrate in slumber, which, having become roused, responds to you with a deep growl. It is even read that some springs bubble over with various wonders, so that some turn drinking animals to different colors, others make flocks white and still others change submerged wood to the hardness of stone. But no rationale comprehends these causes, since it is known that what thus pertains to natural phenomena lies beyond the human intellect. **4.** But let us quickly return to the complaint of the petitioner: when the above-mentioned Nymphadius had taken respite here, he asserts his packhorses were driven off by the cunning of the rustics. It is not becoming to the discipline of our reign that the charm of this place should be rendered disreputable on account of such loss. We want your diligence to search

---

67. Modern Squillace, Cassiodorus's hometown.

with careful examination for what would seem to agree with both the authority of our court and the justice of the laws, so that you may be seen to avenge what a criminal has done. **5.** Let thieves be approached with complete silence, let furtive men be bound in their own snares, so that, as soon as the executioner has bellowed, their hearts will become distraught, they will project their voices in alarm, and throw themselves into disorder with murmuring.[68] Thus will signs determine them to surrender their own waters to punishment.[69] Therefore, let what is exacted from them be fitting, so that these places may be passable. Invite the interest of travelers with strict discipline, lest such a miracle as is known to always gladden the pilgrim should be avoided on account of the excesses of brigands.

LETTER 8.33 (C. 527)

This letter responds to disturbances at a local religious festival in which merchants have been victimized by the agrarian workforce of the area. In order to establish order, the provincial governor is directed to collect sureties from the property owners who manage peasants on their estates. The affair allows Cassiodorus to digress in lavish terms on the abundance of the festival and on the local sacred springs.

King Athalaric to Severus, Vir Spectabilis

1. Just as the wise want to learn unknown things, thus it is foolish to conceal what has been discovered, especially at a time when harmful circumstances are able to find the swiftest correction. Indeed we have learned from repeated attestation that at the assembly in Lucania which received from ancient superstition the name of Leucothea,[70] because there the waters are exceedingly brilliant and clear, the property of merchants has often been vandalized by the hostile plundering and lawless impropriety of rustics, so that those who come for celebrating the most sacred festival of Saint Cyprian and to adorn the countenance of civil harmony with their own merchandise, should depart poor and shamefully destitute. **2.** We believe that this must be corrected with a simple and easy remedy, so that, at a previously designated time, your distinction ought to obtain from the landowners and from the managers of various estates advance sureties for the peace of those attending the assembly, lest punishment utterly consume those whom it finds accused of savage deeds. But if any of the rustics, or a man from any place whatever, attempts a vio-

---

68. Cassiodorus here recycles much of the vocabulary used to describe how the waters respond to sudden disturbance.

69. *Aquas suas,* or "blood"; there is also the sense here that Severus is being told that pursuing the available signs will reveal the thieves, so there would be no excuse for them to remain unpunished.

70. Leucothea was originally a Greek deity associated with initiations, transplanted to southern Italy probably much earlier in the period of Greek colonization.

lent altercation, having been arrested at the very outset, let him be subjected to punishment by cudgeling immediately. Let one who first attempted to excite concealed crime correct his wicked designs with a public spectacle. **3.** Indeed that very gathering is both celebrated by an exceedingly large throng and greatly profitable to the surrounding provinces. For abundant Campania, wealthy Bruttium, cattle-rich Calabria, prosperous Apulia and even its own province of Lucania sends there whatever it has that is excellent, so that you would rightly expect the plenty native to many regions to be gathered there. For there you may see the widest fields bedazzle with booths of the loveliest kind and temporary lodgings woven immediately with charming wickerwork, and the happy commotion of boisterous peoples. **4.** Where it is preferred that you may not view works of urban architecture, nonetheless you may witness the accoutrement of the most celebrated city. Boys and girls are offered for inspection by sex and various ages, those whom liberty, not captivity, brings to be sold. Parents rightly sell them, since they prosper from the very same servitude. Indeed, there is no doubt that slaves who have been transferred from agrarian labor to household service may be improved. What should I say of clothing arrayed by countless variety? What of fattened animals that gleam in their diverse kinds? There everything is displayed at such a price that even the most circumspect buyer would be enticed. Thus, if everything is arranged with proper discipline, nobody departs from that market unsatisfied. **5.** For indeed, the very site extends with the charm of open meadows, a kind of suburb of that most ancient city of Consilinum, which has adopted the name of Marcellianum from the founder of sacred springs. A swell of sweet and clear waters bursts forth here, where the clear liquidity emanates in an apsidal hollow fashioned in the manner of a natural cave, so that you could mistake for an empty pool what you know overflows. Here, clarity persists all the way to the bottom, so that at a glance you would think it appears like air, not water. The most tranquil water emulates clear daylight, for whatever is born into the depths is visible to the eyes with unperturbed clarity. **6.** There plays a school of the happiest fish, which fearlessly approach the hands of those offering food, as though aware they would not be seized. For whoever presumes to dare such a thing is known to immediately attract divine punishment. It would be tedious to describe the wonders of such a spring. Let us come to that most unique portent and sacred miracle. **7.** For when the bishop commences to pour forth the prayer of baptism on holy night,[71] and springs of words flow from that holy mouth, a wave immediately leaps on high, the pool directs the waters, not through their accustomed channels, but by massing them to a height. The unthinking element surges by its own will, and in a kind of solemn devotion prepares itself for the miraculous, so that the sanctity of divine power may be revealed. For while the spring itself extends over five steps and would submerge only these while

---

71. Probably the Saturday evening before Easter Sunday.

placid, it is known to rise above the other two, which it is never known to cover except at that time. It is a great and awe-inspiring miracle that lapping shores would thus stand or rise at human speech, so that you would not doubt them to be an attentive audience. **8.** Let this heavenly spring become venerated in the speech of all; let even Lucania have its own Jordan. Those waters provided a model for baptism; these preserve sacred mysteries in annual devotion. Therefore, reverence for the place and the advantage of the fair ought to recommend holy peace to the people, since the most scandalous who dare to despise the celebration of such days must be held in the judgment of all.[72] Let what we have pronounced be read and posted for the people, so that they will not seek the liberty of complete abandon when they believe it to be unpunished.

---

72. Another affirmation that the leading citizens will be held accountable for indiscretions.

Book 9

In 523, the Vandal king Thrasamund died and was succeeded by Hilderic. Thrasamund's wife and the sister of Theoderic, Amalafrida, led a revolt against Hilderic's rise to power. Her party was defeated and she subsequently died in prison, hence breaking the alliance between Vandals and Ostrogoths. Her death may have coincided with Athalaric's accession in Italy (526), although this letter may also simply serve to apprise Hilderic's court of the new Ostrogothic king's position on the earlier death of his great aunt.

King Athalaric to Hilderic, King of the Vandals

1. We are constrained by a grievously bitter lot, that we, who are known to value tokens of devotion would now attribute the bitterest circumstance to those whom we had formerly called sweet kin. For who does not know that Amalafrida of divine memory, that rare grace of our family, came to a violent fall from splendor by you, and that one who you formerly held as a matron, you could not even allow to live a private life? If this woman seemed to be at odds with the dignified comportment of a kinswoman, a respectable man ought to have returned to us the woman whom he had sought with great entreaties.[1] **2.** It is a kind of parricide that after the king's death you would involve his wife, a kinswoman to you, in unmentionable intrigues. How could a woman deprived of her own husband have merited such a great evil? If the succession of another had been required, how could a

---

1. Hilderic had not sought Amalafrida, but rather the Vandal court had, hence the use of *expetistis* in second person plural.

woman possibly be involved in this course of action? Rather, instead, she ought to be considered as the mother who transferred the kingdom to you. For this, too, would have been advantageous to your nobility, if you would have retained within the line of the Hasdings the purple dignity of Amal blood.[2] Our Goths more correctly understand this to be an insult against them. For one who precipitates the murder of a foreign matron is seen to have wholly despised the honor of her family, when no man would suppose as unavoidable what he knows must be avoided. **3.** And therefore, admonished by moral reason, for now, we await redress from your words through our legates, *ille* and *ille*, anticipating what kind of excuse may be brought to bear for so great a calamity. For no matter what kind of scandal had risen against a woman of such standing, it ought to be intimated to us, so that how she had involved herself in the worst kind of affairs should pass to our judgment. It may be that her death was fashioned from natural causes. We do not say it was impossible, we do not claim that she was young; relate it to *ille* and *ille*, through whom the fact of the matter ought to come to light. Let final judgment over the entire affair be theirs, without war, without slaughter, whether it would satisfy us or render you hated. **4.** If you believe this should be disregarded, or if you do not prepare a reasonable response, being injured, we, who were not held by a bond of alliance, are absolved of the condition of temporary peace. However artfully it was committed, the crime will be punished by supernal majesty, which calls upon the impious slaughter of fraternal blood to reveal itself.[3]

LETTER 9.2 (C. 527)

This is a general edict issued to protect the welfare of the *curiales*. The letter is aimed primarily at persons who have imposed debts upon the properties of the *curiales,* which was held in reserve for the support of municipal taxes. The plight of the *curiales* here may be related to the concern about "urban flight" in *Variae* 8.31, although it is clear from the edict that the *curiales* have also been guilty of oppressing lesser citizens.

Edict of King Athalaric

1. One who longs to stand at the peak of public affairs and maintain position in the republic ought to be attentive to all concerns, since there is no health in a body unless each member is able to enjoy it. Injury to one location impairs the entire system, and so greatly is its strength interdependent that you would believe a single wound to afflict the entire body when it begins to feel great pain. Likewise, the republic does not consist in the care of one city, but rather the provident protection

---

2. The Hasdings were the line of Vandal royalty, as the Amals were of the Ostrogothic royalty.
3. Perhaps a reference to the death of Thrasamund?

of the entire *regnum:* therefore, if anything becomes diminished in the republic, the loss is felt at its source. Hence, it is important to have less of anything by which some portion diminishes. And therefore, being always watchful over diverse cities, we have taken measures lest evils long endured should be able to burden the administration. For a tree that you would see flourishing, that you would behold enjoying the fullest growth, is animated by an unseen source of fertility, drawing to the surface what it holds at the roots. The appearance of people is also adorned with great cheerfulness when they feel the sickness of no grievance in healthy organs. Thus the *regnum* is rightly called a sound whole if nothing has been weakened. This would be the case, if unrestrained license was everywhere expelled, lest the audacity of malicious intention was permitted to sin with reprehensible freedom. The *curiales,* to whom the name was given with provident intention,[4] are said to be stricken with a most severe affliction, so that whatever had been chosen as a reason for distinction for them seems to have become instead an injury. Oh, scandalous crime, oh, insuperable evil! That one who ought to profit by serving the republic should be seen to lose his own liberty along with property! **2.** For this reason, we determined in a proclaimed edict that anyone who has been involved in loss or injury to a *curialis,* or if he has presumed to impose a burden upon his property, excepting those who were ordered by us or by an authority of the palace, whose business it is, that very same person who enacted such a deed with no mind to future affairs will bear the loss of ten pounds of gold, or, if his resources should not satisfy the punishment, he is to be beaten with clubs, and thus render the debt of that punishment which he is unable to pay in money. Nevertheless, when those whom we do not permit to endure the unreasonable demands of others begin owing more of what has been reserved for public weal, let their debts be satisfied with customary attention. **3.** Because the estates of *curiales* are particularly vulnerable to the schemes of low characters, no man may come to possess them through illegal purchase, since a man may not be called bound by contract unless it happens according to the law. Concerning these improprieties, let the *curiales* be protected with the assistance of *saiones* and officials of magistrates. Our authority also defends them from these same moderators, since it is an even more punishable grievance if the man for whom assistance has been delegated is known to sustain damage from that assistance. **4.** Let the hard-pressed straighten their necks; let those burdened with the baggage of evil practices raise their spirits; give attention to recover what you know you lost on account of wickedness. Your city is the republic of each and every citizen. Administer the justice of the cities with an agreeable disposition. Let your class thrive with equity. Do not attempt to burden lesser men, lest those more powerful should rightly be able to oppress you. Such is

---

4. An etymological reference to *cura,* a theme explored earlier in the letter with *cura res publica,* the republic as the care of cities.

the punishment of sinning, that anyone is able to receive what he shamelessly practices against others. Live justly, live moderately, since hardly anyone dares to practice license upon those in whom it is not possible to find fault. **5.** Cranes know how to practice moral concord, among whom none seeks to be foremost, since they do not have an ambition for inequity. They take watch in turn, they protect each other with shared caution, they even eat in turn. Thus distinction is taken away from none, while everything is preserved in common. Even their flight is arranged with equal alternation; the last becomes the leader, and the one that holds first place does not refuse to be last. Thus they are obedient to a kind of shared allegiance without kings; they obey without an overlord and they serve without terror. By serving voluntarily they are free and they protect themselves by being chosen in turn. Writers of natural history, considering the habits of these birds, have noted a certain kind of politic to exist among them, which they recognize to live according to civic affection.[5] **6.** If you would imitate these birds, you should remove all blame from your private affairs. For you, who receive your wishes when honest, hold power over your citizens through laws. For antiquity did not grant the curia to you by accident, not in vain is it named a lesser Senate, calling you the sinew and even the vital organs of the city. What could you lack in power or prestige with such an appellation? For those who are compared to the Senate are excluded from no kind of distinction.

LETTER 9.3 (C. 527)

A fascinating letter ordering the *Comes Patrimonii* to commence mining operations on royal property in Bruttium. The letter offers a discursive treatise on the properties of gold, the lives of miners, and the moral appropriateness of acquiring wealth.

King Athalaric to Bergantinus, Vir Illustris *and* Comes Patrimonii

1. If every specialized labor produces diverse rewards in measure equal to what gold and silver would procure through customary exchange, why should we not diligently search for that very thing by which we are known to exchange other goods? Let wealthy Italy also bear golden fruit for us. A profit is gained everywhere that yellow metal is found. For in what way could the earth become exhausted in its diverse fecundity, if so great a reward is able to be found in it? Nature customarily grants its yield to us with the appropriate amount of industry; vines bear fruit promiscuously; metal is rarely produced, so that it is more eagerly sought out. **2.** Therefore, we order your magnitude to send a surveyor to the Rusticiana estate situated on our property in the province of Bruttium, and if, as is indicated by the

---

5. The "civic" habits of cranes had been noted by Pliny the Elder and, later, Ambrose of Milan.

skill of Theodorus in such matters,[6] the earth is rich in the above-mentioned metals, let the interior of the mountains be duly excavated by instructed crews. Let the earth be delved with the benefit of skill in tunneling and let the wealth of nature be examined as though in its own treasury. For in chambers tunneled with a native presumption, miners imitating molelike animals dig routes which had formerly been permitted to none. Thus, in due course nothing is left concealed, unless they should occasionally sustain an accident. **3.** Men enter stony depths, they live without a sky, being exiled from the sun, and, while they seek profits under the earth, they even forsake the joys of light. Sometimes their own passage is destroyed and those who create paths for their own feet with toiling hands fail to find their return. But for those whose skill is more cautious, life is more fortunate; they enter impoverished and leave wealthy. They seize riches without theft, they penetrate longed-for treasuries without deceit, and they alone among men are seen to attain a profit without any commerce. For as soon as they are restored to heavenly light, they separate the heavier from the lighter portions of mother earth with revealing water and they bake what is uncovered from the clay in a great furnace, until dissolved into a manageable liquid and the resulting rivulets have been cleansed by great tongues of fire, which renders the very beauty which the bowels of the earth had concealed, lest they should be desired. **4.** Nature is conquered when industry softens her. Gold is finer when separated, more useful when baked, since it increases in value the more it has been refined to purity. Its source is indeed noble, but it takes vigor of color from flames, so that you would instead believe it was born from that element, the likeness of which is seen to adorn it. But while flame bestows a splendid ruddiness on gold, it confers the whitest light on silver, so that one substance miraculously accomplishes what is able to be applied to different materials.[7] Thence, let our ordinance provide whatever you know pertains to practicing the skill of this craft, so that in Bruttium, a province which abounds with plentiful products, even the earth is able to pay as taxes what is found within it. For it is fitting that among such great blessings, those which are considered to be the most excellent should not be lacking. For why should that which might be an honest profit be allowed to lie without use? **5.** If indeed it is wrong to seek gold through war, through treachery on the sea, through scandal of falsehood, let it be found justly in nature itself. Gains by which no person grieves are honest, and what is taken from nobody's property is properly acquired. It is often read that griffons dig for gold and rejoice at the sight of this metal, for whom, since it is not an ambition for wealth, they are not said to burn with the sin of cupidity, certainly because each act is related to its nature and what is not done with wanton intention

---

6. Theordorus, otherwise unattested, an *agrimensor* or land surveyor.

7. That is, fire may be applied to both gold and silver for different results.

must not be censured. Therefore, continue the search with diligent work and do not fear infamy; what is called an art is free from criminality.

LETTER 9.4 (C. 526)

A letter fascinating for its disclosure of the problems faced by families of decurial status (for which, cf. *Var.* 8.31 and 9.2), the *Praefectus Praetorio* is here ordered to remove a family from the roster of *curiales,* citing personal financial burden. This family would instead join the ranks of *possessores* as tax payers, rather than collectors. Also curious is the displacement of this letter. *Variae* 8.20 had appointed a new *Praefectus Praetorio* to replace a disgraced holder of the office, presumably the same Abundantius of the present letter.

King Athalaric to Abundantius, Praefectus Praetorio

1. It is a happy request when laws are surmounted by piety, and blessed is the condition of the subjects, if they recognize one among themselves to be more wretched than the others, whom they choose to be favored. For the most sacred laws have not debarred *curiales* from anything, except that only *Principes* may free them; that is, that they should find a gift of forbearance where the lord dissents with his own resolution in amiable strife, when it is a kind of justice of its own that the one who is called dutiful may be held the least by the strictness of the law. For such a ruler is indeed reasonable to separate from the service of their rank those who are proven unequal to their labors. For the *curialis,* if maintained by no strength of substance, is fit only for deception; and what will it avail to continue, if he is known to be lacking in resources? It is quite similar to being an absentee, by whom delegated affairs could not be accomplished. Thence, since the curia enjoys a great number, it should not seem stricken from losses to separate a few from so many. 2. Therefore, let your *illustris* magnificence cause Agenantia, the wife of the learned Campanianus living in the province of Lucania,[8] and their sons, to be immediately erased from the roll of their curia, so that posterity to come may not learn what is forbidden to interpose, since treachery is not perpetrated where a public record is not maintained.[9] Henceforth, let them instead be counted among the populace of landowners, enduring no less the exactions that they themselves had inflicted upon others. 3. Now they will become troubled at the accustomed taxation; now they will dread the appearance of the collector. They will not know rights that come from holding authority. Wearied with their desired ignorance, let it

8. Agenantia may have been a widow with underaged sons, which would account for her request to be removed from the decurial roster.

9. That is, record of decurial obligation should be removed so thoroughly that the family would not be held accountable at a later date.

happen that they dread the exactions for which they had formerly been feared. Still they must be reckoned to have lived out that portion of their lives with good conduct when, once hated, they would bear to live among those who do not recognize them to have earned hatred. Likewise, they would not be vulnerable to abide under those whom they incited with acts of wickedness.[10] Therefore, let them enjoy a favor from the *Princeps;* let those who were ranked by the quality of their own deeds live forgotten in peaceful tranquility.

LETTER 9.5 (C. 527–28)

This letter seeks to address a situation whereby wealthier citizens have bought and stored the bulk of grain in a time of famine, only to release their stores at prices extortionate for poorer *possessores.* The province and responsible citizens are not indicated, but addressing the letter to local bishops and *honorati* suggests that, as the wealthier landowners, they may have been partly responsible.

King Athalaric to Bishops and Honorati

1. We have learned from the complaints of landowners from your region that, beyond the ordinary hardship of the time, certain of your citizens practice an execrable cruelty, when, observing the serious want among the poorer people, they have bought the kind of grain for bread at the beginning of the season and stored it away on their own property, so that they may parsimoniously introduce detestable penury upon restoring the grain, when men situated in danger of famine and seeking grain would offer a price by which they know they have been despoiled. Indeed, there is no negotiation over price in the hardship of poverty, when anyone would suffer what is induced, lest they become beaten down by misfortune. **2.** Therefore, we have sent the present bearers of letters condemning these acts, so that they will be able to find stores of grain, whether in pits or in other places. Let each owner retain as much for his own family as he knows will be needed, sell the rest to the present examiners who have been sent to each property with these notices, and by a fair price, which he will determine appropriate for each province, so that the one who buys should bear nothing excessive and the man who sells should enjoy some compensation. **3.** Therefore, fulfill what has been ordered with a willing spirit, since you ought to consider what would be mutual in your interests, lest, whenever you should complain of excessive want, you would prefer something shameful for yourself rather than endure what you may lack. Therefore, lest anyone lament a sale imposed upon them, let it be known that liberty is not to be found in crime, but there is more profit in good nature than in the haste to succeed. And so let one who

---

10. They had reason to fear reprisal neither from the *possessores* whom they were now joining as tax payers nor from other *curiales* to whom they would now make tax payments.

buys also sell in good conscience. If he should agree, he works to his own advantage; if he disagrees, he makes it a cause for our fame, when it is a good deed for those obeying that justice be imposed upon the unwilling.

LETTER 9.6 (C. 527–28)

This letter grants a *primiscrinius* leave from official duties to recuperate his health at the famous baths of Baiae. The detail given to the natural properties of the region and its baths places the letter on par with others interested in natural wonders (*Var.* 8.32). As a discharge from duty for reasons of health, the letter may also be compared with *Variae* 5.36 and 10.29.

King Athalaric to the Primiscrinius

1. Although you keep vigil with daily labors, you claim you have been grievously wounded by an infirmity of the body, so that you are unable to cope with the traditional demands of service, for which it is fitting that you fasten upon your vow, fearing not that by your absence from these very duties a sweet reward should be withdrawn from you; moreover, you demand that, because you are constrained by the hardship of neglected health, you should be released to the restorative baths of Baiae. **2.** It is clearly merited that we offer the highest among rewards, so that, just as we respond to the desires of the healthy, thus we should also bestow health upon supplicants. Therefore, we both free you from the constraints of fearful labors and we assist you with the gift of the aforementioned baths, so that, first restored with a freedom of the mind, you may more easily recuperate the health of your limbs. Indeed, to grant happiness is a natural cure for an ill man; for to cause the unhealthy to rejoice is healthy. **3.** Therefore, retreat to pleasant places; take yourself, just as I have said, to brighter sun, where the nature of the land is more favorable, tempered by the wholesomeness of the air. There, in deep reflection upon carefully pondered miracles, the human mind converses with the secrets of the world, for what is known to occur there cannot fail admiration: first, the tide of the sea is completely fitted with marine delights, the prudence of nature has interspersed so many ports among recesses of the shore, endowed so many fair islands to the embrace of the sea. There is the pool set in the Avernian Sea, where oysters have been supplied for the pleasure and life of men, and human industry has caused blessings otherwise accidental to appear abundantly everywhere. **4.** The frontier of the sea is becomingly invaded by so many piers! The land projects so many openings into the interior of the sea! Schools of fish play and are easily at hand. Elsewhere, abundant delicacies are enclosed within carefully walled pools; aquatic herds are held captive. Everywhere here, thriving creatures are held under restrained liberty. Additionally, it is so pleasant to undertake fishing that the appearance satisfies the appetite of the one observing before the banquet. For it is a great joy to have seized your desire, but in every way the delight to the eye is even more pleasing than the advantage of the capture. **5.** But let us not wander too far among the marine treasures known to dwell there. Baiae is renowned for its leisure. And so, fattened upon such treasures from delightful exertion, you would hasten to the most beautiful baths, which are both miraculous and precious for the quality of their health. For although the concocted remedies of men are known, they are certainly produced from natural sources. Gathered wood does not heat the furnaces there; perpetual heat operates without continuous flames. Plumes of smoke are unknown here; the airs that assist the steam are the most pure, a sweetly exhaled sweat. What is found more quickly by human industry is provided more wholesomely by nature in connected pools. You would see the waters there to steam with continuous roiling, which easily satisfies the needs of the bather, to the extent that you would believe it regulated by the person's desire. **6.** Let a vaunted reputation be granted to coral-bearing seas, the far-flung fame of the Indian Ocean may rise upon the splendor of pearls. What value is it to me, if the spirit may not enjoy what you desire? Nothing is able to be superior to the shore of Baiae, where it is possible to be fed with finest delicacies and to be satisfied with the gift of priceless health. Therefore, enjoy nothing less than the blessings you have sought. May you arrive at your due recompense through our benefaction; pursue the business of your health in the remedies of Baiae.

LETTER 9.7 (C. 527–28)

This letter appoints a senator as *Praefectus Urbis*, following the eminent public career of his father. The candidate would later be a tragic witness to events in the Gothic War, while his brother became Pope Vigilius (537–55) in the same period.

King Athalaric to Reparatus, Praefectus Urbis

1. The most conspicuous offices are properly conferred upon those who follow after the distinguished services of family, and although it silences the native talent of none to be inactive in the estimation of his own family, it is nonetheless an honorable ambition to want to surpass in public acclaim those of the generation we follow. Furthermore, men cultured by instruction in the ancients should be chosen for increase in the glory of their reputation. For anyone may presume to attain great rewards more abundantly to the extent that he learns to apply himself to the better arts. **2.** And thus, some time ago, the Roman republic took notice of the diligence of your father of illustrious memory. While presiding as *comes* of the largesse, he also worked in the offices of the *Praefectus Praetorio*, and he then performed that office to completion, restoring the curia, remitted taxes to the poor and, although he was unpolished in liberal studies, he did not fail to please by his hard work.[11] Because he was naturally able to be commended for his own good character, he did not seem adorned with accidental qualities. **3.** But what is this in comparison to the fame of your own literary studies? If, indeed, learning separates from the untutored those whom it conjoins in friendly association to the wise, it also confers nobility from obscurity, for which it is quite easy to prepare the well-born. Your father, who made himself continually praised in the conversation of friends for his good character and his honesty, also increases with your own outstanding merits, because such a man for whom it always happened to be spoken of for the integrity of his judgment, for universally good habits, for a singularly good conscience, appointed you in gratitude for your family.[12] Therefore, one who determined to never attach shame to his own reputation must be thought to have shared this quality with his own blood. **4.** And therefore, it is fitting that you come to public honor in youth; after the record of such a man, it would be useless to call you unproven. For if we properly offer favorable ears to suggestions from others, why would we not follow the precedents of those from your own family even more, where those who frequently surpass the deeds of others always eagerly prepare the way for their own? And therefore, let it be happily pronounced that we have conferred upon you the ornaments of the *Praefectus Urbis* for this indiction, so that, just as you would have first rank in the senatorial order, thus may you also be conspicuous in the praise of worthy men. **5.** Indeed, there is hardly anything accomplished in that city that is not offered to the eyes of the world. To whom would a magistrate then ally himself if it offended that Senate of such renown? What will come of your maturity, or of your prudence, you will know through the estimation of that order, whose youngest members are called "fathers" as soon as they advance to that rank. Adolescence commences there because of mature advice; young men attract the old with modesty. There, weight of character permits in youth what elsewhere is hardly produced at a wizened age. **6.** Therefore, conduct yourself as such a man with respect to restrained habits, so that, when you call so many leading men to the curia, the pronouncement of your will may appear worthy before them. Indeed, it is exceedingly difficult to say anything noteworthy among them, because none would want to displease such wise men. And therefore, anyone who might derive a good reputation from that crowd of learned men must not be accounted a man of only one merit. For if it is pleasing to be spoken of even rarely, what of the joy attained by one praised by the esteem of so many nobles? Cherish justice; apply yourself fittingly to the oppressed; render to your posterity the praise that you have received from your forebears.

11. His father Johannus held in succession the offices of *Comes Sacrarum Largitionum,* possibly *consiliarius* to the *Praefectus Praetorio* and then *Praefectus Praetorio.*

12. Although obscure, it seems Reparatus had been appointed to an earlier office or perhaps senatorial rank, probably by Theoderic, on account of his father's service.

LETTER 9.8 (C. 526–27)

This letter reappoints a Gothic *comes* to the provincial command of Dalmatia, with the addition of neighboring Savia. The same *comes* had been active in the region under Theoderic (cf. *Var.* 1. 40, 3.26, 4.9) and should be regarded as a reliable supporter of the Amal regime.

King Athalaric to Osuin, Comes

1. It is our intention to adorn honorable labors with the palm of remuneration, so that, each in turn, the promoted may rejoice, and the idle might be stung and blame themselves that they had not merited the rewards of our acknowledgment in the most benevolent of reigns. And so, with God's blessing, we believe your *illustris* magnitude must be sent again to the provinces of Dalmatia and Savia, so that you would arrange by equitable ordinations whatever you know to be in our advantage and you would cause the people to be loyal and grateful to us through your justice, since it pertains to the praise of the master when an appointed official conducts himself properly. **2.** You require no other example; be mindful of what you will do and do not forget what you have been reminded of. For what could you be in doubt of concerning your own actions, when you recognize your own good works already festoon these very same provinces? In some measure, wanting to offer this is a debt to one whom you know had already praised you.[13] For our intention justly indulges the obedient and to those whom we know to be mindful of your good works, we offer your affection without hesitation a second time. **3.** Your age is indeed advanced, but what could prevail to deprive from you now, who are more mature in your accomplishments and who was never blameworthy as a young man? But you accomplished this in the reign of our lord grandfather; demonstrate such service now, so that you would seem to have reserved for our reign whatever had increased in your probity.

LETTER 9.9 (C. 526–27)

This letter accompanies *Variae* 9.8, announcing to the inhabitants of Dalmatia and Savia the re-appointment of Osuin as *comes* over the territory and the appointment of an accompanying governor.

King Athalaric to All Romans and Goths

1. We want to send such men throughout the provinces granted to us, with God as witness, who are trained with arms and glorified with justice, so that you may forget the dread of foreign nations and not endure treacherous corruption, since it is no

13. Theoderic.

less an evil to avoid war only to fall to the cruelties of civil harassment. For it is the truest kind of security that fears no iniquity from a judge. And so, what should be said with God's guidance, we have decreed the *illustris comes* Osuin, distinguished in our court and noted for his long familiarity with the provincials of Dalmatia, should preside over you. Take care to obey his command for our benefit, since you have tested his justice often before, so that, mindful of the first time, you ought to obey him even without royal insistence. For that man who is just has his own prerogative; for while he is less intent upon the terror of power, he nonetheless is always heard for his persuasive equity. **2.** And likewise, we have determined that the *illustris* Severinus must be sent to you, so that brought together with a consonant will, they would be able to advise you according to matters that would be praiseworthy. For if one song issues from separate reeds, it is much more befitting to wise men that just decrees should persuade with a harmonized voice. **3.** It is true that the commencement of our reign began with oaths offered to us and you at the very limit of the *regnum* should feel your lord to be most kind, so that what had been sought from you for the fourth indiction as increased exaction, we now order the *illustris Comes Patrimonii* to remit. **4.** Beyond conceding this to you, so that, by the grace of God, we would cause the above-mentioned man to return to our service, send such men through whom we may clearly understand by how much the imposed census ought to be adjusted in the future, so that, if we know you to be burdened, we may relieve you of a portion owed to us that we would estimate with careful equity. It thus happens that you, who are already pursuing the course of remedy, even have the promise of future assistance. **5.** Therefore, it is fitting that you serve our advantage, when the munificence of the *Princeps* has conferred more than what you were able to hope for in your greatest prayers. For thus have we learned in following our most clement forebear, that we should not deprive our subjects of assistance. It is clear that the key to ruling is to love what unburdens many, since the republic becomes more secure if the capacity of tax payers remains free of injury.

LETTER 9.10 (C. 526)

This letter concerns the overhaul of tax assessments in Sicily, intended to encourage loyalty to the new regime of Athalaric. All supernumerary taxes formerly instituted by Theoderic are canceled, and oppressed landowners are encouraged to appeal unfair assessments for the regular exaction. This letter initiates a series of communications (*Var.* 9.10–14) concerning corrupt fiscal practices in Sicily.

King Athalaric to the Honorati, Possessores, *and*
Defensores *of Syracuse and to All Provincials*

1. It was indeed some time ago that we decided the commencement of our *imperium* must be announced to you; it is now fitting that a benefaction follow for increasing the happiness of all, so that, to those for whom our accession was most welcome, royal devotion may be liberal in another fashion. We desire all things to increase for us, with God as witness, since that tax assessment is reasonable to us which the landowner pays cheerfully. **2.** Thence we draw away the money that would increase glory and, greedy for praise, we strive to assist cultivators lavishly. Some time ago our lord grandfather of divine memory took great measures for benefactions in his own name; since long peace and the cultivation of fields flourished and the population had increased, he established that a property assessment be required within the province of Sicily, according to the practiced moderation of his wisdom, so that duties would increase with you, whose resources had expanded. But the famous justice of that man prepared a place for our generosity, so that, what was rightly offered to him, we grant with a kind heart as though it is an earned salary; and by a kind of foresight of divine mind he brought about the piety of the man for whom he had prepared *imperium*. **3.** And so, our liberality readily remits for the fourth indiction whatever used to be sought from or paid by you under the title of an increase beyond customary payment.[14] Because even if you are reasonably able to pay, we order you to accept instead the glory of our largesse. **4.** But so that our clemency may be extended further and you should know the sweetness of our rule from allocated benefactions, whatever has been determined by the tax collectors for the next assessment of the fifth indiction, we give them notice to remove, so that, what will have been rightfully estimated, you should produce with an unburdened spirit, since justice served harms none. **5.** But lest you believe you have been burdened on account of a large assessment of the tax assessors, if anyone believes that he will be overwhelmed by what they have assessed, let him hasten to succor of our devotion, so that we who have also kindly conceded unexpected favors may correct those estimating the taxes. For even our lord grandfather of glorious memory had been disturbed concerning the tardiness of those men, so that, having the perception of the highest wisdom, he thought those whom he already commanded to return with repeated orders had resided for too long in the province, to your own burden. **6.** But we, for whom it is fitting to finish anything that man had arranged for equity, now complete those measures begun for you with God's assistance. Return the intention desired from this measure of our generosity, the fidelity of obedience. You have a *Princeps* who has arrived for you with assistance and, what is even sweeter for subjects, who will increase in innate generosity while growing in age. Concerning this, we have seen fit that our *saio* Quidila should be sent, through whom directives may be disclosed to you with God's grace.

14. In other words, Theoderic's increase to property taxes has been repealed, but the basic assessment remained in place.

LETTER 9.11 (C. 526)

This letter communicates to the *comes* of Syracuse the tax reform initiated by *Variae* 9.10, asking for cooperation with the two tax officials sent to Sicily for that purpose.

King Athalaric to Gildila, Vir Sublimis *and* Comes *of Syracuse*

1. We have directed to the tax assessors of the province of Sicily, the *spectabiles* Victor and Witigisclus, our mandate that they should not exact from the landowners whatever had already been determined by them for the taxes of the fourth indiction, since the payment of this tribute is heavy and the justice of this assessment thus far has not been proven. 2. We have, in fact, issued instructions canceling their assessments, so that, if it has been arranged with respect to equity for the men assessed, it should remain moderate, but if it happens to have overburdened anyone beyond fair measure, he may be relieved by our decision; nevertheless, if anything is shown as paid for the fourth indiction, let it be restored to the landowners without any reduction, since an imposed burden that is known must be carried for all time should not cause complaint. 3. Let what is restored now serve to remind your provincials that we have granted assistance to those whom we find devout in all things and that what is owed to a *Princeps* may be paid with a grateful disposition.

LETTER 9.12 (C. 526)

Variae 9.10.5 acknowledged to the provincials of Sicily the recalcitrance of two officials who had evaded Theoderic's attempts to recall them from the province. Here, the fiscal measures initiated at *Variae* 9.10.5 are addressed to the same two officials, who were probably *domestici* assigned to the *comes* of Syracuse (cf. *Var.* 9.13).

King Athalaric to Victor and Witigisclus, Vires Spectabiles

1. Your tardiness rightly caused you to be suspect to our lord grandfather of glorious memory, you whom he believed must be admonished by a second set of dictates, so that you would finally hasten to his court, thus relieving the inconvenience of the provincials. And now the increase of suspicion has made you not want to be present at the commencement of our reign, which an unfettered conscience would prefer. 2. And therefore, we have determined in the present dictate, that, if you have exacted anything from the provincials beyond the tribute of *solidi* assessed for the fourth indiction,[15] you should restore it to them without any

---

15. The additional exactions canceled at *Var.* 9.10.

reduction, since we want them to experience no loss beyond the former assessment for the above-mentioned indiction. **3.** Moreover, we believe that this must be added (because we do not want to find faults attached to the affection of clemency, lest being so constrained, we would instead eliminate what we are not able to conceal from sound justice),[16] that, if you have harmed anyone with depraved ambition, you will pay even more in our judgment, since it is proper to correct, and not to cause, what has been left unresolved. **4.** And lest you should believe, perhaps, that these acts may be passed over, owing to the difficulty of the distance, we have promised to the Sicilians the assurance of one who will succeed you. See now if you are able to bear the complaints that our authority invites. We therefore admonish those for whom it is fitting to be dutiful; let one who has not wanted to be corrected of his own free will be found accused by his own crime.

LETTER 9.13 (C. 526)

In this letter, the fiscal abuses hinted at in *Variae* 9.12 have been ascribed to the cost of officials living abroad in assigned provinces, for which the *Comes Patrimonii* is ordered to increase their salaries by drawing from the income of royals estates.

King Athalaric to Wilia, Vir Illustris and Comes Patrimonii

1. We have learned from the report of your magnitude about the excesses of the *domestici* who serve the *comites* sent abroad, and that the provincials have been burdened by many losses, we think, because of the scantiness of the salary supporting them, since one for whom the necessary things have not been provided is believed to sin almost pardonably. **2.** And so, bestowing an advantage to all with a special privilege, we declare to your magnitude in the present dictate that, in addition to the two hundred *solidi* and ten portions of the *annona* which they have received up to now, from the fifth indiction, you should unhesitatingly cause fifty *solidi* to be added annually for those officials. This ought to be charged to your accounts, so that, when necessity, the mother of crime, is eliminated, the ambition for sinning is removed. **3.** However, if anyone of brazen dishonesty should defy our policies, so that he is involved in any way in either loss to, or harassment of, the provincials, let him do without all salaries, since that man who is known to acknowledge equity is worthy of pursuing rewards; for he thereby receives profit from us, lest he seek it from others. It is our reputation to give; however little, royal gifts do elevate, since the one who is assisted by the reward of a *Princeps* is believed simultaneously to have found gratitude for his merits.

---

16. That is, should Victor and Witigisclus attach any infamy to Athalaric's policies, they would lose their positions.

LETTER 9.14 (C. 527)

The last in a series of letters pertaining to the administration of Sicily (*Var.* 9.10–14), here addressed to the *comes* of Syracuse concerning a wide range of peculation and distortions of comital authority. The tone of the letter suggests correcting these abuses would allow the *comes* to remain in good standing with the royal court.

King Athalaric to Gildila, Vir Sublimis *and* Comes *of Syracuse*

1. It has been reported to us in a complaint of the provincials of Sicily that certain matters have resulted from your exercise of authority, whence it would seem their prosperity has been stricken. But we have taken the report lightly, since they themselves do not want past events to be punished. For a claim yielded by a hostile party is known to be dubious, and one whom the plaintiff prefers to ignore is not legally punishable. But so that we may abrogate suspicion of wickedness in future cases, we have decreed things that must be continually observed according to the present injunction, so that these people need not fear anything in the future, nor may you enact anything for which you would be accused through ignorance. **2.** First, moneys for the reparation of the walls is said to have been extorted from various provincials, whereupon the promised construction has accomplished nothing. If this has been knowingly permitted, either henceforth let the walls be built for their defense, or let each person receive what is proven to have been unreasonably exacted. For it is exceedingly absurd to pledge fortifications for the citizens and to give them shameful waste instead. **3.** Moreover, they maintain that you have distrained the property of certain deceased men under the warrant of caduceus property of the fisc, without any discretion of justice, while this right may be entrusted to you only in the case of foreigners for whom neither an heir nor a legitimate testimony may be found. For it is criminal that a right granted to us should be appropriated by you with injury to our name. **4.** Furthermore, they groan that they have been burdened by every manner of judicial proceeding, such that those who must bring a case to court seem to lose almost as much in fees as they prove themselves to have sustained from the grievance. Indeed the vocation of the judge ought to be the hope of justice, not profit. For such a judge is rightly rendered suspect even before the difficulties of litigants are heard in court. Whence we have decided that if our decrees call for the punishment of litigants, let the court collector receive as much in fees as our most glorious lord grandfather determined, in the prescribed amount that *saiones* ought to receive for the defense of persons according to their rank.[17] For the apportionment ought to be in proper

---

17. These are the fees that a court official could collect from a defeated litigant; the schedule of such fees allowed for legal defense from *saiones* is not elsewhere recorded.

proportion: if it exceeds the measure of fairness, it lacks the virtue of its own name.[18] **5.** If a legal proceeding is convened by your order, precisely in those cases and concerning those persons where the edicts permit your involvement, then let the officer receive half the payment that he would have been able to claim according to royal precepts, since it does not agree with justice that he should be granted as much from your directive as he would be offered for reverence to our command. **6.** However, if anyone has brazenly flaunted such a wholesome constitution, we order fourfold the payment to be remitted, so that what was lost to the delight of greed should be vindicated by the severity of a fine. We certainly want the edicts and general ordinances of our glorious lord grandfather, which he intended for instilling good habits for all in Sicily, to be protected with such strict obedience that whoever, urged by his own brutish motives, would attempt to overthrow the defense of these injunctions should be considered answerable to sacrilege. **7.** You are also said to call cases between unwilling Romans to your court,[19] in which case, if you know this has been done, presume to do so no longer, lest while seeking a judgment where you lack jurisdiction, you would instead find yourself a defendant. You ought to be mindful of the edict before anyone else, since you prefer cases that must follow to be settled by you;[20] otherwise, all authority for deciding cases will be removed from you, if these regulations are preserved the least by you. **8.** Unrestricted authority is retained by the *iudices ordinarii* for their own administration.[21] Let legal contentions be attended by their own designated judges. Do not allow envy of their official role consume you. The preservation of civic harmony is the distinction of Goths. Every honor of reputation will converge upon you if the litigant rarely notices you. You defend state constitutions with arms, let the Romans practice litigation with civil law. **9.** They report that you detain the goods conveyed by ships and from the ambition of hateful greed, you alone determine steep prices; even if this is not a crime in fact, it should not be even remotely mistrusted. Therefore, if, as would be proper, you hasten to avoid a rumor of this sort, let the bishop and people of the city assist as witnesses to your good conscience. Let what necessarily pertains to the fortune of all be pleasing. Prices ought to be determined by shared deliberation, since it is not to the delight of commerce that they are forced upon the unwilling. **10.** Concerning which, we have ascertained that your sublimity must be reminded in the present ordinances, since we do not want those whom we love to transgress, lest we should bear

---

18. *Commodum . . . debet esse cum modo;* a play on the use of *commodum* for "legal fee."

19. Because the *comes* was a military official, cases between civilians should have been heard by a magistrate of the civil administration should they prefer it.

20. The singular *edictum* may be a reference to the *Edictum* of Theoderic, which stipulates the adjudication of legal matters between civilians (Romans) and military personnel (Goths).

21. The regular "circuit judges" who heard civil cases.

anything wicked to be said about such men, through whom we have supposed the conduct of others would be corrected.

LETTER 9.15 (C. 533)

In 532, Pope Boniface II died and was succeeded by the addressee of this letter, John II. The latter's election at Rome was attended by corruption. The main issue seems to have been the sale of church property by clergy and men associated with the church, in order to influence the election for one party or another. The current pope is not implicated directly (his rival party may have been responsible for the abuses), but the king's decree has a flat declarative tone and also refers to a recent *consultum* of the Senate intended to curb current practices.

King Athalaric to Pope John

1. If it was the inclination of ancient *Principes* to scrutinize laws, so that subject peoples may enjoy the delights of peace, it is much more outstanding to decide such matters as may agree with sacred law. Let condemnable profits be lacking from our reign. We can call profit only that which divine judgment is known not to punish. 2. Only recently a *defensor* of the church at Rome approached us with the tearful allegation that, when a bishop was sought for the apostolic seat, certain men exploited the difficulty of the time with an impious scheme and thus moved against the property of the poor with extorted promises so that,[22] even to say it is abominable, sacred vessels were seen exposed for public auction. The deed was committed with as much crassness as the glory gained from the piety to eliminate it. 3. And therefore, let your sanctity be aware that we have established by this ordinance, which we also want to extend to all patriarchs and metropolitan churches, that, from the time of the most holy Pope Boniface, when the fathers of the Senate, mindful of their own nobility, produced a resolution concerning the prohibition of such sales, if anyone is discovered to have promised anything for obtaining the episcopal office, either through his own action or that of any other person, that execrable contract will be deprived of all validity. 4. Moreover, if anyone is caught being involved in this crime, we grant him no representation; but even if someone wants to be repaid for the purchase of church property or does not want to return what they have received, let them immediately be held guilty of sacrilege and restore received property by compulsion of the assigned judge. For even as just laws make legal action available to good people, thus do they close opportunities to people of bad character. 5. Furthermore, we support whatever the Senate decided in its resolution; let it be preserved in every measure against those

22. The property owned by the church that was intended to support a wide range of individuals—the beggars, widows and orphans, monks and nuns, the regular clergy.

who have involved themselves in any way or any intermediary persons in forbidden agreements. **6.** And since it is fitting that everything be moderated by reason, lest something excessive may be considered just, we have decided that when it happens that an accusation concerning the consecration of the apostolic pontiff is made, and the dispute of the people has been brought to our court, those approaching us with a collection of petitions will receive no more than three thousand *solidi*.[23] Nevertheless, we exclude from eligibility for this measure those who are sufficiently wealthy, since it is instead for the poor that a gift of the church must be considered. **7.** But for other patriarchs, we order no more than two thousand *solidi* to be spent on persons for the above-mentioned purpose, when an appointment at their church is drawn to our *comitatus*. Moreover, let them know that they may distribute no more than five hundred *solidi* to the poorest of the people in their own cities.[24] Let the penalty of this edict and of the policy recently determined by the Senate restrain other recipients, but let the severity of church canons harry those giving church property. **8.** You, moreover, who preside over other churches with the office of patriarch, since our decree has freed you from illicit promises, it follows that, imitating good examples, you may present worthy bishops without any loss to the majesty of churches. For it is corrupt that, among you, the purchase of office may hold a place which we have barred to secular office holders out of consideration for divine law. **9.** Therefore, if any chief official of the apostolic church or of the churches of patriarchs believes a bishop must be appointed by the purchase of any votes, either through their own action or that of their relatives, or of any person serving them, we decree that he will return what he has received and he will suffer every measure of what is prescribed by canon law. But if anyone fears to acknowledge what he has given or promised while the same bishop holds office, let the church reclaim it either from the heirs or their representatives, of the one whose sale purchased the ordination of a bishop. Let those surviving heirs be known by no less disgrace of infamy. We order that other ecclesiastical offices, too, will be subject to the same ordinance. **10.** But if, perhaps by the contrivance of a crafty scheme, a person has become obligated by hindering oaths, so that, for the state of his soul's salvation, he may neither be able to prove, nor does he dare to disclose, the offense committed, we grant freedom, to any honorable person,[25] to report this crime, and whatever he will be able to gather as evidence, to the judge assigned to the particular city. So that we may hasten prosecutors to court, let that man who has agreed to prove such a deed receive a third portion of the implicated

---

23. This is a limit to the expenses that any party may impose upon church coffers in order to further their claim with the court at Ravenna.

24. In order to limit suborning the poor to a particular party.

25. With *honestis personis* probably meaning someone of senatorial, decurial, or some other rank determined by public office, such as the *defensor* mentioned at the beginning of the letter.

property; let the remainder of the property profit the same churches from which it is known to have been wrenched, benefitting either the buildings or at least their services. For it is fitting to convert to good use what perverse iniquity wanted to defraud. **11.** Therefore, let the depraved greed of wicked men cease. What may those who have been excluded from the font intend? Let the just condemnation of Simon be recalled and dreaded, he who believed the source of all largesse could be bought.[26] Therefore, pray on our behalf, maintaining our edicts which you know agree with divine mysteries. But so that the will of the *Princeps* may become known more easily to those of every disposition, we have ordered this to be announced to the Senate and the people through the *Praefectus Urbis*,[27] so that the public may recognize that we pursue those who, instead, are hostile to the majesty of the church. You, who rule by the grace of God, will also publish this to all the bishops, lest anyone would be free from blame who was able to acknowledge our ordinances.

LETTER 9.16 (C. 533)

Following *Variae* 9.15, this letter orders the *Praefectus Urbis* to publish the edict correcting corruption during papal elections at Rome.

King Athalaric to Salventius, Vir Illustris *and* Praefectus Urbis

1. It is a pleasant business to publish those rulings beneficial to the future of all, so that what would be a vowed duty may become cause for public celebration. It is otherwise known to be the cause of harm if beneficial rulings are instead concealed. Indeed, a short while ago, the most capable Senate, longing to clean the stain of foulest suspicion from its own splendor, established with provident deliberation that nobody should pollute himself with detestable greed in the consecration of the blessed pope. It furthermore constituted a penalty for one who attempted to undertake such a crime, not with injury, since when money is not loved, then it is the merit of the candidate that is truly sought. **2.** Praising this intervention and expanding upon it, we have sent ordinances to the blessed pope which, having priority over those of the Senate, shine forth so that profane ambition may be removed from the honorability of the holy church. We want you to bring this to the attention of the Senate and the Roman people without any delay, such that what we want to be preserved by the efforts of all may be fixed in the hearts of everyone. **3.** But in order that the favor of a *Princeps* may remain firm in the present and future ages, we command both our regulations and the Senate's resolution to be fittingly engraved on marble tablets and to be posted as public

26. Simon Magus, Acts 8:9–24.
27. Cf. *Var.* 9.16 for the order to publish this edict.

testament before the entrance to the church of the blessed apostle Peter. For it is a place worthy to house both our glorious proclamation and the commendable decrees of that most capable Senate. For this business, we have sent *ille*, by whose return we shall know that our orders have been fulfilled. Indeed, what one orders seems unresolved for one who becomes aware of its achievement only lately.

LETTER 9.17 (C. 533 OR 534)

This letter grants a pardon to two men imprisoned at Rome on allegations of treason since the time of Theoderic's reign. The only treason case known for that period involved Albinus, Boethius, and Symmachus; of the three, only Albinus survived the affair, although his release from confinement is undocumented. Unfortunately, the letter substitutes the names of the two imprisoned individuals with formulaic *ille et ille*.

King Athalaric to Salventius, Vir Illustris and Praefectus Urbis

1. If the ancient *Principes* sought the happiness of the people in the buildings of Rome, lest the citizens in that distinguished place should have anything in common with citizens of other cities, it is scandalous that among so many fair works they should endure long sadness, since the exultation of the city is the chief desire of a *Princeps,* when it is natural for other cities to rejoice, if the head of the world attains joy. 2. Indeed, we have learned from the report from the apostolic Pope John and our leading citizens that the Romans *ille* and *ille* have withered under the punishment of such a long imprisonment only on account of the suspicion of sedition,[28] so that the entire city has drawn together in mourning over the continued suffering of these men, and so that neither the dignity of the city's own name, nor festivals of the calendar, nor anything that is pleasing to us, relieves them. This displeases us on account of the harshness of the fact itself, that men who would prefer the torments of the cross to debts owed to wicked men are reported to have been condemned on the least deliberation. 3. And therefore, we advise your magnitude with the present command that you should not delay releasing them, in whatever place you will have been able to find them. By the above-mentioned pardons, we account those men already released from dread, even if they were clearly implicated by some litigant. But if they plead that they have endured torture as innocent men, we grant free voice to their complaints, so that they may obtain from just laws what they have endured on account of dishonest accusations, since we do not want innocent men to be forced away from the magistrates who are known to be elevated for their defense. 4. Let the hearts of

---

28. This is the first instance in the collection giving evidence of royal authority responding to an appeal from the pope.

Romans now be recalled to former gladness, nor should they believe that we, who chose to treat them with moderated fairness, would be pleased otherwise. Let them know that our forebears ventured laborious dangers on behalf of their peace; moreover, we work at great expense, so that these people should rejoice with boisterous celebration. 5. For even if they had endured anything unjust or harsh up to this point, let them believe nothing would be denied our clemency, we who grant no leisure to ourselves, so that they may enjoy secure peace and quiet happiness. Let them quickly feel how we are unable to love anyone whom they fear from their excesses. For whose favor could those who have earned the displeasure of their own citizens possibly obtain? When they could have had a period of public affection, they acted such that they rightly deserved to be despised.[29]

LETTER 9.18 (C. 533)

An edict aimed at a wide range of civil crimes, including the seizure of property, forgery, adultery, illicit marriages, sorcery, and violence. It is doubtful whether Athalaric's reign had occasioned a sudden rash of infractions against what were ancient codes of conduct, but the attempt at comprehensive treatment has much in common with Theoderic's earlier *Edictum*.

Edict of King Athalaric

Antiquity providently determined that the public be admonished by general edicts, through which every offense is corrected and shame is not a burden to transgressors. For all men assume they have been addressed where it happens that no individual has been exposed and one who has been taken to be cleansed under common law becomes similar to the innocent. Hence our public devotion is also truly preserved, when fear arises from an idle sword and discipline obtains without bloodshed. For we threaten after forgiving, we menace after inactivity and we grow wrathful mildly, while we only condemn vices. It has been a long time that the complaints of diverse persons have sounded in our ears with constant whispering that certain men have determined to live as savage beasts with civil harmony despised, while reverting to primitive brutishness, they consider human law hateful and deadly to themselves. We have now rightly judged that these men must be curbed, so that at the same time we prosecute crimes inimical to good behavior, we also resist enemies of the republic with divine virtue. Both are truly injurious and both must be repelled, but vices that are shown to be domestic range more destructively.[30] The one rests comfortably with

---

29. This seems to be a thinly veiled accusation against persons responsible for the condemnation of the two men, for which responsible parties in public positions earned the displeasure of the people.

30. The contrast here elaborated is between external enemies of the state and the domestic vices of citizens.

the other. Indeed, if we subdue the offenses of our own people, the assaults of enemies fail more easily. **1.** Standing firm in our indignation, we condemn with the
severity of laws that primal crime of the human race, the seizure of property, under
which civic harmony may not be proclaimed or maintained. Thus, let the sanction of
the divine Valentinian,[31] wrongly neglected for a long time, stand against those who,
with the order of law despised, would presume to violently occupy urban or rural
estates either in person or through their familiars, with the lawful owner expelled.
Nor do we want any of its severity to be mellowed by detestable tampering; we add,
moreover, that if any free-born citizen does not hold property sufficient for satisfying the terms of that law, let him submit immediately to the punishment of exile,
since one who knows himself to be unable to bear the penalty otherwise ought to
have more regard for public law. Therefore, the presiding judges, in whose jurisdiction the criminal act is found to pertain, if they should allow the interloper to hold
seized property when they might have removed him, let them be deprived of the
appointed belt of office and let them become liable to our fisc in the amount that the
despoiler would have owed, nevertheless with the laws remaining in effect against
the authors of the deed. But if anyone has been seized by such madness that he
would, with an overbearing spirit, neglect to obey public law, and by virtue of being
more powerful, he scorns the small number assigned to the magistrate's staff, let his
infamy be brought to our attention in the report of the judge, so that one who did not
want to obey legal authority may feel the vengeance of royal force with the warranted
prosecution of *saiones*. **2.** Because even the greatest *Principes* must live under public
law, if anyone has or will presume to post titles of ownership in the name of public
authority but with the process of law omitted, let him be liable to the lawful owner in
the amount claimed by the aforementioned statement. For one who has dared to
burden the majesty of the royal name with the weight of unjust fraud is rightly
stricken with the punishment for sacrilege. Let the person ruled against also pay the
legal expenses, since in this way nourishment is supplied for detestable litigation
when the unrighteous are defeated without injury, and nor does the loss of reputation grieve detractors if they should escape without the loss of assets. **3.** But if someone from our bureau believes a claim against someone must have merit, let him
appraise the amount pertaining to his case, suppressing nothing from his adversary
concerning the following series of ordinances: if he does this, let him lose what he
hoped to gain, or if he should attempt to compel something from him, let it nevertheless be invalid, since we only want those to enjoy our favors whom we know do
not practice cunning ploys. **4.** Let a man who strives to divide the marriage of
another with punishable seduction have his own marriage bond be declared unlawful, so that the malicious man may feel more for himself what he had attempted to
inflict upon another; or if he lacks the dearness of marriage, we deny him the right

---

31. Valentinian II, from *Theodosian Code* 4.22.3.

of future matrimony, since one who dared to assault the marriage bed with division does not deserve to find the reward of respectable marriage. But lest our punishment miss anyone guilty of this crime, if those who have no hope of marriage in the present or future presume against another's bedchamber with cunning trickery,[32] let them be deprived of half their assets, with that portion immediately applied to the benefit of the fisc. But if it is not possible to avenged the property of some on account of poverty's hindrance, let them be bound with the punishment of exile, lest, what is scandalous to say, they may be seen to avoid the menace of public law for the reason that they are known to lie subject to the lowest fortune. But our piety has decreed this concerning the seducers of another's affection. **5.** We want whatever could be decried from holy admonition,[33] to be preserved in the strictest sense against all others involved in adultery. **6.** Let no man be bound to two wives at one time, since he will know that he must be punished by the loss of his property. For this is either lust, and he is rightly not permitted to enjoy it, or it is avarice, and he is condemned by law to poverty. **7.** But if a man prefers to come to the embraces of a concubine, despising an honorable marriage in an excess of unseemly lust, if she is a freeborn woman, let her be delivered to the lawful wife, with her children, into the yoke of servitude in the fullest sense, so that through honorable judgment she may feel herself subject to one whom she believed to be placed above through illicit lust. But if a female slave arrives at such outrage, let her be subject to the vengeance of the wife, with punishment of bloodshed removed, so that she may endure as judge one whose absence she ought to have dreaded. **8.** Let the fear of no person extort property as gifts; let no one desire to acquire property through fraud or accursed licentiousness: only honest profit is correct to desire. With regard to claiming the legality of a bequest, we want that severity of the laws to be preserved which the legal authority of antiquity sanctioned for establishing the truth. For thus, as the very bequest bears witness, no opportunity is open to fraud and the validity increases more with truth. In any other case, we order that nothing is to be considered legitimate which the author made uncertain by not fulfilling what the laws or statutes require. **9.** Let the severity of the laws also pursue sorcerers or those who are known to have sought anything by their nefarious arts, since it would be impious for us to be remiss concerning those whom heavenly devotion does not allow to remain unpunished. For what folly it is to abandon the creator of life and to follow instead the author of mortality! Let shameful conduct be completely removed from magistrates. Let none cause what the statutes condemn, since those who involve themselves in forbidden transgressions must be punished by the stipulated punishment. For what would magistrates condemn in others if they have stained themselves with shameful pollution? Moreover, let people of

32. For example, someone already legally deprived of the right of marriage.
33. Imperial law.

modest means be entirely safe from the wealthy. **10.** Let the insanity of violence be carefully warded. For presumption of the hand is proven to be the conduct of war, especially in those, whom the authority of our patronage protects. But if anyone attempts to act contrary with unjust presumption, let him be regarded a violator of our command. **11.** We do not permit a single case to be appealed from *iudices ordinarii* by a suspect a second time, lest what was intended as a remedy to the innocent would seem a kind of haven for the criminal. But should anyone attempt to repeat what has been forbidden, let him leave deprived of his case. **12.** But lest we should be supposed not to want to preserve laws other than the few touched upon here, we determine all edicts, ours and those of our lord grandfather, which were formulated with respected deliberation, and public ordinances of every kind in regular use, to be observed with rigorous severity. Thus do the laws ward themselves with such protection and are likewise girt with the augmentation of our sworn oath. Why discourse further? The regular use of the laws and the probity of our commands will be observed everywhere.

LETTER 9.19 (C. 533)

This letter orders the Senate and *Praefectus Urbis* to publish the edict from *Variae* 9.18.

King Athalaric to the Senate of Rome

1. Another man's censurable transgression frequently offers opportunities for praiseworthy ordinances and, by marvelous means, adaptations of justice are born from occasions of iniquity. For equity remains silent, if admitted guilt is not voiced, and the nature of a *Princeps* rests idle because some quarrel has not been provoked. **2.** Indeed, urged by grieved voices and stirred by the interruptions of many people concerning certain matters, we have codified certain measures necessary to the peace of Romans, published in an edict of twelve chapters, just as an institute of civil law is read, which should not seem to weaken the preservation of remaining laws, but rather to reinforce them. **3.** Let these be read aloud in the splendor of your assembly and let the *Praefectus Urbis* cause them to be pronounced in the customary fashion for thirty days in the most frequented places, so that, with our public harmony acknowledged, hope may be withdrawn from savage habits. For with what confidence may a violent man undertake what he knows the clemency of the *Princeps* has condemned? Let the love of discipline return to all, by which small affairs increase and the great are preserved. **4.** Indeed, for this reason, we mobilize our army, with God's blessing, for frequent expeditions, so that we may know the entire state to live according to laws. Let this exchange of gifts be returned to us, so that you would know the one occupied with service to the public weal may be battered by only the rarest approach of plaintiffs. Let the magistrates maintain legitimate severity; let them abstain from longing for faithless corruption. Fear will arrange all affairs if the accused finds nothing reproachable in the one judging.

LETTER 9.20 (C. 533)

Similar to *Variae* 9.19, this letter directs provincial governors to publish the edict of *Variae* 9.18.

King Athalaric to All Governors of the Provinces

1. Although we offer you, with God's blessing, to our provinces in annual restoration, lest court services fail to be available throughout the confines of Italy, we have learned that an abundance of legal cases have encountered a scarcity of justice. Indeed, this is known to be the fault of your negligence, to such an extent that men are compelled to demand the blessings of the laws from us. For who would elect to seek at such a long distance what would seem to arrive at his own residence? **2.** But in order to abolish your ingenious excuses and the hard necessities of the provincials, in the detailed publication of an edict we have decided upon certain legal cases thus far neglected by the worst kind of indolence, so that your confidence in judging correctly would increase and malicious audacity gradually would be decreased. Cause this edict to be pronounced in the customary fashion for thirty days in the public assemblies, so that anyone who presumes to remain incorrigible after this remedy will rightly be considered condemned.

LETTER 9.21 (C. 533)

This letter was warranted by apparent adulterations to the salaries and benefits given to professorial chairs of grammar, rhetoric and law at Rome. The Senate has been made responsible for ensuring the continuation of these endowed chairs.

King Athalaric to the Senate of Rome

1. We are known to release the duties of sons to the legal roles of their fathers, so that they may consider the advancement of their sons, for whom it is important to succeed in studies at Rome. For it is not credible that you would be unconcerned for that by which the adornment of your family increases and the deliberation of your assembly advances with unremitting reading. Indeed, as regards our careful concern for you, we have recently learned through certain murmurings that the teachers of eloquence at Rome do not receive the rewards established for their labors and that, by the haggling of some, the payments assigned to masters of schools have been diminished. **2.** Therefore, since it is manifest that rewards nourish the arts, we have judged it scandalous to reduce anything for those teachers of youth, who instead must be encouraged to honorable studies through the increase of their emoluments. **3.** For the initial study of grammar is the noblest foundation of the literary arts, the glorious mother of learning, which knows to be attentive to praise and to speak without fault. Thus this recognizes the discordant blunder in the flow of oration, even as good conduct abominates a crime as alien to itself. For even as the musician creates the sweetest melodies from a harmonizing chorus, thus the grammarian knows how to chant balanced meter with well-arranged accents. **4.** The grammatical mistress of words, the ennobler of the human race, who is known to assist our counsels through training in the most refined reading of ancient authors. Barbarian kings do not employ this; it is known to remain unique among law-minded rulers. For other nations have arms too; eloquence is found only in obedience to masters of the Romans. Thence the jousts of orators sounds the battle call of civil law; thence the most refined speech commends all leading men and, so that we may put it to rest, it is from this whence we speak. **5.** For which reason, conscript fathers, we bestow this concern upon you and, by divine grace, this warrant, that a successor to the school of liberal studies, whether the professor of grammar, rhetoric, or law, may receive from those responsible the emoluments of their predecessors without any reduction. Once a professor has been confirmed by the authority of the first rank of your order and by the rest of the full Senate,[34] provided he is found suitable for the assigned work, he may not suffer improper suit from anyone concerning the transfer or reduction of his *annona*, but he will enjoy the security of his emoluments by your arrangement and patronage, no less than by the protection deputed to the *Praefectus Urbis*. **6.** And lest anything may be left undetermined for the caprice of those paying him, immediately after six months have passed, let the aforementioned masters obtain half of the decreed amount, but let the remaining span of the year be concluded with the payment of the *annona* owed; let those for whom it is a sin to have wasted even a moment of an hour not be compelled to wait upon the aversion of another. **7.** Indeed, we want what has been decreed to be observed only in the strictest sense, so that if anyone should have an interest in deeming this must be deferred as though a tax, that very individual who, with punishable avarice, has refused just payment to those commendably laboring, let him bear a payment in the amount given to moneylenders.[35] **8.** For if we bestow our wealth on actors for the delight of the people and those affairs thus not regarded as necessary are carefully funded, how much more should be offered, without any delay, to those through whom honorable conduct advances and eloquent talent flourishes at our palace! **9.** Furthermore, we order this to be made known to the current masters of studies by

---

34. Members of the Senate actively holding office, followed by the rest of the *illustres*.
35. The payment of interest, probably at the current market rate.

your respected assembly, so that just as they acknowledge our concern for their welfare, thus will they know that we require the strenuous advancement of young men from them. Now, let that opinion of teachers appropriated from querulous satire cease, since the source of talent should not be claimed by two schools of thought. Behold they are now proven to have tolerable accommodations, whence they may now rightly concentrate continually upon a single concern, being transported with full vigor of the mind to studies of the good arts.

LETTER 9.22 (C. 533)

This letter appoints a young member of the politically important and apparently prolific Decian family to the consulship. Celebrated in the following year, this was the last consulship appointed for the West, while the eastern consulship lapsed later in 541. In both cases, the end of the Roman consulship was connected to the Gothic War and the politics of Justinian's reign in the East.

King Athalaric to Paulinus, Vir Clarissimus *and Consul*

1. The conduct of men wanders, confused and undetermined, if there should be neither dread of fault nor rewards for virtue. But when each is enclosed within its own precinct and with its own definition, it is scandalous to hesitate concerning one who has merited election in the judgment of a *Princeps*. For we do not decide anything out of spite, nor do we praise anything, having been appealed to by some flattery. Our choice comes from merits and however much someone approximates the royal disposition, the more he is conjoined in an association with good works. We do not respect the improper, nor could you be roused by complacency in a *Princeps*. 2. Although humanity may be commonplace, it is not possible for the offspring of the Senate to be unknown, when anyone who is attached to good merits, who is abundantly celebrated and who is commended by the witness of reputation, is well known. Therefore, the clear eye of our mind has noticed that you have been long prepared and has seen merit that has not been held in the shadow. Indeed, a celebrated reputation has proclaimed your promotion, giving credibility to the weight of your family's morals, if not to your age.[36] For it would not be proper that that our decision should find anything requiring correction in one who had produced so great a family.[37] 3. The seed of the family has rendered a fruit of strong character. Long years have taken nothing from you; Rome recognizes the ancient Decii in you, I say those Decii, the honored stock from former centuries, the mainstay of liberty, the grace of the curia, the singular fame of the Roman name, by whom, it is particularly noted in the written record, the endangered

---

36. Paulinus was a young man at the time of his appointment.
37. Paulinus's father, Venantius Basilius, consul of 508.

standing of the republic escaped an immense host of enemy and who alone was found, among a multitude of such brave men, to have loved his homeland the most. These examples ever kindle you with quiet reminder, since the praise of forebears is a powerful goad to shame, while we do not suffer those whose parents we have celebrated to be unequal to them. **4.** And therefore, because it has been granted with God's guidance, take for the twelfth indiction the insignia of the consulship, indeed a lofty distinction, but one familiar to your family. For you complete the consular list; let the passage of years declare you often and while aversion to public office may customarily have more advantages, your oft-repeated name will bring glory.[38] To this end, at last, heavenly powers had favored your family by providing a fruitful brood of men for the needs of your fathers. Hence it is that you hardly seem a stranger as a colleague at that summit of public affairs: you will have your own forebears as judges. O singular commendation of the times! The Roman curia is practically filled by your family; behold, it is now truly one body that speaks, when it is known to be blended with the company of close kin. **5.** But do not relax your boldness in confidence of your family, nor should you reckon that what was fitting to celebrate in proclamation concerning them will suffice for you. The heir of a good family accomplishes more when one who is reminded of the virtues of his forebears is compelled without remission. Add to it distinguished acclaim: let your life following hereafter succeed your forebears with a kind of imaginary novelty. For if it is glorious for posterity to attain the property of an elder, how much more outstanding is it to increase the inheritance of virtues! We have praised your character out of familiarity with your family; but it would now be an even more fitting thing to demonstrate in public view whence it is that with you, tender age is not flattery, nor is there anything that fear may challenge or a teacher demand.

LETTER 9.23 (C. 533)

This letter announces the appointment of a new consul to the Senate. This letter and *Variae* 9.22 (to the appointee) are testimonies of the last consulship given in the West. Given the youth of the appointee, this letter dwells more on the qualities of his father and family.

King Athalaric to the Senate of Rome

1. Consider, conscript fathers, what we may think about you, that we would elect to the peak of the highest dignities those men of your families whom we have never seen, with no aversion from a lack of familiarity, but with the presumption of an

---

38. Possibly a reference to the end of the consulship under Justinian in 534, which implies revision of the letter after the fact.

honorable nature. Let what have been deemed uncertainties come to the test: would not anyone assume an appointment must be deliberated for such an affair where nothing of a doubtful nature would be found? **2.** Certainly, our generosity encompasses all things, but we bestow great things from the testimony of truth. Certainly, kindness precedes, but an unimpaired decision follows. For just as your curia is the same as a body, thus you convene with commendable purpose as one. It is, therefore, our decision to choose for you what will increase the growth of liberty and the adornment of our *imperium*. The source of things is always in a seed; born fruit produces new authors and whatever we deserve from divine authority is gathered into fortunate offspring. **3.** Hence it is that we have considered the patrician Venantius with admiration as a man rejoicing with eloquent offspring and a father with so many consulships. For he reared sons who must be praised with no reservation, equal in moderation, identical in the vigor of their native spirit and truly brothers in association of morals, whose infancy was nourished to youth in liberal studies and exercised in arms; he formed their minds with letters and their limbs in the gymnasium, teaching them to show constancy to friends and fidelity to their rulers.[39] And whatever divine grace has granted to this man, you would discern transmitted perfectly intact in his posterity. Let others throw themselves after the possession of property and judge wealth alone to be the greatest good. However, in this house, he has provided not only an inheritance in patrimony, but also in virtues. **4.** It is precisely this that grants true wealth, when nothing could be a better advantage than to have succeeded to the commendation given to ancestors. It is also proven that nothing from these noble stewards lacks in him. Refraining from the property of others and distributing his own with moderation, uncommonly wondrous, this father was a burden to none and produced numerous consulars. Let him, hearing these things, claim the fruit of good deeds; let him reckon himself to have a herald,[40] whom the ruler has praised as outstanding even amid so much brilliance of leading citizens. For if it adorns men to receive the distinction of the palm once,[41] what must be thought of a man who has earned so many consulships in his sons? **5.** And therefore, conscript fathers, we decorate your foster child Paulinus with golden dignity, so that his youth, which blazes with merits, may also shine with the triumphal robe. This honor is not a wonder in the family of the Decii, since the forecourts of their homes are full of laureled *fasces*. It is fitting for this distinction to be rare among others; in the exceptional case of this family, he is practically born into the consulship. **6.** Therefore, conscript fathers, cherish this our gift, who is no less your candi-

---

39. It is interesting that this letter draws attention to the importance of a senatorial father's stewardship over the education of his sons, a theme addressed to the Senate in *Var.* 9.21, concerning the Senate's supervision of professorial salaries.

40. His son, Paulinus.

41. A symbol of victory and award of high office.

date. For it is proper that you are publicly pronounced by all as fathers; in this, too, you are particularly parents. Let him confirm your name with its faithfully rendered meaning, derived from its similarity to "cares";[42] not a word transmitted from common usage, but born from an honored lot. May divine providence grant this felicity to us perpetually, so that, granted that you show kindness to foreigners,[43] you may rejoice more enthusiastically in your offspring.

LETTER 9.24 (C. 533)

This letter announces the appointment of Cassiodorus to his final public post as *Praefectus Praetorio* in 533. Like the letters addressed to his father's elevation as patrician, this letter and the accompanying announcement to the Senate (*Var.* 9.25) provide an intimate glimpse into the political history of the family and its intimacy with Theoderic's reign, including opposition from leading men of court. With deft literary intention, *Variae* 9.24 and 9.25 form a bridge to letters in which Cassiodorus publicly accepts his appointment as *Praefectus* in Book 11 (see *Var.* 11. 1–3), bypassing direct association with letters that he wrote for the kings Theodahad and Witigis in Book 10.

King Athalaric to Senator, Praefectus Praetorio

1. If our inclination had perhaps found you as yet obscure and lacking distinction, we would indeed rejoice at the discovery, but we rightly should have doubted the outcome, since there is more hope than fruit in a new man.[44] But since you glory in the countless promotions and weighty judgment of our lord grandfather, it is unbecoming practice to subject to deliberation one for whom we are scarcely able to express admiration. Indeed, the decisions of so great a *Princeps* must not be scrutinized, but venerated, since it is not possible to be in doubt concerning his deeds, when we are aware that we too were selected by him, who, ever assiduous, chose the deserving with entreaties to divine providence, so that he would accomplish those works that heavenly grace would preserve. **2.** For whom did that man not receive as victorious, having placed him over military affairs, or not prove to be just, having girt him as a judge? You would believe he had intimate knowledge of future affairs: for what his mind conceived always returned accomplished, and by the miraculous intention of wisdom, he never held doubt for what he accurately foresaw as an outcome. **3.** And then, we are able to demonstrate the excellent plan-

---

42. A reference to the connection between the Curia (senatorial assembly) and *curae* ("cares").

43. Probably a reference to the consular colleague appointed in the East.

44. Here Cassiodorus pointedly calls himself a *novus homo*, a designation with a long history of association with both political ambition and incorruptibility, as in the well-known cases of Cato the Elder and Cicero.

ning of the *Princeps* in you. Receiving you in youth, he soon found you endowed with good conscience and mature in knowledge of the laws, enough for the office of *Quaestor*. Without doubt, you were the most praiseworthy accomplishment of the day, so that thus with uninterrupted service you gave peace to a man preoccupied with all affairs, while you sustained the great mass of the royal persona with the force of your eloquence. He considered you charming in composition, unswerving in justice and foreign to avarice. 4. Indeed, you sold none of his favors with scandalous price, so that office brought you to the wealth of reputation, since it was never connected to a bribe. Hence it is that you used to be publicly associated with the affection of the most gloriously just *Princeps*, because you were separated from vices by a known reserve. That wisest judge burdened you with the weight of legal suits and relied so much upon the known discernment of your mind that, in place of your appointed service, without hesitation he would prefer your judgment in seething legal disputes. 5. How many times did he assign senior men of rank to you, when those whom such great longevity had instructed could not compare to your early talents? He clearly promoted what was uncommon in you, a spirit open to furthering kindnesses and closed to the vice of cupidity, when, for what reason I know not, open justice and closed hands are rare among men. 6. Let us come to the office of *Magister Officiorum*, to which you are known for pursuing not with the distribution of cash, but with the advocacy of good character. Set in that office, you always assisted the *Quaestores*. For when a task needed clear eloquence, the case was immediately entrusted to your talent. You used to accomplish for a kind *Princeps* what he knew he had not entrusted to you and by a kind of disadvantageous partiality, he freed others of toil, so that he could cover you with the abundant praise of his approval. 7. For none of the offices preserved their own competences with you, when what truthfully had been accomplished by many court officials was known to be entrusted to your good conscience. Nobody was able to whisper against you, although you nevertheless endured envy from the favor of the *Princeps*. The integrity of your service overcame those desiring to detract; your adversaries were often compelled to admit what the heart did not hold. For any kind of malice dreads to profess anything against manifest good, when it quails to be exposed to public odium. 8. You acted as a personal judge and private advisor to the master of the state. For when he was relieved of public concerns, he would draw the opinions of the wise from your stories, so that he might compare his own deeds to those of antiquity. The keenest investigator, he used to inquire into the course of stars, the contours of the seas and the miracles of springs, so that as the most diligent student of the natural world, he was seen to be a kind of purple-robed philosopher. It would be long, if we related everything; let us turn instead to our preferences, so that what is acknowledged to be a debt from him, you may know to by properly paid to you by the heir of his *imperium*. 9. Therefore, with God's blessing, from which source all things prosper, we confer upon you from the twelfth indiction the insignia and role of *Praefectus Praetorio,* so that the provinces, which we know thus far have been wearied by the service of iniquitous officials, may receive a proven judge without fear. But although you may have the prefecture of your father, celebrated throughout the course of Italy, we nonetheless do not set the examples of others before you; exercise your own good habits and you will fulfill everyone's expectations. **10.** With God's blessing, traverse the field of glory which we know has ever been sought by you. For if, as we believe, this office will also demonstrate your discipline, by this, the ambitions of the age will have been tamed. Indeed, you are not accustomed to sell justice; but now, it is necessary to spend eagerly to assist those wounded by injury. Let your incorruptible temperament watch against hands accustomed to evil; let the designs of the fraudulent be thwarted everywhere, since it is honorable for an honest magistrate to accomplish this. Indeed, we have exhausted the desires of all by postponing this for so long on your behalf, so that we have demonstrated the public good will toward you, and you would arrive even more desired by all. For this concerns the human condition, that something obtained would become despised all the more quickly, since everything precious cheapens when bestowed and, by contrast, what is offered after some delay is received more sweetly. **11.** But we are not limited only by the praise of your time in office. Investigate everything pertaining to the accounts of the prefecture, which the cupidity of others is known to defraud. Let it not be permitted for anyone to glory in thefts or in their miscarriages of justice. We have set you as a lamp upon secret affairs, when none will be able to mock your wisdom or bend your fidelity with any bribe. **12.** Set in order the models for this office, you who have demonstrated examples for wondrous discipline in previous official services. For it is fitting that you have accomplished almost all high offices with consistency, you nonetheless have the intentions of good conscience, where it is appropriate there is no limit. For here it is proper to have no boundary; here ambition is proven honorable, of which even an excess is pleasing. Indeed, however ardently a praiseworthy thing is sought, the more glorious it is found to be.

LETTER 9.25 (C. 533)

This letter announces Cassiodorus's appointment as *Praefectus Praetorio* to the Senate. Whereas the previous letter focused on Cassiodorus's relationship with Theoderic, the present letter provides more details concerning his services to the Amal family.

King Athalaric to the Senate of Rome

1. Indeed, conscript fathers, we have heaped Senator with our favors, a man abundant with virtues, wealthy in good conduct and experienced in the highest offices. If you consider his merits, we owe everything that we have dispensed. For with

what compensation must one who frequently filled the ears of rulers with sparkling oratory be valued, who performed the offices entrusted to him with exceptional seriousness and who has striven to make an age that is rightly praised in the
name of the *Princeps?* The truth and eloquence of his speech enticed the spirit of a
ruler, to whom he related everything thus that the very person who accomplished
the deeds would marvel. **2.** He alone assigned what aided everyone, and while he
brought purple-clad orations to the profit of its own audience, he made our *imperium* pleasing to you.[45] For one who charms the royal summit with pleasing oration commends his own nation, when another from your people will be assumed
to be such a man from whom similar things would be expected. **3.** With what eloquence such a loyal man also proclaimed the father of our clemency in this very
curia of Liberty![46] You recall how the noble orator extolled his deeds, rendering
his virtues more admirable than his office. It is possible to demonstrate what we
say in full. Consider, conscript fathers, with what welcome you were introduced to
one who saw himself thus honored by your assembly. Indeed, public acclamation
is far more pleasing than taxes to glorious rulers, since payment is valued even by
a tyrant, but public praise is due to none except a good *Princeps.* Why, honored
gentlemen, would you believe that he was content only with these services, so that
he would strive to praise the current masters, from whom he perhaps sought a
reward in exchange, when tedium of the task was unavoidable? **4.** He even applied
himself to our ancient lineage, learning from reading what the famous songs of
our ancestors hardly retained. This man led the very kings of Goths, hidden in
long forgetfulness, from the asylum of old age. This man restored the Amals along
with the distinction of his own family, clearly revealing that we had a royal line to
the seventeenth generation. **5.** He made Gothic origins a Roman history, gathering
as though into one garland the blossoms that previously had been dispersed
throughout the fields of literature. **6.** Consider how much one who taught the
people of your *Princeps* a marvel from antiquity will esteem you in our praise.
Now, just as you have always been regarded as noble by your ancestors, so should
an ancient line of kings rule you. We yield, conscript fathers, and if we should want
to relate more, his services overwhelm. **7.** With what labor did he commit himself
to the advent of our reign, when the newness of ruling demanded much to be
arranged? Alone, he was sufficient for all affairs: public correspondence demanded
him, our counsels demanded him and it was done by his labor that *imperium* did
not strain. **8.** Indeed, we found him as *Magister Officiorum,* but he fulfilled the
office of *Quaestor* for us and paying the official salaries with the most just loyalty,
he freely exhibited the care that he had learned from our predecessor for the utility

---

45. The *laudes* ("orations") refer to the panegyrics Cassiodorus recited on behalf of Theoderic and
Eutharic.

46. Eutharic, probably on the occasion of his consulship in 519.

of his heir. But adding something greater to these accomplishments, he supported the beginning of our reign with both letters and arms. For while royal anxieties were assailed by attention to the coasts, suddenly ejected from literary retreat, daringly equal to his ancestors, he assumed a military command, for which, because he lacked an enemy, he triumphed by his outstanding conduct. **9.** For he provisioned the Goths assigned to him from his own expenses, so that he neither troubled the provincials nor did he saddle our fisc with the burden of expenses. His command inflicted no loss on landowners. Truly just, he was the guardian of provincials: for one who protects without harm must properly be called a defender. **10.** But soon, as the season closed the traffic of ships and the concern for war was resolved, he instead exercised his talent as a source of the laws, healing without loss to the litigants what before was known to be inflicted at a price. You will read that such was the military command of Metellus in Asia and Cato in Spain, who were praised more for their own discipline than for battles, and not unjustly, since the outcome is always varied when meeting the enemy, but to protect the measure of good conduct is undoubted glory. **11.** What therefore? How, then, did he boast of himself in exaltation, presuming upon such service, since it is common for men to be extolled when they recognize they have been well admired? Did he not conduct himself with such fellowship—good-natured to all, moderate in prosperity, never knowing wrath, except when excessively provoked—so that it was believed the kindness of the *Princeps* toward him was the only favor possible? While he may be unswerving in justice, this is an austere man, who is not hardened to the forgiveness of angry exchanges. He is uncommonly generous with his own property, and while he may not know how to pursue another's property, he is capable of offering his own abundantly. At first, he strengthened these habits with divine reading, because one always acts well, if respect of the heavens governs human passions. For thence the clear awareness of every virtue derives, thence wisdom is cultivated with the refinement of truth. Thus, one who is steeped in heavenly teaching is rendered humble in all things. **12.** For which reason, conscript fathers, by God's guidance, we confer upon him from the twelfth indiction the office governing the praetorian prefecture, so that with God as witness, he may address with his own integrity all the disputes accumulated through the activities of the untrustworthy and he may bring it about that, so long awaited, he will be able to benefit all. May heavenly powers witness his arrangements, so that one whose wisdom we have tested by long association shall be found fortunate in his own affairs, most faithful to us and useful to the republic; and may he leave to posterity a reputation through which he may bring his family to glory for centuries.

Book 10

LETTER 10.1 (C. 534)

King Athalaric died in 534, leaving his mother, Amalasuntha, as the closest direct link to the line of Theoderic. In order to secure her position, Amalasuntha appointed her cousin, Theodahad, as her ruling colleague. This letter announces his elevation to the eastern emperor. By comparison to other letters to emperors, this is a curious specimen, both for its brevity concerning such a sensitive topic and because Theodahad is never actually named in the letter.

Queen Amalasuntha to Imperator *Justinian*

1. Until now, we have delayed relating to you, most clement *Princeps,* the death of our son of glorious memory, lest we should wound the sensitivity of one loving him through the grief of those bearing the news; but now, by the blessing of God, who is accustomed to commute harsh accidents into something prosperous, we have decided to bring better news to your attention, concerning which you would be able to rejoice with us in shared celebration. **2.** We have brought to the throne a man bound to us in fraternal relation, who, with the strength of shared counsel, would bear the royal office with us, so that he should shine in the purple grace of his own ancestors and so that the comfort of a wise man would support our resolve. Lend your assent now to these felicitous designs, so that, just as we eagerly desire all things to be prosperous in your piety's *imperium,* thus would we wholly appreciate your benevolence to be well-disposed to us. And so with this announcement made, which we believe to be desirable for you for the sake of natural courtesy, we furthermore add the service of a most pleasing legate, so that you would advance the peace, which always occupies your mind and which you already retain for me especially, to be confirmed by the addition to my household. For given that the concord of *Principes* would always be preferred, harmony with you ennobles me absolutely, when a man committed to your glory without reservation is elevated so greatly.[1] **3.** But since the brevity of a letter would fail to explain everything sufficiently, we have entrusted those things that must be related to you by word to our legate, bearing duly reverent greetings, which you should receive in the accustomed manner of your serenity, so that it would be possible to clearly recognize everything that we have shown to be justly promised to us from your generosity. For it is doubtlessly appropriate for you to agree, when we have even sent on this errand those whom you have approved, for the purpose of gaining your support for the kind of matters we know you desire.[2]

LETTER 10.2 (C. 534)

A companion letter to *Variae* 10.1, and of equal length, in which Theodahad announces to the eastern emperor his elevation by Amalasuntha.

King *Theodahad to* Imperator *Justinian*

1. It is customary for new kings to announce the joys of their elevation among diverse peoples, so that they may acquire the affection of a foreign *Princeps* concerning the collegiality of ruling. But when I seek your pleasure, most pious *Imperator*, which I know my most excellent lady sister has pledged with you, divine providence has agreed to make me much more secure. **2.** For I am most determined not to deviate in the least from the judgment of one who shines with the light of such wisdom that she both disposes her own *regnum* with remarkable order and she preserves the agreeability promised to all with firm strength. Therefore did she cause me to be a partner to her cares, to the extent that I too would desire to have such companions deserving respect, whom she, discerning according to the habit of her wisdom, causes to be peaceful with her. Thus, she obtains the friendship of those who have no peers in the whole world. **3.** Indeed, this affection is not new, for if you recollect the deeds of her predecessors, you know that the Amals have always considered friendship with that *imperium* to be a kind of law of custom,[3] which is just as certain as it is ancient, since what has been warded over the long centuries is not easily changed.[4] And so, accept with an affectionate

1. Theodahad.
2. Justinian was apparently familiar with the legates that Amalasuntha sent to Constantinople.
3. *Imperium* here refers to the eastern empire.
4. This may be a reference to the *Gothic History* of Cassiodorus, in which the generations of Gothic kings parallel the progression of Roman imperial history.

disposition both our accession and that of our consort sister, to whom you have been singularly devoted, and favor her decision. **4.** For if you value me similarly, in like manner you make me a king in every way. But since they implore to speak more amply concerning our novel desires, and lettered speech does not permit more to be said, it is therefore proper that we have dispatched, with the full duty owed to salutations, certain things which must be imparted to your piety by the worthy legates bearing our letters, since no man acts more effectively than one who decides to entrust his wishes to your kindness.

LETTER 10.3 (C. 534)

This letter and the following (*Var.* 10.4) parallel the first two letters of book 10 by announcing the elevation of Theodahad to the Senate, first in Amalasuntha's name (the present letter) and then in Theodahad's. The deference shown to Amalasuntha is uniform throughout *Variae* 10.1–4.

Queen Amalasuntha to the Senate of Rome

1. After the tearful downfall of our son of divine memory, affection for the public conquered the temperament of a pious mother, so that she considered, not the sake of her own grief, but rather that of your increase. But that most singular author of chastity and mercy, who had deprived us of a young son, retained affection for a mature brother.[5] **2.** With God's guidance, we have chosen the most fortunate Theodahad as partner in our *regnum,* so that we, who thus far have borne the mass of the republic by our singular deliberation, may now pursue the common weal with conjoined counsels, to the extent that by the efforts of two, we may be known as one in thought. The very stars of heaven are governed by shared assistance, and under their illumination they direct the world by the exchange of shared labors. Likewise, divine providence conferred two hands, paired ears and twin eyes, upon humanity, so that work that must be completed by the agreement of two would be accomplished more effectively. **3.** Rejoice, conscript fathers, and attribute our accomplishment to heavenly inspiration. We who have elected to direct all things with the advice of another have wanted to effect nothing reprehensible. Indeed, a partnership assures the good character of the *regnum,* when one who is constituted with a colleague in power is rightly expected to be moderate. And so, with God's blessing, we have opened the palace to a man conspicuous in the distinction of our family, who, born from the line of the Amals, he would satisfy royal distinction in public service. He is patient in adversity, moderate in prosperity, and, what is the most difficult ability to attain, he is already a master of

---

5. Theodahad was, in fact, her cousin, but as next in the male line of succession, and as Amalasuntha's male colleague in power, he was characterized as "her brother."

himself. **4.** He adds to these good qualities, erudition in literature, which imparts great distinction to a praiseworthy nature. In literature, the wise man finds what renders him wiser; there, the warrior discovers what will strengthen the bold spirit; there, the *Princeps* reads how he may administer the people with equity; nor is it possible to have good fortune in any manner of living which the glorious knowledge of literature would not improve. **5.** Receive now a man greater than what public entreaties had earned. Your *Princeps* is also learned in ecclesiastical literature, from which we are always advised concerning anything pertaining to humanity: to judge appropriately, to recognize goodness, to respect the divine, to think upon future decisions. For it is unavoidable that one who knows that his sentences will be judged would follow the path of justice. I may understand the reading that sharpens wit; divine reading always strives to bring piety. **6.** We come to that bountiful temperance of his private life, which procured such great wealth from gifts, such plenty from banqueting, so that, in consideration to his former habits, he would seem to have nothing new in his *regnum*.[6] He has been prompt to hospitality, most dutiful in charity: thus, although he would spend much, his account increased in heavenly remuneration. Every state should want such a man as we have chosen, who, ordering his own property with proper reason, does not strive for the property of others: for however much *Principes* will have become accustomed to restraining their own property, the need for transgressing does not overwhelm them. **7.** No wonder that inclination is praised which orders a limit to property, since even something good is deemed to displease in excess. Rejoice now, conscript fathers, and give thanks to heaven on behalf of our decision, when I have established as *Princeps* with me such a man who may accomplish good works from our fairness and who may offer the goodness of his own devotion. For the virtue of his own ancestors advises him and his uncle Theoderic stirs him profoundly.

LETTER 10.4 (C. 534)

The companion piece to *Variae* 10.3, whereby Theodahad announced his advancement as king to the Senate. Where Amalasuntha had praised the various merits of Theodahad in *Variae* 10.3, in the present letter, Theodahad does the same for Amalasuntha, thus constructing the image of ideal ruling colleagues.

King Theodahad to the Senate of Rome

1. We providently announce, conscript fathers, both that divine favors have been granted to you, and that glorious matron over the entire realm of affairs has, with

---

6. This seems particularly ironic in that the Theodahad's former habits, as represented in the *Variae*, included allowing his associates to pillage the property of neighbors (cf. *Var.* 3.15, 4.39, 5.12).

great devotion, made me a partner in her own *regnum*, so that she should not lack faithful comfort and an ancestral *imperium* should be bestowed upon us equally. Let what the public is known to wish for be received thankfully: now the wishes of all are revealed without trepidation, so that the whole state acknowledges my elevation, while it may have been dangerous to prefer it.[7] You previously undertook to whisper without my knowledge what you had not been able to claim openly. Whatever I owe you, it is known that you would have hastened that sainted man to bring it about for me,[8] because my spirit would not dare to seek it. **2.** This is new to us, rather than unexpected to you. Therefore, the completion of what seemed to be revealed as quickly as was opportune ought to be received with much gratitude. But if we deserve anything from you, since we nonetheless expect our gratitude to you to increase more, sound out in unison glorious praises to our consort and sister, who wanted the greatness of her *imperium* to be strengthened with our assistance, so that it would be as though one vision in two eyes and no man would believe the agreement of the senses had been divided. **3.** For thus it is for those simultaneously joined by favor and united as family. Disparate dispositions would perhaps find this difficult; it is difficult for those able to agree in the similarity of their good estimations of each other to live otherwise. It is truly the improvident man who declines to follow advice; but that man who possesses the full measure of knowledge seeks wisdom in another. **4.** But among the diverse gifts that divine providence has conferred upon us with royal majesty, it soothes our soul the most that the wisest matron selected us on the scales of great deliberation. I first felt her justice, so that I should arrive first at the grace of her advancement. For, as you know, she caused us to plead our cases with private citizens under common law. Oh, singular nobility of spirit! Behold the wondrous equity of which the world speaks. She did not hesitate to first subdue to public law a kinsman whom she wanted shortly after to administer the very same laws. She thoroughly investigated the conscience of one to whom the regulation of the *regnum* was about to pass, so that she would be recognized as matron of all and it would be deemed justified for me, thus proven, to advance to the *regnum*. **5.** When, with these gifts, when shall we repay that for which we owe such great gratitude? She who ruled alone with a young son has now chosen to govern in partnership with me. The grace of all rulers is in her; in her, the flower of our good family. However we may shine, we receive it from her brilliance, when she confers praise not only upon her family, but she also adorns humanity itself. Who could sufficiently pronounce with how much devotion and with how much weight of character she is imbued? Philoso-

---

7. Amalasuntha's acquiescence cleared the way for the appeasement of a rival faction, who wanted Theodahad brought to power.

8. *Divinitus* is probably a way of saying "Theoderic of divine memory"; there is no other occurrence of the word in the *Variae*.

phers would learn completely new things, if they knew her and they would confess there was less learning stored away in their own books than they could recognize was allotted to her. **6.** Acute in deliberation, she is the most serious in the moderation of her speaking. It is without doubt a royal virtue to quickly ascertain the importance of matters and to pronounce a verdict at the last possible moment. Indeed, one who first determines by his own examination what must be revealed, must know how to say nothing that would be regretted. Hence it is that her remarkable learning flows with great fluency in many languages; her intellect is found so prepared at a given moment, that she does not seem to be of the earth. It is read that a queen of the south came to the Books of Kings in order to learn the wisdom of Solomon; in her case, *Principes* hear what they learn with admiration. She encapsulates infinite meaning in a few words, and what is given shape by others only with long elaboration, she composes with the greatest facility. **7.** Blessed is the republic that boasts the governance of such a matron. It was not that the public should be subject with less freedom, for it is more to her great credit that she and the reverence owed to a *Princeps* would be subject to the public. For by this indulgence do we rule most worthily. For since I obey such wisdom, I yield to every virtue. Indeed, we are not burdened by the weight of the *regnum* under the influence of such an instructor, since if anything should be unknown on account of its newness, it would become familiar to us through her instruction. **8.** It is not shameful to admit the truth for the good of the public.[9] Know, leading men, what may please us most derives from this wisest of women. For either we understand better by asking her, or we profit in imitation of her. Live now as blessed men, live in agreement with God's plan and emulate the grace that you know maintains royal concord.

LETTER 10.5 (C. 534)

Addressed to the *suus homo* of Theodahad, it may be assumed that the recipient was the domestic steward of an estate, whose former habits Theodahad admonishes. Although the letter has more to do with personal domestic matters than of the state, Theodahad may have turned to Cassiodorus (at that time acting as *Praefectus Praetorio*) to draft this letter as a statement of his suitability for public authority.

King Theodahad to His Man, Theodosius

1. We want moderation to be the measure of all conduct of our power, so that, however much divine favor we receive, so much more shall we love fairness. Indeed, private ambitions are demonstrably excluded from our heart, since a

9. The truth that Theodahad's legitimacy derived from Amalasuntha.

master of public life is made guardian of all by the will of God. And therefore, we command by the present order that nobody who is known to pertain to our household and has been entrusted to your supervision, may become arrogant with any demands, since only one who is able to remain untroubled by the laws may be called my own. Increase our reputation by your forbearance.[10] **2.** If anyone will perchance have a claim against another, pass it down to the public courts. Let the forum protect you, not unjust presumption. We want discipline to commence with our domestics, so that others would feel shame to transgress, when we are known not to offer our familiars the freedom to stray. We have exchanged our methods with authority, and if before we defended our rights to the limit, we now temper all things with clemency, since the household of a *Princeps* is not exempt, but whatever we govern, by the will of God, we avow that to be our own. **3.** Therefore, be careful in every way concerning those who were formerly subject to our personal rights: allow none to raise anything against the law. Let praise of you reach us rather than the advance of any quarrels, since a good conscience truly rules then, when it hastens to excel publicly.

LETTER 10.6 (C. 534)

The first of the only two known appointments made by Theodahad (cf. also *Var.* 10.11–12), this letter elevates a candidate as the new *Quaestor*.

King Theodahad to Patricius, Vir Illustris *and* Quaestor

1. It is proven to be necessary for the republic to appoint the kind of people properly suited for offices, so that the one to whom justice is entrusted should not be impeded by poor character. It is otherwise unproductive to expect from a man what he is known to not possess: on the contrary, one seeks confidently for that which is sensed to be present. **2.** And for that reason, it pleases us foremost to behold your moral conduct, without which even the best qualifications can disappoint. For genuine kindness is the adornment of all good men, a quality that is not isolated, since it is known to be engendered from multiple virtues. Preserve the arrangement of our priorities, so that, even as we look for kindness first, thus may we discern you preserving justice before all other things. **3.** A second consideration for us was to inquire after the flow of your eloquence, which, granted that it delights us particularly, we nonetheless rightly place it after good character. For a life is known by the one, the other is only praised on account of speech. But there is such propriety in you, because you are known to possess the company of both qualities. For you bask equally in the glow of good deeds and eloquent speech, so that the will of the *Princeps* may be properly set forth and understood through

---

10. In the sense that Theodosius should remain above being drawn into petty disputes.

you. For certainly, we esteem oratory among other arts, so that we may confess it to be the jewel of all literary attainments. **4.** For whatever is conceived by any other discipline is presented gracefully by this art. Let the philosopher discover something, however great; what does it profit to know, if he is unable to express it in praiseworthy manner? It is innate to find something, but it is for eloquence to fittingly liberate it. For how remarkable is it to speak about anything desired and thus to learnedly say what even the wise would marvel to hear concerning any topic? We know you to be particularly well equipped in this art, so that while you are able to sweetly soothe with your suggestions, you do not know how to involve anything malign with them. **5.** And so, by the grace of divine authority, we grant you the *fasces* of the *Quaestor* for the thirteenth indiction, so that you may sate the wishes of the public by pronouncing the judgment of the administration. Devote yourself entirely to the law; devote yourself entirely to the pronouncements of the jurists. Thus will you serve us best, if you preserve the constitutions of the ancients. Consider how praise for the *Princeps* rests in your words; our reputation is what you will say without hesitation, because you feel it in good conscience. **6.** Know how much would be expected of you, to whom our legal judgment is entrusted. It embraces our subjects and spreads among foreign peoples; through it we are acknowledged where we may not be seen. Our decrees transmit disputation to cities and provinces; those who are loyal to our ordinances are even able to judge as we would. It is therefore known that what can convey our judgment must be preserved with the greatest effort.

LETTER 10.7 (C. 534)

The companion to *Variae* 10.6, announcing the appointment of a new *Quaestor* to the Senate.

King Theodahad to the Senate of Rome

1. After happily announcing the advent of our *imperium* to you, conscript fathers, a cause for public speech fittingly arose for us, so that you may know we have appointed a magistrate whose speech is able to adorn us. For an eloquent *Quaestor* who may best publish our wishes and who protects the laws of the ancients with firm purpose is the grace of the republic. **2.** This man, Patricius, is already truly honored with respect to his name; indeed, one in whose name lies distinction enjoys perpetual praise.[11] Studies at Rome engendered in him a flowing eloquence; he demonstrates skill rightly appropriate to that place. For whoever is steeped in learning there deserves to be praised everywhere. There, Latin is a purified speech; there, clear words become acquainted with complete brilliance. Other

---

11. Here drawing attention to the association of the candidate's name with "patrician."

regions traffic vibrant balms and aromatic resins; Rome traffics eloquence, from which nothing more pleasing may be heard. Thus, having been instructed in the noble arts, he was prepared immediately for the legal chambers, so that he came to resemble in his declamation those orators, whom he would observe with long reflection. **3.** It is also noteworthy that he contended with his own colleagues with such great moderation. His modesty was always present in disputes: seized with the heat of declaiming, he pursued stratagems that were praiseworthy, not because they achieved more, but to avoid insult: one who thus pleads cases with tranquil demeanor always maintains his own good character. For which, it is reported that he defended cases, he did not prosecute them. Indeed, what he accomplished for the legal cases of others, he accomplished for his own reputation. For he was known to win cases thus, that he would be shown not to have harmed the reputation of his opponent. **4.** And so it is no longer proper that such a man should plead for justice, but he should teach it; since it is a virtue of the courtroom to abound in the blessings of eloquence and to preserve temperance of character. Know, conscript fathers, what we expect to happen, when we first privilege good character in judges, especially in that public office which is accustomed to publish the laws. For in our reign, the *Quaestor* is not armed with royal power, but is known to be founded in laws. **5.** Our wish is the inclination of ancient *Principes,* whom we desire to imitate to the extent that they pursued justice. For it is this authority of the ancients, so deserving reverence, that does not waver from the path of rectitude. Indeed, one who involves justice in his own constitutions leaves to posterity the burden of following suit. And therefore, conscript fathers, we have conferred the dignity of the *Quaestor* on the *illustris* Patricius for the thirteenth indiction, so that one who is distinguished in name may also be glorified with office. Respect our faith in him, so that what we have done may be felt by you with no less pleasure.

LETTER 10.8 (C. 534)

This letter commences a series of communications with the eastern court, scattered throughout Book 10, which are increasingly vague and cryptic. The brevity suggests ongoing dialogue, with letters responding only to the matter treated in a previous correspondence. In the present example, Amalasuntha appeals to Justinian for advice or authorization on what sounds like a building project.

Queen Amalasuntha to Justinian, Augustus

1. The kind regard of your devotion so pleases us that we may purpose to openly request of your realm whatever is able to add to our grace, since divine providence has bestowed such blessings upon you that you richly overflow with gifts and you grant those things necessary to the hopeful out of a generous heart. **2.** And therefore, respectfully greeting your kindness, I have sent *ille*, bearing these letters, for the assistance of your excellence, so that through him you may command us to accomplish, with the Lord's favor, that for which we had formerly caused Calogenitus to assemble the marbles and other necessary things,[12] so that we may know ourselves to be prized in a real sense by your devotion, whose entreaties you cause to be answered. For our adornment is to your glory, when it becomes known that you have provided what applies to our praise. For it is fitting that the entire Roman world, which the love of your brilliance illuminates, should gleam with your assistance.

LETTER 10.9 (C. 534)

Addressed to the eastern emperor, this letter's subject, however vaguely expressed, is the same as *Variae* 10.8. Given that the two letters share language, some of it *verbatim*, it may be that the two were intended to demonstrate the agreement of Amalasuntha and Theodahad as royal colleagues.

King Theodahad to Justinian, Augustus

1. It is fair, most wise *Imperator,* that you would cause this to be spent by us with a glad heart, for which we ought to be goaded by your clemency rather than you should remain inactive if we had squandered it. For whatever may happen to be produced by us for the comeliness of Italy without a doubt will be pleasing to you, since it justly contributes to your fame when what pertains to the glory of your republic is seen to increase. **2.** Therefore, expressing the most respectful affection of greeting to your dominion, we have sent the bearer of these letters, in order to present that for which Calogenitus had been formerly sent, so that, even though his role has been removed from human affairs,[13] with the Lord's blessing, your assistance should nevertheless reach us, lest the desire that we had presumed to be secure should be brought to naught.

LETTER 10.10 (C. 534)

Although merely a letter of salutation which introduced the envoys bearing matters of true substance, this letter is nonetheless intriguing as an example of how diplomacy could move through multiple channels at the eastern imperial court, in this case through the wife of the emperor. This is the last letter in the collection

---

12. Calogenitus is otherwise unattested.

13. Apparently whatever Calogenitus had been contracted to accomplish was left incomplete by his death.

from Amalasuntha, whom Theodahad had murdered sometime early in 535, and the first of several addressed to Theodora.

Queen Amalasuntha to Theodora, Augusta

1. While it may be our purpose to seek what is shown to pertain to the glory of a pious *Princeps*,[14] it is proper that you, who are known to continually increase with every kind of blessing, should be offered the respect of an address. Concord is not only had in immediate presence, for on the contrary, those who conjoin themselves with the deepest affection behold each other more truly. And so, rendering the affection of respectful greeting to an *Augusta*, it is my hope that, with the return of those legates whom we have sent to the most clement and glorious *Princeps*, you would cause us to rejoice concerning your approval, since your prosperity is as pleasing to us as our own and it is essential to obtain that hoped-for approval, which we are known to constantly desire.

LETTER 10.11 (C. 535)

This letter confers *primicerius* rank upon a member of the Anicii, a leading senatorial family. In addition, it announces the marriage of the candidate to a woman of the Amal household. Compared with the attention given to marriages with Amal women elsewhere in the collection, the anonymity of the woman is puzzling (cf. *Var.* 4.1 and 5.43). If this promotion followed the death of Amalasuntha (535), it seems likely Theodahad used this opportunity to shore relations with the Senate.

King Theodahad to Maximus, Vir Illustris *and* Domesticus

1. If it is the glory of good *Principes* to elevate untested persons with honors, since it profits rulers to be associated with the celebration of their subjects, how much more excellent is it for us to restore to the noblest of families what we also know it has deserved by lot of birth! For thus do we follow justice, if we do not deny noble heirs the rewards of their parents. For it is fitting that those who have deserved to arrive at our reign should even surpass their forebears. **2.** Indeed, an ancient age engendered the Anicii, a family almost equal to *Principes*: the dignity of their name, channeled in gathered strength from the bloodline, glows restored and more happily celebrated in you. Who, therefore, would leave to posterity fewer honors among those who are known to have been preferred for so long? Let centuries be reproached if such a family should fall into obscurity. Would that longer generations had also preserved the Marii and Corvini for us! The desires of a *Princeps* should almost be satisfied if it would happen that we possessed characters of such merit. How may we, who wish for things past, now neglect their certain

---

14. Here, Justinian is meant.

discovery? **3.** And so, what may be pronounced blissfully, we confer upon you from the fourteenth indiction the distinction of *primicerius,* which is also called the *domesticus.* You will enjoy all the prerogatives which pertain to the service of this rank. Although this honor may seem inferior to such distinguished birth, it is nonetheless known to be more fortunate than all of your former offices, you who have deserved in your lifetime to receive a wife of the royal line, for which you did not presume to wish in your consulship.[15] **4.** Act now, so that, just as it is desired by you, thus will it be rendered agreeable to us. Consider what you have earned and conduct yourself as worthy of relation to us by marriage. For one who is conjoined to the family of a ruler is stationed in the bosom of good reputation. Let a greater service now be given to kindness; let fellowship and generosity be offered to all, so that we may be shown to have chosen such a great man, whom prosperity will not corrupt. Hold a glorified rank with humility, since praise is claimed from moderation, enmity is incited from arrogance. Indeed, envy is doubtlessly the closest neighbor to promotion, which always thrives with strife, but is best conquered by mildness. **5.** Above all other virtues, love patience, handmaiden to the wise: elevated by us, you will be praised for forbearing, rather than for vindicating. Conquer anger; delight in kindness; be concerned lest your good fortune may seem greater than your character. Let one who is conjoined to our family be proven an intimate by glorious services. Indeed, thus far, your family has received acclaim, but it has not been adorned by such a great bond. Your nobility is not beyond further increase. Whatever you will accomplish in public acclaim, you will be considered more worthy of your marriage.

LETTER 10.12 (C. 535)

This letter announces to the Senate the elevation of Maximus to the rank of *primicerius* (cf. *Var.* 10.11), but more importantly announces his marriage to a woman of the Amal family, an event the letter portrays as the union of Senate and Roman people with the Amals. As suggested for *Variae* 10.11, the letter gives the impression of a rather *ad hoc* attempt to leverage loyalty with leading members of the Senate following the death of Amalasuntha.

King Theodahad to the Senate of Rome

1. Let none believe, conscript fathers, that we have not considered due measure in granting offices, because after the insignia of the consulship we would confer an honor less distinguished. On the contrary, because the merits of this candidate please us, let it not seem that one who is known to have received honors of service

---

15. Maximus married a woman of the Amal family, thus granting Theodahad more secure ties with the Anicii after his accession in 535. The woman's identity is unknown.

in his youth now claims something inferior as a mature man. It was indeed an eager *Princeps* who concluded such a great span of life with only one office and therefore offered nothing further, since he was acknowledged as earning the highest office first.[16] But let us instead confer all offices promiscuously: no distinction is inferior, since it is worn well, when it is seen to receive even greater respect from the conduct of the person than from the distinction of the post. These appointments are, moreover, differentiated by grade according to the differences in men to whom they are assigned. For the office always remains equivalent to whatever a consular will have achieved in conduct. Thus does a greater river absorb the names of smaller streams and although your Tiber may receive many tributaries, nonetheless, it does not detract from its own name. **2.** And so, what may be pronounced blissfully, we have bestowed on the *illustris* and magnificent patrician Maximus the distinction of *primicerius,* which is also called the *domesticus,* from the fourteenth indiction, so that he would elevate the mediocrity of the rank by virtue of his appointment. For it is not proper to call lowly what an Anicius bears: this family, famed over the whole world, verily is declared noble, when the respectability of service does not recede from it. **3.** But we add to his honorable distinctions, conscript fathers, so that the shining grace of your order may be commingled in lofty kinship with us. Indeed, it is not possible for only one man to assume to claim for himself the glory that we are granting to the Roman name. Return the fullest regard for our affection. A subject who is worthy enough that his master bestow kinship upon him must be loved more. **4.** But it is also right, conscript fathers, that such a cherished man should be one through whom blessings would extend to you. Rejoice as one and celebrate these nuptials with flowing gladness. What elevates the Roman name ought to be the desire of all. How could entreaties demand of me what my heart has granted of its own accord, so that the men of your order whom we are truly able to call fathers should be bound to us with the distinction of kinship?

LETTER 10.13 (C. LATE 534 OR EARLY 535)

A poignant sample of deteriorating relations between Rome and the Amal court, this letter addresses the responsibility of the Senate to quell unrest at Rome. Although not explicit in the present letter, the companion piece addressed to the citizens of Rome (*Var.* 10.14) makes it clear that the installation of a Gothic garrison at Rome had provoked disturbances. The garrison was possibly a precaution after the deposition of Amalasuntha in 534 or, more likely, the seizure of Syracuse by Belisarius early in 535.

16. Theoderic had appointed Maximus to the consulship of the West for 523 and then died in 526, leaving Maximus without further recognition; for his consulship, cf. the announcement at *Var.* 5.42.

King Theodahad to the Senate of Rome

1. We returned the venerable bishops, with their legation acknowledged, nor did our disposition oppose your petitions, although they were somewhat disagreeable; afterward, certain men traveling to us reported that the city of Rome still labored under absurd apprehension and acted as though, unless our assurance should intervene, it would incite purposed reprisals against itself on the basis of doubtful suspicions. For which, consider who ought to be blamed for the senseless fickleness of the people other than your order, to whom all things submit to be controlled. **2.** Indeed, it is proper that all provinces should be admonished by your wisdom, so that they would be shown to adopt such comportment as would seem to adorn the commencement of our reign. Truly, if Rome errs, what city would not be excused? The lesser hastens to the greater for an example, and that which offers an example of sin rightly bears blame for another's deed. But we give thanks to divine authority, which has provided its own gifts from your transgressions. **3.** Behold, we overlooked your faults before we experienced your loyalty. We owe you nothing, but we absolve you. We grant your favor first, so that later we may find you more grateful. But although the earnestness of our leniency is vindicated in this instance, we nonetheless want to be celebrated only to the extent that courtesy of Rome's loyalty is able to be offered. For we cherish your reputation more than if we are praised for our constant mild manner. **4.** Avoid those suspicions ever uncharacteristic of your order. It is not fitting to correct the Senate, who ought to regulate others with fatherly encouragement. From whom will good conduct have its source, if it should happen that the fathers of the state are wanting? This suffices for nobility, and it certainly suffices for self-conscious men, that we would stimulate eagerness for perfect loyalty in those whom we hold only somewhat responsible for stray suspicions. For even though we have requested your presence, we have dwelled, not on your distress over injury, but on the means of your prosperity, so that you ought to accomplish more eagerly what we know will ease you.[17] **5.** It is a sure reward to see the *Princeps*. We want what is usually sought as a reward to become an advantage to the republic through you. But lest this medicine should seem harsh in any way, we have decided that only certain men should be called to us when affairs require, so Rome would not be denuded of its citizens and our counsels would be assisted by wise men. **6.** Therefore, return to your former loyalty and let my anxieties, which I bear for the state, be assisted instead by your talent, since it was always customary for you to offer your *Principes* a pledge of sincerity, nor to obey from the necessity of fear, but rather from love of your ruler. We have entrusted other matters which must be spoken about in person to *ille*, the

---

17. It seems that in a separate communication Theodahad requested the attendance of some members of the Senate at his court; here the letter emphasizes that the request is not for sureties of good behavior of Rome, but rather to better ascertain the cause of the grievance.

bearer of this letter, so that with all uncertainties dispelled, you ought to trust our assurances.

LETTER 10.14 (C. LATE 534 OR EARLY 535)

This letter to the people of Rome follows the events that triggered *Variae* 10.13, but whereas the previous letter attempted to assuage misgivings concerning the request for senators at Theodahad's court, this letter focuses more on the presence of a Gothic garrison in the city.

King Theodahad to the Roman People

1. Although it should be customary for you to cherish your masters with a clear conscience and to act upon it with obedience, so that you may consider the disposition of the ruler genial, this was, moreover, always characteristic of your ancestors, so that, like limbs to the head, thus would you seem conjoined to your *Principes*. And what may he give in return, he who is defended by the greatest exertion, for whom civic harmony is preserved every day, except that he should esteem beyond anything else those through whom he is shown to command the realm? **2.** For it is uncharacteristic of our reign that we should find anything in you that could provoke our indignation. Instead, let your fidelity clearly demonstrate what manner has governed you thus far. It is not proper that the Roman people should be divided, or vexed or full of sedition. The conduct of wicked men is proven to be adverse to your good name. But it is also remarkable that we are compelled to admonish your sense of dignity, which was always known to be easily perceived. Let no unfitting suspicions, no shadow of fear mislead you. You have a *Princeps* who desires to find in you that zeal for devotion that delights him. Obstruct your enemies, not your defenders. You ought to encourage assistance, not shut it out. **4.** But perhaps this is the feeling of those who know the least about how they should assist the public; return instead to your own good counsel. Did the appearance of some new people frighten you? Why would you dread those you have thus far called family? Those who hastened to you, with families left behind, were instead incited on behalf of your safety. When, I ask, has such a response been received by one who had been owed a reward for guardianship? **4.** Truly, you ought to know what concerns us, since we desire without end, day and night, that what the parent of our reign nourished may be increased further by us with divine assistance. Where, indeed, would the reputation of the ruler be, if, failing at his duty, he permitted you to be harmed? Do not permit yourselves to dwell upon such measures as you are least likely to see us adopt. Even more, if anyone has been subjected to some inequity, do not let him lose hope of a good conscience, when we strive to elevate those whom we have found to practice honest habits. **5.** We also have entrusted other things that must be said to you in person through *ille,* so that, feeling our good intentions everywhere around you, by oaths, as is proper, you ought to be devoted in loyalty and in genuine speech.[18]

LETTER 10.15 (C. 535)

A letter to the eastern emperor, introducing an unnamed representative from the church of Ravenna who was seeking audience with the emperor. Although this may relate to the church's stance on Justinian's theological policy, it is equally possible that Theodahad has involved the church in negotiating on his behalf after the outbreak of the Gothic War.

King Theodahad to the Imperator Justinian

1. It is fitting that the desire of our inclination be satisfied to the extent that wholesome honors will be directed to your devotion, since one who converses with you in genuine thought is always restored with happy rejoicing. And therefore, greeting your clemency with the appropriate pomp, I commend the bearer of these letters coming on behalf of business of the church of Ravenna with a most pleasing petition to you. When such an opportunity is offered for demonstrating where a reward may be easily acquired, those who desire to flourish always seek out your serenity to provide it. For there is no doubt those who offer things justly receive better in return.

LETTER 10.16 (C. 535)

Presumably following the circumstances of *Variae* 10.13–14, this letter announces to the Senate the delivery of Theodahad's oaths of security for Rome.

King Theodahad to the Senate of Rome

1. Our devotion to you, conscript fathers, is an extremely demanding matter, when we, who are not bound by the conditions of other men, are conquered by our own inclination. For while we possess everything by God's will, we permit ourselves only what must be praiseworthy. You know, wise gentlemen, the truth of the words we speak; now acknowledge the kindness that you ought to have permitted yourselves before. Behold that we do not permit those troubles by which we were deemed to be hostile. Thus it is that a deep suspicion must be conquered by the *Princeps*; thus, ought one have regard who does not want to be harmful. Therefore, our authority has decreed the requested oaths to be offered to you by *ille* and *ille*, because it is not a difficult thing for a well-established king to command, since we have thus granted an assurance to you, so that we would be known to have

---

18. It seems Theodahad sent a representative to Rome to either provide or exact oaths to maintain the peace, probably both.

concealed nothing in our purpose. **2.** Indeed, such things as were promised we are already acting on, since we owe those very things to God, not to man. For how could we, who have perused the sacred literature concerning ancient kingdoms, choose anything other than what we feel to have been pleasing to divine authority in other cases? Truly, God himself is the remunerator of all good works; for whatever we do in devotion to our subjects, we have no doubt that he will repay. Therefore, demonstrate good faith for the assurance you have obtained, since after such a thing, affection ought to be repaid for our clemency, rather than promised.

LETTER 10.17 (C. 535)

This letter announces to the citizenry of Rome the delivery of the oaths of security mentioned in *Variae* 10.16.

King Theodahad to the Roman People

1. Know, O Quirites,[19] with what firmness your *Princeps* cherishes you, such that, even tested by harsh behavior, we would not suffer you to be disturbed, nor have we wanted to delay your pledges in the least, which we have always wanted to be celebrated before the great populations of the republic. For your safety is our adornment and we take true pleasure when we feel you are joyous. Therefore, having read your petitions, we have ordered oaths to be offered to you through *ille* and *ille,* so that you should not consider the intention of your king to be unknown. Nor may it be permitted to wander astray under false impressions, when what you trust in your *Princeps* may be palpably grasped. **2.** Consider how much kindness has been expended on you, when the very man who is unable to be compelled swears an oath. For we know the things we have given to be for the relief of all men: we do not disregard healing our subjects. And therefore, granted that it may seem incongruous to our eminence, we have freely acquiesced to bring about what we deem the public has wanted. Know how much your affection weighs upon us: we who are admonished by sacred literature to preserve oaths, even if only spoken, have been bound to you in faith. Now show your devotion; be continually beholden to supernal majesty, so that the peaceful times that we desire you to have may be granted from heavenly munificence.

LETTER 10.18 (C. LATE 534 OR EARLY 535)

It is not clear whether this letter proceeds or follows chronologically those letters dealing with unrest at Rome (*Var.* 10.13–14 and 10.16–17), but it announces the

---

19. An archaic name for "Romans," referring to the Quirinal Hill, supposedly one of the earliest settlements in what became the city of Rome.

dispatch of an extramural garrison and measures for its provisioning at Rome. It is possible to see the hostile reaction to the garrison in light of the assumption (corrected in this letter) that Rome's people would sustain the garrison's material needs, possibly including forced billeting on private property.

King Theodahad to the Senate of Rome

1. We do not permit, conscript fathers, the cure that we have devised for you with dutiful intention to become harmful to you on account of bitter suspicion, since to plan in secret and to demonstrate a different purpose is the same as physical assault. And so, know that our arms have been sent, rather, on behalf of your safety, so that, with divine assistance, the hand of the Goths ought to stand in the way of whoever may attempt to attack you. For if the watchful shepherd prevents treachery within the herd, if the father who loves his household steals the opportunity of theft from burglars, with what precautions do we defend Rome, which is known to be peerless throughout the world? Let the great heights not be cast into ruin because someone who fails to act against adversity is proven to cherish them less. **2.** But, lest that very defense should become a burden to you in any way, we have ordered the *annona* for the army sent for that purpose to be bought at market prices, so that both the hardship of living abroad would be removed from them and a cause for loss would be avoided by you. In respect to this, we have likewise dispatched our *Maior Domo*,[20] Vuacca, who rightly should be respected for the quality of his own virtues in war, by whose role transgressions should be avoided and the instruments of defense should be diligently prepared. **3.** Nonetheless, we have ordered the army to remain in a suitable location, so that there would be armed defense outside the city, and for you, peaceful civic harmony within. Know what comforting capacity of a *Princeps* has devised for you: that a defense should garrison you, lest a hostile hand offer blockade. And we have removed from danger those whom we protect with the blood of our own people. It would truly be a failure if, during our reign, that city, which had been a terror to nations by its reputation alone, should seem to be protected only by walls. Hence do we request from divine assistance that the insult of a siege not spoil what had always been open.[21]

20. This is the only mention in the collection of a "steward" for the royal household, which may have been a dependency of similar distinction and role to the *spatharius* or "shield bearer" (*Var.* 3.43).

21. This statement seems to have double intent—that the garrison would remove threat of siege by enemy, but the city should remain open lest it become necessary for the Goths to invest the city in siege themselves.

LETTER 10.19 (C. 535)

This letter is clearly concerned with preserving peace between Italy and the eastern empire. Whether or not it was written in response to hostilities initiated by Belisarius or prior is uncertain. It is suggestive, however, that the letter claims that Theodahad had requested the pope and Senate to formulate a response for the eastern envoy Peter, perhaps referring to Justinian's insistence on doctrinal conformity in the "Three Chapters" controversy.

King Theodahad to Justinian, Augustus

1. We give thanks to divine authority, from which the tranquility of kings is always received, that you had declared your clemency's pleasure at our elevation. For it is fitting for you to be able to love one whose attainment of kingly eminence you celebrated. It is proper that one who presumed he would be supported by you is thus favored. Bestow, therefore, the example of your kindness on the whole world, so that one who commends himself to you with sincere affection should be known by how much he may be advanced. **2.** For you do not desire petty quarrels among *regna;* unjust conflicts, which are inimical to good conduct, do not delight you, since it befits you to seek nothing other than what could adorn your reputation. For in what way could you be induced to toss aside peace, which, for the sake of your native piety, you are accustomed to impose even upon wrathful nations? Indeed, we need not mention the blessings of your concord. Whatever will be shared with you in praiseworthy affection is considered entirely distinguished. **3.** Even though you are thoroughly wondrous, glorious *Princeps,* something is still gained, even by you, when every *regnum* venerates you. For it is expected to be praised by all in your own *imperium,* but it is something entirely exceptional to find praise for yourself among a foreign people, since apprehension compels none where opinions are open. You are clearly cherished in your own *regnum,* most dutiful *Imperator;* but how much more remarkable is it that you are loved more in the Italian provinces, whence it is known the Roman name was diffused throughout the compass of the world! It is therefore fitting that your peace, which conferred the glorious commencement of our title, should be preserved. **4.** But so that we may be seen to respond in accordance with holy affection, with the most reverent greeting hastened by pious feeling, we have recommended to the blessed pope of Rome and that greatest Senate, advised by our injunction, that the most eloquent legate of your serenity, Peter, being distinguished in the purity of good conscience and elevated by learning, should receive a legal response without any hesitation, lest he should endure any delays contrary to your will, since we desire what should not prejudice your decision to be thoroughly accomplished, especially when we know your piety to be eager for what we feel would benefit us in every way. **5.** For which, we believed our legate must accompany that venerable man, not for the sake of your legate, but rather that you would be able to know our intentions from our own messenger.

LETTER 10.20 (C. 535)

This letter suggests ongoing communication between Theodahad and Theodora, with the intention of finding support for Theodahad with the emperor. Based on a reference to a response requested from the pope and Senate at Rome, which parallels a similar request at *Variae* 10.19.4, the present letter and *Variae* 10.19 should be considered tandem approaches to the same diplomatic issue.

King Theodahad to Theodora, Augusta

1. I have received the letters of your piety with the friendship by which desired things are always claimed, and I have acquired with most reverent satisfaction your verbal message which, loftier than any gift, promises me everything from such serene disposition. Whatever I have been able to desire, I have received from such generous correspondence. 2. For you have encouraged me in order that we would first bring to your attention anything we believe must be sought from your lord husband, the triumphant *Princeps*. Who would now doubt bringing to completion a purpose that such power deems worthy to represent? Indeed, previously we presumed upon the equity of our causes, but now we are fully overjoyed at your promise. For our desires may not be postponed when they involve a patroness who deserves to be heard. Now fulfill your promises, so that you may accomplish with delicacy that purpose for which you have enjoined such certain hope. 3. It also adds to my joy that your serenity has dispatched a man of such distinction as great glory ought to send and who is fitting for your service to retain. For there is no doubt that a woman by whom good conduct is practiced so diligently will select the same, when a mind instructed in good precepts is known to be untroubled. Hence, advised by your reverence, we have given commands that the most blessed pope and that greatest Senate should respond to what you judged must be sought from them,[22] so that your glory, whom an inclination for delay opposed, will not be judged less deserving of reverence, but rather your gracious pledges would increase from the celerity of the deed. 4. For even concerning that person, about whom something tentative reached me by word of mouth, know that what we believe agrees with your designs has been arranged.[23] For such is our desire that,

---

22. This seems to be a reference to the same response from the pope and Senate requested at *Var.* 10.19.4.

23. It has been conjectured that this is a reference to the death of Amalasuntha, which Procopius claimed in his *Anecdoton* occurred through the intrigue of both Theodahad and Theodora; the reference is clearly to a female (*qua*), and the use of *persona* in the *Variae* typically indicates someone with a public role.

with your favor mediating, you may command no less in our *regnum* as in your *imperium*. We also declare that we caused the above-mentioned statement to be issued by the venerable pope before the bearer of these letters, your legate, had been able to leave Rome, lest anything should happen that would obviate your intentions. **5.** Therefore, greeting you with the reverence that ought to be displayed for such merits, we have taken particular care that the respectable gentleman *ille* must be sent to your clemency in the role of our representative. He is capable in conduct and learning, and owed respect for his sacred office, since we believed those persons would be pleasing to you whom we judged to be instructed in the divine mysteries.

LETTER 10.21 (C. 535)

The first of two letters written in the name of Theodahad's wife and royal consort (cf. *Var.* 10.24), it represents both the importance of securing patronage from the imperial family in the east and also Amalasuntha's absence from court affairs.

Queen Gudeliva to Theodora, Augusta

1. It is fitting for you to consider, wisest *Augusta*, how enthusiastically I desire to attain your favor, which my lord husband also desires to obtain with great eagerness. For although this may be entirely dear to him, it is nevertheless known to be a special matter to me, when the love of such a great matron is so able to elevate me that I may come to know something greater beyond a *regnum*. For what could be more pleasing than that I should appear to be a partner in the exchange of affection with your glory, so that, since you shine so abundantly, you would gladly share your own splendor with us, when it does not detract from light to bestow its own brilliant illumination on another? Cherish our desires, which you know by their particular sincerity. Your favor commends us through every *regnum*. For you ought to shed brilliance upon us, we who want to shine with your light. **2.** Therefore, sending the respect of salutations to your serenity, with the presumption of affection, I commend myself to your heart, hoping that your wondrous prudence may arrange all things such that trust, which is committed to us from your heart, may increase more abundantly. For although it would be appropriate for no discord to abide between the Roman *regna*, nonetheless, a situation of importance has emerged which ought to make us even more dependent upon your sense of equity.

LETTER 10.22 (C. 535)

A continuation of attempts to reach a diplomatic solution with the eastern emperor, this letter has an urgent tone suggesting the Gothic War had reached Italy.

King *Theodahad to the* Imperator *Justinian*

1. Our legate and that most learned man Peter, whom your piety recently dispatched to us, both remind you, wisest of *Principes,* with what zeal we desire concord with your august serenity. And now we believe the same attempt must be renewed again through that most blessed man, *ille,* so that you would judge as true and good-natured what you recognize has been sought repeatedly. Indeed, we who have no cause for conflict, seek peace with all sincerity. Therefore, let this great thing come to us, so arranged, so glorious, that we may seem justified in seeking it with such great entreaties. But it would be a failure if what has been conjoined on our behalf should weigh heavily. **2.** Act, rather, that it would be agreeable to us. One who must settle a cause according to reason is not able to show preference for his own advantage; it is to his greater glory to take responsibility for future affairs. Consider too, learned *Princeps,* and recall from the historical testimonials of your books, how much your predecessors strove to depart from their own lawful advantage, so that they could create alliances with our ancestors. Estimate with what gratitude the concessions which were customarily demanded ought to be received. We, who depend upon the truth, do not speak arrogantly. What we strive to demonstrate profits your glory instead, when those who recognize that they are more fortunate than their forebears now seek your favor in addition. Let those whom you formerly bound to yourself for the sake of generosity be tied to your heart in voluntary friendship; let those blessings, which you surpass with abundant kindness and flowing rewards, not be credited only to former times. **3.** And therefore, extending the honor of greeting, we have caused the venerable *ille,* distinguished by priesthood and conspicuous for the fame of his learning, to bear the desires of our embassy to your piety. For trusting in divine virtue, that he will please you abundantly with his merits and obtain the object of an honest petition, we believe that we ought to receive him quickly with the object of these exchanges attained. But since it is not possible to include everything in epistolary correspondence, we have entrusted certain matters which must be disclosed to your sacred attention by mouth, lest the extended reading of documents should be distasteful to you.

LETTER 10.23 (C. 535)

This letter has a tone that is decidedly more optimistic than previous letters to the eastern court, although it is not clear what may have transpired that could have emboldened Theodahad's assessment of the state of affairs. Nonetheless, it is clear that the ratification of a treaty has been entrusted to the intervention of the empress, who is expected to advocate in favor of terms that would not be overly harsh.

King Theodahad to Theodora, Augusta

1. Having received your most eloquent legate, Peter and, what is more honorable than any distinctions, complying with your requests, those things desired by us have flashed like monuments to your august favor, so that we learn through him that what has occurred in this republic is acceptable to you. You have shown that you esteem whatever obviously pertains to justice, when the desired concord, having been cleansed of any suspicion through divine providence, is able to endure. It is rather now that a firm oath and prayed-for harmony may conjoin our *regna*. **2.** And therefore, we believed our legate, the venerable *ille* must be sent in particular to you, for he is truly worthy of your audience, so that, by your careful attention, the grace of peace should be confirmed by your most serene husband, to the extent that the public may clearly know that we have duly attained the blessing of an alliance through the great bond of love. **3.** And since nothing begun well ought to be interrupted by mishap, if there is anything so harsh that should not be imposed upon us, let it be mitigated by the moderation of your wisdom, so that we may increase with perpetual zeal the affection that we have begun to hold for your *regnum*. **4.** Therefore, erect the strength of your wisdom and claim this as your particular laurel of peace, so that, just as the glorious fame of a forgiving *Imperator* is proclaimed on the battlefield, thus in the practice of peace, your reputation will be praised to the admiration of all. Let the bearer of these letters whom I have sent have audience with you regularly and in private, to the extent that one who is clearly sent on the presumption of favor should be able to attain immediate effect. For we hope for things that are just, not onerous, although we know that nothing we entrust to such a glorious patron may seem impossible.

LETTER 10.24 (C. 535)

This letter to the eastern empress from Theodahad's wife and royal consort was probably intended as a companion to the overture made in *Variae* 10.23, much as had been the case with *Variae* 10.20–21.

Queen Gudeliva to Theodora, Augusta

1. With the arrival of wise Peter, the love of your serenity has thus satisfied us, so that we count ourselves as having seen you, whose gracious conversation we have shared. For who, having received such great affability, would not return the bounty of veneration to one, whom loyal service is rightly owed for her own patronage in everything, rather than for the declaration of her rank? **2.** And therefore, we have taken care that the respectable legation of our lord husband must be directed specifically to your healthful eminence through *ille*, so that, returning our affection to your serenity, he may bring delight regarding the preservation of peace and he may cause us to rejoice in celebration of a secured favor. For by such an advantage both the order of affairs is well disposed and the twin affection of your tranquility is increased. Therefore, may we receive the goodness of your heart, since it is a truly royal purpose to enjoy the glorious affection of all people. **3.** We have entrusted certain things that must be related verbally to you through the bearer of these letters, which you should gladly receive and easily grant, with God's assistance, on account of your native kindness.

LETTER 10.25 (C. 535)

A brief note relating to Justinian the fact that Theodahad has forwarded the emperor's letters to the pope in Rome. The content of these letters may be assumed to be theological in nature, as witnessed in the *Collectio Avellana*, upon which peace between East and West, so belabored in previous letters to Justinian, probably depended.

King *Theodahad to the* Imperator *Justinian*

1. The august letter of your serenity has poured illumination upon us through the venerable presbyter Heracleanus, granting the kindly grace of conversation with you and aptly imparting the gift of greeting, so that, in a real sense, it was a great blessing to have earned such sweet conversation with the *Princeps*. We return our response by him with as much affection as we are able, hoping that we may continue to often hear of your well-being and that the happiness of your *regnum* may ever increase, since it is fitting that we harbor such a desire as would continually extend your glory and health. **2.** We also inform you that we have sent letters to the pope of Rome on your behalf, so that he may respond to the bearer of the present letters without any delay, to the extent that anyone who has been directed by you may be attended with the grace of haste. For it is our wish that opportunities arise, in which we shall be able to obey your desires, since thus do we effectively remind you of returning that affection, if we may serve you in any way.

LETTER 10.26 (C. 535)

An interesting perspective of the extent of Justinian's involvement in Italian affairs, Theodahad here responds to reports that have reached Justinian concerning the treatment of men and women of religious orders.

King *Theodahad to the* Imperator *Justinian*

1. We understand that the favor of your serenity is richer than any kind of gift, when you exhort us to do what pertains to our advantage in every way. Such indeed is the wish of one who always loves you, that you would want us to act on opportunities of mercy which would be able to commend us to divine power. **2.** And therefore, we inform your glory concerning a monastery of the servants of God, which was suggested to you to labor with a burdensome allotment of taxes, because in that place where the land of the monastery has been flooded with excessive rainfall, the infection of sterility has diminished it with hostile saturation. Not withstanding, we have given an order to the most eminent *Praefectus Praetorio*, Senator,[24] so that, by his provident administration, he should send a diligent inspector to the estate under dispute and, with the matter examined by reasonable inquiry, whatever burden the property may sustain will be reasonably annulled, so that thus a suitable and sufficient profit will remain for the owners, since we judge that it would truly be a more precious profit to us that we concede to the inclination of your kindness. **3.** Also, regarding the case of Ranilda, concerning which it was worthwhile that your serenity advise me, although it happened long before under the *regnum* of our kinsman, it was nevertheless important to us to settle the business from our own largesse, so that, with such a matter decided, she would not regret the change of religion.[25] **4.** Indeed, we have not presumed to render judgment in her affairs, where we especially lack jurisdiction. For while divine authority permits various religions, we would not dare to impose a single faith. For we recall reading that we must sacrifice willingly to the Lord, not at the command of anyone compelling us: because he who attempts to do otherwise clearly resists heavenly ordinances. Therefore, your piety rightly summons us to that which divine mandate requires of us.

LETTER 10.27 (C. 535–36)

Where the previous letter (*Var.* 10.26) had promised to instruct Cassiodorus to relieve the tax burden of a monastery, here he has been ordered to provide subsidized grain distributions for the provinces of Liguria and Venetia.

King Theodahad to Senator, Praefectus Praetorio

1. Whoever hastens to assist taxpayers in some measure is known not to give relief, but rather to return due payment. For what is more just than conferring on the petitioner that which he himself toiled to produce? It may be that the idle are supported out of compassion; the cultivator of a field is abandoned to future famine, unless he is assisted when necessity requires it. **2.** Therefore, it is said that a surplus has been drawn from the fields of industrious Liguria and from the loyal Venetians: now, let it

---

24. Cassiodorus.

25. Nothing further is known about this case or the woman, who apparently converted to a Christian creed to which Justinian was sympathetic and then petitioned the emperor concerning some unspecified prejudice against her.

instead be harvested from the granaries, since it is exceedingly impious for needy cultivators to hunger on account of chambers brimming with grain. And therefore, your *illustris* magnitude, whose office is read to have been constituted for this purpose, that you would have the power to satisfy from stored surplus the people whom you know are in want, apportion a third measure from the granaries of Ticinum and Dertona to be distributed to the Ligurians, at a rate of twenty-five *modii* per *solidus*. 3. Moreover, cause a third portion from the granaries of Tarvisium and Tridentum to be given to the Venetians at the price set above, so that merciful divine authority will bestow that largess which it recognizes men have practiced with each other. And therefore, assign such men to these distributions that our indulgence may especially reach those who had been least capable of sustaining their own resources.

LETTER 10.28 (C. 535–36)

This letter confirms all subaltern appointments made by Cassiodorus in his capacity as *Praefectus Praetorio*. The letter allows all officials appointed by Cassiodorus to enjoy tenure for five years and assigns penalties for persons who would attempt to discredit or contest those appointments.

King Theodahad to Senator, Praefectus Praetorio

1. What will have been arranged well by magistrates of the palace is appropriate to safeguard royal justice, especially by those whose good conscience is so well-known that they seem incapable of performing recklessly, out of a desire for illegal gain. And therefore, we confirm the appointment of the cashiers of the treasury, the commissaries of grain, wine, and cheese, the stewards of preserved meats and vineyards, the tax agents of the granaries and workshops, and the keepers of provisions and fodder, who pertain to the royal household at Rome and Ravenna, but also those who are known to administer public contracts along the riverbanks of Ticinum, Placentia, or any other places, whomever we find appointed by you, whose judgment we so gladly embrace, that we desire your acts to be observed as though, so to speak, they may be believed to have been ordered by us. Nor do we permit malice of any kind to prevail against those who have received offices of public administration by your judgment. 2. Therefore, let canvassing for the assignment of contracts, always the enemy of justice, fall silent; we hereby properly remove the customary circumstance for intrigue among civil servants; let it not be permitted in any way to attempt to succeed to the aforementioned posts before five years, so long as no criminality rejects those selected by you. Therefore, let those who are, or will be, appointed according to your wish have no fear; let them administer those offices pertaining to them with security; let one whom the probity of service commends not fear to lose their contracts within this five-year period. 3. And so, on account of the scarcity of certain kinds of goods at the present

time, cause the prices to be moderated according to what will have seemed reasonable to your eminence, so that those to whom it is entrusted to discharge each kind of provision should not complain about an unjust burden. But since it is not possible to curtail human ambition except by the dread of loss, if anyone should attempt in any way, whether by canvassing for popular approval or by the petitions of patrons, to obtain those contracts appointed by you, let him bear the penalty of thirty pounds of gold on the spot, which must nonetheless be exacted by you. **4.** But if he is found inadequate to this loss, let one who is unable to meet the above-mentioned fine atone for his transgression with corporal punishment, and anyone who would deceive by his own audacity, who attempts to act contrary to our interdiction by some evasive action, must be branded by the punishment of infamy. For nothing could possibly remain secure and stable if the desires of the envious are continually permitted to enter into illicit plots. But let your magnitude bring this to the attention of all, lest anyone should assume that what he had not known to be prohibited must be excused on account of ignorance.

LETTER 10.29 (C. 535–36)

A particularly interesting specimen of Cassiodorus's interest in natural history (cf. also *Var.* 10.30), this letter grants the *comes* of Ticinum (Pavia) leave of absence from official duties to recuperate from gout at the otherwise unknown natural springs at Bormio. The lurid fascination with the progress of the disease deserves attention, particularly in comparison to other letters concerned with the properties of waters, and the Latin is redolent with comparisons of the human body to the body politic.

King Theodahad to Wisibad, Comes

1. Although the distinguished nobility of your family and the evidence of your great fidelity had recommended you, so that we believed the city of Ticinum must be governed by you as peacefully as you would have defended it in war, being suddenly taken with an invasion of muddy gout, you have instead asked to seek the drying waters of Bormio, and there deliverance from acute suffering. We fulfill your request with a medicinal injunction, so that we might restore with the blessing of a command that health which we rightly expect to find in you. **2.** For it is not right that this disease should disarm such a warlike man with the tyrannies of grievous affliction, a disease which, by miraculous means, forces virile limbs to seize with an infusion of punishing fluid and, growing, fills pliant ligaments with stonelike swelling. When it feels all other parts have been rendered useless, it seeks the hollow cavities of the joints, where, arresting as though in the mire of a swamp, it creates stones from water, and the wandering disease solidly fastens an unsightly rigidity to what nature had granted the grace of flexibility. **3.** This unhealthy suffering and insufferable health binds anything supple, contracts the nerves, and causes a body that has been stricken with no mutilation to shorten. It withers the measure of the body by fastening upon the limbs and, having departed, it is hardly noticed by those made incapable of feeling. The assistance of the limbs is removed from those who survive; the living body is unable to move and thus reduced to senseless members; a man is no longer able to move by his own accord, but is carried by the motion of someone else. The condition is spoken of as a living death worse than any torment, and one who was unable to survive to the final outcome of such punishment is considered to have had the better lot. **4.** For indeed, the sickness departs, but it leaves only a remnant of strength and, in a novel example of misfortune, the suffering seems to withdraw while the diseased man does not cease to be impaired. Even the weighted limbs of debtors are occasionally freed from torture; but the chains of this disease, once it has been able to fasten onto a captive, are known to not release him for the rest of his life. Departing, it leaves a ruinous token of its presence and after the manner of barbarian nations, having claimed the hospitality of the body, it protects its own claim with violence, lest a hostile wholesomeness should perhaps dare to return there, where such a savage entity has laid hold. This is known to be especially hostile in every possible way to those who flourish through the exercise of arms; firm limbs not softened by the waste of sloth and which were unable to be overcome by a foe from without, are instead conquered from within. Therefore, with God's guidance, proceed on your way to the aforementioned place. For it is not right that our warrior should walk at another man's pace. He should be carried on the back of a horse, not by human conveyance, since it is wretched for a brave man to live in this manner, as though unarmed and unable to function. We have related this to you in exaggerated terms, so that you would be seized by an avid desire for pursuits of health. Therefore, use these waters, first in cleansing drink, then in the drying exhalations of the baths, where the indomitable neck of suffering is rightly made to bend, when everywhere within is cleared away with violent purging, everything outside obtains a unrestrained character and it is overcome, as though set in the midst of two gathered armies. Let gifts granted by divine authority be loved for this reason. The advantageous qualities of baths have been given as a defense against this conqueress of humanity, and what is not subdued in a period of ten continuous years, what is not alleviated from within by a thousand concoctions, may be avoided here with the most pleasurable remedy. May divine providence offer the best blessing to one whom we ardently desire to avoid anything that detracts from bodily well-being, so that we may come to know the true reputation of this place rather by your health.

LETTER 10.30 (C. 535 OR 536)

The second of two letters attributed to Theodahad that demonstrate interest in natural history, here the *Praefectus Urbis* has been ordered to restore a bronze statue of an elephant. Although elephants were prominent as symbols of empire, the timing of the decree, in the midst of political unrest at Rome (cf. *Var.* 10.13–14 and 10.16–17), seems questionable, as does the letter's fixation on less ennobling aspects of the animal. Like *Variae* 10.29, the natural history of this letter seems to provide an allegory for the living morbidity of the state.

King Theodahad to Honorius, Praefectus Urbis

1. We learn from the course of your report that along the Via Sacra, which antiquity named on account of many superstitions, the bronze elephants totter near complete ruin, and what would be accustomed to live beyond a thousand years in the flesh seem to endure a lingering death cast in metal. Let your foresight cause the appropriate longevity to be restored to them by strengthening rent limbs with iron fastens; brace also the sagging bellies with a retaining wall, lest that remarkable mass should shamefully give way to ruin. **2.** Even for living elephants, which, while in a kind of genuflection, would lend their enormous limbs to the human occupation of felling trees, a false step is dangerous; those with their full bulk lying prostrate are unable to rise by their own strength, evidently because their feet are not articulated with joints, but they stand continually rigid and unbending in the manner of columns. Whenever such a great mass lies on the ground, then you would believe them to be more crafted of metal, because you would behold living creatures unable to move themselves. They lie overcome as though lifeless bodies: you would deem dead what you should not doubt to be living. And after the fashion of collapsed buildings, they know not how to quit willingly a place that they were able to occupy by their own support. **3.** Such terrible size is unequal to the minutest ant, when it does not enjoy the blessing that is apparently granted by nature to the least animal. They rise with human assistance, by whose skill they are cast down. Even a brute beast, mindful of this favor, knows itself to be restored to its own footing; indeed, it accepts as master the one whom it recognizes as having assisted it. It moves at the pace set by that very governor, willingly takes sustenance from him and, what exceeds the intelligence of all four-legged animals, it does not hesitate to honor on sight the one whom it knows to be the ruler of all affairs; for which reason, if a tyrant should appear, it remains unyielding, nor is it possible to compel this great beast to give to wicked men the attention that it knows to demonstrate to good leaders. **4.** Instead of a hand, it uses a proboscis and gladly accepts rewards offered by the master, since it knows that it survives by his care. It is in fact the handlike proboscis of the aforementioned beast, as I have mentioned, by which it receives things given and transfers victuals to its own mouth. For while it may be the tallest animal, it is formed with a very short neck, so that, because it is not able to crop fodder from the ground, it seems able to satisfy its appetite by this assistance. It always proceeds only with caution, remembering the harmful fall that had been the beginning of its captivity. **5.** Having been coaxed, it exhales its breath, because it is said to be a cure for the human headache. When it approaches water for drinking, it expels the liquid drawn through its hollow proboscis in the manner of a shower and thus it attains what it sought, just as it gladly does what is asked of it. It extends to its master whatever he may demand with diverse movements of the body and it considers the sustenance of its provider to be its own property. Because if anyone has refused to offer what it wants, it is said to discharge such a flood from the opened reservoir of its bladder, so that it would seem to eject a kind of river from its innermost chambers, punishing the contemptuous man with its stench. **6.** For it gladly nurses an insult and is said after a long time to return to the person by whom it feels itself to have been injured. Indeed, it has small eyes, but they move about solemnly. You would believe something regal having been lent its appearance. It despises those playing like fools; anything honest attracts it by its dignity and you would be correct to judge that trivialities displease it. **7.** Its ulcerous skin is furrowed with creases, from which comes the name for the abominable disease of those denied entrance to cities, and which is toughened to such a hardness that you would think the skin to be bony. This hide is torn by no force and penetrated by no point of iron, for which reason did Persian kings lead this beast into battles, in which it never yielded before the onslaught of blows and it terrified enemies by its own mass. **8.** Therefore, it is most pleasing to regard the statues of these creatures, so that those who have not beheld the creature in life may recognize the fabled animal by such a great rendition. And therefore, do not let them perish, when it is on behalf of Roman dignity that the genius of craftsmen store up in that city the wealth that nature is known to have procreated throughout the diverse regions of the world.

LETTER 10.31 (C. 536)

In 536, the Gothic garrison at Rome revolted against Theodahad for his mishandling of the Gothic War in Italy, and he was murdered on a highway fleeing from Rome. In his stead, Witigis was elevated as king, for which this letter serves as notice to other leading Goths requesting legitimation of what had been a coup. According to the *oratio* Cassiodorus gave on the occasion of Witigis's marriage to Amalasuntha's daughter (after Theodahad's death), Witigis had earned military distinction under Theoderic and Athalaric had appointed him *spatharius* (his personal "shield bearer").

King Witigis to All Goths

1. Although every advancement must be attributed to the gift of divine authority, nor is anything consistent with goodness, except what is known to be derived from to that source, nonetheless, the cause of royal office must be particularly connected to supernal judgment, since nothing except that power ordains one whom it is granted that all people obey. Whence, giving thanks to our author with humble satisfaction, we announce that, with the Lord's blessing, our Gothic kinsmen have conferred upon us the royal dignity in the ancestral fashion, by being elevated on a shield among the swords of soldiers, so that arms may grant what a martial reputation prepared. **2.** For you will come to know that I was selected, not in remote chambers, but on the wide and open battlefield; nor was I sought among the refined exchanges of flattering courtiers, but by the resounding of trumpets, so that the Gothic race of Mars, roused by a desire for such uproar, should find for themselves a king of native virtue. For how long could brave men, nourished on the turbulence of war, be expected to bear an unproven *Princeps,* so that however he might labor over their reputation, he could only presume concerning his own courage? For it is necessary that a people deserve to have a ruler whose reputation corresponds with theirs. **3.** For just as you have been able to hear, I was called forth by dangers to our kin and I arrived to undertake a fate shared with you all: but those who were thinking to find a well-practiced king did not permit me to be their military commander.[26] Therefore, approve first divine favor, then the judgment of the Goths, since those who confirm these wishes unanimously make me king over all. Now set aside fear of condemnation, discard suspicions of retribution: under our rule, you need fear nothing adverse.[27] **4.** We who have waged war often know how to cherish brave men. Additionally, I shall stand as witness for each of your men. It is not necessary that another recount your deeds to me, who have come to know everything as a partner to your toils. The Gothic military must never sunder on account of inconsistencies in my command: all that we accomplish will have regard for advantage to our people. We shall not prefer our private affairs; we promise to pursue what adorns the public standing of kings. **5.** Finally, let it be appropriate that we promise that through our *imperium* the Goths should enjoy everything as it had been according to the glorious Theoderic. He was a man uniquely and nobly fitted for the cares of kingship, so that every *Princeps* is rightly considered excellent however much he is known to love that man's examples. On that account, one who is able to imitate his deeds ought to be considered his kinsman. And therefore, with the Lord's blessing, be alert on behalf of the weal of our *regnum* and be untroubled concerning its internal affairs.

LETTER 10.32 (C. 536–40)

With the accession of Witigis in 536, the conflict between Belisarius and the Goths in Italy escalated, including a year-long siege of Rome and culminating with the

---

26. It seems that while the garrison at Rome supported Witigis's elevation, the rest of the Gothic field command may have initially balked.

27. This refers to anxieties that Goths may have had concerning future reprisal for supporting a regicide.

capitulation of Witigis at Ravenna in 540. Diplomatic overtures between Witigis and Justinian would have been few and fraught. This letter may represent an appeal from Witigis as early as his (eventually aborted) siege of Rome or as late as Belisarius's siege of Ravenna.

King Witigis to the Imperator Justinian

1. How valuable the longed-for sweetness of your favor would be to us, most clement *Imperator,* is wholly obvious, as after so many grievous wounds and such great outpouring of blood had been committed, we are nevertheless seen seeking your peace, as though none of your agents should be held accountable for previously harming us. We have endured such things as would shock even those who caused them: harassment without legal redress, hatred without cause, losses without debt. And this should not be ignored as insignificant: this has been inflicted not only in the provinces, but in the very capital of the state.[28] Consider what insults we shirk, so that we would be able to receive your justice. Such a thing has been done, for the world to tell, which deserves to be settled by you so that the public may marvel at your equity. **2.** For if retribution against King Theodahad is sought, I deserve to be cherished: if the praise of Queen Amalasuntha of divine memory is held before your eyes, her daughter ought to be regarded,[29] whom it would have been proper for the effort of all your agents to restore to the *regnum,* so that all nations would be able to acknowledge how you returned such a daughter to a change of fortune. **3.** For truly, this ought to stir you, that by wondrous arrangement, divine authority caused us to know each other before the eminence of *regnum,*[30] so that it bestowed the reason of love on those whom it had conferred the pleasure of meeting. For with what reverence am I able to honor a *Princeps* whom I esteemed when still situated in my previous lot in life? But even now, you are able to restore everything that has happened, when it is not difficult to retain the affection of one who is known to longingly seek your favor. **4.** And therefore, greeting your clemency with the appropriate respect, we inform you that we have sent our legates, *ille* and *ille,* to the wisdom of your serenity, so that you may give thought to everything according to your habit, to the extent that the restored concord between both republics would persevere and so that what was established by *Principes* in times past with commendable report may prosper more in your reign, with divine assistance. But we have entrusted other matters to be communicated to your serenity by word of mouth through the above-mentioned legates, so that they

28. Here referring to the siege of Rome, which could have been ongoing at the time of the letter.

29. Matasuntha, whom Witigis married immediately after claiming the throne.

30. Justinian and Witigis had apparently come into contact before Justinian's accession as emperor, more probably with Witigis acting as envoy for Athalaric to the eastern court in the last year of Justin's reign; on this, cf. *Var.* 10.33.2.

would touch upon anything the brevity of a letter compresses and elaborate our case more fully.

LETTER 10.33 (C. 536–40)

The last letters attributed to Witigis are dedicated to facilitating last-minute diplomacy with Justinian before Belisarius's campaign in Italy eclipsed Gothic kingship at Ravenna. The present piece is a letter of introduction to the *Magister Officiorum* at Constantinople, asking him to facilitate an audience with the emperor for Witigis's legates. Although not named, this official may have been the same Peter the Patrician who had served as envoy to Italy (cf. *Var.* 10.19, 10.22–24) and became *Magister* in 539.

King Witigis to the Magister Officiorum

1. It was fitting that, directing our legates *ille* and *ille* to that most serene *Princeps*, we should also extend through them healthful greetings to your magnitude, so that they would deserve your favor in every way, when they convey the affection of our intent. **2.** And therefore, displaying epistolary gratitude for your merits, we hope that your prudence would support their intention before that most clement *Imperator*, since the things that we seek are so just that they would merit the approval of all wise men. For what should not have been allowed to happen ought to be readily corrected by you. But you are able to arrange everything pleasingly, everything in such a manner as would easily appease, since a favor is accustomed to be sweeter after bitterness has been mollified. It would have been possible for you to refuse an unknown man: I, however, who have seen the adornment of your republic, who have known the noble hearts of so many of your leading men, do not intend to discount myself from the favor of such a pious *Princeps*, if he should want to consider what is just in my case. **3.** For if the other had earned his displeasure,[31] I, who have succeeded that hated man with punishment, ought to be considered most pleasing. I have followed your designs: rewards should be my return, not censure. And therefore, let not that grace to be denied to one upon whom nothing should be grievously blamed. And so also, let the hatred lie buried with the death of the sinner. For even if we should perhaps merit less from you, let Roman liberty be considered, which is stricken everywhere by the tumult of war. It suffices to have said only a few words to your wisdom, since what is extended from deep within the breast, being carefully weighed, is always increased.

---

31. Theodahad.

LETTER 10.34 (C. 536–40)

A brief letter introducing his legates to bishops, from whom they should receive provisions for travel and probably letters of support addressed to the emperor. As Witigis's bishops (*episcopis suis*), it is not clear whether these were Catholic bishops or bishops of the Arian creed (*vobis religione iunctos*).

King Witigis to His Bishops

1. If we owe respect even to priests unknown to us, how much more do we owe to those whom we have regarded with venerable affection! We consider the known and acknowledge the unknown alike. But the affection of those seen is always greater, when one who is conjoined to us in frequent and pleasing conversation is remembered with gratitude. And therefore, through our envoys, the bearers of these letters, whom we have sent to that most serene *Princeps*, we offer to your sanctity the service of owed respect, so that you would deign to speak on our behalf and so that they may find your solace in whatever circumstance required, since it is important that you who are known to be joined to us in religion should wish us well.

LETTER 10.35 (C. 536 OR 537)

This final letter in Witigis's diplomatic mission to Justinian is a letter of introduction meant to facilitate the travel of the envoys from Italy to the eastern court at Constantinople.

King Witigis to the Praefectus of *Thessalonica*

1. We have sent to that most serene *Princeps*, with God's favor, our legates *ille* and *ille*, men through whom it was important to render the affection of greeting to your magnitude, because it is owed to your distinction and wisdom, so that we may enjoy the grace of conversation with you. However, we would prefer of your excellence that those whom you observe us to have sent with all haste should not endure delay, to the extent that we may appeal to your services, should we learn they have encountered the least hindrance.

Book 11

PREFACE (C. 538-54)

The second preface of the collection which introduces the two books of letters written by Cassiodorus in his own name is a rhetorically elaborate document. The primary concern is to defend Cassiodorus against the criticism of future readers, although the preface also signals his intended audience as officials actively engaged in civil service. Whereas many of the main themes have been repeated from the first preface, Cassiodorus also signals the completion of the *Variae* by describing his next literary project, the composition of a *De anima,* a treatise on the nature of the soul and its capacities.

Preface to the Documents of the Prefecture

1. The assistance of a preface commonly arises out of the anticipation of censure, when it would be helpful to the author to alleviate what could hinder the understanding of the reader. And even if this preface avoids commendation, nonetheless, having been extended, it graciously permits forgiveness, since nobody is able demand from those occupied in affairs what those at leisure ought to give.[1] Therefore, it would be scandalous if it were permitted for such an elevated officer to be free of duties, a man whose own private chamber reverberates with the tumult of legal contentions. But a disseminated opinion will hardly have any effect against

---

1. The contrast between *occupati* (persons occupied in the affairs of state) and the *otiosi* (persons at leisure to critique others) is a theme that runs throughout the preface and may have some basis in the opposition Cassiodorus's tenure as *Praefectus Praetorio* (for which, cf. *Var.* 9.24.7 and 11.1.18).

us,[2] because when we are judged as needing to write better, we are also known to have been occupied. **2.** Truthfully, it is more convenient to conceal something blameworthy in darkness, than to spread with bold presumption what should be censured. Indeed, a leisured reader will be able to hold this against me, if I have deployed a word with careless haste, if I have not clothed plain meaning with the charm of rhetoric, if I have not followed precepts of the ancients appropriate to people's public station. An engaged man, however, whose attention is claimed by a diversity of affairs, on whom it continually weighs to return responses and to whom others continually dictate what must be set aright, will not be unfavorable to me, who recognizes himself to be tried in the very same manner.[3] **3.** A man aware of himself is more readily inclined to absolve another: nor do we always prevail in these matters for which we are sometimes deemed capable. A carefree disposition pours forth cunning invention; an occupied mind produces measured words.[4] In some circumstances it is thoroughly proper that a composition is refined, since rhetoric is practiced in our present capacity, so greatly is mental acuity associated with imperial favor. **4.** And so let the unexpected brevity of the books, which no man may defend for long, except one who is expected to instruct well, abide for the purpose of excusing blame. But lest anyone should perhaps be offended, because, having been vested with praetorian authority, I reported fewer things than I had accomplished, let him know that this was done by the presumption of that most wise man, Felix, whose advice I share in every affair.[5] **5.** For indeed, this man was first purified by the sincerity of his good character, exceptional in knowledge of the law, distinguished by the aptness of his diction, young with the maturity of age, a charming disputant, and a man of proportionate refinement in speaking, who neatly discharged the affairs of state by finding a favorable outcome rather than by his own argumentation. Otherwise burdened by such a mass of affairs, I would have either been found unequal to the task or perhaps aloof. But it was better, because, refreshed by his exertion, I attended to royal affairs, so that I had not be found deficient in more taxing matters. **6.** And so I have combined two books of pronouncements from the tenure of my prefecture, so that I, who have acted as the royal spokesman in ten books, should not be considered unknown for my own role, since it would be exceedingly absurd that I, who was

2. This calls to mind Cassiodorus's statement from Horace concerning the volatility of publication *Praefatio* 1.2.

3. From this it is clear that Cassiodorus's intended audience consisted of other public officials.

4. The *laetum ingenium* of Cassiodorus's critics can mean both a "carefree disposition" and a "fertile talent," thus providing agreement with the defense of the first preface, where the contraposition of two extremes (cunning invention paired with leisure and uninspired words paired with political engagement) asks the audience to believe that Cassiodorus was too preoccupied with the affairs of state to include anything worthy of suspicion in the text.

5. Quite possibly the Flavius Felix, consul of *Var.* 2.1–3.

known to have said so much on behalf of others, should fall silent concerning the office I attained. **7.** But after I had concluded the twelve books of my work with the desired end, my friends compelled me to speak about the substance of the soul and its virtues, so that we should be known to say something about that very means by which we had declaimed so much.[6] **8.** Now, learned men, forgive and cherish these imperfect letters: for if I deserve nothing in reward for eloquence, I must at least be considered on account of most dutiful exertion. I was occupied with concerns so important to the republic that if I had been free of pressing cares, I would have glorified myself with Tullian eloquence.[7] For even that font of eloquence, when he was asked to speak, is reported to have excused himself, because he had not read the previous day. What, then, would befall others, if such a praised individual is seen to require the assistance of authors? Even a perfected talent languishes unless it is refreshed with continued reading. Granaries that have not been stocked with careful replenishment are quickly exhausted. **9.** That same treasury is easily squandered if it is not refilled again with money. Thus is the human faculty quickly reduced in its own substance when it is not fattened with influence from another. However, if we are fragrant with anything, it is the blossom of studies, which nonetheless withers, if plucked from the stem of reading. Thence it is possible to be the happiest, whence one is taught and reborn, because everything thrives the fullest at its own source, when it is not removed from its native bosom. Accordingly, it is more forgivable if, not being devoid of reading, we have written, than if, not having read, we are read. But let us now move away from a desire for excuse, lest an overly elaborate defense should offend more.

LETTER 11.1 (C. 533)

The longest letter in the collection, Cassiodorus here addresses the Senate in gratitude for his appointment as *Praefectus Praetorio*. Although Cassiodorus received the office during the reign of Athalaric, the greater portion of the letter is an epistolary panegyric of Amalasuntha, who acted as regent during her son's minority. The letter is also noteworthy for its commentary on relations with other states at the time of Cassiodorus's appointment.

Praefectus Praetorio *Senator to the Senate of Rome*

1. You commend me in my promotion, conscript fathers, if I know you had desired this for your order: for I believe that an outcome so many blessed men had clearly preferred would arrive most propitiously. Indeed, your approval is a premonition

---

6. The *De anima*, which Cassiodorus called the thirteenth book of the *Variae* (at *Expositio Psalmorum* 145.2).

7. A reference to Cicero, also alluded to in *Praefatio* 1.13.

for all good things, when no one is able to receive the commendation of such great men, unless divine authority has arranged for him to be advanced. Receive, therefore, my gratitude, even as you exact obedient service. It is in the nature of things to love a colleague. But truly, you exalt your own reputation, if you applaud an honor that has been given to a Senator.[8] **2.** May concern for the senators drive me unswervingly toward the public weal, so that I may be credited with your acclamation more, when I have earned the pleasure of such solace. After the *Principes,* my next concern is to commend myself to you, since we trust that you love what we feel the masters of the state intend: first, that we judge honesty to be serviceable, so that justice, as though a handmaid, would always attend our public acts and that we not shamefully barter away an office that we received by integrity, without purchase, from a *Princeps.* **3.** You have heard it spoken already, leading men, what a weight of affairs I have assumed.[9] A celebrated entrance to the summit of office requires more than strength. We dare not speak this falsely, but confess the role to be overwhelming: for such judgment does not discover merit, but rather makes it. For we, who know our masters have wanted to elevate humility, neither boast about this, nor should they seem to bestow such remarkable distinction on the unworthy. The blessings of a celebrated reign seize us and invite us, as though parched from long thirst, to a draught of the sweetest savor. **4.** O blessed fortune of the age! With the *Princeps* at leisure, the favor of the mother rules, through whom everything is accomplished in such a way that the good will of the public may be felt covering us. To her, the one whom all resources serve offers glorious obedience,[10] and, by a miraculous admixture of concord between them, he now begins to command his own character before he is able to govern the people. It is easily the most difficult kind of imperial reign, for a young man to rule his own passions. It is an entirely rare blessing for a master to triumph over his own conduct, and in the flush of youth to arrive at what aged modesty is hardly capable of attaining. **5.** Let us rejoice, conscript fathers, and let us give thanks to heavenly majesty in humble devotion, when at the arrival of the right time, clemency will not be difficult for our *Princeps,* who learned to serve in devotion to his subjects in his adolescent years. But let us attribute this wonder to the morals of them both: for the maternal genius is so great in her, whom even a foreign *Princeps* by right ought to serve.[11] **6.** For every *regnum* most properly venerates her, to see her is awesome, to hear her speaking, a marvel. For in what tongue is she shown not to be the most practiced? She is learned in the brilliance of Greek eloquence; she shines in the presentation of Roman discourse;

---

8. An obvious pun on Cassiodorus's own cognomen.

9. A reference to the announcement given in Athalaric's name at *Var.* 9.25.

10. Athalaric.

11. An interesting insight into the view of Amalasuntha's position vis á vis Justinian's prior to Athalaric's death. If Theoderic's reign was understood in truly imperial terms, his appointment by Zeno made his heirs senior to Justinian, after a fashion.

she glories in the wealth of her native speech; she surpasses all in their own languages, while she is equally inspiring in each. For if it is wise to be accomplished in one's native tongue, what would we be able to claim concerning an intellect so great that it preserves so many kinds of eloquence with flawless execution? **7.** Hence, a great and needed assistance comes to diverse nations, because none lack for interpretation in the presence of our wisest matron's hearing. For neither does the envoy suffer delay, nor the petitioner any loss from the slowness of a translator, when both are heard in their native words and are addressed with an answer in their father's tongue. Conjoined to these qualities, as though an extraordinary diadem, is a priceless familiarity with literature, through which, since it teaches the wisdom of the ancients, her royal dignity is ever increased. **8.** But, although she rejoices in such fluency with languages, she is so demure in public events that it may be credited to disinterest. She dissolves tangled litigation with a few words, she settles seething quarrels with calm, she manages the public weal in silence. You do not hear proclaimed what is openly adopted and, by a miraculous restraint, she accomplishes surreptitiously what she knows must be done in great haste. **9.** What similar distinction has antiquity produced? We have learned of Placidia:[12] celebrated by reputation across the world, glorious in a line of a number of *Principes,* she was devoted to her purple-clad son, whose *imperium* diminished shamefully because she administrated it carelessly. At length, she purchased a daughter-in-law for herself by the loss of Illyricum and the union of rulers was accomplished through the lamentable division of provinces.[13] She also sapped the military with excessive inactivity. Warded by his mother, he endured what an abandoned child would hardly be able to bear. **10.** But with this matron, who follows as many kings as she has kinsmen, with God's blessing, our army terrifies foreign peoples: the army is balanced by provident policy, neither ground down with constant campaigning, nor again enervated by long peace. Furthermore, at the very beginning of the reign, when novelty always tests uncertainties, she caused the Danube to be Roman against the will of the eastern *Princeps.* **11.** What the invaders suffered is well known, on which account I judge it must be passed over, lest the spirit of an allied *Princeps* should retain the shame of defeat. For what he felt concerning our territories was made known, when, having been beaten, he conferred a peace which he was unwilling to grant others when prevailed upon. It is added that, so rarely sought, he has furnished so many embassies to us and her unequalled excellence has diminished the awe of eastern grandeur, so that she would elevate the masters of Italy. **12.** Even the Franks, so able in victories over barbarians, how they were thrown into disorder by that

12. Galla Placidia was the daughter of Emperor Theodosius I, the sister of Emperor Honorius and the mother of Emperor Valentinian III, during whose early reign she ruled as regent much as Amalasuntha.

13. This was the marriage of Valentinian III to Licinia Eudoxia, the daughter of the eastern Emperor Theodosius II.

great expedition![14] Those who always wage war on other nations by sudden assault, when challenged, feared to enter battle with our soldiers. Although an arrogant nation, they declined confrontation, but they nevertheless failed to avoid the death of their own king. For that other Theoderic, long glorified by a mighty name, died to the triumph of our *Principes,* overcome by torpor, rather than in battle,[15] I believe by divine arrangement, lest wars between relations by marriage should pollute us, or lest a justly raised army should not enjoy some retribution. Well done sword-girt Goths, more welcome than any good fortune, you, who felled a royal host at the head and endured the death of not the least soldier. **13.** Indeed, the Burgundian too, in order to regain his own territory, has become devoted, surrendering himself completely, while he received something meager in return.[16] Indeed, he decided to obey, with territory intact, rather than resist in a diminished state. He then defended his *regnum* more carefully when he set aside his arms. For he recovered by entreaty what he lost in battle. Blessed are you, matron, in resounding fame, for whom every pretext for conflict is removed by divine favor, when you either conquer adversaries of the republic through heavenly favor or you join them to your *imperium* by unexpected generosity. **14.** Rejoice, Goths and Romans alike, at what all may call a proper marvel. Behold, by God's favor, the fortunate matron has achieved what both sexes consider extraordinary: for she has reared a magnificent king for us and she defends the broadest *imperium* with strength of spirit. **15.** So much of this pertains to war, as it has been reported. But if we want to enter the halls of her devotion, hardly "a hundred tongues and a hundred mouths" would be able to suffice:[17] for her, purpose and justice are equal, but kindness is greater than power. Therefore, let us speak inadequately about weighty matters, a few words about many things. You know how many blessings she has bestowed on our order from heavenly kindness: nothing is in doubt, where the Senate is witness. She has restored the stricken to a better condition, she has elevated with offices the unaggrieved, whom she protects with universal custody, and she has lavished blessings on each. Even now what we declare has increased. **16.** For behold the patrician Liberius,[18] a man practiced in military affairs, beloved by the public, distinguished with merits, attractive in form, but

14. The campaign to eject Franks and Burgundians from southern Gaul after the death of Alaric II in 507.

15. This can only be Theuderic I, the eldest son of Clovis, who inherited the Frankish kingdom of Austrasia in 511 and attempted to reclaim Gothic Gaul before his death in 533 (cf. Gregory of Tours, *Decem libri historiarum* 3.21 and 3.23).

16. Probably Godomar, son of Gundobad; his kingdom of Burgundians was incorporated into the Frankish realm in 534, a year after Cassiodorus became *Praefectus Praetorio.*

17. Virgil, *Aeneid* 6.625.

18. An influential figure in Ostrogothic public life, this interpolation in a panegyric of Amalasuntha is difficult to reconcile, except perhaps as a statement of recent realignment in support for the Amals at this time.

more handsome for his wounds, possessed of the rewards of his own toil, and moreover the *Praefectus Galliarum*: a double honor adorns this outstanding man, so that he would not lose the prefecture which he has managed so well. Acknowledged for merits, for him one reward alone does not suffice. For he has even received the dignity of attending at court,[19] lest one well-deserving should be thought unwelcome for his long absence from the republic. **17.** Oh, the admirable goodwill of the rulers, which has extolled the aforementioned man so greatly that, with the grant of offices, it even deemed his patrimony must be enlarged, which was thus gratefully received by the public, as though everyone believed themselves, rather, to be enriched by his reward, because whatever honor is granted to a deserving man, without doubt is perceived as drawn upon the many. What may I say, therefore, concerning the resolve of her mind, by which she surpasses even widely celebrated philosophers? For an advantageous discourse, and promises abiding in assuredness, issue from the mouth of our matron. **18.** What we say, conscript fathers, is not unproven by us: the one who praises is a true witness, experienced in her virtues. For you know what wishes conspired against me: neither gold nor powerful appeals prevailed; all things were attempted, in order that the glorious constancy of our most wise matron should be proven.[20] **19.** Formal expression demands a challenge to the display of ancient *Augustae* by comparison to her contemporary example. But how would feminine examples be able to compare to one for whom all the fame of men yields? If the royal cohort of her ancestors beheld this woman, they would immediately see their own celebrated qualities, as though in the most refined mirror. For Amalus basked in his good fortune, Ostrogotha in patience, Athala in kindness, Winitarius in equity, Unimundus in beauty, Thorismuth in chastity, Walamer in trust, Theudimer in duty, her illustrious father, as you have already seen, in wisdom. When each individual cause for fame is rightly unable to compare itself with a host of virtues, they would happily confess her to be superior, certainly because, in her, they would recognize each of the whole to be her own. **20.** Think what joy they would have from such an heir, who was able to surpass the merits of each. Perhaps you expect to hear of the good qualities of the *Princeps* separately: one who praises the parent predicts the child abundantly. Next you should recall the exceptional saying of that most eloquent Symmachus,[21] "Happily observing the growth of his virtues, I defer praising his beginnings." Assist me, conscript fathers, and by

19. *Praesentaneam dignitatem*: there were a number of honorary ranks that would provide access to the court and it may be that Liberius assumed the same privilege that Cassidorus's father had received after completing his prefecture (cf. *Var.* 3.28).

20. Here, the general tenor of the preface to Book 11, and *Var.* 9.24.7, all agree in the impression that Cassiodorus's appointment was controversial, possibly as a result of his earlier elevation as *Magister Officiorum*, an office made vacant by Boethius's death.

21. Q. Aurelius Symmachus, consul of 391, was known for eloquent orations; the passage quoted from Cassiodorus does not survive independently.

acting on my behalf, satisfy my debt to our shared masters with your assent: for just as one man is not capable of satisfying the wishes of all, thus are many able to fulfill the requirements of one.

LETTER 11.2 (C. 533)

In this letter, Cassiodorus requests spiritual guidance for the performance of his duties from the pope at Rome. Just as importantly, the letter serves to remind the pope of his responsibility to the needs of the urban populace, for which open communication with the *Praefectus Praetorio* is essential.

Praefectus Praetorio *Senator to Pope John*

1. I must implore you, most blessed father, that the gladness which we receive through you, by God's generosity, we may know to be preserved for us through your prayers. For who would doubt that our prosperity must be attributed to your merits, when we, who have not deserved to be loved by the Lord, attain honor, and in exchange for such things as we have not done, receive the blessings of office? Indeed, by the fasting of clergy, famine is severed from the people; by the tears of grace, foul grief disperses, and through holy men, its departure is accelerated, lest what burdens should drag on longer. 2. And therefore, greeting you with proper formality, which is right, I entreat that you would pray strenuously on behalf of the welfare of those ruling, to the extent that the heavenly *Princeps* may cause their lives to be lengthy, diminish the enemies of the Roman republic, and grant peaceful times. Then, adorning peace, may he bestow needed plenty upon us from the abundance of his granaries. And for me, your son, may he open a spirit of understanding, so that I may follow what is truly useful and avoid what must be shunned. 3. Let that rational strength of the soul offer us counsel; let the face of truth dawn radiantly, lest bodily blindness cloud our mind; let us follow what is within, lest we become lost to ourselves; let wisdom which is wise in its own truth instruct us; let that which shines with heavenly clarity illuminate us. And thus, may public life receive the kind of judge as the universal church would send out as a son. May holy virtue enclose even us among its services, since we are then exposed to the deadly plots of the ancient adversary, when we receive its gifts. 4. Do not leave to me alone the care of that city, which is more secure by your fame. For you preside over the shepherds of the Christian people: in the role of a father, you love all. Therefore, the safety of the urban populace relies upon your reputation, to whom the divinity has entrusted their protection. Therefore, it is appropriate that we have regard for some matters, but you, for everything. Indeed, you pasture the flock entrusted to you spiritually: nevertheless, you are not able to neglect such things as concern the substance of the body. For just as humanity is known by two natures, it is thus for a good father to restore both: first, by holy prayers, avert the seasonal scarcity that

transgressions produce. But if it should befall, would that it doesn't, exigency is properly removed when it has been prepared for under conditions of abundance.[22] **5.** Advise me as to what must be done with urgency. I wish to act well, even by reproof, since the sheep that longs to hear the calls of the shepherd strays with more difficulty, nor does one whom the careful teacher instructs become wicked easily. I am indeed the palatine judge, but I do not desist being your student: for then do we manage affairs properly, if we depart the least from your principles. But since I desire to be advised by your counsel and assisted by your prayers, it must be attributed to you if anything will be found in me other than what is desired. **6.** May that throne, a marvel throughout the world, shield its own cultivators with that affection which,[23] although it may be proffered to the whole world, is known to be more specifically apportioned to us. We hold something particular to the holy apostles, may it not be delivered to another by the sundering force of sins, because Rome has more fortunately deserved to possess in her fold those attestations that the world seeks.[24] **7.** Therefore, with such patrons, we fear nothing, provided the prayers of the bishop are not lacking. It is certainly arduous to satisfy the desires of so many, but divine authority knows how to offer great rewards. May that very authority check the envious; may it make citizens grateful to us by heavenly inspiration, and by your prayers bestow times which may be celebrated as having divine favor.

LETTER 11.3 (C. 533)

Much like *Variae* 11. 2, this letter asks the bishops of the realm to pray on behalf of Cassiodorus's fulfillment of the obligations of his new office, but intriguingly, it also tacitly makes the bishops responsible for reporting to Cassiodorus the actions of subordinate officials whom he sends to act on his behalf. Rather than demonstrating his own subordination to spiritual matters, *Variae* 11. 2 and 11. 3 demonstrate his activation of ecclesiastical networks for the maintenance of public affairs.

Praefectus Praetorio *Senator to Various Bishops*

1. It is a natural habit for a father in the flesh to rejoice in the advancement of his sons, when whatever praise is granted to a distinguished offspring reflects upon the instruction received from the father. You, however, who are spiritual fathers,

---

22. In addition to the obvious spiritual focus of this passage, it may also be an allusive reference to the papacy's role in managing food stores at Rome.

23. The Latin *cultores* could mean both "worshippers" and "husbandmen," in which case it may refer to both the populace of Rome, but perhaps more specifically the clergy of the church.

24. The *sancti apostoli* ("holy apostles") and *confessions* ("attestations") refer to the burial cults of Peter and Paul.

who behold the author of all things with an illuminated mind, do pray diligently to the sacred Trinity on my behalf, so that it may cause the candle waiting in my mind to shine joyously, to the extent that nothing seen within me should be inadequate and that its appearance may incline others toward me. 2. For what does it benefit for a judge to be transparent to others, if he is still rendered obscure to himself? Let one who is worthy to honor a seat of judgment display the dignity of good conscience. Let the judge be untroubled, lest he condemn those wandering astray. Let the Trinity be fortuitously at hand for us, so that unfavorable defects should be rendered absent. Let it bestow its love, so that, having compassion, it would forbid an opportunity for sinning. 3. Therefore, true fathers of the soul, I beseech you in affectionate and honest petition, so that you would pray with silent fasting to the Lord, that he may extend the lives of our *Principes* in a flourishing reign, that as a defender he may diminish the enemies of the republic, that he may give peaceful times, and, for the praise of his own name, he may bring prosperity with tranquility in all affairs, so that he may deign to render me beloved to you. 4. But so that your prayer may also be heard more easily, be attentive to those whom we send concerning various affairs. What we do not know should not be incumbent upon us. Let your testimony accompany their actions, so that a man commended by you should find gratitude in our presence, or blamed, he should find censure. Nor should they be able to impute it to us, if they are not judged to act wrongly when they transgress, so that they may thereby be encouraged to learn inappropriate behavior. 5. Offer to orphans and widows, against harsh circumstances, those comforts pleasing to God; but not so that, what happens through excessive piety when you seek to assist the wretched, you may remove the role set aside for the laws. For if any punishment should perhaps offend, give such admonishments to all alike, so that you would be able to render the laws unnecessary. Exile, holy fathers, the implacable furies of vice to the realm of unclean spirits, temper violence, impoverish avarice, remove theft and isolate luxury, the disease of humanity, from your people. Thus do you thoroughly overcome the author of iniquity, if you remove his enticements from human hearts. 6. Let a bishop teach, lest the judge should punish what he finds. The administration of innocence has been given to you. For if your preaching does not fail, it follows that a punitive course of action may remain idle. And therefore, we who depend less upon secular authority, commend our office to you in full, to the extent that our administration should be conjoined to the prayers of holy men. 7. May what is just please me most intimately. I am not a cunning oath taker; what I promise, I do not willingly unbind. Moreover, I fulfill the obligation of honorable greetings to your sanctity and conclude the text of this letter with an affectionate closing, so that sweeter words might abide in your mind, since the soul commends the last words to itself favorably.

LETTER 11.4 (C. 533)

This letter appoints a *Vices Agens* (deputy assistant) to act as Cassiodorus's viceroy in legal and administrative matters. From the content of *Variae* 11. 5, it appears this agent may have acted as Cassiodorus's representative at Rome.

Praefectus Praetorio Senator to Ambrosius,
Vir Illustris *and* Vices Agens

1. We believe, with God's blessing, our reputation is secure with you, whose good conscience we have proven over a long period through various engagements in the courts. For, if you had shone with the brilliance of justice in the practice of advocacy, what now would you accomplish when advanced to our counsel? Worth truly increases in the one to whom the greater duty is given, when one who has merited presiding over responsibilities at court must already be considered for the role of a judge. Therefore let the voice that resounded in the forum adorn the judge's bench. Thereupon, being absent, you claim the highest honor of cleaving to our side, although what you achieve well on your own will reflect entirely on you. Set in the public eye, you will share both the glory and anxiety with us: but now, we are compelled to attribute only to you whatever praise we have been able to receive in the sight of God. **2.** Therefore, we have decided for you to honor an office that attends to our mandates; we also require your instructions to be obeyed by those justly appointed for the public weal, to the extent that responsibility for discharging the office for the public weal would be yours and no man may claim the audacity of despising that authority. Even if you should decide it necessary to hold anyone liable to legal guarantors, claim the right confidently, since it will be able to lighten our mind more, if we know something has been implemented through you. For in my presence, you would offer only advice; but now that I am absent, deeds are instead required. **3.** The great advantage of such a post is, without a doubt, the fame of good services; but consider what would be required of one upon whom such a title is imposed. Let your labor procure for me solace from the complaints of all. You know what shame neglect will incur. The hazardous reef must be avoided wherever it may threaten. But my sense of precaution brings me to remind you of this, rather than your lack of concern. For we believe that, with God's assistance, you will discharge everything in this duty that we deem to be advantageous for our reputation and for the republic.

LETTER 11.5 (C. 533-35)

This letter directs Cassiodorus's primary agent at Rome to acquire grain for the city. The concluding prayer for a bountiful harvest suggests both crop failure and mismanagement had been at fault.

Praefectus Praetorio *Senator to Ambrosius*,
Vir Illustris *and* Vices Agens

1. I truly trust that you rejoice in these things that we discern your affection to prefer; for in whatever way the affairs of the one man are performed, the wishes of another are fulfilled. But I know that, from the fruit of former friendship, which is even more fortunate for its charm, the sweetness of a pleasant taste will arise, if you would first offer the provisions of the city of Rome through those persons responsible for it, as though it were a distinguished function of our hospitality. **2.** For that reason have we entered upon the inconveniences of travel, for that reason so many anxieties of thought, so that that populace, accustomed to its ancient amenities in the blessed reigns of its rulers,[25] should enjoy freedom from hardships. For it would be far from right that we should be sated with anyone hungering in that city. Their want, because it would be wrong, is our penury. What more need we say? We are incapable of being happy unless we also hear them rejoicing in public. **3.** And so let all kinds of grain, unspoiled with respect to its condition, be gathered, so that baked bread there may be seen displayed for delight, not to inspire grief. Let the proper weights be observed. Let the surplus prevail over desires of the heart; what is sought is not thought to abound. Flee criminal gain and avoid scandalous profit. Whatever is wickedly presumed there plots a personal attack against my soul. Let no man assume that he will be able to claim a profit in that region. We would readily consent to the depletion of our own resources rather than we should allow those of the Romans to diminish, not so that I would capture popular favor and applause, but so that, with God's assistance, I may fulfill my appointed duty through them. **4.** If indeed all citizens must be cherished, then the Romans should merit something more. A city adorned with so many exceptional senators, so greatly blessed with a noble populace, ought to clamor to our *Principes* the praises that a man of a foreign nation would marvel to have heard. For it is proper that the popular adulation which is known to belong to victorious lords should raise itself up there. **5.** Therefore, it must be provided, whatever confidence you may have, whatever great hesitation may appear, since what procures the affection of those citizens for me is truly to our advantage. Those who had been undecided about our ability would celebrate with immediate rejoicing: the prayers and entreaties of those citizens have assisted me and what they had universally claimed to favor profited me in the presence of the lords of state. **6.** Act now, so that this very love should continue with God's assistance, since I fully intend to achieve in return what they thought they had begun auspiciously with me. Let us now seek the wealth of public approval, let us humbly pray for supernal mercy, so that, foremost, divine clemency may grant us the prosperity of the rulers, that negligence should

---

25. The plural *beatissimis regnantium temporibus* may suggest either the reign of Amalasuntha and Athalaric or Amalasuntha and Theodahad.

not diminish the remaining harvest that it offers, and that venality should not detract anything. I promise my trust in you, but I retain the gifts of divine authority with these very things: I offer protection and I exclude the shame of fraudulent trafficking. Moreover, let these things be glorified in the Lord for well-deserved abundance.

LETTER 11.6 (C. 533)

Cassiodorus here appoints a *cancellarius,* or a "bailiff," charged with managing (and screening) admission to the audience hall of the *Praefectus Praetorio.*

Praefectus Praetorio *Senator to Johannus,* Cancellarius

1. Although every public service is discharged according to its own stipulated rank and those who occupy them by appointment of magistrates observe tenures appropriate to each, your distinction is acknowledged not to be held by established practice, for you have deserved to supersede your own superiors. Indeed, those who are known to precede you in official rank render services to you and, in a reversed condition of justice, you appear as one who must be respected by those to whom you clearly ought to be subservient. You conduct this fair inequity, a special ordinance and a particular benefit, with the appearance of a judge, nor is what seems to be claimed from a faultless arrangement able to be reasonably censured. **2.** No man prescribes the nature of your tenure. Your duty is a transgression of the public roster, and you alone confidently ignore what you compel others to observe. But such privileges have been conceded to you on account of your outstanding merits; one known to be our choice ought to be trusted to surpass all men in diligence and good faith. For no man proves himself ready to advance except one to whom a commendable virtue attaches itself; it is shameful to elevate a lesser man, unless he should seem to excel other men in merits. **3.** Therefore, the dignity of a *cancellarius* grants to you this commendable miscarriage of justice, a preferential sentence and a domestic service, from the twelfth indiction, so that you may protect the intimate chambers of our office with complete fidelity. Let those who must be admitted approach through you; let the desires of petitioners become known to our ears through you. May you expedite our orders without attention to private gain and may you accomplish everything else, likewise, so that you would be able to commend our justice. For your service is the reputation of your own judge and just as the interior of a home is able to be known correspondently from its street front, thus the disposition of a head of office is thought to be depicted through you. Cause no insult, since such a thing would cause all men to decide for themselves what kind of a response they should expect. **4.** Would it not be a disgrace to us if the very garments that are placed on our bodies were soiled with some filth? How much more pleasingly are they truly seen to adorn us when they shine with commendable purity! Thus does the secretary before the private chambers of the judge either decorate or besmirch the reputation of his president. Those who oppress others certainly sin against us and when the privilege of the one serving is prostituted, the reputation of the magistrate in office is ruined. **5.** Consider if we ought to ignore how it is that we would come to censure. It is senseless beyond everything that we would not seek to punish one who is known for plotting to our own shame. Behold, by what title you are named.[26] It is not possible to conceal what you will do behind screens. Indeed, you maintain a transparent store front, an open enclosure, windowed doors; and although you may close them carefully, it is necessary that you present yourself to all. For if you were to stand outside, you would not be free of my scrutiny; if you should step within, you would not be able to avoid the observance of those in the court. **6.** See where antiquity determined to place you: you who bask in such brilliance at every turn will be seen from all directions. Thence, turn your ears and heart to our admonition; fix everything that we have ordered in your mind. Let not these words pour through you as though through an empty pipe which appears full only so long as the water flows in it. Be, rather, a receptacle that preserves what is heard because it does not pour out what was received; for it will profit nothing, if whatever words having crossed the thresholds of your ears should please and yet they should not fasten themselves in the chambers of your heart.

LETTER 11.7 (C. 533)

This letter informs officials of the various provinces to notify landowners of the intent to collect land taxes. More importantly, the letter seeks to abolish the exaction of bribes for deferred payments. The letter portrays taxpaying as the joy of citizenship, which corrupt officials deny the landowners.

Praefectus Praetorio *Senator to All Magistrates of the Provincials*

1. What is offered in annual devotion is most justly sought, because what is paid according to public law is known to be a cause almost for celebration. For it is the payment of a tax that causes a subject to be called bountifully dutiful and one who knows that he owes what is duly assessed receives the title of a contributor. What a blessing it is for him to stand unafraid in court, to not fear the public official and who, not compelled to a sense of decency, is allocated an honored position among dutiful men. **2.** For anything that is coerced is dishonorable; nor does one who is compelled to the payment of taxes by the loss of property have the esteem of a contributor; contrary to this, it is worthy of a free man to owe nothing to a debt

---

26. The position of *cancellarius* derived from the *cancellus* ("lattice") that formed a barrier to the presence of a judge.

collector. Only that field is pleasant in which the owner does not fear the unexpected arrival of the collector. Therefore, the proof of payment is rightly called a security, from which not only anxiety but also the property is secured. **3.** And therefore, what is happily announced, we order you and your staff to admonish the landowner, with appropriate moderation, throughout the dioceses of your jurisdiction, so that the devoted subject may complete his payment for the land tax within the constituted amount of time for the twelfth indiction. Thereby, those deferments made through bribery should desist, which are known not for the advantage of the tax payer, but for profit by course of fraud. For whoever claims to alleviate a burden of this sort, imposes an even greater weight of reprehensible bribery.[27] **4.** Let this detestable practice be absent from our tenure and let it be a ploy that must be avoided. Let the landowner pay nothing, except what is owed to the public: for those who strive to cheat us of anything instead work toward their own loss. Therefore, just as we do not want the fiscal burden to become heavier for any reason, thus do we also order, with God's blessing, the predetermined payments to be completed within the constituted amount of time, to the extent that the grateful devotion of the landowners should become known to their masters and the convoluted confusion of deferments should be removed from our accounts. Thence, on each and every occasion, send to our office briefs prepared in the appropriate manner, just as the ancient authority of the laws and the immediate authority of our command is seen to advise you, lest, if you should consider ignoring any portion of this letter, you would cause the danger to yourself to be absolute. **5.** Nonetheless, so that an effect may be more earnestly brought to these most just precepts, we have ordered *ille* and *ille,* men proven by former services, to supervise you and your staff, so that negligence would be able to harm nothing where redoubled care is taken. Whence, act appropriately, if you desire to extend your advancement further. Let ill-gotten gain be unknown to you in every way: you restore the landowner to his duty, if he is not burdened with false debts. It should be accomplished from equity rather than from rapacity. Corrupt practice lives ever in fear of injustice, for what is thought to be gained when good conscience is squandered? In what way is a man able to profit if he is known to have lost his innocence? **6.** Do not ignore the reward that clearly pertains to a good conscience. The agents upon whom we rely have an advocate in us. For I promise to be the remunerator of those whom I will recognize as having conducted themselves with absolute honesty. Take heed, therefore: let praise for you reach me rather than complaints. You could seek no greater profit than if you were to accept no bribes. Only that gain which the taxpayer offers gladly and which the public servant accepts, sure of its legality, should be pursued. I desire not to be your censurer, but your promoter. Have care,

---

27. This is a reference to a common practice by which landowners would bribe collection agents to secure a deferment, thereby compounding their debt by postponement.

then, lest one who covets the role of benefactor should lose patience with you; for one who is compelled against his nature is always more severe in wrath.

LETTER 11.8 (C. 533)

On the surface a general edict, this letter to the provincials acts more as an oration declaiming Cassiodorus's intent to pursue justice, including a brief introductory disquisition on the nature of law. Few specific issues are targeted, rather, the accessibility of the *Praefectus* is elaborated, as is the expectation that the provincials will remain obedient to the laws.

Edict of Praefectus Praetorio *Senator to the Provinces*

1. It was the custom of the ancients to decide new laws, so that they would append whatever seemed lacking for the following generation: now, however, it is sufficient enough for a good conscience to observe the decrees of the ancients. Formerly, the nature of man was roused by this novelty, when they recognized the governance of their own lives to depend on the will of another: but then each law became fixed, because it was not doubted to be soundly constituted by antiquity. Therefore do the laws suffice for us, if their intent should not be exceedingly unclear. What cries of the herald, what troublesome sentences of judges do you attend with expectant ears? **2.** Whoever knows himself to be practiced as a judge of his own character imposes the manner of an upright life. Pay attention to the good acts of all men and you will know nothing that must be dreaded. Refuse the ardor for illicit presumptions: cherish living peacefully; always act without harm. Why would you confound honest things with litigation? Why would you cause what you would immediately fear? If you seek gain, you should instead avoid litigious losses. Nonetheless, if any civil contest should arise, be content with the laws of the fathers: let no man hasten to rebellious behavior, let no man seek refuge in violence. It is a kind of madness to pursue a disorderly purpose in a peaceful age. **3.** But even if this is not true with respect to our magistrates, nevertheless, an understandable hesitancy arises when an untried authority instead attracts fear; it is so much to my purpose, with the blessing of God and of the rulers of state, to promise you everything will be just and moderate. First, because it especially discredits a judge, corrupt bribery will be unknown to me. For my words are not sold in the manner of garments on display. Only a lack of resources, not the cunning of venality, will prompt us to desire anything from you. Nonetheless, where circumstance mitigates, the policy will be moderate; we do not demand what may be purchased, nor do we sequester for appraisal property that is not considered necessary. **4.** Be engaged only in customary practices, untroubled by novelty, since we judge something to be an advantage to us only if, with the Lord's blessing, we preserve you unharmed. No public official will disturb you for his own sake; no collector will burden you with additional exactions. We will keep not only our own hands innocent, but also those of our staff. It is otherwise useless to be a good judge when he refuses personal gain and offers license for it to many others. For they do not thus depart from our policies, so that the practices permitted by others would seem proper. For the favors which, up to this point, used to increase to the detriment of all, have diminished with your love. **5.** We exercise self-restraint in actions, so that, with God's blessing, we are able to require it without shame in public servants. For a declaration that is not supported by example lacks authority, when it would be dishonest to demand good behavior and not to have acted in the same way. Therefore, our administration looks only to the public weal, not private theft. We know what prayers you poured forth on our behalf, with what anxiousness you have been held. It would be unseemly for us to do such things that would cause you to celebrate with less joy. **6.** By the grace of God, our ears are open to receiving the wishes of petitioners. The litigant must be free to see us with his own eyes; he will speak, not with a bribed tongue, but with his own. For neither will a subordinate dictate to us, nor will nobility deserving respect be exhausted by us in court fees. No disgrace, then, will enter our court, no man will leave us less wealthy than he had come. Our personal household knows no difference with the court chambers. Whoever has observed me will find me a judge in each. **7.** Mindful of shame, and with God's blessing, we desire to act according to the mandates we have received from the masters of state. Be dutiful to everything just, so that you would cause me to be a father to the provinces rather than a judge, since the latter grows even more wrathful the less he is given to deeds of impropriety. For if you have offered service to scandalous persons, what should you extend to one whom you know to toil greatly for you? Do not let the established conveniences be denied to the toiling servants of our office, since the very man who does not permit just rewards to be paid opens a way to excess. **8.** Moreover, show obedience to our precepts with equal restraint. Let each man comport his intentions with reason, lest armed terror compel you. The man who recoils from just commands brings hatred upon himself. I will not love one whom I have already compelled. Thus do we want to explain everything that must be done, so that we would not cause you to be diminished by anything compulsory. We desire the blessings granted to you by rulers long ago to be preserved without anything reduced on account of detestable illegality. We want you to experience our elevation only with congratulations and for you to seek blessings from rulers who are known for granting your desires. **9.** Now live in celebration of a fitting security. It will not be necessary to compel one whom you have been able to oblige with willing pledges of good conduct. For whoever hesitates to promise just things under oath to God wants to have the freedom to change, because it has not been promised. Hold, therefore, this suitable assurance of my vow, a mirror of my intention, the likeness of my desire; since I am not known by face, by my vow I may become recognized by the nature of my character. Behold me instead in this report, by which our presence is concealed. My absence is not a loss to you; it is more useful to know a judge in the mind than in the body.

LETTER 11.9 (C. 533)

This letter commands the magistrates of provinces to publish the previous edict (*Var.* 11. 8), in addition to providing a stern reminder of their responsibility to avoid corrupt practices.

Praefectus Praetorio *Senator to Magistrates of the Provincials*

1. Knowing that the opposite may be believed by those who have been ravaged by previous evils, when the human mind easily becomes suspicious concerning what has happened, we have published a notice of our purpose after the fashion of an edict, so that by God's help, we should not burden those whom we wish to be secure with that very concern. For it is no small thing to dread the adversity of future torments, when what is feared is always imagined to appear with more severity. Even the least expectation of censure would be a failure in our reign. The man who is deemed wicked is already defeated in court, since anything will be accepted by the mind when a reasonable suspicion has entered the heart. 2. For which reason, let your command cause this edict to be posted throughout the most frequented places. For it is fitting that just things should be acknowledged by those whom we have determined to be admonished. Let the ardor of all men now be stirred for our happy masters, so that, just as we have not wanted to keep any man in suspense with respect to contrary thoughts, thus should they also show themselves loyal in devotion to those ruling. However, you would bring our honest pledges to effect if you should preside over the provincials equitably. Cherish justice, which may render you beloved and which, by its very nature, may grant an honored advantage. 3. Know the staff assigned to you acts as though a witness to your actions. How great is it to accomplish in the sight of such witnesses what could be proclaimed by the tongues of all men? Know a judgment as though a voice of justice. It does not befit the superior of a magistracy to commit what another man would accuse. What would a litigant fear, when he has witnessed crime ensconced in the public offices? It is only a torment to the wicked if the public office finds them to be contrary to its own character. For it cannot be called discipline, when the very thing will have fled correction. 4. Therefore, strive with us so that good habits may be granted to the provincials, and its scarcity may be removed. It is accomplished with remedies rather than with injury. Whatever becomes a blessing for the distribution of law and is found to be premixed with injuries is a grave evil. Act so that your year might seem brief, since proven justice was found. Let honors be offered to you instead. Indeed, you would abandon the

hardship of political canvassing if you share the same desires as the provincials. We will grant no protection for your actions, nor do we bend the will of the judge to private arbitration. Act accordingly in everything, lest we believe this shameful necessity to then become necessary. **5.** If you would act with the purity of good conscience, you will accomplish the equivalent to our own public position. Obstruct the wicked, and at the same time cherish the innocent. However, should there be anyone who is raised up with bold audacity against your *fasces,* and you are unable to do what is right, either immediately send a messenger with your report, or, if he lacks the strength for coming, let the case be declared in a dispatched report, whenever you have access to the public post, and whenever it would be suitable to hear such matters. And therefore, the case of every kind of excuse has been taken away from you, when you are able either to act upon a problem correctly through your official position, or to announce to us what the troubles may be.

LETTER 11.10 (C. 533–38)

This letter orders provisions by which the personal servant of one of the Amal rulers (it is unknown which) should travel to Mount Lactarius to partake in the natural healing qualities of the locale. The letter dilates on the nature of bodily infirmity, but with more interest in the natural history of the cure, for which this letter offers a stark contrast to *Variae* 10.29. The position of the letter's recipient is unknown, although it could be the *exceptor* of *Variae* 11. 30.

Praefectus Praetorio *Senator to Beatus,* Vir Clarissimus

1. When the clemency of the master of the state, whose wish it is to rejoice for the well-being of all, considered the health of his own servant, Danus, he ordered him to seek the remedies of Mount Lactarius, so that the widely known benefit of the place would assist one for whom human healing profited nothing. This man, resounding with a frequent cough, wasted his limbs with the exhalation of his breast, when natural ministrations failed to restore his own strength to health, enfeebled as it was by excessive shaking. Even the food offered in assistance to the human body, since he could not properly consume it, was rendered useless. Nor does it matter in such a case whether food is consumed or fasting sustained. Day by day, the living substance of the body fails and, as though a cracked jar gradually leaking until empty, is exhausted. **2.** Therefore, for this reason, the divine providence of this mountain has granted a cure for terrible suffering, where the health of the air, harmonizing with the fecundity of fertile meadows, produces a grass stored with the sweetest quality. Herds of cows stuffed from pasturing on this fodder confect a milk of such wholesomeness that this draught alone seems to offer what the counsels of physicians could not produce, restoring the firm vigor of natural health to its former state. **3.** It fills out wasted limbs, revives exhausted strength and thus assists the infirm with a kind of restoration in the same manner as you would banish fatigue with sleep. And so it is a wonder to see these herds exhausted in the midst of such abundant fodder, so that the milky humor proven to restore the afflictions of the human body does not benefit its own source, and in a wondrous manner the animals do not benefit from the herbage whence the limbs of men are enriched. Meager of body, they wander around the thickets of the mountain, appearing slender and as though they suffered the affliction for which they are the remedy. However, the milk is so rich that it coheres to the fingers when it is expressed into containers. **4.** For which reason, offer him the allotted *annona* and necessary conveyance for travel, so that, in the aforementioned place, he may restore his youth with the same provisions by which his infancy was nourished, by suckling on the pasturage of herds. Let spirits laboring from such a disease rise: you need not tremble at the thought of the sweet life on account of bitter antidote. Drink happily what you will feel to be most healthful. It is a kind of happiness to be cured there, where a man sick at heart can freely be fulfilled.

LETTER 11.11 (C. 533–38)

This brief notice announces the publication of a list of set prices, intended to alleviate the inflationary prices of unspecified goods at Ravenna. A list (no longer extant) of the goods and prices was attached to the notice.

Edict Concerning Prices That Must Be Preserved at Ravenna

1. The sale of provisions ought to be subject to a reckoning of conditions of the time, so that an exorbitant price may not be demanded from scarcity, nor cheapness from abundance, but that both the suffering of the buyers and the burden upon querulous merchants should be alleviated with carefully weighed equity. **2.** And therefore, we have attached below the prices of various goods, compared with careful consideration of equality on all scales, so that the protected prices should remain free of all ambiguity. However, if anyone selling goods should not follow what the contents of the present edict indicates, he will find himself compelled to pay the amount of six *solidi* for each infraction and liable to be subjected to corporal punishment, to the extent that dread of loss may frighten him and the threatened penalty may severely vex him.

LETTER 11.12 (C. 533–38)

A curious letter requiring all proprietors of inns and hostels along the Via Flaminia to refrain from fleecing travelers with exorbitant prices.

Edict Concerning Prices along the Via Flaminia

1. If the leisured people of each town are curbed by the justice of prices, how much more assistance should there be for workers, lest the profitability of traveling to and fro should be impaired by the hazards of chance. And therefore, the enterprise of traveling ought to be a respite from worries, lest what is known to be intended for recuperation should instead inflict a reprehensible hardship. Let a guest be refreshed at a fixed price: someone invited for courtesy should not suffer the iniquity of avarice, when it is a shameful practice to attract their business and then terrify them with the enormity of the prices. **2.** One who desires to cheat with a false guise is similar to a brigand: for both the brigand and the proprietor are known to willingly plunder others and to have no regard for justice. Do you not know how much you could gain with moderation? Those who recognized that you conducted business fairly would come to your accommodations from afar. Therefore, let none assume himself to be shielded by the forgetfulness of distance, because he is always familiar to those traveling when those who have endured your commerce come to us daily. **3.** Let you, who grasp with the longing of gain, instead beware the loss of much. For if anyone should be suspected of charging anything other than the prices that our official, sent for that purpose, has agreed upon with the citizens and the bishop of each place, he will find himself sustaining a fine of six *solidi,* and he must be discouraged by flogging. For honest gain from fellow citizens ought to suffice for anyone, lest the highways should instead seem besieged by thieves.

LETTER 11.13 (C. 535)

This letter serves as the Senate's formal request that Justinian recognize Theodahad's kingship. The reference to Libya's liberty indicates the letter should be placed after the Vandalic War (c. 534) and the plea from the personification of Rome suggests that it was written after the death of Amalasuntha (c. 535), when Belisarius's actions had threatened stability in Italy.

The Senate of Rome to Justinian, Augustus

1. It seems a quite honorable and important charge to beseech a dutiful *Princeps* on behalf of the safety of the Roman republic, since it is proper to seek from you what is able to advance our liberty. For among the other blessings that divine providence has conferred upon you especially, nothing more glorious is manifest than that you are everywhere recognized as preeminent. Therefore, we entreat you, most clement *Imperator,* and we extend hopeful hands from the breast of the curia, so that you may offer your most enduring peace to our king, lest we, who have ever been known to be the recipient of your concord, should be allowed to become deserving of your hostility. **2.** If you truly have regard for the Roman name, thus will you concede this kindness to our masters. Your favor exalts and protects us, and we know that what appeals to your disposition is deserved. Therefore, let your agreement bind tranquility for Italy, since we are then loved, if promised affection is conjoined through you. If our prayers still do not seem sufficient for this goal, imagine our country bursting into this pleading speech: **3.** "If at any time I have been pleasing to you, most dutiful of *Principes*, love my protectors. Those who rule me ought to have concord with you, lest such things would begin to happen in my realm as they know would depart from your wishes. For you, who have always bestowed the joys of life, would not be the cause of my cruel destruction. Behold how I have united my fosterlings to your peace, behold how I have radiated the honors to my citizens.[28] If you suffer me to be injured, where then would you extend the reputation of your devotion? For what would you attempt to accomplish more grandly for me, whose religion is yours and which is known to flourish thus? My Senate grows in honors, it ceaselessly increases in resources. **4.** Do not allow what you ought to defend in war to be dismantled in discord. I have had many kings, but none of such literary talent; I have had prudent men, but none so vigorous in learning and piety. I prize the Amal nourished at my breast, a brave man formed in my association, dear to Romans for wisdom, respected among other nations for virtue. Indeed, truly unite your intentions, share your counsels, so that your glory may increase if we attain any prosperity. Do not intend to call upon me in such a way that you would not be able to find me. I am no less in your affection, if you cause none to rend my limbs. **5.** For if Libya deserved to receive liberty through you, it is cruel that I lose what I have always been known to possess. Peerlessly triumphant, control the tumult of your wrath. What the public voice seeks is greater than your temperament being conquered by the wound of some ingratitude." **6.** Rome utters these words, while she implores you through her senators. But if this is as yet of minor importance, consider the most holy petition of the blessed apostles Peter and Paul. What will you, a *Princeps*, not offer on behalf of the merits of those who have often been proven to defend the security of Rome from enemies? But so that all these things may be found agreeable to your reverence, we have decided that our entreaties must be poured forth through the venerable bishop, *ille*, the legate of our most devoted king, sent to your clemency so that many things may be accomplished which, individually, would be possible to obtain in the presence of pious souls.

LETTER 11.14 (C. 533–38)

A charming letter responding to complaints about the burden of the *cursus publicus* upon residents around the region of Lake Como. The exact nature of relief to

---

28. Here the reference to *alumni* ("fosterlings") and *cives* ("citizens") is analogous to Goths and Romans.

be provided is not specified, but the delights of the natural geography of the region receive full attention.

Praefectus Praetorio *Senator to Gaudiosus,*
Cancellarius *of the Province of Liguria*

1. Since the city of Como is sought by many roads, its landowners report that they are exhausted from the constant provision of transport animals,[29] so that they themselves are in fact trampled down by the passage of too many steeds. We extend to them the benefit of a royal indulgence to be perpetually maintained, lest that city, attractively habitable from its location, should become depopulated through the frequency of the damage. For, beyond the distant mountains and the vast expanse of the clear lake is a kind of wall for the Ligurian plain. Although it is evidently a key defense of the province, it unfolds such beauty that it seems to be formed for pleasure alone. **2.** Beyond protection, it disseminates supplies of the cultivated plains, on account of both its aptness for comfortable travel and its generous supply of food. Along the shore, it enjoys the amenity of sixty miles of sweet water, so that the spirit is gratified with delightful refreshment, while the supply of fish is not driven away by storms. Rightly, therefore, it has received the name of Como, rejoicing in the gifts that make it comely. Here the lake is truly enfolded in the depth of a great valley; exquisitely imitating the shape of a shell, it is dappled with white on its foamy shores. **3.** Around it the beautiful peaks of lofty mountains gather like a crown; its coasts are exquisitely adorned by great and gleaming villas, and are enclosed as though by a belt with the perennial greenery of a forest of olives. Above this, leafy vines climb the mountainsides. But the summit itself, curled, so to speak, with thick growth of chestnut trees, is painted by adorning nature. Thence torrents that shine with snowy whiteness are hurled downward by the height, and fall to the levels of the lake. **4.** Into its bays, flowing from the south, the River Adda is received with open jaws. It thus takes such a name because, being fed from a double source, it flows down as though into a sea of its own.[30] Such is the speed with which it enters the waves of the vast expanse that, retaining its form and color, it pours northward in a swollen bellied stream. You would think that a kind of dark line had been drawn across the pale waters and, by miraculous means, the discolored nature of the influx, which is supposed blend with similar fluids, is visible. **5.** This also happens even with the waves of the sea where rivers debouche: but the reason itself is commonly known, as headlong torrents, polluted with muddy filth, differ in color from the glass-clear sea. But this will be rightly thought something astonishing,

29. The *paraveredi* or animals provided at the changing stations of the *cursus publicus.*

30. The Adda rises in the Alps, flows south into Lake Como and then continues south until joining the Po; Cassiodorus has used the river's dual-contact points with the lake to supply an etymology for the Latin name *Addua* ("at two places").

because you may see an element move at great speed through standing water similar in so many characteristics, so that you would imagine a stream, which is unable to commingle in color with foreign waters, to decant through standing fields.[31] **6.** Therefore, it rightly should be used sparingly, for the residents of these regions, when everything charming is too delicate for toiling and those who are accustomed to enjoy sweet delights easily feel the burden of strain. Therefore, let them enjoy a royal gift in perpetuity, so that, just as they rejoice in native luxuries, thus may the munificence of the *Princeps* cause them to celebrate.

LETTER 11.15 (C. 534–35)

This letter announces monetary assistance for the cities of Liguria in the wake of unspecified distress. Given Liguria's location on a frontier with Gaul, it is plausible that the disturbance was an incursion of Franks. The reference to plural *domini* suggests the letter dates to the joint rule of Amalasuntha and Theodahad. The letter indicates that local town councils were responsible for the equitable distribution of aid.[32]

Praefectus Praetorio *Senator to the Ligurians*

1. A royal gift ought to be a joy obtained for all, so that you would be called to better works, when you illustrate those things granted to you to be most pleasing. For if it is always the place of a loving citizen to assist, in what way would you, who have been relieved of duress, be obliged? But lest we delay your happiness with a long preamble, since the swiftest acknowledgment of good things is always preferred, your most glorious masters, having regard for the hardships of the devoted Ligurians with their accustomed piety, send one hundred pounds of gold from their own privy chamber by means of *ille* and *ille,* so that, whichever case is the most worthy in your judgment, let each be gladdened with a portion of the award in measure appropriate to however much it was burdened by hardship, lest an uninjured man appropriate what is awarded for the afflicted; instead, let those who falter under the pressing obligation of losses rise up with renewed strength. **2.** However, the city of Hastensis, which sustained molestation beyond the others, should be assisted in particular by the justice of your arrangements, so that it may enjoy the advantage of the gift in measure according to its loss. Claim this payment of devotion, O tax-bearing citizens, and consider the clemency of your masters; in a reversal of condition, you find yourselves receiving from the treasury what you are accustomed to pay. But so that the blessings of your masters may increase with

---

31. The confluence of bodies of water is described in similar terms by Ammianus Marcellinus, *Res gestae* 15.4.3–6.

32. For possibly analogous events, cf. Gregory of Tours, *Decem libri historiarum* 3.31–32 (on the Frankish reprisal against the death of Amalasuntha).

the hindrance of tax payments removed, let your swift report inform us what you deem must be remitted from the total in each case, so that we may cause an amount to be suspended from the first payment of taxes as the dispatched report will have made clear to us.[33] Therefore, render to your most devoted rulers those prayers of goodwill which you owe, so that the measure of your supplication may accomplish what the citizenry would acknowledge it has received on its own behalf.

LETTER 11.16 (C. 534-35)

With reference to the assistance rendered in *Variae* 11. 15, this letter directs additional attention to securing the loyalty of Ligurians by ordering a review of the weights and measures used in the payment of taxes and by ordering all praetorian officials to submit their tax accounts for thorough review.

Praefectus Praetorio *Senator to the Ligurians*

1. It is proper for us to eagerly encourage those whom royal devotion has determined to assist: for with regard to the subjects on whom the clemency of our rulers is wont to descend, it is, moreover, right to offer them these things out of regard for their worth. You recently gave me thanks because I had conferred hope for good things as a kind of harvest. You have encouraged me to kindness, since you received vowed assistance with great gratitude. I have discharged the duty of a sworn magistrate. What had been promised is now proven to be fulfilled. **2.** We shall, therefore, begin with the weights, since the pronouncement of a magistrate ought to commence there, where it is right to strive for good conscience. Hence it is that you have reported that you are aggravated by weights and measures.[34] And therefore, our attention will make provision, so that the iniquity of none will be able to trouble you further in that regard, since we judge it a grave crime that measures transgress the standard and that weights not have the integrity of fair weight. **3.** Moreover, we have caused the officials of our office, not only the tax assessors but also the collectors, about whom you bemoan having sustained severe losses, to be summoned by our command, so that, with the accounts explained to clarity, they may pay without delay if anything fraudulent is found: for we declare it to be inimical to our tenure in office that one should rejoice at the disadvantage of another. **4.** Now turn prayers to the preparation of that grandest army, procuring everything needed without dispute or any delay. For you effectively constrain me to every kindness, if you joyfully fulfill what has been ordered. Let one whom the public cause urges gladly obey. Only those losses ought to be regretted which

33. That is, the first of three payments made in a given tax cycle.

34. These would be the weights and measures by which taxes would be commuted from commodities and paid in coin value.

the eagerness of cupidity is seen to impose. For what is required for the needs of the state does not trouble the temperament of the wise.

LETTER 11.17 (C. 533-38)

This letter commences a series of brief letters (*Var.* 11. 17–35) which may be thought of as *formulae* for promotion and discharge within the cohorts of officials serving the *Praefectus Praetorio.* The present letter announces the advancement of all praetorian officials to the next available rank on Christmas day, in effect, the award of a Christmas bonus. The theme of staged successions within the bureaucratic hierarchy, with promotions creating vacancies filled by junior colleagues, is illustrated in the following letters.

Annual Promotions of the Praetorian Staff, Which Occur on the Birthday of the Lord

1. If we find living cure on this singular day of redemption, if hope of salvation is offered from a heavenly blessing, it is also fitting for us to apply the medicine of joy to those exhausted from long service, so that the supernal blessings which are gathered for those making trial of secular life may be widely appreciated. It is otherwise a kind of sacrilege to want to rejoice among saddened men and for one who does not attend the grief of others to shun the affection of humanity. It would be much better should he rouse himself on behalf of common happiness, when it is an inducement to great cheer to see so many people rejoicing! **2.** Hence it is that wise men have declared humanity to be of one kind, since each person wants his own change of circumstance to be inseparable from everyone else's. Therefore, let each man share in your appointment, according to his rank on the roster, so that one whose position determines it may receive a degree of advancement. Let one man step forth so that all may follow. He draws the entire corps of men following to promotion when he leaves a post that he performed previously.

LETTER 11.18 (C. 533-38)

This letter confirms the promotion of a *cornicularius* to the position of *tribunus et notarius,* with honorary senatorial rank of *spectabilis.*

Concerning One Who Leaves the Office of Cornicularius

1. The pleasure of advancement that repays the vigils of the deserving so well must be embraced, since the hope of service is granted to young recruits when the opportunity is made available by the veterans. And therefore, let Anthianus, who is reported to have served in praetorian service faultlessly, advance to the honored sight of the *Principes* among the *tribuni et notarii,* so that, according to custom, he may be decorated with the insignia of a *spectabilis* in the royal presence.

LETTER 11.19 (C. 533–38)

This letter confirms promotion to *cornicularius,* a position recently vacated by the promotion of *Variae* 11.18.

Concerning One Who Receives the Office of Cornicularius

1. Let Optatus be assigned to better things, obtaining the consequence of his own name.[35] And therefore, we have decided that the above-mentioned man should claim a duty appropriate to his diligent labors, so that one who blamelessly performed the vigils of recruits should rightly assist the chief officers.

LETTER 11.20 (C. 533–38)

Similar to *Variae* 11. 18, this letter confirms the promotion of a *primiscrinius* to the position of *tribunus et notarius,* with honorary senatorial rank of *spectabilis.*

Concerning One Who Leaves the Office of Primiscrinius

1. You formerly earned the positive assessments, indeed, fulfilling the orders of many others so efficiently: but now, commended even by divine favor, you will be elevated, because you demonstrate yourself to be accomplished in the labors of service. Therefore, come to adore the awe-inspiring purple, supported among the *tribuni et notarii* with the distinction of *spectabilis* rank, so that the legitimacy of your public distinction may sustain you in the sacred company of your *Princeps.*

LETTER 11.21 (C. 533–38)

Similar to *Variae* 11. 19, this letter confirms promotion to *primiscrinius,* a position recently vacated by the promotion of *Variae* 11. 20.

Concerning One Who Receives the Office of Primiscrinius

1. We do not suffer the rewards of the dutiful to be delayed, so that we may direct the attention of all to the exertions of good service. Let us, therefore, grant what is appropriate for those serving, so that by the advancement of senior men, we shall kindle the hearts of those following. And so let Andreas, who is known to have obeyed the praetorian office faultlessly, rise happily in rank as *primiscrinius,* so

---

35. A play on the meaning of recipient's name, *Optatus ad optata.*

that he should rejoice to have found by his own upright conduct a post which cunning knows not how to attain.

LETTER 11.22 (C. 533–38)

This letter promotes an official to the position of *scriniarius*.

Concerning the Scriniarius Actorum

1. One who is commended for accomplishing business entrusted to him justly advances to greater responsibilities. And therefore our authority orders Castellus, whose position on the roster has caused him to rise, to also accept responsibility as *scriniarius actorum*.

LETTER 11.23 (C. 533–38)

This letter promotes an official (*exceptor*) to the maintenance of public correspondence (*cura epistularum*).

Concerning the Office of Correspondence

1. It is permitted that the attainments of Constantinianus claim many things; let our confirmation also commend him. The integrity of mind in him is so truly great that he deserves to be praised with the testimony of his judge. Let this man, thus far advanced, also receive the custody of the records of correspondence, so that he may fully provide evidence of his own integrity, when he beholds the truth of the public record to be entrusted to him.

LETTER 11.24 (C. 533–38)

This letter promotes an official to a position that presumably handled the accounts for military payments.

Concerning the Scriniarius of the Office of Military Affairs

1. The probity of service aptly betokens the increase of distinction, nor should it be otherwise for one who often happens to be proven effective. Hence it is that we have ordered Lucinus to be *scriniarius* of military affairs; let him demonstrate that loyalty rightly attributed to him without hesitation.

LETTER 11.25 (C. 533–38)

This letter promotes an official to the head of a department of legal secretaries (*exceptores*).

Concerning the Primicerius *of the* Exceptores

1. It is fitting that we continually bestow the ascent of promotion that assiduous toil in public service deserves. For just as it is fair to deny the rewards of laboring to the slothful, thus is it appropriate to grant the best kind of remuneration to the vigilant. And therefore Patricius will know himself to have been vested by us as *primicerius* of the *exceptores,* so that, having advanced to such a duty, he may rejoice at enjoying the rewards of his own services.

LETTER 11.26 (C. 533–38)

This letter promotes an official of previously unknown designation to a position among the palace guardsmen (*scholarii*). Unlike the *excubitores,* who protected members of the royal household, this was more or less an honorary dignity.

Concerning the Sixth Cohort of Scholarii

1. It is right for one who merits the approval of many leading officials to be promoted by our judgment. Indeed, it is pleasing for one who has satisfied judgment on many occasions to occasionally be a recipient. Therefore let Iustus, soon to find the reward of service, know himself to be installed in the grade of the sixth cohort of *scholarii,* since he has striven to associate himself with faithful service.

LETTER 11.27 (C. 533–38)

This letter promotes a former *cancellarius* to the honorary rank of *praerogativarius.* This official's former appointment was announced at *Variae* 11. 6.

Concerning the Rank of Praerogativarius

1. Who would consider that Johannus should not rightly be promoted, a man who previously claimed from our judgment the office of *cancellarius* and who then already deserved the privilege owed to good conscience, when he received charge of the judge's private chamber? And so let one who is known to have pleased us with commendable conduct enjoy with celebration both rank and privilege. Therefore our decision confirms him as *praerogativarius,* so that, possessed of earned rank, he may observe public commands with a more devoted spirit.

LETTER 11.28 (C. 533–38)

A fairly obscure letter that appoints an official to the role of *commentariensis,* in which function he would be assigned to a judge to execute legal sentences.

Concerning the Commentariensis

1. It is a great delight to answer the petitions of the deserving with delegated assistance, so that one who has deserved preference should be accommodated by more devoted intention. Therefore, Heliodorus will enjoy the duty of *commentariensis*. Indeed, we have rightly entrusted to his integrity what we deem must be safeguarded.

LETTER 11.29 (C. 533–38)

This letter advances an official to the position of *regendarius* (or *regerendarius*), a senior role in the management of the *cursus publicus*.

Concerning the Regendarius

1. It seems appropriately equitable, if a worthy change of circumstance should be offered to those praised for effective service. For one who is known to advance a fortunate career with well-considered vigilance has his own glory. Hence it is that we order Carterius to happily claim the post of *regendarius,* so that, spurred by hope for the future, he would be able to more eagerly apply himself to praetorian duties.

LETTER 11.30 (C. 533–38)

This letter promotes two men as head (*primicerius*) of their respective departments; the *deputati* and the *augustales* were two distinct cohorts of *exceptores*.

Concerning the Primicerius Deputatorum *and*
the Primicerius Augustalium

1. It is fitting that the fruit of labors should attend the wishes of the faithful and that the better man should claim positions which the practiced integrity of former accomplishments would commend. Hence it is that we have decided Ursus should be the *primicerius deputatorum* and Beatus the *primicerius augustalium,* so that those who are seen to be advanced to greater duties should follow previously established examples of good conscience.

LETTER 11.31 (C. 533–38)

A letter similar to *Variae* 11. 26, an official retires from his position as department head of palatine heralds, for which he earns the titular honor of rank equal to those who attend the royal family (*domestici*) and palace guards (*protectores*), without fulfilling those services.

Concerning One Who Leaves the Office of Primicerius Singulariorum

1. It is fitting for those who are known to have completed sworn public services to follow the rewards of victory, since continuous labor claims for itself what untested nobility is hardly able to acquire. And therefore, since Urbicus is known to have discharged the office of *primicerius* during his own tenure, let him ascend to the adoration of the sacred purple among the *domestici* and *protectores,* so that, distinguished by the company of those requiring respect, he may rejoice to be liberated from the vigils of service.

LETTER 11.32 (C. 533–38)

In consequence of the position vacated in *Variae* 11.31, this letter appoints an official as department head (*primicerius*) of palatine heralds.

Concerning One Who Receives the Office
of Primicerius Singulariorum

1. The integrity of the one acting as magistrate is present in the service of his staff, since he gladly pays what he knows to be justly owed. Therefore, let Pierius know himself to be made *primicerius singulariorum* by our authority. If there is any other news, let it be faithfully reported,[36] since there is no fear of stammering where the dictation of the magistrate is not corrupt.

LETTER 11.33 (C. 533–38)

This letter represents the kind of document (a *delegatoria*) that would have authorized the release of various emoluments (salary or *annona*) owed to members of the civil service. The present version is addressed to a recipient of the *delegatoria* (cf. *Var.* 11.35 also).

Concerning Those Who Must Be Granted a Delegatoria

1. He anticipates delays, whom the habit of giving constrains, since that man who is urged by native kindness is compelled even more to generosity. Nor is it at all proper that we ought to be dissimilar to our own record of achievements, when it would be better to increase in the number of beneficent acts for one whose quality of administration is known to be enhanced. And therefore, our generosity bestows an increase in rations to you with the present letter, so that you would then enjoy the advantage of your reward, even when you reach the end of your exertion. We do not hold you in anxious suspense, nor do we weary you with tortuous delays.

---

36. This seems to refer to the frequent practice of messengers verbally reporting "other matters" not included in a letter.

Let there be one end to toil and to cares. For who would think it must be deferred, if he should not want to sell his own services again?

LETTER 11.34 (C. 533–38)

Perhaps the most obscure letter of the collection, it serves to acknowledge receipt of a petition from an official recently retired from service (cf. *Var.* 11. 18). The letter appears to concern the security of arrangements made upon his discharge from service. The reference to an *alpha* seems to be an allusion to a person.

A Response to the Petition of Anthianus

1. The office will retain your petition, until we seek the approval of those following, when the opportunity permits, since what must be substantiated by many is only recklessly accepted by one. All promoted men advance. Each is proven with good fortune. You never had doubt, while every opinion held uncertainty. The alpha alone embraced you, where that letter is not feared. For in as much as each man had not depended on the judgment of another, he thus exercised his own will.

LETTER 11.35 (C. 535)

Whereas *Variae* 11. 33 presented the recipient of a *delegatoria* with notification of his award, this letter is addressed to the official who would have paid the pension from a portion of the taxes. Like *Variae* 17–34, this letter should be considered a *formula* for such an award as it lacks an addressee and the recipient of the *delegatoria* is unstated.

A Delegatoria

1. If the driver of an Olympian chariot snatches the prize after his labors, if the struggle of disreputable brutes is accustomed to swiftly crown the victors, what speed of remuneration is deserved for one by whom the oaths of service are commendably executed? For why should an official of the department of *agentes in rebus* endure anything insecure after such uncertainties of service? Such a man has vowed to preserve the reputation of the *Princeps* by being vigilant in repeated duties, since he surpasses others in observing oaths of service. **2.** For he has continually obeyed imperial commands and as he used to exalt the honor of the praetorian seat, he entered the service of that office as soon as he began holding leading rank.[37] Therefore, to hinder such a man is sinful, since no man should be vexed after victory. What a man receives in sadness is not able to be called repayment

---

37. That is, he began service under the *Praefectus Praetorio* when he was awarded the rank of *Princeps Augustorum*.

for service. Let those absolved from service dread no burdens, lest a safe haven should bring upon the liberated what a storm is wont to do to the distressed. **3.** Therefore, let your trustworthiness pay, without delay, the amount of *solidi* from the third payment of the taxes from that province, which provident antiquity determined for the *Princeps Augustorum,* and which you know must be entered into the accounts of the thirteenth indiction. But beware venal impediments, shun condemnable contempt, so that you, who would desire to pursue similar favors, should not seem to set a precedent for your own loss. Indeed, for what reason would you reject the one entreating, if you constrain yourself by the nature of your action? Veterans must be considered truly honorable by all, but especially by those who are occupied in the labor of service. Therefore, you offer yourself what you permit to another, when the compensation of the predecessor instead becomes the profit of the successors.

LETTER 11.36 (C. 533–38)

Elaborating on the *formula* for a *delegatoria* (*Var.* 11.35), this letter provides a specific example, ordering a *cancellarius* to disperse a pension to an official following his discharge from service. The pension was paid out of the tax revenues of Samnium. The letter includes a digression from natural philosophy and a testimonial to Cassiodorus's own record as a magistrate.

Praefectus Praetorio *Senator to Anatolicus,*
Cancellarius *of the Province of Samnium*

1. The one who invented laborious vigils and duties, requiring great exertion, quite reasonably also established limits of tenure, so that the reward set for the term of active service should have no uncertainty. Who would otherwise be able to continually serve and attend, when the very light withdraws itself from mortal affairs? For which reason, civil service is certain in an uncertain life, lest one who deserves to reach that appointed term without offense should be apprehensive about what he holds.[38] **2.** The very stars, as astronomers claim, although they revolve in ceaseless repetition, preserve the set paces of their courses. What is held confined by its own fixity cannot be inconsistent. Saturn travels the course of the heavens appointed to it in thirty years. The star of Jove illuminates the region assigned it in twelve years. The heavenly body of Mars, seized by fiery celerity, traces its determined course in eighteen months. The sun passes the signs of the zodiacal belt in the span of a year. The star of Venus arches over the space given it in fifteen months. Mercury, girt with speed, rides through the span set for it in thirteen months. The moon, closer to us in our own neighborhood, accomplishes in thirty days what the

---

38. That is, lest he fear being discharged from service without pension.

golden, circumscribing sun completes in the span of a year. **3.** Mortals, therefore, rightly find an end to labor when, as the philosophers say, even those bodies which are unable to perish except with the world have received, quite reasonably, limits to their course; nevertheless, with this distinguishing difference, that they end their own work, so that they may return to the beginning, whereas humankind serves so that it may rest when labors are accomplished. **4.** And therefore, disperse without any hesitation to *ille*, who blamelessly completed the office of *cornicularius*, the seven hundred *solidi* that established custom assigned to him, from the third payment of taxes for *illa* indiction in the province of Samnium: since it is not possible to question the reward of one whom the formal and genuine discharge of a magistrate commends. For, acknowledged for praiseworthy service, he supervised the judicial chambers of the praetorian bureau, whence his title is derived.[39] By his assistance, we signed in ink, uncompromised, what used to be done with preference to weighty bribes, we gave preference to those whom the law favored, we rejected those to whom justice offered no surety. **5.** No one grieved for his own victory, since he obtained it with his resources secure, not sold, when the verdict arrived in his favor. You know all that we say, for your personal assistance was not conducted in our private chambers; what we did, the bureau knew. No doubt, we caused grievances as a private citizen, but we represented honor as a magistrate. Our discipline was considered in words and our kindness was felt in deeds. We became wrathful for peace, we threatened harmlessly and, so that we would not be able to do harm, we were seen wielding terror. As you were accustomed to say, you have a magistrate of the greatest purity; I leave you as the most uncorrupted witness.

LETTER 11.37 (C. 533–38)

This letter is a type similar to *Variae* 11.36, ordering a *cancellarius* to award the emoluments of discharge from public service to a *primiscrinius* from the tax revenues of Campania. The letter served as an opportunity for Cassiodorus to wax effusively on the virtues of state service.

Praefectus Praetorio *Senator to Lucinus,* Vir Clarissimus *and* Cancellarius *of Campania*

1. It has been well provided by ancient regulation that those who serve the public weal should receive in return the value of their services, lest anyone who must be commended for upstanding duty should be passed over. For from what office would remuneration be expected, if rewards are withheld from praetorian

---

39. The *cornicularius* acted as chief legal aid to the *Praefectus Praetorio;* Cassiodorus associates the title with the *cornua,* or "judicial bench."

servants? For almost everything that is accomplished in the republic is completed with their exertion, for this office requires every other to comply, thus that it may not be permitted to transgress; and, what is the most difficult kind of service, it attends the needs of the army, it is subject to armed forces and carries favor there, where another office would find censure. **2.** How would we order tax payments, planned with great precision, to be collected by complex procedure? And who exacts from those whom none dare to offend? Not only must the rations that are stored for distribution at a distance be attributed to their exertions, but without complaint they gather at the royal city those goods native to the provinces, so that when something is sought at the appropriate moment, it is not considered a loss to the one giving. **3.** The service of such men is our glory, the reputation of our tenure, the effective strength of our commands and whatever we receive for the sake of any obligated kindness, we justly attribute to their preparations. Those assigned to toil gleam with the practice of that very thing, which always renders men educated; labors, let me call them harsh masters and relentless teachers, through which anyone may be made more careful, when dangers are feared to be incurred. Let someone be educated in oratory, and another be taught in some other discipline; nonetheless, that man who is honed in the devotion of continuous service is rendered the more learned. **4.** And therefore, what is deserved by such men must be paid with honor, so that one who had always acquired profit for the republic may at some point receive it for himself. Concerning which, we order you to give to that *primiscrinius* already discharged from the labor of service the appropriate amount of *solidi* from the taxes of the third payment from the province of Campania, so that man may fully enjoy just labors and his successors may find an example of willing servitude, when they know him to have been well accoutered on account of his own fidelity.

LETTER 11.38 (C. 535)

Identical in purpose to *Variae* 11. 36–37, this letter orders the award of a pension to an unnamed administrative assistant (*subadivva*) from the taxes of Tuscany. This letter, however, offers one of the most charming digressions in the collection: a natural history of papyrus intended to remind the addressee that all public affairs are documented.

Praefectus Praetorio *Senator to Johannus,*
Canonicarius *of Tuscany*

1. The governess of all affairs, antiquity, diligently prepared so that the abundant supply of documents should not fail, since our archive must be consulted by many people, to the extent that, when magistrates should resolve future affairs for the many, sweet benefactions would not experience hateful delays. This service is granted to petitioners, lest they should be constrained by avarice to pay for what is known to be provided from public largesse. Shameless opportunity for extortion has been deprived, a benefit the humanity of the *Princeps* has granted to those whom it removes from loss. **2.** Clever Memphis conceived a worked material handsomely plain, so that what the delicate work of a single place has woven should clothe every archive. On the Nile rises a forest without branches, a grove without leaves, a watery crop, comely hairs of the marsh, more pliant than a thicket and hardier than grass. I know not how, but the material is filled with emptiness, and light from its length, an absorbent tenderness, a spongy wood, the durability of which, in the nature of an apple, is in the exterior skin. Soft in the interior, tall and slender, but it supports itself, the most beautiful fruit of a filthy flood. **3.** For what crop is produced of such a kind anywhere, which there preserves the thoughts of the wise? Before this, the sayings of the wise, the ideas of ancestors, were imperiled. For by what means would it have been possible to quickly write what could hardly be expressed on the resistant hardness of bark? No doubt the inspiration of the mind endured awkward delays and when words were distracted, their genius was forced to grow cool. **4.** Hence, antiquity named the works of the ancients *libri,* for even today we call strips of green wood *libri*. It was unseemly, I confess, to entrust learned tracts to rough tablets and to impress on unrefined, woody scraps what exquisite sensitivity was able to discern. With hands burdened, few were inspired to record, nor would one to whom such a page was offered be enticed to speak much. But this was becoming to primitive times, when a rude beginning ought to use such a contrivance that would challenge the ingenuity of those following. The sweet allure of documents is amply attested, where there is no apprehension for the shortage of material. **5.** For this uncovers a field for eloquent composition on a white surface, it always supports abundant writing and, by which means it becomes easily manageable, it gathers into its own roll, although it may be unfolded into great treatises. Joined without seams, it extends by reducing; the white interior of green reeds, a face for writing which accepts black ink for adornment, where, with elevated letters, the transplanted crop of fertile words returns the sweetest fruit to the mind, as often as it strikes the reader's fancy: faithfully preserving a testimony of human deeds, hostile to forgetfulness, it speaks of past events. **6.** For even if our memory retains material, it changes the words: but there the memory reposes secure, because it may always be read in the same terms. Therefore, we order you to offer to the administrative assistant *ille,* the assigned amount of *solidi* from the third payment of taxes of the province of Tuscany, charged to the accounts of the thirteenth indiction, to the end that the public archive ought to preserve in commendable perpetuity the integrity of its own trustworthiness. Because, not knowing the failure of mortal affairs, the public archive ever increases with annual accumulation, constantly receiving new materials and preserving the old.

LETTER 11.39 (C. 533–38)

This letter orders a reduction of the tax burden for citizens of Lucania and Bruttium, with the additional treat of Cassiodorus's digression into the history of how these provinces contributed to the provisioning of Rome.

Praefectus Praetorio *Senator to Vitalianus,* Vir Clarissimus *and*
Cancellarius *of Lucania and Bruttium*

1. It becomes apparent how great was the population of the city of Rome, as it was fed from abundant provisions from even distant regions, to such an extent that the immediately surrounding provinces sufficed for the victuals of visiting foreigners, while imported plenty served the city itself. For how could those who possessed dominion over the world manage to be small in number! 2. For the vast span of the walls, the strained circuit of spectacles, the wondrous mass of the baths and the numerousness of water mills, which is known to be associated especially with provisioning, all bear witness to the crowds of citizens. For if this last apparatus had not been useful, it would have no importance, when it is neither able to furnish ornament nor to complement any other part of the city. In sum, these things are thus tokens of cities, as though the precious garments of bodies, since none rest from creating the excesses that are known to advertise themselves by their great cost. 3. For hence it was that mountainous Lucania provided pigs, hence that Bruttium offered herds of cattle from its native wealth. No doubt both are wondrous, that these provinces would suffice for such a city and that, by their services, such a full city should have no lack of provisions. Indeed, it was their glory to supply Rome: but it was known that they were able to deliver at great loss what was offered by weight through so many journeys, while nobody was able to reckon what was proven to decrease! 4. The levy was reduced to a payment, because it was neither diminished by traveling, nor stricken by exertion. Let the provinces know their own blessings. For if their ancestors were loyal even in loss, why would these today not be generous in paying from profits?[40] And therefore, your diligence will direct both assessments to the public taxes, now reduced to the established payments, lest those who had obeyed nonresident officials with commendable integrity should seem to be neglected during my tenure. 5. For although I have endeavored to restore other provinces as well, nonetheless, nothing has been accomplished in these provinces that I would wish to claim. These provinces have experience of me as their governor, and those whom I represented as a private citizen, following my grandfather and great grandfather, I tenaciously strove to assist in my official

---

40. The tax was formerly paid in kind with the delivery of livestock to Rome and the journey naturally reduced the weight (and value) of the animals; later, with the tax value converted from weight to a set price, the provincials satisfied their tax burden from profits received after the sale of livestock locally.

capacity, so that those whom I noticed rejoicing with well-intended adulation at my promotion should acknowledge I retained affection for my homeland. Therefore, let them obey not from any compulsion, but from love, when I have reduced for them even the amount that was customarily offered. For while twelve hundred *solidi* had been dispersed in annual payment, I have reduced the payment again, to a thousand *solidi*, through royal generosity, so that they may celebrate, with an increase of joy from the diminishment of their burdens.

LETTER 11.40 (C. 533–38)

This letter serves as a "dispensation" or "amnesty," a general edict ordering the release of prisoners. An exploration of ethics and natural history provides material for the justification of the order, including an address to the personification of indulgence. A reference to what may have been a religious holiday focused on redemption suggests the edict may have been prompted by Easter celebrations. The theme of redemption makes it a pair with the last letter of Book 12, which focuses on fiscal remission.

Indulgentia

1. Although the very title of judge would seem to speak of justice and we may bid the course of the entire year to tread on paths of equity, nonetheless, on these days we rightly turn aside from duty to the household, so that we may approach the redeemer of all men along the path of forgiveness. Indeed, from this virtue we pluck the sweetest fruit and by freeing others do we save ourselves. For we, who are harshly just, forgive always in a time of security. Therefore, we renounce punishment, we condemn torture, and we are then truly a judge. 2. Rejoice, Indulgence, you who are exceptional and who unbind. You, the patroness of humanity; you, the unique medicine to those afflicted by circumstance. Who is not in want of your service, when sinning is a universal condition? You assault hardship for all, when that hope of freedom is claimed under you, which was not had under justice. For while you may share the grace of heaven with three other sisters and you are bound together in a loving embrace, and although they too are virtues, they honorably yield everything to you when they recognize you to be the salvation of humanity.[41] But how do we proclaim such a thing from earthly discourse? It is piety that rules even the heavens. Oh, if it were permitted to reside with you for a longer extent of

---

41. Although it would be easier to equate Indulgence with either the Hope or Charity of the three Graces, the reference to three other sisters suggests Cassiodorus has in mind the four cardinal virtues (Prudence, Temperance, Fortitude, and Justice), in which case he may have intended Indulgence to serve as Justice.

time![42] Every man accused would be excused, and by being forgiven it would happen that he was given leave to forgive. **3.** But most providently, such a sacred service seems to be granted only at certain times, so that the world would receive this blessing more gratefully, because it rejoiced for the unexpectedness of the thing. Therefore, O *lictor,* refrain from the hated ax, by which it is permitted to commit with impunity what you would see punished in others; love for a short while steel that is polished, not gory. Let your chains, moistened with tears, cheerfully take on rust; lock away what was instead accustomed to confine. Let the sound of feral voices be exchanged for a better condition. Thus in a real sense you would preserve a title without grief to others.[43] Why do you continually labor in the dungeons? Even you must occasionally serve the heavens. An act of clemency means leisure for you. Let kind piety disarm him, for whom it is necessary to keep vigil over ceaseless justice. **4.** And therefore, let the chambers of groaning, the house of sadness, a place blinded with perpetual night, let them shine with a flood of light, among those beyond the hospitality of Pluto, where not a single condemned man endures torment. He is thought to be lost to heavenly assistance even before he may meet a violent end. First the fetter cripples with the unbearable suffering of heaped chains; groans and lamentation of other men torment the hearing; long fasting debilitates the taste; pressing weights fatigue the touch; vision obscured with continual darkness becomes enfeebled. There is not just one death for the confined; one tormented in the squalor of the prison is permitted death in many ways. **5.** Now, therefore, set free those condemned to your Avernus;[44] let those who had suffered things infernal for a long portion of the year return to things heavenly; let your halls be filled with emptiness. May a place formerly of endless tears lose its native sadness. Those people are happy who are not there, where there would be a kind of grace, if it would appear abandoned. Come forth prisoners, men growing ever pale with death's company; return to the light, those whom the depths of darkness possessed, those for whom nothing could be better than a merciful death, except that you were already dead. **6.** But you, who ought to be deceived by no ambition now, forsake crime with the chains, be absolved with the blessings of these days. Live honestly now, you who have learned to prevail over death. Learn how good habits may be beneficial: one manner of living knows how to bestow splendid liberty, the other confers foul prison. The one offers such things as you would want to enjoy; the other grants such as you would choose to perish. If the laws bind you, no man will imprison you further. Take fright at hidden chambers; come into the forum without trepidation. **7.** You justly flee that by which you had come to sadness. Let free men marvel at you, whom they saw condemned. You

---

42. Another reference to what was probably a Christian holiday.
43. Here *nomen custodis* has the double meaning of "you preserve the title" and "title of jailor."
44. "Hell."

should have despised what leads you to death. Even cattle knows to avoid what they have learned will harm them; they do not follow again those paths where they have fallen into snares. The cautious bird avoids tangling snares and those perceiving the glue of lime do not perch. The pike buries itself in soft sand, so that it may avoid entanglements of weighted lines; since the above-mentioned nets scrape across its back to no effect, it leaps nimbly into the waves and, now free, acknowledges the joy of the avoided danger. **8.** The wrasse lured by bait, when it begins to enter its reedy prison, as soon as it recognizes it has been lead to its own death, glides its back tail first, gradually retracting itself from the narrow confines. If another of the same species recognizes the entangled fish, it draws its tail by the teeth, so that the fish unable to help itself in captivity may be shown escape with the assistance of another. Thus too, a clever species of mackerel noted for its speed, when they have driven themselves into snares, knit themselves together into a kind of rope and then, drawing backward with full strength, they attempt to free their captive companions. There are many such examples, if they are sought. Indeed, everything that has an enemy would easily meet its ruin, if it lacked the means of its own salvation. **9.** To you, master jailor, we repeat our words to open your penal chamber and to be innocently hidden. You are indeed tormented because no man is afflicted; you derive grief from public rejoicing, when you must be comported with raging jealousy that the shared grace of the sun is not for you a pardon. You, who experience happiness at the affliction of many, endure your loss from the safety of all. But so that we may also console your lamentation, claim entirely for yourself those whom the welcome law of devotion may not free, lest, when it would spare the most savage men, it would open the way for the most grievous deeds. Let us, therefore, absolve all fettered for secular offenses. Let each man suffer the company of those who hasten to escape the dangers of bondage. Let the cells disperse convicted men; let us loosen the bonds of impure intent.

Book 12

LETTER 12.1 (C. 533–38)

The first three letters of Book 12 constitute a triad mobilizing the fiscal apparatus for the annual collection of taxes. The first is a forceful letter addressed to the *cancellarii* who acted as praetorian representatives administrating tax collection in each province. The letter focuses on mutual responsibility for a shared reputation that corruption might impair. The designation of the indictional date as *illa* may imply the letter was intended as a *formula* that would have been dispatched to *cancellarii* on an annual basis.

Praefectus Praetorio *Senator to the Various*
Cancellarii *of Individual Provinces*

1. How could someone who is sent from the inner counsels of his judge not be considered important, since anyone is thought to love justice more, in proportion to how often he is known to have audience there? The judge is known by his public servants and, just as students spread the teaching of the master, thus does the conduct of our servants expose us. The precipitate man is not thought to have heeded a careful one; the greedy man is not believed to have obeyed a man of restraint; the fool is not considered to have attended men of wisdom. **2.** I confess that we are judged by our actions, if you follow bad intentions and, what effects none but you, the scandal of other men spreads to our disgrace. We endure such a downfall as we could not inflict upon others and the law, by which all men prosper, would not be a safeguard to us. But, on the other hand, we have consolation through the role played by others, because your good deeds are accounted as our mandates and whatever glory develops from your service is attached to us without effort. **3.** For if anyone should observe you acting wisely, it immediately exalts the reputation of your teacher, since the type of deeds witnessed are likewise assumed to have been learned. However you happen to be judged will be the unanimous opinion of the people concerning your judge. And so, particular care must be taken, lest the one whose reputation you have previously damaged should begin judging you. Whatever you release to common gossip will be avenged with punishments, and whatever a goaded populace amplifies will be exacted from you with torments. How dangerous it is to endure a justifiably wrathful judge and for him, whom you have grievously incited, to decide your future well-being. Therefore, take great care, so that you will instead be praised by our voice, since just as the negative sentence of a judge is capable of oppressing you, thus may a favorable decision elevate you. **4.** Therefore, hasten to that province for this indiction with God's blessing, decorated with the ostentation of a *cancellarius* and girt with a dignified severity.[1] Though you be far away, know the honor of our presence. For what baseness would you, who serve in office, dare to attempt? The *fasces* of magistrates obey you, and while you are thought to bear the orders of the praetorian seat, you assume some measure of that very authority by the reverence due to you. Above all, observe our edicts; demonstrate the best course to those serving under you. For whose responsibility is it to preserve the mandates of the magistrate, if our servants are seen to ignore things properly decreed? **5.** Flee avarice, that queen of shameless vices, whom all crimes service with reprehensible devotion; who, once she has crossed the threshold of a man's heart, also admits a crowd of wicked attendants. Once received, she cannot be removed, since she knows not how to be solitary. She has the most flattering troop of followers, she takes up arms from money and sweetly overcomes those whom she captivates with bitter deception. Accordingly, be on guard for the public weal; discharge your obligations with moral vigor. Someone insistent upon reason accomplishes more than a dreaded man is able to coerce. Let your role be one of refuge to the oppressed, protection for the weak, and defense for one stricken by any calamity. For thus do you properly administer our legal domain, if you open the impious closures to the stricken.[2]

LETTER 12.2 (C. 534)

The second of a triad (cf. *Var.* 12.1 and 12.3), this letter was directed to the provincial governors and orders the commencement of tax collections. It also announces

---

1. On the execution of this command, cf. *Var.* 12.2.6.

2. Cassiodorus here reminds the *cancellarius* of his role as warden of the court, by contrasting the "legal domain" of the *Praefectus* (*nostros cancellos*) with illegal closures (*impia claustra*) that would exclude the needy.

the arrival of the *cancellarii* from *Variae* 12.1, for the purpose of supervising the collection process.

Praefectus Praetorio *Senator to All Governors of the Provinces*

1. I return thanks to divine authority, since I have both advised what the provincials have accomplished and I have fulfilled all that I have promised. For nobody has felt me to be befouled by any venality; nor have I suffered disloyal subjects. We have considered in every situation what we ought to esteem in our servants: we shall acquire the most complete distinction, should they rediscover loving magistrates. And so, let us accomplish what we have begun with God as witness. Let the landowner pay the public taxes to me gladly; I shall discharge this debt to him in the assembly of justice. 2. Moreover, what is felt to be administered truthfully by you is recalled favorably, when great hope is given for future affairs out of respect for past conduct. For you have been approved because we have compelled no man to give what would not be proper for him to offer. Neither in public affairs, nor in private, has anyone been driven to loss by me. We have caused the terrors of foreclosures to be unknown. Nor have we, who would prefer everything to be conducted according to the laws, asked for extraordinary payments. But neither should you be dissimilar to this in any way. Legal authority wants governors to be imitators of our office and it has conferred upon them almost the same jurisdiction as ours in the provinces. 3. Let no man be rejected for pursuing justice; it ennobles everyone whom it elevates by its very practice. Only that man who would part from justice accomplishes less. Why would we attend to desires for profit? One who is called wealthy receives no glory; on the contrary, one who is proclaimed just is decorated with every praise. We desire instead what makes us more valuable than the richest men. We have taken up the *fasces* so that we ought to be burdened; let us mount the judge's tribunal so that we might preside over the path to good conduct. 4. No baseness, no avarice may touch magistrates. For they render their own distinction soiled, if those upon whom many depend should become polluted with any blame. It is more advantageous to be unseen than to be marked by the scorn of all. Therefore, we, who seek every eminence of human company, renounce the baseness of vices. Let our conscience be clear, so that we would be able to correct the sins of others. Crime levels all distinction among those who sin, and therefore the one who judges ought to be set apart from one accused. It is appropriate for us to say this in our annual address, since there is no satiety in good acts. I confess the longing of my desire: I want myself to be seen in you. 5. We come now to the usual matters, which nonetheless ought to be undertaken gladly, because they are known to be customary. Therefore, what should be pronounced happily, we order you and your staff to remind the landowners, with God's blessing, that they may pay the taxes of the thirteenth indiction with a devoted spirit, to the extent that they discharge their obligation to the republic within the prescribed

limit of three payments. The prescribed period for payment should be observed, but nonetheless, even though none should bemoan experiencing the injury of an untimely payment, do not permit the condemnable generosity of a deferment to offer an inroad to shameful venality. For a delay of payment would become cause for greater loss, when it illegally suspends what should not be evaded with procrastination.[3] **6.** Moreover, you will hasten to send to our office, with the usual care, a full and faithful report of expenses every four months, so that complete clarity, cleansed of the fog of error, would appear in the public accounts. For if you should do otherwise, anticipate for yourselves the same losses that have been inflicted upon the public weal through your negligence. And so that you would be able to more easily accomplish, God willing, what is constituted in law, we have ordered *ille* and *ille,* public servants of our office,[4] to supervise you and your staff in the usual manner, to the extent that our ordinance should be flawlessly put into effect. Beware, therefore, lest you show yourself unequal to our admonitions, since it would be very unbecoming if we should find that what is commendable has instead fallen short.

LETTER 12.3 (C. 533–38)

The final letter in a triad aimed at mobilizing the tax collection process, this letter advises the *saiones* who accompanied and assisted the *cancellarii* dispatched to each province.

Praefectus Praetorio *Senator to All* Saiones
Who Are Assigned to Cancellarii

1. It is truly becoming that all things are accomplished peacefully, however it may be possible that they happen according to good character. But in the republic there is such a great variety in the kinds of conduct that no man may succeed in defending the laws, unless terror should be known to moderate some kinds of behavior. There is no one cure for sick men; some are restored with nourishment, others are offered a remedy through fasting; this man seeks a soothing bath for his wounds, another the scalpel; and varied degrees of illness require diverse treatments. Thus, one who is recognized to preside over the people should not be found equipped with only one course of action. Violent men must be repressed with punishment, men tame of heart must be admonished with civility; the cunning must be treated with caution, the guileless with forbearance. And so prudence is proven to be necessary in each case, since a suitable plan is seen to apply to each case. **2.** Therefore,

---

3. A common form of corruption in fiscal practices: officials would allow taxpayers to defer payments after a bribe, eventually resulting in tax arrears beyond the ability of the landowner to satisfy.

4. Presumably two *cancellarii* who had been recipients of *Var.* 12.1.

we have chosen your devotion for the customary duty of assisting our distinguished *cancellarius,* so that you would rise up against none other except one who would despise to obey the laws. Drag to the courts those who do not accept just decisions; refrain from wrath with restraint and discretion. We want you to be feared as much as approved, since it will especially reflect upon your vigor, if the *cancellarius* should be cheated by the presumption of none. **3.** The faithful collection of public taxes should be exacted before any other consideration. Let scorned debt be your concern. The coerced man may produce what he refused to pay willingly. Set yourself to resolve only such cases. If you adhere to these precepts, you will not follow errant courses. One who would accomplish mandates should be free of blame. It is the worst thing in an agent, if he should abandon the direction of a judge. Do not throw your weight about, because it is not possible for you to be denied, lest you want to adopt an arrogance because the humble condition of many fears you. Brave men are always unassuming in peace and those who have often waged battles cherish justice greatly. **4.** It would be pleasing if, having returned to your kin, you do not bring with you the scandal of brawls, but that they recognize you to have conducted yourself in such a manner that respected men are known to adopt. Moreover, we gratefully welcome one arriving with praise, and we do not permit one whom we feel has acted appropriately to lack reward. Furthermore, the master of the state concedes greater things to those whose usefulness is known to be accomplished with good conscience. How many things are there that wise men are able to extol! No man acquires more abundant reward than one who has comported himself with good conduct.

LETTER 12.4 (C. 533–38)

An order for a shipment of the famous *acinaticium,* a wine of Verona, for the royal table, this letter becomes a tribute to the wine and the apparently famous glass goblets that must accompany it.

Praefectus Praetorio *Senator to the* Canonicarius *of Venetia*

1. It is appreciated that the opulent provisioning of the royal table is not a slight adornment to the republic, since, however much the master feasts upon rare delicacies, he is believed to possess such resources. It is the lot of a private individual to enjoy what the local area contains; with the dining of a *Princeps,* it is perfectly proper to search for what ought to be admired. Let the Danube send its carp, let the *ancorago* come from the Rhine, and let Sicily offer its *exormiston* by any means necessary. Let the sea of Bruttium send its sweet *acernia;* let succulent fish be transported from far-flung shores.[5] Thus is it fitting to provender a king, so that

5. The fish given in Latin are unidentifiable by English names.

he may be reckoned by the legates of foreign nations to possess practically everything. 2. And so wines must be procured that only fertile Italy nourishes, lest we,
who should be able to obtain foreign stores, should seem to have no regard for our
own. Thus, it has been disclosed in a report of the *Comes Patrimonii* that the wine
acinaticium, the name of which is derived from the small grape, has become
depleted in the royal cellars. 3. And since each magistrate ought to supply in turn
the necessary resources that are known to be fitting for the rulers of the state, we
order you to approach the landowners of Verona, where the cultivation of this
wine is renowned, under the condition that none should hesitate to sell at an
acceptable price what ought to be offered for the gratitude of a *Princeps.* It is clearly
a noble vintage, about which Italy may boast. For although clever Greece may
commend itself with various subtleties of careful preparation and either perfume
its wines with scents or flavor them with rosemary, on close inspection, it is nonetheless found to have nothing similar. 4. For this wine is pure, with the color of
kings and with the flavor of distinction, so that you would either think the color to
be tinged from the very source of blood or that its essence may be thought to be
expressed from purple dye. In that wine, sweetness is experienced with indescrib-
able pleasure. I know not what strength ripens it on the stake: its body is tinged
with texture, so that you may call it either a liquid flesh or an edible drink. It is fitting to report how the cultivation of this wine seems to be so singular. Gathered
from the vines in autumn, the clusters are hung upside down from the eaves of
houses, it is preserved in its own receptacles, protected in natural casings. They
become wrinkled with age, not putrid. Then, with insipid humors seeping out, it
becomes sweeter. 5. It is drawn down in the month of December, when the season
of winter reveals its ripeness, and in a wondrous manner, it becomes renewed
when found aged in every storehouse. Wintry fresh, the chilled blood of the bunch,
a frosty vintage and bloody liquid, drinkable purple and violet nectar, it first quick-
ens in its own source and when it has been able to mature, it begins to enjoy perpetual youth. It is not insultingly trodden under feet, nor is it darkened with the
blending of any impurity, but, however it happens, it produces such noble character. It flows when water hardens with ice. It is fruitful, when every fruit of the field
fails. It decants a gemlike clarity. I know nothing else that pours pleasant tears and,
other than the delights of its sweetness, the exceptional beauty of the wine is in its
appearance. 6. Found as quickly as possible and set with a compensatory price, it
must be surrendered to those agents who are placed in charge of this business. Nor
should you suppose it may be forgotten that the wine grows bright in frosted goblets, when it is more remarkable because you will have discerned it with greater
difficulty. When combined, the whiteness is graceful and the clarity pure, such that
the one is thought born from roses and the other from lilies. It is indeed dissimilar
in color, but complementary in taste. Each is unlike in appearance but alike in
charm. For in addition to the fact that it tastes sharp and it restores strength

quickly, it is commonly recognized by those goblets, although the difference between them is great. In one, you would behold red cheer; in the other, you see its festive clarity. And therefore, the procurement of these things ought to be quick, when what is known to contain the wine is also expected.

LETTER 12.5 (C. 535 OR 536)

This letter should be dated to the final days of Theodahad's reign, with preparations to repulse Belisarius's arrival in Italy. The letter communicates to the provincial governor of Lucania and Bruttium the means to allow landowners to commute to tax credits those supplies seized by the Gothic army sent to the region. The real concern of the letter seems to be maintaining the loyalty of the countryside in time of war.

Praefectus Praetorio *Senator to Valerianus,* Vir Spectabilis

1. It is indeed fitting that the most successful public defender should spread favors widely, since one who is known to preside over all affairs is expected to assume costs for the profit of all. But, by obligation to nature, we owe more to those who are conjoined to us by some relationship, when it would seem to be a kind of righteous purpose to depart from equality. **2.** For we display modesty before colleagues, we offer reverence to our fathers, we owe common decency to fellow citizens, but a particular affection to our children; and the force of this compulsion is so great, that none would judge himself despised, if he learns the offspring of another have been preferred to him. And so, there is no injustice in being more solicitous with regard to one's native land, especially at such a time when we are found capable of alleviating dangers to it. For we are deemed to love those more whom we hasten to deliver from danger. **3.** Therefore, a vast army arriving in Lucania and Bruttium, known to be sent for the defense of the republic, is said to despoil cultivated property and to diminish the prosperity of the regions with enthusiastic plunder.[6] But since it is necessary for some to give and others to take according to the condition of the times, know that the prices which ancient administration established have been moderated by order of royal governance, so that supplies ought to be charged to public taxes at a price more fixed than that at which you would be accustomed to sell, to the extent that neither the landowner will sustain a loss, nor will the toiling army endure want. **4.** Therefore, do not be agitated. You have avoided the hand of compulsory exactions; the present provision removes your taxes. But so that your ordinance may be more readily accessed, we have decided the sums of credits must be copied in brief lists below, so that none may sell you a benefit that you

---

6. This is likely the force mentioned by Procopius, commanded by Theodahad's nephew, who capitulated to Belisarius shortly after the latter crossed from Sicily in 535.

know has been conferred from public largesse. Restrain, therefore, the reckless agitation of the landowners. Let those whom none have hurled to an uncertain fate love tranquility. While the Gothic army wages war, let the Roman be at peace. What is imposed is the desire of productive citizens, lest the rustics, a coarse species of men, are carried away to lawless audacities when they escape the tedium of laboring and lest those whom you are barely able to govern in peace begin rising against you. **5.** Therefore, admonish by royal command the individual estate managers and prominent landowners,[7] so that they organize nothing barbarous in the conflict, lest they hasten, not so much to assist with the war, but to disturb the peace. Let them seize iron, but that used to cultivate the fields; let them take up pikes for driving cattle, not for armed rage. It is particularly to the praise of the soldiers if, while they are seen defending the aforementioned regions, the peasants would not fail to cultivate their ancestral lands. **6.** Let the strength of the magistrates be in the laws; the judicial benches may not cease to thunder against wicked conduct. Let the bandit fear that judgment he has always dreaded; let the adulterer tremble at the pronouncement of the judge; let the forger find terror in the voice of the bailiff. Do not let the thief find the court ridiculous, since liberty rejoices then, if such things do not bring delight. For thus, you will not feel a war being waged successfully, if the consensus concerning civic harmony is complete among those serving you. None may oppress the poor; trespass against trespassers, harass those who persecute. Waging the public campaign is for you. You will restore everything to a pacified state if you check the crimes of war leaders. Be truly careful in reckoning the distribution of the *annona*, lest it be possible for cunning of any sort to cheat someone. **7.** Know, also, that this has been communicated by the rulers through my letter to the officers of the army, so that, when it has become necessary to be advised by you, it ought to assist those burdened by harm.[8] Let them ward discipline no less, whence the best-forged army is ever equipped. It is, furthermore, added by royal command that, as a kind of benefit, the divine household may not be found exempt from the present offer, but everything that is decreed for the public should be supported in common.[9] **8.** Now, therefore, rise to the occasion with your countrymen and provide what is needed with every precaution, so that the publication of such a document will benefit the noblest homeland in a true sense. For even men of modest intelligence are able to govern in peaceful times and to administrate provinces by usual practice; but "this is the task, this the toil";[10] it is greater to govern what is unable to control itself alone. For the skill of

---

7. The *possessores* and *conductores*.

8. The governor had the authority to work with military leadership in restoring property to civilians.

9. That properties of the royal household should also be subject to supply levies for the army.

10. Virgil, *Aeneid* 6.129.

sailors is idle on calm seas, nor is the name conferred upon practitioners, except that it will have been with the great strain of danger. **9.** You, therefore, have an opportunity in which you could acquire the reputation of wise men and, with God's blessing, serve commendably in every way. Nevertheless, far be it that I commend my countrymen beyond others, since the outcome that we want for our familial hearth,[11] we desire for all. For after I began to ponder public safety, concern for my own affairs melted away. I wish my own well, but that it would be a shared prosperity, since it is a kind of weighty injustice for a judge to want something for himself which the public is unable to enjoy.[12]

LETTER 12.6 (C. 533–38)

This letter follows the theme of *Variae* 10.28, by confirming administrative contracts made by the *Praefectus Praetorio*. The main concern is that agents of the prefecture should not fear being defrauded of their posts, nor should they sell their appointed offices.

Praefectus Praetorio *Senator to All Agents*
Administrating Contracts for the Prefecture

1. Although what has been commanded by the innate piety of the ruler of state should suffice abundantly, nonetheless, we redouble the threats to the insolent and punishments applied to the foolish, so that those who fail to blush with shame should at least restrain themselves out of fear. For who is honored for his own presumption, when, having flaunted an interdiction, is about to squander his reputation? Let the blind ambition of covetous men be checked; let shameless audacity be restrained. Let one who seeks profit from wickedness be dismayed by the promised punishment; let one who desires public position through impious deeds be vexed instead by lost reputation. **2.** In addition, criminal profits will not increase during our tenure, nor will one who knows himself to be condemned purchase his pardon. Opportunity does not lie open to perverse fraud; we will prosecute, not sell, exceptions. Where now, you thieving malefactors, will you find hope, when the rulers of state and your magistrates threaten you? However, those whom our selection brought to public administration, trust in the honesty of your deeds, since no bribery will hamper you, if the probity of your service has restrained you. **3.** Be resolved in your service to the public weal, because no private losses will shake you. Reserve the change of posts for my judgment; since I have not caused

---

11. Cassiodorus here refers to the fate of his own hometown of Squillace (*nostris laribus*).

12. The sentiment expressed here with *magnae iniustitiae genus* contradicts the notion introduced at the beginning of the letter that nature allowed for preference to be given to one's own (*quoddam genus recti propositi*).

you to be burdened by payment for office, you may strive to be praised for my acts on your behalf. And so, you know the period assigned to appointment by the rulers of state must be preserved, so that thus, you ought to give attention to and fulfill what has been decreed for you on behalf of the public weal.

LETTER 12.7 (C. 536)

An interesting order to grant remission from taxes following an attack by the Suevi. This letter departs from similar directives in that the petitioners have not been named (*ille et ille*), and further instructions have been relegated to a separate (nonextant) document. Presumably, the present letter simply provides the authorization of the *Praefectus Praetorio*, who delegated the language of the individual tax exemptions to another official.

Praefectus Praetorio *Senator to the* Canonicarius *of the Veneti*

1. It is proper that nothing happens by chance with regard to the clemency of a good *Princeps*, because those who have determined to give aid fortuitously rectify bad circumstances. For in what manner could a man stripped of possessions endure both barbarian savagery and the severity of a *Princeps*, when, having been despoiled, he rightly refuses what he had been instructed to contribute while prosperous. And so, royal serenity has conceded to *ille* and *ille*, devastated by the incursion of the Suevi,[13] the payment of the fifteenth indiction, just as the attached injunction will instruct you. **2.** Whence for the present indiction, preferring obedience, you will not exact taxes from the above-mentioned landowners for those estates that you determine have been plundered; but let the remaining properties prepare the accustomed payment, so that you may pay the remaining amount to our treasury within the constituted amount of time. Beware, therefore, lest you should become more severe than the enemy, if you should wish to strip bare those already deprived. Those whom bare weapons have terrified should not grow fearful of the official robe of the civil servant; let them not experience rapine after brigandage. They had produced valid receipts of payment against you;[14] their own calamity has granted them an absolute guarantee. Violence has stolen what you seek. It is evident that one for whom apparently nothing remains should be free from taxes.

---

13. This particular incursion is otherwise unknown. Procopius, *Wars* 5.25.26, mentions the Suevi as a people living north of Venetia (beyond the Alps and Danube), although at *Wars* 5.26.9, Witigis has recruited from the Suevi to fight Justinian's forces in Dalmatia.

14. Based on this, it seems the *canonicarius* may have already attempted to collect from the ruined properties; the "attached injunction" (*relecta praeceptio*) possibly included the original receipts.

LETTER 12.8 (C. 533–38)

In response to another anonymous petition (cf. *Var.* 12.7), this letter grants a land-owner the privilege of paying taxes directly to the praetorian treasury, rather than to local tax collectors, whom he accuses of unspecified "irregularities."

Praefectus Praetorio *Senator to the* Consular
of the Province of Liguria

1. It seems to be a new kind of profit for petitioners to gain and their benefactors to experience no loss. For the gift is received by one man in such a way that it is not possible to be lost by the other. It is given without expense, it is conferred without reduction and holds the name generosity, which never departs from the rights of the ruler. **2.** Therefore, *ille* has reported that the revenues of his properties located in that province, which the attached brief details below, are vexed by the irregularity of the tax collectors. He wishes instead to make the owed payment to our treasury officials without any loss to the public weal. We, who are known to enjoy losses to none, gladly consent to this, provided that obligations to the fisc are paid according to the scheduled requirement, since it is a good intention to interrupt what illegal intentions would perpetrate. **3.** For which reason, with the *curiales* and collectors informed, and also whomever else are known to be involved, your *spectabilis* will cause the collection from the above-mentioned properties to be canceled for *illa* indiction, on the condition that, if before the first of the month, the amount that is owed has not been paid to the treasury, the scheduled exaction should be conducted in the province, unless he will have shown the obligation of his promised payment to be discharged with receipts from treasury officials, then the designated estates should be freed from any disquiet from collectors, since what is known to be offered with a willing spirit, without risk of loss, ought to be preferred. For tax payment without the compulsion of a collector, that the loyal citizen should give what the compelled man is hardly able to fulfill, is pleasing to us. Would that the landowner should voluntarily remove the hardship of delays from me and that he would deprive himself of losses by scheduled payments! For that man who delays offering what is established makes enforcement necessary.

LETTER 12.9 (C. 533–35)

This letter orders the restoration of property rights to someone (Afer, or "the African") from North Africa. The letter seems to describe diplomatic conditions between Italy and Vandalic North Africa and contrasts the ease of acquisition of those rights in Italy to the difficulties a Roman of Italy would face in North Africa. The potential for cultivating the petitioner as a diplomatic broker is explored, indicating that he still maintained status in North Africa.

Praefectus Praetorio *Senator to Paschasius,* Praefectus Annonae

1. It is wholly in good faith to obligate a foreign people with public benefactions and to permit the acquisition of property, not only to people of common blood, but also to invite newcomers to that same privilege. It is a heredity without relations, a succession absent parents, in which pronouncing the speech of the homeland is the only connection to kinship. For thus does the African seek benefaction, so that he may claim those rights formerly withdrawn from him. Since the name was first conferred upon a family, so that it could afterward be applied to the title of those following, a gift without obligation to the recipient, generosity beyond public entitlement.[15] **2.** Hence it is that they claim foreign inheritances by a certain right and what the Roman is not able to obtain in similar circumstances seems only to apply to them.[16] They do not have such a privilege in their own country, but here all citizens are family in such a circumstance. The entire nation is one family, insofar as it pertains to the privilege of succession. **3.** Concerning which, let your able-mindedness review the requests of the appellant with careful consideration and if in truth that man,[17] whom he claims to have passed from this light, has not left sons, nor may it rightfully be owned by another, let your office permit the introduction of the aforementioned case, by virtue of frequent practice, to the extent that the ancient duty of the present rulers would restore the privileges of owners and he would be able to entreat on behalf of those from whom he knows his wishes deserved more.[18] Let him reclaim that property he had pined for as lost. One who has claimed the best countryside will not be able to call himself a foreigner any longer. Let him have distinction like that of landowners and let one who sought an opportunity from foreign hands, now restored, bear taxes. **4.** Let him rejoice that he has accomplished this for himself, so that he may contribute what is known to pertain only to ownership in particular. Since he may not alienate what he has succeeded in gaining, he is inferior to other owners only in this condition. But we consider he has attained this too with great fairness, as one who succeeds to the role of a caretaker would rightly protect his own property in foreign lands with the affection of a father. Having been fed with compassion, he now feeds others; it happens fortunately for him both to enjoy captivity in a celebrated Roman city and to share in the privileges of Africans.

---

15. Cassiodorus here seems to be making a connection between rights of the "African" to Roman citizenship, and the adoption of the title Africanus by some ancient Romans.

16. That is, a Roman from North Africa may claim legal rights in Italy, while a Roman from Italy could not do the same in Vandalic North Africa.

17. "Your able-mindedness" is *tua experientia.*

18. It may be that it was thought the petitioner could strengthen lines of communication between the Ostrogothic and Vandalic courts.

LETTER 12.10 (C. 533–38)

This letter warns about a familiar form of peculation: officials accepting bribes to defer the payment of taxes, resulting in spiraling debt for landowners and the state. Here, *cancellarii* charged with collecting taxes in the provinces are threatened with the loss of personal property and degrading removal from office should the practice persist.

Praefectus Praetorio *Senator to the Various* Cancellarii *of the Provinces*

1. The neglected portions of public accounts must be compared to an unfortunate sickness. What burdens also enfeebles, unless quickly discharged. Indeed, it is a kind of condemnation to be in debt, nor is it possible for one who is known to be indebted to truly be called free. The wise man compels himself; less careful is the man who is urged by another. For what does harassment endured for an entire year accomplish? The amount owed consumes the payment of future indictions. **2.** You do not spare them by holding back payment; you weigh them down by releasing them, and when you seek delays purchased with bribery, you double the burden of taxation. Abandon, then, this cruel mercy, a kindness completely steeped in accursedness. One who connives by being kind strikes more severely, and one who delays collecting taxes within the accustomed time injures with generosity. And so, desist from selling the losses of the landowners at any time, since you render entirely constrained by disadvantages what you disregard with harmful postponements. For after such practices, do not expect that you will be warned again with words, but that you will be compelled by irrevocable distraint. **3.** Therefore, if you have neither sent to our treasury on *ille* day the amount that is annually required from the provincials, nor have you balanced the difference in the accounts from your own resources, you will instantly be dishonorably discharged from the province where you know you have been dilatory, since it is exceedingly corrupt that the public account should fall to your negligence and that the treasurer should constantly pay out money borrowed from public use.

LETTER 12.11 (C. 533–37)

This letter appoints a magistrate to manage the supply and distribution of preserved foods (*opsonia*) to the residents of Rome. The letter includes an interesting parable on the nature of purity and a curious, near-monastic characterization of the people of Rome.

Praefectus Praetorio *Senator to Peter,* Vir Clarissimus *and Distributor of Preserved Foods*

1. One who is appointed to distribute the favors of a *Princeps* ought to be of proven good conscience, lest what flows with such liberality should whither with the corruption of greed. For the hands of grasping men will adulterate any beneficence whatever and just as the purity of a spring is spoiled by mud, thus is the affluence of a good king changed by greedy distributors. Even gold, when melted into a liquid state, unless it is received into the cleanest vessel, becomes tainted, when only material that is not darkened with the admixture of filth preserves its purity. How pleasing to see streams coursing through snowy channels and, in a manner, for that very purity to enjoy the freedom of nature because, uncompromised,[19] it is sullied by no blemish. Thus should gifts from the ruler of state not be darkened with any pollution, but their bounty ought to reach the Romans just as pure as when it originated from him. **2.** For granted that any fraud is known to be serious, but that which acts against the populace of Rome is rendered unbearable. It is a crowd abiding in peace, a people that is unheard except when celebrating, a clamor without sedition, an uproar lacking fury, whose only contention is to flee poverty while not cherishing wealth. For they know not how to be fond of gain, nor would they torment themselves with the fervor of commercial enterprise; they live modestly in wealth and lavishly in good character. Would it not be impious to steal from such people, who know not how to cheat others? **3.** Therefore, we grant to you, by divine grace, the preserved foods that must be distributed to the Roman people from this indiction, so that what the royal court has generously promised could be attained without any obstruction. Beware, lest some other person take what the people deserve, rendering you a stranger to our gratitude if you should lapse in civic affection. Do not let someone who does not hold the rights of that city by birth become Latian for a price.[20] What that name grants to the people must always be respected, because it grants to human affairs an ability to be noted with distinction. Such a reward belongs to the Quirites.[21] Let not servile fortune steal the place of a free man. That man who defiles the purity of that blood with the company of servants sins against the majesty of the Roman people.

LETTER 12.12 (C. 533–38)

A charming letter requisitioning a particular cheese and wine for royal banquets. The letter is an homage to the gustatory delights of Cassiodorus's home province. For similar "self-portraits," *Variae* 12.14 and 12.15. What these letters lack by way of explaining the administration of the region, they more than compensate as explanations for Cassiodorus's later retirement there.

19. Cassiodorus here uses *iniuriata*, probably as a reference to the oaths of conduct taken by magistrates.

20. The distribution of the *annona*, of which preserved foods was a considerable part, was strictly limited to freeborn residents of Rome, here figuratively named "Latian."

21. The ancestral name of Romans, used elsewhere only rarely in the collection.

Praefectus Praetorio *Senator to Anastasius,*
Cancellarius *of Lucania and Bruttium*

1. While we dined at a formal event with the lord of state, the various provinces were praised for their individual delicacies and, with conversation continuing as is wont, it arrived at the wines of Bruttium and the sweet cheese of Sila, which, by benefit of the grasses there, is produced with such natural pleasantness that you would not believe a flavor that you observe as unmixed with any substance should lack honey. There, slight coaxing expresses milk from pipelike udders and, from the richness of nature, when collected in flasks, as though into second stomachs, it does not rain in drops, but pours almost in rapid torrents. It emits a sweet and complex odor; the pasture of cattle is detected by the nose, which, scented with diverse qualities, is thought to exhale something similar to frankincense. **2.** To this, such richness is blended, that you would deem something similar to Pallas's liqueur flowed,[22] except that it is distinguished from the meadow-green of the olive by its snowy whiteness. Then, that miraculous supply received by the delighted herdsman in wide-open jars, when by admixture it begins to thicken and harden to a tender solidity,[23] it is fashioned into the shape of a beautiful sphere, which, when stored for a short time in an underground storehouse, causes the substance to be long-lasting cheese. You will send ships loaded with this cheese as soon as possible, so that by a small gift, I may be seen to satisfy royal wishes. **3.** Search, too, for the wine, which antiquity called the *Palmatianum,*[24] wishing to confer praise, because it is not dry or bitter, but pleasing with sweetness. For although it may seem the most remote among Bruttian wines, it has nevertheless been made distinguished practically in popular opinion. For there, it is considered equal to Gazan, and similar to Sabine, noted for its weighty aroma. **4.** But since it has claimed the noblest reputation for itself, let the choicest vintage in this wine be selected, lest the wisdom of the ancients should seem to have named something inappropriately. For it is gently dense with rich sweetness, full and lively, with a forceful bouquet, also white and clear, which diffuses such flavor in the mouth that it rightly seems allocated a name from the palm. **5.** It binds faltering bowels, dries weeping wounds, restores a faint breast, and what a skillfully brewed remedy barely succeeds in treating, this offers naturally and unaccompanied. But take care that you would send the exact varieties described above, since we, who recall this with patriotic integrity, are not able to be deceived; for up to this point, we have offered what was desired from our own cellars. You, however, will produce at your own risk anything dissimilar to what you know is still held in traces.

22. Olive oil.
23. An admixture of rennet.
24. "Award winning."

LETTER 12.13 (C. 533–38)

This letter responds to a situation in which *canonicarii* have been collecting taxes from churches by falsely claiming to execute the authority of fiscal accountants (*numerarii*). The churches in question had received certain unspecified fiscal immunities by earlier imperial decree, and Cassiodorus seeks to distance these actions from the policies of his prefecture through repudiation.

An Edict

1. The largesse distributed by our rulers ought to be preserved by the effort of all, when what they are shown to accomplish by the inducement of divine authority is necessary to benefit all people. Indeed, the devotion of the *Principes* safeguards the entire *imperium* and, provided that fitting compensation is returned to them, the limbs of the republic are preserved intact. Some time ago, indeed, imperial decrees assisted the holy churches of Bruttium and Lucania by a particular offering of gifts. But as it is habitual for sacrilegious intentions to sin even against divine reverence itself, the *canonicarii* have been removing a considerable portion in the name of the *numerarii,* making the property of clergy a profit for the laity. **2.** But the *numerarii* of our office, repudiating this detestable abomination, report that nothing that impious hands have embezzled by such crime has been paid to them. To what length will you assay with inhuman audacity, if you extend thefts even there, where you know you are least able to be concealed? That you may perhaps toy with human witnesses, however shamefully, nevertheless seems to be a particular presumption. But one who assumes he may perpetrate what divine authority may not condone has been condemned to such great blindness! **3.** But lest similar presumption should perchance violate further or repeated transgressions should challenge divine patience, we have determined in the formula of an edict that anyone who is involved further in this fraud shall be deprived of official rank and shall lose the enjoyment of his own property. Indeed, one who has extended his own audacity no less than to injury of the divine must be seriously stricken with punishment. Let the poor hold the gifts of those ruling; let those who have no property possess something. **4.** Why should the resources of another, established by royal generosity, be plundered? The possession of it is the gift of the *Princeps*. In what way may a subject presume to seize what he beholds the humility of the ruler offering to God? Moreover, not giving to such men is stealing from them; and rightly, when one capable of assisting the hungry condemns them if he does not feed them. Let it be a shame to rob from those whom we are commanded to support. Desiring to become wealthy from the poverty of the needy is beyond all perfidy. Let honest profit be loved, let damnable gains be feared. Thus, let no man dare to pilfer what is able to scatter gathered blessings. One who acquires by withholding perishes by increasing and he instead draws poverty upon himself if he does not reject the money of the needy.

LETTER 12.14 (C. 533-38)

Similar to *Variae* 12.12 and 12.15, this letter is an excuse to wax nostalgically on Cassiodorus's native region. Here, Regium is excused from the payment of taxes on grain and other products not available owing to the peculiar environmental regime of the area. Less is said of fiscal instructions than the natural geography, in which Cassiodorus clearly delights.

Praefectus Praetorio Senator to Anastasius,
Cancellarius of Lucania and Bruttium

1. The citizens of Regium, the most distant in Bruttium, whom at some point in the past the blows of the violent sea detached from the body of Sicily (whence their city derives its name, for it is called a "division," ῥήγιον, in the Greek language), have reported themselves to be exhausted by the unfair seizures of the tax collectors. They plead for assistance, appealing to things known to us not by the ears, but with our eyes, which know that what is required of their region is not to be had. For the earth is thin in rocky mountains, parched for pasturage, but undulating with vineyards. It is hostile to corn, yet suitable for olive trees; and therefore, the entire cultivation is with a light hoe, since the dryness of the topsoil does not permit seeds to take root from above.[25] A barren field there is clothed with labor of the back rather than by nature. **2.** For country that is acknowledged as the most arid is covered only in the greenery of Pallas's tree. Indeed, in such locales, these trees prosper, which penetrate the earth deeply with extensive roots. Corn fields are irrigated, so that they may thrive and, by an alternate method, that growth which is available in olives produces grains of corn. How much corn can be cultivated by hand? Rarely does a farmer there return from the threshing floor with burdened shoulders, so that he is hardly able to fill a few baskets from the entire reaping, much less gather a harvest in granaries. **3.** However, a productive yield is had in the gardens of the rustics, since every vegetable there is tasty when sprinkled with sea spray; the savor customarily produced by human effort is received while the vegetables are nurtured. Contrary to the opinion of Maro, however, the fibers of the endive from this place are the sweetest,[26] which grows in tight masses of snarled leaves with a tough fragility, whence, having been plucked, it snaps something like glass when removed from fertile earth. **4.** If you would know, this region is rich in such foods. For it also enjoys a pleasant harvest in marine delicacies, since both the upper and lower seas unite there along a curved bay that produces the delicacies of both seas gathered into a single haven with its own encircling current. Hence it is necessary that the fish there remain in motion, where it

---

25. The seeds must be planted and buried in worked furrows, rather than "broadcasting" the seeds on the surface.

26. Virgil, *Georgics* 1.118–21, explains that the endive is a bitter plant.

is even possible for the wave to be torn away. **5.** There is also the *exormiston*, a kind of king among fish,[27] similar in body to an eel, but differing in color, with bristled nostrils, possessing a delicious tenderness, succulent with sweet and oily fluid. It is eagerly sought for its fatty flesh, when it attempts to escape churning waves in the exposure of air and fails to return to I know not what lair. I believe that, either forgetful of its return or weakened by extreme age, it is unable to descend through the rising waves with opposing effort. It is carried as though a lifeless body, in danger from no exertion and avoiding by no stratagem, and it is believed not to return because it is utterly lacking in strength, since it seems unable to flee. This fish is clearly distinguished as the sweetest, such that no other fish compares to it. **6.** These things of which we speak are from the shore of Regium, which we know not by referring to another writer, but which we remember with the proof of our own eyes. Therefore, we have decided that at no time is grain or lard to be demanded in the name of taxes, since what is not available as a natural blessing of the place is required with excessive maliciousness. A defense of the truth and the testimony of a magistrate ought to suffice, therefore, since it is an especially execrable wickedness that, if, when something is known in good conscience, the tongue should declare something different. It is added, moreover, that the city is wearied with the arrival of so much frequent travel, it is worn down with such a great turbulence of expeditions, that whatever is known to be produced there should understandably be remitted to them.

LETTER 12.15 (C. 533–38)

The final piece in a "tryptic" of portraits of Cassiodorus's native region, this letter revels in the natural resources of Scyllaceum (modern Squillace) in order to justify the cancellation of its contribution to the local *cursus publicus*. For a treatment of Como for the same reason, see *Variae* 11. 14.

Praefectus Praetorio *Senator to Maximus*, Vir Clarissimus *and* Cancellarius *of Lucania and Bruttium*

1. It is reported that Scyllaceum, the foremost city of Bruttium, which, it is read, had been founded by Ulysses, the destroyer of Troy, is unreasonably troubled by an excess of unauthorized seizures; it is not fitting that this occur during our tenure, since we are compelled to feel attacks against it more acutely, inasmuch as it obviously affects us with patriotic affection. The city, situated above the Adriatic gulf,[28] hangs from the foothills like a cluster of grapes, not that it may gloat over the

---

27. Mentioned previously at *Var.* 12.4.1.

28. The modern Ionian Sea; Cassiodorus describes the Adriatic Sea as extending south between Greece and Sicily.

perilous climb, but so that it may view with pleasure the verdant fields and the dark-blue cover of the sea. **2.** It beholds the sun rising from its very cradle, where the approaching day does not dispatch morning light in advance, but suddenly, as it becomes visible, an erupting flash reveals its torch. It views Phoebus rejoicing, and there glitters back with the splendor of its own illumination, so that you would deem this more to be the homeland of the sun, with the reputation of Rhodes surpassed. It prospers in clear light and has been gifted with moderate seasons: it feels warmed winters, cooled summers, and completes seasons without sorrow, where foul weather is not feared. Hence it is even the case that men are more unimpeded in perception, since all passions are moderated. **3.** Indeed, a boiling homeland makes men excitable and fickle, a chilled climate makes them slow-witted and untrustworthy: it is only the temperate climate that fashions the character of men with its own nature.[29] Hence it is that the ancients called Athens the seat of the wise, which, anointed with the purity of its air, by blessed benevolence equipped the clearest minds for the contemplative life. For does it not matter that a body swallows down muddied waters, on the one hand, and sips at the clarity of the sweetest spring, on the other? Thus, the force of the soul is oppressed when it is restrained by heavier airs. For, by necessity, we are subject to the nature of such things when sadness is caused by overcast weather and again, naturally, we rejoice at bright weather, since the heavenly substance of the soul delights at everything pure and unspoiled. **4.** The city also enjoys an abundance of marine delicacies, since it possesses nearby tidal pools which we made; indeed, at the foot of Mount Moscius, we admitted an appropriate flow of Nereus's currents into pits excavated in the stone, where a school of fish, playing in free captivity, both restores temperaments with amusement and soothes with the marvel of the sight.[30] They rush eagerly to the hands of men and, before they become food, they seek morsels. A man nourishes his own delicacies and while he holds what he may claim in his power, it often happens that, contented, he releases them all. **5.** Furthermore, residents in the city are not deprived of the fine spectacle of their labors. Satisfyingly abundant grape harvests are descried, the heaped chafe of the threshing floors is evident, and the features of green olives are also in view. Nothing of the pleasantness of the countryside is lacking for one who is able to view everything from the city. For this reason it has no walls, that you will think it a rural city, that you will believe it an urban villa and, situated between both, it becomes known in praise as being abundantly wealthy. **6.** Since travelers frequently desire to visit this place, because they long to find refuge from the weariness of labor in the charm of the city, the citizens are exhausted by the expense of their own provisioning of trans-

29. This is a common ethnographic conceit evident from Aristotle to Vegetius.

30. The "fish ponds" for which Cassiodorus later named his monastic school Vivarium; cf. Cassiodorus, *Institutiones*.

port animals and the *annona*. Therefore, lest its own charm injure the city or the fact of its fame become a cause for expense, we have determined that the provisioning of transport animals and the *annona* based on allotted travel warrants should be charged to the public taxes. 7. Moreover, utterly cutting the gratuities of the judge, we have decided that the *annona* should be offered to a governor for three days only, according to ancient stipulations, with delays made in travel at their own expense. For those executing the laws intended them to be a remedy, not a burden. For which reason, it is for the courts to relieve our city with the sight of equity; what we grant to you will not be revoked. Live in the justice of the times and, by God's guidance, with the privileged joy of security. Others may speak of the Islands of the Blessed,[31] but I would rather the designation apply to your home.[32]

LETTER 12.16 (C. 537)

This is a summons to all provincial officials to commence the new tax cycle. Attention given to necessity of stable institutions in times of duress nod to the ongoing military conflict in Italy (the Gothic War).

A Canonicaria

1. Time continually instructs us to adapt to human needs, while, by our seizing an opportune moment, it even reconciles us to calamitous events; thus do we revive attention to the payment of taxes in annual celebration, when the administration of the republic is understood to hold together by such an institution. And what is provided for the utility of all is rightly promised by oath. Such a policy whence the republic is seen to be at its strongest must be cherished; provided that it is readjusted by a returning census, it is maintained by the firmest vigor of its own condition.[33] 2. Therefore, demonstrated loyalty is important at any time, but greater appreciation is rendered then, when there is more need. Accordingly, let the landowners offer payments for the future of their own good standing. Indeed, a debt that may not be avoided always ought to be offered with an agreeable disposition, so that what is known to be paid without compulsion may become a benefit. 3. And so, may it be happily announced, for the first indiction, we command you to remind the landowner in your diocese that a loyal subject may pay the amount of taxes in three separate installments, to the extent that none may groan over

---

31. A legendary place in Greek mythology inhabited by heroes.

32. Mommsen's edition indicates two possible lacunae in the text of this letter which the Fridh edition does not acknowledge. The lacunae do not impede translation.

33. In other words, the economic policies maintained by the state and the state itself are interdependent.

collection by unexpected compulsion, nor again may anyone claim themselves to be exempted by a prolonged release from payment. Let none transgress the amount of the correct weight and let the scales be thoroughly just; if it should be appropriate for the weights to be adulterated, there will be no limit to grasping. **4.** And so, you will send to our secretariat, on schedule, an accurate account of each four-month period, so that truth of expenses may shine forth from the public accounts, with the shadow of any error scrubbed clean.[34] But whereby you would more easily be able to complete what is assigned, we have ordered *ille* and *ille*, public servants of our office, mindful of their own risk, to supervise you and your staff, to the extent that the order you acknowledge may be shared for the purpose of completing it blamelessly. Therefore, beware, lest you assume culpability for either corrupt bribery or idle neglect, and lest what you decline to accomplish may bring loss to your fortune.

LETTER 12.17 (C. 533–34)

An intriguing command to improve the defenses of Ravenna, this is the only letter which clearly seems misplaced in the collection. As a letter written in the name of Athalaric, it properly belongs to either Book 8 or 9, although Cassiodorus may have written it while serving as *Praefectus Praetorio,* before Athalaric's death in 534.

King Athalaric to Johannis, Siliquatarius *of Ravenna*

1. The certain defense of a city is the hope of all, when what is truly to be feared in battle is learned from foreign people in a time of peace. For the habitation of each city is full of men from diverse nations.[35] Who knows with what nation conflict may happen? And so, everyone ought to consider what would discourage the approach of a future enemy. Therefore, you will take care to admonish the landowners by our command, so that the wide mouths of trenches would be extended near the hill of Caprarius and the encircling area outside the walls and that such a gap should remain open there, so that no entrance would be gained. Why, abominable men, do you scrutinize the illegal access points when entrance may be freely gained at the gates? I know not what you, who do not desire to enter openly, would think to conceal. **2.** An upstanding conscience holds to the public ways, appreciates the placement of obstacles and, when it agreeably follows various pursuits, is not burdened with the fatigue of anxiety. However, anonymity is the companion of

---

34. One imagines that Cassiodorus is being figurative by *obscuritate detersa,* although the literal sense of scrubbing documents clean of any fraud is probably also true.

35. The meaning of this obscure statement is unclear, referring perhaps to rumors of war brought to Ravenna by immigrants, or perhaps to the fear of the city's betrayal by new residents.

a criminal and one who counterfeits good conscience conceals his tracks. Thence, let the ancient through fares be recalled to common use, lest, when criminals seek an advantage for their pains, they should suffer the loss of their lives. For that man should justly be considered an enemy who strives to violate the defenses of the city.

LETTER 12.18 (C. 535)

A letter in which Cassiodorus has delegated a wide range of tasks including highway repairs and provisioning of the army to an official of unknown title. As a "most capable gentleman" (*vir experientissimus*), the recipient probably lacked the rank of a provincial governor and may have been assigned to preparations for the movement of Theodahad's *comitatus* from Ravenna to Rome in 535. The following letter, ordering preparations at Rome, strengthens this interpretation.

Praefectus Praetorio *Senator to Constantinianus,* Vir Experientissimus

1. Just as the royal administration announces warnings to the negligent, thus does it provide support for those toiling strenuously, since the reward of a good life is to serve under the gaze of a master, from whom it is possible neither to conceal a good deed nor to hide blame. How pleasing it is, having been sent on a journey to pass without any obstacle, to behold signs of diligence, to pass doubtful places without fear, to easily ascend mountainous steps, and to traverse a route on bridges with no trembling in the movement of beams, so that everything would demonstrate agreement with purpose! You transcend your own allotted service if you are able to please the ruler of state. For we strive to obey one who grants great advancement, if you should deserve to come to his attention in high regard. **2.** Concerning which, the Via Flaminia has been ploughed up by the furrows of streams. Bind the widest gaps in the embankments with the addition of bridges and clear away the boundaries of the road overgrown with wild trees. Let the stipulated number of transport animals with choice quality of body be procured and let the produce of the designated *annona* be gathered without any detriment to the landowners, since thus do you render everything pleasing, if you should sin in no way. Only one instance may mar an entire enterprise, and it is thought to wholly fail when the least complaint stirs severity. **3.** Beyond the goods normally requisitioned, seek with great attention the ingredients that should appear on a king's table. For what does it benefit to satisfy the army, if it happens that you have failed in provisioning the rulers? Let the provincials obey your admonitions; let the particular cities indicated supply the goods declared in the attached reports. For however much it satisfies the pleasure of the *Princeps,* they may confidently request his favors. Moreover, know that I judge your actions in person: whether rejoicing, I render the ruler's gratitude to you, or wrathful, I extend the censure of the *Princeps.* Act, therefore, lest your transgressions should be imputed to me, since I shall recompense from your property every harm that I endure by your fault. Let the entire army instead pay its gratitude to me. It will mean great glory for you and render me secure to earn good opinions from such assignments.

LETTER 12.19 (C. 535)

Where *Variae* 12.18 seeks a range of preparations for the king's departure from Ravenna, the present letter seeks to mobilize resources at Rome for his arrival, including the repair of bridges on the Tiber and organizing the Senate for a proper greeting.

Praefectus Praetorio *Senator to Maximus,* Vicarius *of Rome*

1. Certainly, you are able to learn of the arrival of kings from the very frequency of travelers, since it is given that a great event should always send forth the appropriate indications. The rise of Lucifer announces the coming day;[36] a favorable wind precedes the approach of clear skies; we learn of the immediacy of good things by a kind of prophesizing of the mind and a task that is declared by the least hint of indications is accomplished with the greatest difficulty. **2.** Thus do we admonish by necessity that you should properly clothe the flood of the Tiber with connecting bridges, to the extent that chaining boats together may offer a crossing of fixed tremulousness and the river may offer the speed of its rushing by its own immobility. It should not be operated with slow cables, as is usual; such a mass should not be subject to drawing by hand. Let fastened boats instead permit a speed that they had not previously offered when moving.[37] Let hordes of travelers walk across in perfect safety, not sail. Let a current divided convey us. It would befit the conveyance of the king if he ought to be greeted by a kind of novelty. **3.** Planks bound fast ought to offer the requisite firmness, so that it should remove the fear of attempting the current by its similarity to earth. Indeed, when a bridge is crossed so harmlessly, one wishes it were longer. The protection of railing should be fitted to the right and left; good fortune is granted to crossing when bitter accident has been avoided. You know you are to be confronted: see that you prepare whatever else is in your interest. For it is thus important not to be found blameworthy before such a great assembly! One who withholds anything necessary to a king afflicts all in common since, when gladdened, the king is welcomed by all, but it casts a shadow over all if he should be found harmed. **4.** It is additionally noteworthy to be praised upon meeting the Senate, for a *Princeps* to be received thus, that all may know nothing is amiss, and that before the ruler arrives, all know he is gladdened rather than perturbed by any consternation. It is an unexpected blessing, if the man who

---

36. "Light bringer," the morning star.
37. The Tiber should be fordable by pontoon bridge as opposed to ferry.

is prone to the being mistrusted should procure for himself the benefit of gratitude. In which case, know that we have sent *ille*, an agent of our office,[38] who ought
to assist you and your staff, to the extent that he would report all preparations to
us, since what is known to assign danger to us may not be entrusted to an accident.

LETTER 12.20 (C. 536)

Early in 536, Theodahad funded an embassy to Constantinople by Pope Agapitus,
who died at the eastern capital. It would have been normal practice for the royal
court to provide envoys with money to distribute as gifts, although envoys would
provide some form of surety for the sum entrusted to them. In this case, the church
of Rome had submitted expensive liturgical vessels, which the treasury agents
addressed by the letter are commanded to restore.

Praefectus Praetorio *Senator to Thomas and Peter,*
Viri Clarissimi *and* Arcarii

1. You remember along with me, faithful gentlemen, that the holy pope of Rome,
Agapitus, when by royal command he was sent for the courtesy of an embassy to the
eastern *Princeps*, received *tot* pounds of gold from you with securities given by a
promissory note as custom requires,[39] so that our provident master would also spur
to haste the departure of the one whom he had commanded. Truly, the ruler gave
the money on loan in necessity, initially offering it in kindness;[40] but how much
more glorious will he become to furthermore bestow as a gift what would have been
returned with the obligation of gratitude. 2. Necessity was conquered without loss;
the hand of the pope distributed what his property could not afford and a journey
known to be full of giving was rendered debt-free. How wonderful, I declare, it was
to see the bishop pour largesse upon the needy and for the church to feel no damage! The king was a benefactor rather than a lender, since the act inevitably should
be credited to the one whose resources were expended. What would such an
embassy, dispatched in such unparalleled manner, not rouse in a devoted *Princeps*?
3. Therefore, advised by our instruction and assured by royal command, restore
without any delay to the agents of the holy apostle Peter the sacred vessels, with the
written pledge, so that their prompt return may be seen to advantageously achieve
what is desired. Let accoutrements known across the whole world be returned to
the hands of deacons. Let the bishop be given what was his own, since what he

38. If this letter addresses the same occasion as *Var.* 12.19, it is possible that this agent is the recipient of *Var.* 12.19.

39. The amount of gold entrusted to Agapitus is not disclosed.

40. This may indicate that the initiative for the embassy had come from the church of Rome, which
was currently attempting to negotiate its doctrinal position with Justinian.

obligated to the laws, he justly recovers as largesse. **4.** It is beyond the example that we recounted with great purpose in our history.[41] For when King Alaric, glutted from the sack of Rome, received the vessels of the apostle Peter among his share of the spoils, as soon as he came to know the nature of the property from his customary inquiry, he ordered them to be returned to the sacred precincts in the hands of the plunderers. In this way, greed, which had permitted a crime in the course of the sacking, blotted the transgression with the most generous devotion. But is it any wonder that one who had enriched himself from such spoliation of the city would not want to ravage the holy property of the saints? **5.** Our king, however, has restored out of religious principle the vessels that were made his own by lawful pledge. And so, let frequent prayer be offered for such a deed, since we believe it possible to receive happiness when we seek remuneration for good acts.

LETTER 12.21 (C. 533–38)

This letter appoints a scribe to serve in the secretariat at Ravenna. Although a letter of appointment in every other regard, this specimen is somewhat unusual in that it states only indirectly that the recipient has been given the post of scribe.

Praefectus Praetorio *Senator to Deusdedit*, Scriba *at Ravenna*

1. The office of scribes is accustomed to be the safeguard of all, when the legal right of each person is preserved by its care. For some documents are consumed in flame, furtive theft claims others, and negligence sometimes loses what the careful author has collected; but whatever is lost by private citizens may most assuredly be restored where it concerns public trust. **2.** The attentions of this office are more diligent with the documents of others than they can be with regard to their own; without reminder, the scribe accomplishes what another scarcely completes upon request, and the audited man is unable to deny what would be in his best interest to profess having lost. This man's strongbox is the fortune of all, and the protection of all is rightly claimed where the record of all business is found. He transcends paternal duties, since uncorrupted truth is his preserve. For just as the diligent father preserves so that his successor may inherit free of care, thus, this testator permits no portion to be cheated for his own advantage. **3.** And we expect the warden of such great importance to be thus continually, and so you, who thus far have been pleasing with respect to your integrity, ought to become tainted with no inconsistency. See what ancient trust and daily efficiency is expected from you. You separate the claims of disputing parties; it is rather you, who loosens the entanglements of cases, who decides from

---

41. A reference to Cassiodorus's lost *Gothic History;* the example referred to here, for which Cassiodorus's source was probably Orosius, did not survive in the iteration produced by Jordanes, cf. *Getica* 156.

your charge what will be tried among judges. This noble grace, this indisputable testimony, the ancient voice of documents, when it arrives incorrupt from your sanctum, advocates respectfully yield and litigants, however dishonest, are nevertheless compelled to obey. And although it may be proper for a published sentence to be suspended, it is not permitted for you to be obstructed. **4.** For which reason, you may not enjoy bribery. The wicked flattery of one who purchases favors is the worm of documents, for they seek to consume what they know impedes them. Let the comely publication of the truth nourish you; let integrity be held as your property. Grant to petitioners what has already been enacted. Be a transcriber, not an inventor, of ancient enactments. Copy the transcript as a signet ring upon wax, so that, just as the face is unable to avoid the indications expressed on it, thus should your hand refrain from differing with the original. **5.** Because if the litigant draws you into any kind of miscarriage of justice, how may he trust, in other cases, one whom he knows to be capable of corruption? He will accuse and easily convict for his own fraud, you, whom he has already entrapped in one case. Love justice, about which none complain, so that even the wrathful man, who in vain tempts you to deviate, would be able to provide sure testimony. Whether you are found praised in gratitude or condemned for offense, everything that you will accomplish is public.

LETTER 12.22 (C. 537–38)

A letter ordering an increase in taxes from the province of Istria, owing to the bounty of cultivation there. Additionally, the letter orders the delivery of gold to purchase a larger portion of the crop than usually required as taxes, presumably because, with the advance of the Gothic War, the court has lost control of tribute paying regions in central and southern Italy. Instructions to officials tasked with executing this directive follows in *Variae* 12.23 and 12.24.

Praefectus Praetorio *Senator to the Provincials of Istria*

1. Public expenses, fluctuating with diverse variations throughout the year, can be held in check by this means: if the appropriateness of demands accords with the yield of each region. Certainly, collection is easy there, where profit is more bountiful. For if the indication of sterile poverty is ignored, then the province is harmed and the desired result is not obtained. Consequently, we have learned by the attestation of travelers that the province of Istria, so named with praise from three outstanding crops, rejoices in fertility this year, being laden by divine gift with wine, oil, and grain. And so, let the mentioned commodities, given in payment of taxes in the amount of *tot solidi*,[42] be charged to you for the current first indiction; but the remainder we leave on behalf of the customary expenses of a loyal province.

---

42. The amount is not given.

2. But since an amount greater than what we had stipulated must be obtained from you, we have also sent *tot solidi* from our treasury, so that the necessary goods may be productively gathered without loss to you. For often, when you are compelled to sell to strangers, you are accustomed to experience a loss, especially at a time when the foreign purchaser is suddenly absent and it is rare to receive gold when you know merchants are not on hand. But how much better it is to obey your rulers than to provide for distant people, and to pay taxes with crops, than to bear the contempt of purchasers. **3.** We have caused, moreover, from a love of justice, what you would want to suggest to us, since, while we are not burdened by furnishing ships, we would not adulterate the price. For your region is situated the closest to us across the gulf of the Ionian Sea, covered with olive groves, adorned with grain fields, abundant in vines, where all crops flow forth in optimum fertility as though from three teats of surpassingly rich generosity. Not without warrant is the region called the Campania of Ravenna, the storehouse of the royal city, an exceedingly pleasurable and delightful retreat. **4.** Being set in the north, it enjoys an admirable commingling of climate. It even has its own Baiaes of a sort[43]—I do not claim this recklessly—where the turbulent sea enters inlets of the shore, calming it to a lovely surface with the quality of a lake. These places also furnish much fish sauce and they glory in the bounty of fish. Not one Avernus is located here.[44] Conspicuous are the numerous Neptuniae,[45] in which oysters spawn everywhere unbidden with even lax diligence. Thus, it is proven that there is neither effort in nourishing nor uncertainty in catching with these delicacies. **5.** You may perceive extensive residences scattered far and wide, shining like pearls, so that here it may reveal what kind of discernment was had by the ancestors of this province, which is known to be adorned with such buildings. Moreover, added to the shore is the most beautiful arrangement of islands, which are positioned with lovely utility, both warding ships from danger and enriching cultivators with great fertility. The region clearly restores the attendants of our *comitatus,* it adorns the *imperium* of Italy, it feeds leading men with delicacies and the humble with its payment of stores, and what is produced there is possessed almost entirely in the royal city. Let the loyal province offer its abundance more willingly now; let it obey fully when it is desired, since it used to produce gladly when it was called upon the least. **6.** But lest any uncertainty should proceed from our commands, we have sent with the present directive the most proven gentleman, Laurentius, approved by us in great toil for the republic. Thus, according to the brief attached below, he may unhesitatingly accomplish what he knows to be enjoined upon public expenses. Now procure

43. Cassiodorus returns to the comparison of Istria with Campania, where Baiae was a famous seaside resort.

44. A lake in Campania famous for villae and vinyards.

45. Salinated ponds.

what has been ordered. For you make public service loyal, when you freely undertake a command. 7. But I shall publish the prices determined for you on a subsequent opportunity,[46] when the bearer of the present letter has estimated by sent report the measure of your harvest. For nothing can be appraised for taxes justly, unless the amount of resources can be clearly investigated. It is indeed an unfair assessor who produces a judgment in ignorance and one who decrees without deliberation is shown to be aware of his own bad character.

LETTER 12.23 (C. 537-38)

Following a lengthy directive to the provincials of Istria (*Var.* 12.22), this letter dispatches a praetorian official to assess the capability of the province to sustain increased taxes.

Praefectus Praetorio *Senator to Laurentius,* Vir Experientissimus

1. The deliberation of a magistrate ought to bring proven men to public service, so that it would be easy to satisfy what is clearly needed from the insufficiency of the time. A single person is able to extricate himself from any manner of difficulties in a period of plenty; it is a task for carefully selected public officials, when the pressure of hardship prevails. And so, we order your proven ability, being most pleasing by your devotion to our company, to hasten to the province of Istria, so that you would procure supplies of wine, oil, and grain equivalent to *tot solidi* in taxes; but with another *tot solidi,* which you will claim from our treasury, you will hasten to buy as much from merchants as from the landowners, just as the requisition prepared by the *numerarii* has instructed you. **2.** Therefore, now, raise your spirit for what must be obeyed, you who have been approved for such services by unhesitating selection. Let the example of your first responsibility admonish you, since it is exceedingly egregious for a veteran to fail in his duty, when as a recruit he was known to err under no circumstance. Such a man, however, by honesty toward us, will open himself to favors well beyond the wealth of the aforementioned commodities, so that we may trust what reports indicate concerning you, and so that we may establish as standard practice what neither harms the provincials nor is able to burden public expenses.

LETTER 12.24 (C. 537-38)

The last in a series concerning Istria (*Var.* 12.22-24), this letter directs the ship masters (here addressed as *tribuni maritimorum*) to prepare the transport of

---

46. Prices at which the inhabitants of Istria may sell their surplus after surrendering the portion owed in taxes.

supplies from Istria to Ravenna. The subject afforded a delightful excursus on sea-faring and the Venetian districts that were apparently home to many of the ship masters.

Praefectus Praetorio *Senator to the* Tribuni Maritimorum

1. We previously determined in a published command that Istria should gladly direct to the court at Ravenna the commodities of wine, oil, and grain, of which it enjoys a generous abundance in the current year. But you, who have numerous ships on the border of the province, will provide them with equally pleasing dependability, so that you may strive to convey with speed what has been prepared there for delivery. Indeed, the high regard will be the same for both parties upon accomplishing this, when one sundered from the other would not permit the work to be completed. Therefore, be ready for a neighboring province, you who often cross boundless distances. **2.** You, who sail through your own homeland, travel, after a fashion, to your own reception. It also happens, to your advantage, that another route is available to you, one calm with perpetual safety. For when the sea is closed by savage winds, the way through the most pleasant river courses is opened to you. Your keels are not alarmed at rough gales; they trace the shore with great fortune, and what regularly dashes against the seas knows not how to floun-der. At a distance, you would suppose the ships were carried upon meadows, when it happens their channel is not visible.[47] Ships that are accustomed to stay afloat with rigging are drawn by cables, and by changed condition, men assist their own ships on foot; they draw the maidens of transport without toil and they use the more secure steps of sailors out of fear of the sails. **3.** It is a pleasure to relate how we have seen your homes situated. The Venetians, once greatly famed for cele-brated men, border Ravenna and the Po to the south, enjoying the pleasantness of the Adriatic shores to the east, where, in alternation, the withdrawal of the tide now closes, and the returning flood now opens, access to the sea. Here, a home for you is after the fashion of aquatic birds. For you are now perceived as land-locked, and then as an islander, so that you would consider your homes to be more like the Cyclades,[48] where you behold the appearance of places change suddenly. **4.** Indeed, similar to the islands, homes are seen scattered far into open waters made by nature, but which the ingenuity of men colonized. For here, the solidity of earth is accumulated by mooring pliant osiers, and there is no uncertainty in such a fragile rampart opposing the marine surge, when it is evident that the shallows of the coast are unable to thrust heaps of waves forward and waters not supported by the assistance of depth are carried without force. **5.** Accordingly, there is one source of

---

47. That is, when the ships follow the river courses.

48. Islands of the Greek Aegean that were reported to float and change position in popular literature.

wealth for the inhabitants, so that they may be glutted on fish alone. There, poverty dines with wealth in equality. One food nourishes all, one dwelling shelters all alike, the inhabitants know not how to envy ancestral homes and, abiding under these conditions, they avoid a vice for which the entire world appears guilty. **6.** On the contrary, the sum of your rivalry is in the salt works. Instead of plows and pruning hooks, you roll grinding stones; from this, all your profit is produced, when in this very industry, you possess what you do not make. In this, a kind of dietary coin is struck. Every wave is favorable to your craft. Some are able to seek gold less, there is no one who does not desire to acquire salt, and rightly, when each meal is owed to this, which makes the meal satisfying. **7.** Prepare with diligent care, then, the ships that you tether to your walls in the manner of animals, so that, when that most proven gentleman Laurentius, who has been sent to procure commodities, appears to advise you, you will hasten to set upon your task, to the extent that you, who are able to select an advantageous route on the basis of the quality of weather, would not delay necessary payments with difficulties.

LETTER 12.25 (C. 536)

This letter was directed to the deputy assistant of the *Praefectus Praetorio* to order the storage of additional food stuffs in light of the effects of an unidentified volcanic eruption on crop production. Much of the letter is a poignant meditation on change and the natural order. If the *Vices Agens* acted as the praetorian representative at Rome (cf. *Var.* 11. 4–5), it is also possible the letter was a response to the rupture in food supplies to Rome occasioned by the advance of the Gothic War in southern Italy. In this case, *Variae* 12.22–24, concerning the requisition of commodities from Istria, may also have been a response to exigencies at Rome. The letter's enumeration of the eruption's impact on the winter, spring and summer place it in the autumn of 536, before Belisarius entered Rome in December.

Praefectus Praetorio *Senator to Ambrosius,*
Vir Illustris *and* Vices Agens

1. Those who observe the changing order of the world frequently become agitated, since such things often presage what is shown to be contrary to habit. For nothing happens without provocation, nor does the world operate by casual accident, but whatever we see reach a conclusion is known to be a divine plan. Men are held in suspense when kings alter their own policies, and if problems should proceed other than how their practice had prepared them.[49] But who would not be troubled with great curiosity about such events, if, in a way contrary to precedents,

---

49. This may be a reference to Witigis's decision to abandon Rome after Theodahad's assassination earlier in 536.

something mysterious should seem to come from the heavens? For just as there is a certain comfort in observing the course of seasons in their own particular succession, thus are we filled with great curiosity when such things are thought to be altered. **2.** What does it mean, I ask, to intently gaze upon the most conspicuous star and not witness its usual brilliance;[50] to observe the moon, the splendor of night, in its full circumference, but absent its natural luster? Together, we all still perceive a kind of sea-colored sun; we marvel that physical bodies lack shadows at midday and that the strength of the sun's fullest exposure attains only the dullness of a cooling tepidness, which has happened not in the momentary lapse of an eclipse, but for the duration of almost a full year. **3.** What a terror it is, therefore, to endure daily what usually frightens people only in the swiftest moment! And so, we have had winter without storms, spring without mingled weather, summer without heat waves. How is it now hoped to possibly attain the proper season, when the months that had ripened crops before have cooled intemperately with the northern winds? For what may produce fertility, if the earth does not warm in the summer months? How may buds appear, if the progenitress, rain, does not resume her place? Of all the elements, we find these two opposed, a perpetual chill and a difficult drought. The seasons have changed by not changing and what usually happens with the commingling of showers cannot be procured through dryness alone. **4.** And therefore, let your prudence overcome future scarcity with previous stores, since there was such blessed abundance in the previous year that provisions may suffice for even the coming months. Let everything that is needed for food be stored. The private citizen will easily find necessary things when public provision has been completed. **5.** But, lest the present circumstance torments you with great hesitation, return to a consideration of the nature of things and let what seems uncertain to the gaping crowd become understandable by reason. For it is known to be thus disposed by divine arrangement: just as the stars of the current year have assembled in their own domains for cooperative administration, thus winter has been rendered colder and drier than usual. Hence, air laden with snow from excessive cold is not converted to dryness by the heat of the sun, but abiding its acquired density, it blocks the heat of the sun and deflects the view of human frailty. For matter of the middle air governs our ability to see, and we are able to see through this substance only as much as the thinness of its matter allows. **6.** For this great void, which spreads in the manner of a liquid element between heaven and earth, truly extends our vision, provided it happens to be pure and washed with the brightness of the sun. But, if it is condensed with some mixture, then, as though with a kind of taught membrane, it allows neither particular colors nor the heat of celestial bodies to penetrate. This has also happened frequently in other eras by means of a cloud cover. Hence it is that the rays of stars have been darkened daily

---

50. The sun.

by strange color, that the reaper dreads the novel cold, that fruits have hardened at the approach of the season and that the ripening of grapes on the vine is bitter. **7.** But if this is ascribed to divine providence, we are not to fret, since by command of that very power, we are forbidden from asking for prodigies.[51] Nevertheless, we are certain that this is hostile to products of the earth, when we no longer see proper foods nourished according to their own demands.[52] Accordingly, let your solicitude behave so that the unfruitfulness of one year may not appear to disturb us, since it was foreseen by the founding rector of our office,[53] that the abundance of a previous year would suffice to soften the penury to follow.

LETTER 12.26 (C. 537-38)

This letter remits payments from taxes in wine and grain for citizens of the Veneto owing to widespread crop failure, possibly under the same circumstances as *Variae* 12.25. The collection agent is ordered to correct the imbalance in supplies collected for the army from the surplus at Istria (cf. *Var.* 12.22–24).

Praefectus Praetorio *Senator to Paulus,* Vir Strenuus

1. The public weal is frequently served by brief examples of duty, when what is alleviated by the intervention of good men acquires something more. And so the venerable gentleman Augustine, distinguished by his way of life and his name, coming to us, has revealed the hardships of the Venetians in a tearful report, maintaining that supplies of neither wine, wheat, nor millet have been produced by them, and that the fortunes of the provincials have reached such penury that they are unable to endure the hazards of life, unless royal devotion should provide for them with its accustomed kindness. It seems cruel to us to require anything from petitioners and to request that which a province is known to lack. For one who imposes what is not possible collects only tears from such people. **2.** And so, moved by the report of such a man, by the present dictate, we remit the wine and grain that we had ordered you to collect in the military storehouses at Concordia, Aquileia, and Forum Iulii; thereafter, they will provide only the meat, as the brief given to you maintains. For we shall send a sufficient supply of wheat there, when it will be necessary. **3.** And since we have learned that wine has been produced abundantly in Istria, thereafter, demand from there however much had been requested from the above-mentioned cities, according to the price of the commodities found in the market. Thus, the Istrians will not be harmed, when just

---

51. A reference to the biblical treatment of portents, at Matthew 16.1–4.

52. *Lege propria,* may also be given as "natural law," although it may be important that Cassiodorus did not simply use *ius naturale* or another more common variant.

53. The biblical Joseph, for which see *Var.* 6.3, 8.20, 12.28.

prices are kept for them. Therefore, let you ensure that the present generosity must be appraised with no profit motive, so that, in as much as the remedy will be free of cost, it will nonetheless be able to emerge gloriously. For you know that you will be submitted to serious punishment, if what is forbidden to be prostituted should be found in your possession.

LETTER 12.27 (C. 535–36)

Possibly related to the crop failure reported at *Variae* 12.25–26, this letter requests that the bishop of Milan supervise the distribution of grain at state-subsidized prices. The primary concern is that an unscrupulous manager would accept bribes to reserve the grain for buyers who could afford to horde and then resell the grain for a profit.

Praefectus Praetorio *Senator to Datius, Bishop of Milan*

1. It profits less to order something good, unless we intend to accomplish it through the most holy men. For the righteous inclination of just men increases the benefit and whatever is done without fraud truly attaches to the merits of the one giving. For it is proper that the purity of a priest should accompany the generosity of a *Princeps*. For one whose desire it is to do something good from his own resources is able to commendably fulfill the wishes of another. **2.** And so, we approach your sanctity, whose purpose it is to facilitate divine commands, so that a third of the supply of millet from the granaries of Pavia and Dertona would be distributed to a starving people, just as it has been commanded by the *Princeps*, at twenty-five *modii* per *solidus*.[54] Let this be done under your supervision, lest by anyone's venality this benefit should reach those who are known to be capable of supporting themselves with their own resources. Let one who has less receive the largesse of the *Princeps*. The directive is given to provide assistance to the needy, not the wealthy. One who places wealth in a full vessel instead pours it out, for only what is collected in empty vessels is actually stored. **3.** Therefore, let your sanctity not deem the duty of pity an outrage, since everything is worthwhile for you, where piety is found; indeed, to faithfully act on the wishes of another is the accomplishment of your own good purpose. In order to attend to this business, with God's blessing, we have taken care to dispatch *ille* and *ille,* who, following the directions of your sanctity, will do nothing of their own accord, but will only strive to obey you. But declare to us in your report how many *solidi* have been collected from the above-specified amount of millet, so that they may be held in the treasury and reserved for restoring the above-mentioned commodity at a future time, God willing. After the fashion of repairing a garment, the mending of which is the

---

54. A *modius* was a dry measure, equivalent to a peck, or two dry gallons.

unraveling of threads, so that it may instead be woven into a form new with brilliant elegance.

LETTER 12.28 (C. 535–36)

Last letter of the collection, Cassiodorus here communicates a royal decree to remit half of the taxes normally imposed upon the provinces of Liguria and Aemilia. The letter dwells on the themes of warfare and famine, thus connecting it both to the environmental conditions that preoccupied *Variae* 12.22–27 and also to the politics of maintaining loyalty in Italy during the Gothic War.

An Edict

1. Who does not know that divine providence elects to remove certain things from our use, so that it will be able to test the integrity of humanity? For if it should happen that nobody was in deep need, then generosity would have no place. Penury is given to provincials for the praise of our king; fields have been made barren, so that the fruitfulness of our ruler might become manifest. It would be a less appreciated gift, except that some hardship had preceded it. Rejoice, provincials! Give thanks instead for your misfortunes, when you have proven the spirit of the *Princeps* to be such that that he yields before no adversity. Behold such remarkable duty, which everywhere opposes our disadvantages. **2.** For when the savagery of the tribes had roused itself in a previous time, as you will doubtlessly remember, your Aemilia and Liguria was troubled by an incursion of the Burgundians and a war of raids was waged across the border, the fame of the present *imperium* immediately shone forth as though from a rising sun.[55] Having been forced out with arms, the enemy lamented his own presumption, when he recognized that man to be the ruler of a celebrated people, whose excellence he had tested in the capacity of a soldier.[56] How often did the Burgundian wish he had not left his own boarders, so that he would not contend with our *Princeps* as an adversary, whose presence it was permitted for him to avoid, once relieved of spoils, so that even the downtrodden should incur some blessing? **3.** For as soon as the Goths gathered themselves together with their native vigor for pressing war, thus was the band of raiders cut down in victorious battle, as though it had happened with unarmed men arrayed on one side, and armed men on the other. By the equity of divine judgment, the plunderer fell in the very fields that he had presumed to lay waste. Rejoice, O

---

55. It seems likely that by *praesentis imperii,* Cassiodorus describes the current administration during the Gothic War, in which the Franks had been induced to make incursions into Italy (Procopius, *Wars* 5.1.13); the reference to "Burgundians" may be explained by the fact that the Franks had annexed the Burgundian kingdom by 534.

56. Witigis.

province, adorned with the corpses of your adversaries; find cheer in the heap of dead that the ruin of your enemy clearly created. Liguria is better cultivated, having been denied its own crops, the enemy now provides a harvest of grain;[57] for even though your tribute had been reduced, you have demonstrated triumphs blessedly conceived in your province. **4.** To these events may be added the raid of the Alamanni, routed some time ago, which was proven to be overwhelmed in its very initial attempt, so that it simultaneously combined arrival and departure, as though purged by the salutary operation of a scalpel, to the extent that both the wicked disregard of those transgressing law was punished and the plundering of subjects did not spread unchecked. I could easily enumerate for you how many hosts of enemy have fallen in other places, but being eager for your happiness, after the nature of the human heart, you will want us to speak only about that which you feel pertains specifically to you. **5.** Therefore, let us return to the delightful edict of the *Princeps,* since one who has defended you from the blows of war could not permit the dangers of poverty to abide; for one who ejects the enemy from the province likewise commands famine to depart. Oh, struggle proclaimed throughout the world! The humanity of a glorious *Princeps* fights against cruel indigence, whose heaped granaries truly are military camps, which, if he purposed to keep closed, then would an unbearable enemy enter; but because he has opened them more, he has already routed a cruel adversary. **6.** I know not for which war the world admires our *Princeps* more. Nonetheless, let me say what I feel. It is in the nature of brave men to conclude battles favorably, but it is clearly beyond human strength to conquer poverty. But even with these great feats and such favors, nothing has prevailed to satisfy the prayers of the needy, for which he has seen fit to remit half the payment of the taxes, lest he should cause grief in some region where he has already bestowed so much happiness. **7.** Thus we read that Joseph gave permission for grain to be sold even in the face of a disastrous famine, but the price had been such that, being eager to render assistance, he was about to trade himself rather than sell the food.[58] What a time it was, I declare, to live then in such miseries, from which it was a bitter release to sacrifice one's own liberty, where the free man groans no less than the captive would weep! I believe the holy man was constrained by this necessity, that he should both satisfy a greedy *Princeps* and he should assist an endangered populace. Let me speak by leave of such a father:[59] it is so much more excellent to sell wholesome grain in liberty and to relax taxes on account of impoverishment! **8.** Such is a pleasant kind of bribery, when it thus both yields to those buying and imposes a price that would please you. And so

---

57. This either refers to Burgundian slaves or, more gruesomely, the fertilization of Ligurian fields with Burgundian dead.

58. Genesis 41:41–44.

59. That is, Joseph.

public munificence will sell the amount of twenty-five *modii* for the price of ten, whenever the landowner is unable find it. Humanity has altered the nature of the world; we are ordered to sell cheaply, when the man desirous of food would be prepared to purchase more dearly. Oh, strange outcome of a proclamation! By the acceptance of a loss, both a sale is made and it is the wish of the seller to lose even more, so that by selling he ought to find profit. It is perfectly fitting for the king to conduct commerce such as this; such commerce agrees with the exercise of devotion, so that he should consent to receive less when the purchaser is predisposed to offer more. **9.** It is fitting to remark what affection you should have for the one ruling, since he first consented to the amount he believed necessary and now he has doubled again what was requested. It was shameful for you to hope for anything after such gifts, when the kindness of the *Princeps* had thus far been held in reserve for favors. He does not despise things requested, when he himself has witnessed the sight. It is a fortunate calamity that first finds a pitying man as witness, so that he should not afterward consider a harsh judgment. Therefore rejoice, O Ligurian, already accustomed to favor, a second blessing arrives for your use. For you have surpassed the Egyptians compared to you by your remarkable good fortune; you have avoided a time of hardship and have not lost the gift of freedom. In contrast to that time, you have been rendered free of enemies, when you are also known to be secure from the peril of famine. **10.** However the aforementioned story honors you, it is surpassed by the present measure. For it is read that Joseph had returned the price paid to his brothers only in bags of money. Does it surprise us that by nature's compulsion he is seen to have been kinder to his own kindred? This ruler, however, has sold generously to all men, he has abandoned claim to an owed obligation and has conferred more to taxpayers in common than the other is known to have offered to his brothers alone. Let broadly cast blessings be proclaimed briefly: hence, may the state learn of its own good fortune, when our age is compared, not to that of kings, but of prophets. But lest we delay the object of royal kindness any longer, know that our instructions have been published for those whom it concerns, so that according to the tenor of the command, you may obtain the generosity of the *Princeps*.

BIBLIOGRAPHY OF RELATED READING

STUDIES OF THE *VARIAE*

Amici, Angela. "Cassiodoro a Costantinopoli: Da *Magister Officiorum* a *Religiosus Vir*." *Vetera Christianorumb* 42 (2005): 215–31.

Barnish, Samuel. *Cassiodorus: Variae*. Liverpool: Liverpool University Press, 1992.

———. "Sacred Texts of the Secular: Writing, Hearing and Reading Cassiodorus' *Variae*." *Studia Patristica* 38 (2001): 362–70.

Bjornlie, Shane. *Politics and Tradition between Rome, Ravenna, and Constantinople: A Study of the Cassiodorus and the Variae, 527–554*. Cambridge: Cambridge University Press, 2013.

———. "The Rhetoric of *Varietas* and Epistolary Encyclopedism in the *Variae* of Cassiodorus." In *Shifting Genres in Late Antiquity*, ed. Geoffrey Greatrex, Hugh Elton, and Lucas McMahon, 289–303. Burlington: Ashgate, 2015.

———. "Virtues in a Time of War: Administrative Writing, Dialectic, and the Gothic War." In *The Collectio Avellana and Its Revivals*, ed. Rita Lizzi Testa and Giulia Marconi, 425–62. Newcastle: Cambridge Scholars Publishing. 2019.

———. "What Have Elephants to Do with Sixth-Century Politics? A Reappraisal of the 'Official' Governmental Dossier of Cassiodorus." *Journal of Late Antiquity* 2, no. 1 (2009): 143–71.

Fauvinet-Ranson, Valerie. "Portrait d'une regent: Un panegyrique d'Amalasonthe (Cassiodorus, *Variae* 11.1)." *Cassiodorus* 4 (1998): 267–308.

Fridh, Åke. *Études critique et syntaxiques sur les Variae de Cassiodore*. Göteborg: Elanders, 1950.

———. *Magni Aurelii Cassiodori Senatoris Opera, Pars I*. Turnhout: Brepols, 1973.

———. *Terminologie et formules dans les Variae de Cassiodore: Études sur le développement du style administrative aux derniers siècles de l'antiquité*. Stockholm: Almqvist & Wiksell, 1956.

Giardina, Andrea., et al., eds. *Cassiodoro: Varie*. Vols. 1–5. Rome: L'Erma di Bretschneider, 2014–17.

Gillett, Andrew. "The Purposes of Cassiodorus' *Variae*." In *After Rome's Fall: Narrators and Sources of Early Medieval History*, ed. Alexander C. Murray, 37–50. Toronto: University of Toronto Press, 1998.

Kakridi, Christina. *Cassiodors Variae: Literatur und Politik im ostgotischen Italien*. Munich: Saur, 2005.

Skahill, Bernard. *The Syntax of the Variae*. Washington, D.C.: Catholic University of America, 1934.

Suelzer, Mary J. *The Clausulae of Cassiodorus*. Washington, D.C.: Catholic University of America, 1944.

Vidén, Gunhild. *The Roman Chancery Tradition: Studies in the Language of the Codex Theodosianus and Cassiodorus' Variae*. Göteborg: Acta Universitatis Gothoburgensis, 1984.

Viscido, Lorenzo. *Studi sulle Variae di Cassiodoro*. Calabria: Calabria Letteraria, 1987.

STUDIES OF CASSIODORUS

Barnish, Samuel. "The Work of Cassiodorus after His Conversion." *Latomus* 48 (1989): 157–87.

Croke, Brian. "Cassiodorus and the *Getica* of Jordanes." *Classical Philology* 82, no. 2 (1987): 117–34.

Giardina, Andrea. *Cassiodoro Politico*. Rome: Erma di Bretschneider, 2006.

Halporn, James W., and Mark Vessey. *Cassiodorus: Institutions of Divine and Secular Learning; On the Soul*. Liverpool: Liverpool University Press, 2004.

Krautschick, Stefan, *Cassiodor und die Politik seiner Zeit*. Bonn: Habelt, 1983.

Leanza, Sandro, ed., *Atti della Settimana di Studi su Flavio Magno Aurelio Cassiodoro*. Soveria Mannelli: Rubbettino, 1986.

———. *Cassiodoro: dalla Corte di Ravenna al Vivarium di Squillace: Atti del Convegno Internazionale di Studi*. Soveria Mannelli: Rubbettino, 1993.

Momigliano, Arnaldo, "Cassiodorus and the Italian Culture of His Time." *Proceedings of the British Academy* 41 (1955): 207–36.

O'Donnell, J. *Cassiodorus*. Berkeley: University of California Press, 1979.

Van de Vyver, André. "Cassiodore et son oeuvre." *Speculum* 6 (1931): 244–92.

STUDIES OF OSTROGOTHIC ITALY

Amory, Patrick. *People and Identity in Ostrogothic Italy, 489–554*. Cambridge: Cambridge University Press, 1997.

Arnold, Jonathan. *Theoderic and the Roman Imperial Restoration*. New York: Oxford University Press, 2014.

Arnold, Jonathan, Shane Bjornlie, and Kristina Sessa, eds. *A Companion to Ostrogothic Italy*. Leiden: Brill, 2016.

Barnish, Samuel, "Pigs, Plebeians and *Potentes*: Rome's Economic Hinterland, c. 350–600." *Papers of the British School* 55 (1987): 157–85.

Barnish, Samuel, and Federico Marazzi, eds., *The Ostrogoths from the Migration Period to the Sixth Century: An Ethnographic Perspective*. Woodbridge: Boydell, 2007.

Bjornlie, Shane., "Law, Ethnicity, and Taxes in Ostrogothic Italy: A Case for Continuity, Adaptation and Departure." *Early Medieval Europe* 22, no. 2 (2014): 138–70.

Jones, A. H. M. "The Constitutional Position of Odoacer and Theoderic." *Journal of Roman Studies* 52 (1962): 126–30.

Lafferty, Sean. *Law and Society in the Age of Theoderic the Great: A Study of the Edictum Theoderici*. Cambridge: Cambridge University Press, 2013.

Marazzi, Federico. "The Destinies of the Late Antique Italies: Politico-Economic Developments of the Sixth Century." In *The Sixth Century: Production, Distribution, and Demand*, ed. Richard Hodges and William Bowden, 119–59. Leiden: Brill, 1998.

Moorhead, John., "Cassiodorus on the Goths in Ostrogothic Italy." *Romanobarbarica* 16 (1999): 241–59.

———. *Theoderic in Italy*. Oxford: Oxford University Press, 1992.

O'Donnell, J. "Liberius the Patrician." *Traditio* 37 (1981): 32–71.

———. *The Ruin of the Roman Empire*. New York: Ecco, 2008.

References to either the PLRE or Pietri are provided for individuals where additional information is available, excepting emperors and legendary or mythical figures.

Johannus, *arcarius*: *PLRE II*, "Ioannes 71," 611; Var. 5.6–7

Johannus, *cancellarius* and *praerogativarius*: *PLRE III*, "Ioannes 18," 637; *Var.* 11.6, 11.27

Johannus, *canonicarius*: *PLRE III*, "Ioannes 17," 637; *Var.* 11.38

Johannus, claimant in property dispute: *PLRE II*, "Ioannes 54," 607; *Var.* 4.32

Johannus, court physician: *PLRE II*, "Ioannes 56," 607; *Var.* 4.41

Johannus, governor of Campania: *PLRE II*, "Ioannes 67," 609–10; *Var.* 3.27, 3.30, 3.31, 4.10

Johannus, merchant: *Var.* 3.7

Johannus, Pope (John II): *Var.* 9.15–16, 9.17, 11.2

Johannus, *referendarius*, recipient of Castrum Lucullanum: *PLRE II*, "Ioannes 72," 611; *Var.* 8.25

Johannus, *siliquatarius* of Ravenna: *PLRE III*, "Ioannes 13," 635; *Var.* 12.17

John II, Pope: *Var.* 9.15–6, 9.17, 11.2

Joseph, Biblical character: *Var.* 6.3.1–2, 8.20.3, 12.28.7–10

Jove, Roman deity: *Var.* 6.2.1, 7.15.4

Jovinus, condemned *curialis*: *Var.* 3.47

Julianus, *Comes Patrimonii*: *PLRE II*, "Iulianus 24," 640–41; *Var.* 1.16

Julianus, petitioner: *Var.* 3.14

Juno, Roman deity: *Var.* 7.18.2

Justin, eastern Emperor: *Var.* 8.1

Justinian, eastern Emperor: *Var.* 10.1–2, 10.8–9, 10.15, 10.19, 10.22, 10.25–26, 10.31–35, 11.13

Laetus, magistrate in Spain: *PLRE II*, "Laetus 2," 654; *Var.* 5.39.10

Laurentius, praetorian official: *PLRE III*, "Laurentius 1," 766; *Var.* 12.22.6, 12.23, 12.24.7

Laurentius, presbyter: Pietri 2.2, "Laurentius 34," 1252; *Var.* 4.18

Leodefrid, *saio*: *PLRE II*, "Leodefridus," 666; *Var.* 3.48

Leontius, petitioner: *Var.* 3.52

Leucothea, Greek deity: *Var.* 8.33.1

Liberius, *Praefectus Galliarum*: *PLRE II*, "(Petrus Marcellinus Felix) Liberius 3," 677–81; *Var.* 2.15–16, 3.35, 8.6, 11.1.16–17

Liberius, Gallic *spectabilis*: *PLRE II*, "Liberius 2," 676; *Var.* 4.12, 4.46

Licinia Eudoxia, western Augusta: *Var.* 11.1.9

Liuvirit, *comes*: *Var.* 5.35, 5.39

Lucinus, *cancellarius*: *PLRE III*, "Lucinus 1," 797–98; *Var.* 11.37

Lucinus, *scriniarius*: *PLRE III*, "Lucinus 2," 798; *Var.* 11.24

Mannila, *saio*: *PLRE II*, "Mannila," 705–6; *Var.* 5.5

Marabadus, *comes*: *PLRE II*, "Marabadus," 706; *Var.* 3.34, 4.12, 4.46

Marcellus, *advocatus fisci*: *PLRE II*, "Marcellus 4," 713; *Var.* 1.22

Marcellus, ancient author: *Var.* 3.53.4

Marcianus, *clarissimus*: *PLRE II*, "Marcianus 14," 716; *Var.* 4.42

Marcianus, *spectabilis*: *PLRE II*, "Marcianus 15"; *Var.* 5.35

Marcus, debtor: *Var.* 5.31

Marii, ancient family of the republic: *Var.* 10.11.2

Marinus, petitioner: *PLRE II*, "Marinus 4," 726; *Var.* 4.32

Mars, Roman deity: *Var.* 8.10, 10.31.2

Martinus, victim of parricide: *Var.* 2.14

Matasuntha, daughter of Amalasuntha: *PLRE III*, "Matasuentha," 851–52; *Var.* 10.31.2

Maurentius, orphan: *Var.* 4.9

Mausolus, legendary king: *Var.* 7.15.4

Maximianus, *illustris*: *PLRE II*, "Maximianus 6," 739; *Var.* 1.21, 4.22

Maximus, *cancellarius*: *PLRE III*, "Maximus 2," 867; *Var.* 12.15

Maximus, *clarissimus*: *PLRE II*, "Maximus 17," 747; *Var.* 4.42

Maximus, consul: *PLRE II*, "Fl. Maximus 20," 748–49; *Var.* 5.42, 10.11–12

Maximus, *vicarious* of Rome: *PLRE III*, "Maximus 1," 866; *Var.* 12.19

Memnon, ancient architect: *Var.* 7.15.4

Mercury, Roman deity: *Var.* 2.40.14, 8.12.4–5

Metellus, war hero of Roman Republic: *Var.* 9.25.10

Metrobius, otherwise unknown classical scholar: *Var.* 7.5.4

Moniarius, petitioner: *Var.* 1.11

Montanarius, official: *PLRE II*, "Montanarius," 765; *Var.* 2.8

Moses, biblical founder: *Var.* 4.31.2, 7.46

Musaeus, mythic character: *Var.* 2.40.7

Muses, mythic characters: *Var.* 2.40.14

Nanduin, *saio*: *PLRE II*, "Nanduin," 772; *Var.* 1.24.2

Neoterius, litigant in inheritance dispute: *PLRE II* "Neoterius 3," 776; *Var.* 1.7

Nereus, Roman deity: *Var.* 12.15.4

Nero, Emperor: *Var.* 2.39.6, 3.51.9

Neudes, *comes*: *PLRE II*, "Neudis," 780; *Var.* 5.29

Nicomachus, classical Greek philosopher: *Var.* 1.45.4

Nymphadius, traveler of senatorial rank: *PLRE II*, "Nymphadius," 788; *Var.* 8.32

Oenomaus, ancient king of Elis: *Var.* 3.51.3

Odoacer, king of Italy from 476–93: *PLRE II*, "Odoacer," 791–93; *Var.* 1.4.6, 2.16.2–3, 4.38, 5.41.5, 8.17.2

Olybrius, *Praefectus Praetorio*: *PLRE II*, "Olybrius 5," 795–96; *Var.* 8.19.5

Opilio, *Comes Sacrarum Largitionum* under Athalaric: *PLRE II*, "Opilio 4," 808; *Var.* 8.16–17

Opilio, *Comes Sacrarum Largitionum* under Odoacer: *PLRE II*, "Opilio 3," 807–08; *Var.* 5.41.5

Oppas, soldier: *PLRE II*, "Oppa," 809; *Var.* 5.29

Optatus, *cornicularius*: *PLRE III*, "Optatus," 956; *Var.* 11.19

Orpheus, mythic character: *Var.* 2.40.6, 2.40.17

Ostrogotha, legendary Gothic king: *Var.* 11.1.19

Osuin, *comes*: *PLRE II*, "Osuin," 815; *Var.* 1.40, 3.26, 4.9, 9.8–9

Pallas, Roman deity: *Var.* 8.31.5, 12.12.2, 12.14.2

Pan, Roman deity: *Var.* 6.18.6

Paschasius, petitioner: *PLRE II*, "Paschasius II," 835; *Var.* 3.52

Paschasius, *Praefectus Annonae*: *PLRE III*, "Paschasius," 969; *Var.* 12.9

Patricius, *primicerius*: *PLRE III*, "Patricius 2," 971–72; *Var.* 11.25

Patricius, *Quaestor*: *Var.* 10.6–7

Patza, soldier: Amory, *People and Identity*, 404; *Var.* 5.32–33

Paul, the apostle: *Var.* 11.13.6

Paula, orphan: *Var.* 4.9

Paulinus, consul: *PLRE III*, "(Decius) Paulinus 1," 973–74; *Var.* 9.22–23

Paulinus, patrician: *PLRE II*, "Paulinus 11," 847; *Var.* 1.23, 2.3.5, 3.29

Paulus, praetorian official: *PLRE III*, "Paulus 2," 975; *Var.* 12.26

Persephone, mythical character: *Var.* 5.42.3

Peter, the apostle: *Var.* 11.13.6, 12.20.3–4

Peter, *arcarius*: *PLRE III*, "Petrus 4," 994; *Var.* 12.20

Peter, bishop: Pietri 2.2, "Petrus 44," 1750; *Var.* 3.37

Peter, curator of preserved foods at Rome: *PLRE III*, "Petrus 3," 993–94; *Var.* 12.11

Peter, eastern envoy ('the Patrician'): *PLRE III*, "Petrus 6," 994–98; *Var.* 10.19, 10.22–24, 10.32

Peter, *illustris* and consul of 516: *PLRE II*, "Fl. Petrus 28," 871; *Var.* 4.25

Peter, *spectabilis*: *PLRE II*, "Petrus 21," 868; *Var.* 4.27–28

Pharaoh, described as King of Egypt: *Var.* 6.3.1

Phidias, classical sculptor: *Var.* 7.15.4

Philagrius, *spectabilis*: *PLRE II*, "Philagrius 3," 874; *Var.* 1.39.1

Philistio, ancient Greek author: *Var.* 4.51.10

Phoebus, Roman deity: *Var.* 12.15.2

Phoroneus, legendary king: *Var.* 7.18.2

Pierius, *Primicerius Singulariorum*: *PLRE III*, "Pierius," 1041; *Var.* 11.32

Pitzia, *comes*: *PLRE II*, "Pitzias," 886–87; *Var.* 5.29

Plato, classical Greek philosopher: *Var.* 1.45.4

Pliny the Younger, early imperial senator: *Var.* 8.13.4

Plutianus, minor in inheritance dispute: *PLRE II*, "Plutianus," 894; *Var.* 1.7

Polymnia, Greek Muse: *Var.* 4.51.8

Polyphemus, a cyclops: *Var.* 7.5.2

Pompeius Magnus, republican general: *Var.* 4.51.12, 6.18.3

Praetextatus, senator accused of sorcery: *PLRE II*, "Praetextatus 4," 904; *Var.* 4.22–23

Priam, mythic character: *Var.* 2.22.2

Priapus, Roman deity: *Var.* 6.21.2

Probinus, patrician: *PLRE II*, "Petronius Probinus 2," 909–10; *Var.* 2.11, 4.40

Probus, tax auditor: *PLRE II*, "Probus 5," 911; *Var.* 4.38

Procula, soldier's wife: *Var.* 5.32–33

Proteus, mythic character: *Var.* 5.34.4

Prusias, ancient king of Bithynia: *Var.* 3.47.5

Ptolemy, Hellenistic Greek astronomer: *Var.* 1.45.4

Publianus, senator: *PLRE II*, "Publianus 1," 928; *Var.* 8.15

Pythagoras, classical Greek philosopher: *Var.* 1.45.4

Quidila, *prior* of Nursia and Reate: *PLRE II*, "Quidila 1," 932; *Var.* 8.26

Quidila, *saio*: *PLRE II*, "Quidila 2," 932; *Var.* 9.10

Quirinus, mythic Roman founder: *Var.* 1.45.4

Ranilda, petitioner with grievance over religion: *Var.* 10.26.3–4

Regina, soldier's wife: *Var.* 5.33

Renatus, petitioner: *Var.* 4.37

Reparatus, *Praefectus Urbis*: *PLRE II*, "Reparatus 1," 939–40; *Var.* 9.7

Romulus, mythic founder of Rome: *Var.* 1.45.3, 3.51.3, 6.4.7, 8.10

Romulus, accused of parricide: *Var.* 2.14

Romulus, western emperor: *PLRE II*, "Romulus Augustulus 4," 949–50; *Var.* 3.35

Sabinus, charioteer: *Var.* 2.9

Sabinianus, *spectabilis*: *PLRE II*, "Sabinianus 6," 968; *Var.* 1.25

Salventius, *Praefectus Urbis*: *PLRE III*, "Salventius," 1108; *Var.* 9.16, 9.17

Samiramis, queen of Babylon: *Var.* 7.15.4

Saturninus, *spectabilis*: *PLRE II*, "Saturninus 5," 980; *Var.* 1.19

Senarius, *Comes Patrimonii*: *PLRE II*, "Senarius," 988–89; *Var.* 4.3–4, 4.7, 4.11, 4.13

Servandus, royal agent: *PLRE II*, "Servandus," 997; *Var.* 5.35

Servatus, *dux*: *PLRE II*, "Servatus 2," 997; *Var.* 1.11

Servius, legendary king of Rome: *Var.* 7.32.4

Severinus, *illustris* governor: *PLRE II*, "Severinus 4," 1001; *Var.* 5.14, 5.15, 9.9

Severus, bishop: Pietri 2.2, "Severus 18," 2060; *Var.* 2.8

Severus, governor of Lucania and Bruttium: *PLRE II*, "Severus 16," 1004; *Var.* 8.31–33

Sibia, father of *prior* of Nursia and Reate: *PLRE II*, "Sibia," 1007; *Var.* 8.26.1

Simeon, *comes*: *PLRE II*, "Simeonius" 1013; *Var.* 3.3.25–26

Simeonius, debtor: *Var.* 5.31

Simon Magus, biblical character: *Var.* 9.15.11

Simplicius, deceased clergy: Pietri 2.2, "Simplicius 7," 2082; *Var.* 3.45

Solomon, ancient Hebrew king: *Var.* 10.4.6

Speciosus, *comitiacus*: *PLRE II*, "Speciosus 2," 1025; *Var.* 1.27, 2.10

Spes, *spectabilis*: *PLRE II*, "Spes," 1026; *Var.* 2.21

Stabularius, *comitiacus*: *PLRE II*, "Stabularius," 1027; *Var.* 5.6

Starcedius, *spectabilis* soldier: *PLRE II*, "Starcedius," 1027; *Var.* 5.36

Stephanus, *Comes Sacrae Vestis*: *PLRE II*, "Stephanus 20," 1031, *Var.* 1.2.1

Stephanus, murdered by slaves: *Var.* 2.19

Stephanus, *Comes Primi Ordinis*: *PLRE II*, "Stephanus 21," 1031; *Var.* 2.28

Stephanus, petitioner: *Var.* 4.44

Suna, *comes*: *PLRE II*, "Suna," 1040; *Var.* 2.7, 3.15

Sunivadus, Gothic *comes*: *PLRE II*, "Sunhivadus," 1040; *Var.* 3.13

Superbus, *referendus curiae*: *PLRE II*, "Superbus," 1041; *Var.* 3.33

Symmachu, Quintus Aurelius, senator: *PLRE I*, "Q. Aurelius Symmachus Eusebius 4"; *Var.* 11.1.20

Symmachus, patrician and father-in-law of Boethius: *PLRE II*, "Q. Aurelius Memmius Symmachus iunior 9," 1044–46; *Var.* 1.23, 2.14, 4.6, 4.22, 4.51

Tacitus, historian: *Var.* 5.2

Tanca, landowner: *Var.* 8.28

Tancila, *comes*: *PLRE II*, "Tancila," 1052; *Var.* 2.35

Tata, *saio*: *PLRE II*, "Tata," 1053; *Var.* 5.23

Terence, Roman play write: *Var.* 2.40.9

Theodagunda, *illustris* woman of Amal family: *PLRE II*, "Theodagunda," 1067; *Var.* 4.37

Theodahad, Gothic king in Italy from 534–36: *PLRE II*, "Theodahadus," 1067–68; *Var.* 3.15, 4.39, 5.12, 8.23, 10.1–7, 10.9, 10.11–20, 10.22–23, 10.25–30, 10.31.2, 10.32.3, 11.13, 12.5, 12.18–20

Theoderic, Gothic king in Italy from 493–526: *PLRE II*, "Fl. Theodericus 7," 1077–84; *Var.* 1.1–5.44, 8.1–8.12 (*passim*), 8.14–8.17 (*passim*), 8.21.3, 8.25.1, 8.26.1–2, 8.29.1, 8.30.1, 9.8.3, 9.10, 9.12.1, 9.14, 9.18.12, 9.24.1, 10.31.5, 11.1.12

Theodora, eastern Augusta: *PLRE III*, "Theodora 1," 1240–41; *Var.* 10.10, 10.20–21, 10.23–24

Theodorus, land surveyor: *Var.* 9.3

Theodorus, patrician: *PLRE II*, "Fl. Theodorus 62," 1097–96; *Var.* 1.27

Theodosius, estate manager: *Var.* 10.5

Theodulus, *spectabilis* awarded a pottery contract: *PLRE II*, "Theodulus 4," 1106; *Var.* 2.23

Theon, *spectabilis*: *PLRE II*, "Theon 6," 1107, *Var.* 1.2

Theudimer, early Gothic king: *PLRE II*, "Theodemer 2," 1069–70; *Var.* 11.1.19

Thomas, *arcarius*: *PLRE III*, "Thomas 7," 1315–16; *Var.* 12.20

Thomas, charioteer: *Var.* 3.51

Thomas, *clarissimus*: *PLRE II*, "Thomas 10," 1114; *Var.* 5.31

Thomas, debtor: *PLRE II*, "Thomas 9," 1114; *Var.* 5.6–7

Thomas, father of petitioner: *Var.* 3.37

Thorismuth, legendary Gothic king: *PLRE II*, "Thorismud," 1116; *Var.* 11.1.19

Thorodon, performer: *Var.* 1.20.4

Thrasamundus, Vandal King: *PLRE II*, "Thras-amundus 1," 1116–17; *Var.* 5.43–44, 9.1

Titus, Roman Emperor: *Var.* 5.42.5

Trajan, Roman Emperor: *Var.* 8.3.5, 8.13.4–5

Trivuila, *saio*: *PLRE II*, "Triwila," 1126–27; *Var.* 3.20

Tufa, proscribed *magister militum* of Odoacer: *PLRE II*, "Tufa," 1131; *Var.* 4.32

Tuluin, Gothic patrician: *PLRE II*, "Tuluin," 1131–33; *Var.* 8.9–12, 8.25

Tutizar, *saio*: *PLRE II*, "Tutizar," 1134; *Var.* 4.27

Ulpianus, senator: *Var.* 2.13

Ulysses: *Var.* 1.39.2, 2.40.10–11, 7.5.2, 12.15.1

Umbisuus, *spectabilis*: *PLRE II* "Umbisuus," 1182; *Var.* 1.19

Unigis, *spatharius*: *PLRE II*, "Unigis," 1182; *Var.* 3.43

Unimundus, legendary Gothic king: *Var.* 11.1.19

Unscila, bishop: Pietri 2.2, "Unscila," 2339; *Var.* 1.26.2

Urbicus, *Primicerius Singulariorum*: *PLRE III*, "Urbicus 1," 1394; *Var.* 11.31

Ursus, *primicerius*: *PLRE III*, "Ursus," 1395; *Var.* 11.30

Valentinian II, western emperor: *Var.* 9.18.1

Valentinian III, western emperor: *Var.* 1.4.10, 11.1.9

Valeria, woman in legal case: *Var.* 3.46

Valerianus, *spectabilis* of Syracuse, governor of Lucania and Bruttium: *PLRE II*, "Valerianus 5," 1142; *Var.* 4.6, 12.5

Venantius, senator: *PLRE II*, "Venantius 4," 1153; *Var.* 1.7, 2.13

Venantius, *Comes Domesticorum*: *PLRE II*, "Ve-nantius 2," 1153; *Var.* 2.15–16

Venantius, governor of Lucania-Bruttium: *PLRE II*, "Venantius 3," 1153; *Var.* 3.8, 3.36, 3.46, 3.47

Venantius, consul and father of consul: *PLRE II*, "Basilius Venantius iunior 5," 1153–54; *Var.* 9.22–23

Venerius, *colonus* (?): *Var.* 8.28

Venus, Roman deity: *Var.* 4.51.9, 6.21.2

Veranus, *saio*: *PLRE II*, "Vera," 1154–55; *Var.* 5.10

Victor, tax collector: *PLRE II*, "Victor 10," 1159–60; *Var.* 9.11–12

Victorinus, bishop: Pietri 2.2, "Victorinus 7," 2294; *Var.* 8.8

Virgil, Roman poet: *Var.* 2.40.7, 5.4.6, 5.21.3, 12.14.3

Vitalianus, *cancellarius*: *PLRE III*, "Vitalianus 1," 1379; *Var.* 11.39

Vivianus, *spectabilis*: *PLRE II*, "Vivianus 1," 1179; *Var.* 4.41

Volusianus, western consul of 503: *PLRE II*, "Volusianus 5," 1183–84; *Var.* 4.22, 4.22

Vuacca, *maior domo*: *PLRE III*, "Wacces," 1397; *Var.* 10.18.2

Vuandil, military commander: *PLRE II*, "Wandil," 1149; *Var.* 3.38

Walamer, early Gothic king: *PLRE II*, "Valamer," 1135–36; *Var.* 11.1.19

Wilia, *Comes Patrimonii*: *PLRE II*, "Wilia 1, 2," 1166–67; *Var.* 1.18, 5.18–20, 5.23, 9.13

Wiliarit: *PLRE II*, "Wiliarit 1," 1167; *Var.* 1.38

Wiligis: *PLRE II*, "Wiligis," 1167; *Var.* 2.20

Wilitancus, *dux*: *PLRE II*, "Wilitancus," 1167; *Var.* 5.33

Winitarius, legendary Gothic king: *PLRE I*, "Vinitharius," 968; *Var.* 11.1.19

Wisibad, *comes*: *PLRE III*, "Wisibadus," 1407; *Var.* 10.29

Witigis, king of the Goths in Italy from 536–40: *PLRE III*, "Vitigis," 1382–87; *Var.* 10.31–35, 12.22–28

Witigisclus, tax collector: *PLRE II*, "Witigisclus," 1178; *Var.* 9.11–12

Zeno, eastern emperor: *Var.* 1.43.2

INDEX OF CONCEPTS, PEOPLES, AND TERMS

cancellarius, 1.35, 11.6, 11.14, 11.27, 11.36, 11.37, 11.39, 12.1–3, 12.10, 12.12, 12.14, 12.15

canonicaria, 3.8.2, 12.16

canonicarius, 6.8.5, 11.38, 12.4, 12.7, 12.13

Catalienses (Catali), 1.14

Chaldaeans, 3.51.8, 3.52.3

chartarius, 7.43

church, affairs and personnel, 1.9, 1.26, 2.17, 2.29, 2.30, 3.14, 3.37, 3.45, 3.47.1, 4.17, 4.18, 4.20, 4.24, 4.44, 8.8, 8.15, 8.24, 9.15–16, 10.15, 10.19–20, 10.22.3, 10.25.1, 10.26.2, 11.2–3, 12.13, 12.20

classical references or digressions, preface 1.2, 1.3.3, 1.10.3–6, 1.17.2, 1.20.5, 1.27.5, 1.30.5, 1.39.2, 1.45.2–11, 2.3.4, 2.22.2, 2.28.1, 2.39.4, 2.40, 3.6.3, 3.31.4, 3.47.5, 3.51, 3.52, 3.53, 4.35, 4.51.2–12, 5.2, 5.17.2–4, 5.21.3, 5.34.4, 5.42, 6.2.1, 6.4.7, 6.5.3, 6.18.3–7, 6.21.2, 7.5.2–4, 7.7.3, 7.15.2–5, 7.32.3, 7.32.4, 8.12.4–5, 9.3.5, 9.25.10, 10.11.12, 10.17.1, 12.11.3, 12.12.2, 12.14.1–3, 12.15.1–7

comes and *dux* (as primarily military commands), 1.5, 1.11, 1.40, 2.7, 2.12, 2.29, 2.35, 3.13, 3.23–24, 3.25–26, 3.34, 3.36, 3.42, 3.45, 4.5, 4.9, 4.12, 4.13, 4.16, 4.17, 4.18, 4.20, 4.22–23, 4.27–28, 4.43.2, 4.45, 4.46, 4.49, 5.14.8, 5.29, 5.30, 5.33, 5.35, 5.39, 6.22–25, 7.1, 7.3, 7.4, 7.9, 7.13, 7.14, 7.16, 7.24–28, 8.2, 8.10, 9.8–9, 9.11, 9.13, 9.14, 10.29

Comes Archiatrorum, 6.19

Comes Domesticorum, 2.15–16, 6.11, 8.12

Comes Formarum, 7.6

Comes Patrimonii, 1.16, 1.18, 4.3–4, 4.15, 5.7.3, 5.18–20, 5.23, 6.9, 8.23, 9.3, 9.9.3, 9.13, 12.4.2

Comes Primi Ordinis, 2.28, 6.12, 6.13

Comes Privatarum, 3.12.3, 3.53, 4.7, 4.11, 4.13, 6.8

Comes Sacrarum Largitionum, 2.31, 3.8.2, 3.12.2, 5.40–41, 6.7, 7.20–22, 8.13.2, 8.16–17, 8.21, 8.24.5, 9.7.2

comitiacus, 1.27, 2.10, 5.6, 6.13, 7.31, 8.27

commentariensis, 11.28

commerce, and merchants, 1.34, 2.4, 2.12, 2.14.2, 2.26, 2.30, 2.38, 3.50, 4.5, 4.7, 4.19, 5.1, 5.2, 5.16, 5.35, 5.39, 6.7.7–8, 7.9, 7.11, 7.12, 7.14, 7.23, 7.29, 8.33, 9.14.9, 11.11, 11.12

conductores, 1.16, 2.25.2, 5.39.6

consul, appointment to, 2.1–3, 3.5.5, 3.39, 5.42, 6.1, 6.10.2, 9.22–23

consularis. See governors

contracts, awarded for various public works, 1.6, 1.36, 1.45, 2.4, 2.21, 2.23, 2.30, 2.32–33, 2.40, 3.19, 3.29, 4.30, 7.44, 10.28, 12.6, 12.11

cornicularius, 11.18–19, 11.36

Curator Civitatis, 7.12

Curator Palatii, 7.5, 7.15

curiales, 1.19, 2.17, 2.18, 2.24.2–4, 2.25.2–4, 3.9, 3.47, 3.49, 4.8, 4.11, 4.45, 4.49, 5.14, 6.24, 7.12, 7.27, 7.47, 8.29, 8.31, 9.2, 9.4

cursus publicus, 1.29, 2.31, 4.15, 4.47, 5.5, 5.39, 6.6.3, 11.14, 11.29, 12.15.6

Cyclopses, 7.5.2

defensores, 2.17, 2.30, 3.9, 3.45, 3.49, 4.45, 4.49, 5.14, 7.11, 9.10, 9.15.2

diplomatic letters, 1.1, 1.45–46, 2.1, 2.6, 2.40, 2.41, 3.1, 3.2, 3.3, 3.4, 4.1, 4.2, 4.45, 5.1, 5.2, 5.43–44, 7.33, 8.1, 9.1, 10.1–2, 10.8–10, 10.15, 10.19–20, 10.21–26, 10.31–35

domestici, 9.13, 11.31

donative, 2.31, 4.14, 4.20, 5.26–27, 5.36, 11.17, 11.33, 11.35–38

edicts, 2.24–26, 2.33, 2.35–36, 4.10, 4.27, 5.5, 7.3, 7.42, 8.3, 9.2, 9.14–16, 9.18–20, 11.8–9, 11.11, 11.12, 11.40, 12.1, 12.13, 12.16, 12.28

Etruscans, 7.15.3

exceptores, 11.23, 11.25, 11.30

family, elite family histories, 1.3–6, 1.4.5, 1.43, 2.1–3, 2.15–16, 3.5–6, 3.12.2, 4.39.2, 5.3.1–4, 5.4.4–5, 5.41.5, 8.10, 8.16.2–4, 8.17, 8.19, 8.21, 8.23, 9.1, 9.4, 9.7, 9.22–23, 10.2, 10.11–12, 11.1.19

formulae, preface 1.14, 6.1–25, 7.1–47

Franks, 2.40, 2.41, 3.1, 3.2, 3.3, 3.4, 8.10, 11.1.12

Gepids, 5.10, 5.11

Goths, see *Ostrogoths* or *Visigoths*

governors, of provinces, 1.4.16, 2.24.2, 2.25.2, 2.28.5, 3.8, 3.16–17, 3.23–24, 3.25–26, 3.27, 3.46, 3.47, 4.10, 4.32, 5.8, 5.14, 5.24, 5.35, 5.39, 6.3.3, 6.6.5, 6.12, 6.20–21, 7.1, 7.2, 7.20, 7.24, 8.31–33, 9.9, 9.20, 11.7, 11.9, 12.2, 12.5, 12.8, 12.15.7

grain, 1.34–35, 2.20, 2.26, 3.41, 4.7, 4.19, 5.16, 5.35, 6.18, 8.19.1, 9.5, 10.27, 10.28, 11.5, 12.14, 12.15.5, 12.22–24, 12.26, 12.27, 12.28, 12.28.7

Greek, language, 1.45.4, 2.39.4, 4.51.5, 5.40.5, 5.42.5, 11.1.6, 12.14.1

Greeks, 3.53.4, 5.17.3, 8.12.5

Haesti, 5.2

Herules, 3.3, 4.2, 4.45

honorati, 2.17, 3.49, 4.8, 4.12.3, 6.21.3, 6.24, 7.27, 8.29, 9.5, 9.10

INDEX OF PLACES

Founded in 1893,
UNIVERSITY OF CALIFORNIA PRESS
publishes bold, progressive books and journals
on topics in the arts, humanities, social sciences,
and natural sciences—with a focus on social
justice issues—that inspire thought and action
among readers worldwide.

The UC PRESS FOUNDATION
raises funds to uphold the press's vital role
as an independent, nonprofit publisher, and
receives philanthropic support from a wide
range of individuals and institutions—and from
committed readers like you. To learn more, visit
ucpress.edu/supportus.